OXFORD PRIVATE INTERNATIONAL
LAW SERIES

GENERAL EDITOR: JAMES J. FAWCETT

Professor of Law
University of Nottingham

SUBSTANCE AND PROCEDURE IN PRIVATE INTERNATIONAL LAW

OXFORD PRIVATE INTERNATIONAL LAW SERIES

General Editor: James J. Fawcett

The aim of the series is to publish work of quality and originality in a number of important areas of private international law. The series is intended for both scholarly and practitioner readers.

ALSO IN THIS SERIES

Employment Contracts in Private International Law
LOUISE MERRETT

The Arrest of Ships in Private International Law
VERÓNICA RUIZ ABOU-NIGM

Intellectual Property and Private International Law
Second edition
JAMES J. FAWCETT and PAUL TORREMANS

The Rome II Regulation
ANDREW DICKINSON

Cross-Border Divorce Law
MÁIRE NÍ SHÚILLEABHÁIN

The Anti-Suit Injunction
THOMAS RAPHAEL

Agreements on Jurisdiction and Choice of Law
ADRIAN BRIGGS

Civil Jurisdiction Rules of the EU and their Impact on Third States
THALIA KRUGER

Cross-Border Consumer Contracts
JONATHAN HILL

Insolvency in Private International Law
Second edition
IAN F FLETCHER

Conflict of Laws Within the UK
KIRSTY J HOOD

The Transfer of Property in the Conflict of Laws
JANEEN M CARRUTHERS

International Sale of Goods in the Conflict of Laws
JAMES J FAWCETT, JONATHAN M HARRIS, and MICHAEL BRIDGE

Choice of Law for Equitable Doctrines
T M YEO

Procedural Law in International Arbitration
GEORGIOS PETROCHILOS

Foreign Law in Civil Litigation
SOFIE GEEROMS

Shares and Other Securities in the Conflict of Laws
MAISIE OOI

Forum Shopping and Venue in Transnational Litigation
ANDREW S BELL

Cross-Border Enforcement of Patent Rights
MARTA PERTEGÁS SENDER

Res Judicata, Estoppel, and Foreign Judgments
PETER BARNETT

Corporations in Private International Law
STEPHAN RAMMELOO

The Enforcement of Judgments in Europe
WENDY KENNETT

Claims for Contribution and Reimbursement in an International Context
KOJI TAKAHASHI

The Hague Convention on International Child Abduction
PAUL BEAUMONT and PETER MCELEAVY

SUBSTANCE AND PROCEDURE IN PRIVATE INTERNATIONAL LAW

RICHARD GARNETT

*Professor of Law, The University of Melbourne,
Consultant, Freehills*

OXFORD
UNIVERSITY PRESS

OXFORD
UNIVERSITY PRESS

Great Clarendon Street, Oxford, ox2 6DP,
United Kingdom

Oxford University Press is a department of the University of Oxford.
It furthers the University's objective of excellence in research, scholarship,
and education by publishing worldwide. Oxford is a registered trade mark of
Oxford University Press in the UK and in certain other countries

© Richard Garnett, 2012

The moral rights of the author have been asserted

First Edition published in 2012

Impression: 2

All rights reserved. No part of this publication may be reproduced, stored in
a retrieval system, or transmitted, in any form or by any means, without the
prior permission in writing of Oxford University Press, or as expressly permitted
by law, by licence or under terms agreed with the appropriate reprographics
rights organization. Enquiries concerning reproduction outside the scope of the
above should be sent to the Rights Department, Oxford University Press, at the
address above

You must not circulate this work in any other form
and you must impose this same condition on any acquirer

Crown copyright material is reproduced under Class Licence
Number C01P0000148 with the permission of OPSI
and the Queen's Printer for Scotland

British Library Cataloguing in publication Data
Data available

Library of Congress Cataloguing in Publication Data
Library of Congress Control Number: 2012932745

ISBN 978–0–19–953279–7

Printed and bound by
CPI Group (UK) Ltd, Croydon, CR0 4YY

Links to third party websites are provided by Oxford in good faith and
for information only. Oxford disclaims any responsibility for the materials
contained in any third party website referenced in this work.

General Editor's Preface

The *Oxford Private International Law Series* contains a number of works which fall within the ambit of what are referred to in the textbooks as preliminary or procedural matters. There is Richard Fentiman's *Foreign Law in English Courts* and Sophie Geerom's companion monograph, *Foreign Law in Civil Litigation*. There is also Georgios Petrochilos' *Procedural Law in International Arbitration*. What was needed was a monograph to examine procedural law in civil litigation. We now have Richard Garnett's *Substance and Procedure in Private International Law* to fill this gap. This book is not only welcome as dealing with one of the most fundamental and essential distinctions in private international law but is also very timely.

In Australia and Canada, the theoretical basis for drawing the distinction between substance and procedure has gone through a re-assessment in recent years. The differences in approach from that recently adopted at common law in England by the House of Lords makes particularly interesting reading. For the United Kingdom, the Europeanization of the law applicable to contractual and non-contractual obligations under the Rome Convention and Rome I and Rome II Regulations has meant that old classifications have had to be re-examined.

The emphasis in the book is on substance and procedure in common law jurisdictions and contains an impressively wider examination of the position not only in Australia, Canada, England (at common law), New Zealand, and the United States but also in Hong Kong and Singapore. At the same time, the position under the Rome Convention and Rome I and Rome II Regulations is fully considered. The book provides a practical guide for dealing with concrete situations but also a choice of law framework for procedural questions.

The stated aim of the *Oxford Private International Law Series* is to publish works of high quality and originality in a number of important areas of private international law. *Substance and Procedure in Private International Law* palpably fulfils these criteria and is an excellent addition to the Series.

James Fawcett
Nottingham
September 2011

Preface

Procedure has long been a significant factor in cross-border disputes, as can be seen from the increasing volume of decisions, particularly in the common law world, on matters such as service of process, jurisdiction, taking of evidence, interim measures of protection, and the recognition and enforcement of foreign judgments. The question of the law to be applied to procedural matters has always been assumed to be the law of the forum of adjudication of the dispute, given that forum's greater familiarity with and expertise in applying its own procedural rules. While granting the forum exclusive control over procedural matters may be generally accepted where procedure is narrowly defined, it becomes much more contentious where—as has traditionally occurred in common law countries—procedure has been expansively interpreted. The controversy arises from the fact that a wide view of procedure in private international law necessarily means a more restricted role for foreign law and greater opportunities for forum shopping. This book aims to explore the applicable law dimensions of procedure through three lines of inquiry. The first is the distinction between matters of 'substance' and matters of 'procedure', which remains inconsistent and contested across common law jurisdictions; the second examines procedure in the light of other approaches in private international law for referring matters to forum law, such as public policy and overriding mandatory rules; and the third considers, in the context of matters which are wholly 'procedural', whether the exclusive application of forum law is accurate and justified. A substantial part of the book involves an examination of these three inquiries in a number of situations commonly arising in transnational litigation, such as the admissibility and exclusion of evidence, service and jurisdiction, judicial administration, limitation of actions, and remedies.

The book aims to provide scholars and practitioners with clear guidance not only as to the current state of the law but also as to how it may develop and be applied in future cases. While the major focus of the book is the decisions of courts in England, Australia, Canada, New Zealand, Singapore, Hong Kong, Malaysia, South Africa, and the United States, important aspects of EU law, such as the Rome I and II Regulations and the literature and decisions of European civil law countries, are also examined. While the book is predominantly directed at lawyers from common law countries, the suggested framework for applicable law and procedure is equally relevant to a global audience.

This book has been enhanced by the discussions I have had with scholars and practitioners in England and Australia, many of whom also read and commented upon the manuscript. I wish to acknowledge in particular the assistance of Andrew Bell SC, Andrew Dickinson, Dion Fahey, Perry Herzfeld, Kathryn Howard, Mary Keyes, James McComish, and Danielle Sirmai. I wish to thank the Honourable Sir Anthony Mason for writing such a gracious and insightful foreword and also Professor James Fawcett, the General Editor of the Series, who read the entire manuscript before publication and made many valuable suggestions. I also wish to thank Jessica Huntley at Oxford University Press whose patience and encouragement were unstinting. Finally, I would like to acknowledge the great support and encouragement provided by my family during the writing of this book, in particular my wife Linda and children Thomas and Isabelle. The book is dedicated to the memory of William Young, my grandfather, whose destiny is hopefully fulfilled in these pages. The law in this book is stated, as best known to me, as at 30 June 2011.

Richard Garnett
Melbourne
30 June 2011

ADDENDUM

Since the completion of this manuscript for publication, the European Court of Justice (ECJ) has delivered its judgment in Case C-412/10 Homawoo v GMF Assurance (17 November 2011) on the temporal effect of the Rome II Regulation (Regulation (EC) No. 864/2007). The ECJ held that the Regulation only applies to events giving rise to damage occurring after 11 January 2009.

Foreword

The publication of this work will fill a gap in the library shelf devoted to private international law. The distinction between substance and procedure, so fundamental in this area of law, is the central concern of the book. The author argues convincingly in favour of a narrow 'process' concept of procedure—the regulation of court proceedings—in preference to the broader concept of remedy; an argument which, if accepted, will promote uniformity across jurisdictions and inhibit forum-shopping, thereby achieving desirable policy goals at the expense of more parochial considerations.

Professor Garnett seeks also to establish a more comprehensive choice of law framework for the consideration of a broad range of procedural questions than that offered by the inadequate traditional law of the forum/ law of the cause of action dichotomy. In doing so, the author maintains a focus on cross-border litigation excluding international commercial arbitration. Although the author's focus is mainly on the rules applicable in Commonwealth countries, he refers as well to United States and European materials.

This work is not just an admirable statement of the law as it currently stands; it identifies and engages with deeper underlying issues and offers persuasive solutions to them. In addition, it presents a penetrating analysis of the existing rules and the decided cases.

The Hon. Sir Anthony Mason AC, KBE
Chief Justice of Australia 1987–95
Justice of the High Court of Australia 1972–87
15 December 2011

Contents

Table of Cases xiii
Table of Legislation xlix
Table of Conventions and Treaties lix
Table of Principles and Restatements lxv
List of Abbreviations lxvii

Chapter 1 INTRODUCTION 1

Chapter 2 THE SUBSTANCE AND PROCEDURE DISTINCTION: ORIGINS, RATIONALE, AND DEFINITION 5

    A. History and Origins 2.01
    B. The Rationale for Forum Law Governing Procedure 2.09
    C. Contemporary Approaches to Substance and Procedure 2.17
    D. Conclusion 2.59

Chapter 3 CHARACTERIZATION, ALTERNATIVE METHODS OF FORUM REFERENCE, AND HARMONIZATION 45

    A. Characterization 3.02
    B. Alternative Methods of Forum Reference 3.15
    C. Harmonization 3.31

Chapter 4 SERVICE AND JURISDICTION 71

    A. Service 4.01
    B. Jurisdiction 4.41

Chapter 5 PARTIES TO LITIGATION 117

    A. Capacity 5.01
    B. The Proper Party 5.09
    C. Individual Issues 5.16

Chapter 6 JUDICIAL ADMINISTRATION 143

    A. Court Proceedings 6.02
    B. Costs and Lawyers' Fees 6.31
    C. Statutory 'No Action' Clauses 6.40
    D. Priorities and Rights of Creditors 6.59
    E. Judgments and Orders 6.77

xii   *Contents*

Chapter 7 EVIDENCE I: GENERAL PRINCIPLES   189
    A. Introduction   7.01
    B. Admissibility   7.03
    C. Burden of Proof and Presumptions   7.15
    D. Individual Topics within Evidence   7.26
    E. Estoppel   7.36

Chapter 8 EVIDENCE II: TAKING EVIDENCE ABROAD, PRIVILEGE,
              AND OTHER BARS ON DISCLOSURE   223
    A. Taking of Evidence Abroad   8.01
    B. Privilege and Other Bars on Disclosure   8.20

Chapter 9 STATUTES OF LIMITATION   261
    A. The Common Law Position   9.01
    B. The UK Statutory Regime   9.12
    C. Further Issues   9.35

Chapter 10 REMEDIES I: GENERAL PRINCIPLES, NON-MONETARY
               RELIEF, AND STATUTORY RESTRICTIONS   295
    A. The Nature of the Remedy   10.01
    B. Interim and Provisional Remedies   10.06
    C. Final Non-Monetary Relief   10.20
    D. Set-Off and Counterclaim   10.25
    E. Statutory Restrictions on Remedies   10.32

Chapter 11 REMEDIES II: DAMAGES AND
               STATUTORY COMPENSATION   315
    A. The Common Law Position   11.02
    B. The EU Instruments   11.52
    C. The US Position   11.68

Chapter 12 CONCLUSION   361

Bibliography   365
Index   375

Table of Cases

Abbott Laboratories v Takeda Pharmaceutical Co Ltd 476
   F 3d 421 (7th Cir 2007) 4.59
Abdel Hadi Abdallah Al Qahtari & Sons Beverage Industry
   Co v Antliff [2010] EWHC 1735 (Comm); [2010]
   All ER (D) 172 (Jul)............................. 7.39, 11.04–11.05
ABF Capital Corp v Grove Properties Co 126 Cal App 4th 204
   (CA Cal 2005) 6.34
Ackermann v Levine 788 F 2d 830 (2nd Cir 1986) 4.38
Acrux, The [1965] P 391.. 6.66
Activate No 1 Pty Ltd v Equuscorp Pty Ltd [1999] FCA 619......... 2.33
Adams v Cape Industries plc [1990] Ch 433 .... 6.83, 7.23
Addison v Brown [1954] 1 WLR 779............................. 3.18
Adhiguna Meranti, The [1987] 1 HKLR 904................. 2.35, 4.49
AE Inc v Goodyear Tyre & Rubber Co 168 P 3d 507
   (SC Colo 2007)... 11.72
Airbus Industrie GIE v Patel [1999] 1 AC 119 (HL)................ 4.63
AK Investment CJSC v Kyrgyz Mobil Tel Ltd [2011]
   UKPC 7 .... 4.43, 5.34
Akai Pty Ltd v People's Insurance Co Ltd (1996) 188 CLR 418....... 4.56
Akai Pty Ltd v People's Insurance Co Ltd [1998]
   1 Lloyd's Rep 90... 6.82
Al Jedda v Secretary of State for Defence [2011]
   2 WLR 225.. 4.67–4.68
Al Mowahidine v Chatar [1989] ECLY 161 (Trib Liv Liège,
   30 November 1988) 7.06
Albemarle Corp v Astrazeneca UK Ltd 628 F 3d 643
   (4th Cir 2010) 4.59
Allan J Panozza and Co Pty Ltd v Allied Interstate (Q)
   Pty Ltd [1976] 2 NSWLR 192 .... 6.22, 9.44
Allegheny Energy Inc v DQE Inc 171 F 3d 153 (4th Cir 1999) 10.20
Allen v Hay (1922) 69 DLR 193 .... 7.52
Allen v Kemble (1848) 6 Moo PC 314 (PC)....................... 10.26
Allianz Ins Co v Guidant Corp 869 NE 2d 1042
   (CA Ill 2007) 8.31–8.32
Allstate Life Insurance Co v Australia and New Zealand
   Banking Group Ltd (No 4) (1996) 64 FCR 61 .... 8.17
Amaca Pty Ltd v Aartsen [2011] NSWSC 676 .... 7.49, 11.28
Amaca Pty Ltd v Frost (2006) 67
   NSWLR 635........................... 3.10, 4.68, 6.57–6.58, 11.15

Amchem Products Inc v British Columbia Workers'
  Compensation Board [1993] 1 SCR 897.................2.35, 11.51
America Online Inc v Superior Court 90 Cal App 4th 1
  (CA Cal 2001) 5.28
American Endeavour Fund Ltd v Trueger [1997] JLR 18............8.18
Amusement Industry Inc v Stern 693 F Supp 2d 327
  (SDNY 2010)...10.21
Anderson v Johnson (1877) 1 Knox (NSW) 1 (SC NSW)............5.27
Andres Bonifacio, The [1993] SGCA 70.............................4.60
Andrews v Traynor [2003] QSC 292 ....11.32
Andrico Unity, The [1989] 4 SA 325 (A) 6.60, 6.67, 6.72
Annecca Inc v Lexent Inc 345 F Supp 2d 897 (ND Ill 2004)..........7.52
Annesley, Re [1926] Ch 692.......................................3.14
Anthes Equipment Ltd v Wilhelm Layher GmbH (1986) 53
  OR (2d) 435 (Ont HC) 4.55
Anton Piller KG v Manufacturing Processes Ltd [1976]
  Ch 55 (CA)..10.06
Antonio Gramsci Shipping Corp v Oleg Stephanovs
  [2011] EWHC 333 (Comm) 4.56
Aosta Shipping Co Ltd v Gulf Overseas General Trading
  LLC 2007 BCSC 354 ....10.13
Apache Village Inc v Coleman Co 776 P 2d 1154 (Colo App 1989)....6.39
Application concerning s 80 of the Supreme Court Act and
  sections 119 and 128 of the Evidence Act, Re [2004]
  NSWSC 614...8.58
Application of Robert William Whitton [2007] NSWSC 606 ....8.05
Arab Monetary Fund v Hashim [1993] 1 Lloyd's Rep 543
  (Comm) (affd [1996] 1 Lloyd's Rep 589 (CA))..............9.20, 9.22
Arab Monetary Fund v Hashim (No 9) (1994) *The Times*,
  11 October (EWHC)..5.18
Aramarine Brokerage Inc v OneBeacon Ins Co 307 Fed
  Appx 562 (2nd Cir 2009)......................................7.27
Arhill Pty Ltd v General Terminal Coy Pty Ltd (1990)
  23 NSWLR 545 ....8.05
Aries v Palmer Johnson Inc 735 P 2d 1373 (Ariz CA 1987) 6.34
Armacel Pty Ltd v Smurfit Stone Container Corp (2008)
  248 ALR 573 ....7.41
Arros Invest Ltd v Nishanov [2004] EWHC 576 (Ch)...............4.16
AS Hydrema Danmark v Euman SA (Supreme Court of Spain,
  8 April 2005) 7.04, 7.07
Asbestos Insurance, Re [1985] 1 WLR 331 ....8.14
Ashby v White (1703) 2 Ld Raym 938; 92 ER 126 ....2.05
Ashland Chemical Co v Provence 181 Cal Rptr 340 (CA Cal 1982)...9.46

Asian Plutus, The [1990] 1 SLR 543 (Sing HC)................ 2.11, 4.54
ASML Netherlands BV v Semiconductor Industry Services
    GmbH (Case C-283/05) (ECJ 14 December 2006) 4.26
Astra Aktiebolag v Andrx Pharmaceuticals Inc 208 FRD 92
    (SDNY 2002) 8.29
Astrazeneca UK Ltd v Albemarle International Corp [2010]
    EWHC 1028 (Comm)................................. 4.55–4.56
Atchison Casting Corp v DOFASCO Inc 1995 WL 655183
    (D Kan 1995).. 6.34
Attorney-General (United Kingdom) v Heinemann Publishers
    Australia Pty Ltd (1988) 165 CLR 30........................ 2.13
Australian Continental Resources Ltd v ATS (1974)
    8 SASR 127 (SC SA) 6.42
Australian Iron and Steel v Hoogland (1962)
    108 CLR 471... 9.01
Australian Securities Commission v Bank Leumi Le-Israel
    (1995) 134 ALR 101 (affd (1996) 69 FCR 531) 8.47
Australian Zircon NL v Austpac Resources NL (2010)
    243 FLR 423... 7.13
Austrian Lloyd Steamship Co v Gresham Life Assurance
    Society [1903] 1 KB 249 (CA) 4.55
Avenue Properties Ltd v First City Development
    Corporation Ltd (1986) 32 DLR (4th) 40 (BCCA) 6.46
Axis Management Inc v Alsager (2000) 197 Sask R 234 .... 5.41

B v B 29 July 2008 (QBD).. 11.41
Bacci v Kaiser Permanente Foundation Health Plan 278
    F Supp 2d 34 (DDC 2003) 11.70
Bachand v Roberts (1996) 7 CPC (4th) 93........................... 6.31
Bacon v Nacional Suiza Cia Seguros y Reseguros SA [2010]
    EWHC 2017 (QB) 11.01, 11.65
Bain v Whitehaven and Furness Junction Railway (1850)
    3 HLC 1 .... 7.01, 7.03, 7.31
Baker v General Motors Corp 522 US 222 (US Sup Ct 1998).......... 6.80
Baldry v Jackson [1977] 1 NSWLR 496 .... 5.18
Baltic Flame, The [2001] 2 Lloyd's Rep 203 .... 5.18
Bamco 18 v Reeves 685 F Supp 414 (SDNY 1988) 8.29
Banco Latino SACA v Gomez Lopez 53 F Supp 2d 1273
    (SD Fla 1999)....................................... 4.14, 4.36
Bank Gesellschaft Berlin International SA v Raif Zihnal
    16 July 2001 (Com Ct) 8.57
Bank Julius Baer and Co Ltd v Wikileaks 2008 WL 413737
    (ND Cal) 4.37

Bank of America v Maas 2010 ONSC 4546 (affd 2010
  ONCA 833) 9.06, 9.15, 9.39, 9.41
Bank of Credit and Commerce International SA v Ali [2006]
  EWHC 2135 (Ch) 9.13
Bank of Credit and Commerce International SA (No 10), Re
  [1997] Ch 213...3.23, 10.31
Bank of Crete SA v Koskotas [1991] 2 Lloyd's Rep 587 .... 8.04
Bank of Ireland v Pexxnet Ltd [2010] EWHC 1872 (Comm) 10.21
Bank of Nova Scotia v Beynon Ontario District Court,
  3 April 1987... 10.33
Bank of Valetta plc v National Crime Authority (1999) 164
  ALR 45 (affd [1999] FCAFC 1099) 8.46
Bankers Trust International plc v PT Dharmala Comm Ct,
  19 October 1995 .... 8.17
Bannister v Bemis Co Inc 2008 WL 2002087 (D Minn 2008)........... 6.33
Banque Indosuez v Madam Sumilan Awal [1997] SGHC 2.......7.05–7.06
Banque Internationale de Commerce de Petrograd v
  Goukassow [1923] 2 KB 682 (CA) 5.02
Bargain Harold's Discount Ltd v Paribas Bank of Canada
  (1992) 113 NSR (2d) 434 (NSSC)............................. 5.26
Barrett v Universal-Island Records Ltd [2006] EWHC 1009 .... 7.39
Barros Mattos v MacDaniels Ltd [2005] EWHC 1323 (Ch) 9.17, 9.32
Bas Capital Funding Corporation v Medfinco Ltd [2004]
  1 Lloyd's Rep 652.. 4.21
Baschet v London Illustrated Standard Co [1900] 1 Ch 73.......... 10.04
Base Metal Trading Ltd v Shamurin [2005]
  1 WLR 1157 .... 5.38, 6.07, 6.22
Bateman & Litman Real Estate Ltd v Big T Motel Ltd (1964)
  44 DLR (2d) 474 (Sask QB) (affd 49 DLR (2d) 480) 6.42–6.43
Baxter v RMC Group plc [2003] 1 NZLR 304..................... 11.45
Bayat Telephone Systems International Inc v
  Lord Michael Cecil [2011] EWCA Civ 135 .... 4.02, 4.07, 4.21
BDO Seidman LLP v British Car Auctions Inc 802 So 2d 366
  (CA Fla 2001).. 6.33
Beals v Saldanha [2003] 3 SCR 416; (2003) 234 DLR
  (4th) 1 (SCC)...6.83, 11.51
Beckford v Wade (1805) 17 Ves J 87............................... 9.01
Beckkett Pte Ltd v Deutsche Bank AG [2005] SGCA 34.............. 8.57
Bell Group Ltd (in liq) v Westpac Banking Corp (2000)
  104 FCR 305.. 2.33
Bellezza Club Japan Co Ltd v Matsumura Akihiko [2010]
  2 SLR 342.. 7.41
Benefit Strategies Group Inc v Prider (2005) 91 SASR 544.......... 11.02

Table of Cases

Bernkrant v Fowler 360 P 2d 906 (Cal 1961)..................... 7.27
Berriman v Cricket Australia (2007) 17 VR 528.................. 9.16
Betty Ott, The [1992] 1 NZLR 655 .... 6.70–6.71
Bezan v Van der Hooft [2004] ABCA 44 .... 11.37
BHP Billiton Ltd v Schultz (2004) 221
    CLR 400............2.34–2.35, 3.05, 4.05, 6.19, 7.48–7.49, 11.11, 11.28
BHP Billiton Ltd v Utting [2005] NSWSC 260..................... 7.48
BI (Contracting) Pty Ltd v Haylock [2005] NSWSC 592............. 7.48
Black v Yates [1992] 1 QB 526................................... 7.39
Black-Clawson International Ltd v Papierwerke
    Waldhof-Asschaffenburg AG [1975] 1 AC 591.............2.05, 2.46
Blanton v Kenneth Littlefield 2010 RI Super Lexis 107
    (Super Ct RI)... 8.31
Block Bros Realty Ltd v Mollard (1981) 122 DLR
    (3d) 323 (BCCA).......................................2.29, 6.43
Blue Sky One Ltd v Mahan Air [2010] EWHC 631 (Comm)......... 3.11
Boardwalk Regency Corp v Maalouf (1992) 88 DLR (4th)
    612 (Ont CA)... 6.43
Bodner v Paribas 202 FRD 370 (EDNY 2000).................... 8.55
Boele v Norsemeter Holding AS [2002] NSWCA 363............... 6.83
Boersma v Amoco Oil Company 658 NE 2d 1173
    (Ill App Ct 1995)................................. 6.04, 6.15, 7.22
Boise Tower Associates LLC v Washington Capital Joint Master
    Trust Mortgage Income Fund 2007 WL 4355815 (D Idaho)....... 6.34
Bominflot Inc v The MV Heinrich S 465 F 3d 144 (4th Cir 2006) 6.76
Bonsall v Cattolica Assicurazioni [2010] IL Pr 45 (Winchester
    County Court).. 11.01
Boone v Royal Indemnity Co 460 F 2d 26 (10th Cir 1972)............. 7.33
Botanic Ltd v China National United Oil Corp [2008] HKCFI 721.... 9.07
Bourns Inc v Raychem Corporation [1999] 3 All ER 154 (CA) 8.24
Boyd Rosene and Associates Inc v Kansas Municipal Gas
    Agency 174 F 3d 1115 (10th Cir 1999)......................... 6.34
Boys v Chaplin [1971] AC 356 ....2.18, 9.37, 11.02, 11.05,
                                                  11.40, 11.43, 11.45
BP plc v AON Ltd [2005] EWHC 2554 (Comm).................... 9.32
BP plc Derivative Litigation, Re 507 F Supp 2d 302 (SDNY 2007) 5.47
Brannigan v Davison [1997] AC 238 ....8.42–8.43, 8.46, 8.53, 8.57–8.58
Brear v James Hardie & Co Pty Ltd (2000) 50 NSWLR 388
    (NSWCA)... 9.11
Breavington v Godleman (1988) 169 CLR 41
    (High Ct) 2.14, 6.56, 11.02
Brewer v Dodson Aviation 447 F Supp 2d 1166
    (WD Wash 2006)....................................... 11.68, 11.71

Bridgestone/Firestone Inc, Re 190 F Supp 2d 1125
  (SD Ind 2002). 4.50
Brill v Korpaach Estate (1997) 200 AR 161 . . . . 9.06
Brinkerhoff Maritime Drilling Corp v PT Airfast
  Services Indonesia [1992] 2 SLR 776 (Sing CA) 2.35, 4.49
Bristow v Sequeville (1850) 5 Exch 275 . . . . 7.03
Britannia Steamship Insurance Association v Ausonia
  Assicurazioni SpA [1984] 2 Lloyd's Rep 98 . . . . 7.54
British American Tobacco (Investments) Ltd v
  United States [2004] EWCA Civ 1064 . . . . 8.24
British American Tobacco Services Ltd v Eubanks (2004)
  60 NSWLR 483 . . . . 8.14
Britton v O'Callaghan (2002) 62 OR (3d) 95 (Ont CA) 11.11
Brown v Thornton (1837) 6 Ad and El 185 . . . . 7.03, 7.12
Brunei LNG Sendirian Berhad v Interbeton BV [1996]
  BNHC 32 . . . . 11.04
Buckby v Lloyd Aviation Jet Charter Ltd (1992)
  58 SASR 269. . . . . 11.38
Bulmer Aircraft Services Ltd v Bulmer 2005 NBQB 396 . . . . 9.36
Bumper Development Corporation v Commissioner of the
  Police of the Metropolis [1991] 1 WLR 1362 (CA) 5.01, 5.08
Bundesgerichtshof [1984] ECLY 74 . . . . 6.38
Bundesgerichtshof 29 June 1989 [1990] ECLY 160. . . . . 7.15
Bundesverfassungsgericht 1994 [1997] IL Pr 325. . . . . 4.12
Bundesverfassungsgericht 2007 [2008] ECLY 99 . . . . 4.12
Bundesverfassungsgericht 2007 [2010] ECLY 151 . . . . 4.12
Bushkin Associates v Raytheon Co 473 NE 2d 662
  (Sup Jud Ct Mass 1985). 7.27
Butler v Stagecoach Group plc 72 AD 3d 1581
  (SCNY App Div 2010) 11.68
Byers v Higgen (1993) 80 BCLR (2d) 386 (BCSC) 11.51
Byrnes v Groote Eylandt Mining Co Pty Ltd (1990)
  19 NSWLR 13 (NSWCA). 9.01

Caltex Refineries (Qld) Pty Ltd v Stavar [2008] NSWSC 223. . . . . 7.48
Calvert v Estate of Calvert 259 SW 3d 456 (CA Ark 2007) 6.34
Campeau v Campeau 2004 Can LII 42942 (ONSC). 4.33
Canada Trust Co v Stolzenberg *The Times*, 10 November
  1997 (Ch D) 8.40, 8.43
Canadian Acceptance Corporation v Matte (1957)
  9 DLR (2d) 304 (Sask CA) 10.32
Canales Martinez v Dow Chemical Co 219 F Supp 2d 719
  (ED La 2002) 4.50

Table of Cases

Cardile v LED Builders Pty Ltd (1999) 198 CLR 380. . . . . 10.13
Carl Zeiss Stiftung v Rayner and Keeler Ltd (No 2) [1967]
   1 AC 853. . . . . .7.37–7.39
Carslake v Gadens Lawyers [2006] SASC 9 . . . . 9.16
Caspian Construction Inc v Drake Surveys Ltd (2004)
   184 Man R (2d) 284. . . . . .9.06, 9.41
Casterbridge Properties, Re [2002] BPIR 428 (Ch D). 8.43
Castillo v Castillo [2005] 3 SCR 870. . . . . .9.40–9.41
Chaff and Hay Acquisition Committee v JA Hemphill &
   Sons Pty Ltd (1947) 74 CLR 375 . . . . 5.01
Chagos Islanders v The Attorney-General [2003] EWHC
   2222 (QB) (affd [2004] EWCA Civ 997) 9.21
Chan Mei Yiu Paddy v Secretary for Justice (No 2) [2008]
   HKCFI 337. . . . . 8.14
Channar Mining Pty Ltd v CMIEC [2003] WASC 253 . . . . 4.29
Charm Maritime Inc v Kyriakou [1987] 1 Lloyd's Rep 433 . . . . 7.43
Chase Manhattan Bank NA v Israel-British Bank
   (London) Ltd [1981] Ch 105 . . . . .2.05, 3.03, 3.06,
                                                                            10.21–10.22, 11.31
Chin v Chrysler LLC 538 F 3d 272 (3rd Cir 2008). 6.33
Chomos v Economical Mutual Insurance Co (2002)
   216 DLR (4th) 356 . . . . .3.05, 11.15
Chrysler Financial Canada v Morris 2009 SKQB 510 . . . . 10.34
Circosta v Lilly (1967) 61 DLR (2d) 12 (Ont CA) 8.23
City of Gotha v Sotherby's *The Times*,
   8 October 1998 (QBD) 9.21–9.22
City of Harper Woods Employees Retirement System v
   Olver 589 F 3d 1292 (DC Cir 2009). 5.47
Claim by a Polish Producer of Zinc and Copper Products,
   Re [1998] IL Pr 727 (Oberlandesgericht Cologne
   9 September 1996) 4.54
Clayton v Burnett 522 SE 2d 785 (CANC 1999). 5.14
Club Méditerranée NZ v Wendell [1989] 1 NZLR 216 (CA) 2.35
Clyde & Co v Sovrybflot [1998] CLY 586 QBD,
   16 February 1998 . . . . 4.18
CMIA Partners Equity Ltd v O'Neill 29 Misc 3d 1228A
   (Sup Ct NY 2010) 5.45
Cobham Hire Services Ltd v Eeles [2009] EWCA Civ 204 . . . . 11.28
Coburn v The Auxiliary Insurance Fund for Covering Liability
   Arising from Car Accidents [2008] IL Pr 9 (Areios Pagos
   17 November 2006) 6.32
Cochran Consulting Inc v Uwatec USA Inc 102 F 3d 1224
   (Fed Cir 1996) 8.55

Cohn, Re [1945] Ch 5 . . . . 3.02–3.03, 3.06, 7.18, 7.48
Collavino Inc v Yemen (Tihama Development Authority)
  (2007) 9 WWR 290 . . . . .5.50–5.51
Colorado, The [1923] P 102 (CA) 6.62–6.63, 6.65, 6.68
Comaplex Resources International Ltd v Schaffhauser
  Kantonalbank (1991) 84 DLR (4th) 343 (Ont CJ). 8.50
Comexter Inc v Westminster County (Official Administrator)
  BCCA, 17 July 1987 . . . . 8.50
Commercial Money Center Inc, Re 627 F Supp 2d 786
  (ND Ohio 2009). 10.20
Commonwealth v Cryer 689 NE 2d 808 (Mass 1998) 7.11
Commonwealth v Miller 15 Mass L Rptr 11 (Mass
  Superior Court 2002) 7.10–7.11
Commonwealth v Sanchez 716 A 2d 1221 (Pa 1998). 7.10
Compagnie Francaise d'Assurance v Phillips Petroleum
  Co 105 FRD 16 (SDNY 1984). 8.55
Compagnie Noga d'Importation v Russian Federation
  361 F 3d 676 (2nd Cir 2004). 5.54
Computerized Radiological Services Inc v Syntex Corp 595
  F Supp 1495 (EDNY 1984). 7.33
Compuware Corp v Moody's Investors Services Inc 222
  FRD 124 (ED Mich 2004) 8.32
Conagra International Fertiliser Co v Lief Investments Pty
  Ltd [1997] NSWSC 511. . . . . 4.47
Connecticut Retirement Plans and Trust Funds v Buchan 2007
  ONCA 462 . . . . 8.13
Connolly Data Sys Inc v Victor Technologies Inc 114 FRD 89
  (SD Cal 1987). 8.29
Connolly v RTZ Corp plc (No 3) [1999] CLC 533 . . . . 9.22
Consolidated Oil and Gas Inc v Suncor Inc (1993)
  140 AR 188. . . . . 7.41
Consul Corfitzon, The [1917] AC 550 . . . . .8.41–8.42
Cook v Parcel BCSC, 11 July 1996 (affd (1997) 143 DLR (4th)
  213 (BCCA)) 8.28
Cooley v Ramsey [2008] EWHC 129 (QB) 11.50
Cooper-Standard Automotive Canada Ltd 2009
  ONSC 51188 . . . . 10.21
Cope v Doherty (1858) 4 K & J 367 . . . . 11.22
Corporacion Salvadorena de Calzado SA v Injection Footwear
  Corp 533 F Supp 290 (SD Fla 1982) 4.38
Cortes v Yorkton Securities Inc (2007) 278 DLR (4th) 740 . . . . 6.83
Coupland v Arabian Gulf Petroleum Co [1983] 1 WLR 1136 . . . . 11.10
Coutts & Co v Ford 1997 1 ZLR 440 (Harare High Court). 9.09–9.10

Coutu v Gauthier (Estate) (2006) 264 DLR (4th) 391 (NBCA)......... 4.44
Crafton v Union Pacific Railroad Co 585 NW 2d 115
 (Neb Ct App 1998).. 7.03
Craig v Allstate Insurance Co of Canada (2002) 59 OR
 (3d) 590 .... 11.26
Credit Suisse Fides Trust SA v Cuoghi [1998] QB
 818 (CA)................................... 8.04, 8.57, 8.64, 10.13
Crown Resources Corp SA v National Iranian Oil Co (2006)
 273 DLR (4th) 65 (Ont CA)................................. 4.55
Cruickshank v Mid-Continent Casualty Co 355 BR 391
 (D Mass Bank 2006)....................................... 5.31
CSR Ltd v Cigna Insurance Australia Ltd (1997) 189 CLR 345....... 4.63
CSX Transportation Inc v Howell 675 SE 2d 306 (CA Ga 2009)...... 7.46
Cuba Railroad Co v Crosby 222 US 473 (1912) 3.29

Dachser v Waco [2000] NSWSC 1049 .... 5.13
Dahya v Second Judicial District Court of the State of
 Nevada 19 P 3d 239 (SC Nev 2001) 4.14
D'Almeida Aranjo Ida v Sir Frederick Becker &
 Co Ltd [1953] 2 KB 329 .... 11.16
Damberg v Damberg (2001) 52 NSWLR 492 .... 3.29
Danklef v Wilmington 429 A 2d 509 (Super Ct Del 1981) 8.32
Darcy v Medtel Ltd (No 3) [2004] FCA 807 .... 9.06
Davidson v State 25 SW 3d 183 (Tex Crim App 2000) 7.10
Davis v Turning Properties Pty Ltd (2005) 222 ALR 676
 (NSW Sup Ct).. 8.04
Dawson v Broughton (2007) 151 Sol Jo 1167 (Manchester
 County Court)............................. 7.16, 7.21, 11.12, 11.41
DC Utrecht, 30 August 1978 (affd CA Amsterdam 13 May
 1982) 1983 NIPR 204 .... 7.15
De Gortari v Smithwick [1999] IESC 51 .... 6.20–6.21
De James v Magnificence Carriers Inc 654 F 2d 280
 (3rd Cir 1981).. 4.09
De La Mata v American Life Ins Co 771 F Supp 1375
 (D Del 1991)... 4.38
De La Vega v Vianna (1830) 1 B & Ad 284 ....2.12, 6.78
De Loach v Alfred 960 P 2d 628 (Sup Ct Ariz 1998) 9.46
De Santis v Wackenhut Corp 732 SW 2d 29 (CA Tex 1987) 7.19
Decision of the Oberlandesgericht, Frankfurt of
 21 February 1991 .... 4.02
Decision XaZR 19/08 (German Bundesgerichtshof, 9 July 2009).... 11.01
Dee-K Ent Inc v Heveafil Sdn Bhd 174 FRD 376
 (ED Va 1997) 4.35–4.36

DEF and the Protected Estates Act 1983, Re (2005) 192 FLR 92....... 2.33
Dehsabzi v John Fairfax Publications Pty Ltd (No 2) [2008]
    NSWDC 77 .... 6.14
Delaire v Delaire (1996) 147 Sask R 161 (SCQB) 6.79
Dempsey v Staples 2011 ONSC 1709.............................. 9.36
Deripaska v Cherney [2009] EWCA Civ 849 .... 4.43
Dernick Resources Inc v Wilstein 2007 WL 2688900
    (D Neb 2007)... 6.33
Devon Canada Corp v PE-Pitsfield LLC (2008) 303
    DLR (4th) 460, 2008 ABCA 393 .... 5.03
Diamond Waterproofing Systems Inc v 55 Liberty
    Owners Corp 826 NE 2d 802 (NY 2005) 9.48
Didisheim v London and Westminster Bank [1900] 2 Ch 15.....5.06, 5.26
Diehl v Ogorewac 836 F Supp 88 (EDNY 1993).................... 7.04
Discover Bank v Superior Court 134 Cal App 4th 886
    (CA Cal 2005) 5.28
Dixon v Royal Insurance Australia Ltd (1991) 105
    ACTR 1 (SC ACT).. 6.47
Dobson v Festi, Rasini & Co [1891] 2 QB 92 (CA).................. 4.03
Doczi v Zurich Forsikring [1992] ECLY 2398..................... 11.30
Doe v Canada (2001) 204 DLR (4th) 80 (Alta CA) 5.01
Doetsch, Re [1896] 2 Ch 836 .... 5.31
Dofasco Inc v Ucar Carbon Canada Inc (1998) 27 CPC (4th) 342...... 4.33
Dombrovski v Sirius International Ins Corp 2007 WL
    2624804 (ND Oh) 6.39
Don v Lippmann (1837) 5 Cl & Fin 1............................. 2.05
Donohue v Armco Inc [2002] 1 All ER 749 (HL) 4.57, 4.63
Dornoch Ltd v Westminster International BV [2009]
    EWHC 1782 (Adm) 7.53, 7.55
Douglas v Hello! Ltd (No 3) [2006] QB 125 ....3.26, 10.20
Drews v Insurance Corp of British Columbia (1998)
    55 BCLR (3d) 281 .... 5.20
DS Langdale Two LLC v Daisytek (Canada) Inc
    (2004) 6 CPC (6th) 363..................................... 6.78
Dubai Bank v Abbas Commercial Court, 15 October 1997 .... 9.22
Duncan, Re, Garfield v Fay [1968] 2 All ER 395.................... 8.36
Durham v T & N Noble plc CA, 1 May 1996..................9.22, 9.37
Dynasty Apparel Industries Inc v Rentz 2007
    WL 641825 (SD Ohio)..................................... 10.20
Dynasty Line Ltd v Sukamto SIA [2009] HKCA 197................ 4.43
Dyno Wesfarmers Ltd v Knuckey [2003]
    NSWCA 375 ....5.25, 6.04, 9.05, 9.31

Table of Cases

889457 Alberta Inc v Katanga Mining Ltd [2008]
   EWHC 2679 (Comm) 4.46
East Asia Satellite Television (Holdings) Ltd v
   New Cotai LLC [2010] HKCFI 615 .... 5.40
Ebbage v Manthey [2001] QSC 4 (SC Qld) 5.42
Eby v York-Division 455 NE 2d 623 (CA Ind 1983) 7.54
ED Miller Sales & Rentals Ltd v Caterpillar Tractor Co
   (1988) 22 CPR (3d) 290 (Alta CA) 8.50
Edmunds v Simmonds [2001] 1 WLR 1003 (QBD) 11.27, 11.41–11.42
Education Resources Institute Inc v Orndorff
   (Circ Ct Virginia 18 December 2008) 2.58
Edwards v Aetna Life and Casualty 690 F 2d 595 (6th Cir 1982) 7.46
Eisai Ltd v Dr Reddy's Laboratories Inc 406 F Supp 2d 341
   (SDNY 2005) 8.29
Elbe Shipping SA v The Ship Global Peace [2006] FCA 954 .... 6.73
Elberta Crate & Box Co v Cox Automation Systems LLC
   2005 WL 1972599 (MD Ga 2005) 6.34
Enforcement of a United States Judgment for Damages,
   Re (Bundesgerichthof Case IX ZR 149/91 4 June 1992)
   [1994] IL Pr 602 .... 6.32
Ennstone Building Products Ltd v Stanger [2002]
   1 WLR 3059 (CA) 9.37
EPlus Technology Inc v Aboud 155 F Supp 2d 692 (ED Va 2001) 4.14
Equitable Life Assurance Society v McKay 760 P 2d 871
   (S Ct Ore 1988) 7.31
Equity Residential Properties Management Corp v Kendall
   Risk Management Inc 246 FRD 557 (ND Ill 2007) 8.31–8.32
Erie Railroad Co v Tompkins 304 US 64 (1938) 2.55
Erinodikeio Limiras 25/2002 [2003] ECLY 729 .... 7.06
Estate of Agioritis, Re 80 Misc 2d 108 (Surr Ct NY 1974) 5.05
Estate of Blanton 824 So 2d 558 (Miss 2002) 5.25
Estate of Gilmore, Re 946 P 2d 1130 (NM App 1997) 5.25
Estate of Louis Riso, Re 48 Va Cir 352 (Circ Ct Va 1999) 5.25
Evans Marshall & Co v Bertola SA [1973] 1 WLR 349 .... 4.55
Everest Canadian Properties Ltd v CIBC World Markets
   Inc 2008 BCCA 276 .... 5.41–5.42
Expedition Helicopters Inc v Honeywell Inc (2010) 100 OR
   (3d) 241 (Ont CA) 4.55
Export-Import Bank of the US v Asia Pulp and Paper Ltd
   2005 WL 1123755 (SDNY) 4.37

FAI Allianz Insurance Ltd v Lang [2004] NSWCA 413 .... 11.32

FAI General Insurance v Ocean Marine Mutual Protection
and Indemnity Association (1997) 41 NSWLR 117 ....4.54–4.55
Fairmont Supply Co v Hooks Industrial Inc 177 SW 3d 529
(Tex App 2005) 6.34
Farmers Exchange Bank v Metro Contracting Services
Inc 107 SW 3d 381 (CA Mo 2003)...................... 6.80
Farquharson v Balfour (1823) Turn & R 184...................... 8.03
Farquharson Pty Ltd v FAI General Insurance Co Ltd
[1998] VSC 106 (SC Vic)..................................... 6.47
FDC Co Ltd v The Chase Manhattan Bank [1990] 1 HKLR 277 ...... 8.60
Feng v GMS Fulfilment Service Ltd (2004) 50 ACSR 527
(SC NSW)... 5.02
Ferguson v Arctic Transportation Ltd (1998) 147 FTR 96............ 9.06
Ferranti Packard Ltd v Cushman Rentals Ltd (1981) 115
DLR (3d) 691 (Ont HCJ) 5.49
Fesco Angara, The [2010] EWCA Civ 1050........................ 6.75
Fiden Electrical Engineering Sdn Bhd v Nippon Seiko KK
[2004] 7 MLJ 231 (High Court)............................... 4.32
Filter Solutions Ltd v Donaldson Australia Pty Ltd
[2006] NZHC 762 .... 7.13
Fiona Trust and Holding Corp v Privalov [2010]
EWHC 3199 (Comm)......................... 7.15, 7.18, 9.26, 10.04
First Laser Ltd v Fujian Enterprises (Holdings) Co
Ltd [2011] HKCA 1..7.41, 7.53
Fitzpatrick v International Railway 169 NE 112 (1929) (NYCA)....... 7.16
Flack v Holm (1820) 1 Jac & W 405 .... 6.78
Fleming v Marshall [2011] NSWCA 86............................. 9.06
Fluor Australia Pty Ltd v ASC Engineering Pty Ltd (2007)
19 VR 458..5.18–5.19
Fondazione Banco di Sicilia v Mauritius Commercial Bank Ltd
(Court of Cassation, 30 September 2005) [2006] ECLY 121 ...... 7.06
Ford v Newman 396 NE 2d 539 (Sup Ct Ill 1979) 7.04
Ford v State Farm Insurance Co 625 So 2d 792 (Miss 1993).......... 5.12
Ford Motor Co v Leggatt 904 SW 2d 643 (Tex 1995)................ 8.32
Foresight Shipping Co v Union of India 2004 FC 1501............... 5.49
Forsyth v Cessna Aircraft Co 520 F 2d 608 (9th Cir 1975)............. 6.05
Fortis Bank (Nederland) NV v MV Shamrock 379 F Supp 2d 2
(D Me 2005).. 6.76
Fortune Hong Kong Trading Ltd v Cosco Feoso (Sing) Pte Ltd
[2000] 2 SLR 717 (Sing CA).................................. 4.06
Foss v Harbottle (1843) 2 Hare 461 (Ch)......................5.35–5.36
Four Embarcadero Center Venture v Mr Greenjeans Corp (1988)
64 OR (2d) 746 (affd (1988) 65 OR (2d) 160 (Ont CA)) 7.41

Table of Cases xxv

Fournier v The Ship Margaret 'Z' [1999] 3 NZLR 111 (HCNZ) 6.63
Freehills Re New Tel Ltd (in liq) (2008) 66 ACSR 311 . . . . 4.28
Frick v Oklahoma 634 P 2d 738 (Okla Crim App 1981) 7.10
Friction Division Products Inc and EI Du Pont de Nemours
 & Co Inc (1986) 56 OR (2d) 722 . . . . 8.14
Frischke v Royal Bank of Canada (1977) 17 OR (2d) 388 . . . . 8.49–8.50
Frodyma v Royal Adelaide Hospital [2006] NSWDDT 11 . . . . 7.48
Fuld's Estate (No 3), Re [1968] P 675 . . . . 2.18, 7.25
Fuller v K & J Trucks [2006] NSWCA 88 . . . . 11.49

G + H Montage GmbH v Irvani [1990] 1 WLR 667 (CA) 7.27
Gaetano and Maria, The (1882) 7 PD 137 (CA) 7.02, 7.18
Galustian v The Skylink Group of Companies 2010 ONSC 292 . . . . . . 4.45
Gambazzi v Daimlerchrysler Canada Inc (Case C-394/07)
 [2009] 1 Lloyd's Rep 647 . . . . 3.18, 8.61
Gao v Zhu [2002] VSC 64 . . . . 8.05
Garb v Republic of Poland 440 F 3d 579 (2nd Cir 2006) 5.54
Garcia v GMC 990 P 2d 1069 (CA Ariz 1999) 7.45
Garpeg Ltd v US 583 F Supp 789 (SDNY 1984) 8.55
Garsec Pty Ltd v His Majesty the Sultan of Brunei (2008)
 250 ALR 682 (NSWCA) 2.37, 3.11, 3.13, 4.66, 4.68–4.70
Gater Assets Ltd v NAK Naftogaz Ukrainy [2008]
 EWHC 1108 (Comm) 11.06
General Steam Navigation Co v Guillou (1843) 11 M & W 877 . . . . 5.31
Genira Trade and Finance Inc v CS First Boston and
 Standard Bank (London) Ltd [2001] EWCA Civ 1733 . . . . 8.13–8.14
George v Gubernowicz (1999) 44 OR (3d) 247 . . . . 11.11
Gerling Global General Insurance Co v Canadian
 Occidental Petroleum Ltd (1998) 230 AR 39;
 1998 ABQB 714 . . . . 5.03, 5.06, 7.41
Ghosn v Principle Focus Pty Ltd & Ors (No 2) [2008]
 VSC 574 . . . . 7.06
Gill v Conamex Trucking System Inc (2001) 16 CPC (5th) 320 . . . . 11.37
Gill v Gill [2000] BCSC 870 . . . . 11.37
Gillars v US 182 F 2d 962 (DC Cir 1950) 8.09
Ginter v Belcher 536 F 3d 439 (5th Cir 2008) 4.59
Giuseppe di Vittorio, The [1998] 1 Lloyd's Rep 136 . . . . 4.61
Global Container Lines Ltd v Bonyad Shipping Co [1999]
 1 Lloyd's Rep 287 (Com Ct) 5.05
Global Partners Fund Ltd v Babcock & Brown Ltd (in liq)
 [2010] NSWSC 270 (affd (2010) 79 ACSR 383; [2010]
 NSWCA 196) 4.55, 4.57
Godin v Godin [2003] WADC 21 . . . . 11.21

Goede v Aerojet General Corp 143 SW 3d 14
  (CA Mo 2004) 11.68, 11.70
Goh Suan Hee v Teo Cher Teck [2009]
  SGCA 52. .... 11.30–11.32, 11.35, 11.51
Goldamere v Metso Minerals [2007] NSWSC 980. .... 11.03
Golden Trade Srl v Lee Apparel Co 143 FRD 514 (SDNY 1992) 8.29
Gonzalez v State 45 SW 3d 101 (Tex Crim App 2001). 8.32
Good Challenger, The [2003] EWHC 10 (Comm) (affd [2004]
  1 Lloyd's Rep 67) 7.39
Good Earth Agricultural Co Ltd v Novus International
  Pte Ltd [2008] SGCA 13. .... 4.49
Gosche v Boucher 2009 ABQB 277. .... 11.03
Gotch v Ramirez (2000) 48 OR (3d) 515 .... 9.36
Gouge v BAX Global Inc 252 F Supp 2d 509 (ND Ohio 2003). 6.05
Gould v State Bank of NSW SC NSW, 28 February 1996. .... 8.06
Grand Entertainment Group Ltd v Star Media Sales
  Inc 988 F 2d 476 (3rd Cir 1993). 4.35
Grand Jury Subpoena, Re 218 F Supp 2d 544 (SDNY 2002). 8.55
Grant v Grant 2003 BCSC 649. .... 4.33
Grant v McAuliffe 264 P 2d 944 (Cal 1953). 5.24
Gredd v Arpad Busson [2003] EWHC 3001 .... 8.14
Greenwood v Hildebrand 515 A 2d 963 (SC Pa 1986). 7.04
Grupo Torras SA v Al-Sabah [1999] CLC 1469. .... 5.34
Guaranty Trust Co of New York v New York 326 US 99 (1945) 2.55

Habib Bank v Central Bank of Sudan [2007] 1 WLR 470 .... 4.19, 4.24
Hal Commodities Cycle Management v Krish (1993)
  17 CPC (3d) 320 (Ont Ct Gen Div). 5.05
Halcyon Isle, The [1981] AC 221 (PC) 6.60, 6.63, 6.66–6.68, 6.70–6.74
Halley, The (1886) LR 2 PC 193 .... 5.22
Hamill v Hamill 24 July 2000. .... 11.41–11.42
Hamilton v Merck and Co Inc (2006) 66
  NSWLR 48. .... 2.55, 3.05, 3.07, 6.12, 6.25–6.30
Hamlyn & Co v Talisker Distillery [1894] AC 202 (HL) 1.04, 4.55–4.56
Hanlan v Sernesky (1998) 38 OR (3d) 479 (Ont CA). 11.37
Harbour Assurance Co (UK) Ltd v Kansa General International
  Insurance Co Ltd [1993] QB 701 (CA). 4.54
Hardie Rubber Co Pty Ltd v The General Tire & Rubber
  Co (1973) 129 CLR 521. .... 8.06
Harding v Wealands [2004] EWHC 1957 (QB); [2005] 1 WLR 1539
  (revd [2007] 2 AC 1 (HL)) 2.01, 2.09, 2.14, 2.36–2.47,
      2.55, 3.03–3.04, 3.06, 3.15, 5.38, 5.42, 6.14, 6.47, 7.16,
          7.21, 11.07, 11.09–11.10, 11.12, 11.15–11.16,
              11.18–11.29, 11.37, 11.42, 11.50, 11.54, 11.63, 12.02

Table of Cases xxvii

Harley v Smith [2010] EWCA Civ 78. .... 9.22
Harper v Delaware Broadcasters Inc 743
    F Supp 1076 (D Del 1990) 7.45
Harper v Harper 600 SE 2d 659 (CA Ga 2004). 7.45
Harris v Quine (1869) LR 4 QB 653 .... 9.02, 9.14
Hartmann v Konig (1933) 50 TLR 114 (HL) 5.09
Harty v Sabre International Security Ltd [2011]
    EWHC 852 (QB) 4.68
Hartz Canada Inc v Colgate-Palmolive Co (1988)
    27 CPC (2d) 152 .... 8.36
Harwood v Priestley (1997) 6 Tas R 383 .... 8.06
Hatfield v Halifax plc 564 F 3d 1177 (9th Cir 2009) 9.48
Hausman v Buckley 299 F 2d 696 (2nd Cir 1962) 5.42, 5.44–5.45
Hearn v Commonwealth [2000] NSWDDT 12. .... 7.48
Heavner v Uniroyal Inc 305 A 2d 412 (NJ 1973) 9.46
Heidberg, The [1993] 2 Lloyd's Rep 324. .... 8.12, 8.42
Hein v Taco Bell Inc 803 P 2d 329 (Wash Ct App 1991) 9.46
Helmsing v Malta Drydocks [1977] 2 Lloyd's Rep 444. .... 11.07
Henderson v Henderson (1843) 3 Hare 100; 67 ER 313 .... 7.42, 7.44–7.45
Henderson v Merrett Syndicates Ltd [1994] 2 AC 145 .... 6.07
Henry v Henry (1995) 185 CLR 571. .... 4.47
Herbert v District of Columbia 808 A 2d 776 (DC 2002). 11.70
Hertz Corp v Piccolo 453 So 2d 12 (SC Fla 1984). 5.12
Heyting v Dupont [1964] 1 WLR 843 .... 5.36, 5.41
HJ Heinz Co Ltd v EFL Inc [2010] EWHC 1203 (Comm). 7.39
Hodgson v Dimbola Pty Ltd [2009] ACTSC 59 .... 6.29
Hoeper v Air Wisconsin Airlines 2009 WL 3764080 (CA Colo). 6.15
Hoerter v Hanover Telegraph Works (1893) 10 TLR 103 .... 4.55
Hof's-Hertogenbosch [2008] LJN BD 3905
    (Dutch Court of Appeal). 9.11
Hoiles v Alioto 461 F 3d 1224 (10th Cir 2006) 6.36
Holiday v Ford Motor Co 2006 WL 178011 (Ohio App Dist). 7.35
Holt Cargo Systems Inc v ABC Container Line NV
    (Trustees of) [2001] 3 SCR 907. .... 6.68
Homawoo v GMF Assurance SA [2010] EWHC 1941 (QB) 11.01, 11.65
Hong Kong Housing Authority v Hsin Yieh Architects
    and Associates Ltd [2005] 2 HKC 201 (HKCFI). 4.31
Hooper v Robinson [2002] QDC 80. .... 6.28
Hornsby v James Fisher Rumic Ltd [2008] EWHC 1944 (QB). 9.38
Horseshoe Club Operating Co v Bath [1998]
    3 WWR 128 (BCSC) 2.30, 6.43, 6.50
HR 24 January 1986 NJ 1987 56 (Dutch Supreme Court). 9.04
Hrynenko v Hrynenko (1997) 37 BCLR (3d) 35 (affd (1998)
    168 DLR (4th) 437 (BCCA)) 9.34

Hubbard v City of Edmonton (1917) 37 DLR 458 (Alta CA) 6.14
Huber v Steiner (1835) 2 Bing NC 202. .... 2.05, 9.02
Hughes Electronics Corp v Citibank Delaware 15 Cal
    Rptr 3d 244 (CA Cal 2004). 9.48
Hulse v Chambers [2001] 1 WLR 2386 .... 11.27–11.28, 11.42
Humble v Gill 2009 WL 151668 (WD Ky). 4.14
Huntington v Attrill [1893] AC 150. .... 3.06, 6.82
Huynh v Chase Manhattan Bank 465 F 3d 992 (9th Cir 2006) 9.46
HWC v The Corp of the Synod of the
    Diocese of Brisbane [2008] QSC 212 .... 9.06

Idoport Pty Ltd v National Australia Bank
    Ltd [2001] NSWSC 838 .... 8.06
Igra v Igra [1951] P 404 .... 6.83
Imperial Oil Ltd v Petromar Inc 2001 FCA 391 .... 6.69
Imperial Park Country Club Properties Ltd v Audencia
    Provincial de Alicante (Constitutional Court First
    Division 162/2002, 16 September 2002) 4.10
In the Goods of Schulhof [1948] P 66. .... 7.20
In the Marriage of Wilton and Jarvis (1996) 133 FLR 355. .... 2.33
Independent Petrochemical v Aetna Cas and Sur
    Co 117 FRD 292 (DDC 1987). 8.32
Inglis v Commonwealth Trading Bank of Australia
    (1972) 20 FLR 30 (ACTSC). 9.01
Instituto Nacional de Commercializacion Agricola
    (Indeca) v Continental Illinois National Bank and
    Trust Co 858 F 2d 1264 (7th Cir 1988). 7.45
Intel Corp v Advanced Micro Devices Inc 542 US 241 (2004) 8.16
Intercontinental Planning Ltd v Daystrom Inc 248
    NE 2d 576 (NYCA 1969) 7.30
International Association of Science and Technology for
    Development v Hamza (1995) 122 DLR (4th) 92 (Alta CA) 5.01
Investors Group Trust Co Ltd v Capital City Savings and
    Credit Union Ltd (1991) 118 AR 254 (Alta QB) 2.30, 4.68, 6.51
Ioannis Daskalelis, The [1974] SCR 1248 (Sup Ct Can). 6.63, 6.68
Iowa v Eldrenkamp 541 NW 2d 877 (Iowa 1995) 8.31–8.32
Isabelle Lancray SA v Pieters und Sickert KG [1991] IL Pr 99. .... 4.26
Ishikazi Kisen Co v US 510 F 2d 875 (9th Cir 1975) 7.19
Ismail bin Sukardi v Kamal bin Ikhwan [2008] SGHC 191 .... 11.51
ITC Global Holdings Pte Ltd (in liq) v ITC Ltd [2011]
    SGHC 150 .... 4.32, 4.43

J Barber & Sons v Lloyds Underwriters [1987] QB 103 .... 8.13

Table of Cases xxix

Jackson v Chandler 61 P 3d 17 (Az 2003) 9.46
Jacobs v Motor Insurers Bureau [2010] EWHC 231 (QB)
    (revd [2010] EWCA Civ 1208; [2011] 1 All ER 844) 11.01, 11.63,
                                                              11.66–11.67
James Hardie & Co Pty Ltd v Barry (2000) 50 NSWLR 357 .... 7.48
James Hardie & Co Pty Ltd v Hall (1998)
    43 NSWLR 554 .... 6.25, 11.15
Janred Properties Ltd v Ente Nazionale Italiano per Il
    Turismo [1989] 2 All ER 444 .... 7.52
Jarguh Sawit, The [1997] SGCA 59. .... 4.49, 4.60
Jenton Overseas Investment Pte Ltd v Townsing (2008)
    21 VR 241 (Sup Ct Vic). 3.18
Jet Holdings Inc v Patel [1990] 1 QB 335. .... 6.83
John Pfeiffer Pty Ltd v Rogerson (2000) 203 CLR 503. .... 2.01, 2.08,
              2.21, 2.24–2.25, 2.28, 2.31, 2.36–2.38, 2.41–2.45,
              2.48, 3.03, 3.07, 4.42, 4.66, 6.01–6.03, 6.13, 6.18,
              6.25, 6.73, 6.78, 7.27, 7.48, 9.05–9.06, 9.44, 10.01,
              11.20–11.21, 11.23, 11.25, 11.31–11.32, 11.46, 11.49
Johnson v Continental Airlines Corp 964 F 2d 1059
    (10th Cir 1992) 11.72
Johnson v Helicopter and Airplane Services Corp 404
    F Supp 726 (D Md 1975) 5.02
Johnson Matthey & Wallace Ltd v Ahmed Alloush (1984)
    135 NLJ 1012 (CA) 5.32
Jones v Assurances Generales de France (AGF) SA
    [2010] IL Pr 4. .... 5.12
Jones v Dunkel (1959) 101 CLR 298 (Aust H Ct) 7.22
Jones v Prince George's County 835 A 2d 632 (CA Md 2003) 5.16
Jones v Trollope Colls Cementation Overseas Ltd *The Times*,
    26 January 1990 (CA). 9.22
Jones v Winnebago Industries Inc 460 F Supp 2d 953
    (ND Iowa 2006). 11.70
Joss v Snowball (1969) 72 SR (NSW) 218 .... 5.22
Joyce v Sunland Waterfront (BVI) Ltd (2011) 281 ALR 54 .... 8.08
J-Squared Technologies Inc v Motorola Inc 364 F
    Supp 2d 449 (D Del 2005) 7.54
Judgment of Milan Court of Appeal, 24 November 2010 .... 8.61
Judgment upon case concerning judgment of a foreign court as
    provided in Article 24 of the Law on Civil Enforcement and
    the judgment of Hong Kong High Court ordering the payment
    of court costs [1998] JPSC 24 (28 April 1998) 6.32
Julia Farr Services Inc v Hayes [2003] NSWCA 37 .... 2.26, 6.17, 6.19
Jupiters Ltd v Lim Kin Tong [2005] MLJU 534. .... 6.44

Kammerer v Western Gear Corp 618 P 2d 1330
 (CA Wash 1980) 11.68
Kamouth v Associated Electrical Industries International
 Ltd [1980] 1 QB 199 .... 5.26
Kansas v Hartford Accident and Indemnity Co 426 SW 2d 720
 (Mo KC Ct App 1968) 6.03
Kantonsgerichtpräsident, Zug (19 April 1990) [1992]
 ECLY 4330 .... 10.12
Kapitan Temkin, The [1998] SGHC 427 .... 4.60, 7.04
Karam v Australia and New Zealand Banking Group Ltd
 (2000) 34 ACSR 545 .... 5.42
Kase v Salomon Smith Barney Inc 218 FRD 149
 (SD Tex 2003) 10.20
Kaupthing Singer and Friedlander Ltd (in Administration),
 Re [2010] EWCA Civ 518 .... 10.31
Kelly v Selwyn [1905] 2 Ch 117 .... 6.64
Kelner Pilatus Center v Charest 2007 ONSC 20782 .... 9.36
Kennedy v Anderson (1991) 50 DLR 105 (Sask CA) 7.31
Kennedy v Wallace (2004) 213 ALR 108 (Fed Ct) 8.23, 8.36
Kensington International Ltd v Republic of the Congo
 [2005] EWHC 2684 (Comm) 5.52
Kent Trade and Finance Inc v JP Morgan Chase Bank
 [2008] FCA 399 .... 6.68–6.69
Keybank National Association v The Ship 'Blaze' [2009]
 2 NZLR 271 .... 6.71
Khalij Commercial Bank Ltd v Woods (1985) 17 DLR (4th)
 358 (Ontario High Court) 10.03
Kilberg v Northeast Airlines Inc [1961] 2 Lloyd's Rep 406
 (NYCA) 5.25
Kim v Co-operative Centrale Raiffeisen-Boerenleenbank BA
 364 F Supp 2d 346 (SDNY 2005) 7.45
Kim v Hayes Lemmerz International Inc 2007 WL 1566713
 (CA Cal) 6.34
Kingsway General Insurance Co v Canada Life Insurance
 Co (2001) 149 OAC 303 .... 5.20
Knauf UK GmbH v British Gypsum [2002] 1 WLR 907 .... 4.21
Knight v Axa Assurances [2009] EWHC 1900 (QB) 11.03
Knorr-Bremse Systems for Commercial Vehicles Ltd v
 Haldex Brake Products GmbH [2008] EWHC 156 (Pat) 4.55
Ko Lai Kuen v Li Tak Ming [2011] HKCFI 304 .... 4.55
Kohnke v Karger [1951] 2 KB 670 .... 11.27
Kok v Sheppard [2009] NSWSC 1262 .... 3.07, 6.29
Komarek v Ramco Energy plc [2002] All ER (D) 314 (Nov) 4.65–4.66

Komninos S, The [1990] 1 Lloyd's Rep 541 (revd [1991]
    1 Lloyd's Rep 370) 9.20, 9.22
Konamaneni v Rolls Royce Industrial Power (India)
    Ltd [2002] 1 WLR 1269 (Ch) 5.37–5.38, 5.41–5.44
Korner v Witkowitzer [1950] 2 KB 128 .... 7.12–7.14
Kos v State 15 SW 3d 633 (CA Tex 2000)......................... 8.32
Kraut AG v Albany Fabrics Ltd [1977] QB 192 .... 6.77
Kuhn & Kogan Chtd v Jeffrey C Mensh & Assocs Inc 77 F
    Supp 2d 52 (DDC 1999)...................................... 8.32
Kuhne & Nagel AG Zurich v APA Distributors (Pty) Ltd 1981
    3 SA 536 (High Court of Witwatersrand) 9.08, 9.10
Kuwait Airways Corp v Iraqi Airways Co (Nos 4 and 5)
    [2002] 2 AC 883................................. 3.18, 4.69, 9.21
Kuwait Oil Tanker Co SAK v Al Bader *The Independent*,
    11 January 1999... 11.04

Labuda v Langford [2001] ACTSC 108........................... 11.32
Labuda v Langford [2001] ACTSC 126 .... 6.31, 11.03
Lacey v Cessna Aircraft Co 862 F 3d 38 (3rd Cir 1988) 4.50
Laconian Enterprises Ltd v Agromar Lineas Ltd 1986
    3 SA 509 (Durban High Court)......................... 9.08–9.10
Landsman & Funk PC v Skinder-Strauss Associates 636
    F Supp 2d 359 (DNJ 2009)................................... 5.29
Lashburn AG Ventures Ltd v Western Grain Cleaning &
    Processing Ltd (2003) 241 Sask R 97 .... 10.29
Latreefers Inc v Hobson [2002] EWHC 1696 (Ch)................. 9.32
Laurens v von Hohne 1993 2 SA 104 (High Court
    of Witwatersrand) 9.08, 9.10
Laxton v Coglon (2006) 61 BCLR (4th) 127 (BCSC) 8.50
Laxton v Jurem Anstalt 2011 BCCA 212 .... 4.44
Lazard Bros & Co v Midland Bank Ltd [1933] AC 289.............. 5.02
Le Meilleur v Trehout (Court of Cassation 1e Ch Civ,
    23 January 2001) [2002] ECLY 1188 .... 7.06
Lego v Stratos Lightwave 224 FRD 576 (SDNY 2004)............... 8.29
Lehndorff Property Management Ltd v McGrath [1984]
    3 WWR 187 (BCSC) 7.28
Lemme v Wine of Japan Import Inc 631 F Supp 456
    (EDNY 1986)... 4.14
Lemons v Cloer 206 SW 3d 60 (CA Tenn 2006) 11.70
Leroux v Brown (1852) 12
    CB 801 .... 3.03, 3.06, 6.41, 7.26–7.27, 7.29–7.30
Lesecq v Ottawa Montessori School (2008) 89
    OR (3d) 62 (Ont SCJ) 6.37

Lesotho Highlands Development Authority v Impregilo
   SpA [2002] EWHC 2435 (Comm).......................... 11.07
Letendre v SYSCO Food Service of Atlantic Canada 2008
   NSSC 105 (Sup Ct Nova Scotia)............................ 6.37
Lewincamp v ACP Magazines Ltd [2008] ACTSC 69.............. 11.13
Li Yuen Ling v Tang Kwong Wai Thomas [2009] HKCFI 1164 .... 7.06
Lifetime Investments Pty Ltd v Commercial (Worldwide)
   Financial Services Pty Ltd [2006] FCA 696................... 8.58
Lilydale Cooperative Ltd v Meyn Canada Inc (2007) 84 OR
   (3d) 621 (affd 2008 ONCA 126)............................. 9.36
Limited Stores Inc v Pan America World Airways Inc 600
   NE 2d 1027 (Sup Ct Ohio 1992) 7.54
Linde v Arab Bank plc 463 F Supp 2d 310 (EDNY 2006) 8.55
Liverpool Marine Credit Co v Hunter (1868) LR 3 Ch App 479..... 10.04
Livesley v Horst [1924] SCR 605 (Sup Ct Can) 11.02, 11.07, 11.16
Livingston v Baxter Health Corp 313 SW 3d 717
   (Mo App 2010) 11.68
Locals 302 and 612 of the International Union of Operating
   Engineers v Blanchard 2005 WL 2063852 (SDNY).............. 6.54
Loewen Group Inc, The v United States ICSID Case
   No ARB (AF)/98/3 (26 June 2003) 6.13
Lou v Lotis Elevator 933 NE 2d 140 (Mass App Ct 2010)........... 11.72
Loucks v Standard Oil Co of New York 224 NY 99 (1918).......3.17, 9.21
Loutchansky v Times Newspapers Ltd (Nos 2 to 5)
   [2002] QB 783 .... 7.02
Lowland Yachts BV v Firma Dahm International GmbH (District
   Court of the Hague) (23 February 1989) [1991] IL Pr 350....... 10.12
Lucas v Coupal [1931] 1 DLR 391 .... 5.10
Lucas v Gagnon (1994) 120 DLR (4th) 289........................ 11.15
Lyons v Bell Asbestos Mines Ltd 119 FRD 384 (DSC 1988) 8.55

Ma v Continental Bank NA 905 F 2d 1073 (7th Cir 1990) 4.38
MacFarlane v Norris (1862) 2 B & S 783......................... 10.26
McGowan v Summit at Lloyds [2002] SC 638 .... 4.55
McGrath v National Indemnity Co [2004] NSWSC 391 .... 4.28
McGregor v Potts (2005) 68 NSWLR 109 .... 11.32
McGuid v Office de Commercialisation et d'Exportation [1999]
   NSWSC 931... 4.55
McIntyre v Eastern Prosperity Investments Pte Ltd (No 6)
   (2005) 218 ALR 401 (Fed Ct)................................ 5.02
McKain v RW Miller & Co (South Australia) Pty
   Ltd (1991) 174 CLR 1 .... 2.08–2.09, 2.11, 2.19–2.20, 2.22,
                              2.34, 2.36, 2.41, 2.43, 2.48, 9.02

Table of Cases xxxiii

MacKinnon v Donaldson, Luffkin Jenrette Securities
  Corporation [1986] Ch 482 .... 8.03, 8.05, 8.42
MacMillan v Bishopsgate Investment Trust plc (No 3)
  [1996] 1 WLR 387 .... 3.03, 3.06
McMillan v Canadian Northern Railway Co [1923] AC 120 .... 11.14
McNeilly v Imbree [2007] NSWCA 156..................... 11.21, 11.38
Maddison v Alderson (1883) 8 AC 467 .... 7.27
Mahadervan v Mahadervan [1964] P 233..................... 7.20, 7.48
Maharanee of Baroda v Wildenstein [1972] 2 QB 283 (CA).......... 4.01
Maher v Groupama Grand Est [2009] EWHC 38 (QB)
  (affd [2010] 1 WLR 1564)............... 3.03, 11.01, 11.03, 11.05, 11.08
Major v Commonwealth 275 SW 3d 706 (SC Ky 2009).............. 8.32
Makassar Caraka Jaya Niaga III-39, The [2011] 1 SLR 982
  (Sing HC)... 4.60
Maldonado, Re [1953] 2 All ER 300.............................. 3.06
Maltas v Maltas 197 F Supp 2d 409 (D Md 2002) 7.31
Marie v Garrison 13 Abb N Cas 210 (NY 1883).................... 7.29
Marillo v Benjamin Moore & Co 32 AD 3d 1313 (NYAD 2006)...... 11.70
Marine Midland Bank v Surfbelt Inc 532 F Supp 728
  (WD Pa 1982) 6.80
Marks v Alfa Group 615 F Supp 2d 375 (ED Pa 2009) 4.36
Marlex Petroleum Inc v The Har Rai [1984] 2 FC 345
  (affd [1987] 1 SCR 57)....................................... 6.68
Martin v Kelly (1995) 22 MVR 115 (Sup Ct Vic)................... 3.07
Martyn v Graham [2003] QDC 447 (Dist Ct Queensland).......... 6.77
Mason v Lynch 878 A 2d 588 (CA Md 2005)...................... 7.04
Mason v Murray's Charter Coaches and Travel Services
  Pty Ltd (1998) 88 FCR 308................................... 9.16
Maspons v Mildred, Goyeneche & Co (1882) 9 QBD 530 (CA)...... 10.26
Masri v Consolidated Contractors International Company SAL
  [2008] EWHC 2492 (Comm); [2011] EWHC 1024 (Comm)....... 8.44
Mastondrea v Occidental Hotels Management SA 918 A 2d 27
  (NJ Super Ct App Div 2007)................................. 11.71
Mathers v Bruce 2002 BCSC 210 .... 4.33
Maurice Bidermann Zylberberg v RHI Holdings Inc [1996]
  IL Pr 189 (Paris Court of Appeal 9 March 1995) 6.80
Maxwell v Murphy (1957) 96 CLR 261 .... 2.55
Mayoral-Amy v NHI Corp 180 FRD 456 (SD Fla 1998) 4.35
Mazzella v Philadelphia Newspapers Inc 479 F Supp 523
  (EDNY 1979).. 8.32
Melbourn, ex parte (1870) LR 6 Ch App 64 .... 3.23, 6.62
Melville v American Home Assurance Co 584 F 2d 1306
  (3rd Cir 1978) 7.20

Menendez v Perishable Distributors Inc 329 SE 2d 149
(SC Ga 1985) 7.13
Meredith v Missouri Pacific Railroad 467 SW 2d 79
(Mo Sup Ct 1971) 6.15
Merkle v Robinson 737 So 2d 540 (Fla 1999) 9.46
Merwin Pastoral Co Pty Ltd v Moolpa Pastoral Co Pty
Ltd (1933) 48 CLR 565 .... 9.06
Metaxas v Ship Galaxias (No 2) (1988) 19 FTR 108 .... 6.68
Metaxas v Ship Galaxias (No 5) (1990) 35 FTR 40
(Fed Ct Can) 11.33
Meyer v Dresser (1864) 16 CB (NS) 646 .... 10.25, 10.29
Meyer v Paschal 498 SE 2d 635 (SC 1998) 9.47
Michael Wilson and Partners Ltd v Nicholls (2008) 74
NSWLR 218 .... 8.23, 8.40, 8.47
Michalski v Olson (1997) 123 Man R (2d) 101 .... 9.06, 9.23
Mid East Trading Ltd, Re; Lehman Bros Inc v Phillips
[1998] 1 All ER 577 (CA) 8.05, 8.43
Middle Eastern Oil LLC v National Bank of Abu Dhabi
[2008] EWHC 2895 (Comm) 4.55
Middleton v Caterpillar Industrial Inc 979 So 2d 53
(SC Ala 2007) 7.46
Midland International Trade Services v Sudairy
Financial Times, 2 May 1990 .... 11.04
Midwest Grain Products of Illinois Inc v Productization
Inc 228 F 3d 784 (7th Cir 2000) 6.33
Midwest Medical Supply Co LLC v Wingert 317 SW 3d 530
(Tex App 2010) 6.34
Miliangos v George Frank Textiles Ltd [1976] AC 443 .... 6.77
Miliangos v George Frank Textiles Ltd (No 2) [1977]
QB 489 .... 11.03, 11.07
Miller Farm Equipment (2005) Inc v Shewchuk (2009)
335 Sask R 111 (Sask Ct QB) 7.27
Minera Aquiline Argentina SA v IMA Exploration Inc 2006
BCSC 1102 (affd 2007 BCCA 319) 10.21
Ming Lai Siu Fun v Tsang Hung Kong [2010] HKCFI 381 .... 5.40
Minnesota Mining & Manufacturing Co v Rennicks
(UK) Ltd (No 1) [1991] FSR 97 (Ch D) 8.36
Minpeco SA v Conticommodity Services Inc 116
FRD 517 (SDNY 1987) 8.55
Mitzel v Westinghouse Electric Corp 72 F 3d 414
(3rd Cir 1995) 6.33, 6.36
ML Ubase Holdings Co Ltd v Trigem Computer Inc [2005]
NSWSC 224 .... 4.28

Modern Computer Systems Inc v Modern Banking Systems
   Inc 871 F 2d 734 (8th Cir 1989). 10.08
Monokandilos v Générale des Carriers et des Mines SA
   [2010] ZAGPPHC 184 (Pretoria High Court). 9.08, 9.10
Monteiro v Toronto Dominion Bank 2006 Can Lll 124 (ONSCDC)
   (affd (2008) 89 OR (3d) 565) 7.41
Monterosso Shipping Co Ltd v International Transport
   Workers Federation [1982] 2 Lloyd's Rep 120 . . . . 7.27
Morales v Ford Motor Co 313 F Supp 2d 672 (SD Tex 2004) 4.50
Morgan Stanley & Co International Ltd v Pilot Lead
   Investments Ltd [2006] HKCFI 497 . . . . 6.82
Morlines Maritime Agency Ltd v The Proceeds of Sale of
   the Ship 'Skulptor Vuchetich' [1997] FCA 432 . . . . 6.73
Morris v Banque Arabe et Internationale d'Investissement
   SA [2001] IL Pr 37 (Com Ct) 8.44
Morris v Baron & Co [1918] AC 1 (HL). 7.27
Motorola Credit Corp v Uzan (No 2) [2004] 1 WLR 113 (CA). 8.04
Mount Albert Borough Council v Australasian Temperance and
   General Mutual Life Assurance Society [1938] AC 224 (PC). . . . 11.03
M/S Bremen & Unterweser Reederel GmbH v Zapata
   Offshore Co 407 US 1 (Sup Ct 1972) 4.59
Mudd v Goldblatt Bros Inc 454 NE 2d 754 (App Ct Ill 1983) 7.16
Mueller v Hubbard Milling Co 573 F 2d 1029 (8th Cir 1978) 7.13
Murakami v Wiryadi (2010) 268 ALR 377; [2010]
   NSWCA 7 . . . . 3.26, 10.20–10.21
Muscutt v Courcelles (2002) 60 OR (3d) 20
   (Ont CA) 4.43–4.44, 4.48, 6.48, 6.51

Nalpantidis v Stark (1996) 65 SASR 454 (Full Court Sup Ct SA) 3.07
Nasser v United Bank of Kuwait [2002] 1 WLR 1868 (CA) 6.37
National Commercial Bank v Wimborne [1978] 5
   BPR 11,958. . . . . .3.23, 3.26
Naughton v Bankier 691 A 2d 712 (Ct Spec App Md 1997) 6.15
Nazym Khikmet, The [1996] 2 Lloyd's Rep 362 (CA). 4.61
NCC Sunday Inserts Inc v World Color Press Inc 759 F
   Supp 1004 (SDNY 1991) 7.54
Neilson v Overseas Projects Corp of Victoria Ltd (2005)
   223 CLR 331. . . . . 2.27, 3.09–3.14, 3.25, 3.28, 3.30, 4.70, 6.06,
                              6.55, 6.57, 7.17, 9.15, 9.28, 9.42, 11.32, 11.46
Nemaha Energy Inc v Wood and Locker Inc (1985)
   68 BCLR 187 (BCSC) 6.48
Nicholls v Michael Wilson and Partners Ltd (2010)
   243 FLR 177 (NSWCA) 7.41

Nierman v Hyatt Corp 808 NE 2d 290 (Sup Jud Ct Mass 2004) 9.46
Nieuwersteeg v Colonia Versicherungs AG [1997] ECLY 732
  (Hohe Raad 1996)... 4.10
NIFSMBC-V200651 Investment Ltd Partnership v Gainday
  Investments Ltd [2009] HKCFI 17........................... 5.06
Nikolay Malakhov Shipping Co Ltd v Seas Sapfor Ltd (1998)
  44 NSWLR 371 (NSWCA).............................. 6.04, 9.31
Nokia Corporation v Interdigital Technology Corporation
  [2004] EWHC 2920 (Pat) 8.18
Nominal Defendant, The v Bagot's Executor and Trustee
  Co Ltd [1971] SASR 346 (revd (1971) 125 CLR 179) 5.18
Nord Resources Corporation v Nord Pacific Ltd (2003)
  263 NBR (2d) 205 (NBQB)................................... 6.54
Norfolk Southern Railway Co v Trinity Industries Inc 2009
  WL 856340 (ND Tex) 7.52
Norton v Florence Land and Public Works Co (1877) 7 Ch D 332 .... 6.64
Nouvion v Freeman (1889) 15 App Cas 1................ 6.82, 7.38, 8.64

Oates v Consolidated Capital Services Ltd [2008] NSWSC
  464 (affd (2009) 76 NSWLR 69).............................. 5.43
Obégi Chemicals LLC v Kilani 2011 ONSC 1636................... 8.04
Obergericht Thurgau [2001] ECLY 1315......................... 11.30
Oberlandesgericht Brandenburg (31 May 2000) [2001] ECLY 464 .... 5.04
Oberlandesgericht Düsseldorf 1992 [1992] ECLY 4831 .... 4.12
Oberlandesgericht Düsseldorf 1996 [1998] ECLY 1030.............. 4.12
Oberlandesgericht Düsseldorf 1999 [2002] IL Pr 7 .... 4.27
Oberlandesgericht Frankfurt (23 June 1999) [2001] ECLY 890....... 5.04
Oberlandesgericht Frankfurt 2002 [2003] ECLY 878 .... 4.27
Oberlandesgericht Hamm (16 October 2000) [2002]
  ECLY 1191 .... 6.32
Oberlandesgericht Karlsruhe 1999 [2001] IL Pr 17 .... 4.27
Oberlandesgericht Koblenz [1998] ECLY 1003.................... 6.38
O'Brien v Tanning Research Laboratories Inc (1988) 84
  ALR 221 (NSWCA) 7.43
Oceanic Sunline Special Shipping Co v Fay (1988)
  165 CLR 197...3.06, 11.51
O'Driscoll v J Ray McDermott SA [2006] WASCA 25
  (Western Australian Court of Appeal) 3.12–3.13, 9.06–9.07, 9.28
Odishelidze and Employee Benefits Associates Inc v Agora
  Inc 1996 WL 655787 (D Puerto Rico)........................ 10.20
Office des Poursuites et des Faillites de Nyon (OPF) v
  Dumartheray [2007] IL Pr 29 (French Court of Cassation
  First Civil Chamber, 30 October 2006) 6.80

Table of Cases

Oil Shipping (Bunkering) BV v Sonmez Denizcilik ve
   Ticaret AS 10 F 3d 1015 (3rd Cir 1993) 6.76
Oilworld Supply Co v Audas BCSC, 23 May 1985 .... 8.23
Olafsson v Gissurarson [2006] EWHC 3162 (QB) 4.06
Olafsson v Gissurarson [2008] 1 WLR 2016 .... 4.23–4.24, 4.29
O'Leary v Illinois Terminal Railroad Co 299 SW
   2d 873 (Sup Ct Mo 1957) 7.16
Ollanescu v Culacov (Court of Cassation 1e Ch Civ D,
   5 January 1999) [1999] ECLY 1195 .... 7.06
Omega Group Holdings Ltd v Kozeny [2002] CLC 132 .... 8.17
Orbusneich Medical Co Ltd v Boston Scientific Corp 694
   F Supp 2d 106 (D Mass 2010) 2.58
Otal Investments Ltd v M/V Clary Mineral Shipping
   Co 494 F 3d 40 (2nd Cir 2007) 7.19
Oteng v Golden Star Resources Ltd 615 F Supp 2d 1228
   (D Colo 2009) 5.45
Owens Bank Ltd v Bracco [1992] 2 AC 443 (HL) 6.83
Owens-Corning Fiberglas Corp v Martin 942 SW 2d 712
   (Ct App Tex 1997) 6.15
Owners of Eleftheotria v Despina R [1979] AC 685 .... 6.77
Owners of Sailing Ship 'Fortunato Figari' v Steamship
   'Coogee' (1904) 29 VLR 874 (Sup Ct Vic) 7.02, 7.19
Owusu v Jackson [2005] QB 801 .... 4.53, 11.51
Oxnard Financing SA v Rahn [1998] 1 WLR 1465 (CA) 5.06
OZ-US Film Productions Pty Ltd (in liq) v Heath
   [2000] NSWSC 967 .... 3.23

Pacific Assets Management Ltd v Chen Lip Keong [2005]
   SGHC 228 .... 4.32
Pacific Electric Wire & Cable Co Ltd v Texan Management
   Ltd [2007] HKCU 1298 (HKCA) 4.31
Pacific International Sports Club Ltd v Soccer Marketing
   International Ltd [2009] EWHC 1839 (Ch) 7.43
Pacific Petroleum Corp v Nauru Phosphate Corp [2002]
   QSC 389 .... 4.48
PAE Govt Services Inc v MPRI Inc 514 F 3d 856 (9th Cir 2007) 7.54
Painewebber Inc v Ras 767 F Supp 930 (ND Ill 1991) 7.45
Pan Pacific Specialities v Shandong Machinery and
   Equipment I/E Corp 1999 BCSC 5755 .... 4.33
Paramasivam v Flynn (1998) 90 FCR 489 .... 3.23
Pardo v Bingham (1868) LR 6 Eq 485 .... 6.61
Park v Citibank Savings Ltd (1993) 31 NSWLR 219 .... 8.06
Parker v TUI UK Ltd [2009] EWCA Civ 1261 .... 3.28

Paulownia Plantations de Panama Corp v Rajamannan 793
    NW 2d 128 (SC Minn 2009)................................... 4.50
Paulson v Shapiro 490 F 2d 1 (7th Cir 1973) 7.27
Pavacic v Estate of Nicely (2008) 91 OR (3d) 49................... 4.45
Pawlus v Banque Nationale de Paris (Canada) (2001)
    277 AR 80 (CA).. 9.06
PCH Offshore Pty Ltd v Dunn (No 2) (2010) 273 ALR 167 .... 7.43
Peat's Trusts, Re (1869) LR 7 Eq 302 .... 9.01
Pederson v Young (1964) 110 CLR 162 .... 9.01
Penny (Litigation Guardian of) v Bouch (2009) 310 DLR
    (4th) 433 (NSCA).. 11.51
People v Allen 336 Ill App 3d 457 (CA Ill 2003)................8.31–8.32
People v Burge 443 SW 2d 720 (Tex Crim App 1969) 7.10
People v Flores 28 Misc 3d 1213A (SCNY 2010) 7.10
People v Orlosky 40 Cal App 3d 935 (CA Cal 1974)................. 7.11
People v Ostas 179 AD 2d 893 (SCNY 1992) 7.10
People v Saiken 275 NE 2d 381 (Ill 1971) 7.10
Pepsico Inc v Baird, Kurtz and Dobson LLP 206 FRD 646
    (ED Mo 2002) 8.29
Pera Tourism Inc v Savile Row Tours and Travel Ltd
    [1998] IL Pr 407 (Central London County Court) 6.38
Peregrine Fixed Income Ltd v JP Morgan Chase Bank [2005]
    HKCFI 71..6.31, 9.07
Pergamon Press Ltd v Maxwell [1970] 1 WLR 1167 .... 5.37
Petroleo Brasiliero SA v Mellitus Shipping Inc [2001]
    EWCA Civ 418 .... 4.46
Phillips v Audio Active Ltd 494 F 3d 378 (2nd Cir 2007)............. 4.59
Phillips v Eyre (1870) LR 6 QB 1 .... 2.08, 3.16, 3.23, 3.25, 11.14
Phillips v Phillips 285 SE 2d 52 (CA Ga 1981) 6.80
Phillips v Symes (No 3) [2008] 1 WLR 180 (HL) 4.22–4.24, 4.29, 4.32
Phrantzes v Argenti [1960] 2 QB 19....... 10.01, 10.03, 10.05, 10.09, 10.20
Pinnacle Communications International Inc v American Family
    Mortgage Corp 417 F Supp 2d 1073 (D Minn 2006) 10.20
Piper Aircraft v Reyno 454 US 235 (1981)......................... 4.50
Plamondon v Aviva Canada Inc 2008 ONSC 61240 .... 11.15
Plozza v South Australian Insurance Co Ltd [1963] SASR 122....... 5.12
Pocket Kings v Safenames Ltd [2009] EWHC 2529 (Ch) 4.25
Poh Soon Kiat v Desert Palace Inc [2009] SGCA 60 .... 6.82
Polensky v Continental Casualty Co 397 F Supp
    2d 1164 (DND 2005)....................................... 5.12
Pordea v Times Newspapers Ltd [2000] IL Pr 763 (Court of
    Cassation 16 March 1999).................................. 6.32
Port of Melbourne Authority v Anshun Pty Ltd (1981)
    147 CLR 589.. 7.42

Powell Duffryn plc v Petereit [1992] ECR I-1745. 4.56
PPG Industries Inc v Central Industrial Maintenance
   Inc 2006 WL 752982 (WD Pa) 7.19
Precourt v Driscoll 157 A 525 (NH 1931) 7.16
Prediwave Corporation v New World TMT Ltd [2006]
   HKCA 391 . . . . 8.14
Preferential Trade Area Bank v ESCOM
   (High Court of Malawi 2003) 6.31
Prekons Insaat Sanayi AS v Rowlands Castle Contracting
   Group Ltd [2006] EWHC 1367 (Comm) 10.26
PreWitt Enterprises Inc v OPEC 353 F 3d 916 (11th Cir 2003). 4.35, 4.37
Province of Alberta Treasury Branches v Granoff (1984)
   15 DLR (4th) 295 (BCCA) 2.55
Prudential Assurance Co Ltd v Prudential Insurance
   Co of America [2003] EWCA Civ 1154 . . . . 8.25
PT Garuda Indonesia Ltd v Australian Competition and
   Consumer Commission [2011] FCAFC 52;
   (2011) 277 ALR 67. . . . . 5.53
Pulido v RS Distributions Pty Ltd [2003] ACTSC 61 . . . . 9.16
Puttick v Tenon Ltd (2008) 238 CLR 265. . . . . 2.35, 4.51, 11.51

R v Harrer (1995) 128 DLR (4th) 98. . . . . 7.09
R v Newall (No 1) (1982) 67 CCC (2d) 431 (BCSC) 7.09
R v Thomas (2005) 199 CCC (3d) 188 . . . . 7.09
Rahim v Crawther (1996) 25 MVR 190 (Full Court Sup Ct WA). 3.07
Rainbow Line Inc v MV Tequila 480 F 2d 1024 (2nd Cir 1973) 6.76
Randall v Arabian American Oil Co 778 F 2d 1146 (5th Cir 1998) 6.52
Randwick Labor Club v Amalgamated Television
   Services Pty Ltd [2000] NSWSC 906 . . . . 11.32
Rasmussen v Eltrax Systems Pty Ltd [2006]
   NSWIR Comm 225. . . . . 4.28
Rawat v Navistar International Corp 2010 WL 1417840 (ND Ill) 8.32
Reach v Pearson 860 F Supp 141 (SDNY 1994) 11.70
Recyclers of Australia Pty Ltd v Hettinga Equipment Inc
   (2000) 100 FCR 420 (Fed Ct Aust) 4.55
Reefer Creole, The [1994] 1 Lloyd's Rep 584 . . . . 4.09
Reeves v Sprecher [2007] EWHC 117 (Ch) 4.46
Regie Nationale des Usines Renault v Zhang (2002) 210
   CLR 491 . . . . 2.35, 2.37, 2.43, 3.28, 4.47, 11.21, 11.32, 11.46, 11.51
Reichsgericht 4 January 1882 RGZ 7 . . . . 9.03
Reinsurance Co of America Inc v Administratia Asigurarilor
   de Stat 902 F 2d 1275 (7th Cir 1990) 8.55
Remington Products Inc v N Am Philips Corp 107 FRD 642
   (D Conn 1984). 8.55

Table of Cases

Renfield Corp v E Remy Martin & Co SA 98 FRD 442
(D Del 1983)... 8.62
Republic of India v Indian Steamship Co Ltd (No 2)
[1998] 1 AC 878.. 7.53
Resource Ventures Inc v Resources Management
International Inc 42 F Supp 2d 423 (D Del 1999)............... 4.36
Rice v Dow Chemical Co 875 P 2d 1213 (Wash 1994)............... 9.46
Rich v Kis-California Inc 121 FRD 254 (MDNC 1988).............. 8.55
Richard Crookes Constructions (Qld) Pty Ltd v Wendell
[1990] 1 Qd R 392... 4.28
Rickshaw Investments Ltd v Nicolai Baron von
Uexkull [2006] SGHC 70 (revd [2006] SGCA 39;
[2007] 1 SLR 377 (Sing CA))................. 3.26, 4.49, 4.55, 10.20
Rimini Ltd v Manning Management and Marketing Pty Ltd
[2003] 3 NZLR 22 (High Ct).................................... 6.53
Rimkus Consulting Group Inc v Cammarata
255 FRD 417 (SD Tex 2008)..................................... 10.08
Rimpacific Navigation Inc v Daehan Shipbuilding Co
Ltd [2009] EWHC 2941 (Comm)................................... 7.54
Ringfree USA Corp v Ringfree Co Ltd 2008 WL 4691046
(CD Cal).. 10.20
Rio Properties v Rio International Interlink 284 F 3d
1007 (9th Cir 2002)... 4.37
Rio Tinto Zinc Corp v Westinghouse [1978] AC 547....... 8.13–8.14, 8.62
RLS Associates Inc v United Bank of Kuwait plc 464 F
Supp 2d 206 (SDNY 2006)....................................... 6.34
Roberta, The (1937) 58 Lloyd's Rep 159.......................... 7.15
Roberts v Home Insurance Indemnity Co 48 Cal App 3d
313 (CA Cal 1975)... 5.12
Rockwell v Raytheon Corp 2006 WL 305411 (CA Mich 2006)......... 6.08
Roerig v Valiant Trawlers Ltd [2002] 1 WLR
2304 (CA)........................... 3.22, 11.09–11.11, 11.44, 11.56
Rogers v Markel Corp [2004] EWHC 1375 (QB).................... 11.07
Ross v Ross [2010] NZCA 447..................................... 3.18
Rothwells Ltd (in liq) v Connell (1993) 119
ALR 538 (Qld CA)... 7.05–7.06
Rowe v Hoffmann-La Roche Inc 892 A 2d 694
(NJ Superior Court 2006)...................................... 7.19
Roy v North American Leisure Group Inc (2004) 73 OR (3d) 561.... 9.37
Royal Bank of Scotland v Hicks [2011] EWHC 287................. 8.18
Royal Bank of Scotland plc v GBS Gold International
Inc [2009] FCA 1596... 4.28
Royal Trust Co v Kritzwiser [1924] 3 DLR 596 (Sask CA).......... 6.78

Table of Cases

Ruwenzori Enterprises v Waji 2004 BCSC 741 (affd (2006)
274 DLR (4th) 696)..................................... 9.39

S & R Davis v Yemen 218 F 3d 1292 (11th Cir 2000)............... 5.54
SA General Textiles v Sun & Sand Ltd [1978] 1 QB 279............ 11.02
Sabell v Liberty Mutual Ins Co (1973) 38 DLR (3d) 113 (BCSC)...... 5.12
Saint Anne's Development Coy LLC v Trabich 2009
WL 324054 (D Md)....................................... 8.32
Saleba v Schrand 300 SW 3d 177 (SC Ky 2009).................. 8.32
Salt and Light Development Inc v Sjtu Sunway Software
Industry Ltd 2006 HKCFI 384 .... 8.23, 8.57
Salminen v Emerald Taxi Ltd OSCJ 14 October 1999 .... 11.11
Samarni v Williams [1980] 2 NSWLR 389 (NSW Sup Ct)........... 4.01
Samina North America Inc v H3 Environmental LLC 2004
Can LII 65382 (ONSC).................................. 4.33
Samra v Shaheen Business & Investment Group Inc 355 F
Supp 2d 483 (DDC 2005)................................ 7.27
Samson v Holden [1963] SCR 373 .... 5.10
Sanderson v Halstead [1968] 1 OR 749 (Ont HCJ) 5.10
Sandria Saqui v Pride International 2007 WL 528193 (SD Tex)....... 4.50
Scarel Pty v City Loan and Credit Corp Ltd (No 2)
(1988) 17 FCR 344...................................... 5.42
Schmidt v Won [1998] 3 VR 435............................. 4.47
Schnabel v Yung Lui [2002] NSWSC 15 (SC NSW)............ 6.82, 7.38
Schreiber v Mulroney (2007) 88 OR (3d) 605 .... 9.36
Schwartz v Twin City Fire Insurance Co 492 F
Supp 2d 308 (SDNY 2007)................................ 11.72
Scott v Seymour (1862) 1 H & C 219 .... 5.34
Scotts Co v Hacienda Loma Linda 2 So 3d 1013 (CA Fla 2008)....... 4.50
Seaworld Parks and Entertainment LLC v Marineland of
Canada Inc 2011 ONSC 4084 .... 7.13
SEC v Anticevic 2009 WL 361739 (SDNY) 4.37
SecretHotels2Ltd v EA Traveller Ltd [2010] EWHC 1023 (Ch) 10.29
Servicios Comerciales Andinos SA v GE del Caribe 145
F 3d 463 (1st Cir 1998).................................... 6.34
Shaik Sahied v Sockalingam Chettiar [1933] AC 342 (PC)........... 2.09
Shanghai Electric Group Co Ltd v PT Merak Energi
Indonesia [2010] SGHC 2 .... 10.09–10.10, 10.17
Shaps v Provident Life & Accident Insurance Company 826
So 2d 250 (SC Fla 2002) 7.16
Sheludko v Sheludko [1972] VR 82............................ 3.29
Shiblaq v Sadikoglu [2004] EWHC 1890
(Comm) 4.13, 4.20–4.21, 4.23–4.24

Ship 'Mercury Bell', The v Amosin (1986) 27 DLR (4th) 641 .... 3.29
Ship Nordems, The [2010] FC 332 (affd [2011] FCA 73) 6.68–6.69
Siegel v Novak 920 So 2d 89 (CA Fla 2006) 5.14
Sigurdson v Farrow (1981) 121 DLR (3d) 183 (Alta Ct QB) 10.32
Sim Snowboards Inc v Kelly 863 F 2d 643 (9th Cir 1988) 10.11
Sinochem International Oil (London) Co Ltd v Mobil Sales
 and Supply Corp [2000] 1 Lloyd's Rep 670 .... 4.55
Sky One, The [1988] 1 Lloyd's Rep 238 (CA) 4.18, 4.22, 4.29, 4.31, 4.33
SMBD-Jewish General Hospital v Kummermann 2004
 QCCS 13776. .... 5.26
Smith v Strongbuilt Inc 393 F Supp 2d 1254 (WD Okla 2005)........ 5.12
Smithco Engineering Inc v International Fabricators Inc
 775 P 2d 1011 (Sup Ct Wyo 1989). 6.33
Smither v Asset Acceptance LLC 919 NE 2d 1153 (CA Ind 2010) 9.48
Société Française Hoechst v Allied Colloids Ltd [1991]
 RPC 245 (Pat Ct). 8.36
Société Internationale pour Participations Industrielles et
 Commerciales SA v Rogers 357 US 197 (1958). 8.52, 8.55
Société National Industrielle Aerospatiale v US District Court
 for the Southern District of Iowa 482 US 522 (1987) 8.12
Société Nationale de Recouvrement v Y [2003] ECLY 724
 (Court of Cassation, First Civil Chamber, 3 June 2003) 9.04
Société Vandel v Sociétés ZF France and ZF Passau GmbH (Court
 of Cassation 1e Ch Civ, 4 July 2007) [2008] ECLY 52. .... 7.34
Society of Lloyds v Price 2006 5 SA 393 .... 9.08–9.10
Society of Lloyds v Romahn 2006 4 SA 23 (Cape High
 Court). 9.09–9.10
Society of Lloyds v X (French Court of Cassation,
 22 October 2008) [2009] IL Pr 12. .... 6.08
Sodeca NA v NE Investments [2002] EWHC 1700 .... 8.25
Somers v Fournier (2002) 60 OR (3d) 225
 (Ont CA) 2.28, 6.31, 11.03, 11.24–11.25, 11.33, 11.37
South Carolina Insurance Co v Assurantie Maatschappij de
 Zeven Provincien NV [1987] AC 24. .... 8.16–8.17
Southeastern Health Care Inc v Payton Health Care Facilities
 Inc 1988 WL 71209 (ND Ill). 7.13
Southern New England Telephone Co v Zrihen 2007 QCCS 1391 .... 8.60
Spencer v The Queen (1983) 145 DLR (3d) 344 (affd [1985]
 2 SCR 278) 8.49–8.50
Spiliada Maritime Corp v Cansulex Ltd [1987]
 AC 460 .... 2.08, 2.35, 4.46, 4.49, 9.35, 11.50
Spink & Son Ltd v General Atlantic Corp Ltd 167 Misc 2d 120
 (NYSC 1996) 7.27, 7.30

Standard Reserve Holdings Ltd v Downey 2004 WL 3316264
    (Md Cir Ct) 6.37
Stangvik v Shiley Inc 819 P 2d 14 (SC Cal 1991) 4.50
Star City Pty Ltd v Tan Hong Woon [2002] 2 SLR 22 .... 6.44
State v Bridges 925 P 2d 357 (Hawaii 1996) 7.10
State v Briggs 756 A 2d 731 (RI 2000) 7.10
State v Heaney 689 NW 2d 168 (Sup Ct Minn 2004)............ 8.31–8.32
State v Lipham 910 A 2d 388 (Sup Jud Ct Me 2006) 8.32
State v Lynch 969 P 2d 920 (Mont 1998) 7.10
Stavar v Caltex Refineries (NSW) Pty Ltd [2008]
    NSWDDT 22 .... 7.48–7.49
Stemcor (A/Asia) Pty Ltd v Oceanwave Line SA [2004]
    FCA 391 .... 8.05
Stephens v National Distillers and Chemical Corp 1993
    WL 228851 (SDNY) 6.39
Sterling Financial Management LP v UBS Paine and
    Webber 336 Ill App 3d 442 (2002)...................... 8.31–8.32
Stern v Dill 442 NW 2d 322 (Minn 1989) 9.43
Stern v National Australia Bank [1999] FCA 1421............ 3.18, 6.83
Stevens v Head (1993) 176 CLR 433 .... 2.37, 3.06, 11.20,
                                                      11.24–11.26, 11.28
Stewart v Honey [1972] 2 SASR 585 .... 5.18
Stewart v Stewart (1997) 30 BCLR (3d) 233 (BCCA)........... 9.06, 9.16
Stoeterau v Crowsnest Air Ltd (1995) 5 BCLR (3d) 251 (BCSC) 6.51
Strandhill, The [1926] SCR 680................................... 6.68
Strauss v Credit Lyonnais SA 242 FRD 199 (EDNY 2007) 8.55
Stricklin v Soued 936 P 2d 398 (CA Ore 1997) 10.33
Sturge v Naatra Rotterdam BV [1993] ECLY 601
    (RB Rotterdam)... 4.09
Subbotovsky v Waung (1968) 72 SR (NSW) 242 (NSWCA)...... 5.33, 9.02
Sun Oil Co v Wortman 486 US 717 (1988)................... 2.55, 9.45
Super Tire Engineering Co v Bandag Inc 562 F Supp 439
    (ED Pa 1983) 8.29
Sweedman v Transport Accident Commission (2006) 226 CLR 362... 5.18

243930 Alberta Ltd v Wickham (1990) 75 OR (2d) 289 .... 10.33
T & N Ltd, Re [2005] EWHC 2990 (Ch)................. 6.14, 11.29, 11.58
Talacko v Talacko [1999] VSC 81 .... 7.41, 7.43
Talacko v Talacko [2009] VSC 349 .... 10.13
Tavoulareas v Tsavliris [2007] 1 WLR 1573 .... 4.27
Taylor v LSI Logic Corporation 715 A 2d 837 (SC Del 1998) 5.45, 6.54
Teleglobe Communications Corp, Re 392 BR 561
    (Bank D Del 2008)..................................... 8.31–8.32

Telesis Technologies Inc v Sure Controls Systems
 Inc 2010 ONSC 5288.............................. 2.11, 4.54, 10.10
Texaco Inc v Pennzoil Co 784 F 2d 1133 (2nd Cir 1986).............. 6.80
Thompson v Evanoss [2000] ACTSC 73 .... 11.32
Thompson v Hill (1995) 38 NSWLR 714......................... 3.07
Thor Shipping A/S v The Ship 'Al Dulhail' [2008]
 FCA 1842... 4.61
Thorburn v Steward (1871) LR 3 PC 478 (PC) 6.62
Through Transport Mutual Insurance Association (Eurasia)
 Ltd v New India Assurance Association Company Ltd
 [2004] EWCA Civ 1598; [2005] 1 Lloyd's Rep 67 .... 3.03
Thwaites v Aviva Assurances [2010] IL Pr 47 .... 5.12
Tietloff v Lift-A-Loft Corp 441 NE 2d 986 (CA Ind 1982)............. 7.16
Tipperary Developments Pty Ltd v The State of Western
 Australia (2009) 38 WAR 488 ....7.27–7.28
Tisand Pty Ltd v The Owners of the Ship MV Cape Moreton
 (ex Freya) (2005) 143 FCR 43................................ 4.61
TMR Energy Ltd v State Property Fund of Ukraine (2003)
 244 FTR 1 (revd (2005) 250 DLR (4th) 10) 5.50–5.51
To Group Co Ltd Xiamen King v Eton Properties
 Ltd [2010] HKCFI 236 .... 10.21
Tolofson v Jensen (1994) 120 DLR (4th) 289 (Supreme Court
 of Canada)....................... 2.08, 2.28–2.29, 2.48, 3.25, 8.23,
 9.05–9.06, 9.23, 9.34, 9.36–9.37,
 9.39–9.43, 11.24, 11.45
Toronto-Dominion Bank v Martin (1985) 39
 Sask R 60 (Sask QB) 2.30, 2.55, 6.50–6.51, 6.58
Tournier v National Provincial and Union Bank
 of England [1924] 1 KB 461.................................. 8.60
Townsend v Sears, Roebuck & Co 858 NE 2d 552
 (Ill App Ct 2006).. 11.71
Trade Development Bank v Continental Insurance
 Co 469 F 2d 35 (2nd Cir 1972)................................ 8.55
Trans Grupo Vialle Iberica (Société) v X [2011] ECLY 29
 (French Court of Cassation, 12 July 2010)..................... 9.11
Transaero Inc v La Fuerza Aera Boliviana 30 F
 3d 148 (DC Cir 1994) 5.54
Travelers Casualty and Surety Co v Insurance Co of
 North America 609 F 3d 143 (3rd Cir 2010).................... 11.72
Travelers Casualty and Surety Co of Europe Ltd v Sun
 Life Assurance Co of Canada (UK) Ltd [2004]
 EWHC 1704 (Comm)...................................... 11.02
Treat America Ltd v Nestlé Canada Inc 2011 ONSC 617 .... 8.14

Trent Partners and Associates Inc v Digital Equipment
    Corp 120 F Supp 2d 84 (D Mass 1999)........................ 7.54
Treuhand und Rechtspraxis Ulrich Diener-Hafner AG v
    Fuchsl [1992] ECLY 4351 (Cass Luxembourg 1991).............. 4.09
Tripodi v Local Union No 38, Sheet Metal Workers International
    Association 120 F Supp 2d 318 (SDNY 2000).................. 6.10
Trumpet Vine Investments NV v Union Capital Partners
    Inc 92 F 3d 1110 (11th Cir 1996)................................ 7.27
Turner v Grovit [2005] 1 AC 101 .... 4.53

Union Discount Co Ltd v Zoller [2002] 1 All ER 693 (CA)............ 6.31
United States of America v One Silicon Valley Bank Account
    549 F Supp 2d 940 (WD Mich 2008)........................... 10.21
United States Surgical Co v Hospital Products International
    Pty Ltd [1982] 2 NSWLR 766 .... 3.23
University of Calgary v Colorado School of Mines (1995)
    179 AR 81... 5.49
Uranium Antitrust Litigation, Re 480 F Supp 1138 (ND Ill 1979)..... 8.55
US v Balsys 524 US 666 (1998) 8.59
US v Chase Manhattan Bank 584 F Supp 1080 (SDNY 1984).......... 8.55
US v Davis 767 F 2d 1025 (2nd Cir 1985) 8.55
US v First National City Bank 396 F 2d 897 (2nd Cir 1968).......... 8.55
US v First National City Bank of Chicago 699 F 2d 341
    (7th Cir 1983) 8.55

Valois of America v Risdon Corp 183 FRD 344 (D Conn 1997)........ 8.55
Van Breda v Village Resorts Ltd (2010) 98 OR (3d) 721 .... 4.44
Van Opdorp v Compagnie Belge d'Assurance Credit
    [1991] IL Pr 316 (CA Luxembourg) 4.09
Vanier v Ponsoldt 833 P 2d 949 (SC Kan 1992) 6.15
Vaughn v LJ International Inc 174 Cal App 4th 213
    (Cal Ct App 2009)... 5.45
Vervaeke v Smith [1983] 1 AC 145................................. 7.39
Vest v St Albans Psychiatric Hospital Inc 387
    SE 2d 282 (W Va 1989).................................6.23, 11.49
Victorian Workcover Authority v Orientstar Shipping
    Corp [2003] VSC 311 .... 4.28
Viktor Overseas Ltd Deuilemar Compagnia di
    Navigazione SpA 1997 FC 6298 .... 11.07
Villet v Bosch [2006] WADC 8 .... 11.32
Virgtel Ltd v Zabusky [2006] 2 Qd R 81 (SC Qld) 5.42
Vital State Canada Ltd v Dreampak LLC 303 F
    Supp 2d 516 (DNJ 2003) 10.08

Vitamins Antitrust Litigation, Re 120 F Supp 2d 45
  (DDC 2000) 8.10, 8.12
Vitol SA v Capri Marine Ltd (No 2) [2010] EWHC 458 (Comm)...... 6.78
Vivendi Universal SA Securities Litigation, Re 242 FRD 76
  (SDNY 2007) 2.14, 4.52
Vivendi Universal SA Securities Litigation, Re 618 F
  Supp 2d 335 (SDNY 2009)....................................... 8.55
VLT Corp v Unitrode Corp 194 FRD 8 (D Mass 2000) 8.29
Vogler v Szendroi (2008) 290 DLR (4th) 642 .... 6.03, 9.17
Volksbank Schwabisch Gmund eG v Werner Qld CA,
  1 September 1999 .... 8.25
Volkswagenwerk Aktiengesellschaft v Schlunk 486
  US 694 (US Sup Ct 1988)......................... 4.09–4.10, 4.34
Von Hellfeld v Rechnitzer [1914] 1 Ch 748 (CA).................... 5.01
Vorhees v Fischer and Krecke GmbH 697 F 2d 574
  (4th Cir 1983) 4.09
Vostok Shipping Co Ltd v Confederation Ltd [2000]
  1 NZLR 37 (NZCA) 4.61
Voth v Manildra Flour Mills Pty Ltd (1990) 171 CLR 538 .... 2.35, 4.43
Voyage Co Industries Inc v Craster 1998 BCSC 1776 .... 6.54

Waddington Ltd v Chan Chun Hoo Thomas [2008]
  HKCFA 63 .... 5.40, 6.47
Wakim, Re; ex parte McNally (1999) 198 CLR 511 .... 2.33
Walker v Newmont Australia Ltd [2010] FCA 298 .... 8.05
Wall v Toll Transport Pty Ltd [2010] VSC 522 .... 9.16
Wallaby Grip Ltd v Gilchrist [2007] NSWSC 1181 .... 6.17, 11.28
Waller v Max Resources Ltd (in liq) HCNZ, 21 June 2004........... 8.57
Walpole v Canadian Northern Railway Co [1923] AC 113 .... 11.14
Walters v Rockwell International Corp 559 F Supp 47
  (ED Va 1983) 5.25
Ward Associates Ltd v Public Services Mutual Insurance
  Co EWHC, 5 December 2000 .... 4.46
Warner Brothers Pictures Inc v Nelson [1937] 1 KB 209............ 10.04
Warren v Warren [1972] Qd R 386 (Sup Ct Qld) 5.23
Washburn v Soper 319 F 3d 338 (8th Cir 2003) 9.46
Washington v Brown 940 P 2d 546 (Wash 1997) 7.10
Washington v Donahue 18 P 3d 608 (Wash CA 2001).......... 8.31–8.32
Waterhouse v Australian Broadcasting Corporation (1990)
  A Def R 50-070 .... 6.14
Wayfarer Holidays Ltd v Hoteles Barcelo (1993) 12 OR (3d) 208 ..... 6.79
Wayte v Wayte [2005] WADC 192 (Dist Ct WA) 6.56

Wear v Farmers and Merchants Bank of Las Cruces 605
   P 2d 27 (SC Alaska 1980) 10.27
Weber v US Sterling Securities 924 A 2d 816 (Sup Ct Conn 2007) 5.29
Weiss v National Westminster Bank 242 FRD 33 (EDNY 2007) 8.55
Weitz Company LLC v Travellers Cas & Suty Co 266 F
   Supp 2d 984 (SD Iowa 2003) 9.46
West Tankers Inc v Ras Riunione Adriatica Di Sicurta
   SpA [2005] EWHC 454 (Comm) 5.20
Wheeler v SDS Ausminco Ltd [2001] VSC 261 .... 6.09
Wicken v Wicken [1999] 2 WLR 1166 (Fam D) 7.05–7.06
Wiedemann v Walpole [1891] 2 QB 534 (CA) 7.03
Williams v Lips-Heerlen BV SC NSW, 1 November 1991 .... 4.28
Williamson Pounders Architects PC v Tunica County 597
   F 3d 292 (5th Cir 2010) 7.30
Wimpey Construction (UK) Ltd v Martin Black & Co
   (Wire Ropes) Ltd [1988] SLT 637 .... 6.31
Windsurf Holdings Pty Ltd v Leonard [2009] NSWCA 6 .... 6.08
Wong v Lee (2002) 58 OR (3d) 398 (Ont CA) 9.06, 11.15, 11.37
Wong v Wei (1999) 65 BCLR (3d) 222 .... 11.24–11.25
Wong Zhong Lan-Xiang v Wong [2002] HKCFI 50 .... 7.20
Wooley v Lucksinger 14 So 3d 311 (CA La 2008) 6.33
World Wide Imports Inc v Bartel 145 Cal App 3d 1006
   (CA Cal 1983) 6.15

X v Australian Crime Commission (2004) 212 ALR 596 .... 8.58
X v Société JA Delmas Export [2006] ECLY 136 (French Court
   of Cassation First Civil Chamber 31 January 2006) 6.83
X1, X2 and X3 v Y Tokyo High Court, 25 January 2001 (2002)
   45 Japanese Annual of International Law 155 .... 11.30
XAG v A Bank [1983] 2 All ER 464 .... 8.60
XL Insurance Ltd v Owens Corning [2001] 1 All ER
   (Comm) 530 .... 1.06

Yates v Thompson (1835) 3 Cl and F 544 .... 7.03
Yavuz v 61 MM Ltd 465 F 3d 418 (10th Cir 2006) 4.59
Yoon v Song (2000) 158 FLR 295 (SC NSW) 6.83
Young v Keong [1999] 2 Qd R 335 (QCA) 6.26
Yu Ge v River Island Clothing Pty Ltd [2002] NSWSC 28 .... 11.30
Yugraneft v Abramovich [2008] EWHC 2613
   (Comm) 3.26, 5.34, 6.10, 7.46, 9.13, 9.22, 10.20
Yugraneft Corporation v Rexx Management Corporation
   [2010] 1 SCR 649; 2010 SCC 19 .... 9.41

Zardo v Ivancic (2001) 161 FLR 228.............................. 11.12
Zhang v Jiang (2006) 82 OR (3d) 306.............................. 4.33
Zi Corporation v Steinberg 2006 ABQB 92 (Alb QB) 6.54
ZI Pompey Industrie v ECU-Line NV [2003] 1 SCR 450 .... 4.55
Zigurds, The [1932] P 113 .... 6.66

Table of Legislation

Australia
Admiralty Act 1988 (Cth)
   s 17 . . . . 4.60

Choice of Law (Limitation Periods) Act 1993 (NSW) 9.06, 9.32
   s 6 . . . . 9.16
Choice of Law (Limitation Periods) Act 1993 (Vic) 9.06
Civil Law (Wrongs) Act 2002 (ACT)
   s 95(1) 7.21
   s 135 . . . . 11.13
Civil Liability Act 1936 (SA)
   s 37(1) 7.21
Civil Liability Act 2002 (NSW)
   s 5G(1) 7.21
   s 50(1) 7.21
   Pt 4 . . . . 5.21
Civil Liability Act 2003 (Qld)
   s 14(1) 7.21
   s 47(1)–(3) 7.21
   Ch 2, Pt 2 . . . . 5.21
Competition and Consumer Act 2010 (Cth) 10.01

Dust Diseases Tribunal Act 1989 (NSW) 3.05, 7.47
   s 11A 11.28
   s 12A 9.11
   s 12D 11.11
   s 17 . . . . 4.05
   s 25(3) 7.49
   s 25B 7.47–7.49
   s 32 . . . . 6.17, 6.19

Evidence Act 1958 (Vic) 2.33
Evidence Act 1995 (Cth) 2.33
   s 128 . . . . 8.58
   s 128(4)(a) 8.58
Evidence (Audio and Audio Visual Links) Act 1998 (NSW)
   s 5C(2) 8.37

Table of Legislation

Evidence (Miscellaneous Provisions) Act 1958 (Vic)
    s 42E 8.37

Federal Court of Australia Act 1976 (Cth)
    s 47A 8.08
    Pt IVA 5.27
Federal Court Rules 4.28–4.29
    r 10.43(6) 4.28
    r 10.43(7)(b)(iii) 4.28
    r 10.46 .... 4.28
Foreign Corporations (Application of Laws) Act 1989 (Cth)
    s 7(3)(e) 5.42
Foreign Evidence Act 1994 (Cth)
    s 42(1)(a) 8.62
Foreign Judgments Act 1991 (Cth)
    s 7(4)(b) 4.58
Foreign States Immunities Act 1985 (Cth) 4.66, 5.53

Jurisdiction of Courts (Cross-Vesting) Act 1987 (Cth)
    s 11(1)(c) 2.33–2.34
Jurisdiction of Courts (Cross-Vesting) Act 1987 (NSW)
    s 5(2)(b)(iii) 2.35

Motor Accidents Compensation Act 1999 (NSW) 2.37, 3.03–3.04, 3.06,
                                                                                               11.19, 11.38
    s 123(1) 11.38
    s 132(1) 11.49
    Pt 3.4 .... 11.49
Motor Accident Insurance Act 1994 (Qld) 6.25
Motor Accidents Act 1988 (NSW)
    s 42 .... 6.28
    s 66 .... 11.12
Motor Accidents (Compensation) Act 1979 (NT)
    s 5 .... 6.56

Personal Injuries Proceedings Act 2002 (Qld) 6.29
    s 7(1) 3.07
    s 9(1) 6.24–6.25
    s 18(1)(a)(c) 6.26
    Ch 2, Pt 1, Divisions 1, 1A, 2, 4 .... 3.07

Rules of the Supreme Court 1971 (WA)
    O 10, r 10(2) 4.29
    O 10, r 10(3)(a) 4.28

Supreme Court Act 1970 (NSW)
  s 125 .... 3.29
Supreme Court Act 1986 (Vic)
  Pt 4A... 5.27
Supreme Court Civil Rules 2006 (SA)
  r 41(2), (3)... 4.29
Supreme Court (General Civil Procedure)
    Rules 2005 (Vic) 4.29
  r 7.03.. 4.28
  r 9.06.. 6.09

Trade Practices Act 1974 (Cth) 10.01
Transport Accident Act 1986 (Vic)
  s 93(20).. 3.07

Uniform Civil Procedure Rules 1999 (Qld)
  s 129(2).. 4.29
Uniform Civil Procedure Rules 2005 (NSW) 4.29
  rr 6.42–6.45 .... 3.29
  r 11.6.. 4.28

Workers Rehabilitation and Compensation Act 1986 (SA) 11.38
  s 6 .... 11.38
  s 54 .... 11.38
Workplace Injury Management and Workers Compensation
    Act 1998 (NSW)
  s 315 .... 6.29
Wrongs Act 1936 (SA)
  s 35a(7).. 3.07
Wrongs Act 1958 (Vic)
  Pt IVAA 5.21

Brunei

Constitution 3.13

Canada

Business Concerns Records Act (Quebec) 8.55
  s 2 .... 8.60

Chattel Mortgage Act 1979 (BC)
  s 23 .... 10.33
Civil Code (Quebec)
  art 3130.. 7.02
  art 3131.. 9.04

Code of Civil Procedure (Quebec)
  art 59..5.26

Farm Security Act 1989 (Sask)
  s 55..10.34

Insurance Act (Ont)
  s 267(1)..11.15

Judicature Act 1970 (Alta)
  s 34(17)..10.32

Land Contracts (Actions) Act 1978 (Sask)
  s 2(b)..6.49, 6.51
  s 3(1)..6.49, 6.51
Law of Property Act 1980 (Alta)
  s 41..10.33
Law of Property Act 2000 (Alta)
  s 40(1)..10.32
Limitation Act 1996 (BC)
  s 13(1)...9.39
Limitations Act 2000 (Alta)
  s 12..9.40–9.41
  s 12(1), (2)...9.41
Limitations Act 1995 (Newf and Lab)
  s 23..9.40
Limitations Act 2002 (Ont)
  s 23..9.42
Limitations Act 2004 (Sask)
  s 27..9.40
Limitation of Civil Rights Act 1953 (Sask)
  s 18(1)..10.32
Limitation of Civil Rights Act 1978 (Sask)
  s 18(1)..10.32

Real Estate Act 1979 (BC)
  s 62..6.46
Rules of Civil Procedure (Ont)
  r 17.05(2)..4.33

Supreme Court Civil Rules (BC)
  r 4–5(10)...4.33

France

'Blocking Statute' of July 1980 . . . . 8.39, 8.44, 8.55, 8.62
    art 1 *bis* 8.39

Germany

Code of Civil Procedure
    art 328. . . . . 4.02

Hong Kong

Rules of the High Court
    O 11, r 5(2) 4.31

Iraq

Coalition Provisional Authority 17 . . . . 4.67–4.68
    s 2(3). 4.67

Ireland

Constitution
    art 34.1 . . . . 6.21

Italy

Legge di 31 Maggio 1995 n 218
    art 12. . . . . 2.02
    art 25(1) 5.04

Jordan

Companies Law (No 12 of 1964)
    s 19 . . . . 5.32

Netherlands

Civil Code
    art 3:322(2). 9.11

New Zealand

Accident Insurance Act 1998
    s 394(1). 6.57
Accident Rehabilitation and Compensation Insurance Act 1992 . . . . . 6.25

Contractual Remedies Act 1979 . . . . 6.53, 7.13

Limitation Act 2010
    s 55(2). 9.07

Limitation Act 2010 (*cont.*)
  s 55(3) 9.16
  s 56(3) 9.07

Ship Registration Act 1992
  s 70 .... 6.71

Papua New Guinea
Lord Cairns Act 9.31

Russia
Civil Code 10.04
  art 1064(2) 7.15

Singapore
Civil Law Act 1999
  s 5(2) 6.44
Rules of Court
  O 11, r 3(2) 4.32
  O 11, r.4(2)(c) 4.32

South Africa
Prescription Act 1969 .... 9.08

Spain
Ley Enjuiciamiento Civil (2000)
  art 3. .... 2.02

Switzerland
Bank Law
  art 47. .... 8.39, 8.52, 8.55

Penal Code
  art 271. .... 4.18
  art 273. .... 8.39, 8.42–8.43, 8.47, 8.50, 8.52, 8.55, 8.62

Statute of Private International Law
  art 148(1) 9.04

United Kingdom
Civil Evidence Act 1968
  s 14(1)(a). 8.57

Table of Legislation

Civil Jurisdiction and Judgments Act 1982
    s 32 . . . . 4.58, 6.82
    s 33 . . . . 6.82
Civil Liability (Contribution) Act 1978 . . . . 5.18–5.19
Civil Procedure Rules 1998 . . . . 4.16–4.18, 4.22, 4.24, 4.26, 4.29
    r.3.10 . . . . 4.17–4.18, 4.20, 4.22
    r 6.15 . . . . 4.17, 4.19, 4.21
    r 6.16. . . . . 4.17, 4.20–4.23
    r 6.36. . . . . 4.46
    r 6.40. . . . . 4.20
    r 6.40(3) 4.16
    r 6.40(3)(a)(i) 4.15
    r 6.40(3)(a)(ii). 4.16
    r 6.40(3)(b) 4.09, 4.16
    r 6.40(3)(c) 4.16, 4.35
    r. 6.40(4) 4.16, 4.19
    r 6.42(1)(b) 4.16
    r 6.44. . . . . 4.25
    r 17.4. . . . . 9.32
    r 19.5. . . . . 9.32
    r 19.9. . . . . 5.38
    r 31.6. . . . . 8.03
    r 34.13(4) 8.06
    PD 6B 4.46
Companies Act 2006
    s 260 . . . . 5.38, 6.47

Employment Rights Act 1996 . . . . 3.22
Evidence (Proceedings in other Jurisdictions) Act 1975
    s 1 . . . . 8.19

Fatal Accidents Act 1976 . . . . 11.09
    s 4 . . . . 11.09
Foreign Limitation Periods Act 1984 . . . . 9.09, 9.12–9.13, 9.15,
                                                        9.17–9.21, 9.24–9.35, 9.47
    s 1 . . . . 9.13, 9.24
    s 1(1) 9.27
    s 1(2) 9.13
    s 1(3) 9.17, 9.32
    s 1(4) 9.16
    s 1(5) 9.27
    s 2 . . . . 3.19, 9.21, 9.24, 9.26

Foreign Limitation Periods Act 1984 (*cont.*)
  s 2(1) 9.21
  s 2(2) 9.22
  s 2(3) 9.18
  s 3 .... 9.14
  s 4 .... 9.24
  s 4(1)(a) 9.16
  s 4(2) 9.15
  s 4(3) 9.19
  s 8 .... 9.24

Gaming Act 1845 .... 6.43
  s 18 .... 6.44

Law of Property Act 1925
  s 53(1)(a), (b) 7.26
Limitation Act 1980
  s 33 .... 9.22
  s 35 .... 9.32–9.33
  s 35(3) 9.32

Merchant Shipping Act 1894
  s 419(4) 7.19
Motor Vehicles (Compulsory Insurance Information Centre
    and Compensation Body) Regulations 2003 .... 11.66
  reg 13(1) 11.66
  reg 13(2)(a) 11.66
  reg 13(2)(b) 11.66–11.67

Prescription and Limitation (Scotland) Act 1984 .... 9.12
Private International Law (Miscellaneous Provisions)
    Act 1995 .... 2.08, 2.38, 2.42–2.43, 2.45–2.46, 3.25, 9.13,
                   9.38, 11.18, 11.36–11.37, 11.40, 11.56, 11.58, 11.64
  s 9(4) 2.44
  s 11 .... 3.25, 4.67, 9.38, 11.19, 11.40–11.42, 11.53
  s 11(1), (2) 11.40
  s 12 .... 3.25, 9.38, 11.40–11.42, 11.44, 11.62–11.63, 11.70
  s 12(1) 11.40
  s 13 .... 3.23, 9.13, 11.40
  s 14 .... 2.38, 2.41–2.43, 2.46
  s 14(3)(a)(i) 11.37
  s 14(3)(b) 2.37, 2.44, 11.19

s 14(4)	11.38
Pt III	2.37
Protection of Trading Interests Act 1980	8.55

Senior Courts Act 1981

s 31(3)	5.16
s 32A	11.28
s 35A	11.03–11.05, 11.08
State Immunity Act 1978	5.52
s 12	4.25
Statute of Frauds 1677	3.03, 6.41, 7.26

Unfair Contract Terms Act 1977	3.22

United States

Assistance to Foreign and International Tribunals and Litigants before such Tribunals Act 28 USC § 1782	8.16–8.19

Conflict of Laws Code 1991 (Louisiana)

art 3549	9.46
Constitution	4.50, 9.45

Federal Rules of Civil Procedure	4.34, 8.10
r 4	4.38
r 4(f)	4.37
r 4(f)(1)	4.34
r 4(f)(2)	4.35
r 4(f)(2)(A)	4.34–4.35
r 4(f)(2)(C)	4.36
r 4(f)(2)(C)(i),(ii)	4.34
r 4(f)(3)	4.34–4.35, 4.37
Fifth Amendment to Constitution	8.23

New York Civil Practice Law and Rules

§ 901(b)	5.29

Trading with the Enemy Act 1917	8.52

Uniform Conflict of Laws Limitations Act 1982	9.46
§ 2	9.46
§ 4	9.46

Uniform Foreign Money Judgments Recognition Act 1962.......... 4.38
   § 4(b)(1) 4.38
Walsh Act 28 USC § 1783... 8.09

Venezuela

Ley de derecho internacional (1998)
   Art 56 .... 2.02

Table of Conventions and Treaties

Bustamante Code 1928
   art 314. . . . . 2.02

Convention of 15 November 1965 on the Service Abroad of
   Judicial and Extrajudicial Documents in Civil or
   Commercial Matters (Hague Service Convention),
   see Hague Service Convention
Convention of 18 March 1970 on the Taking of Evidence
   Abroad in Civil or Commercial Matters (Hague Evidence
   Convention), *see* Hague Evidence Convention

European Convention of Human Rights
   art 6. . . . . .3.31, 6.83
   art 6(1) 4.27, 6.32

Hague Choice of Court Convention 2005. .4.56–4.57
   art 3(b) 4.55
   art 6(a), (c) 4.56
Hague Convention of 4 May 1971 on the Law Applicable to
   Traffic Accidents
   art 8(8) 9.04
Hague Convention of 2 October 1973 on the Law Applicable
   to Products Liability
   art 8(a) 9.04
Hague Evidence Convention 3.31, 7.34, 8.01–8.02, 8.07,
                                                      8.10–8.16, 8.60, 8.62
   art 1. . . . . .8.13, 8.62
   art 3. . . . . 8.62
   art 9. . . . . .8.13, 8.62
   art 10. . . . . 8.13
   art 11. . . . . .8.13, 8.25, 8.37, 8.62–8.63
   art 11(2) 8.63
   art 12. . . . . .8.13, 8.62
Hague Service Convention. 3.31, 4.04, 4.07–4.17, 4.20–4.21, 4.24,
                                             4.28, 4.33–4.34, 4.37, 4.39–4.40, 9.17
   art 4. . . . . 4.12
   art 5. . . . . .4.11, 4.13
   art 5(b) 4.11

Hague Service Convention (*cont.*)
   art 8. . . . . 4.13
   art 9. . . . . 4.13
   art 10(a), (b), (c). 4.13
   art 13. . . . . 4.12
   art 15. . . . . 4.12
   art 15(1), (2) 4.12
   art 19. . . . . 4.13–4.14

International Regulations for the Prevention of Collisions
   at Sea 1897 . . . . 7.19

United Kingdom–Turkey Convention 1931
   art 12. . . . . 6.38
United Nations Convention on the International Sale of
   Goods 1980 . . . . 3.31

EU Instruments

Brussels Convention 2.08, 4.26
   art 27. . . . . 8.61
   art 27(2) 4.26–4.27
Brussels I Regulation 2.08, 3.31, 4.23–4.24, 4.26–4.27, 4.40, 4.53,
                                                                                           4.57, 11.51
   art 23. . . . . 4.55–4.56
   art 23(1) 4.55
   art 27. . . . . 4.53
   art 30. . . . . 4.53
   art 34(2) 4.26–4.27

Convention of 27 September 1968 on Jurisdiction and the
   Enforcement of Judgments in Civil and Commercial
   Matters (Brussels Convention), *see* Brussels Convention
Convention of 16 September 1988 on Jurisdiction and the
   Enforcement of Judgments in Civil and Commercial
   Matters (Lugano Convention), *see* Lugano Convention
Convention of 19 June 1980 on the Law
   Applicable to Contractual Obligations
   (Rome Convention), *see* Rome Convention
Council Directive (EEC) 77/249 of 22 March 1977 to Facilitate
   the Effective Exercise by Lawyers of Freedom to
   Provide Services 6.32

Council Regulation (EC) 44/2001 of 22 December 2000
   on Jurisdiction and the Enforcement of Judgments in
   Civil and Commercial Matters (Brussels I Regulation),
   see Brussels I Regulation
Council Regulation (EC) 1206/2001 of 28 May 2001 on
   Cooperation between the Courts of the Member States in
   the Taking of Evidence in Civil or Commercial Matters (EU
   Evidence Regulation), *see* EU Evidence Regulation
Council Regulation (EC) 1393/2007 of 13 November 2007 on
   the Service in the Member States of Judicial and Extrajudicial
   Documents in Civil or Commercial Matters [2007]
   OJ L324/79 (EU Service Regulation), *see* EU Service Regulation

Directive 2000/26 (Fourth Motor Insurance Directive) 11.66
   art 1. . . . . 11.66
   art 1(4) 11.66

EC Treaty
   art 12. . . . . 4.27
EU Evidence Regulation 8.01–8.02, 8.11, 8.15
   art 10(2), (3), (4). 8.15
   art 14. . . . . 8.63
EU Service Regulation. 4.04, 4.07–4.08, 4.15–4.17, 4.24, 4.27
   art 1(1) 4.15
   art 7(1) 4.15
   art 14. . . . . 4.15
   art 15. . . . . 4.15
EU Treaty
   art 49. . . . . 6.32
   art 50. . . . . 6.32

Lugano Convention 4.24, 4.26, 4.40, 11.51

Regulation (EC) 864/2007 of 11 July 2007 on the Law Applicable
   to Non-Contractual Obligations (Rome II), *see* Rome II
   Regulation
Regulation (EC) 593/2008 of 17 June 2008 on the Law
   Applicable to Contractual Obligations (Rome I), *see*
   Rome I Regulation
Rome Convention 3.08, 6.74, 9.09, 9.11–9.12, 9.20, 9.24–9.26,
                    9.30, 9.34–9.35, 10.02, 10.19, 10.23, 11.01, 11.22,
                                    11.52, 11.58–11.59

Rome Convention (*cont.*)
- art 1(2)(h) 3.08
- art 7(2) 9.11
- art 10(1) 3.08
- art 10(1)(c) 6.74, 10.02, 10.19, 10.23, 11.22, 11.58
- art 10(1)(d) 9.24
- art 13(1) 5.20
- art 13(2) 5.19
- art 14(2) 7.28
- art 15 .... 9.30
- art 16 .... 9.26

Rome I Regulation 2.07, 2.51, 2.53, 3.08, 3.16, 3.18, 3.22, 6.74, 7.01,
          7.35, 9.11–9.12, 9.20, 9.24–9.27, 9.30–9.31, 9.34–9.35, 10.02,
              10.19, 10.23, 10.28–10.29, 11.01, 11.22, 11.52
- art 1(3) 2.51, 3.08, 7.07
- art 9 .... 3.22, 7.30, 9.11, 11.61
- art 11(1) 2.51
- art 11(2) 7.07
- art 12(1) 3.08
- art 12(1)(c) 2.51, 6.74, 9.24, 10.02, 10.19, 10.23, 11.22, 11.58
- art 12(1)(d) 2.51, 9.24
- art 15 .... 5.20
- art 16 .... 5.19
- art 17 .... 10.28–10.29
- art 18(1) 2.52, 3.08, 7.17
- art 18(2) 2.52, 7.07, 7.14, 7.28, 7.34
- art 20 .... 9.30
- art 21 .... 3.18, 9.26

Rome II Regulation 2.07–2.08, 2.46, 2.51, 2.53, 3.08, 3.16,
          3.18, 3.22, 3.25–3.26, 4.62, 5.23, 6.13, 6.74, 7.01, 7.35,
          9.11–9.13, 9.20, 9.24–9.27, 9.30–9.31, 9.34–9.35, 9.38,
          10.02, 10.18–10.19, 10.23, 11.01, 11.28, 11.30, 11.35–11.36,
          11.42–11.43, 11.52, 11.59–11.60, 11.64–11.67
- recital 6 .... 11.65
- recital 12 .... 5.11
- recital 32 .... 11.60–11.61
- recital 33 .... 11.59
- art 1(3) 2.51, 3.08, 7.07
- art 2 .... 10.15
- art 4 .... 11.53
- art 4(1) 3.25, 11.62–11.63
- art 4(2), (3) 3.25, 9.38, 11.53, 11.62–11.64
- art 15 .... 3.08

art 15(a)	5.11
art 15(b)	5.19, 11.54
art 15(c)	2.51, 9.24, 10.24, 11.53–11.59, 11.63, 11.65–11.66
art 15(d)	2.52, 6.74, 6.81, 10.02, 10.15–10.17, 10.23–10.24, 11.53, 11.55, 11.57
art 15(e)	5.24
art 15(f)	5.11
art 15(g)	5.22
art 15(h)	2.51, 9.24, 9.33
art 16	3.22, 5.19, 7.30, 9.11, 11.61, 11.67
art 18	5.12
art 19	5.20
art 20	5.19
art 21	2.51
art 22(1)	2.52, 3.08, 7.17, 7.24
art 22(2)	2.52, 7.07, 7.14, 7.28, 7.34
art 24	9.30
art 26	3.18, 9.26, 11.60

Table of Principles and Restatements

American Law Institute/UNIDROIT Rules and Principles of
    Transnational Civil Procedure (2004) 3.32–3.33
    R 1.2 .... 3.33
    R 7.1 .... 3.33
    R 11.2 .... 3.33
    R 20.3 .... 3.33
    R 22.1 .... 3.33
    R 25.1 .... 3.33
    R 27.1.1 .... 3.33, 8.21
    R 32.3 .... 3.33
    P 10.2 .... 3.33
    P 16.1 .... 3.33

Restatement (First) of Conflict of Laws 1934 .... 2.54
    § 94 .... 8.51
Restatement (Second) of Conflict of Laws 1971 .... 2.54, 2.56–2.57,
                                                                                                                                    3.08, 8.33
    § 95 comment g 7.45
    § 99 .... 6.80
    § 122 .... 6.01
    § 122 comment a 2.09, 2.22, 2.54, 6.11, 6.33
    § 122 comment b 2.54
    § 123 .... 6.02
    § 124 .... 6.05
    § 124 comment a 5.24, 6.05
    § 124 illustration 2 .... 5.24
    § 125 .... 2.25, 5.14
    § 125 comment a 5.06, 5.12
    § 126 .... 6.03
    § 127 .... 6.08
    § 127 comment a(2), (3) 6.04
    § 127 comment a(4) 5.17, 6.09
    § 127 comment a(5) 6.11, 7.34
    § 127 comment a(6) 7.34
    § 127 comment a(7) 6.77
    § 127 comment a(9) 6.16
    § 128 .... 10.27
    § 129 .... 6.15
    § 130 .... 6.80, 10.13

Restatement (Second) of Conflict of Laws 1971 (*cont.*)
  § 130 comment a 6.37, 6.39
  § 131 .... 6.80
  § 131 comment a 6.80
  § 132 .... 6.80
  § 133 .... 2.25, 7.16
  § 134 .... 2.25, 7.18–7.19
  § 135 .... 7.32
  § 135 comment b 7.22
  § 137 .... 7.31
  § 138 comment a 7.03
  § 139 .... 8.30, 8.32
  § 139(1), (2) 8.30, 8.32
  § 139 comment b 8.30
  § 139 comment d 8.32
  § 139 comment e 8.31
  § 140 .... 7.13
  § 141 .... 7.27
  § 142 .... 9.46
  § 142(1), (2) 9.46
  § 155 .... 6.10
  § 171 .... 11.68, 11.72
  § 171 comment a 11.68
  § 171 comment b 11.70
  § 171 comment f 11.69
  § 173 .... 5.18
  § 177 .... 5.25
  § 177 comment a 5.25
  § 302 comments b, c, g 5.47
Restatement (Second) of the Foreign Relations Law 1965
  § 40 .... 8.53
Restatement (Third) of the Foreign Relations Law 1987
  § 442 .... 8.53
  § 442(1)(c) 8.53

List of Abbreviations

GENERAL

ALI	American Law Institute
CPR	Civil Procedure Rules
ECJ	European Court of Justice
FLPA 1984	Foreign Limitation Periods Act 1984
FRCP	Federal Rules of Civil Procedure
HSC	Hague Service Convention
LA 1980	Limitation Act 1980 (UK)
MACA 1999	Motor Accidents Compensation Act 1999 (New South Wales)
PILA 1995	Private International Law (Miscellaneous Provisions) Act 1995
PIPA 2002	Personal Injuries Proceedings Act 2002 (Queensland)
UCLLA	1982 Uniform Conflict of Laws Limitations Act (US)
UNIDROIT	International Institute for the Unification of Private Law

PUBLICATIONS

AJCL	American Journal of Comparative Law
BYBIL	British Yearbook of International Law
ECLY	European Current Law Yearbook
JPIL	Journal of Private International Law
ICLQ	International Comparative Law Quarterly
LMCLQ	Lloyd's Maritime and Commercial Law Quarterly
LQR	Law Quarterly Review
NYU L Rev	New York University Law Review
OUCLJ	Oxford University Commonwealth Law Journal
UCLA L Rev	University of California, Los Angeles Law Review
YBPIL	Yearbook of Private International Law

1
Introduction

1.01 Procedure is highly important in transnational disputes, both in the context of litigation and arbitration. Many cases are decided not on the basis of the applicable substantive law or the merits of the action but because one party has secured or been granted a procedural advantage over the other. Most of the legal literature and court decisions on procedural issues in private international law have focused on individual topics within the broad realm of procedure, such as service of process and jurisdiction, the taking of evidence, or interim or provisional measures. A question that has so far been little explored is the question of applicable law or choice of law in procedural matters. Indeed, the statement of one English commentator, made over 40 years ago, still remains valid: 'The basic question which has seldom been faced by English writers and courts is whether procedure in cases of private international law should be linked to rules of private international law or confined to those of municipal law or municipal jurisdiction. This question deserves consideration . . .'[1]

1.02 The principal reason for this gap in the discourse to date is that procedural matters have been governed by a single choice of law rule, common to all legal systems, whose status has been rarely, if ever, questioned. The rule provides that *'lex fori regit processum'*, that is, the law of the forum governs procedure. Courts, legislatures, and writers (at least in the common law world) have been almost universal in their approval of this rule with the result that the choice of law dimensions of procedure have only been appreciated in one real respect: the need to distinguish between matters of procedure (governed by the law of the forum) and matters of substance (governed by the law of the cause of action). According to this view, the rule *lex fori regit processum* is absolute and the only issue to be resolved by a court is whether a matter falls within the rubric of 'procedure'. If a matter is classified as substantive, then the ordinary choice of law rules or approaches of the forum with respect to cases involving a foreign element will be employed to determine the applicable law; if considered procedural, then the law of the forum is applied. The distinction

---

[1] R Graveson, 'Review of I Szászy, *International Civil Procedure: A Comparative Study*' (1968) 17 ICLQ 534; see also R Graveson, *Conflict of Laws* (Sweet & Maxwell, 7th edn, 1974) 593.

between substance and procedure will be analysed in detail in this book. In particular, there will be an examination of the rationale for the distinction and an assessment of whether a general classification is possible or whether the content of the distinction can only be elucidated on a case-by-case basis.[2] The argument will be made that the concept of procedure should be generally limited to matters relating to the mode, conduct, or regulation of court proceedings rather than being based on any concept of 'remedy'. A substantial part of the book considers how the distinction has been applied by courts and legislatures in important areas of doctrine such as evidence, damages, statutes of limitation, and matters concerning the process of the courts. The aim is to give practitioners a clear picture not only of the current state of the law but also as to how it may develop and be applied in future cases. The primary focus will be on the rules applicable in Commonwealth countries but reference will also be made to recent choice of law instruments of the European Union, as well as US commentary and decisions and some materials from European civil law countries.

1.03 Any examination of the distinction between substance and procedure must, however, also take into account the wider choice of law context in Anglo-Commonwealth private international law. Key objectives of private international law have long been the pursuit of uniformity of outcome in decisions of different national courts and the discouragement of forum shopping. Such aims are compromised when national systems of choice of law allow too wide a scope for the operation of forum law at the expense of foreign rules. Therefore, any consideration of the scope of the law of the forum in procedural matters must also examine the nature of forum interests in choice of law more generally, as well as other methods or devices of 'forum reference', such as *lex fori*-specific choice of law rules, overriding mandatory rules, public policy, mechanisms for displacing the applicable law, and the failure to plead and prove foreign law. Ultimately, therefore, any recommendation as to the appropriate scope of 'procedure' in Commonwealth choice of law must take into account the place of the law of the forum in Anglo-Commonwealth choice of law systems as a whole.

1.04 A further important point to note is that most writers, courts, and legislatures have largely assumed that no choice of law problems can ever arise *within* the context of procedure. Such a conclusion flows from the equation made at 1.02 between procedure and forum law. The implications of this view are that the procedural law of the forum can never come into

---

[2] See Ch 2.

Introduction

conflict with another country's procedural rules and foreign procedural rules can never be admitted into the forum.[3] Hence, if a matter is classified as procedural, then the reference to the law of the forum is absolute; there is no scope whatsoever for the recognition of other foreign laws by the forum. As will be argued in this book this position is flawed both in practice and principle. First, there are increasing instances where, in the context of applying forum procedural law, *foreign* procedural law is also applied or at least recognized by English and other Commonwealth courts, such as in the areas of taking of evidence abroad (where laws in the country where the evidence is located, which prevent disclosure, may call for recognition) and jurisdiction (where a court may, in determining whether to exercise jurisdiction, examine whether a foreign court would have done so under its laws). Secondly, there are circumstances where the scope and reach of the procedural rules of the forum are qualified and limited by reference to foreign laws, for example where a forum court refuses to allow service of process in a foreign country because it would violate the laws of that state or where a forum court will recognize service of process in a foreign country if it was effected according to the procedural rules governing service in that country. Some scholars have recognized that even where forum law is not *replaced* by foreign law but is modified to take account of foreign rules or elements, a type of choice of law process is at work. Kahn-Freund's doctrine of the 'enlightened *lex fori*'[4] and Kay's concept of foreign law as 'datum'[5] where the forum takes cognisance of foreign laws in the context of applying forum law, are examples of this idea, practical illustrations of which will be considered throughout this work.

A further aim of this book therefore, apart from identifying the precise scope of substance and procedure and considering its application in various practical situations, is to establish a more complete choice of law framework for procedural questions. In developing this framework it may be necessary to suggest further, more precisely tailored choice of law rules in addition to the traditional law of the forum/law of the cause of action dichotomy. Questions relating to the capacity of persons, the formal validity of documents and acts, rights to privilege, and quantification of damages are all areas where the dichotomy is arguably inadequate and alternative choice of law rules may be required. Relevantly, an examination will be made of the position in the United States, where the perceived

1.05

---

[3] See eg Australian Law Reform Commission, *Choice of Law* Report No 58 (1992) 122, para 10.2; *Hamlyn & Co v Talisker Distillery* [1894] AC 202, 210 (Lord Herschell LC): 'the parties cannot, in a case where the merits fall to be determined in the Scotch Courts, insist, by virtue of an agreement, that those Courts shall depart from their ordinary course of procedure'.
[4] O Kahn-Freund, *General Problems of Private International Law* (Sijthoff, 1976) 227.
[5] H Kay, 'Foreign Law as Datum' (1965) 53 California L Rev 47.

limitations of the substance / procedure distinction has led to it being increasingly discarded and subsumed within a broader general choice of law inquiry, based on the concept of the law which has the 'most significant relationship' to an issue. The work of organizations such as the American Law Institute and UNIDROIT, which have proposed harmonized models of procedural rules for transnational cases, will also be considered to determine whether harmonization can overcome the problem of applicable law.

1.06 The focus of this book will be on cross-border litigation, excluding international commercial arbitration. Not only has the topic of procedure in international arbitration been thoroughly covered in a recent work in the present series[6] but the choice of law analysis in arbitration, especially in procedural matters, is different from litigation due to the absence of a 'forum' and the interplay between arbitral tribunals and the courts.[7] Overall, the aim of the book is to provide guidance to lawyers on a topic which has had only limited attention in the literature to date but which is of important practical significance.

---

[6] G Petrochilos, *Procedure In International Arbitration* (OUP, 2004).
[7] As was noted by an English judge: 'Arbitration law is all about a particular method of resolving disputes. Its substance and processes are closely intertwined. The Arbitration Act contains various provisions which could not be readily separated into boxes labelled substantive arbitration law or procedural law, because that would be an artificial division'; *XL Insurance Ltd v Owens Corning* [2001] 1 All ER (Comm) 530, 541 (Toulson J).

2
The Substance and Procedure Distinction: Origins, Rationale, and Definition

A. History and Origins	2.01
1. The European Civil Law Model	2.02
2. The Common Law Right-Remedy Approach	2.03
B. The Rationale for Forum Law Governing Procedure	2.09
1. Convenience	2.09
2. Natural Justice	2.11
3. Public Law	2.13
4. Territorial Sovereignty	2.14
C. Contemporary Approaches to Substance and Procedure	2.17
1. Case by Case	2.18
2. Convenience	2.19
3. The Australian Reappraisal	2.21
4. Canada Takes a Similar Path	2.28
5. Australia: Further Developments	2.31
6. England: The Contemporary Position	2.36
7. A New Approach?	2.48
8. EU Instruments on Choice of Law	2.51
9. The US Position	2.54
D. Conclusion	2.59

A. HISTORY AND ORIGINS

2.01 While choice of law in general is a highly contentious and disputed area in almost every national system of private international law, one rule is universally accepted and applied: matters of procedure are governed by the law of the forum. The corollary of this rule is that courts of the forum do not apply foreign procedural law and it is notable that in the majority of decisions from common law countries the focus has been on whether foreign law should be denied application because it is procedural[1] rather than

---

[1] See eg *Harding v Wealands* [2007] 2 AC 1; *John Pfeiffer Pty Ltd v Rogerson* (2000) 203 CLR 503.

whether 'forum law covers the field and . . . leaves no place for the application of foreign law'.[2]

1. THE EUROPEAN CIVIL LAW MODEL

2.02 The rule that forum law governs procedure has a long history, being apparently first pronounced by Balduinus of the 'glossator school' in the thirteenth century. He drew the distinction between norms which were *'ad ordinandam litem'*—the rules by which the judge conducted the proceedings—and those which were *'ad decidendam litem'*—the rules by which the judge resolved the dispute before the court.[3] This is the first recorded articulation of what is now known as the procedure/substance distinction. The rule that forum law governs procedure was also applied in the thirteenth century by the Parlement de Paris where the defendant pleaded a foreign custom as a defence to non-appearance in a French court. The tribunal rejected the defence on the basis that the question of appearance was procedural and so governed exclusively by the law of the forum.[4] Later writers such as the Italian Bartolus, in the fourteenth century, asserted the same principle, and it continued to be endorsed throughout the next four centuries by European writers on private international law and remains the 'universally admitted'[5] position today in civil law countries. A number of such jurisdictions have even codified the 'forum law governs procedure' principle,[6] although such a statement on its own is unenlightening; it is abstract and begs the question as to *which* issues are procedural,[7] leaving the content of the concept to be determined by the courts on a case-by-case basis.[8] Some codifications have sought to give examples of what is procedural but none are particularly comprehensive.[9] The other

---

[2] M Keyes, 'Substance and Procedure in Multistate Tort Litigation' (2010) 18 Torts LJ 201, 214.

[3] E Spiro, 'Forum Regit Processum' (1969) 18 ICLQ 949–50.

[4] E Ailes, 'Substance and Procedure in the Conflict of Laws' (1941) 39 Michigan L Rev 392, 396–7.

[5] B Audit, *Droit International Privé* (Economica, 3rd edn, 2005) para 14.

[6] See eg Italy: Legge di 31 Maggio 1995 n218, art 12; Spain: Ley Enjuiciamiento Civil (2000) art 3; Venezuela: Ley de derecho internacional (1998) art 56; Bustamante Code (1928) art 314 (adopted by Bolivia, Brazil, Chile, Costa Rica, Cuba, Dominican Republic, Ecuador, El Salvador, Guatemala, Haiti, Honduras, Nicaragua, Panama, Peru, and Venezuela).

[7] J Gonzalez Campos, 'Les Liens Entre La Compéténce Judiciaire et La Compéténce Législative en Droit International Privé' (1977) 156 *Hague Recueil* 227, 292–3.

[8] Art 12 of the Italian law, for example, simply states that 'the civil trial that takes place in Italy is governed by Italian law'.

[9] See eg Bustamante Code, art 314 which states that 'the law of each contracting state determines the competence of the courts, the organisation and forms of prosecution, the execution of judgments and appeals against such decisions'.

A. History and Origins

problem with these formulations is that they all rely on the false assumption that foreign law can never apply to procedural issues;[10] this misconception will be fully examined in this work.

2. THE COMMON LAW RIGHT-REMEDY APPROACH

The acceptance of the rule that forum law governs procedure in English law came much later, in the eighteenth century, after a private international law jurisprudence, where foreign laws were recognized and applied, had emerged. Until that time the English courts heard few foreign cases due to the fact that the courts had no personal jurisdiction over a defendant resident abroad and uncertain subject matter jurisdiction over events outside English territory.[11] In addition, English courts did not recognize rights granted under foreign law: the law of the forum was applied to both substance and procedure in all cases.[12] Yet, even after a system of choice of law developed from the late eighteenth century, with scope for admission and reception of foreign laws, English courts provided their own interpretation of the *lex fori regit processum* rule. This approach can also be explained by historical factors. In the English common law, procedure has always occupied a highly central place in the legal system to the extent that a legal right was not recognized as existing in the abstract but only in the context of the procedural framework in which it could be enforced. The concepts of substance and procedure were therefore often blurred and overlapping, with *enforcement* of the substantive right (and remedy obtained thereby) being, in practice, more significant than the right itself. Such a view is confirmed in the comment by Maine that in English law 'substantive law . . . [is] secreted in the interstices of procedure'.[13] 2.03

The central focus of English law on enforcement and remedy had a direct effect on the way in which English courts were to classify matters of substance and procedure in private international law. As noted above, Balduinus had originally drawn a distinction between rules relating to the conduct of proceedings and those relevant to the determination of the merits of the case. This analysis appears to have escaped the attention of English courts, which instead provided their own interpretation of 2.04

---

[10] P Carlier, *L'Utilisation de la* Lex Fori *dans La Résolution des Conflits de Lois* (doctoral thesis, Université de Lille 2 2008) para 43.

[11] Ailes (n 4 above) 400 citing J Beale, 'The Jurisdiction of Courts over Foreigners' (1913) 26 Harvard L Rev 283, 289.

[12] ibid 400.

[13] H Maine, *Dissertations on Early Law and Custom* (first published 1886, Arno Press, 1975) 389; T Main, 'The Procedural Foundation of Substantive Law' (2009) 87 Washington L Rev 801, 807.

the dichotomy, driven by the primacy that English domestic law attached to remedy and enforcement. Consequently, instead of the concept of procedure having an administrative connotation, as something relating to judicial machinery or protocol (as Balduinus most likely intended), it was interpreted to embrace all aspects of relief and enforcement in a suit ('the remedy'). The consequence of such an approach was that a much *wider* definition of procedure was created; leading accordingly to a greater scope of operation for the law of the forum in actions brought before English courts. It was only matters involving the abrogation of 'the right', by contrast, which were classified as substantive and had the potential of being governed by foreign law.

2.05 Furthermore, in many cases the remedy or enforcement aspect of a legal action was considered indispensably connected with the substantive right which suggested, in practice, a limited role for the latter: 'if the plaintiff has a right he must of necessity have a means to vindicate and maintain it, and a remedy if he is injured in the exercise or enjoyment of it; and indeed it is a vain thing to imagine a right without a remedy, for want of right and want of remedy are reciprocal'.[14] So, with the practical 'remedy' being regarded as equally, if not more, significant than the right of action, and both being closely linked in any event, it is perhaps not surprising that English courts interpreted procedure so broadly. Indeed, the right-remedy dichotomy continued to be applied by English courts until at least the late twentieth century as can be seen in the endorsement by the House of Lords in 1975[15] of the following statement by Tindal CJ in *Huber v Steiner*:[16]

> The distinction between that part of the law of the foreign country where a personal contract is made, which is adopted and that which is not adopted by our English courts of law is well known and established; namely that so much of the law as affects the rights and merit of the contract, all that relates *ad litis decisionem* is adopted from the foreign country; so much of the law as affects the remedy only, all that relates *ad litis ordinationem*, is taken from the *lex fori* of that country where the action is brought.

2.06 What is noticeably absent from all these statements is any concern that a wide definition of procedure, with its large reservation of matters to the law of the forum, is undesirable because it would compromise uniformity of outcome and the discouragement of forum shopping. One explanation

---

[14] *Ashby v White* (1703) 2 Ld Raym 938, 953; 92 ER 126 (Lord Holt); see also *Chase Manhattan Bank NA v Israel-British Bank (London) Ltd* [1981] Ch 105, 124 (Goulding J).
[15] *Black-Clawson International Ltd v Papierwerke Waldhof-Asschaffenburg AG* [1975] 1 AC 591, 630 (Lord Wilberforce).
[16] (1835) 2 Bing NC 202, 210; see also *Don v Lippmann* (1837) 5 Cl & Fin 1, 13 (Lord Brougham).

A. History and Origins

for the long adherence to the right-remedy view is that English courts preferred the easy accessibility and familiarity of local law over the uncertainty and difficulty of applying foreign rules, particularly from European civil law countries. The European states by contrast, all with a common Roman law inheritance, may have felt less unease in recognizing each other's laws.[17] The retention (to this day) of the principle that the pleading and proof of foreign law is not mandatory but at the discretion of the parties is consistent with this traditionally 'hands off' approach to foreign law. By contrast, the much earlier development of choice of law rules on the European continent may well have influenced European scholars to provide a more confined and closely-tailored view of procedure—so as to allow greater scope for the operation of foreign law.

2.07 Considerable time has been spent describing the traditional English approach to substance and procedure because it is not clear that this position has been abandoned. Indeed, it is strongly arguable that the right-remedy approach to substance and procedure still represents the law in some Commonwealth countries, apart from Australia and Canada, and a number of states in the United States. By contrast, EU instruments on choice of law,[18] which grant a wider field of operation to the substantive law, implicitly reject the forum-centredness of the right-remedy test. Recent attempts to redefine the substance / procedure distinction with a narrower field allocated to the law of the forum are discussed later in this chapter.[19]

2.08 As mentioned earlier, the key reason why the traditional English view remained uncontested for so long was that the uniquely English domestic law view of procedure based on remedy was applied, with little dissent, to cases with a foreign element. Yet in the past twenty years there has been a dramatic increase in transnational litigation in both English and other Commonwealth courts and with that a much greater awareness of foreign laws and institutions. The adoption of a more even-handed approach to the exercise of jurisdiction in the 1980s, as evidenced by the implementation of the Brussels Convention[20] (and later, the Brussels I Regulation[21])

---

[17] E Lorenzen, 'The Statute of Frauds and the Conflict of Laws' (1923) 32 Yale LJ 311, 327.

[18] See eg the Regulation (EC) 593/2008 of 17 June 2008 on the law applicable to contractual obligations (Rome I) and Regulation (EC) 864/2007 of 11 July 2007 on the law applicable to non-contractual obligations (Rome II). The temporal application of Rome I and II is discussed at 11.01 below.

[19] See 2.21–2.30 below.

[20] Convention of 27 September 1968 on Jurisdiction and the Enforcement of Judgments in Civil and Commercial Matters.

[21] Council Regulation (EC) 44/2001 of 22 December 2000 on jurisdiction and the enforcement of judgments in civil and commercial matters.

and the acceptance of a doctrine of *forum non conveniens*,[22] as well as the emergence of more balanced, less forum-centric choice of law rules in tort,[23] have signalled a clear movement away from unqualified forum dominance. Such developments may suggest that it is time for a reconsideration of the traditionally wide view of procedure in English private international law. The link between the tradition of forum control in English private international law and the expansive view of procedure has been noted by Australian judges. Mason CJ said that an historically wide view of procedure was articulated at a time when 'the importance of international judicial comity may not have been given the same recognition it nowadays commands and when the notion of forum shopping was not considered as objectionable a practice as it now is'.[24] By contrast, more recently there has been a greater concern to ensure that actions are brought in the most appropriate place to resolve them and that choice of law rules should operate to fulfil, not frustrate, foreign rights.[25] A narrow view of procedure is more consistent with this objective.[26] The impact of this new awareness in common law countries can arguably be seen in the profusion of new approaches to the substance / procedure distinction. Before examining these approaches in detail and assessing their value it is important to consider the rationale for matters of procedure being reserved to the law of the forum.

B. THE RATIONALE FOR FORUM LAW GOVERNING PROCEDURE

1. Convenience

2.09 Under the traditional right-remedy view, the rationale for forum law applying to procedure appears not to have been directly addressed by English courts, although English and foreign commentators and Australian judges have considered the issue. The most commonly cited modern rationale for procedural matters being governed by forum law is that it suits

---

[22] *Spiliada Maritime Corp v Cansulex Ltd* [1987] AC 460.
[23] See for the UK, Private International Law (Miscellaneous Provisions) Act 1995 and Rome II Regulation; for Australia, *John Pfeiffer Pty Ltd v Rogerson* (2000) 203 CLR 503 (High Court of Australia); and for Canada, *Tolofson v Jensen* (1994) 120 DLR (4th) 289 (Supreme Court of Canada), all replacing the rule in *Phillips v Eyre* (1870) LR 6 QB 1 (with the exception of defamation claims in England).
[24] *McKain v RW Miller & Co (South Australia) Pty Ltd* (1991) 174 CLR 1, 22–3.
[25] ibid 23 (Mason CJ), 50 (Deane J).
[26] R Fentiman, *Foreign Law in English Courts* (OUP, 1998) 36.

B. The Rationale for Forum Law Governing Procedure

the convenience and efficiency of the forum court.[27] The idea is that courts are established according to local custom and tradition and a number of their practices and rituals would be difficult for foreign judges, unfamiliar with such rules, to replicate.[28] For example, it would be difficult for a court to adopt the language and etiquette of the foreign tribunal, particularly if it was significantly different from its own. More formal methods of trial, such as the use of juries, may also be impracticable to adopt in, for example, a civil law country. In addition, it is likely that there would be certain procedural rules the employment of which by a foreign court would be highly expensive, time-consuming, and burdensome.[29] Courts owe a duty not only to the state which constituted them but also to litigants to conduct proceedings efficiently and expeditiously.[30] The use of the same procedures in every case by courts will further these objectives; by contrast, the employment of unfamiliar foreign procedures may frustrate them.

Some writers have been critical of the focus on convenience and practicality as the rationale for applying forum law to procedural issues. It has been suggested that convenience gives undue weight to 'administration of justice concerns', which are normally downplayed in English private international law, and that this 'displays an overtly parochial tendency' inconsistent with the notion of judicial comity in private international law.[31] While such observations have force, it must be acknowledged that there are some institutions of a country's legal system (such as a jury) which simply cannot be replicated in another system and any attempt to do so would be at best artificial and at worst disastrous. More likely, requests to do so will simply be ignored. Further, it should also be remembered that all that is being considered at this stage is the *rationale* of the forum law governs procedure rule. As discussed at 2.18–2.30, courts and most writers have not suggested that convenience should be the sole test for determining whether a matter is procedural; it will be argued in this

2.10

---

[27] See eg W Cook, '"Substance" and "Procedure" in the Conflict of Laws' (1933) 42 Yale LJ 333, 343–4; L Collins (ed), *Dicey, Morris and Collins on the Conflict of Laws* (Sweet & Maxwell, 14th edn, 2006) para 7.004, citing a number of decisions including *Shaik Sahied v Sockalingam Chettiar* [1933] AC 342, 346 (PC); G Panagopoulos, 'Substance and Procedure in Private International Law' (2005) 1 JPIL 69, 71; J Carruthers, 'Substance and Procedure in the Conflict of Laws: A Continuing Debate in Relation to Damages' (2004) 53 ICLQ 691, 692–3; *Harding v Wealands* [2007] 2 AC 1, paras 9, 11 (Lord Woolf); and *McKain v RW Miller & Co (South Australia) Pty Ltd* (1991) 174 CLR 1, 22, 26–7 (Mason CJ), 49 (Deane J), and 56 (Gaudron J).

[28] *McKain v RW Miller & Co (South Australia) Pty Ltd* (1991) 174 CLR 1, 22 (Mason CJ).

[29] US Restatement (Second) of Conflict of Laws, § 122 comment a.

[30] *McKain v RW Miller & Co (South Australia) Pty Ltd* (1991) 174 CLR 1, 22 (Mason CJ); M Whincop and M Keyes, *Policy and Pragmatism in the Conflict of Laws* (Ashgate, 2001) 41.

[31] Keyes (n 2 above) 217.

chapter that, at most, it remains useful as one factor to be considered in that determination.

2. Natural Justice

2.11 Another suggested rationale for the forum law governs procedure rule, although less widely advocated, is natural justice. One writer has argued that 'it is a postulate of justice that the courts of a given country follow the general rules of procedure irrespective of whether the subject matter of the litigation is governed by foreign law or by the law of the country'.[32] If the court were to apply foreign procedural laws this would 'not only be inconvenient... but would also entail injustice through the unequal treatment of the parties in the suit in question on the one hand and the parties in other lawsuits on the other'.[33] There are two distinct elements to this justification. The first is that the parties have an expectation that once the jurisdiction of a court is invoked, the procedures of that court shall apply. The second is that it is inequitable and discriminatory for different procedural rules to be applied to wholly domestic cases on the one hand and cases with a foreign element on the other. The 'expectation' argument has been supported by other writers who even argue that a choice of forum jurisdiction or court clause in a contract amounts to a selection by the parties of local procedural law.[34] The implication here is that if a court does not apply its own procedural rules it is not honouring the terms of the parties' agreement. Such a view, however, assumes that the preference for local procedures is the main factor in parties agreeing to enter a choice of jurisdiction clause. It is more likely that broader questions of convenience are influential, such as the costs for a party of having to litigate at great distance from its place of business or the greater risk of being subject to an unfamiliar or undesirable substantive law if a suit were brought in a court other than that of the party's choosing. 'Party expectations' in procedural law is therefore a difficult factor to assess accurately although it is probably true that if parties turned their minds to the issue, they would assume that local procedures would apply to a suit in the forum. Yet the 'party expectations' view is stretched too far when it is said that the application

---

[32] M Wolff, *Private International Law* (OUP, 2nd edn, 1950) 230.
[33] ibid.
[34] *The Asian Plutus* [1990] 1 SLR 543, para 19 (Sing HC); *Telesis Technologies Inc v Sure Controls Systems Inc* 2010 ONSC 5288, para 9; and Keyes (n 2 above) 222, who argues that in such a circumstance 'it is less objectionable for forum law to be applied to matters of procedure'. cf E Crawford and J Carruthers, *International Private Law: A Scots Perspective* (Thomson West, 3rd edn, 2010) para 8.01, who reject the view that parties may make a choice of procedural law in a contract.

B. The Rationale for Forum Law Governing Procedure

of forum law to procedure can be justified on the basis of the plaintiff's choice of forum and the defendant's submission to jurisdiction—particularly where the defendant has contested jurisdiction.[35]

The further argument that the use of foreign procedures somehow amounts to inequitable or discriminatory treatment of the parties (when compared to domestic cases where local procedure is exclusively applied)[36] must be rejected since foreign and domestic cases are not identical. If it is generally accepted that cases involving a foreign element may require resolution by application of foreign substantive law, then it should equally be no surprise that in such cases foreign procedural rules may also be relevant. In principle, a party in a cross-border case has no greater right to have its local procedural law applied than its local substantive law. The comparison with wholly domestic cases, where there is no scope for foreign law of any kind to apply, is therefore flawed.[37]

2.12

3. PUBLIC LAW

A third rationale for the forum law governs procedure rule, which is not referred to in the common law literature or decisions but is frequently cited in French and Italian texts, is that procedure is part of the administration of justice of the state entrusted to the courts and so is a 'public law' matter which can only be governed by the laws of that state.[38] This approach is said to be supported by principles of public international law, pursuant to which the nation state has complete sovereignty over its organs, including the operation of its courts.[39] The problem with such an argument is that it ignores the interests of the parties to the litigation and their advisers, who (apart from the judge) are the principal actors in the process and who may have little or no connection with the state. Moreover, at least under common law rules of private international law, it is unlikely that foreign procedural rules would come within the rubric of foreign penal or public laws or 'governmental interests'[40] which are not recognized

2.13

---

[35] Keyes (n 2 above) 218; cf *McKain v RW Miller & Co (South Australia) Pty Ltd* (1991) 174 CLR 1, 22 (Mason CJ).

[36] *De la Vega v Vianna* (1830) 1 B & Ad 284.

[37] I Szászy, 'The Basic Connecting Factor in International Cases in the Domain of Civil Procedure' (1966) 15 ICLQ 436, 446–7.

[38] See especially P Mayer and V Heuze, *Droit International Privé* (Montchrestien, 9th edn, 2007) para 492; and R Baratta, 'Processo Civile (Legge Regolatrice)' in R Baratta (ed), *Dizionari del Diritto Privato Diritto Internazionale Privato* (Giuffrè Editore, 2010) 290.

[39] Carlier (n 10 above) para 47.

[40] *Attorney-General (United Kingdom) v Heinemann Publishers Australia Pty Ltd* (1988) 165 CLR 30.

14   *Chapter 2: The Substance and Procedure Distinction*

by the forum. As has been already noted, it is not accurate to describe such laws as solely embodying such interests.[41] Rather, procedural rules are designed to smooth the conduct of business in the courts; while there is a state interest in this process in terms of providing just, efficient, and expeditious proceedings, in practice these concerns also reflect and respond to the needs of private litigants. The degree of intrusion of sovereignty on the forum state by applying the procedural rules of another country is therefore likely to be minimal.

4. Territorial Sovereignty

2.14 A final justification for the forum law governs procedure rule, which is referred to in some judgments from common law courts[42] and European civil law texts,[43] is territorial sovereignty. The idea here is that the law of the forum exclusively applies because procedure is a matter wholly connected to acts or events within the forum's territory. While as an empirical observation it is true that most procedural acts relating to litigation occur within the territory of the adjudicating court, there is an increasing range of procedural conduct which has an extraterritorial aspect. As was mentioned in Chapter 1, many procedural acts either occur or have effects in foreign territories, for example service of process or the taking of evidence which may require consideration of the procedural rules of such territories *in combination with* local rules. Other examples would be where a court considers the jurisdictional rules of a foreign country before granting a stay of proceedings on appropriate forum grounds[44] or where it examines the rules on recognition and enforcement of foreign judgments of another country before certifying a class action involving claimants resident in such country.[45] Yet, as will be seen later,[46] questions of territoriality may be relevant in the context of substance and procedure, as a number of Canadian courts have relied upon the territorial scope of a statute as an alternative approach to the substance / procedure distinction in determining whether forum law applies.

2.15 A variant on the territorial sovereignty justification is to say that procedural rules of the forum are 'overriding mandatory rules' and so must be applied in every case. Yet in common law systems at least, the scope of

---

[41] cf E Sykes and M Pryles, *Australian Private International Law* (LBC, 3rd edn, 1991) 267.
[42] *Harding v Wealands* [2007] 2 AC 1, paras 73–75 (Lord Rodger); *Breavington v Godleman* (1988) 169 CLR 41, 136 (Deane J).
[43] For Italy see Baratta (n 38 above) 289.
[44] See eg for Canada 4.44–4.45 below.
[45] *Re Vivendi Universal SA Securities Litigation* 242 FRD 76 (SDNY 2007).
[46] See 2.30.

C. Contemporary Approaches to Substance and Procedure

such rules in private international law is generally limited to forum statutes[47] with a clear and explicit intention to apply in transnational cases. Only some forum procedural rules would fall within this category. In those cases there is much to be said for the use of overriding mandatory rules as a transparent, policy-based method for applying forum law in procedural matters. This issue is explored further at 3.22.

2.16 To conclude on the question of rationale, while convenience is properly the most accurate justification for the rule that forum law governs procedure, in most cases, a number of the arguments are likely to reinforce one another. So, for example, the imposition of a jury trial on a court in a civil law country is not only likely to be inconvenient and impractical for the court but also a source of injustice, as parties have to employ a procedure with which the forum is completely unfamiliar. The identification of the appropriate rationale for the substance-procedure rule does not, however, resolve the key problems that may arise. The first and most obvious is the issue of how to determine what is substantive and what is procedural, a question which may require an answer both at the abstract level and in application in specific cases. A second question that may arise even if a matter is found to be procedural, is whether it is nevertheless appropriate to apply forum law exclusively without regard to other foreign laws that may be relevant to the dispute. The third question is whether further choice of law rules, beyond the law of the forum and the law of the cause of action, may need to be developed for specific issues. Finally, there may be circumstances where, although a matter is classified as substantive, there are compelling reasons of public policy for applying forum law to the case.

C. CONTEMPORARY APPROACHES TO SUBSTANCE AND PROCEDURE

2.17 While modern text writers now almost unanimously condemn the right-remedy test as a basis for applying the substance / procedure distinction, it is not clear that all Commonwealth courts have rejected this view. Moreover, even among those writers and judges who have advocated

---

[47] Some commentators have suggested that such overriding provisions may also include common law rules, see T Hartley, 'Mandatory Rules in International Contracts: The Common Law Approach' (1997) 266 *Hague Recueil* 337, 351–3, J Fawcett and J Carruthers, *Cheshire, North and Fawcett Private International Law* (OUP, 14th edn, 2008) 736–7, but so far there has been limited recognition of this view in judicial decisions.

different tests, there is no unanimity as to what approach should be taken.[48]

1. Case by Case

2.18 One view, which has the support of leading English and Canadian text writers[49] and the Australian Law Reform Commission,[50] is that it is impossible to elucidate a test in abstract terms, given the diversity of foreign laws and circumstances which may have to be considered. Consequently, courts must determine what is substantive and what is procedural on an issue-by-issue basis. Clear evidence of this approach appears in the following statement:[51] 'When is a question one of substantive law? When is a question merely one of evidence and procedure? I attempt no general answer to these questions for answer can only be made after an analysis of the specific questions calling for decision, its legal background and factual context.' To the same effect are the comments of Lord Pearson:[52] 'I do not think there is any exact and authoritative definition of the boundary between substantive and procedural . . . law . . . the boundary remains to be settled by further decisions in particular cases.' The argument in favour of this approach is that, as a matter of reality, substance and procedure cannot be relegated to clear-cut categories with a preordained line discoverable by logic.[53] If this position were widely adopted it would have the benefit of liberating English courts from the rigid right-remedy dichotomy and provide more flexibility to choose the rule which best meets the needs of the particular case. Yet the problem with this approach is that it provides no guidance or criteria as to where the distinction should be drawn and so uniformity and predictability will be hard to accomplish. Under this approach courts may be tempted to rely on their own often unarticulated policy assumptions as to whether local or foreign law should apply, with the risk that the historical dominance of forum law (at least in

---

[48] Consequently, it is interesting that some Australian writers have said, in relation to the substance / procedure distinction, that 'what used to be a very controversial part of the conflict of laws is now likely to be regarded as both settled and sensible'; M Tilbury, G Davis, and B Opeskin, *Conflict of Laws in Australia* (OUP, 2002) 328. The material covered in this work will reveal, however, that, at least in the Commonwealth as a whole, the position remains fluid and contentious.

[49] *Cheshire, North and Fawcett* (n 47 above) 78; J Walker, *Castel & Walker Canadian Conflict of Laws* (LexisNexis Butterworths, 6th edn, 2005) para 6.2. See also Main (n 13 above).

[50] At least in respect of international, as opposed to intra-federal, conflicts, see *Choice of Law* Report No 58 (1992) para 10.15.

[51] *Re Fuld's Estate (No 3)* [1968] P 675, 695 (Scarman J).

[52] *Boys v Chaplin* [1971] 1 AC 356, 395.

[53] Cook (n 27 above) 335–6; *Cheshire, North and Fawcett* (n 47 above) 78.

C. Contemporary Approaches to Substance and Procedure

common law countries) will remain strong. Also, under this view, there is no recognition that a matter may be classified as procedural yet not subject to the law of the forum or that new choice of law rules may need to be created to resolve procedural disputes. Moreover, while the task of formulating an abstract test is certainly difficult, the great advantage of some general principle is that it provides at least some guidance for courts, parties, and their advisers in future cases; limits the potential for arbitrary and inconsistent decision-making; and promotes certainty and settlement.

2. Convenience

2.19 Other writers and courts have also sought to restrict the scope of procedure in private international law, motivated by an increasing concern to deter forum shopping and to give effect to foreign laws and institutions. The view of one US author, Cook, has recently been endorsed by leading English and Canadian text writers.[54] Cook[55] argues that as convenience is the most popularly accepted rationale for the rule that forum law governs procedure, so should it also constitute the test for determining when local law should apply. In his view, the forum should apply all the rules of the law of the cause of action as long as it is practicable and convenient to do so. The idea here, which has been acknowledged by some Australian judges,[56] is that a foreign rule which is 'readily available' and whose application does not 'depend on knowledge and reference to factors peculiar to the enacting state' should normally be applied by the forum. The cost and delay involved in having to prove foreign law as a fact by expert evidence probably also underlies this view. An example of readily transferable rules may be a foreign statute of limitation or a principle of admissibility of evidence, whereas the language, dress code in a foreign court, or method of assigning judges to a particular case would obviously be things more peculiar to that jurisdiction and so impractical, if not impossible, for the forum to replicate. 'A judge can never apply foreign rules which regulate the judge's office.'[57] Another example of impracticality would be where the law of the cause of action provided remedies which required a particular local infrastructure to administer or supervise. Such types of relief would be beyond the powers or competence of the forum court to order and so highly 'inconvenient'. Beyond these rather extreme and obvious examples, however, the notion of impracticality or inconvenience is difficult to apply. Indeed, on one view, inconvenience has the danger of

---

[54] *Dicey, Morris and Collins* (n 27 above) para 7.004; Walker (n 49 above) para 6.2.
[55] Cook (n 27 above) 343–4.
[56] *McKain v RW Miller & Co (South Australia) Pty Ltd* (1991) 174 CLR 1, 26 (Mason CJ).
[57] O Kahn-Freund, *General Problems of Private International Law* (Sijthoff, 1976) 294.

being elevated to a general test of 'unfamiliarity' which could have the effect of excluding the vast majority of foreign laws. Obviously, such an outcome would destroy Cook's worthy intention of restricting the concept of procedure to allow wider operation of foreign law in the forum.

2.20 In summary, while convenience may be a useful, broad rationale for understanding why courts are keen to adhere to their local procedural rules, its vagueness and uncertainty render it problematic as the *sole* test for drawing the line between substance and procedure.[58] At most, it may be a useful factor (among a number of others) in resolving the classification. Moreover, some of the examples of foreign rules often suggested as too 'inconvenient' to apply may nevertheless demand to be recognized by forum courts on comity and sovereignty grounds. Matters such as service of process, jurisdictional rules, evidence, and the enforcement of judgments may all once have been regarded as wholly within the concern of the forum. As will be seen, however, in many of these issues forum law may come into contact with the procedural regimes of other countries, raising the question as to whether such laws should be applied by the forum or at least used as limits on the scope of operation of forum law. So, convenience is an inadequate concept, by itself, for defining what procedural laws should be admitted in the forum.

3. THE AUSTRALIAN REAPPRAISAL

2.21 Recognizing this problem, the High Court of Australia and the Supreme Court of Canada in a series of cases, have sought to create a new principle for classifying rules as procedural or substantive. While these courts have recognized the difficulty of identifying 'some unifying principle' or 'bright line'[59] which would assist in making the distinction with 'the dividing line [being] sometimes doubtful or even artificial', they nevertheless see the task as important enough to warrant an attempt. In their view, the correct approach grows out of one of the primary reasons for the rule that forum law governs procedure, that is, the efficiency of litigation.

(a) Mode or Conduct of Court Proceedings (Procedural)

2.22 Applying this ethos, some Australian High Court judges, in particular Mason CJ in *McKain v RW Miller & Co (South Australia) Pty Ltd*,[60] have suggested

---

[58] *McKain v RW Miller & Co (South Australia) Pty Ltd* (1991) 174 CLR 1, 26 (Mason CJ).
[59] *John Pfeiffer Pty Ltd v Rogerson* (2000) 203 CLR 503, paras 97 (Gleeson CJ, Gaudron, McHugh, Gummow, and Hayne JJ) and 133 (Kirby J).
[60] (1991) 174 CLR 1, 26–7; see also 56 (Gaudron J).

C. Contemporary Approaches to Substance and Procedure

that 'the essence of what is procedural may be found in those rules directed to governing or regulating the mode or conduct of proceedings' with all other rules or provisions to be classified as substantive. A distinguished US author had proposed a similar test almost eighty years earlier when he defined procedure as 'that branch of law which governs the process of litigation'.[61] Such a test has the advantage of significantly reducing the number of cases which will be automatically referred to the law of the forum, when compared with the right-remedy distinction. It also supports one of the key objectives of private international law, namely, the pursuit of uniformity of outcome and deterrence of forum shopping. The test also arguably sits more comfortably with the idea of practicality or convenience,[62] although, as some have argued,[63] convenience may be compatible with almost any definition of procedure. The test also appears similar to some observations in the US Second Restatement of the Conflict of Laws where it was suggested that rules relating to 'how the forum's judicial machinery functions and [the] administering [of] the court's processes' would normally be governed by the law of the forum.[64] Note, however, that the drafters of the Restatement did not intend these criteria to be the sole test by which all applicable law questions involving substance and procedure were to be determined. These elements were to be merely guidelines which could be departed from in an appropriate case such as where another country's law had a stronger claim to application. The Mason mode or conduct of proceedings test, by contrast, is expressed as a more universal, abstract standard to be applied in every case where delimitation between substance and procedure is required.[65]

2.23 The concept of rules 'directed to regulating the mode of proceedings' will, however, not be easy to apply in every case. For example, rules regulating the assessment of damages while not obviously relating to the conduct of court proceedings, may nevertheless involve local features (for example the court appointment of an assessor or expert) unique to that particular jurisdiction and difficult to replicate elsewhere. In such a case application of forum law may be exceptionally justified either on the ground of practicality or, possibly, public policy. Another 'gap' in the test, which is common to all substance/procedure delineations, is that it again appears to preclude the possibility of laws other than that of the forum or the cause of action being applied or of foreign rules being used to modify the scope and operation of forum law, for instance, in cases of service or taking evidence

---

[61] Lorenzen (n 17 above) 325.
[62] Tilbury (n 48 above) 333.
[63] E Schoeman, 'Rome II and the Substance-Procedure Dichotomy' [2010] LMCLQ 81, 89–90.
[64] Restatement (Second) of Conflict of Laws, § 122 comment a.
[65] The Australian Law Reform Commission recommended adoption of this test in intra-federal disputes within Australia (n 50 above) para 10.13.

abroad. Hence, even if it is accepted that procedure is best defined in terms of those rules which regulate court proceedings, in some cases forum law should not necessarily be automatically applied. Any test which is limited to substance and procedure does not allow for such possibilities. These arguments are reinforced when the second part or corollary of the rule is considered: any matter which does not involve the regulation of court proceedings will be classified as substantive and submitted to the law of the cause of action. Once again, such a view ignores the possibility of other laws being relevant: for example the law of the place of the act (for formal validity of certain documents), or the law of the domicile of the parties, or the law of the country of incorporation (for questions of capacity). This test therefore arguably gives too wide an operation to the law of the cause of action at the expense of other choice of law possibilities.

2.24 A slightly different version of this test was proposed by another Australian High Court judge, Callinan J, in *John Pfeiffer Pty Ltd v Rogerson*:[66] 'what should be regarded as procedural are the laws and regulations which are reasonable and necessary in the lex fori for the conduct of the action only'. The judge then gives the following examples of such laws: '[those] relating to procedures such as the initiation, preparation and prosecution of the case, the recovery processes following any judgment and the rules of evidence'. Examining this version of the test, while again it is likely that the law of the forum will have predominant application to questions of 'initiation, preparation and prosecution of the case', this cannot deny the relevance of other laws, especially where those acts have an extraterritorial impact outside the forum. The same comment could be made about subjecting the whole body of the law of evidence to the law of the forum. First, as has been noted, there are often cases where the taking of evidence will involve acts and effects in another country. Secondly, there may also be situations where a rule of evidence is not necessary for the conduct of the action but still has a profound impact on the rights of the parties and the outcome of the litigation (for example a question of admissibility) and so should arguably be governed by a law other than that of the forum—for example the law of the cause of action.

(b) Outcome Determinative (Substantive)

2.25 Another recent version of the substance / procedure distinction seeks to define what is *substantive* as opposed to what is procedural. This approach, which emanates from the decision of the High Court of Australia in the

---

[66] *John Pfeiffer Pty Ltd v Rogerson* (2000) 203 CLR 503, para 192.

C. Contemporary Approaches to Substance and Procedure

Pfeiffer case,[67] provides that 'matters that affect the existence, extent or enforceability of the rights or duties of the parties to an action' are substantive, with everything else being (presumably) procedural.[68] Writers have interpreted the 'existence, extent or enforceability of rights or duties' test as an 'outcome determinative' formulation,[69] whereby any rule which has the effect of altering the result of a given case will be classified as substantive. Interestingly, the High Court in *Pfeiffer* suggested[70] that this 'outcome determinative' test may be the functional equivalent of (or at least lead to the same results as) the 'mode or conduct of court proceedings' test proposed by Mason CJ in the *McKain* case. As noted later,[71] however, this conclusion is unlikely to be correct in all cases. There is some evidence of adoption of an 'outcome determinative' approach in the US Second Restatement where, for example, the issues of the burden of proof[72] and presumptions[73] are referred to the law of the forum 'unless the primary purpose of the relevant rule of the *lex causae* is to affect decision of the issue'. A similar approach is taken to the question of who should be a party to litigation.[74]

2.26 While a number of European[75] and American[76] scholars have supported a test based on 'outcome determination' for substance and procedure, it has a clear flaw. This is that potentially any procedural rule in a given context may affect the rights and duties of the parties and so alter the result.[77] The decision to use a jury rather than have trial by judge alone may affect both the existence and extent of a defendant's liability and the size of any award of compensation. A rule which requires each party to pay its own legal costs in a suit, regardless of the result, may encourage the commencement of actions which would otherwise not have been brought. It follows,

---

[67] (2000) 203 CLR 503.
[68] ibid para 99 (Gleeson CJ, Gaudron, McHugh, Gummow, and Hayne JJ).
[69] M Davies, A Bell, and P Brereton, *Nygh's Conflict of Laws in Australia* (LexisNexis Butterworths, 8th edn, 2010) para 16.5.
[70] (2000) 203 CLR 503, para 99.
[71] See 2.26.
[72] Restatement (Second) of Conflict of Laws, § 133.
[73] ibid § 134.
[74] ibid § 125.
[75] H Niederländer, 'Materielles Recht und Verfahrensrecht im Internationalen Privatrecht' (1955) 20 *Rabels Zeitschrift* 1, 34.
[76] R Sedler, 'The *Erie* Outcome Test as a Guide to Substance and Procedure in the Conflict of Laws' (1962) 37 NYU L Rev 813; G Stumberg, *Principles of the Conflict of Laws* (Foundation Press, 3rd edn, 1963) 155.
[77] Ailes (n 4 above) 408–9, 413; Australian Law Reform Commission (n 50 above) para 10.7; Main (n 13 above) 819, 826; L Brilmayer, 'The Role of Substantive and Choice of Law Policies in the Formation and Application of Choice of Law Rules' (1995) 252 *Hague Recueil* 9, 95–6.

therefore, that many laws regulating the mode or conduct of court proceedings (for example for joinder of parties) may also have a material effect on the outcome of a case. Compared to the right-remedy test, the outcome determinative approach therefore goes too far in the opposite direction: it gives too much operation to the law of the cause of action. Consequently, in this work it will be argued that while the 'outcome determinative effect' is a useful factor in determining whether an issue or provision is substantive or procedural, it should not be applied in isolation. Nor should the concept generally be applied where to do so would conflict with the 'mode or conduct of proceedings' principle. It will be argued that where a matter clearly falls within the scope of 'mode or conduct of proceedings', the fact that it may also be outcome determinative should not disturb its primary procedural characterization. This contention is supported by one of the surprisingly few decisions in which the possible conflict between the two criteria was identified. In *Julia Farr Services Inc v Hayes*[78] the New South Wales Court of Appeal noted the problem in the context of classifying a provision permitting a right of appeal. The court held that the fundamentally procedural nature of the right, because of its intimate connection with court proceedings, should be recognized despite the fact that the issue may also have an outcome determinative effect.[79] A further concern with the outcome determinative test is that, in a similar way to the regulating court proceedings principle, it does not appear to contemplate the operation of rules other than the law of the cause of action or the law of the forum, nor of the possible application of foreign procedural rules in the forum.

2.27 The position of the High Court of Australia in failing to acknowledge the role and relevance of foreign procedural rules may, however, have changed recently. In 2005, in *Neilson v Overseas Projects Corporation of Victoria Ltd*,[80] the High Court adopted a novel approach to choice of law which requires an Australian court to seek uniformity of outcome to prevent parties from obtaining an advantage by suing in Australia. Consequently, where foreign law is selected as the law of the cause of action the Australian court should apply the choice of law rules of the foreign country and any approaches to *renvoi* under that law to ensure that the same result is reached. A likely consequence of this view[81] is that where, for example, a foreign legal system classifies a matter as procedural but Australian law

---

[78] [2003] NSWCA 37.
[79] ibid para 52.
[80] (2005) 223 CLR 331.
[81] The various interpretations of *Neilson* and their relevance to the substance and procedure distinction are discussed more fully at 3.09–3.14 below.

C. Contemporary Approaches to Substance and Procedure

views it as substantive, the forum should nevertheless apply the foreign law because the foreign court itself would have done so had it adjudicated the same facts. Such a result may therefore be seen as an example of foreign procedural rules being applied in the forum—in the sense that the forum applies the same rules which the foreign court would apply if it were hearing the matter regardless of their characterization by the foreign court. It will be argued in this work that the *Neilson* approach does no harm when the Australian and foreign choice of law rules do not conflict. Where, however, a conflict does exist, for instance where under the choice of law rules of the law of the cause of action, a third country's law (and any *renvoi* doctrine) is selected, the position as to what law is to be applied by an Australian court becomes extremely complex.

4. Canada Takes a Similar Path

(a) Machinery Versus Outcome Determination

2.28 A slightly different version of the two Australian tests, although similar in effect, has been proposed by the Supreme Court of Canada in *Tolofson v Jensen*.[82] According to this view, procedure and substance are fused into a single test but defined in a similar way to the formulations discussed at 2.22–2.25. Procedural rules are those which 'make the machinery of the forum court run smoothly' and substantive provisions are those 'determinative of the rights of both parties'.[83] While the 'machinery' test may be similar in effect to Mason CJ's 'mode, conduct and regulation of court proceedings' principle, it arguably lacks the precision of the Mason version. In addition, as has already been shown, many highly process-oriented rules can nevertheless determine the rights of parties. This last point shows the danger of combining these two elements in one test. Such an approach even more clearly assumes that there is a stark line of difference between the two elements, whereas again it is highly possible that a rule for smoothing the machinery may also determine the rights of the parties. In such a case, the test would be rendered meaningless. Finally, and in a similar way to the Australian models, the Canadian formulation of substance and procedure also appears not to recognize any scope for application of rules other than the law of the forum to procedural matters. The same general observations may be made about the later, more detailed version of the

---

[82] (1994) 120 DLR (4th) 289.
[83] ibid 321 (La Forest J) (with whom Gonthier, Cory, McLachlin and Iacobucci JJ agreed); this view was endorsed by Kirby J in *John Pfeiffer Pty Ltd v Rogerson* (2000) 203 CLR 503, para 133.

substance-procedure test articulated by the Court of Appeal of Ontario in *Somers v Fournier*.[84] According to the court:

> Substantive law creates rights and obligations and is concerned with the ends which the administration of justice seeks to attain whereas procedural law is the vehicle providing the means and instruments by which those ends are attained. It regulates the conduct of courts and litigants in respect of the litigation itself whereas substantive law determines their conduct and relations in respect of the matters litigated.

(b) Statutory Interpretation

2.29 There are two other Canadian decisions in which interesting observations have been made regarding the substance and procedure distinction. In *Block Bros Realty Ltd v Mollard*,[85] a 1981 decision of the British Columbia Court of Appeal which was referred to with approval by the Supreme Court in *Tolofson v Jensen*,[86] the rather radical view was expressed that, in determining whether a legislative provision was substantive or procedural, the enactment 'should be categorized as procedural only if the question is beyond any doubt. If there is any doubt, [it] should be resolved by holding that the legislation is substantive'.[87] This statement is remarkable given that it was made at a time when the right-remedy position was well entrenched in Canada and so presumably had some influence on the Supreme Court in its reshaping of the law in the *Tolofson* case. Yet the comment does not provide an adequate test for drawing the line between substance and procedure since no guidelines are provided for determining in which category a provision must fall.

2.30 A possibly more instructive approach was suggested by a Saskatchewan court in *Toronto-Dominion Bank v Martin*.[88] In that case the court held a statutory provision of the forum to be substantive on the basis that application of the provision would destroy the claimant's rights to enforce a contract governed by foreign law. The court emphasized that the scope of procedure should be restricted 'so as not to frustrate the fundamental purposes of conflict laws',[89] one of which is the recognition of foreign rights. Such an approach certainly reflects the more contemporary Commonwealth view of substance and procedure. Of greater interest was the court's suggestion that statutory provisions of the forum should not be

---

[84] (2002) 60 OR (3d) 225, para 14.
[85] (1981) 122 DLR (3d) 323 (BCCA).
[86] (1994) 120 DLR (4th) 289, 318.
[87] *Block Bros Realty Ltd v Mollard* (1981) 122 DLR (3d) 323, 328.
[88] (1985) 39 Sask R 60 (Sask QB).
[89] ibid para 5.

C. Contemporary Approaches to Substance and Procedure 25

subject to the substance and procedure classification at all but applied purely on the basis of whether, as a matter of construction, they were intended to govern. Similarly to the approach taken to determine whether a forum enactment may apply as an overriding mandatory rule, the court here suggested that a forum statutory provision may, by contrast, *not* be applied in the forum *even where it is classified as procedural under the forum's rules of private international law*.[90] There is some evidence of this approach being taken in later Canadian decisions,[91] which is a beneficial development since unlike the traditional substance-procedure dichotomy, it focuses on the policy underlying the law rather than its abstract classification.

5. Australia: Further Developments

The High Court of Australia in the *Pfeiffer* case also made two other general observations in relation to the substance / procedure distinction which are significant to note in this context. The Court said:[92] **2.31**

> ... litigants who resort to a court to obtain relief must take the court as they find it. A plaintiff cannot ask that a tribunal which does not exist in the forum (but does in the place where a wrong was committed) should be established to deal, in the forum, with the claim that the plaintiff makes. Similarly the plaintiff cannot ask that the courts of the forum adopt procedures or give remedies of a kind which their constituting statutes do not contemplate any more than the plaintiff can ask that the court apply any adjectival law other than the laws of the forum.

The first part of this statement is uncontroversial. Obviously a plaintiff must accept the court and tribunal structure of the forum, including the allocation of subject matter jurisdiction between the courts, for example the fact that certain courts can only hear matters below a certain monetary limit or have exclusive jurisdiction over particular subject matter such as labour disputes. Presumably though, since it is the plaintiff who has invoked the jurisdiction of the forum's courts, it must be assumed that the party is aware of such conditions or else it would have sued elsewhere.

The second part of the passage requires closer examination, particularly the statement that the courts of the forum cannot adopt procedures or give remedies uncontemplated by their constituting statutes. The clear intent of this statement is that an Australian court has no power to adopt foreign procedures or award foreign remedies. In the case of procedures, it has **2.32**

---

[90] ibid para 14.
[91] *Investors Group Trust Co Ltd v Capital City Savings and Credit Union Ltd* (1991) 118 AR 254 (Alta QB); *Horseshoe Club Operating Co v Bath* [1998] 3 WWR 128 (BCSC).
[92] (2000) 203 CLR 503 para 99 (Gleeson CJ, Gaudron, McHugh, Gummow, and Hayne JJ).

already been noted that there are circumstances where a Commonwealth court may have regard to foreign procedural law and so this proposition is too wide. The final wording in the passage at 2.31, '. . . any more than the plaintiff can ask that the court apply any adjectival law other than the laws of the forum' reveals the same misconception. In the case of remedies, as will be discussed in Chapter 10, it is true that the forum cannot award a remedy which does not exist in the forum's own armoury but once this is established then foreign law will govern all other aspects of whether the relief may be granted. The role of forum law in remedies is therefore now very circumscribed under both common law and EU law principles. The High Court may also have been adverting in the passage to the fact that certain practices or relief granted by a foreign court may be inconsistent with the forum's public policy and so not enforceable on that basis. This view is important, because it provides an explanation for the application of forum law based on inconsistency with local policies and interests of the forum rather than simply because an issue happens to fall within the category of 'procedure'. It will be argued in this work that public policy, particularly when expressed through overriding mandatory rules of the forum, has the advantage of transparency since it makes clear the basis for excluding the otherwise applicable foreign law.

(a) A Legislative Solution?

2.33 Before leaving the Australian material it is useful to note that a small legislative step has been taken towards weakening the forum law governs procedure rule. Section 11(1)(c) of the uniform cross-vesting legislation[93] provides:

> (1) Where it appears to a court that the court will, or will be likely to, in determining a matter for determination in a proceeding be exercising [cross-vested] jurisdiction . . . (c) the rules of evidence and procedure to be applied in dealing with that matter shall be such as the court considers appropriate in the circumstances, being rules that are applied in a superior court in Australia.

'Cross-vested jurisdiction' is a difficult concept, the intricacies of which are beyond the scope of this work, but it suffices to say that such jurisdiction normally only arises to fill the gap which occurs where an Australian court lacks subject matter jurisdiction over an action[94] or where a matter has been transferred from one Australian court to another under

---

[93] See eg Jurisdiction of Courts (Cross-Vesting) Act 1987 (Cth).
[94] D Kelly and J Crawford, 'The Cross-Vesting Scheme' (1988) 62 Australian LJ 589. The legislative vesting of state jurisdiction in federal courts (where not otherwise within the accrued jurisdiction of such courts) was declared unconstitutional in *Re Wakim; ex parte McNally* (1999) 198 CLR 511.

C. Contemporary Approaches to Substance and Procedure

the cross-vesting legislation. It is important to note that section 11(1)(c) confers a discretion on an Australian court to apply the rules of evidence and procedure it considers appropriate in all the circumstances[95] rather than simply those of the forum under the traditional common law choice of law rule. For example, the provision could allow a transferee court to apply a rule of evidence or procedure under the law of the *transferor* court 'where there would be otherwise an unfair advantage for the party who obtained the transfer'.[96] Further, courts have recognized that a tribunal is not required to select 'a single set of rules of evidence and procedure' but may apply some rules from the forum and some from another jurisdiction.[97] It is clear, however, that a court of one Australian state exercising the jurisdiction of another state under the cross-vesting legislation is under no *obligation* to apply the rules of practice and procedure of the second state.[98]

Therefore, section 11(1)(c) is certainly a statutory acknowledgement that 'it would not be unduly inconvenient to apply the procedural laws of the cause [of action]'.[99] It is apparent, also, that the common law choice of law dichotomy between substance and procedure 'does not necessarily control the interpretation of para (c)'.[100] A court may therefore give a very wide definition of procedure under the provision not, as has been normally the case, in order to restrict the admission of foreign laws into the forum but rather to expand their operation. The provision would also conceivably allow the application of the procedural laws of a third jurisdiction *other than* the laws of the cause of action or the forum, although in no decision has this occurred. Despite these encouraging sentiments about section 11(1)(c), the reality is that the provision has rarely been invoked, although this is probably a result of the limited number of occasions on which cross-vested jurisdiction has been exercised. The opportunity for greater importation of foreign procedural laws into the forum has therefore not been realized although one question does remain: would the Australian legislatures ever consider extending the principle in section 11(1)(c) to proceedings apart from cross-vested jurisdiction, including those involving non-Australian laws? Given the limited record in using the provision

2.34

---

[95] *Bell Group Ltd (in liq) v Westpac Banking Corp* (2000) 104 FCR 305, 356; *Activate No 1 Pty Ltd v Equuscorp Pty Ltd* [1999] FCA 619, para 15 (suggestion that provisions of Evidence Act 1995 (Cth) could be applied by the court instead of those under the Evidence Act 1958 (Vic) (the rules of the forum) under s 11(1)(c)); G Griffith, D Rose, and S Gageler, 'Choice of Law Rules in Cross-vested Jurisdiction: A Reply to Kelly and Crawford' (1988) 62 Australian LJ 698, 703.
[96] Australian Law Reform Commission (n 50 above) para 10.12.
[97] *In the Marriage of Wilton and Jarvis* (1996) 133 FLR 355.
[98] *Re DEF and the Protected Estates Act 1983* (2005) 192 FLR 92, paras 34–35.
[99] *McKain v RW Miller & Co (South Australia) Pty Ltd* (1991) 174 CLR 1, 26 (Mason CJ).
[100] *BHP Billiton Ltd v Schultz* (2004) 221 CLR 400, para 54 (Gummow J).

28   *Chapter 2: The Substance and Procedure Distinction*

to apply the procedural laws of other Australian states and territories, it seems unlikely that Australian legislatures or courts would rely upon it as a model more generously to apply foreign procedural laws.

(b) A Jurisdictional Solution?

2.35 Another relevant point which emerges from the Australian jurisprudence is the awareness that the problem of distinguishing substance from procedure can also be avoided, at least in common law countries, by jurisdictional strategies. Three judges of the Australian High Court, for example, have noted that a robust use of the mechanism for transferring cases from one Australian court to another (in the 'interests of justice')[101] may be particularly justified where it has the effect that, in the transferee forum, the law of the cause of action and the law of the forum coincide. In such a case, no resort to the substance / procedure classification is required.[102] This idea of jurisdictional control of choice of law in order to subject a matter to a single law in this context is worthy of consideration although, paradoxically, it may have limited operation in *international* cases in Australia, given the High Court's restrictive 'clearly inappropriate forum' test[103] which is not only excessively weighted in favour of claimants but places little reliance on choice of law considerations.[104] By contrast, in other Commonwealth jurisdictions such as England,[105] Canada,[106] Singapore,[107] Hong Kong,[108] and New Zealand,[109] where the broader and more flexible 'more appropriate forum' test applies for stays of proceedings, there would seem to be greater scope for taking such a principle into account and so possibly reducing the instances where the classification has to be made.

6. ENGLAND: THE CONTEMPORARY POSITION

2.36 As discussed at 2.03–2.06, English courts, in their typically pragmatic way, have generally refrained from analysing the theoretical basis of the substance / procedure distinction or attempting to create a test based on any

---

[101] See eg Jurisdiction of Courts (Cross-Vesting) Act 1987 (NSW), s 5(2)(b)(iii).
[102] *BHP Billiton Ltd v Schultz* (2004) 221 CLR 400, para 99 (Gummow J), para 177 (Hayne J), and para 244 (Callinan J).
[103] *Voth v Manildra Flour Mills Pty Ltd* (1990) 171 CLR 538.
[104] *Regie Nationale des Usines Renault v Zhang* (2002) 210 CLR 491; *Puttick v Tenon Ltd* (2008) 238 CLR 265.
[105] *Spiliada Maritime Corp v Cansulex Ltd* [1987] AC 460.
[106] *Amchem Products Inc v British Columbia Workers' Compensation Board* [1993] 1 SCR 897.
[107] *Brinkerhoff Maritime Drilling Corp v PT Airfast Services Indonesia* [1992] 2 SLR 776 (CA).
[108] *The Adhiguna Meranti* [1987] 1 HKLR 904.
[109] *Club Méditerranée NZ v Wendell* [1989] 1 NZLR 216 (CA).

C. Contemporary Approaches to Substance and Procedure

such rationale. Instead, as was noted, English courts rather uncritically applied the right/remedy distinction for many years before some individual judges[110] replaced it with a test which made the classification depend entirely on the individual facts of each case. However in a recent decision, *Harding v Wealands*,[111] there is the first sign, particularly in the judgments of the Court of Appeal, of an approach to the substance / procedure distinction which is closer to that of the High Court of Australia in the *McKain* and *Pfeiffer* cases.

(a) *Harding v Wealands* Court of Appeal

Harding v Wealands involved an action for damages arising from a road accident in the state of New South Wales in Australia. One of the questions which the court had to resolve was, on the assumption that New South Wales law was the law of the cause of action of the tort, whether all the provisions in the New South Wales Motor Accidents Compensation Act 1999 should nevertheless apply in the English proceeding on the basis that they were substantive and not procedural. Significantly, however, the question of classification was not considered in the context of the common law rules of choice of law but in interpreting section 14(3)(b) of the Private International Law (Miscellaneous Provisions) Act 1995 (UK). Section 14(3)(b) provides that 'nothing in this Part [III] affects any rules of evidence, pleading or practice' or 'authorises questions of procedure in any proceedings to be determined otherwise than in accordance with the law of the forum'. The trial judge in the *Harding* case[112] acknowledged the various views expressed by the Australian High Court regarding the delineation of substance and procedure but expressed no clear preference for any particular approach, noting 'the elusive nature of the ... distinction and how far it depends on the context in which the issue arises'.[113] To that extent, the judge could be said to support a Pearson-Scarman contextual analysis. On appeal to the Court of Appeal, a variety of opinions were expressed. Waller LJ noted that it was clear that under the provision 'questions of procedure went beyond evidence, pleading and practice' and so presumably a narrow view of procedure was not intended by the legislative drafters. Consistent with this approach, he rejected the analyses of the minority judges in *Stevens v Head* and the majority in *Pfeiffer* on the basis 'that they were concerned only with the [Australian] federal context and not the

2.37

---

[110] See 2.18 above.
[111] [2005] 1 WLR 1539 (revd [2007] 2 AC 1).
[112] [2004] EWHC 1957 (QB), para 52.
[113] ibid.

international context'.[114] Waller LJ also referred to the subsequent reservation expressed by the High Court in *Regie Nationale des Usines Renault v Zhang*[115] as to the application of the *Pfeiffer* principle 'in cases of *foreign tort*'.[116] Yet analysis of the High Court's statement in *Zhang* reveals that the reservation was solely directed at the remark in *Pfeiffer* that all questions relating to *damages* should be considered substantive *not* the revised definition of substance and procedure.[117] Indeed, in Australian decisions since *Zhang* involving international torts or causes of action, the *Pfeiffer* test of substance and procedure (usually expressed in terms of the 'outcome determinative' principle) has been applied without question, and so confirms this view.[118] Ultimately, however, Waller LJ avoided providing a general definition of 'procedure' in the *Harding* case. The judge decided the case on the basis of precedent to the effect that once heads of damages have been established all questions going to the assessment of damages are procedural and so governed by the law of the forum.

2.38 Arden LJ discussed the issue of how to define 'procedure' much more fully. She agreed with Waller LJ that the *Harding* case did not require a comprehensive definition of procedure but only one in the particular context of section 14 of the Private International Law (Miscellaneous Provisions) Act 1995. Moreover, the definition of procedure had to be elucidated 'on a case-by-case basis' with particular regard to the context in which it was being sought.[119] Such a view is reminiscent of the Pearson-Scarman aversion to abstract definitions with the concept of procedure only capable of being understood in the context of the precise issue for determination by the court. Yet Arden LJ also expressed sympathy for the view of the majority in the *Pfeiffer* case that procedure should be 'reined in' in the context of choice of law, as a matter of principle. In a key passage her Ladyship states that:[120]

> In the context of section 14 a principled approach requires the court to start from the position that it has already decided that the proper law of the tort is not the law of the forum . . . On this basis a reference to the law of the forum must be the exception and it must be justified by some imperative which relative to the imperative of applying the proper law has priority.

---

[114] [2005] 1 WLR 1539, para 25.
[115] (2002) 210 CLR 491, para 76 (Gleeson CJ, Gaudron, McHugh, Gummow, and Hayne JJ).
[116] [2005] 1 WLR 1539 para 26 (emphasis added).
[117] Lord Rodger clearly recognized this in the appeal to the House of Lords: [2007] 2 AC 1, para 69.
[118] See eg *Garsec v The Sultan of Brunei* (2008) 250 ALR 682 (NSWCA).
[119] [2005] 1 WLR 1539 para 52.
[120] ibid.

C. Contemporary Approaches to Substance and Procedure 31

Hence, according to Arden LJ, under the scheme of the 1995 Act once foreign law has been chosen as the law of the cause of action it should only be in rare and exceptional circumstances that such law should be displaced because it is considered procedural. This view recalls the concern of Mason CJ at 2.08, that too wide a definition of procedure ultimately stultifies the operation of choice of law rules and limits the scope for admission and reception of foreign law.

Arden LJ then proceeded to identify the circumstances where the law of the forum may be entitled to 'priority' over the foreign law of the cause of action:[121] **2.39**

> It may, for instance, be appropriate to apply the law of the forum where the court cannot put itself into the shoes of the foreign court. This would arise where it has no power to award damages on a structured basis, even though such a power exists in the court of the jurisdiction which is the proper law. It would also arise where the court cannot put itself into the shoes of the foreign court of the [lex causae] in the sense that it cannot do justice unless it applies its own law.

Here Arden LJ acknowledges the incapacity or incompetence point mentioned earlier: sometimes a foreign remedy or procedure will be so alien to the forum that it cannot be sensibly or realistically applied. Her Ladyship appears to make the same point later in her judgment where she says that[122] 'in the context of conflicts of laws when the court says that a particular issue is one of procedure rather than substance ... the court is really saying that it cannot, for whatever reason, apply the relevant foreign law to that issue'. While the logic of this argument is hard to refute on the basis that certain procedures may simply be beyond the practical competence of a court to adopt, it is hoped that such a test of incapacity would be narrowly construed and not used as a device simply to avoid any foreign law on the ground that it was different or unfamiliar. Interestingly and hearteningly, the trial judge in the *Harding* case was mindful of this danger, noting that unfamiliarity, by itself, is an insufficient basis for excluding foreign law.[123]

Arden LJ also notes in the quoted passage at 2.39, that 'justice' may be a basis for applying forum law. While she does not expand on this idea it would be assumed that, again, such an exception should apply only rarely given the primacy Arden LJ attaches to the operation of choice of law rules. Significantly though, this comment is a frank acknowledgement that a decision to label an issue as 'procedural' as opposed to substantive **2.40**

---

[121] ibid.
[122] ibid para 60.
[123] [2004] EWHC 1957 (QB), para 61.

reflects a broader policy choice on the part of the court as to when forum law should apply.

2.41 Finally, it should be noted that Arden LJ expresses approval of both the majority of the High Court's approach in the *Pfeiffer* case and the minority opinion of Mason CJ in the *McKain* case. While noting that the central issue in *Harding* was the interpretation of section 14 of the 1995 UK legislation, Arden LJ nevertheless endorsed the principle in *Pfeiffer*, namely that substantive rules are those which 'bear upon the existence, extent or enforceability of remedies, rights and obligations'[124] and the view of Mason CJ 'that procedure covers matters as to the mode and conduct of trial'.[125] In Arden LJ's view, these observations on the common law position apply equally in the interpretation of section 14. So, while her Ladyship was at pains earlier in her judgment to stress that she was only making a contextual analysis of procedure in interpreting section 14, in fact her ultimate approach mirrors that of the Australian High Court.

2.42 By contrast, the judgment of Sir William Aldous in the *Harding* case is far more explicit in its adoption of the *Pfeiffer* approach. In interpreting the word 'procedure' in section 14 Sir William Aldous said that the expression 'should be given its natural meaning namely the mode or rules used to govern and regulate the conduct of court proceedings'. This view, he said, was supported not only by *Dicey and Morris* and 'persuasive authority' (namely the *Pfeiffer* case from which the quotation came) but also by the need to avoid 'forum shopping' which was 'an aim of the 1995 Act'. The *Pfeiffer*/Mason approach was preferable, the judge said, because it was 'consistent with the purpose of differentiating between substance and procedure'[126] and it was 'illogical' to suggest that this approach was not intended to apply in an international context. Sir William Aldous's primary concern, therefore, was with combating forum shopping and ensuring that, where possible, the same law should be applied wherever the case was litigated.[127] In his view the narrow approach to procedure taken by the High Court of Australia, in focusing on rules 'which regulate the mode or conduct of court proceedings', best supports that objective.

(b) *Harding v Wealands:* House of Lords

2.43 A further appeal in *Harding v Wealands* was taken to the House of Lords,[128] with Lords Hoffmann and Rodger delivering the leading speeches

---

[124] [2005] 1 WLR 1539, para 54.
[125] ibid para 61.
[126] ibid para 95.
[127] ibid paras 97, 105.
[128] [2007] 2 AC 1.

C. Contemporary Approaches to Substance and Procedure

(with whom Lords Bingham, Woolf, and Carswell agreed). The approach taken by the House of Lords to the meaning of procedure was, in this author's respectful view, disappointingly regressive.[129] Both Lords Hoffmann and Rodger first found that the meaning of 'procedure' in section 14 had to be interpreted in the light of the common law meaning which existed at the time of the enactment of the Private International Law (Miscellaneous Provisions) Act 1995.[130] According to Lord Hoffmann 'the terms "remedy" and "procedure" had been regularly used interchangeably' in private international law and this view was intended to be codified in the Act.[131] While procedure could be interpreted more narrowly on the lines of the approach in *Pfeiffer* and of Mason CJ in *McKain*, it was the clear intention of Parliament to adopt the 'equation between matters relating to remedy and matters of procedure' in the Act as, 'this is the sense in which the term has always been used in English private international law'. Significantly, Lord Hoffmann may have also thought that the *Pfeiffer* test of substance and procedure was of no application in the international context but one 'required by the constitutional imperatives of Australian federalism'.[132] In support of this view his Lordship appeared to rely upon the subsequent reservation to the *Pfeiffer* position by the High Court in the *Zhang* case.[133] For the reasons mentioned at 2.37, this analysis was, with respect, mistaken.

2.44 Lord Rodger thought that, in the UK legislation, there was no warrant for reading the reference to 'questions of procedure' in section 14(3)(b) as an 'exception' to the general choice of law rule for torts in section 9(4) 'for which some overriding imperative must be found' before it could be applied, since such an approach would, in effect, relegate the law of the forum to secondary status. Secondly, while the *Pfeiffer* definition of procedure 'in many contexts might well be regarded as the appropriate meaning', here, however, the expression 'questions of procedure' is being used within a statute on *private international law* [and] it is a fair assumption that Parliament meant the expression to be understood in the way it would be understood in the field of private international law'.[134] Accordingly, Lord Rodger also found that the right-remedy test must be applied to resolve questions of substance and procedure both under the Act and at common law.

---

[129] A Briggs, 'Decisions of British Courts Involving Private International Law' (2006) 77 BYBIL 554, 568, 572.
[130] [2007] 2 AC 1, paras 32, 65.
[131] ibid paras 32, 36.
[132] ibid para 48.
[133] (2002) 210 CLR 491, para 76.
[134] [2007] 2 AC 1, para 65 (emphasis added).

2.45 Lords Carswell and Woolf agreed with Lords Hoffmann and Rodger in separate speeches. Lord Carswell however acknowledged that the *Pfeiffer* view of procedure was closer to the 'natural meaning' of the term but that a 'special meaning' of the word existed in private international law which Parliament intended to adopt.[135] Lord Woolf expressly disagreed with Lord Carswell on this point, finding that the meaning of the term 'procedure' adopted by their Lordships, as being codified in the 1995 Act, was the 'natural' rather than a special meaning.[136]

2.46 The overall approach of the House of Lords to the definition of procedure was surprising, particularly in the light of Lord Wilberforce's remark[137] thirty years earlier, that 'for English law to abolish the distinction between substance and procedure . . . might be an intelligible objective'. Instead, the House of Lords in the *Harding* case chose to rehabilitate the right-remedy distinction for defining substance and procedure, which had seemed dead and buried. While their Lordships' remarks were addressed to the statutory context of section 14 of the 1995 Act, it is clear that they saw the provision as codifying the common law definition of procedure existing in 1995, which in their view was the right-remedy dichotomy. According to the court, this approach had always been used in English private international law and so should inform the interpretation of the Act. Consequently, it is arguable that their Lordships' definition of 'procedure' was intended to apply beyond the Act across all areas of choice of law. As has been discussed at 2.18, however, analyses of substance and procedure in English private international law by 1995 were far less monolithic than the House of Lords suggested, with a number of judges suggesting that the distinction should be considered on a case-by-case basis. In any event, to find that the development of the concept of 'procedure' under the Act was confined to its definition at the time of enactment would operate to stifle any possible judicial development in England of the substance-procedure rule in relation to torts,[138] unless new legislation appeared (which did, of course, happen with the Rome II Regulation).

2.47 Secondly, what is not clear from the speeches in the *Harding* case is whether the Lords would have taken a different approach if they had been considering the common law as it stood in 2006 (the time the appeal was heard in the House of Lords) rather than 1995 (the time of enactment of the legislation). Given their reluctance, however, even to consider the merits of

---

[135] ibid para 83.
[136] ibid paras 7–9.
[137] *Black-Clawson International Ltd v Papierwerke Waldhof-Asschaffenburg AG* [1975] 1 AC 591, 632.
[138] Briggs (n 129 above) 569.

C. Contemporary Approaches to Substance and Procedure

an alternative approach to procedure or the wider choice of law policies involved (such as the deterrence of forum shopping and willingness to accept foreign law on the one hand compared with the need to protect local residents from alien procedures on the other) the adoption of an approach based on the mode or conduct of court proceedings (procedure) or outcome determination (substance) seems unlikely. Indeed, their Lordships' apparent reliance on the right-remedy distinction, without any attempt to support the test in principle, is highly reminiscent of the traditional approach to procedure in private international law. On one view, therefore, the House of Lords approach in *Harding* leaves the meaning of procedure in private international law completely unchanged since the nineteenth century, which is surprising given the developments outlined in this chapter. The effect of the decision is to create great uncertainty in both English and Commonwealth law.

7. A New Approach?

The modern tests for delineating substance and procedure such as have been provided by Mason CJ in *McKain*, the High Court of Australia in *Pfeiffer*, and the Supreme Court of Canada in *Tolofson* are significant improvements on the right-remedy distinction in their narrowing of the scope of procedure. Yet, as already noted, both old and new approaches suffer from the same weakness since they appear to contemplate the application of only two laws, the law of the cause of action (substance) and the law of the forum (procedure), to all questions. There is no scope for the application of other laws, such as the law of the domicile of an entity or the law of the place where an act is to be performed, or a recognition that choice of law problems may sometimes arise *within* the concept of procedure, possibly requiring the application of a law other than that of the forum. Civil law commentators, by contrast, have for many years shown a greater awareness of the relevance of foreign law to matters which may be clearly classified as procedural, noting that issues such as service of process abroad, parties to litigation, and the taking of evidence in a foreign country may all involve the forum court applying the procedural rules of a foreign country, if not exclusively, then in tandem with forum law.[139]

2.48

---

[139] Gonzalez Campos (n 7 above) 295–6; M-L Niboyet, 'Contre le dogme de la *lex fori* en matière de procédure' in *Vers de nouveaux équilibres entre ordres juridiques mélanges en l'honneur d'Hélène Gaudemet-Tallon* (Dalloz, 2008) 363; A Caravaca and J Carrascosa González, *Derecho Internacional Privado: Vol 1* (6th edn, Editorial Comares, 2005) ch 13; M Feuillade, 'Ley que Rige el Proceso en Casos Iusprivatistas Internacionales' 72 (165) *La Ley* 28 August 2008, 1 (Argentina).

Given this empirical reality, some writers have argued that the forum law governs procedure rule is too restricted and should be replaced.[140]

2.49 Acknowledgement of the deficiencies in the existing common law model may therefore require a new approach. One option would be to create further and additional choice of law rules to supplement the basic forum law governs procedure rule at the same time as redefining the circumstances in which forum law should be applied, for example where the issue concerns the mode or conduct of court proceedings. In determining the proper scope of forum law in procedural matters, reference would also be made to the other choice of law mechanisms or 'homing devices' for applying forum law, such as public policy. Another option would be to abolish the forum law governs procedure rule entirely and replace it with a series of distinct choice of law rules applying to specific issues, recognizing directly that many different laws can apply to procedural questions. A leading adherent of this second view is the Hungarian scholar, Szászy,[141] whose writings were cited with approval by the English scholar Graveson.[142] Szászy argues that procedural questions are currently excluded from mainstream private international law analysis because of the blanket acceptance of the procedure (forum)/substance (cause) dichotomy, particularly in common law countries. Yet, given the diversity of questions involving procedure frequently presented, it is too limited, imprecise, and arbitrary to apply only these two laws to all such issues. What is needed, therefore, is a more inclusive and nuanced set of choice of law rules to apply to procedural matters. Szászy proposes a rule based on the Savigny idea of 'centre of gravity', that is, the law which has the closest connection to the proceedings, the act or matter to be judged, or the legal relationship in question.[143] Szászy then applies this principle to a range of issues (evidence, limitation, capacity of parties, validity of documents, defences, service of process, jurisdiction, and provisional measures) which commonly arise before the courts. In some cases the law of the forum is found to be the law most closely connected to the issue, in others it is the law of the cause of action, in others it is the personal law of the party, and in yet others it is the law of the place where the act was performed.

---

[140] See Niboyet, (n 139 above) ibid, and especially I Szászy, *International Civil Procedure: A Comparative Study* (Sijthoff, 1967) and n 37 above.

[141] ibid.

[142] See (1968) 17 ICLQ 534 and *Conflict of Laws* (Sweet & Maxwell, 7th edn, 1974) 593. See also *Cheshire, North and Fawcett* (n 47 above) 75 n 1 and the review by M Cappelletti in (1968) 16 AJCL 624, 626, which describes Szászy's work as 'original and extraordinary'.

[143] Szászy (n 37 above) 449, 452.

C. Contemporary Approaches to Substance and Procedure

The Szászy view has a logical attraction in that it directly addresses the policy reasons why forum law should be applied in a given case and also recognizes the possibility that other laws might apply to procedural questions. Yet a wholesale adoption of this approach is not recommended for a number of reasons. First, the forum law governs procedure rule is well entrenched not only in Commonwealth jurisprudence but also in civil law countries. It is unrealistic to expect such systems to reject this rule entirely; an approach, however, which redefines the scope of forum law in procedural matters and adds further choice of law rules where necessary is more likely to be accepted. Secondly, it is likely that the same results can be reached under the Szászy view as under a model which retains a version of the forum law governs procedure rule. Specifically, a court will refer a matter to forum law or the law of the cause of action in a similar manner to the Szászy model but where conflicts of law arise *within* the field of procedure, such as in service of process, jurisdiction, or the taking of evidence abroad, then new choice of law rules can be created where necessary or alternatively limitations placed on the exclusive application of forum law. Ultimately, therefore, it is preferable to retain the forum law governs procedure rule as a basic starting point while recognizing that it will not be the appropriate or exclusive choice of law rule in all cases involving procedure. **2.50**

8. EU INSTRUMENTS ON CHOICE OF LAW

Some evidence of lesser reliance on the generic substance-procedure classification model can be seen in a number of major EU instruments on choice of law, specifically the Rome I and Rome II Regulations. The provisions in both instruments dealing with choice of law in matters at the interface of substance and procedure are almost identical, with the drafters conspicuously not including a general definition of procedure. Instead, certain issues are subjected to the applicable law of the obligation under the instrument (for example the existence, nature and assessment of damage,[144] and limitation of actions[145]) and others, for example formal validity, to the law of the obligation or the law of the country of performance of the act (*lex loci actus*).[146] Such a 'direct' approach creates greater certainty than the substance-procedure classification.[147] Matters relating **2.51**

---

[144] Rome II, art 15(c); Rome I, art 12(1)(c).
[145] Rome II, art 15(h); Rome I, art 12(1)(d).
[146] Rome II, art 21; Rome I, art 11(1).
[147] M Illmer, 'Neutrality Matters—Some Thoughts about the Rome Regulations and the so-called Dichotomy of Substance and Procedure in European Private International Law' (2009) 28 Civil Justice Quarterly 237, 241.

to 'evidence and procedure' are excluded from the scope of both instruments.[148] As will be discussed throughout this work, the overall effect of the EU instruments is to reduce the scope of the law of the forum, at least when compared to English common law private international law rules. Such an outcome is consistent with the intention of the drafters of the texts, namely 'to promote uniformity of result [within the EU] and leave less [to] depend on the procedural peculiarities within a forum'.[149] This approach, at least in terms of outcome, conforms to the general trend in recent Australian and Canadian jurisprudence to classify more matters as substantive.

2.52 Note, however, that while the drafters of the EU texts have generally sought to avoid employment of the substance / procedure distinction, the classification is still relevant in the case of presumptions of law and the burden of proof,[150] where rules of the law of the obligation which are classified as procedural under such law will not be applied in the forum. Further, in some provisions (for example mode of proof[151] and remedial measures[152]) there is an awkward combination of forum law and law of the obligation, with little guidance as to how both should be applied. Finally, the limited scope of the instruments—confined to contractual and non-contractual obligations—means that many choice of law issues will continue to arise which will require resolution according to general principles.

2.53 This last observation is borne out by the exclusion of 'evidence and procedure' from the instruments and the lack of any autonomous definition provided for these terms.[153] The result is that national law will have to be applied to determine both the meaning to be given to these words and what law should be applied to an individual issue (assuming it falls outside the scope of the instrument). Significantly, the drafters do not stipulate that the law of the forum *must* be applied to matters falling within 'evidence and procedure', even though that would be the position in many cases under English common law principles. It is possible, therefore, that a national court may classify a matter falling outside the scope of either instrument (for example admissibility of evidence) as substantive and so governed by the law of the cause of action. Alternatively, a matter may be

---

[148] Rome II, art 1(3); Rome I, art 1(3).
[149] Schoeman (n 63 above) 88.
[150] Rome II, art 22(1); Rome I, art 18(1); *Cheshire, North and Fawcett* (n 47 above) 89, *Dicey, Morris and Collins* (n 27 above) paras 7-028, 7-029 Fentiman (n 26 above) 37; cf Schoeman ibid, 84–6, 91, who suggests that the substance-procedure classification has been entirely ousted from the Rome II Regulation.
[151] Rome II, art 22(2); Rome I, art 18(2).
[152] Rome II, art 15(d).
[153] Illmer (n 147 above) 242–3.

C. Contemporary Approaches to Substance and Procedure

classified as procedural but still governed (even in part) by a law other than that of the forum, for instance in a case involving the taking of evidence in a foreign country. Considerable scope of operation is therefore left to national choice of law rules under the Regulations. Some writers, in particular Illmer, have bemoaned this position, saying that the application of national law to matters of evidence and procedure, where the law of the cause of action falls under the Regulations, will lead to disharmony of court decisions and is incompatible with a European system of private international law. Accordingly, Illmer argues, an autonomous view of 'evidence and procedure' is required, based on the idea of 'neutrality',[154] which means that a national court must apply the law of the cause of action to any issue which is 'concerned with' or 'directed at' 'the decision on the merits' (which apparently is different from 'affecting' the decision on the merits)[155] and requires the law of the forum to be applied to any matter which concerns the mode or conduct of court proceedings. A response to this view is that there is no evidence that the exclusion of 'evidence and procedure' from the Regulations was an oversight by the drafters but was arguably instead the result of a conscious policy to allocate such matters to national choice of law rules.[156] Until European drafters create a text specifically addressing choice of law issues in procedure it is perhaps premature to remove the matter from the laws of the Member States. Nevertheless, the present author considers that whether or not an autonomous definition of 'procedure' is adopted to matters falling outside the scope of the Regulation, it should be based on the narrow mode and conduct of court proceedings view espoused by the Australian courts rather than the right-remedy test.[157] It is hoped that English courts can reach this conclusion themselves without the need for it to be imposed from above ('autonomously') by the European Union. Finally, however, there remains the same problem mentioned at 2.48 with any test of choice of law and procedure based solely on the substance-procedure dichotomy: that is, there may be limited scope for a court to apply or recognize laws other than those of the forum or the cause of action.

---

[154] ibid 246–7.

[155] The present author finds this distinction difficult to draw.

[156] cf Dickinson, who sees the concepts of 'evidence' and 'procedure' as 'matters that define the scope of the Regulation' which must therefore be given a uniform, autonomous meaning, 'independent of the forum's notions'; A Dickinson, *The Rome II Regulation* (OUP, 2008) para 14.57.

[157] Dickinson suggests adoption of such a test: ibid para 14.60.

9. THE US POSITION

2.54 In US private international law it is true that there is no universally dominant approach to choice of law in procedural matters. For example, some states still adhere to the First Restatement of Conflict of Laws approach of the 1930s, under which the right-remedy version of the substance / procedure distinction is applied, although a clear majority of states and scholars now reject this view.[158] Perhaps the most widely accepted approach in the United States to choice of law in procedural matters is that taken in the 1971 Second Restatement of Conflict of Laws. Under the Second Restatement, no attempt is made to classify issues according to whether they are substantive or procedural but, instead, the focus is on defining the scope of operation of the law of the forum in respect of individual issues. It is necessary to 'face directly the question whether the forum's rule should be applied'.[159] It is likely that this approach was taken for a number of reasons. First, the categories of substance and procedure are difficult to define (as has been noted), secondly, they can be used as conclusory labels to conceal the real reason for applying forum law,[160] and thirdly, they prevent courts from applying laws other than the law of the forum and the law of the cause of action to a given issue. Matters such as limitations, the burden of proof, jurisdiction, etc are considered separately from the point of view of the law to be applied in each case. Yet interestingly, while the Second Restatement makes no express reference to the substance-procedure dichotomy, it nevertheless, in certain provisions, resembles key elements of the modern Australian/Canadian approach, discussed at 2.22–2.28, in determining the governing law. Hence, where the purpose of the provision is found to 'affect the decision of the issue' or 'the ultimate result' (ie is outcome determinative),[161] it will be referred to the law of cause of action. Where instead, a provision merely concerns the 'conduct of the trial' or where the 'effort to apply the rules of judicial administration of another jurisdiction would impose an undue burden on the forum',[162] then forum law will apply.

---

[158] See eg R Weintraub, *Commentary on the Conflict of Laws* (Foundation Press, 4th edn, 2001) E Scoles, P Hay, P Borchers, and S Symeonides, *Conflict of Laws* (Thomson West, 4th edn, 2004) and L McDougal, R Felix, and R Whitten, *American Conflicts Law* (Transnational Publishers, 5th edn, 2001).

[159] Restatement (Second) of Conflict of Laws, § 122 comment b.

[160] As one US commentator has noted, '"procedural"' in conflicts jargon is simply shorthand for saying that the forum's rule applies': R Weintraub, 'Choice of Law for Quantification of Damages: A Judgment of the House of Lords Makes a Bad Rule Worse' (2007) 42 Texas Intl LJ 311, 311.

[161] Restatement (n 159) § 122 comment a.

[162] ibid.

C. Contemporary Approaches to Substance and Procedure

Another important matter which has been noted in the US literature is that the substance / procedure distinction has also been applied in areas outside private international law, in circumstances where the purposes are arguably very different. For example, a substance and procedure test is also used in the United States (and Commonwealth countries) to determine whether a provision in a statute should be applied retrospectively[163] (if the provision is classified as substantive then it will not be applied) and also in deciding whether an issue is governed by federal law (if it is classified as procedural) as opposed to state law (if it is classified as substantive).[164] It is obvious that these areas are very distinct from choice of law analysis in private international law, the purpose of which is to resolve conflicts between the laws of equal sovereigns: in the international context, nation states; and in the federal context, states or provinces. Cook, the US writer referred to earlier in this chapter,[165] warned correctly of the 'heresy' of automatically applying a definition of substance and procedure from a context or for a purpose outside choice of law to the choice of law inquiry. This point is of great significance and has been recognized by English,[166] US,[167] Canadian,[168] and Australian[169] judges, as well as common law[170] and civilian[171] scholars—although it has also sometimes been overlooked.[172] Consequently, it will be important in this work to identify decisions (in particular of Commonwealth courts) in which the 'heresy' has been employed.

2.55

The drafters of the US Second Restatement therefore sought to introduce more flexibility into the choice of law inquiry in procedural matters while at the same time limiting the scope of the law of the forum when compared to the traditional right-remedy formulation. In this last respect the objective

2.56

---

[163] *Maxwell v Murphy* (1957) 96 CLR 261.

[164] *Erie Railroad Co v Tompkins* 304 US 64 (1938). Another possible example may be a rule which allows parties a right of appeal in respect of a judgment on the merits (substantive) but requires leave of the court for an appeal in respect of an interlocutory (procedural) judgment; Spiro (n 3 above) 951.

[165] Cook (n 27 above) 341–3.

[166] *Harding v Wealands* [2005] 1 WLR 1539, para 52 (Arden LJ).

[167] *Guaranty Trust Co of New York v New York* 326 US 99, 108 (1945) (Frankfurter J): 'Neither "substance" nor "procedure" represents the same invariants. Each implies different variables depending upon the particular problem.' The US Supreme Court has also rejected the idea of an 'equivalence' between what is substantive under *Erie v Tompkins* and what is substantive for the purposes of the conflict of laws: see *Sun Oil Co v Wortman* 486 US 717, 726 (1988).

[168] *Toronto-Dominion Bank v Martin* (1985) 39 Sask R 60, 63, paras 8–9; *Province of Alberta Treasury Branches v Granoff* (1984) 15 DLR (4th) 295, 302–3 (BCCA Esson JA).

[169] *Hamilton v Merck and Co Inc* (2006) 66 NSWLR 48, para 54 (Spigelman CJ).

[170] Cheshire, North and Fawcett (n 47 above) 79; Walker (n 49 above) para 6.2.

[171] F Jaeckel, *Die Reichweite der lex fori im internationalen Zivilprozeßrecht* (Duncker & Humblot, 1995) 62; Illmer (n 147 above) 246.

[172] See, eg, *Hamilton v Merck and Co Inc* (2006) 66 NSWLR 48 paras 132–133 (Handley JA).

is similar to the modern Australian/Canadian approach; however, the technique employed is different. Instead of seeking to create a single, abstract principle to resolve all disputes, the US drafters have relied on guidelines for courts in the context of specific issues. The Second Restatement also envisages, to a greater extent than Commonwealth approaches, that laws *other than* the law of the forum and the law of the cause of action may apply in a given situation. This second aspect of the US experience will be recommended in this work for adoption in Commonwealth countries.

2.57 A further important approach adopted in the United States for resolving choice of law disputes concerning procedural questions is the doctrine of interest analysis.[173] While there are a variety of different versions of this principle, in broad terms, the forum court is required to select and apply the law which has the greatest interest or whose policies will be most affected in respect of the particular issue in dispute. Such a test, being expressed at such a high level of generality, obviously provides much less certainty than the Second Restatement model, given the absence of any specific guidelines as to what law should be applied. However, what interest analysis has in common with the Second Restatement approach is a capacity to consider the claims of all possibly relevant countries to having their laws applied. Again, unlike the position in England and other Commonwealth countries, it is not simply a matter of choosing between the law of the forum and the law of the cause of action; potentially any law may be relevant. The interest analysis model, however, provides little certainty and guidance for courts and litigants in choosing the applicable law and for this reason has not generally been embraced outside the United States.

2.58 Finally, of possible interest to Commonwealth lawyers may be two recent US decisions from jurisdictions in which the substance-procedure dichotomy is applied where it has been suggested that it may be possible for parties to 'contract out of' the substance / procedure distinction. Suppose, for example, that parties agree a choice of a law clause that provides that 'the law of X governs this contract without regard to conflict of laws rules'. One interpretation of such a clause would be that it excludes the doctrine of *renvoi* so that when a court seeks to apply X law it is directed to apply X's domestic law, not X's choice of law rules. Such an approach would be logical in that it would prevent another country's law applying in circumstances which might defeat the parties' expectations. By contrast, in two US decisions,[174] courts took the view that the above choice of law clause

---

[173] The leading work is B Currie, *Selected Essays on the Conflict of Laws* (first published in 1963, William S Hein & Co, 1990).
[174] *Education Resources Institute Inc v Orndorff* (Circ Ct Virginia 18 December 2008); *Orbusneich Medical Co Ltd v Boston Scientific Corp* 694 F Supp 2d 106 (D Mass 2010).

operated to exclude the substance / procedure distinction from the choice of law rules of the forum. The effect of this interpretation was that the law of X in its entirety, both substantive and procedural, applied in the forum. While in both decisions the approach had the relatively uncontroversial effect that a foreign statute of limitations was admitted into the forum, the potential was created for a much wider transplant of foreign procedural rules. Would, for example, these American courts have adopted the language, court attire, and rituals of the courts of the law of the cause of action? Intriguing as this approach is, it may be wondered whether its full implications were appreciated by the courts.

D. CONCLUSION

The substance-procedure dichotomy continues to be a central plank in Commonwealth choice of law doctrine, although its precise scope remains contested. The recent steps taken to restrict the scope of procedure in Australia and Canada are welcome in that they provide more scope for the operation of foreign laws and consequently further the goals of uniformity of outcome and deterrence of forum shopping. Yet all tests based on substance and procedure insufficiently recognize the possibility of applying a law other than that of the forum or the cause of action or that conflicts may arise within procedure. A preferable approach may therefore be to retain the substance-procedure classification for most cases with a narrow referral of matters to forum law but at the same time, where necessary, to develop discrete choice of law rules for individual issues. In Chapters 4–11 this suggestion will be further considered in the context of providing a detailed analysis of how the substance / procedure distinction applies in Commonwealth law in important areas of doctrine such as evidence, damages, statutes of limitation, and matters concerning the process of the courts. Where the current law is considered to be outdated, such as where it involves the application of the right-remedy test rather than the modern consensus as to what is procedural, then this will be noted. Also, where the appropriate basis for applying forum law rests on another 'homing device', such as public policy or overriding mandatory rules rather than a procedural classification, this will also be identified. An important objective of this work, therefore, is to provide practitioners with a clear framework for addressing issues that arise in this area.

2.59

3

Characterization, Alternative Methods of Forum Reference, and Harmonization

A. Characterization		3.02
	1. Rule of Law or Issue?	3.02
	2. Global or Provision-Specific?	3.04
	3. Applicable Law	3.06
	4. Self-Characterizing Provisions	3.07
	5. Avoiding Characterization	3.08
	6. Uniformity of Outcome/No Advantage	3.09
B. Alternative Methods of Forum Reference		3.15
	1. Public Policy of the Forum	3.16
	2. Overriding Mandatory Rules of the Forum	3.22
	3. Forum Law-Specific Choice of Law Rules	3.23
	4. Pleading and Proof of Foreign Law	3.28
	5. No Advantage/Uniformity of Outcome	3.30
C. Harmonization		3.31

The focus of this chapter is on three important issues relating to the study **3.01** of choice of law and procedure. The first topic is characterization or classification, which examines the method(s) by which a Commonwealth court resolves choice of law questions generally and which will have particular relevance when examining the distinction between substance and procedure. The second issue to be addressed is the other means by which matters may be referred to the law of the forum in Commonwealth private international law—apart from the procedural classification. Such an inquiry is important to provide a fuller understanding of the scope of forum interests in choice of law and the extent to which a procedural classification is still needed in cross-border disputes or whether other methods (such as public policy) can (or should) instead perform the task. This discussion is also important because the judicial decisions have at times been ambiguous about why the law of the forum has been applied, with courts relying on unarticulated policy assumptions through the mask of a procedural classification. The final issue examined in this chapter concerns the attempts to harmonize the law of procedure transnationally and the extent

A. CHARACTERIZATION

1. Rule of Law or Issue?

3.02 Where an issue of conflict of laws arises, characterization is the first step in determining the appropriate choice of law rule to apply. The first stage of characterization is that the forum court must characterize the cause of action, that is, assign the set of facts to the appropriate legal category, whether it be tort, contract, etc.[1] This process is conducted according to the principles of the law of the forum.[2] Once this process is complete the forum court must then apply the relevant choice of law rule to determine the law of the cause of action. Once this law has been identified, the forum may have to make a further characterization to ascertain whether a rule is substantive or procedural. This process only arises when a foreign law is the law of the cause of action, since if forum law is the law of the cause of action there can be no conflict between substance and procedure as the law applicable to both is the same. Where, however, foreign law is the law of the cause of action, the conflict can arise in two distinct ways. First and most commonly, a party may argue that elements of the foreign law are procedural and so cannot be applied in the forum or alternatively a party may seek to rely on provisions of forum law as a defence, with such provisions only being applicable to the action if they are considered procedural. While the majority of writers and the decided cases proceed on the assumption that the forum characterizes a *rule of law* of the foreign country or the forum,[3] some writers have argued that this technique is flawed and that courts should characterize *the issue in dispute* between the parties.[4]

---

[1] J Fawcett and J Carruthers, *Cheshire, North and Fawcett Private International Law* (OUP, 14th edn, 2008) 42.

[2] ibid 43; J Harris, 'Does Choice of Law Make Any Sense?' (2004) 57 Current Legal Problems 305, 309, 313.

[3] *Cheshire, North and Fawcett* (n 1 above) 45–50; L Collins (ed), *Dicey, Morris and Collins on the Conflict of Laws* (Sweet & Maxwell, 14th edn, 2006) paras 2.018, 2.040; C Forsyth, 'Characterisation Revisited: An Essay in the Theory and Practice of the English Conflict of Laws' (1998) 114 LQR 141; A Robertson, *Characterization in the Conflict of Laws* (Harvard University Press, 1940) 59–66; M Davies, A Bell, and P Brereton, *Nygh's Conflict of Laws in Australia* (LexisNexis Butterworths, 8th edn, 2010) para 14.7.

[4] See especially O Kahn-Freund, *General Problems of Private International Law* (Sijthoff, 1976); S Eiselen, '*Laconian* Revisited: A Reappraisal of Classification in Conflicts Law' [2006] South African LJ 147.

A. Characterization

The distinction between the two schools of thought is said to have practical significance in particular cases. If a rule of law approach is adopted, the forum may face a difficulty if confronted by conflicting rules under forum law and foreign law, such as in the famous *Re Cohn* case. The first problem which may arise is where the foreign rule is procedural and the forum rule substantive, in which case no rule is applied—there is a 'gap' in the applicable law. Alternatively the situation may ensue that the forum rule is classified as procedural and the foreign rule substantive, in which case both rules apply—the problem of 'cumulation'.[5] While in reality courts would strive to avoid such absurd results, the potential nevertheless exists under the 'rule of law' method. Under the 'issue' approach these problems are said to be avoided since the forum court only has to identify the matter in dispute and then apply a single law to it.[6] It must, however, be acknowledged that at times it will be difficult and arbitrary to identify the precise 'issue' for determination; at least with rules of law the material to be classified is clear.

In terms of the decided cases, English courts have generally appeared to support the 'rule of law' approach with a good recent example being *Harding v Wealands*.[7] In that case the English courts had to determine whether certain restrictions on damages imposed by New South Wales legislation, the Motor Accidents Compensation Act 1999 (MACA 1999), were substantive or procedural. Both the Court of Appeal and the House of Lords construed the foreign provisions alone without seeking to distil any abstract issues for classification from the case presented. A similar approach was taken in *Leroux v Brown*[8] in classifying the English version of the Statute of Frauds and in *Chase Manhattan Bank NA v Israel-British Bank (London) Ltd*[9] in construing US law. By contrast, in *MacMillan v Bishopsgate Investment Trust plc (No 3)*,[10] a case not involving the substance / procedure distinction, a majority of the Court of Appeal[11] spoke of characterizing the issue rather than rules of law. This view was approved in two

3.03

---

[5] Kahn-Freund (n 4 above) 224–5.
[6] G Panagopoulos, 'Substance and Procedure in Private International Law' (2005) 1 JPIL 69, 74–5; A Scott, 'Substance and Procedure and Choice of Law in Torts' [2006] LMCLQ 44, 47.
[7] [2005] 1 WLR 1539 (CA) (revd [2007] 2 AC 1).
[8] (1852) 12 CB 801.
[9] [1981] Ch 105, 122.
[10] [1996] 1 WLR 387.
[11] ibid 391, 393 (Staughton LJ); 417 (Aldous LJ) but cf 407 (Auld LJ) (issue and rules of law).

subsequent decisions of the Court of Appeal.[12] The decision in *Re Cohn*,[13] however, in which the question arose as to the order of death between a mother and her daughter, is contested territory in terms of characterization. While some writers have argued that this case was an example of a court classifying rules of law, specifically the German and English legislative provisions on survivorship,[14] others[15] have argued that in fact the judge purported to classify *the issue* of the effect of the testamentary disposition of property made by the mother. Since this issue was governed by German law, so too was the question of survivorship. The Australian case of *John Pfeiffer Pty Ltd v Rogerson*[16] has also been cited[17] as an example of a court applying an issue-specific approach to classification, although in truth it would not have mattered which view was adopted since the court only had to consider the legislation of one jurisdiction—that of the law of the cause of action, New South Wales—which limited damages for non-economic loss. Consequently, in the vast majority of cases it will not matter whether a rule of law or issue approach is adopted; where there are conflicting statutes of the forum and a foreign country which both demand to be applied, ultimately a choice must be made as to which law best meets the needs of justice in the individual case. Arguably the same process is involved when the court defines the 'issue' for choice of law purposes.

2. Global or Provision-Specific?

3.04 Related to the discussion of whether it is proper to characterize an issue as opposed to a rule of law is the question of whether foreign legislation, when selected by the forum as part of the law of the cause of action, should be classified in terms of their individual provisions or 'as a package'.[18] This matter arose acutely in the English decision of *Harding v Wealands*,[19] where the court had to determine whether the provisions of the MACA 1999 were substantive or procedural. The Act, however, dealt with many issues, such as: limits placed on the amounts recoverable for general damages for

---

[12] *Through Transport Mutual Insurance Association (Eurasia) Ltd v New India Assurance Association Company Ltd* [2004] EWCA Civ 1598, [2005] 1 Lloyd's Rep 67, para 57; and *Maher v Groupama Grand Est* [2009] EWCA Civ 1191, [2010] 1 WLR 1564, paras 8–11.
[13] [1945] Ch 5.
[14] *Cheshire, North and Fawcett* (n 1 above) 50; Forsyth (n 3 above) 147–8; *Dicey, Morris and Collins* (n 3 above) para 2.16; Davies (n 3 above) para 14.29.
[15] Kahn-Freund (n 4 above) 224; Panagopoulos (n 6 above) 74.
[16] (2000) 203 CLR 503.
[17] Panagopoulos (n 6 above) 74–5.
[18] J Carruthers, 'Damages in the Conflict of Laws—the Substance and Procedure Spectrum: *Harding v Wealands*' (2005) 1 JPIL 323, 327.
[19] [2005] 1 WLR 1539 (CA) (revd [2007] 2 AC 1 (HL)).

A. Characterization

non-economic loss, for loss of earnings, for gratuitous care; a prohibition on an award for the first five days' loss of earning capacity; and a discount rate on damages in respect of future economic loss. The Court of Appeal in *Harding v Wealands* split on this question, with Waller LJ[20] and Sir William Aldous[21] taking the 'package' approach and construing the legislation as a whole but Arden LJ[22] classifying each provision individually. A similar division occurred in the House of Lords, with Lords Woolf[23] and Hoffmann[24] taking a holistic approach but Lord Rodger[25] considering the provisions separately. Lord Woolf felt that the global approach was justified since the MACA 1999 'contains . . . a detailed statutory code . . . [and] . . . [to] have different parts of that code dealt with by different systems of law would not be an attractive result and in some cases . . . would produce an impractical result . . . The greater part of the code is clearly procedural and those parts which could be arguably regarded as substantive should be treated as being procedural as well'.[26]

3.05 While at first glance the individual provision approach appears more nuanced and capable of precise results, there may be circumstances where its use is inappropriate as Lord Woolf suggests. For example, a country may establish an administrative no-fault compensation scheme for accidents which contains provisions allowing suits for damages in extreme cases where losses meet a certain threshold. If such a provision were classified in isolation from the remaining provisions in the scheme and then subjected to a law other than that which created the scheme, the legislative framework could be seriously undermined. The Ontario Court of Appeal in *Chomos v Economical Mutual Insurance Co*[27] recognized this concern, finding that the above quantification provision in a no-fault scheme should receive the same classification as the remainder of the legislation. The provision did not alter the fundamentally substantive nature of the scheme; it was 'integral' to it.[28] The court in *Chomos* therefore also took a holistic approach to characterization.[29] In the case of legislation, however, which does not constitute a single codified scheme but addresses a number of

---

[20] ibid paras 30, 33.
[21] ibid para 85.
[22] ibid para 66.
[23] [2007] 2 AC 1, para 11.
[24] ibid paras 42, 48 ('all the provisions of the MACA . . . should be characterised as procedural').
[25] ibid paras 73–77.
[26] ibid para 11.
[27] (2002) 216 DLR (4th) 356.
[28] ibid para 51.
[29] For further evidence of such an approach, see *Hamilton v Merck & Co Inc* (2006) 66 NSWLR 48, paras 61, 67–69 (Spigelman CJ).

distinct issues, a more provision-specific approach to classification, such as that advocated by Arden LJ, may be more desirable. Interestingly, however, Callinan J of the High Court of Australia in *BHP Billiton Ltd v Schultz*[30] adopted an individual provision approach to characterization of the Dust Diseases Tribunal Act 1989 (NSW) despite such legislation being a unique code for the resolution of dust-related litigation.

3. Applicable Law

3.06 Another question which has arisen in the literature on characterization is whether it should occur according to the law of the forum or the law of the cause of action. While, as noted at 3.02, there is general consensus that at the initial stage of assigning a set of facts to a legal category, forum law should apply, there is less agreement at the later stage when a foreign or a forum rule of law or an 'issue' is being assessed. While some writers have argued for forum law to apply at this stage as well,[31] the more persuasive view from the perspective of comity and also preventing distortion in the application of the foreign law is to apply the rule in the setting from which it emanates.[32] A clear risk of such distortion would exist if the forum court had to classify a rule or concept either unknown to the forum or with no close analogy.[33] Classification of the governing law according to its own principles is also more consistent with uniformity of outcome. While it has to be acknowledged that this approach has not occurred in many cases,[34] significantly, the House of Lords in *Harding v Wealands*[35] characterized[36] the relevant provisions of the MACA 1999 by reference to the interpretation made of the same legislation by the High Court of Australia in *Stevens v Head*.[37] Most Commonwealth courts, however, no doubt for reasons of convenience, have chosen to apply forum standards of classification to all

---

[30] (2004) 221 CLR 400, paras 226–253.

[31] W Beckett, 'The Question of Classification in Private International Law' (1934) 15 BYBIL 46, 49–57; E Lorenzen, *Selected Articles on the Conflict of Laws* (Yale University Press, 1947) 91–3; and Robertson (n 3 above) 25–38. Forsyth notes that for the forum to do otherwise would be to cede control of its choice of law rule to a foreign legal system; see (n 3 above) 152.

[32] *Cheshire, North and Fawcett* (n 1 above) 49–50; Harris (n 2 above) 309–10. Kahn-Freund proposes a middle view between the two positions based on his concept of the 'enlightened *lex fori*'. While forum law governs the characterization process it must take into account the characterization used by the law of the cause of action (and other relevant foreign legal systems) with a view to developing a set of internationally accepted concepts; see (n 4 above) 227 et seq. Forsyth appears to support this view (n 3 above) 153–4.

[33] Forsyth (n 3 above) 151.

[34] Two exceptions may be *Re Maldonado* [1953] 2 All ER 300; and *Re Cohn* [1945] Ch 5.

[35] [2007] 2 AC 1.

[36] ibid para 40 (Lord Hoffmann), para 72 (Lord Rodger).

[37] (1993) 176 CLR 433.

aspects of the case,[38] although such a position is unlikely to apply in Australia in the context of a cause of action governed by the law of a foreign country. In such a case, the Australian court must apply the 'whole law' of that country, as discussed later in this chapter.[39]

4. SELF-CHARACTERIZING PROVISIONS

The issue of the law to be applied to characterization has indirectly arisen in Australia due to the enactment of several 'self-characterizing' provisions which typically involve a legislature stating that a particular provision or provisions in personal injury legislation are substantive. The objective of such a provision has been to encourage courts in other Australian states to apply the enactment whenever their choice of law rules selected the law of the enacting state as the law of the cause of action. Provisions of this nature were first enacted in the area of quantification of damages[40] before the High Court in *Pfeiffer v Rogerson* adopted a substantive classification under the common law rules of private international law. More recently, there have been provisions such as section 7(1) of the Personal Injuries Proceedings Act 2002 (Qld), which provides that 'the provisions of Chapter 2, Part 1 Divisions 1, 1A, 2 and 4 are . . . substantive as opposed to procedural law'. The experience with respect to all such self-characterizing provisions in Australia is that they have generally been given little weight by courts outside the place of enactment when conducting characterization. One reason given for this conclusion is constitutional: while the legislature of one Australian state has the power to alter the common law choice of law rules in the context of litigation before its own courts, it has no power to modify the common law choice of law rules as applied in other states' courts.[41] Consequently, such provisions have no effect outside the state of enactment and should not even 'be given weight in the task of statutory

3.07

---

[38] See eg *Leroux v Brown* (1852) 12 CB 801; *Huntington v Attrill* [1893] AC 150; *Harding v Wealands* [2005] 1 WLR 1539 (CA) (revd on other grounds [2007] 2 AC 1); and *MacMillan v Bishopsgate Investment Trust plc (No 3)* [1996] 1 WLR 387, 392 (Staughton LJ), 407 (Auld LJ) (although possibly an 'enlightened' version of forum law), and 417 (Aldous LJ); *Oceanic Sunline Special Shipping Co v Fay* (1988) 165 CLR 197, 225 (Brennan J). In *Chase Manhattan Bank NA v Israel-British Bank (London) Ltd* [1981] Ch 105 Goulding J left open the question of whether it was permissible to characterize an issue by the law of the cause of action; both parties assumed that the law of the forum applied.
[39] See 3.09 below.
[40] See eg Wrongs Act 1936 (SA), s 35a (7); Transport Accident Act 1986 (Vic), s 93(20).
[41] *Hamilton v Merck & Co Inc* (2006) 66 NSWLR 48, para 44 (Spigelman CJ) (with whom Handley JA, para 163 and Tobias JA, para 165 agreed); *Kok v Sheppard* [2009] NSWSC 1262, para 39.

interpretation'.⁴² Such a view does not of course address the broader question as to whether a forum (in the absence of any constitutional bar) may ever have reference to a classification made by the legislature of the law of the cause of action. In other Australian decisions, the suggestion has been made that although it is for the law of the forum to determine the issue of classification, the intention of the foreign legislature legitimately informs the forum's resolution of the issue and should be consulted.⁴³ Of course, this intention will be reinforced where there is a prior authoritative decision by a court in the country of the law of the cause of action characterizing its own laws as substantive.⁴⁴ Such a view suggests a Kahn-Freund 'enlightened *lex fori*' approach to characterization, with the forum applying its principles but in a manner mindful of the views expressed under the law of the cause of action. Such an approach has the advantage of avoiding the problems of distortion and unintended dépeçage in the application of foreign law. Hence, in the absence of any constitutional impediment under the law of the forum (an issue which is beyond the scope of this work), it is suggested that such an approach is worthy of general adoption in Commonwealth countries.

5. Avoiding Characterization

3.08 EU instruments on choice of law, such as the Rome Convention and the Rome I and Rome II Regulations, seek to reduce the need for courts to make characterizations by identifying specific matters to be governed by the law of the contractual or non-contractual obligation. The classification of many such matters as substantive or procedural may have been controversial under Member States' rules of private international law but they are now placed within the 'scope of the applicable law'⁴⁵ under each instrument. Some parallel can be seen with the approach taken under the US Second Restatement, where issues are generally subjected to particular laws rather than first characterized as substantive or procedural. Yet, the drafters of the EU instruments have not entirely eliminated the need for substance-procedure characterization. First, the distinction remains relevant

---

⁴² *Hamilton v Merck & Co Inc* (2006) 66 NSWLR 48, para 47 (Spigelman CJ) (with whom Handley JA, para 163 and Tobias JA, para 165 agreed).

⁴³ *Nalpantidis v Stark* (1996) 65 SASR 454, 458 (Full Court Sup Ct SA) applied in *Rahim v Crawther* (1996) 25 MVR 190, 198 (Full Court Sup Ct WA); cf *Martin v Kelly* (1995) 22 MVR 115, 124 (Sup Ct Vic Ashley and Hedigan JJ) where it was said that such a provision 'might possibly aid construction in a doubtful case'.

⁴⁴ *Thompson v Hill* (1995) 38 NSWLR 714, 728–31 (Kirby P).

⁴⁵ See Rome Convention, art 10(1); Rome I, art 12(1); and Rome II, art 15.

A. Characterization

in the case of presumptions of law and the burden of proof,[46] where rules of the law of the obligation which are classified as procedural under such law will not be applied in the forum. Secondly, matters relating to 'evidence and procedure' are excluded from the scope of each instrument[47] but no definition is provided of such terms. It will therefore be left to national law rules to determine the meaning of 'evidence and procedure' and the law applicable to an individual issue which falls within the scope of these terms.

6. Uniformity of Outcome/No Advantage

3.09 The process of characterization may also be affected, at least in Australia, by the High Court's recent adoption of the no advantage or uniformity of outcome approach to choice of law in *Neilson v Overseas Projects Corporation of Victoria Ltd*.[48] *Neilson* concerned an action in Western Australia in respect of a tort occurring in China which was alleged to be statute barred under Chinese limitation law. Since the tort occurred in China, application of the Australian choice of law rule for torts—the law of the place of the wrong—would have selected Chinese law. However, the High Court held that whenever application of Australian common law choice of law rules point to a foreign law, the Australian court must also apply the choice of law rules of that country (as well as any doctrine of *renvoi* existing under that law). The aim of this approach is to prevent parties from obtaining an advantage by choice of forum. Such an advantage should be nullified by the Australian court adopting the same approach on choice of law and so striving to reach the same outcome as the foreign court of the law of the cause of action. Application of the Chinese choice of law rules in *Neilson* led to the matter being referred back to the substantive law of Western Australia, including its limitation period, and so the action was not barred. Two judges of the High Court in *Neilson* took the principle of 'no advantage' even further, noting that the requirement that the Australian forum court apply the choice of law rules of the law of the cause of action also extends to adopting that country's rules on *characterization*.[49] So where the law of the forum and the law of the cause classify an issue differently—for example tortious as opposed to contractual—then the forum should adopt

---

[46] Rome I, art 18(1); Rome II, art 22(1), *Cheshire, North and Fawcett* (n 1 above) 89, *Dicey, Morris and Collins* (n 3 above) paras 7.028, 7.029; R Fentiman, *Foreign Law in English Courts* (OUP, 1998) 37; cf E Schoeman, 'Rome II and the Substance-Procedure Dichotomy' [2010] LMCLQ 81, 84–6, 91, who suggests that the substance-procedure classification has been entirely ousted from the Rome II Regulation.
[47] Rome II, art 1(3); Rome I, art 1(3); Rome Convention, art 1(2)(h).
[48] (2005) 223 CLR 331.
[49] ibid paras 105–107 (Gummow and Hayne JJ).

the foreign position, again to further the goal of uniformity of outcome.[50] The impact of the *Neilson* 'no advantage' approach on choice of law in procedural matters is not entirely clear but is of potentially great significance not only to Australian lawyers but also to Commonwealth scholars and practitioners, in the event that a similar approach is adopted in their countries. An attempt will now be made to explain the effect of the 'no advantage' test on substance and procedure questions.

3.10 The first (and easiest) situation is where an issue is classified as substantive by both the law of the cause of action and the law of the forum. Obviously in such case no conflict arises and the forum will apply the rule selected by both sets of choice of law rules. This outcome would have occurred in the *Neilson* case itself, had the Chinese choice of law rule not referred the matter back to Western Australian substantive law. Indeed, the expert evidence of Chinese law in *Neilson* suggested that the Chinese limitation period would have been classified as substantive, not procedural, which accorded with the Australian characterization.[51] In the absence of the application of the 'no advantage' principle, therefore, the Australian court would have applied the Chinese limitation period. Another example of this situation arose in *Amaca Pty Ltd v Frost*,[52] where the New South Wales Court of Appeal had to consider a tort action in New South Wales governed by New Zealand law. The question for decision was whether the action was barred by a New Zealand statutory provision which prevented proceedings being brought 'in any court in New Zealand'. The New South Wales court held that the provision barred the proceedings for two reasons. The first arose from the application of the *Neilson* 'no advantage principle', which requires 'single actionability', that is, a wrong must be actionable in the place of the tort to be capable of being sued upon in Australia.[53] Here, because the provision precluded suit in New Zealand, it must also bar proceedings in New South Wales. Implicit in this reasoning is that the New Zealand provision was classified as substantive as a matter of Australian choice of law rules (the law of the forum) and so found applicable in New South Wales as part of the law of the cause of action. The second reason relied upon by the court was that expert evidence of New Zealand law showed that the New Zealand Parliament did not intend to allow actions in courts outside New Zealand and that, consequently, the provision 'should be understood to prohibit the institution of proceedings [in general] without giving separate effect to the reference . . . to

---

[50] ibid.
[51] ibid para 187 (Kirby J).
[52] (2006) 67 NSWLR 635.
[53] ibid para 66.

A. Characterization

New Zealand courts'.[54] It is implicit in this analysis that, as a matter of *New Zealand law*, the provision was to be characterized as substantive and so applicable whenever New Zealand law was the law of the cause of action, not merely when proceedings were brought in a New Zealand court. Once again, therefore, there was no conflict between the characterizations of the law of the forum and the law of the cause of action and so the foreign provision was applied in the forum.

3.11 The next situation to consider is where a matter is classified as procedural by the law of the forum but substantive by the law of the cause of action. On a strict and literal view of the *Neilson* case, a conflict between forum procedure and foreign substantive law must be resolved in favour of the foreign law; at least where the plaintiff would gain an advantage by the application of local procedure. According to the same approach, in a case where a foreign law of the cause of action is selected, forum procedures must bow to foreign *procedures* in the court of the country of the law of the cause of action if a local advantage exists to the plaintiff in having forum procedures applied. Such conclusions, however, are extreme and absurd in that they would involve the complete jettisoning of the forum's procedural rules in every case where foreign law was the law of the cause of action. Consequently, in lower court decisions since *Neilson*, it has not been suggested that the 'no advantage' test requires the ousting of local rules of procedure.[55] An English court recently reached the same conclusion in the context of considering whether the doctrine of *renvoi* should apply to the transfer of title to movables.[56]

3.12 The third situation that may arise is where the matter is classified as substantive by the law of the forum but procedural by the law of the cause of action. In this category of case the forum court is required to place itself entirely in the shoes of the foreign court (of the country of the law of the cause of action) and strive to reach the identical result that the foreign court would; in other words, to apply all substantive and procedural rules that the foreign court itself would apply. In a sense, this view is the purest version of the 'no advantage' principle because the forum court seeks to replicate both the approach and result of the foreign court. Under this approach, regard may be had to both forum and foreign law classifications of the issue to ensure that the outcome is the same in each tribunal. This view was adopted in *O'Driscoll v J Ray McDermott SA*[57] where the Western Australian Court of Appeal had to consider a breach of contract action

---

[54] ibid para 130.
[55] See eg *Garsec Pty Ltd v His Majesty the Sultan of Brunei* (2008) 250 ALR 682.
[56] *Blue Sky One Ltd v Mahan Air* [2010] EWHC 631 (Comm) para 176.
[57] [2006] WASCA 25.

56   *Chapter 3: Characterization, Methods of Forum Reference*

with Singapore law as the substantive law. The action was barred under the Singapore statute of limitation but not under the law of Western Australia. Under Australian common law choice of law rules, the application of statutory limitation periods is considered a substantive matter, governed by the law of the cause of action, whereas under Singapore choice of law rules (according to the expert evidence), such an issue is classified as procedural and governed by the law of the forum. In this case, however, the plaintiff derived 'no advantage' from suing in Western Australia as opposed to Singapore since the outcome of applying both local and foreign choice of law rules was the same: the Singapore limitation period applied. Moreover, it would not have mattered *what* classification was made by Singaporean law since the limitation would have applied in any case in any Singapore proceedings and so would therefore have to be applied in Australia.

3.13 The same result was reached in *Garsec Pty Ltd v His Majesty the Sultan of Brunei*,[58] although in that case the court saw no need to consider the classification of the issue under the law of the cause of action, once it had determined that the issue was substantive under forum law. The *Garsec* case involved claims for breach of contract and tort which were both governed by the law of Brunei, according to Australian choice of law rules. The court held that the Sultan was entitled to immunity from suit in the Australian court under the Constitution of Brunei on the basis that such immunity was substantive and not procedural as a matter of Australian choice of law rules.[59] Further, and most importantly, the court held that it was irrelevant to consider whether the immunity would also be characterized as substantive or procedural under Brunei law,[60] once it was determined that the matter was substantive under the choice of law rules of the forum. Again the reason for this conclusion is likely to be that, similarly to *O'Driscoll*, after establishing that immunity was substantive under Australian law it mattered not how Brunei law would classify the plea; it would apply in Brunei proceedings regardless and so must also apply in New South Wales.[61]

3.14 There are, however, complications which may arise under *Neilson* if the choice of law rules of the foreign law of the cause of action (Ruritania) select the law of a third country or the law of an Australian state (for example Victoria) as the substantive law. In such a case the Australian

---

[58] (2008) 250 ALR 682.
[59] ibid para 132; for an analysis of whether state immunity is substantive or procedural, see 4.64–4.70 below.
[60] ibid para 151.
[61] ibid para 131.

court would have to apply the law of the third country or Victorian law to matters of substance and Ruritanian procedural rules (assuming the Australian court would characterize such rules as substantive). The picture becomes even less clear if Ruritania also has a doctrine of *renvoi*. If the version used is 'double *renvoi*' the application of which would remit the matter back to the law of a third country or Victorian law (which also adopts double *renvoi*), then there may be an inextricable circle or perpetual reference. If the version employed in Ruritanian law is 'single *renvoi*', then much will depend upon whether the matter is referred back to Victorian law (which would then probably remit the issue back to Ruritanian domestic law)[62] or referred to the law of a third country. Either way, the position can become very complex and unpredictable—which suggests that true uniformity of outcome may be an unattainable goal. On balance, therefore, the approach in *Neilson* is not recommended for export to other Commonwealth countries.

B. ALTERNATIVE METHODS OF FORUM REFERENCE

The purpose of this section[63] is to examine the other means in Commonwealth private international law by which matters may be referred to the law of the forum. Such an inquiry is important in order to assess the role and purpose of the procedural classification within the broader context of 'homing devices' or mechanisms for applying forum law. While the existence of most such devices in national laws is accepted, many commentators have criticized the tendency among some courts to give them an excessive interpretation, given the threat posed to decisional harmony.[64] The right-remedy approach to substance and procedure, discussed in Chapter 2, is a good example. Commentators have also noted the relationship between the procedural classification and other methods of forum reference,[65] suggesting that a court's attitude to what is procedural in a given case has been and should be shaped by the absence of an alternative (and arguably more appropriate) vehicle for applying forum law.[66] Further, suggestions have occasionally been made that the use of a procedural

3.15

---

[62] This would have been the outcome in *Neilson* itself had Chinese law been found to have adopted the 'single *renvoi*' principle and did occur in *Re Annesley* [1926] Ch 692.

[63] See generally C Fassberg, 'The Forum: Its Role and Significance in Choice of Law' (1985) 84 *Zeitschrift für Vergleichende Rechtswissenschaft* 1.

[64] T De Boer, 'Facultative Choice of Law: The Procedural Status of Choice of Law Rules and Foreign Law' (1996) 257 *Hague Recueil* 223, 393.

[65] R Mortensen, 'Homing Devices in Choice of Tort Law: Australian, British and Canadian Approaches' (2006) 55 ICLQ 839.

[66] See eg A Briggs, 'The Legal Significance of the Place of a Tort' (2002) 2 OUCLJ 133, 136.

classification may have been a subterfuge for other, undisclosed policy interests, such as the protection of local residents from less generous foreign laws.[67] Consequently, this discussion is also important because at times in the judicial decisions the precise basis for the application of forum law has been uncertain and an analysis of the proper sphere of operation of each method of forum reference is therefore desirable.

1. Public Policy of the Forum

3.16 The first alternative method of forum law control to consider is the doctrine of forum public policy. While there has occasionally been dispute as to whether forum law applies by default once a matter arising under foreign law is found to violate local public policy or whether the foreign law applies alone without the 'offending' portion, the first view is most widely accepted in Commonwealth jurisprudence.[68] It has been noted that the public policy doctrine 'has assumed far less prominence in the English conflict of laws than have corresponding doctrines in the laws of foreign countries, eg France and Germany'.[69] Clearly, at least part of the explanation for this position rests with the traditionally broad conception of procedure in English law as implemented through the right-remedy distinction, which gave forum law a fairly wide scope of operation compared to that adopted in civil law countries. Another explanation was that in a number of areas, most famously torts, the common law choice of law rule was weighted in favour of the law of the forum.[70] Yet in some Commonwealth cases examined in this work it is difficult to identify the precise basis for application of the law of the forum by a court—was it because the matter was classified as procedural or because a foreign rule offended English public policy—and so an understanding of the public policy doctrine is necessary. It was also noted in Chapter 2 that the right-remedy approach to substance and procedure has now been rejected in some Commonwealth countries, such as Australia and Canada. A question which therefore arises is whether public policy may enjoy an enhanced role in Commonwealth choice of law rules in the future as courts seek to 'fill the gap' left by a more limited role given to the law of the forum in procedural matters. This inquiry is particularly pertinent in relation to EU instruments such as the Rome I and Rome II Regulations, which grant a

---

[67] For a salient recent example, see *Harding v Wealands* [2007] 2 AC 1.
[68] See J Carruthers and E Crawford, 'Kuwait Airways Corp v Iraqi Airways Co' (2003) 52 ICLQ 761, 772, who criticize the House of Lords in the said case for not applying English law by default according to the traditional approach.
[69] *Dicey, Morris and Collins* (n 3 above) para 5.004.
[70] *Phillips v Eyre* (1870) LR 6 QB 1.

B. Alternative Methods of Forum Reference

wide scope of operation to the law of the cause of action when compared to common law principles. Alternatively, courts may view these recent developments to limit the role of the forum in procedural matters as indicative of a more general trend to reduce the scope and influence of forum law; in which case public policy should similarly be kept under restraint.

Certainly, the traditional scope of the doctrine of public policy in English and Commonwealth law as a basis for refusing to apply a foreign law of the cause of action has been very limited. Writers and courts have generally agreed that foreign law should only be excluded where it offends fundamental values and principles of the forum and that public policy in transnational cases should have a more restrictive operation than in domestic law.[71] This idea is best expressed in the often quoted statement of Cardozo J:

3.17

> The courts are not free to refuse to enforce a foreign right at the pleasure of the judges, to suit the individual notion of expediency or fairness. They do not close their doors, unless help would violate some fundamental principle of justice, some prevalent conception of good morals, some deep-rooted tradition of the common weal.[72]

While there is broad agreement as to the narrow scope of public policy in English and Commonwealth private international law, it is more difficult to identify precisely the situations when it should be applied. It is beyond the scope of this work to explore the doctrine of public policy in complete detail but for present purposes it suffices to note the following situations suggested by one commentator where the doctrine may be invoked:[73]

3.18

(1) where the basic principles of English justice and fairness are affronted;[74]
(2) when English conceptions of morality are infringed;
(3) where a transaction prejudices the interests of the United Kingdom or its good relations with foreign powers; and
(4) when there is a fundamental breach of human rights or public international law.

It is apparent that these categories, even when considered as a whole, represent a far less significant intrusion into the scope of foreign law than the right-remedy version of substance and procedure. In particular, it is clear that a mere difference between the law of the forum and a foreign law of

---

[71] A Mills, 'The Dimensions of Public Policy in Private International Law' (2008) 4 JPIL 201.
[72] *Loucks v Standard Oil Co of New York* 224 NY 99, 111 (1918).
[73] *Cheshire, North and Fawcett* (n 1 above) 142–6.
[74] *Kuwait Airways Corp v Iraqi Airways Co (Nos 4 and 5)* [2002] 2 AC 883, para 18 (Lord Nicholls); P Carter, 'The Role of Public Policy in English Private International Law' (1993) 42 ICLQ 1.

the cause of action is insufficient to trigger the public policy exception.[75] Australian courts have described the test in similarly narrow and exceptional terms, requiring that for the doctrine to be applied, there must be a 'substantial injustice either because ... of a repugnant foreign law or a repugnant application of the law in a particular case'[76] or 'a fundamental question'[77] of moral or ethical policy, fairness of procedure, or illegality involved. A possibly even narrower version of public policy is found in EU instruments such as the Rome I[78] and Rome II Regulations,[79] where it is provided that the applicable law may only be excluded if its application 'is manifestly incompatible' with the public policy of the forum. The European Court of Justice has suggested that the defence should only be available to exclude a foreign law or judgment where a 'fundamental principle of the legal order of the country in which enforcement is sought' would be violated.[80]

3.19 As mentioned at 3.16, it is likely that the wide scope given to forum law under the right-remedy approach has meant that in a number of cases public policy has not been needed to engage the law of the forum. Public policy, as illustrated by the examples, is also a more principled basis for invoking the law of the forum than the right-remedy test for substance and procedure because the reasons for applying forum law are more transparent. Further, public policy also only operates as an exception or modification to the rule that foreign law applies and only excludes so much of that law that the *application* of which is offensive to local values; the classification of a law as 'procedural', by contrast, in operating at a more abstract level, may exclude a wider portion of the foreign law. Consequently, as a vehicle for vindicating forum interests, the traditional procedural classification is, by comparison, less nuanced and calibrated in its application.[81] Hence, if, as suggested in Chapter 2, the operation of the law of the forum in procedural matters should be kept confined to issues relating to the functions and operation of the court system, then such a view would sit much more comfortably with the current scope of the doctrine of public policy. There would be less potential for overlap and public policy would have greater opportunity to perform its important role in protecting parties from unjust and unconscionable foreign laws. To take an example, if statutes of limitation were classified as substantive (which

---

[75] *Addison v Brown* [1954] 1 WLR 779.
[76] *Jenton Overseas Investment Pte Ltd v Townsing* (2008) 21 VR 241, para 22 (Sup Ct Vic); see also *Ross v Ross* [2010] NZCA 447.
[77] *Stern v National Australia Bank* [1999] FCA 1421, para 143.
[78] Rome I, art 21.
[79] Rome II, art 26.
[80] *Gambazzi v Daimlerchrysler Canada Inc* C-394/07 [2009] 1 Lloyd's Rep 647, para 27.
[81] Harris (n 2 above) 347; A Briggs 'Conflict of Laws and Commercial Remedies' in A Burrows and E Peel (eds), *Commercial Remedies Current Issues and Problems* (OUP, 2003) 271, 276.

B. Alternative Methods of Forum Reference

is the case now in many Commonwealth countries), the law of the cause of action presumptively applies. Yet if such a law had a ridiculously short time period and imposed a great hardship on the claimant, arguably such a provision should be disallowed because basic principles of the forum's justice and fairness are compromised.[82] In this way, closer attention is paid to the *detail* of the foreign law and why certain aspects of it should not be applied in the forum rather than simply excluding it entirely because it is classified as 'remedial'.

Public policy may also have an important function to perform in the area of procedure by protecting parties from unjust foreign *procedural* laws, the possible application of which in the forum was discussed in Chapter 2. As was noted at 2.48, the procedural rules of the forum may also be qualified or limited by reference to foreign rules of procedure, such as where a forum rule permitting discovery gives way to a right of privilege or duty to disclose under foreign law. If, for example, such a duty were granted in circumstances that would be considered seriously unjust or oppressive by the forum, public policy could provide a principled basis for excluding such law or at least diminishing its significance. Another example of public policy being employed to override a foreign procedural law would be where a foreign judgment would not be enforced by a Commonwealth court because, for example, it was granted in circumstances where the defendant had no notice of the foreign proceedings. **3.20**

Overall, it is suggested that courts should continue to construe public policy narrowly so as to maintain consistency with the recent trend in the Commonwealth of greater receptivity to foreign law. Also, unlike the previous position where the right-remedy distinction reduced the need for the doctrine, if the law of the forum is now to be more narrowly employed in procedural matters, public policy is likely to have a greater role to play in protecting forum interests from offensive foreign laws. Such a result will be more consistent with the original basis of the doctrine. Also, in the discussion of specific issues in Chapters 4–11, reference will be made to decisions where public policy arguably formed the true basis for the application of the law of the forum or where perhaps it *should* have. **3.21**

2. Overriding Mandatory Rules of the Forum

Another basis for applying forum law in Anglo-Commonwealth private international law is through the operation of overriding mandatory rules, which are domestic legislative (and possibly also common law)[83] rules of **3.22**

---

[82] See eg Foreign Limitation Periods Act 1984 (UK), s 2.
[83] T Hartley, 'Mandatory Rules in International Contracts: The Common Law Approach' (1997) 266 *Hague Recueil* 341, 351–3.

the forum 'regarded as so important that as a matter of construction or policy, they must apply in any action before a court of the forum, even where the issues are in principle governed by a foreign law selected by a foreign choice of law rule'.[84] Overriding mandatory rules of the forum are recognized as an exception to the application of foreign law in all Commonwealth countries and also in EU instruments such as the Rome I[85] and Rome II[86] Regulations. Essentially, whether a given statutory provision applies to override a foreign law of the cause of action is a matter for judicial interpretation of parliamentary intent.[87] Commonly, overriding mandatory rules in a statute do not exclude the entire foreign law but only so much of that law which is inconsistent with the legislation. In this way, the operation of such rules is similar to the public policy doctrine in providing a transparent but limited referral of matters to the law of the forum. Hence, such an approach sits comfortably with the narrow view of the law of the forum advocated at 3.21, for both procedure and public policy. Moreover, overriding mandatory rules have often arisen in the context where certain categories of party need protection from unconscionable transactions, such as consumers and employees.[88] There have been few instances of such laws being found by courts to mandate the operation of local procedures in transnational cases, although this position may change as Commonwealth lawyers become more familiar with the concept of overriding rules. Nevertheless, in the specific situations considered in Chapters 4–11, there are decisions where application of the law of the forum can perhaps best be explained as an example of a court giving effect to overriding mandatory rules of the forum rather than applying a procedural classification.[89]

3. Forum Law-Specific Choice of Law Rules

3.23 In most areas of Anglo-Commonwealth private international law there have always been some forum law-specific choice of law rules, that is, rules which select the law of the forum directly with little or no scope for application of another law. Such rules have existed, until recently, in the

---

[84] Law Commission Working Paper No 87 (1984) para 4.5.
[85] Rome I, art 9.
[86] Rome II, art 16.
[87] Fassberg (n 63 above) 29.
[88] See eg in England, the Unfair Contract Terms Act 1977 and Employment Rights Act 1996.
[89] See eg *Roerig v Valiant Trawlers* [2002] 1 WLR 2304.

B. Alternative Methods of Forum Reference

areas of tort,[90] equity,[91] aspects of insolvency,[92] and family law.[93] The reason why the law of the forum has applied as the choice of law rule in each of these areas has often been unexplained and ambiguous. For example, in the case of family law[94] and insolvency,[95] public policy has sometimes been cited as the reason for forum preference, while in equity application of forum law is said to be based on the fact that it operates *in personam* and on the conscience of the defendant.[96] In court decisions, however, little attention has been given to justifying the application of forum law; its operation has largely been assumed, much like the right-remedy rule for substance and procedure as noted in Chapter 2.

It is important to note the use of forum law-specific choice of law rules for the present study because it makes the substance-procedure classification redundant as forum law applies to both procedure and substance. Such an approach therefore reinforces the tradition of forum dominance in Commonwealth choice of law, similar to the right-remedy distinction. Yet in the same way that the right-remedy test is now under challenge, it is significant to note that in two of the above areas, tort and equity, there has been a movement away from the law of the forum in recent years to more flexible and nuanced choice of law approaches. In these fields, therefore, there is likely to be an enhanced need for the substance-procedure classification and, consequently, a greater need to characterize the two distinctly and correctly. Further, any suggestions made for (re)defining the substance-procedure boundary should ideally take account of the trend towards diminution in the status of the law of the forum across the wider choice of law system. **3.24**

---

[90] *Phillips v Eyre* (1870) LR 6 QB 1 which continues to apply in a number of Commonwealth countries, such as New Zealand and Singapore, as well as in England for defamation claims; see Private International Law (Miscellaneous Provisions) Act 1995 (UK), s 13.

[91] See *National Commercial Bank v Wimborne* [1978] 5 BPR 11,958, 11,982; *United States Surgical Co v Hospital Products International Pty Ltd* [1982] 2 NSWLR 766, 796–9; *Paramasivam v Flynn* (1998) 90 FCR 489; and *OZ-US Film Productions Pty Ltd (in liq) v Heath* [2000] NSWSC 967, para 22.

[92] See eg winding up of companies: *Re Bank of Commerce and Credit International SA (No 10)* [1997] Ch 213 and administration of a bankrupt's estate: *Ex parte Melbourn* (1870) LR 6 Ch App 64.

[93] See eg divorce and judicial separation (*Dicey, Morris and Collins* (n 3 above) R 77(1)); financial relief and maintenance of wives and children (ibid R 91(7)); and guardianship and custody of children (ibid R 97(10)).

[94] *Dicey, Morris and Collins* (n 3 above) para 5.004.

[95] I Fletcher, *Insolvency in Private International Law* (OUP, 2nd edn, 2005) para 2.79; this author also attributes the dominance of forum law in insolvency to the fact that much of the law is statutory with undefined territorial scope.

[96] *National Commercial Bank v Wimborne* (1978) 5 BPR 11,958, 11,982.

3.25 For example, in the case of torts it remains the situation in all Commonwealth countries that the law of the forum applies exclusively as substantive law in respect of a wrong which has occurred in the forum. Where the wrong takes place outside the forum, the common law choice of law rule was (and remains in many Commonwealth countries) based on the decision in *Phillips v Eyre*.[97] According to this rule, the law of the forum is applied to determine liability in relation to a foreign tort, where the events give rise to an actionable wrong under both the law of the forum and the law of the place of the tort. The Commonwealth choice of law position, however, is changing. Canada, Australia, and England have all but entirely abandoned the rule in *Phillips v Eyre*. In Canada[98] (for all torts) and in England[99] (for torts other than defamation) there is now a presumptive law of the place of the wrong rule, subject to displacement in favour of another law in various circumstances. In Canada, the applicable foreign law may be avoided where it could 'work an injustice' in the circumstances of the case,[100] while in England displacement may occur under the Private International Law (Miscellaneous Provisions) Act 1995 if it is 'substantially more appropriate' for another country's law to apply and under Rome II where the tort is 'manifestly more closely connected with a country' other than that indicated in article 4(1) or (2) of the Regulation.[101] Under Rome II the applicable law may also be excluded where the parties share a common habitual residence in another country.[102] As will be seen in Chapter 11, Commonwealth courts have, apart from the common habitual residence context, been generally reluctant to displace the law of the place of the wrong. In Australia, while there is also a basic law of the place of the wrong rule, the forum must further apply the choice of law rules of the foreign country and any doctrine of *renvoi* existing under that law.[103] Yet in most cases, the consequence of the Australian test will be that the domestic law of the place of the wrong will still apply since application of that country's choice of law rules will also select its law to govern a local wrong. It will only be where the choice of law rules of the law of the place refer the

---

[97] (1870) LR 6 QB 1.
[98] *Tolofson v Jensen* (1994) 120 DLR (4th) 289 (Sup Ct Can).
[99] Private International Law (Miscellaneous Provisions) Act 1995 (UK), s 11. According to the majority of English commentators and courts, the Rome II Regulation applies to events giving rise to damage on or after 20 August 2007, where legal proceedings in respect of such events are commenced after 11 January 2009. The issue of the temporal operation of the Regulation is, however, currently the subject of a reference to the European Court of Justice. See decisions and commentary cited at 11.01 below.
[100] *Tolofson v Jensen* (1994) 120 DLR (4th) 289, 314 (La Forest J), 326 (Major J).
[101] PILA 1995, s 12; Rome II, art 4(3).
[102] Rome II, art 4(2).
[103] *Neilson v Overseas Projects Corp of Victoria Ltd* (2005) 223 CLR 331.

B. Alternative Methods of Forum Reference

matter back to the law of the forum (remission) or to a third country (transmission) that a different substantive law may be selected. Alternatively, where the foreign law also has a doctrine of 'double *renvoi*', an 'inextricable circle' may arise where no substantive law can be chosen but this situation has not yet occurred in a decided case. Hence, application of the law of the forum in tort cases is also now rare in Australia.

In equity, similarly, there has been a recent move away from strict application of the law of the forum (a position long held in Australia)[104] to a position that equitable claims should be subjected to choice of law analysis, either by identifying the nearest established category (for example tort, contract, or restitution)[105] or by creating separate choice of law rules.[106] In the case of England, this development is again demonstrated in the Rome II Regulation, where a number of equitable doctrines are likely to fall within the scope of 'non-contractual obligations'.[107]   **3.26**

The effect of these developments in tort and equity is to increase the probability of a foreign law being selected as the law of the cause of action and, consequently, for the forum court to have to consider whether an issue is substantive or procedural. If the increased willingness of the courts and legislatures to expand the operation of foreign law in these areas by the creation of new choice of law rules is not to be undermined, it may be argued that a correspondingly restrictive approach to applying the law of the forum in procedural matters should be adopted. Otherwise, there is scope for the law of the forum to reappear 'through the back door', as has happened under the right-remedy doctrine.   **3.27**

4. Pleading and Proof of Foreign Law

Another method by which an issue may be referred to the law of the forum is by a party's failure to plead or prove the applicable foreign law. The general principle remains in Commonwealth private international law that a court cannot take judicial notice of foreign law even where such law has been selected by the forum's choice of law rules.[108] Moreover, unless foreign law is pleaded and proven by the party wishing to rely on it, the   **3.28**

---

[104] *National Commercial Bank v Wimborne* (1978) 5 BPR 11,958, 11,982.
[105] T Yeo, *Choice of Law For Equitable Doctrines* (OUP, 2004); *Dicey, Morris and Collins* (n 3 of this chapter) paras 34-033–34-041; *Rickshaw Investments Ltd v Nicolai Baron von Uexkull* [2007] 1 SLR 377 (CA); *Yugraneft v Abramovich* [2008] EWHC 2613 (Comm); *Douglas v Hello! Ltd (No 3)* [2006] QB 125, para 97; *Murakami v Wiryadi* (2010) 268 ALR 377; [2010] NSWCA 7.
[106] *Cheshire, North and Fawcett* (n 1 above) 769.
[107] A Dickinson, *The Rome II Regulation* (OUP, 2008) para 4.99.
[108] *Regie Nationale des Usines Renault v Zhang* (2002) 210 CLR 491, para 66; Fentiman (n 46 above).

court applies the law of the forum by default either on the basis of a presumption that such law is the same as the law of the forum or that the foreign law has been insufficiently established.[109] In effect, the party seeking to rely on foreign law bears the onus of proving both its content and that it is different from the law of the forum. Often foreign law will not be pleaded out of ignorance as to its potential application or because neither party sees any tactical advantage in doing so. The consequence of otherwise applicable foreign law not being put before the court is similar to that observed in the case of the forum law-specific choice of law rules mentioned at 3.23–3.27. The substance-procedure classification is rendered redundant as the law of the forum has exclusive application.

3.29 This position may be contrasted with that taken in some European civil law countries where choice of law rules are regarded as mandatory, with courts having a duty to apply foreign law where applicable.[110] There is evidence of a movement towards this approach in some Commonwealth cases where courts have refused to apply the presumption that local and foreign laws are identical. Instead, where such laws are likely to be very different and not to rest 'on great and broad principles likely to be part of any given system',[111] a party who fails to prove the applicable foreign law may be deemed not to have proven a constituent element in its case. In such a situation the claim (or defence) based on foreign law will be dismissed rather than referred to the law of the forum by default. While some writers have supported a general obligation to prove foreign law because it provides greater incentive for the admission of foreign law and so assists the goal of uniformity of outcome,[112] others have noted that it could cause unnecessary cost and injustice to a claimant particularly where the foreign law is difficult to ascertain.[113] The traditionally forum-centric approach to pleading and proof of foreign law has also been modified recently in the Australian state of New South Wales. In that state, the Supreme Court has revised its rules of court[114] to adopt a procedure for referral of matters (with the consent of the parties) involving foreign law to a relevant foreign

---

[109] *Neilson v Overseas Projects Corp of Victoria Ltd* (2005) 223 CLR 331; *Parker v TUI UK Ltd* [2009] EWCA Civ 1261, paras 22–23.

[110] See eg Germany and Austria: Fassberg (n 63 above) 11, n 23.

[111] *Damberg v Damberg* (2001) 52 NSWLR 492, 522 (Heydon JA) (with whom Spigelman CJ and Sheller JA agreed). See also *The Ship 'Mercury Bell' v Amosin* (1986) 27 DLR (4th) 641, 650 (Marceau J) and 651–2 (Husson J). Examples include taxation (*Damberg v Damberg* (2001) 52 NSWLR 492) and the validity of marriages (*Sheludko v Sheludko* [1972] VR 82). For a US example, see *Cuba Railroad Co v Crosby* 222 US 473 (1912).

[112] Fassberg (n 63 above) 12.

[113] See generally Fentiman (n 46 above) chs 3–4 and J McComish, 'Pleading and Proving Foreign Law in Australia' (2007) 31 Melbourne University L Rev 400, 441.

[114] Uniform Civil Procedure Rules 2005 (NSW), rr 6.42–6.45; Supreme Court Act 1970 (NSW) s 125.

court for determination. Memoranda of understanding have been entered into with courts in Singapore and New York for this purpose.[115] A major contention of this work is that the scope and operation of the law of the forum in procedural matters should be reduced and that, in some cases, new choice of law rules should be created so as to provide wider opportunities for the reception of foreign law. Again, such a proposal will be assisted by measures which limit and deter easy resort to the law of the forum and evasion of otherwise applicable foreign law.

5. No Advantage/Uniformity of Outcome

3.30 Another choice of law method of reference to forum law may arise from the adoption by the High Court of Australia of the 'no advantage' or 'uniformity of outcome'[116] approach to choice of law. Such a result occurred in the *Neilson* case itself where the High Court applied the choice of law rules of China, the law of the cause of action, and found that application of such rules would send the matter back to Australian substantive law. Such an approach, however, may not be a reliable method of applying forum law in future cases since it depends upon the foreign country's choice of law rules being interpreted to select forum law as opposed to the country's own domestic law or the law of a third state. Significantly, in no case since *Neilson* has an Australian court applied forum law following application of the choice of law rules of a foreign country.

C. HARMONIZATION

3.31 The final topic to be explored in this chapter is the extent to which measures of harmonization on a transnational scale may overcome the problem of choice of law in procedural matters. Certainly in areas of substantive law, such as contract, harmonization can significantly reduce the need for choice of law rules as each member state to a particular instrument must, at least in theory, apply the same law to a single set of facts. The 1980 United Nations Convention on the International Sale of Goods is a good example of such a text. In the area of procedural law, given the strong connections between procedure and the social, political, and economic mores of a country and the consequent greater differences in procedural laws between countries,[117]

---

[115] J Spigelman, 'Proof of Foreign Law by Reference to the Foreign Court' (2011) 127 LQR 208, 215.

[116] *Neilson v Overseas Projects Corp of Victoria Ltd* (2005) 223 CLR 331.

[117] A Lowenfeld, 'Introduction: The Elements of Procedure: Are They Separately Portable?' (1997) 45 AJCL 649, 652; C Hodges, 'Europeanisation of Civil Justice: Trends and Issues' (2007) 26 Civil Justice Quarterly 96, 109.

harmonization has proved difficult with only a few, limited regional examples such as the EU Council Regulation on Jurisdiction and Judgments. The Hague Service and Evidence Conventions (discussed in Chapters 4 and 8 respectively) make an important contribution but cover narrow fields and leave many issues to be determined by domestic law. The European Convention on Human Rights also plays a role in converging procedures with article 6 creating a right of access to an independent court for the vindication of a person's rights. Yet, overall, the result is that in most cases the procedural law of states has only been slightly affected by international harmonization measures.

3.32 One of the most ambitious recent efforts to address the harmonization of procedure has been the 2004 American Law Institute/UNIDROIT Rules and Principles of Transnational Civil Procedure. The aim of this project was to create sets of rules and principles for transnational commercial disputes, representing a middle ground between, or combination of, common law and civil law approaches to civil litigation. The Rules and Principles were intended to be comprehensive, covering all stages of the litigation process as well as dealing with ethical issues such as the independence of judges. A key rationale of the Rules and Principles was that they would assist in ensuring that the same procedural rules would apply to a dispute wherever it may be adjudicated. Such an outcome would promote decisional harmony between courts and discourage forum shopping. While the ALI Rules and Principles have not yet been adopted in national legislation, it may be that their influence will be more subliminal in encouraging courts to apply their procedural laws in a more enlightened and less parochial way. In that sense, a less direct form of harmonization may occur.

3.33 Yet the major question explored in this work—the distinction between substance and procedure—is not likely to be made redundant by the Rules and Principles. While the drafters cover many highly important issues in procedure and resolve some significant transnational conflicts, such as adopting the 'loser-pays' rule in costs over the US model,[118] providing limited rights of discovery,[119] and creating a general rule of admissibility of evidence based on relevance,[120] it was not possible for the Rules and Principles to address every issue which can arise, even within the topics covered. Accordingly, in both the Rules and Principles there is a general statement at the outset that 'the procedural law of the forum governs

---

[118] Rules and Principles of Transnational Civil Procedure, R 32.3.
[119] ibid R 22.1.
[120] ibid R 25.1, P 16.1.

C. Harmonization

matters not addressed in these Rules'.[121] This statement is slightly unfortunate since it purports to articulate a forum-specific choice of law rule for all procedural matters not covered by the Rules which, as this work attests, may not be accurate in all cases. Significantly, there may be many matters to which laws other than that of the forum apply. Yet, in practice, such a provision is unlikely to preclude a country which has adopted the Rules and Principles from applying its own choice of law rules to procedural matters not addressed. In a similar vein, the drafters allocate certain issues to the domestic law of the forum, such as the availability of interim or provisional measures,[122] how court orders may be enforced (including what sanctions may be used),[123] whether illegally obtained evidence should be admitted,[124] and the competence of witnesses.[125] As will be seen, however, it is by no means clear that forum law would apply exclusively to all these issues under both common law and EU choice of law principles. By contrast, on other matters, the Rules and Principles wisely preserve the operation of the forum's choice of law rules. For example, in the case of privilege, it is stated that 'evidence may not be elicited in violation of the legal profession privilege of confidentiality under forum law, including choice of law'[126] and, in relation to the attorney-client relationship, it will 'ordinarily [be] governed by rules of the forum *including choice of law rules*'.[127] In these cases as well as where other 'gaps' in the Rules exist, forum choice of law rules, including the substance / procedure distinction, should remain relevant. Another example is rule 11 which provides for filing and service of process. While the rule mentions that 'the time of lodging the complaint with the court determines compliance with the statute of limitations',[128] it does not specify which such statute should apply. A similar choice of law 'gap' may arise in the case of service of process and the taking of evidence abroad. As discussed in Chapters 4 and 8, while both such issues are procedural and governed by the Rules and Principles and forum law,[129] a conflict may nevertheless arise with *another* legal system's rules, such as the law of the country where the service is performed or evidence is taken. This problem is not addressed in the

---

[121] ibid R 1.2; see also Commentary P-A.
[122] ibid Commentary R-17A, P-8A.
[123] ibid R 20.3; Commentary P-17A.
[124] ibid R 25.1.
[125] ibid Commentary R 25D.
[126] ibid R 27.1.1; Commentary P-18A.
[127] ibid Commentary P-4C.
[128] ibid R 11.2, P 10.2.
[129] ibid R 7.1; Commentary R-11B, P-10B.

Rules and Principles.[130] These observations are not intended as a criticism of the Rules and Principles but rather to reflect the fact that total harmonization of procedure is unlikely ever to occur[131] and so choice of law analysis remains important.

---

[130] J Dolinger and C Tiburcio, 'The Forum Rule in International Litigation—Which Procedural Law Governs Proceedings to be Performed in Foreign Jurisdictions: *Lex Fori* or *Lex Diligentiae*?' (1998) 33 Texas Intl LJ 425.

[131] T Main, 'The Procedural Foundation of Substantive Law' (2010) 87 Washington University L Rev 801.

4
Service and Jurisdiction

A.	Service	4.01
	1. Introduction	4.01
	2. Choice of Law Rules under International Instruments	4.08
	3. Choice of Law Rules under Domestic Law	4.16
B.	Jurisdiction	4.41
	1. Personal Jurisdiction	4.43
	2. Jurisdiction or Choice of Court Clauses	4.54
	3. *In Rem* Jurisdiction	4.60
	4. Anti-Suit Injunctions	4.62
	5. Immunities from Jurisdiction	4.64

A. SERVICE

1. INTRODUCTION

It is well established in all systems of private international law that the **4.01** manner of effecting service of originating process on a defendant is governed by the law of the forum court. Indeed, the basic common law rule of personal jurisdiction is that a defendant will be subject to local jurisdiction where he or she has been served with originating process while present in the forum.[1] In determining whether the defendant has in fact been 'served', the forum court will apply its own procedural rules. However, the question of whether the parties have entered into an agreement with respect to service or the validity of such agreement is governed by the proper law of the agreement.[2] A complication arises where the defendant is located in a country or place outside the forum. In common law systems jurisdiction over such a person is established by service out of the jurisdiction, which will normally only be available where there is some link between the defendant or the claimant's cause of action and the forum. If a question arises in the forum court as to the validity of such service, it is again undisputed that the court will apply its own procedural rules to resolve the issue.

---

[1] See eg *Maharanee of Baroda v Wildenstein* [1972] 2 QB 283 (CA).
[2] *Samarni v Williams* [1980] 2 NSWLR 389 (NSW Sup Ct).

4.02 Yet service out of the jurisdiction has one fundamental difference to service upon a defendant present within the forum. Where the defendant is located in a foreign jurisdiction the act of service may involve conduct by the forum in another country's territory, which engages the interests of that state.³ For example, the state in which service is to be performed may view any act on its territory, including service of process of a foreign court, as constituting a violation of its sovereignty, even where, for example, the service was performed by a private agent and not by an official of the forum country. On a practical level, the cooperation of the country in which service is to be performed may be required not only to effect service but also to enforce any judgment against the defendant and local assets. So if, for example, the claimant effected service by a method which violated the criminal law of a foreign country, that country's courts may well be hesitant to recognize any judgment of the forum court on the ground that the public policy of the state has been infringed by a failure to take into account local rules in the country where service was performed.⁴

4.03 The laws of most countries now⁵ recognize, therefore, that from both a principled (respecting the sovereignty of the foreign country) and pragmatic (the need to enforce any orders against the foreign defendant) standpoint, service—at least when it takes place abroad—cannot be entirely subjected to the rules of the law of the forum. To varying degrees the law of the country in which service is to be performed⁶ must also be taken into account. Hence, again, the maxim *lex fori regit processum* is not accurate to the extent that it implies *exclusive* forum control over service. While it is true that the topic—service of process—is wholly procedural, it

---

³ *Bayat Telephone Systems International Inc v Lord Michael Cecil* [2011] EWCA Civ 135, para 61 (Stanley Burnton LJ) (with whom Rix LJ, para 112 and Wilson LJ, para 72 agreed); D McClean, *International Co-operation in Civil and Criminal Matters* (OUP, 2002) 12.

⁴ See eg G Born and P Rutledge, *International Civil Litigation in US Courts* (Aspen Publishers, 4th edn, 2007) 855, citing the German Code of Civil Procedure, art 328; see also the decision of the Oberlandesgericht, Frankfurt of 21 February 1991 (cited by McClean (n 3 above) 13, n 2), in which an English judgment was not enforced where the method of service employed was held to be incompatible with German law.

⁵ Earlier court decisions and statutory rules reveal a marked reluctance to recognize foreign laws in the area of service; see *Dobson v Festi, Rasini & Co* [1891] 2 QB 92 (CA).

⁶ Two Brazilian writers suggest that a dual choice of law rule operates in the case of service abroad: the law of the forum and the *lex diligentiae*, the law of the place where the act of service is to be performed: see J Dolinger and C Tiburcio, 'The Forum Rule in International Litigation—Which Procedural Law Governs Proceedings to be Performed in Foreign Jurisdictions: Lex Fori or Lex Diligentiae?' (1998) 33 Texas Intl LJ 425. See also I Szászy, 'The Basic Connecting Factor in International Cases in the Domain of Civil Procedure' (1966) 15 ICLQ 436, 453, who considers that the '*lex loci actus*' applies in cases of 'service abroad of the judicial process of the forum'.

does not preclude the operation of foreign laws, even though, conceptually, such laws may be seen only as 'connecting factors' under the law of the forum rather than selected pursuant to a distinct choice of law rule. Nevertheless, only a few scholars note the relevance of foreign law in service disputes.[7]

Sometimes the law of the country where service is to be effected will be expressly referred to in the rules of the law of the forum. In other situations, both countries will be parties to an international instrument such as the Hague Service Convention (HSC) or the EU Service Regulation (the Service Regulation), which impose autonomous rules requiring the forum court to apply the law of the country of service to certain issues. In terms of choice of law analysis, the reference to foreign law in service abroad cases under both domestic choice of law rules and international instruments can be viewed in similar yet distinct ways. On one view, foreign law can be seen as applying *in addition to* local law. In that respect, a 'double actionability' type of choice of law is effectively created, requiring reference to both local and foreign law.[8] Alternatively, the reference to foreign law can be seen as a qualification or modification of the scope of the law of the forum in a way suggested by Kahn-Freund to produce an 'enlightened' law of the forum.[9] Rather than simply applying the law of the forum's rules for service that would be engaged in a purely domestic case, the rules are instead adapted to take account of the impact of foreign interests and laws. Either way, however, it is not correct to describe the choice of law position as one of strict application of the law of the forum in service abroad cases. The foreign law of the country of service either demands recognition in its own right or reshapes the law of the forum. **4.04**

Also, in proceedings to recognize or enforce a judgment in the country of service, it may be insufficient for the claimant to show that service was performed according to the rules of the country where judgment was delivered. In such a case, the law of the country of service may use its own rules of service or public policy more generally to preclude recognition. Therefore, again, the assumption that because service is a procedural matter it is exclusively governed by forum law in all situations is inaccurate. The circumstances and degree to which foreign law may qualify or limit the law of the forum's control is explored later separately in the case of England, Commonwealth countries, and the United States. While differences in statutory wording exist between the jurisdictions, all regimes **4.05**

---

[7] See Dolinger and Tiburcio, and Szászy (n 6 above); also Born and Rutledge (n 4 above) 816 and McClean (n 3 above).
[8] Dolinger and Tiburcio (n 6 above).
[9] O Kahn-Freund, *General Problems of Private International Law* (Sijthoff, 1976) 227.

offer some scope for the operation of foreign laws. An example of where public policy of the enforcing country may also be engaged to preclude recognition of a forum judgment would be where the law of the forum dispensed with service and so allowed judgment to be given against a defendant who was unaware of the proceedings.[10]

4.06 Before exploring these principles and the degree to which a choice of law system exists in the case of service a comment should also made about harmonization. As noted earlier,[11] harmonization of domestic law by international instruments and the development of supranational, autonomous concepts can represent alternatives to a choice of law methodology. While there is only limited evidence of such measures so far, a few common law judges have sought to identify an autonomous concept at the heart of service, which may form the basis of future development in the area. An English court has said that:[12]

> ... the overriding objective and the general reason for service *pervading all jurisdictions* ... [is a] need to ensure that the defendant had received the [court] process, that the court should be aware that he had done so and that the defendant should appreciate that ... [such process] required some response from him.

In a similar vein are the views of a Singaporean court:[13]

> The purpose of service of process is to notify the defendant of the proceedings that have been commenced against him/her and the modern view in most common law countries is to focus on whether the method is sufficient to bring to the attention of the defendant such proceedings rather than the abstract acceptability of the method itself.

4.07 The concept of notification of the defendant is an important objective of service which many legal systems would share. The reality, however, is that countries still seek to achieve this goal by a variety of methods leading to possible conflicts. International instruments can also perform a key role in harmonization, potentially eliminating the need for choice of law rules to select the applicable law. Yet, as will be seen at 4.08–4.15, in the case of the HSC and the Service Regulation the amount of harmonization accomplished by both instruments is relatively modest, with many issues left to national law, either the law of the forum or the law of the country

---

[10] *BHP Billiton Ltd v Schultz* (2004) 221 CLR 400, para 252 (Callinan J), citing Dust Diseases Tribunal Act 1989 (NSW), s 17.
[11] See 3.31–3.33 above.
[12] *Olafsson v Gissurarson* [2006] EWHC 3162 (QB), para 12 (emphasis added).
[13] *Fortune Hong Kong Trading Ltd v Cosco Feoso (Sing) Pte Ltd* [2000] 2 SLR 717 (Sing CA), para 34.

A. Service

where service is to be performed. Hence, choice of law problems remain in the area of service abroad, which is perhaps not surprising given that such service is also still regarded by some courts as an exercise of the forum's sovereignty within a foreign state.[14]

2. Choice of Law Rules under International Instruments

4.08 Before examining the particular domestic law provisions on service in each of these jurisdictions, two important international instruments will be considered. The first is the HSC, ratified by sixty-four parties, including the United Kingdom, many Commonwealth countries, and the United States, and the second is the Service Regulation, which applies solely to EU Member States. The HSC and the Regulation create systems of authorities or agencies which administer the transfer of documents from the sending state (the forum state of adjudication) to the receiving state, the country in which service is to be performed. Both instruments provide considerable scope for the operation of the law of country of service, especially the HSC. Such an observation is not surprising, given that the Regulation (by contrast) was designed for the closed system of the European Union where greater trust and recognition between legal systems is to be expected.

(a) The Hague Service Convention

4.09 Taking the HSC first, it is generally accepted that where service is to be performed in a contracting state to the Convention, the provisions of the Convention prevail over the internal rules of the forum as to service of process and must be used.[15] In this respect the law of the forum only applies to the extent the Convention permits. Yet on a number of issues, the HSC reserves considerable scope to the law of the forum. First, the HSC only applies to the issue of *how* service abroad is to be effected. It does not affect the rules of jurisdiction of the forum state or give permission or authorization to a claimant to effect service abroad,[16] nor alter any provisions on procedural time limits. The topic of procedural time limits and statutes of limitations is explored more fully in Chapter 9, but in the context of limits with regard to service the rules of the law of the forum

---

[14] *Bayat Telephone Systems International Inc v Lord Michael Cecil* [2011] EWCA Civ 135, para 61 (Stanley Burnton LJ) (with whom Rix LJ, para 112 and Wilson LJ, para 72 agreed).

[15] *Volkswagenwerk Aktiengesellschaft v Schlunk* 486 US 694, 699 (1988); *Vorhees v Fischer and Krecke GmbH* 697 F 2d 574 (4th Cir 1983). Service under the Convention is provided for in English law in CPR, r 6.40(3)(b).

[16] *De James v Magnificence Carriers Inc* 654 F 2d 280, 288–9 (3rd Cir 1981).

76   *Chapter 4: Service and Jurisdiction*

will normally have exclusive operation. Thus in *The Reefer Creole*[17] the court had to consider what time period applied to the service of a writ. Under English law, the law of the forum, the writ had expired but under Greek law, the law of the country of service, it was still valid. The court held that the law of the forum exclusively governed this question; the law of the country in which service was to be performed could only be relevant if the law of the forum made reference to it.[18] The procedural rules of the forum state also exclusively govern the issues of the required form and validity of documents to be served.[19]

4.10 Further, the HSC provides no universal autonomous rule as to *when* service abroad is required so as to engage the provisions of the HSC. In a series of US, Dutch, and Spanish decisions it has been established that the HSC allows the law of the forum to determine when service abroad is required. So even where a defendant is resident abroad, if a claimant can effect service on an entity within the forum which is linked to the defendant and such service is valid under forum law, the HSC does not apply.[20] While such an approach may be criticized for its undermining of the HSC and encouragement to claimants to evade the law of the country where service is to be performed, it seems too well established to change. Indeed, the Special Commission of 2009 of the Hague Conference of Private International Law confirmed that it is a matter for forum law to determine whether a document must be transmitted for service abroad[21] to engage the provisions of the HSC. Yet the warning to claimants at the outset of this chapter should be noted. While this approach may allow avoidance of a foreign law on service, if recognition of the judgment is sought in such country, the foreign court may well reimpose its own law as to service (or public policy) and refuse recognition. To that extent, the law of the country

---

[17] [1994] 1 Lloyd's Rep 584.

[18] For a criticism of this decision, based on the fact that Greek law had the closest connection to the issue of service and so should have been applied, see K Kerameus, 'Enforcement in the International Context' (1997) 264 *Hague Recueil* 179, 391–2.

[19] *Van Opdorp v Compagnie Belge d'Assurance Credit* [1991] IL Pr 316 (CA Luxembourg); *Treuhand und Rechtspraxis Ulrich Diener-Hafner AG v Fuchsl* [1992] ECLY 4351 (Cass Luxembourg 1991); *Sturge v Naatra Rotterdam BV* [1993] ECLY 601 (RB Rotterdam).

[20] *Volkswagenwerk Aktiengesellschaft v Schlunk* 486 US 694 (1988); *Nieuwersteeg v Colonia Versicherungs AG* [1997] ECLY 732 (Hohe Raad 1996); *Imperial Park Country Club Properties Ltd v Audencia Provincial de Alicante* (Constitutional Court First Division 162/2002, 16 September 2002) cited in J Forner, 'Service of Judicial Documents Within Europe and in Third States' in A Nuyts and N Watte (eds), *International Civil Litigation in Europe* (Bruylant, 2005) 391, 413–14.

[21] Conclusions and Recommendations of the Special Commission (2009), para 12, at <http:/www.hcch.net/upload/wop/jac_concl_e.pdf> (accessed October 2011).

A. Service

of service may reappear 'through the backdoor'. The choice of law position is therefore more fluid than appears at first glance.

Assuming the HSC applies, the basic choice of law rule under the Convention is that service must generally be performed in accordance with the law of the country of service. This rule is implemented in article 5 by granting to the central authority of the receiving state, the country of service, the power to choose to serve the document either by the method prescribed by its internal law for the service of documents in actions brought against defendants within the jurisdiction or by delivery to the defendant where it has accepted service voluntarily. However, where the claimant requests a particular method of service, the central authority of the receiving state will honour such request,[22] unless to do so would be inconsistent with the law of the receiving state. 4.11

Further control is vested in the law of the country of service by articles 4 and 13. Article 4 provides that if a central authority in the receiving state considers that a request for service does not fall within the scope of the HSC it may reject the request. Article 13 provides further that a receiving state may reject a request for service (falling within the scope of the HSC) where it would compromise the state's sovereignty or security. Such a defence was, however, intended to have only limited application and operate as a residual public policy exception under the law of the receiving state. Consequently, in the history of the HSC few requests have been rejected,[23] although in one case a German court refused to serve English court process in which an anti-suit injunction was sought.[24] While German sovereignty and public policy would be infringed by allowing service of this particular process, service in the context of US actions where punitive damages have been claimed has been upheld.[25] The courts noted that if public policy in the law of the country where service is to be performed was too widely asserted, it would weaken the effectiveness of the HSC by giving the law of that country excessive operation. The HSC seeks to balance the interests of both the law of the country of origin (the forum of adjudication) and the law of the country where service is to take place. The 'safeguards' under the HSC also reveal the need to protect the foreign 4.12

---

[22] HSC, art 5(b).
[23] McClean (n 3 above) 33.
[24] Oberlandesgericht Düsseldorf 1996 [1998] ECLY 1030.
[25] See Oberlandesgericht Düsseldorf 1992 [1992] ECLY 4831, Bundesverfassungsgericht [1997] IL Pr 325 and Bundesverfassungsgericht 2007 [2008] ECLY 99. See also Bundesverfassungsgericht 2007 [2010] ECLY 151 where it was held that US law rules providing for pre-action discovery and the non-recovery of costs by the successful party did not infringe German sovereignty and security.

defendant and the sovereignty of the country of service by giving that country's law a further role to play at the time of adjudication by the forum (requesting) state. Article 15 provides that where a defendant has not appeared in a proceeding to which the HSC applies, judgment will not be given until it is established that (a) the writ was served by a method prescribed by the internal law of the country of service for service of documents in domestic actions upon persons who are within its territory, or (b) the document was actually delivered to the defendant by another method provided in this Convention. Article 15(2) allows non-compliance with article 15(1) if the writ has been transmitted by one of the methods provided under the Convention. In practice, therefore, for a default judgment to be valid, service must either comply with the rules of the country of service or the autonomous rules of the HSC.

4.13 The significance of the law of the receiving state under the HSC can also be seen in the alternative mechanisms for service under the Convention. While the basic mechanism for service is found in article 5, a claimant is also entitled to effect service (i) through the diplomatic channel,[26] (ii) through the courts of the country where service is to be performed,[27] (iii) by sending documents by mail,[28] (iv) through 'a competent person' in the state of destination (which would include a lawyer),[29] or (v) in accordance with any method permitted by the law of the country where service is to be performed for documents coming from abroad for service within its territory.[30] In interpreting article 10(a), courts have generally read the provision as preserving the operation of foreign law, so that service by mail is only possible where the foreign state has not objected under the HSC to service by such means.[31]

4.14 Article 19 makes the most explicit reference to the law of the country where service is to be performed but has not yet, at least according to US decisions, received a settled interpretation. Some US courts have interpreted the article as allowing claimants to use any method of service available under US law, provided that such mechanism is not expressly prohibited by the law of the country where service is to be performed. If the foreign law is silent on the question, then article 19 will allow

---

[26] HSC, arts 8, 9.
[27] HSC, art 10(b).
[28] HSC, art 10(a).
[29] HSC, art 10(c); this provision would, for example, allow service of English process by an agent in another common law country: L Collins (ed), *Dicey, Morris and Collins on the Conflict of Laws* (Sweet & Maxwell, 14th edn, 2006) para 8.047.
[30] HSC, art 19.
[31] *Dicey, Morris and Collins* (n 29 above) para 8.045; *Shiblaq v Sadikoglu* [2004] EWHC 1890, para 27.

A. Service

such service.[32] This approach gives a wide scope of operation to the law of the forum in matters of service at the expense of the law of the country where service is to be effected. Other US courts have, however, disagreed with this view, stating that the plain English text of article 19 requires a claimant only to use methods 'expressly sanctioned' by the law of the country where service is to be performed.[33] Such an approach embodies more respect for foreign state sovereignty.[34] Thus in *EPlus Technology Inc v Aboud*[35] service by a private non-resident process server was held invalid because such method was not permitted under the law of the country where service occurred. A third, even more restrictive approach requires not only that the method of service be permitted under the law of the country of service but that it be a method specifically designated for foreign process being served from abroad. Consequently, a claimant cannot make use of a service mechanism available in purely domestic cases.[36] What both the second and third approaches have in common is that they give determinative weight to the law of the country where service is to be performed and so do not allow an expansive operation of the law of the forum to undermine the HSC. Arguably, the second and third approaches are also desirable since they reduce the scope for challenges to service in the event that enforcement of any judgment is sought in the country where service is to be performed.

(b) EU Service Regulation

The other major international instrument in the area of service to which **4.15**
the United Kingdom is a party is the EU Service Regulation.[37] The provisions on choice of law in the Regulation provide for less supervision and control by the law of the country of service when compared with the HSC. The scope of the operation of the Regulation is similar to the HSC: it applies whenever transmission of a document from one EU Member State to another, in a civil or commercial matter, is required.[38] Again similarly to the HSC, the Regulation requires that the agency in the receiving state must itself serve the document either in accordance with the law of the

---

[32] *Banco Latino SACA v Gomez Lopez* 53 F Supp 2d 1273, 1280 (SD Fla 1999); *Lemme v Wine of Japan Import Inc* 631 F Supp 456, 462-3 (EDNY 1986).
[33] *EPlus Technology Inc v Aboud* 155 F Supp 2d 692, 699 (ED Va 2001); *Dahya v Second Judicial District Court of the State of Nevada* 19 P 3d 239 (SC Nev 2001).
[34] *Dahya v Second Judicial District Court of the State of Nevada* 19 P 3d 239, 243 (SC Nev 2001).
[35] 155 F Supp 2d 692 (ED Va 2001).
[36] *Humble v Gill* 2009 WL 151668 (WD Ky).
[37] Council Regulation (EC) 1393/2007 of 13 November 2007 on the service in the Member States of judicial and extrajudicial documents in civil or commercial matters [2007] OJ L324/79.
[38] EU Service Regulation art 1(1). The Regulation is given effect in English law in CPR, r 6.40(3)(a)(i).

receiving state or by a particular method requested by the transmitting state unless such method is incompatible with the law of the receiving state.[39] Also, like the HSC, other methods of service are preserved by the Regulation, such as postal service[40] or direct service through the judicial officers, officials, or other competent persons of the receiving state, provided that such direct service is permitted under the law of the receiving state.[41] Unlike the HSC, however, there is no scope for an agency or a court in the receiving state to refuse to set aside service on the ground that the sovereignty or security of the state is impaired. To that extent, the Regulation permits less derogation from the rules of the law of the forum than the HSC.

3. Choice of Law Rules under Domestic Law

(a) England

4.16 In the case of England, assuming neither the HSC nor the Service Regulation applies, the law of the forum still does not have exclusive operation in the case of service abroad. Under the Civil Procedure Rules (CPR) service of a claim form (originating process) outside England may be made in the following ways. First, service may be performed by any method permitted by the law of the country in which service is to be performed.[42] Secondly, if the country where service is to be performed is a party to a civil procedure convention, then service may be effected by any method permitted in that convention.[43] Thirdly, if the country in which service is to take place is not a party to a relevant convention and if the law of such country permits, service can be performed through the government or judicial authorities of the country or a British consular authority.[44] In the case of the first situation, English courts, while accepting that the provision must be applied 'flexibly', have nevertheless been careful to ensure that foreign law is correctly applied. Specifically, the claimant must show that the desired method of service would have been available had the proceedings been filed in the courts of the foreign country.[45] Most significantly, there is also a provision in the CPR which states that 'nothing in [r 6.40(3)] or in any court order may authorize or require any person to do anything [in the

---

[39] EU Service Regulation, art 7(1).
[40] EU Service Regulation, art 14.
[41] EU Service Regulation, art 15.
[42] CPR, r 6.40(3)(c).
[43] CPR, r 6.40(3)(b).
[44] CPR, rr 6.40(3)(a)(ii), 6.42(1)(b).
[45] *Arros Invest Ltd v Nishanov* [2004] EWHC 576 (Ch), para 25.

country where the claim form is to be served] which is contrary to the law of [that] country'.[46]

4.17 The above English rules therefore appear concerned to ensure strict compliance with the law of the country in which service is to be performed. Yet there exist three other provisions in the CPR which have the potential to reassert the primacy of the law of the forum in service matters, not only as regards the law of the country of service but also the HSC and the Service Regulation. Under CPR, rule 6.15 where there is a good reason, the court may authorize service by an alternative method not permitted by the rules, under CPR, rule 6.16 the court can dispense with service of a document altogether, and finally under CPR, rule 3.10 the court may remedy any procedural defect or error in service. The key question for present purposes is to consider how English courts have applied these principles in cases involving service abroad. Specifically, have they been adequately mindful of the need to give effect to the law of the country where service is to be performed or have they interpreted the rules in a way which gives predominant control to the law of the forum?

4.18 In an earlier pre-CPR case (although involving almost identical rules) the English High Court held[47] that where a method of service used was contrary to the law of the country of service, Switzerland, service should be set aside in England. Under Swiss law it is a criminal offence to serve or assist in serving foreign legal process on Swiss territory.[48] Other countries, such as France, Germany, and Austria, have similar provisions, which some commentators regard as outdated.[49] Yet when confronted with such evidence of foreign law, the English court in *The Sky One* set aside service. The claimant in the case also argued that the predecessor to CPR, rule 3.10 should be employed to 'cure' the default but the court declared that it would require a very strong case not to set aside service where it was expressly prohibited in the law of the country of service. Such a case may arise, for example, where the defendant expressly represented that service according to the desired method was lawful.[50] Overall, once service is found to be *prohibited* under the law of the country of service, then it will be a rare case where it will not be set aside by an English court. Yet, before doing so, English courts have required clear evidence that service is actually contrary to the law of the foreign country in which service is to be performed. Specifically, the defendant must show that the manner of service

---

[46] CPR, r 6.40(4).
[47] *The Sky One* [1988] 1 Lloyd's Rep 238 (CA).
[48] Swiss Penal Code, art 271.
[49] Born describes such provisions as 'medieval ritualism' (n 4 above) 833.
[50] *The Sky One* [1988] 1 Lloyd's Rep 238, 244.

Chapter 4: Service and Jurisdiction

is either a criminal offence or violates the civil law of the foreign country. An example would be that foreign law allows only one method of service, such as through the diplomatic channel.[51] The limited role of foreign law on service questions in English courts can also be seen in more recent decisions.

4.19 In *Habib Bank v Central Bank of Sudan*[52] the court made an order for alternative service under the equivalent of CPR, rule 6.15, where the method was neither expressly permitted nor expressly prohibited by the law of Sudan, the country of service. The court emphasized that the equivalent of rule 6.40(4) did not require that the method of service be *permitted* by the law of the country where service is to be performed, only that such method should not *contravene* such law. The court seems to suggest that the interests of comity and the protection of foreign defendants which underlie the reference to foreign law in the rules are adequately met by requiring that the service method chosen should not violate foreign law. Put another way, the law of the forum will generally regulate questions of service abroad unless the public policy of the law of the country of service is infringed. In terms of choice of law, however, it would arguably go too far to require the claimant actually to effect service according to one of the methods provided by foreign law. Not only would this substantially supplant the law of the forum on the issue of service abroad, it would also impose an excessive burden on claimants wishing to vindicate their rights.

4.20 Recent decisions have been inconsistent with regard to the balance between foreign and forum law in service disputes. In *Shiblaq v Sadikoglu*[53] the court refused to apply rule 3.10 and the equivalent of rule 6.16 to overcome defects in service under Turkish law. Turkey was a party to the HSC and objected to direct service of foreign proceedings under the Convention. In relation to the application to remedy the error in service under rule 3.10 the court held that this method could not be used where 'it had the result of impleading a defendant outside the jurisdiction in circumstances where the method of service actually adopted was impermissible under the law of the country . . . [of service] [or under any international convention]'.[54] Note again the court's concern to preserve the operation of the law of the country of service, which although not explicitly referred to in rule 3.10 is implicitly part of the service regime in rule 6.40.[55]

---

[51] *Clyde & Co v Sovrybflot* [1998] CLY 586 (QBD, 16 February 1998).
[52] [2007] 1 WLR 470.
[53] [2004] EWHC 1890 (Comm).
[54] ibid para 41.
[55] ibid para 31.

A. Service

The application under the equivalent of rule 6.16 to dispense with service **4.21**
met a similar fate. Here the court was strongly influenced by comments in
Bas Capital Funding Corporation v Medfinco Ltd.[56] The *Bas Capital* case
involved service of an English claim form in Malta in circumstances where
the service complied with neither English nor Maltese law. The court felt
that 'in international cases, where the basis of jurisdiction is service' it
would 'hesitate before ordering service by an alternative method under
r [6.15] or dispensing with service under r [6.16]'. In the *Shiblaq* case the
court applied this observation to the context where the defendant was
resident in an HSC country. In such a case, neither rule 6.15 nor rule 6.16
should be used 'if their deployment is for the purpose of substituting a
form of service or avoiding a defect in service which is inconsistent with a
service convention binding as between this country and the country of
service'. This conclusion was an 'emanation of the fundamental principle
of international comity'.[57] Again, there is a clear concern expressed not to
allow the law of the forum to be applied in an absolutist way in service
abroad cases where the interests of both the foreign defendant and the
country of service dictate that foreign law be recognized, whether under
domestic choice of law rules or through the operation of an international
service convention such as the HSC. Similarly, in *Knauf UK GmbH v British
Gypsum*[58] the Court of Appeal refused to allow service to be made by an
alternative method under the equivalent of rule 6.15 in circumstances
where such form of service was not permitted under the law of the country
where it was to be effected (Germany). The court suggested that it would
only be in an exceptional case, such as where there was great practical difficulty in effecting service in the country in question,[59] that the court might
consider allowing service by an alternative method under forum law.

By contrast, in other decisions, the primacy of the law of the forum has **4.22**
been reasserted in service questions, at least where the non-compliance
with foreign law is merely technical. *Phillips v Symes (No 3)*[60] concerned
service of English process on a defendant in Switzerland. Service complied
with Swiss law in all respects apart from the fact that the English language
claim form was erroneously removed from the bundle of documents to be
served by the Swiss authorities, although the German translation was present.

---

[56] [2004] 1 Lloyd's Rep 652.
[57] [2004] EWHC 1890 (Comm), para 57.
[58] [2002] 1 WLR 907, paras 47, 59.
[59] An example of such a situation would be where the defendant seeks to avoid personal service and that is the only method permitted under foreign law: *Bayat Telephone Systems International Inc v Lord Michael Cecil* [2011] EWCA Civ 135, para 68 (Stanley Burnton LJ) (with whom Rix LJ, para 112 and Wilson LJ, para 72 agreed).
[60] [2008] 1 WLR 180 (HL).

The House of Lords granted both an order to dispense with service under the equivalent of rule 6.16 and an order to cure the defect under rule 3.10 notwithstanding non-compliance with Swiss law. According to Lord Brown, who gave the leading speech, while the power to grant such orders is exceptional and 'to be exercised sparingly' this was a special case[61] for two reasons. First, the defendant had 'suffered no prejudice whatsoever' by the failure to serve the original claim in the correct manner but 'rather sought to exploit it' and, secondly, the fault lay with the Swiss authorities rather than the claimant.[62] In such a case, using the rules of the law of forum to overcome the failure to adhere to the law of the country of service was permissible. It would be a different case, according to Lord Brown, where there had been no service whatever or presumably, as in *The Sky One* decision, where service violated the criminal law of the foreign country. Of course, if the law of the forum could be used to salvage such situations, then the references in the CPR to foreign law would be rendered almost meaningless and forum law would effectively have exclusive operation in cases of service abroad.

4.23 The decision in *Phillips v Symes* was applied and explained by the Court of Appeal in *Olafsson v Gissurarson*.[63] The *Olafsson* case involved service of English process in Iceland where, again, careful steps were taken to ensure that the method chosen was permissible under local law. However, the service failed to comply with such law, because although the documents were read and understood by the defendant, he signed no declaration confirming receipt of the documents. Similarly to the *Phillips* decision the court felt that this was an exceptional case where an order to dispense with service under the equivalent of rule 6.16 was justified. Specifically, the court found that the claimant was entitled to assume, given the careful efforts to choose a permissible method under the law of the country where service was to be performed, that valid service had in fact occurred. While the method of service was allowed by the law of the country of service, its execution was ineffective.[64] To allow the defendant to overturn service on the basis of a minor, technical breach of the foreign law would be unreasonable, particularly where the purpose of service—that is, to inform the defendant of the contents of the claim form and the claimant's case—had been complied with. In a sense, therefore, the court in *Olafsson* appears to be moving away from a strict view that questions relating to service are governed by the rules of one state and/or another but instead is examining

---

[61] ibid para 37.
[62] ibid para 38.
[63] [2008] 1 WLR 2016.
[64] ibid para 29.

A. Service

the concept in an autonomous, transnational light which almost supplants choice of law. This trend is also evident in the approach to service in the context of recognition and enforcement of judgments under the Brussels I Regulation.[65] Notwithstanding this last observation, the court in *Olafsson* did note that the effect of the *Phillips* and *Olafsson* decisions is to strengthen the role of the law of the forum in cases involving service of English process abroad. Further, and more specifically, the comment by Colman J in *Shiblaq* that the equivalent of rule 6.16 should not be used to overcome deficiencies under the law of the country of service or an applicable convention was rejected by the court as being too wide.

While the concerns of comity and respect for foreign laws relating to service remain paramount in cases where leave is required to serve the originating process out of the jurisdiction and service is the basis of jurisdiction, the position is arguably different where jurisdiction is obtained as of right under the Brussels I Regulation[66] or the Lugano Convention.[67] Where a case involves jurisdiction under those instruments, courts may feel much less restrained in using the procedural rules of the forum to overcome defects under the law of the country of service given that service is not the basis of jurisdiction. It may be, therefore, that outside the Brussels/Lugano context a claimant will not be able to use the CPR to overcome deficiencies in service under the law of the country of service, although the *Habib Bank* case shows that, even in that context, a claimant can choose a method which avoids the foreign rules altogether, as long as it does not violate such rules. Where such foreign laws are free standing, that is, not made applicable in an English court by reference to international instruments such as the HSC or the Service Regulation, but rather by local choice of law rules, then an English court's ignoring of defects under foreign law may be seen as less injurious to comity.[68] Where, however, the HSC or the Service Regulation makes such laws directly applicable in English law, the approach in *Olafsson* and *Phillips* is less tenable given that both instruments require compliance with such laws. While it may be argued that the absence of any reference to dispensing with service or curing of defects in the instruments suggests a residual role for the law of the forum on such issues,[69] it is more likely that the drafters of the rules intended that foreign law would exclusively apply. To that extent, the cases in which an expansion of the

4.24

---

[65] See 4.26 below.
[66] Council Regulation (EC) 44/2001 of 22 December 2000 on jurisdiction and the enforcement of judgments in civil and commercial matters.
[67] Convention of 16 September 1988 on jurisdiction and the enforcement of judgments in civil and commercial matters.
[68] *Shiblaq v Sadikoglu* [2004] EWHC 1890 (Comm), para 57.
[69] See *Phillips v Symes (No 3)* [2008] 1 WLR 180, para 33 (Lord Brown).

law of the forum was permitted can be seen as arguably contrary to the United Kingdom's international obligations and giving insufficient weight to foreign law in cases involving service abroad.

4.25 Service on a foreign state under English law is governed by section 12 of the State Immunity Act 1978 (UK) and CPR, rule 6.44. Section 12 is mandatory in its terms, with no additional requirement on a claimant to comply with the law of the foreign state.[70]

4.26 The question of the law to be applied to service has also arisen at the stage of recognition and enforcement of foreign judgments, although interestingly only where recognition has been sought under EU instruments such as the 1968 Brussels Convention,[71] not at common law. No doubt this difference can be explained by the fact that under article 27(2) of the Convention a default judgment could only be recognized in another contracting state if there had been 'due service' under the law of the country in which the judgment was given.[72] The Brussels I Regulation has replaced the Convention in all EU Member States since 2007, and since 2008 the revised Lugano Convention (in similar terms to the Regulation) has applied to all European Economic Area members. Significantly for the present discussion, article 27(2) of the Convention has been replaced by article 34(2) of the Regulation. Article 34(2) no longer requires that the defendant be 'duly' served; what is required now is that the defendant has been served with notice, in sufficient time and in such a way as to enable him or her to arrange for their defence.[73] The intention behind this change was to reduce emphasis on the service requirements of the law of the country of adjudication and to move to a more autonomous, less technical notion of 'service'. A similar trend was noted at 4.16–4.24, in the recent English court practice on service abroad under the CPR. The result is that a mere formal irregularity in the process of service, such as where translation of a document was not included, will not preclude recognition[74] even though it may have done so under article 27(2) of the Brussels Convention.

---

[70] *Pocket Kings v Safenames Ltd* [2009] EWHC 2529 (Ch), para 26.

[71] Convention of 27 September 1968 on jurisdiction and the enforcement of judgments in civil and commercial matters.

[72] See *Isabelle Lancray SA v Pieters und Sickert KG* [1991] IL Pr 99 where the ECJ confirmed that the question of whether service was valid and proper was referred to the law of the country of origin (the original forum of adjudication).

[73] Case C-283/05 *ASML Netherlands BV v Semiconductor Industry Services GmbH* [2006] ECR I-12041 (ECJ 14 December 2006), para 20.

[74] ibid.

A. Service

The question which remains, however, is the extent to which choice of law considerations have been completely ousted by article 34(2) of the Brussels I Regulation. Here there is a difference of opinion. One view is that the procedural rules of the country of origin remain relevant even if formal irregularities under such law may now be ignored. Another view is that the rules for service under the Service Regulation may be relevant.[75] Either way, it seems clear that a court in the country of recognition will want to maintain some control over the question of service, for example by use of the public policy defence to recognition under the Brussels I Regulation. Defendants need to be protected from abuses of rights by 'gross irregularit[ies] in service'[76] and total deference to the law of the country of origin may compromise this goal. In support of this view, it is noteworthy that German courts in a number of cases declined to recognize judgments under article 27(2) of the Convention where the method of service employed, although valid under the law of the country of adjudication, violated the public policy of the state of recognition.[77] Public policy was said to include other relevant treaty provisions such as article 12 of the EC Treaty which prohibits discrimination on the ground of nationality (and also presumably article 6(1) of the European Convention on Human Rights which provides for a right of access to a court). It will be interesting to see whether these sentiments—which represent a reassertion of control by the law of the country where service is performed—are maintained in the context of recognition under article 34(2) of the Regulation.

4.27

(b) Australia

In Commonwealth countries, a similar approach is taken to that adopted in the English rules and decisions examined in 4.16–4.27: the law of the forum of adjudication has dominant control over the issue of service, with only a limited role provided for the law of the country where service is to be performed. Australia has recently become a party to the Hague Service Convention and so where the Convention applies service must proceed according to its terms. Where, however, the HSC does not apply, there have been a range of approaches adopted, although most give primacy to the law of the forum. The rules of the Federal Court of Australia are the most generous of all the Australian jurisdictions, in their recognition of foreign law in service matters. Under these rules, the court will approve

4.28

---

[75] *Tavoulareas v Tsavliris* [2007] 1 WLR 1573, para 8.
[76] *Dicey, Morris and Collins* (n 29 above) para 14.214.
[77] See eg Oberlandesgericht Düsseldorf 1999 [2002] IL Pr 7 (refusing recognition of Dutch judgment); and Oberlandesgericht Karlsruhe 1999 [2001] IL Pr 17 (refusing recognition of French judgment). cf Oberlandesgericht Frankfurt 2002 [2003] ECLY 878 (public policy not infringed merely because court of origin failed to comply with procedural law of country of recognition).

the service of originating process abroad only if the court is satisfied that service is permitted under the law of the country of service.[78] In the absence of evidence as to foreign law, the court will not authorize service.[79] In other Australian jurisdictions, more latitude is given to the law of the forum. Under the rules of court of some Australian states, including New South Wales,[80] Victoria,[81] and Western Australia,[82] it is provided that where originating process is to be served out of Australia it 'need not be served personally as long as it is served in accordance with the law of the country in which service is to be effected'. In a number of cases, foreign defendants have argued that this provision imposes an obligation on claimants to effect service in accordance with the rules of the law of the country where service is to occur. New South Wales and Victorian courts are divided on this issue. Some courts have held that the reference to foreign law in the provision does not impose a mandatory requirement on claimants which must be satisfied for valid service but is merely an *alternative* mode of service to procedures under forum law. According to this view, where a claimant can effect valid personal service under the rules of the forum, it does not have to employ a method under the law of the country of service.[83] Similarly, service has been held to be valid where the method used complied with the law of the country where service was to be performed even though it did not amount to valid service under the rules of the forum.[84] The effect of this view is to consign the issue of service almost entirely to the law of the forum by making adherence to foreign law optional. The opposing interpretation of the provision is that it *requires* compliance with the service rules of the law of the country of service, an approach which is similar to the position under the Federal Court Rules.[85]

4.29 Significantly, in neither the Federal Court Rules nor the rules of New South Wales and Victoria, is there a provision similar to that under the English CPR, which provides that no rule or order may authorize or require the doing of anything which is contrary to the law of the country in which service is to be performed. Such a provision is, however, found in the rules

---

[78] FCR, rr 10.43(6), (7)(b)(iii), 10.46.

[79] *Freehills Re New Tel Ltd (in liq)* (2008) 66 ACSR 311, para 34; *Royal Bank of Scotland plc v GBS Gold International Inc* [2009] FCA 1596, para 13.

[80] Uniform Civil Procedure Rules 2005 (NSW), r 11.6.

[81] Supreme Court (General Civil Procedure) Rules 2005 (Vic), r 7.03.

[82] Rules of the Supreme Court 1971 (WA) O 10, r 10 (3)(a).

[83] *Williams v Lips-Heerlen BV* SC NSW, 1 November 1991; *Victorian Workcover Authority v Orientstar Shipping Corp* [2003] VSC 311; and *ML Ubase Holdings Co Ltd v Trigem Computer Inc* [2005] NSWSC 224.

[84] *Richard Crookes Constructions (Qld) Pty Ltd v Wendell* [1990] 1 Qd R 392, 397.

[85] *McGrath v National Indemnity Co* [2004] NSWSC 391; *Rasmussen v Eltrax Systems Pty Ltd* [2006] NSWIR Comm 225; in both cases, service was found to be valid under foreign law.

of court of two Australian states, Queensland[86] and Western Australia.[87] The effect of this provision is that service must be set aside where the law of the country of service prohibits the method of service employed.[88] Such an approach is therefore similar to that adopted in England in *The Sky One* decision at 4.18, and represents a middle ground between applying the law of the country of service in its entirety and ignoring such law. Although there is no direct authority on this point, it is unlikely that such a provision would be used to invalidate service for mere technical breaches of the foreign law, such as where there is a page missing in the served documents[89] or where there is no signed declaration by the defendant confirming receipt of the material (where receipt has nevertheless been shown to have occurred).[90] In the state of South Australia[91] the status of foreign law on the issue of service is even less clear, given the different wording used. There, it is provided that 'subject to the law of the country in which service is to be effected, originating process is to be served outside Australia in the same way as if it were served within Australia' and 'the court may give any direction as to service outside Australia that may be appropriate (a) to avoid conflict with the law of the country in which service is to be effected'. The effect of such provisions may be either to require compliance with the law of the country of service in all respects or only where such law prohibits the method of service employed.

Unfortunately, there appears to be no consistent choice of law position with respect to service abroad in Australia, with some jurisdictions giving little or no operation to the law of the country of service, others taking it into account only when it prohibits the method of service used, and yet others requiring full compliance with foreign law. **4.30**

(c) Hong Kong

In other Commonwealth jurisdictions there also appears to be no uniform position regarding choice of law in the matter of service abroad. Hong Kong courts have held that a claimant is not required to use a method of service under the law of the country of service to confer jurisdiction on a Hong Kong court; it will be sufficient if the method employed is valid under Hong Kong law. Consequently, it does not matter if the law of the **4.31**

---

[86] Uniform Civil Procedure Rules 1999 (Qld), r 129(2).
[87] Rules of the Supreme Court 1971 (WA) O 10, r 10 (2).
[88] *Channar Mining Pty Ltd v CMIEC* [2003] WASC 253, para 28.
[89] cf *Phillips v Symes (No 3)* [2008] 1 WLR 180.
[90] cf *Olafsson v Gissurarson* [2008] 1 WLR 2016.
[91] Supreme Court Civil Rules 2006 (SA), r 41(2), (3).

country of service would recognize the service as valid.[92] Yet the courts have also noted that an exception similar to that identified in *The Sky One* case may apply if the method of service used would be illegal under the penal code of the foreign country. In such a case service may not be authorized, even where it was valid under the law of the forum.[93]

(d) Singapore

4.32 Singapore, by contrast, appears to give wider operation to the law of the country where service is to be performed. Although its courts have stressed that matters relating to the service of originating process are governed by the law of the forum,[94] Singapore rules provide that service abroad can be performed in accordance with any 'method of service authorised by the [law of the country of service] for service of any originating process issued by that country',[95] and that the court may not make any order which 'shall authorise or require the doing of anything in a country in which service is to be effected which is contrary to the law of that country'.[96] In *ITC Global Holdings Pte Ltd (in Liquidation) v ITC Ltd*,[97] service was found not to comply with the law of the country of service where an individual was served neither personally nor through an agent. Yet the Singapore forum, following the House of Lords decision in *Phillips v Symes (No 3)*,[98] agreed to 'cure' the irregularity because the defendant had suffered no prejudice, having been apprised of the proceedings and taken steps to contest them, and the claimant had done all it could do to effect service.[99]

(e) Canada

4.33 Canada also displays a variety of approaches to choice of law in service abroad cases but in general reserves strong control in the law of the forum. In Ontario, where service is made on a defendant not resident in an HSC state, it may be performed 'in the manner provided by [the] rules for service in Ontario *or* in the manner provided by the law of the jurisdiction

---

[92] *Pacific Electric Wire & Cable Co Ltd v Texan Management Ltd* [2007] HKCU 1298 (HKCA); *Hong Kong Housing Authority v Hsin Yieh Architects and Associates Ltd* [2005] 2 HKC 201 (HKCFI).
[93] See Hong Kong Rules of the High Court, O 11, r 5(2); *Hong Kong Housing Authority v Hsin Yieh Architects and Associates Ltd* [2005] 2 HKC 201, para 86.
[94] *Pacific Assets Management Ltd v Chen Lip Keong* [2005] SGHC 228, para 14.
[95] Rules of Court, O 11, r 4(2)(c). The position under Malaysian law is similar, see *Fiden Electrical Engineering Sdn Bhd v Nippon Seiko KK* [2004] 7 MLJ 231, paras 5, 13 (High Court).
[96] Rules of Court, O 11, r 3(2).
[97] [2011] SGHC 150.
[98] [2008] 1 WLR 180.
[99] *ITC Global Holdings Pte Ltd (in liq) v ITC Ltd* [2011] SGHC 150, para 49.

A. Service

where service is made . . . if service made in that manner could be reasonably expected to come to the notice of the person to be served'.[100] In effect, this provision gives a claimant the option to ignore the rules of the law of the country of service entirely in favour of the service mechanism of the law of the forum. Also, even where a claimant resorts to the rules of the law of the country of service, the law of the forum imposes a public policy gloss such that the foreign rules can only be applied 'if service . . . could reasonably be expected to come to the notice of the person to be served'. In the case of service on a defendant in an HSC country, by contrast, Ontario courts have generally rejected plaintiffs' arguments that because service under the HSC is inconvenient or impractical, substituted service under the law of the forum should be ordered,[101] especially where the form of service would be invalid under the law of the country of service. To that extent, the law of the forum is subordinated to the Convention where the HSC applies. In British Columbia, the only other Canadian jurisdiction with decisions on service abroad, the position is weighted even more heavily in favour of the law of the forum. Under the rules[102] a document may be served outside the province (a) in a manner provided by the rules for service of the forum, (b) in a manner provided by the law of the place where service is made if, by the manner of that service, the document could reasonably be expected to come to the notice of the person to be served, or (c) in a state that is a contracting state under the HSC, in a manner provided by or permitted under the HSC. In a consistent body of decisions, British Columbia courts have held that these rules allow service abroad by three alternative means.[103] In effect, regardless of whether the defendant is located in an HSC country, a claimant may always have resort to the service rules of the law of the forum. Presumably such rules can be applied even where service was prohibited under the law of the country of service, as in *The Sky One* case. If this analysis is accurate, then the approach in British Columbia amounts to an exclusive reference to the law of the forum, even to the extent of overriding the Convention.

---

[100] Rules of Civil Procedure (Ont), r 17.05(2).

[101] *Campeau v Campeau* 2004 Can LII 42942, para 57 (ONSC); *Dofasco Inc v Ucar Carbon Canada Inc* (1998) 27 CPC (4th) 342, para 16; *Samina North America Inc v H3 Environmental LLC* 2004 Can LII 65382 (ONSC) but cf *Zhang v Jiang* (2006) 82 OR (3d) 306 (substituted service under the law of the forum ordered where the claimant had exhausted all possible methods under the law of the country of service and the claim alleged serious human rights violations in that country).

[102] See, as of 1 July 2010, Supreme Court Civil Rules, r 4–5(10).

[103] *Grant v Grant* 2003 BCSC 649; *Mathers v Bruce* 2002 BCSC 210; *Pan Pacific Specialities Ltd v Shandong Machinery and Equipment I/E Corp* 1999 BCSC 5755.

(f) United States

4.34 US practice in service abroad disputes reflects a strong inclination towards application of the law of the forum. The Federal Rules of Civil Procedure (FRCP) provide that service may be made by 'any internationally agreed means reasonably calculated to give notice'.[104] Such means include the HSC,[105] which is mandatory in all cases to which it applies.[106] If no internationally agreed means of service is available service may be made: (i) by any method prescribed by the law of the foreign country for service in that country in an action in its own courts,[107] (ii) unless prohibited by law of the foreign country, by personal delivery to an individual or by any form of mail requiring a signed receipt dispatched to a party,[108] or (iii) by any other means not prohibited by international agreement as may be directed by the court.[109]

4.35 FRCP, rules 4(f)(2) and 4(f)(3) have been the subject of much judicial interpretation. Service under rule 4(f)(2)(A) is similar to the English CPR, rule 6.40(3)(c) in that this provision allows a claimant to select a method of service available under the law of the country of service. It is insufficient that the method chosen does not *violate* foreign law; the means of service must actually *exist* under the law of the country of service.[110] In a number of cases, however, US courts have given a more restrictive interpretation of when a method of service is 'prescribed by' foreign law under rule 4(f)(2)(A). According to these decisions, it is not enough that the method of service is available for *domestic* actions in the courts of that country. Instead, it must be a method of service prescribed for actions filed *outside* the foreign country in which the claimant seeks to serve a defendant within the country.[111] Hence, a claimant in a US action can only have access to a method of service under Ruritanian law where such law provides a method for claimants in foreign actions seeking to serve defendants in Ruritanian territory. While such an approach has been justified on the ground of US respect for the sovereignty of foreign courts,[112] it will ironically result in less reliance on foreign law by claimants, given the likely difficulty of showing that under that law there is a method of service specifically

---

[104] FRCP, r 4(f)(1).
[105] ibid.
[106] *Volkswagenwerk Aktiengesellschaft v Schlunk* 486 US 694, 705 (US Sup Ct 1988).
[107] FRCP, r 4(f)(2)(A).
[108] FRCP, r 4(f)(2)(C)(i), (ii).
[109] FRCP, r 4(f)(3).
[110] *Dee-K Ent Inc v Heveafil Sdn Bhd* 174 FRD 376 (ED Va 1997); *Mayoral-Amy v BHI Corp* 180 FRD 456 (SD Fla 1998).
[111] *PreWitt Enterprises Inc v OPEC* 353 F 3d 916, 925 (11th Cir 2003).
[112] *Grand Entertainment Group Ltd v Star Media Sales Inc* 988 F 2d 476, 487 (3rd Cir 1993).

designed for claimants in foreign actions. It would surely be simpler and just as respectful of foreign law if a claimant could use the means of service provided under foreign law for domestic cases in that country.[113]

FRCP, rule 4(f)(2)(C) restores some control to the law of the forum. This provision permits service by a method that may not be available under the law of the country of service, provided the means is not *prohibited* by such law and falls within one of the two categories in rule 4(f)(2)(C).[114] Further, the notion of when a means of service is 'prohibited' by foreign law is to be interpreted narrowly: there must be a provision in the foreign law which states that service 'must be effected' by a specific means or that the law 'requires' such a method.[115] **4.36**

FRCP rule 4(f)(3), in allowing service 'by any other means not prohibited by international agreement', has also been the subject of differing judicial opinions. While on its face this provision would seem to allow for an almost unqualified operation of the law of the forum in service abroad, at least in cases where the HSC is not relevant, the drafters of the provision may not have intended such an outcome. In 1993, the Advisory Committee noted that in applying rule 4(f)(3) courts should make 'an earnest effort . . . to devise a method of . . . [service] that minimizes offense to foreign law'. Furthermore, scholars[116] have noted the general presumption that where a US statute is ambiguous, it should be interpreted consistently with principles of international law and the laws of other countries. The instruction from the Advisory Committee was quoted with approval in one Circuit Court of Appeals decision where it was stated that the general purpose of rule 4(f) is to provide great deference to foreign law.[117] Consequently, the court refused to authorize a method of service under rule 4(f)(3) where such method was prohibited by the law of the country of service. This analysis seeks to preserve the operation of the law of the country of service by ensuring that in no case can a US court authorize a method of service which would contravene foreign law. Unfortunately, other US courts have been less accommodating of foreign laws in their interpretation of rule 4(f)(3). In *Rio Properties v Rio International Interlink*[118] it was held that the only limitation on a US court authorizing a method of service under **4.37**

---

[113] Born and Rutledge (n 4 above) 851.
[114] *Dee-K Ent Inc v Heveafil Sdn Bhd* 174 FRD 376, 380 (ED Va 1997) (service by courier not prescribed by foreign law but not prohibited and so valid); *Resource Ventures Inc v Resources Management International Inc* 42 F Supp 2d 423, 430 (D Del 1999); *Banco Latino SACA v Gomez-Lopez* 53 F Supp 2d 1273, 1278 (SD Fla 1999).
[115] *Marks v Alfa Group* 615 F Supp 2d 375 (ED Pa 2009).
[116] Born and Rutledge (n 4 above) 836.
[117] *PreWitt Enterprises Inc v OPEC* 353 F 3d 916, 927 (11th Cir 2003).
[118] 284 F 3d 1007, 1014 (9th Cir 2002).

94   *Chapter 4: Service and Jurisdiction*

rule 4(f)(3) was that provided in the literal text itself, namely that the method should not be prohibited by international agreement. Consequently, where the HSC does not apply, a method of service under forum law may be approved by a US court which is in clear violation of the law of the country of service. Such an approach is inimical to comity and recognition of foreign laws. Regrettably, the *Rio* decision has been followed in some later cases,[119] although it should be noted that in none of these decisions was the method of service found to be prohibited by the law of the country of service.

4.38 It was mentioned at 4.26–4.27, in the discussion of EU law, that the problem of applicable law in relation to service abroad has also arisen at the stage of recognition and enforcement of foreign judgments. Specifically, the claimant seeks recognition of its judgment in the country where service was performed and the local courts have to decide whether to defer to the findings of the court of origin on the issue of service or impose their own standards. Recognition and enforcement of foreign judgments in the United States is governed by both common law standards and statute.[120] Under both common law principles and the Act, a well accepted ground for non-recognition of a foreign judgment is that there was no 'due citation' of the defendant, that is, he or she 'did not receive notice of the proceedings in the foreign court in sufficient time to enable them to defend'.[121] This test suggests a due process type inquiry as to the suitability of service, namely, whether the defendant received adequate notice of the proceedings, regardless of the method of service employed in the court of origin. Yet in some US cases, courts have held that in addition to this adequacy of notice requirement, the service of process must also satisfy the US rules for service under FRCP, rule 4 before the judgment can be enforced.[122] Other courts have, however, rejected this view, saying that adequate notice is all that is required and the 'niceties of [US] domestic jurisprudence' on service need not be investigated.[123] Still other US courts have required that service of process comply with the *country of origin's* own rules before a foreign judgment can be recognized.[124] Such a view may appear to be an example of

---

[119] See eg *Export-Import Bank of the US v Asia Pulp and Paper Ltd* 2005 WL 1123755 (SDNY); *Bank Julius Baer and Co Ltd v Wikileaks* 2008 WL 413737 (ND Cal); *SEC v Anticevic* 2009 WL 361739 (SDNY).

[120] See eg the Uniform Foreign Money Judgments Recognition Act (1962) <http://www.law.upenn.edu/bll/archives/ulc/fnact99/1920_69/ufmjra62.pdf> (accessed October 2011).

[121] ibid s 4(b)(1).

[122] *Corporacion Salvadorena de Calzado SA v Injection Footwear Corp* 533 F Supp 290, 296–297 (SD Fla 1982).

[123] *Ma v Continental Bank NA* 905 F 2d 1073, 1076 (7th Cir 1990).

[124] See eg *De La Mata v American Life Ins Co* 771 F Supp 1375, 1385–6 (D Del 1991); *Ackermann v Levine* 788 F 2d 830 (2nd Cir 1986).

A. Service

overreaching by the enforcing US court given that it involves second-guessing a foreign court as to the application of its own rules on service. Yet again though, in none of the cases mentioned did the US court find service to be invalid under the law of the country of origin. Such a conclusion suggests that the adequacy of notice issue will be the key concern of US courts at the stage of recognition and enforcement rather than compliance with the technical requirements of service in the country of origin or the place of enforcement. To that extent, choice of law concerns will ordinarily be minimized.

4.39 Overall therefore, US practice reveals a similar pattern to the English and Commonwealth material already discussed; on the face of the statutory rules there is a clear recognition of foreign law in matters of service abroad but in the interpretation of the rules the courts have sometimes acceded to claimants' demands and consequently conferred considerable scope of operation on the law of the forum. Even the existence of treaties such as the HSC has not completely ousted the rules of the forum: as was noted, in England, Canada, and the United States, courts have occasionally been willing to authorize or dispense with service even where to do so could violate the international instrument. Perhaps, after all, the principle of *lex fori regit processum*, which applies to many aspects of service of process generally, is also dominant in service abroad. Yet the law of the country where service is to be performed remains relevant in most jurisdictions and, to that extent, there is some evidence of a choice of law analysis or at least an 'enlightened *lex fori*' in the case of service abroad.

4.40 An alternative to employing choice of law rules in the area of service abroad is to harmonize domestic rules through international instruments or the recognition of autonomous, supranational concepts. The international instruments that have been developed so far, in particular the HSC, have harmonized domestic law to some extent but still rely on choice of law rules to apply the law of the forum and/or the law of the country of service to discrete issues. Such an approach was no doubt thought appropriate for instruments whose goal was to create a mechanism for cooperation and coordination between legal systems. By contrast, the recent revisions to the Brussels I Regulation and the Lugano Convention (in the context of recognition of foreign judgments) suggest a small move towards accepting an autonomous concept of service focusing on whether the method chosen has adequately informed the defendant of the existence of proceedings, rather than simply whether national law requirements have been complied with. Some US court practices on recognition point in a similar direction. As noted at 4.06, similar sentiments have been expressed by English and Singaporean judges, which may be indicative of a new trend in this area.

B. JURISDICTION

4.41 Jurisdiction is a topic which, like service of process, is often assumed to involve only the application of one law—the law of the forum—because of its procedural nature, based on the closeness of the issue to the foundation of the court's proceedings and enlivening of its powers. Increasingly, however, as will be seen, other laws may also be relevant. Such reference to foreign law is not made pursuant to a substance-procedure classification but rather because forum law uses foreign procedural law as a preliminary step or 'connecting factor' in determining whether jurisdiction should be exercised under the rules of the forum. This inquiry shows again, therefore, that forum law does not have exclusive operation in this area.

4.42 The concept of jurisdiction is frequently used in two distinct senses. The first is subject matter jurisdiction, which refers to the capacity of a court to pronounce upon the issues raised before it. For example, the forum legislature may reserve certain disputes to specialist courts or tribunals or place monetary limits on the actions which can be brought in a particular court. Obviously subject matter jurisdiction in this sense is clearly an issue for the exclusive operation of forum law: a claimant must take the court it sues in as it finds it.[125] While application of forum law to subject matter jurisdiction may be based on the general classification of jurisdictional issues as procedural, it may equally be justified as an example of overriding mandatory rules. Yet, in private international law there are limitations on a forum court's subject matter jurisdiction which may not be wholly resolved by forum law, for example where a defendant pleads an immunity from the jurisdiction of the forum courts. The possible relevance of foreign law to this topic is explored at 4.64–4.70. The second sense in which the term jurisdiction is used is in referring to *personal* jurisdiction, which is the court's adjudicatory power or competence over a defendant. The relevance of foreign law to this latter topic will first be examined.

1. Personal Jurisdiction

4.43 Under Commonwealth common law rules, personal jurisdiction is established by service of process upon the defendant while present in the forum. As noted in the material on service at 4.01 above, the law of the forum exclusively applies to determine the validity of service *within* the forum, with foreign law being irrelevant. The position, however, regarding service out of the jurisdiction was shown to be more complex, with the law of

---

[125] See *John Pfeiffer Pty Ltd v Rogerson* (2000) 203 CLR 503, para 99.

B. Jurisdiction

the country where service is to be performed at times having a role to play. There are also further rules of the forum which must be complied with before jurisdiction can be established based on service out of the jurisdiction. Under the statutory rules of most Commonwealth countries, the claimant must obtain leave to serve the defendant and satisfy two matters. The first requirement is that the cause of action is connected with the forum, for example that the contract was made there or the tort occurred locally, and the second element is that the forum is an appropriate jurisdiction for trial. Individual Commonwealth countries express this second requirement in slightly different ways, but in each case a broad discretionary test is involved. Under English,[126] Hong Kong,[127] and Singapore law,[128] the claimant must show, in order to obtain permission to serve outside the jurisdiction, that England, Hong Kong, or Singapore (as the case may be) is the clearly appropriate forum for trial (or *forum conveniens*), while in Australia, the claimant must establish that the Australian court is not a 'clearly inappropriate' forum.[129] By contrast in Canada, the first and second elements are subsumed into one test, where the claimant must show that the cause of action has 'a real and substantial connection' with the forum before the court will agree to adjudicate the matter.[130] Similar discretionary principles also apply when the defendant seeks to set aside service or to stay the forum court's proceedings on appropriate forum grounds.

(a) Canada

4.44 In the Commonwealth rules for service out of the jurisdiction (apart from Canada), the law of the forum appears to apply exclusively. For example, in determining whether a tort has been committed in the forum or a contract was made or breached there, no reference to any other law is made. Under the Canadian 'real and substantial connection' test, however, the position is more complicated.[131] According to the leading authority on this issue, *Muscutt v Courcelles*,[132] eight criteria must be applied to determine whether the Canadian court has a real and substantial connection to the action sufficient to found jurisdiction, with one of the eight criteria making

---

[126] *AK Investment CJSC v Kyrgyz Mobil Tel Ltd* [2011] UKPC 7, para 71 (Lord Collins); *Deripaska v Cherney* [2009] EWCA Civ 849, para 20 (Waller LJ).
[127] *Dynasty Line Ltd v Sukamto SIA* [2009] HKCA 197, para 29.
[128] *ITC Global Holdings Pte Ltd (in liq) v ITC Ltd* [2011] SGHC 150, para 11.
[129] *Voth v Manildra Flour Mills Pty Ltd* (1990) 171 CLR 538.
[130] *Muscutt v Courcelles* (2002) 60 OR (3d) 20 (Ont CA).
[131] Note, however, that this test for personal jurisdiction is not accepted in all Canadian provinces, see eg British Columbia: *Laxton v Jurem Anstalt* 2011 BCCA 212, para 42 and New Brunswick: *Coutu v Gauthier (Estate)* (2006) 264 DLR (4th) 391 (NBCA).
[132] (2002) 60 OR (3d) 20.

express reference to foreign procedural law: 'comity and standards of jurisdiction, recognition and enforcement prevailing elsewhere'. There are two aspects to this inquiry. The first is that the Canadian court should examine whether the competing, foreign forum would have exercised jurisdiction *under its own rules* had it been presented with a reciprocal set of facts. Secondly, the Canadian court should consider whether the foreign court would recognize and enforce any judgment of the Canadian court. In a recent restatement of the *Muscutt* principles, the Ontario Court of Appeal confirmed that, in applying the real and substantial connection test, reference to foreign jurisdictional rules was desirable:[133] 'it is entirely appropriate to take foreign law into account in an area of law that has such obvious and immediate application to foreign litigants . . . I view it as helpful to know how foreign courts treat like cases when determining the appropriateness of extending the reach of Ontario law against a foreign litigant'.

4.45 Hence, a Canadian court, in determining whether jurisdiction exists, should consider both foreign law rules of jurisdiction and recognition and enforcement of foreign judgments. A choice of law rule, similar to the 'incidental' or preliminary question, is created where forum law makes reference to foreign procedural rules as a *precondition* to finding jurisdiction existing in the forum. Once again, the result has echoes of a Kahn-Freund 'enlightened *lex fori*' approach, where the scope of operation of forum law is modified or qualified by reference to foreign elements. An illustration of this principle occurred in *Pavacic v Estate of Nicely*,[134] where an Ontario court found no real and substantial connection to exist between Ontario and a tort action by an Ontario claimant against a Georgian (US) defendant arising from an accident in Georgia. Application of the criterion in 4.44 led the Ontario court to accept evidence that under US jurisdictional rules, a Georgian court would not have assumed jurisdiction over a claim by a Georgian claimant against an Ontario defendant, had the accident occurred in Ontario. Secondly, it was likely that the Georgian court would not have recognized and enforced an Ontario judgment arising out of the current action before the court.[135] Satisfaction of the forum's rules of jurisdiction was therefore made dependent on compliance with foreign procedural rules on jurisdiction and judgment recognition.

---

[133] *Van Breda v Village Resorts Ltd* (2010) 98 OR (3d) 721, para 107.
[134] (2008) 91 OR (3d) 49.
[135] See also *Galustian v The Skylink Group of Companies* 2010 ONSC 292, para 64, where jurisdiction was found not to exist where the foreign court would not enforce the Canadian court's orders.

(b) England

There is some evidence of a receptive approach to foreign law in the prac- **4.46** tice of other Commonwealth countries. In England, at the second stage of the service out inquiry, where the claimant must show that England is the clearly appropriate forum or in a stay application, where the defendant must establish that a foreign court is more appropriate, there may be some reference to foreign law. The English test of *forum non conveniens* comes from the *Spiliada* case[136] and requires the court to identify the forum in which the case can be suitably tried for the interests of the parties and the ends of justice.[137] A key element in the defendant being able to obtain a stay of English proceedings or an English court refusing leave to serve out under CPR, rule 6.36 and PD 6B is that there exists another 'available' forum abroad with 'competent jurisdiction' to try the case.[138] What the defendant must therefore show is that a foreign court would have jurisdiction over both the parties and the subject matter of the action. Normally the requirement that the foreign court should have personal jurisdiction is satisfied by the defendant agreeing to submit to the foreign court's jurisdiction, which obviates the need to lead evidence of foreign law. However, in the rare case where the defendant fails to submit to the foreign jurisdiction, the burden rests on that party to show that the foreign court would reject arguments that it was an inappropriate forum. In effect, the defendant must show that the foreign court would unquestionably have exercised jurisdiction under its own rules. No case has yet arisen where a defendant has sought to establish such a fact as, understandably, they have been content to rely on their submission to the jurisdiction of the foreign court. Further, in determining whether a 'submission' to the jurisdiction of the foreign court has occurred, the English court applies its own law exclusively.[139] Yet a possible circumstance where foreign rules of jurisdiction could be relevant to an English stay application is where the foreign court has already declined jurisdiction over the action so as to render it an 'unavailable' forum or where the foreign rules would not allow a suit to be brought regardless of whether the defendant had submitted. In such a case the English court may be much less willing to stay the action because the effect of the foreign jurisdictional rules is to leave only one possible forum.

---

[136] *Spiliada Maritime Corp v Cansulex Ltd* [1987] AC 460.
[137] ibid 480.
[138] ibid 476; see also *Reeves v Sprecher* [2007] EWHC 117 (Ch), para 15; *Petroleo Brasiliero SA v Mellitus Shipping Inc* [2001] EWCA Civ 418, para 35; *889457 Alberta Inc v Katanga Mining Ltd* [2008] EWHC 2679 (Comm), para 33.
[139] *Ward Associates Ltd v Public Services Mutual Insurance Co* EWHC, 5 December 2000.

(c) Australia

4.47 In Australia, as in England, the rules for service out of the jurisdiction allow for some reference to be made to foreign law in determining whether service will be authorized. Once service is approved, however, there is no test equivalent to that in Canada which requires, in addition, that an Australian court should investigate whether the foreign court would have accepted jurisdiction on the same facts as a condition to the forum's acceptance of jurisdiction. There may, however, be some scope for Australian courts to consider foreign jurisdictional rules where a defendant asks the court to decline jurisdiction on discretionary grounds. While in a number of early decisions discretionary stays were refused because of the failure by the defendant to show that a foreign forum existed with jurisdiction over the matter and the parties,[140] in more recent cases the issue of foreign jurisdictional rules has not been raised. Instead, Australian courts have focused simply on whether the defendant has shown that the proceedings in the forum amount to vexation and oppression 'in the sense of . . . harassment'.[141] It seems, therefore, that the matter is now exclusively resolved by the law of the forum. Yet, in the related area of applications to stay proceedings on the basis of foreign pending proceedings abroad or *lis pendens*, there seems a greater willingness among Australian courts to refer to foreign procedural rules as a factor in deciding whether a stay should be ordered. In *Henry v Henry*[142] the High Court held that a factor in determining whether it would grant a stay of local proceedings on the basis of a pending foreign suit was whether the foreign court had jurisdiction over the matter or had stayed its proceedings. This principle has been applied in subsequent decisions but so far there has been little willingness to consider foreign jurisdictional rules outside the situation of pending proceedings.

4.48 It has been suggested also[143] that under the 'uniformity of outcome' approach to choice of law an Australian court might, by analogy with the *renvoi* doctrine, consider evidence as to whether the courts in the country of the law of the cause of action would have exercised jurisdiction on the

---

[140] *Schmidt v Won* [1998] 3 VR 435; *Conagra International Fertiliser Co v Lief Investments Pty Ltd* [1997] NSWSC 511.
[141] *Regie Nationale des Usines Renault v Zhang* (2002) 210 CLR 491, para 78.
[142] (1995) 185 CLR 571.
[143] M Davies, 'Case Note *Neilson v Overseas Projects Corp of Victoria Ltd* Renvoi and Presumptions about Foreign Law' (2006) 30 Melbourne University L Rev 244, 254–7.

B. Jurisdiction

same facts. Although such an approach requires the forum to ascertain the applicable law before determining the jurisdictional question, this process is increasingly common in international litigation. Adoption of this approach would mean that a key influence in the forum's decision to hear an action would be that the foreign court itself would not have had or would have declined jurisdiction. Such an approach has some similarity with the Canadian *Muscutt* principle[144] and would represent a wider use of foreign procedural law in Australian jurisdictional determinations, although it is acknowledged that making accurate predictions of how a foreign court would exercise its discretion on jurisdiction questions would not be easy.

(d) Singapore

4.49 Singapore, by contrast, has adamantly affirmed the proposition that the law of the forum has exclusive control in jurisdictional matters:

> The question of jurisdiction must always be determined by the *lex fori*. To classify a jurisdictional dispute as a substantive issue is to accept the possibility that the law governing a jurisdictional dispute is the *lex causae* and not the *lex fori* a proposition which merely begs the question as to what would be the connecting factor in such a case. Clearly the scope of judicial power must be determined by the law of the state which confers the power, i.e. the *lex fori* and cannot be determined by reference to the laws of another state.[145]

Such a statement is categorical in its assertion that the law of the forum has exclusive application in jurisdictional matters and appears to preclude any reference to foreign law. While the first part of the statement is correct in that jurisdiction is procedural and that, in principle, reference is not made to the *law of the cause of action* on such questions, it is not accurate to say that foreign law is entirely irrelevant. First, as was discussed earlier,[146] Singapore law does have regard to the law of the country in which service is to be performed in determining whether service abroad will be authorized. In that respect, the application of forum law is modified to accommodate the foreign rules and not simply applied in the same way as would occur in a wholly domestic case. Secondly, Singapore courts follow the *Spiliada* principle of *forum non conveniens*[147] and so it would be expected

---

[144] Some evidence of this approach can be seen in *Pacific Petroleum Corp v Nauru Phosphate Corp* [2002] QSC 389, para 17, where an Australian court granted a stay after being presented with evidence that the foreign court would have had jurisdiction over the parties and the subject matter of the action.
[145] *The Jarguh Sawit* [1997] SGCA 59, para 31.
[146] See 4.32 above.
[147] *Brinkerhoff Maritime Drilling Corp v PT Airfast Services Indonesia* [1992] 2 SLR 776; *Rickshaw Investments Ltd v Nicolai Baron von Uexkull* [2007] 1 SLR 377 (both Sing CA).

that its courts may consider, in determining whether to order a stay, whether the competing foreign court had, and would exercise, jurisdiction over the matter.[148] Consequently, despite the above quotation, the Singapore position is likely to be closer to the mainstream Commonwealth view, which recognizes that while it is correct to say that jurisdiction is inherently procedural and subject to general control by the law of the forum, reference to such law is not exclusive.

(e) United States

4.50 In the United States foreign jurisdictional rules have been given a more prominent role in determining whether a US court should adjudicate a matter. Indeed, the effect of some recent decisions is that as a matter of choice of law a US court must apply both local and foreign jurisdictional rules in a type of 'double actionability' test before allowing the matter to proceed. While US rules of personal jurisdiction, which are influenced strongly by the due process clause of the US Constitution, make no reference to foreign jurisdictional rules, it is under the US doctrine of *forum non conveniens* that they assume importance. Under the US doctrine of *forum non conveniens*, to obtain a dismissal of the action the defendant must show that there is another available forum in a foreign country in which the plaintiff's action may be tried.[149] A forum is generally considered adequate and available if the defendant is subject to personal jurisdiction there.[150] Consequently, similar to the position under Commonwealth practice, where a defendant consents to jurisdiction in the foreign court, this will often be considered sufficient to render the foreign forum available.[151] The problem, however, which has arisen in US practice but not in Commonwealth countries, arises from the fact that a number of South American countries have enacted jurisdictional 'blocking statutes'. Such statutes are based on the Roman law doctrine of pre-emptive jurisdiction which provides that once the court has found jurisdiction to exist it cannot subsequently decline to adjudicate a matter. The legislation therefore precludes a local court from hearing an action which has been previously commenced in another country such as the United States, but has been dismissed on *forum non conveniens* grounds. The aim of these blocking

---

[148] See eg *Good Earth Agricultural Co Ltd v Novus International Pte Ltd* [2008] SGCA 13. The position in Kong Kong, where *Spiliada* is also applied, is likely to be similar: *The Adhiguna Meranti* [1987] 1 HKLR 904.

[149] *Piper Aircraft v Reyno* 454 US 235, 249–56 (1981); *Lacey v Cessna Aircraft Co* 862 F 3d 38, 44–5 (3rd Cir 1988).

[150] ibid 255 n 2.

[151] *Stangvik v Shiley Inc* 819 P 2d 14, 17 n 2 (SC Cal 1991).

B. Jurisdiction

statutes is to prevent a US court from finding that an alternative forum exists to hear the plaintiff suit regardless of whether the defendant has consented to trial in the local forum. US courts have disagreed over whether such blocking statutes should be recognized in determining whether the foreign court is available. In *Re Bridgestone/Firestone Inc*[152] a US court refused to dismiss an action where a Venezuelan statute blocked access to its local courts. The same result was reached in respect of statutes in Costa Rica[153] and Mexico.[154] In other decisions, however, US courts have ignored foreign blocking statutes, claiming that to do otherwise would be to support 'plaintiff forum shopping' and 'unilateral authority regarding choice of forum'.[155] In terms of choice of law, under the first view, local exercise of jurisdiction by the forum is effectively determined by the operation of foreign jurisdictional rules. Hence the law of the forum loses its exclusive application in jurisdictional matters and is now qualified by the law of the competing jurisdiction. The second view, however, represents the traditional position on choice of law in jurisdictional matters: the law of the forum applies exclusively and foreign rules or practice are irrelevant.

4.51 In principle, there is much to be said for the view that the resolution of jurisdictional questions should take into account the parallel rules of a competing forum or forums. While the issue of jurisdiction is obviously a matter in which the interest of the forum is paramount, given that it concerns the willingness of a court system to accept a proceeding for adjudication, this does not mean that there are no foreign interests involved. Reference to foreign jurisdictional rules, as the Canadian and US experience shows, enables the forum to gain a fuller picture. Also, jurisdiction is a matter which plainly affects the rights of the parties and can be outcome determinative; it is well known that many suits are settled after the issue of jurisdiction has been decided.[156] There is a good argument, therefore, for the matter to be determined in part by reference to foreign law.

4.52 Finally, it is worth noting that a similar tendency to apply foreign procedural rules can be seen in US decisions in which the rules on recognition and enforcement of foreign judgments of other countries have been examined, before certifying a US class action involving claimants resident in

---

[152] 190 F Supp 2d 1125 (SD Ind 2002).
[153] *Canales Martinez v Dow Chemical Co* 219 F Supp 2d 719 (ED La 2002).
[154] *Sandria Saqui v Pride International* 2007 WL 528193 (SD Tex).
[155] *Morales v Ford Motor Co* 313 F Supp 2d 672, 676 (SD Tex 2004); *The Scotts Co v Hacienda Loma Linda* 2 So 3d 1013 (CA Fla 2008); *Paulownia Plantations de Panama Corp v Rajamannan* 793 NW 2d 128 (SC Minn 2009).
[156] See eg *Puttick v Tenon Ltd* (2008) 238 CLR 265.

such countries.[157] The rationale here is that defendants to a class action proceeding should be protected from further, individual litigation in those countries on the same facts and issues by claimants who were not bound by the original class action judgment. A class action, therefore, will not normally be certified under US law where the judgment would not be binding and enforceable in the claimants' countries of residence.

(f) EU law

4.53 Where a defendant is domiciled in a Member State of the European Union, the jurisdictional rules of the Brussels I Regulation apply. Under the rules of the Regulation there is no discretion to decline jurisdiction on *forum non conveniens* grounds[158] or to grant an anti-suit injunction to restrain proceedings in another Member State's court.[159] The rules of the Regulation are autonomous in that they are common to all EU Member States and designed to achieve uniform outcomes. The drafting of the rules has also largely eliminated any scope for the operation of forum or foreign procedural rules. A good example is article 27 of the Regulation which requires a Member State court to stay its proceedings where another Member State's court is 'first seised' of proceedings involving the same cause of action and parties, with the expression 'first seised' receiving an autonomous, EU law definition in article 30.

2. Jurisdiction or Choice of Court Clauses

(a) Commonwealth

4.54 An issue which has so far received limited attention in the decided cases in the Commonwealth but is growing in significance in the United States is the applicable law to choice of court or jurisdiction clauses. The context for this issue is where a claimant sues in the forum and establishes jurisdiction but the defendant argues that the court should stay its proceedings and decline jurisdiction because the parties had entered a contractual clause whereby the parties agreed to resolve their disputes in the courts of

---

[157] See eg *Re Vivendi Universal SA Securities Litigation* 242 FRD 76 (SDNY 2007).
[158] *Owusu v Jackson* [2005] QB 801.
[159] *Turner v Grovit* [2005] 1 AC 101.

B. Jurisdiction

another country or state. Alternatively, some courts[160] and writers[161] have described a jurisdiction clause as a choice of the procedural law of the country whose courts are stipulated, with the forum court being asked, in a stay application, to enforce the parties' choice of procedure. In any case, in common law countries there is a distinction between a 'non-exclusive' or 'permissive' choice of court clause where the parties nominate a country's courts for dispute resolution but do not preclude suit elsewhere and an 'exclusive' or 'mandatory' choice of court clause where the parties have entered a binding contractual obligation to submit their dispute to a particular forum. The other important point to note is that while a jurisdiction clause is invariably physically part of a larger contract, it is regarded as a legally 'separable' agreement under the laws of most Commonwealth countries.[162]

In determining whether the proceedings in the forum should be stayed in deference to the choice of court clause, three main issues arise for choice of law purposes: first, the interpretation and meaning of the clause; secondly, the formal and essential validity of the clause; and thirdly, the enforceability of the clause. There are two distinct aspects to the issue of interpretation: the first is whether the clause is 'exclusive' or non-exclusive' and the second is whether the clause, as a matter of scope, applies to the claims pleaded by the claimant against the defendant in the forum. On the first aspect of interpretation, exclusivity, Commonwealth courts have almost always applied the law of the forum,[163] although it is not clear whether this approach has been taken because the issue is considered 'procedural' or simply because it has never been asserted that any other

4.55

---

[160] *The Asian Plutus* [1990] 1 SLR 543, para 19 (Sing HC); *Telesis Technologies Inc v Sure Controls Systems Inc* 2010 ONSC 5288, para 9. There is German authority to the same effect: *Re Claim by a Polish Producer of Zinc and Copper Products* [1998] IL Pr 727 (Oberlandesgericht Cologne 9 September 1996), para 3.

[161] M Keyes, 'Substance and Procedure in Multistate Tort Litigation' (2010) 18 Torts LJ 201, 222; see also M Illmer, 'Neutrality Matters—Some Thoughts about the Rome Regulations and the so-called Dichotomy of Substance and Procedure in European Private International Law' (2009) 28 Civil Justice Quarterly 237, 252–3.

[162] See eg *FAI General Insurance v Ocean Marine Mutual Protection and Indemnity Association* (1997) 41 NSWLR 117; *Harbour Assurance Co (UK) Ltd v Kansa General International Insurance Co Ltd* [1993] QB 701 (CA).

[163] For England see *Austrian Lloyd Steamship Co v Gresham Life Assurance Society* [1903] I KB 249 (CA) (Budapest courts clause); *Sinochem International Oil (London) Co Ltd v Mobil Sales and Supply Corp* [2000] 1 Lloyd's Rep 670 (Hong Kong courts clause); and *Middle Eastern Oil LLC v National Bank of Abu Dhabi* [2008] EWHC 2895 (Comm) (UAE courts clause); and for Australia see *FAI General Insurance v Ocean Marine Mutual Protection and Indemnity Association* (1997) 41 NSWLR 117, 126–7 (English courts clause); and *McGuid v Office de Commercialisation et d'Exportation* [1999] NSWSC 931 (Casablanca courts clause).

law should apply and forum law has been applied by default.[164] In one case, *Evans Marshall & Co v Bertola SA*,[165] Kerr J applied the law governing the clause to determine this issue but this approach seems to have been overlooked in later cases.[166] On the second aspect, the scope of the clause, there is longstanding authority[167] to the effect that this issue is to be determined according to the law governing the clause which, in the absence of an express choice of such law, will in most cases be the law governing the principal contract in which the clause is contained. The same approach applies to jurisdiction clauses falling within the terms of article 23 of the Brussels I Regulation.[168] Despite this conclusion, in relatively few Commonwealth decisions have courts applied foreign law to determine the issue of scope.[169] Again the explanation for this may be that parties have simply not been aware of the choice of law issue or saw no advantage in pleading foreign law.[170] Further, it is suggested that the first aspect of interpretation referred to earlier, that is, whether the clause is exclusive or non-exclusive, should also be subject to the law governing the clause as a substantive matter. General principles of contract choice of law arguably

---

[164] Recently a Hong Kong court suggested that this issue was governed by the law of the principal contract in which the clause was contained but ultimately the court did not apply foreign law because it was not pleaded by the parties: *Ko Lai Kuen v Li Tak Ming* [2011] HKCFI 304, para 27.

[165] [1973] 1 WLR 349, 361–2 (affd on other grounds CA).

[166] But see *McGowan v Summit at Lloyds* [2002] SC 638, para 15, where the Scottish Extra Division court applied foreign law to determine whether a clause was exclusive. There is also some evidence of a similar approach being taken by the Singapore High Court in *Rickshaw Investments Ltd v Nicolai Baron Von Uexkull* [2006] SGHC 70, para 16 (revd on other grounds [2006] SGCA 39).

[167] *Hamlyn & Co v Talisker Distillery* [1894] AC 202 (HL); *Hoerter v Hanover Telegraph Works* (1893) 10 TLR 103, 104.

[168] *Knorr-Bremse Systems for Commercial Vehicles Ltd v Haldex Brake Products Gmb H* [2008] EWHC 156 (Pat), para 30.

[169] Examples of decisions where foreign law was applied include: *Astrazeneca UK Ltd v Albemarle International Corp* [2010] EWHC 1028 (Comm), paras 83–87; *Recyclers of Australia Pty Ltd v Hettinga Equipment Inc* (2000) 100 FCR 420, 430–4 (Fed Ct Aust); and *Global Partners Fund Ltd v Babcock & Brown Ltd (in liq)* (2010) 79 ACSR 383 [2010] NSWCA 196, para 51. The choice of law issue does not seem to have been discussed recently in Canada, where the law of the forum has been applied to all issues involving jurisdiction clauses; see *ZI Pompey Industrie v ECU-Line NV* [2003] 1 SCR 450; *Crown Resources Corp SA v National Iranian Oil Co* (2006) 273 DLR (4th) 65; and *Expedition Helicopters Inc v Honeywell Inc* (2010) 100 OR (3d) 241 (both Ont CA). In an earlier decision, however, an Ontario court held that that the question of whether a choice of forum clause is exclusive is determined by the law governing the contract in which the clause is found: see *Anthes Equipment Ltd v Wilhelm Layher GmbH* (1986) 53 OR (2d) 435 (Ont HC).

[170] See eg *Middle Eastern Oil LLC v National Bank of Abu Dhabi* [2008] EWHC 2895 (Comm).

dictate this conclusion.[171] Where, however, the jurisdiction clause falls within the Brussels I Regulation, article 23(1) provides an autonomous presumption on this issue: 'such jurisdiction [in the clause] shall be exclusive unless the parties have agreed otherwise'.[172]

Issues concerning the formal and essential[173] validity of jurisdiction clauses as well as separability[174] are also, in principle, governed by the law applicable to the clause but some qualifications must be noted. First, on the issue of formal validity, article 23 of the Brussels I Regulation provides a uniform, autonomous EU law rule for choice of court clauses in actions which fall under the terms of the Regulation and so no reference to domestic law is required.[175] Secondly, at least in the case of essential validity, reference to the law governing the contract is subject to the overriding public policy of the forum as expressed in mandatory rules.[176] So, for example, if a forum mandatory statute in the area of insurance declared a foreign jurisdiction clause to be invalid, then this rule must be applied regardless of the governing law.[177] This last case is an example of forum law applying to a jurisdiction clause not because the issue is procedural but through the medium of public policy. Note that the 2005 Hague Choice of Court Convention (not yet in force) is consistent with this view by subjecting the validity of a choice of court clause to the law of the country of the chosen court[178] except where to do so would be 'manifestly contrary' to the public policy of the enforcing court.[179] Some residual scope for forum control is therefore maintained. **4.56**

The third issue in respect of jurisdiction or choice of court clauses, enforceability, has historically involved primary reference to the law of the forum, except for clauses falling within the terms of the Regulation (or the Hague Choice of Court Convention), where the autonomous rules of those instruments will apply. A *foreign* jurisdiction clause is typically enforced in **4.57**

---

[171] *Ko Lai Kuen v Li Tak Ming* [2011] HKCFI 304, para 27; see also A Briggs, *Agreements on Jurisdiction and Choice of Law* (OUP, 2008) paras 4.08, 4.13, 4.33, although the author does not go so far as to say that the question of whether a clause is 'exclusive' should be subjected to the governing law of the clause.

[172] The 2005 Hague Choice of Court Convention (2005), art 3(b) is to the same effect.

[173] *Astrazeneca UK Ltd v Albemarle International Corp* [2010] EWHC 1028 (Comm), para 41; *Antonio Gramsci Shipping Corp v Oleg Stephanovs* [2011] EWHC 333 (Comm), para 31; *Hamlyn & Co v Talisker Distillery* [1894] AC 202 (HL).

[174] *Astrazeneca UK Ltd v Albemarle International Corp* [2010] EWHC 1028 (Comm), para 88.

[175] *Powell Duffryn plc v Petereit* [1992] ECR I-1745.

[176] *Astrazeneca UK Ltd v Albemarle International Corp* [2010] EWHC 1028 (Comm), para 41.

[177] For an Australian example, see *Akai Pty Ltd v People's Insurance Co Ltd* (1996) 188 CLR 418.

[178] Hague Choice of Court Convention (2005), art 6(a).

[179] ibid art 6 (c); see generally R Garnett, 'The Hague Choice of Court Convention: Magnum Opus or Much Ado about Nothing?' (2009) 5 JPIL 161.

Commonwealth courts by the defendant applying to stay or dismiss proceedings brought by the claimant in the forum in breach of the clause. Enforcement of a *forum* jurisdiction clause, by contrast, usually occurs by a defendant seeking an anti-suit injunction to restrain the claimant from pursuing proceedings abroad. In both categories of case Commonwealth courts have generally enforced such clauses and granted a stay or anti-suit injunction unless the claimant can show 'strong reasons' for the forum to retain or decline jurisdiction in each case.[180] While in the case of both remedies, there is a connection with the forum's interest in determining access to its courts, the forum court is also being asked to enforce a contract of the parties with clear outcome determinative effect. It is therefore arguable that the issue of enforceability of jurisdiction clauses is primarily contractual rather than jurisdictional and so should also be treated as substantive and governed by the law applicable to the clause.[181] Yet, even if Commonwealth courts continue to apply forum law to enforceability, there is still scope for the admission of foreign law on the question of jurisdiction. For example, the forum may consider it relevant, in determining whether to enforce a foreign jurisdiction clause, to inquire whether the foreign court would itself have jurisdiction over the dispute. Such an approach was recently taken by a New South Wales court in enforcing an English exclusive jurisdiction clause.[182] On this view, while the matter of enforceability is procedural, it may not be wholly subject to forum law. A substantive approach to enforceability, by contrast, would resolve the question entirely by reference to the law applicable to the clause, subject only to forum public policy and overriding mandatory rules.

4.58 Similarly, a Commonwealth court may also consider it important to have regard to the *law of the country in which enforcement of the judgment* may occur in deciding whether to exercise jurisdiction. A number of countries[183] have provisions which prevent enforcement of a foreign judgment where it was obtained in a court in breach of an exclusive jurisdiction clause and so it would be prudent for a forum, at the jurisdictional stage, to take such rules into account.

---

[180] Such reasons were found to be present in *Donohue v Armco Inc* [2002] 1 All ER 749 (HL).

[181] A Briggs, 'The Unrestrained Breach of an Anti-Suit Injunction: A Pause for Thought' [1997] LMCLQ 90; T Yeo, *Choice of Law for Equitable Doctrines* (OUP, 2004) paras 4.55, 4.70; cf F Sparka, *Jurisdiction and Arbitration Clauses in Maritime Transport Documents: A Comparative Analysis* (Springer-Verlag, 2010) 97–8.

[182] *Global Partners Fund Ltd v Babcock & Brown Ltd (in liq)* [2010] NSWSC 270, para 132 (affd (2010) 79 ACSR 383; [2010] NSWCA 196).

[183] See eg in England, Civil Jurisdiction and Judgments Act 1982, s 32 and in Australia, Foreign Judgments Act 1991 (Cth), s 7(4)(b).

(b) United States

The earlier analysis finds some support in recent developments in the United States. While traditionally, all matters in relation to jurisdiction or choice of court clauses were subjected to the law of the forum,[184] in a number of recent decisions this position has changed. So, in *Yavuz v 61 MM Ltd*,[185] the US Tenth Circuit Court of Appeals held that the issue of the scope of a Swiss jurisdiction clause was governed by the law applicable to the clause, in this case the law of Switzerland. The court persuasively argued that to apply forum law to the issue of scope risked the words of the parties' agreement being subjected to different interpretations depending upon where the suit was brought and so would create the possibility of forum shopping. Such an approach also makes it difficult for parties to anticipate at the contract drafting stage what law will be actually applied.[186] The court in the *Yavuz* case did, however, suggest that the issue of enforceability of the clause—that is, whether a discretionary order of dismissal of forum proceedings should be made—remains a question exclusively for the law of the forum as the earlier US Supreme Court decisions[187] had indicated. In later cases, US Circuit Courts of Appeal have been divided on the role of foreign law in respect of jurisdiction clauses. While some courts have asserted that the law of the forum applies both to questions of scope and enforceability,[188] others have followed the approach in *Yavuz* of applying foreign law to scope but retaining forum law for enforceability on the basis that the latter is a procedural issue.[189] Other courts have approved the reasoning in *Yavuz* and applied the governing law to the issue of the essential validity of a jurisdiction clause.[190] Still other courts have suggested that all questions of interpretation of the clause, including whether it is exclusive (mandatory) or non-exclusive (permissive), should be governed by the law applicable to the clause.[191] So, in *Albemarle Corporation v Astrazeneca UK Ltd*,[192] the US Fourth Circuit Court of Appeals applied English law to determine that an English jurisdiction clause was exclusive, even though the clause would only have been considered 'permissive'

4.59

---

[184] No other law was suggested as being applicable in the leading US Supreme Court case *M/S Bremen & Unterweser Reederel GmbH v Zapata Offshore Co* 407 US 1 (Sup Ct 1972).
[185] 465 F 3d 418 (10th Cir 2006).
[186] ibid 431.
[187] See eg *M/S Bremen v Zapata Offshore Co* 407 US 1 (1972).
[188] See eg *Ginter v Belcher* 536 F 3d 439, 441 (5th Cir 2008).
[189] *Phillips v Audio Active Ltd* 494 F 3d 378, 384–6 (2nd Cir 2007).
[190] *Abbott Laboratories v Takeda Pharmaceutical Co Ltd* 476 F 3d 421 (7th Cir 2007) (although the law of the forum was also the governing law of the clause in that case).
[191] *Albemarle Corp v Astrazeneca UK Ltd* 628 F 3d 643, 651 (4th Cir 2010).
[192] ibid.

Chapter 4: Service and Jurisdiction

under the law of the forum. This approach goes beyond the Commonwealth position in its amenability to foreign law and is arguably more consistent with the restricted notion of procedure espoused in recent Canadian and Australian decisions.

3. IN REM JURISDICTION

4.60 In admiralty matters, it is common for a claimant to arrest a ship of the defendant and retain it as security in a personal action against that party, such as for breach of a charterparty contract. The court's powers to order arrest fall within a statutory *in rem* jurisdiction in Commonwealth countries with a common basis of such jurisdiction being that the defendant in the personal action is the 'owner' of the ship.[193] Commonwealth courts have taken different approaches to determining the question of ownership. Singapore courts classify the issue as one of *jurisdiction* which is governed by the law of the forum exclusively; an approach consistent with the quotation from *The Jarguh Sawit* case at 4.49, that jurisdictional matters are procedural. On this view, any evidence of foreign law on the issue of ownership may be ignored.[194]

4.61 Other Commonwealth courts have taken a less parochial approach, one which is more consistent with the view that jurisdictional questions benefit from the input of foreign law. Thus English courts[195] have expressed the view that reference should be made to the law of the domicile of the person who is alleged to be the owner of the ship on the issue of ownership before then considering whether the position under foreign law satisfies the English law concept. Again there are echoes here of an enlightened *lex fori* or 'preliminary question' reference to foreign law. The English approach has been endorsed by the New Zealand Court of Appeal[196] and the Full Court of the Federal Court of Australia,[197] with the Australian tribunal importantly adding that where an assignment or transfer of ownership in the ship has occurred reference to the *lex situs* of the ship or the law of the country of registration may be appropriate as an alternative foreign law

---

[193] See eg for Australia, Admiralty Act 1988 (Cth), s 17.

[194] *The Andres Bonifacio* [1993] SGCA 70; *The Kapitan Temkin* [1998] SGHC 427 but see *The Makassar Caraka Jaya Niaga III-39* [2011] 1 SLR 982, para 9 (Sing HC), where the issue was stated to be governed by forum law but the forum could, in the context of foreign ships, 'take into account relevant aspects of . . . foreign law for a better picture of how ships may be owned or transferred'.

[195] *The Nazym Khikmet* [1996] 2 Lloyd's Rep 362 (CA) and *The Giuseppe di Vittorio* [1998] 1 Lloyd's Rep 136.

[196] *Vostok Shipping Co Ltd v Confederation Ltd* [2000] 1 NZLR 37 (NZCA).

[197] *Tisand Pty Ltd v The Owners of the Ship MV Cape Moreton (ex Freya)* (2005) 143 FCR 43.

B. Jurisdiction

reference.¹⁹⁸ The key point to note is that in all these decisions the courts, while accepting that the matter was one of jurisdiction and so governed by forum law as a procedural matter, again clearly rejected the view that such law should apply exclusively. Foreign law was (correctly) seen as relevant in providing the court with a full picture of the various national interests in determining whether jurisdiction exists.

4. Anti-Suit Injunctions

The anti-suit injunction is a remedy commonly sought in jurisdictional disputes, involving the restraint of one party from commencing or continuing proceedings against another in a foreign country. While the law of the forum has also traditionally been applied to the grant of such injunctions, this position may also have been reached in part because injunctions are *equitable* in nature and subject to English principles of equity. In more recent scholarship and judicial decisions, however, it has been asserted that equitable rights should be subjected to a more sophisticated choice of law analysis, which should not necessarily result in application of the law of the forum in every case.¹⁹⁹ The impact of the Rome II Regulation, where many equitable doctrines will now be classified as 'non-contractual obligations' falling within the scope of the Regulation, will give added momentum to this trend. **4.62**

There are a number of different categories of case in which anti-suit injunctions have been sought. One category is where the injunction is sought to protect the integrity of the forum court's own processes, such as where the foreign proceeding would interfere with a local action or local administration of an estate or insolvency.²⁰⁰ In this case it is clear that forum law should apply to determine the grant of the injunction, given the clear connection between the matter and the conduct of local proceedings. Alternatively, public policy may provide a justification for application of forum law. A second category of case is where an anti-suit injunction has been sought to enforce a forum exclusive jurisdiction clause.²⁰¹ For the reasons mentioned at 4.57, this issue should be treated as substantive and governed by the law applicable to the clause. In the final category of case where an anti-suit injunction is sought, to protect equitable rights such as where foreign proceedings are unconscionable,²⁰² a substantive **4.63**

---

¹⁹⁸ ibid para 140. See also *Thor Shipping A/S v the Ship 'Al Dulhail'* [2008] FCA 1842, paras 48–51.
¹⁹⁹ See especially Yeo (n 181 above).
²⁰⁰ See eg *CSR Ltd v Cigna Insurance Australia Ltd* (1997) 189 CLR 345.
²⁰¹ See eg *Donohue v Armco* [2002] 1 All ER 749 (HL).
²⁰² See eg *Airbus Industrie GIE v Patel* [1999] 1 AC 119 (HL).

112 *Chapter 4: Service and Jurisdiction*

classification is also warranted, given the clear scope for impact on the parties' rights and obligations. While this conclusion in the last category of case has led to some contention as to which choice of law rule should be applied,[203] such disagreement should not be an argument for re-imposing a procedural classification, especially not one based on the right-remedy view of substance and procedure.[204]

5. Immunities from Jurisdiction

4.64 There are other forms of jurisdictional challenge in Commonwealth countries which arise in transnational litigation. For example, the defendant may argue that an English court lacks subject matter jurisdiction over the action because the defendant is entitled to foreign state or diplomatic immunity from English jurisdiction under forum law. In such cases it has not been doubted that English law as the law of the forum exclusively applies to such pleas on the basis that they are matters of procedure.[205] Alternatively a defendant may seek to rely in English proceedings on an immunity granted by *foreign* law which, if also classified as procedural, would be unavailable to block proceedings in the forum. In both cases, however, a finding of immunity has the effect of barring the court's jurisdiction and so is clearly determinative of outcome, particularly where the claimant cannot proceed against the defendant in any other country (including the defendant state itself). While, as noted at 4.41, questions of jurisdiction are normally best regarded as procedural, exceptionally in the case of immunity because of its drastic impact on the rights of the parties, a substantive classification may be warranted. There have been English and Australian decisions which have considered the classification of immunities in private international law.

4.65 *Komarek v Ramco Energy plc*[206] involved an attempt to rely on immunity under foreign law in an English action for libel arising out of the publication of material to the British ambassador in the Czech Republic. In determining whether the wrong was actionable under Czech law for the purposes of the 'double actionability' choice of law rule for torts, the court disregarded the fact that the document containing the alleged libel may have attracted diplomatic immunity under Czech law. The court held that such immunity, whether it is 'personal immunity or the inviolability of

---

[203] cf Briggs (n 181 above) and J Harris, 'Anti-Suit Injunctions—A Home Comfort?' [1997] LMCLQ 413.

[204] cf T Raphael, *The Law of Anti-suit Injunctions* (OUP, 2008) para 4.08.

[205] See eg (in the case of Scotland) E Crawford and J Carruthers, *International Private Law: A Scots Perspective* (Thomson West, 3rd edn, 2010) para 8.05.

[206] [2002] All ER (D) 314 (Nov).

B. Jurisdiction

archives, documents or correspondence is properly to be classified as procedural'[207] and 'barring only of remedies rather than the absence of a right'. The court therefore appeared to apply the right-remedy distinction to classify the matter of immunity as procedural rather than any more limited test based on the link between immunity and the mode or conduct of the forum's proceedings.

4.66 A recent Australian case took a different approach to the classification of immunities under foreign law. In *Garsec v The Sultan of Brunei*[208] claims were brought in contract and tort to recover an artefact from the Sultan of Brunei, with the defendant Sultan pleading immunity, although not under Australian foreign state immunity legislation[209] but under Brunei law, which was the law of the causes of action. The New South Wales court, on an application to stay proceedings on appropriate forum grounds, had to consider whether the immunity under foreign law was substantive under Australian choice of law rules, in which case it would have applied in proceedings in both New South Wales and Brunei; or procedural, in which case it would only have applied in an action in Brunei. Applying the narrow view of the substance-procedure classification from *Pfeiffer v Rogerson*,[210] the court concluded that immunity is a substantive matter because it related to the existence and enforceability of rights of the parties and so was applicable to bar proceedings in New South Wales. Such an approach (and result) is plainly inconsistent with the 'remedial' view of immunity espoused in the *Komarek* case.

4.67 A more nuanced view of immunity under foreign law, although still partly retaining the procedural classification, was taken by the English Court of Appeal in *Al Jedda v Secretary of State for Defence*.[211] The case concerned an action for damages for unlawful imprisonment based on the claimant's detention by British forces at a military detention centre in Iraq. It was accepted that Iraqi law applied to the action as the country where the claimant suffered injury[212] but the UK government defendant sought to avoid liability by relying upon a provision of Iraqi law, Coalition Provisional Authority (CPA) 17, which provided in section 2(3) that: 'All multinational force personnel shall be subject to the exclusive jurisdiction of their Sending States. They shall be immune from any form of arrest or detention other than by persons acting on behalf of their Sending States'.

---

[207] ibid para 25.
[208] (2008) 250 ALR 682 (NSWCA).
[209] Foreign States Immunities Act 1985 (Cth).
[210] (2000) 203 CLR 503.
[211] [2011] 2 WLR 225.
[212] Private International Law (Miscellaneous Provisions) Act 1995 (UK), s 11.

114   *Chapter 4: Service and Jurisdiction*

The court, however, held that the provision, which conferred immunity on multinational forces serving in Iraq, only applied to actions before *Iraqi* courts, not foreign tribunals. This conclusion was reached by two routes. First, the wording of the provision made it clear that the immunity did not apply to actions in foreign courts.[213] Otherwise, the provision would have little scope for operation, since the exclusive jurisdiction which was conferred on sending states could not in practice be activated as almost all claims against multinational forces would be likely to involve application of Iraqi law.[214] Secondly, according to Elias LJ, the provision did not provide a 'substantive defence to the claim' but only a 'procedural bar' and so was inapplicable in English proceedings.[215] In effect, CPA 17 was akin to a rule of state immunity under Iraqi law whereby Iraqi courts could not hear actions against a foreign state.

4.68 In reflecting upon the *Al Jedda* decision, it is suggested that the result is defensible but only on the ground of statutory interpretation. It seems likely, as the court suggests, that the intention of the drafters of CPA 17 was not to preclude all actions against multinational forces wherever instituted but simply to remove the matters from the jurisdiction of the Iraqi courts—otherwise the provision would have little or no work to do. The second reason relied upon by Elias LJ, that the provision was procedural and not substantive, is less persuasive. If, as was argued earlier and upheld in the New South Wales decision of *Garsec*, a plea of immunity directly affects the rights and liabilities of the parties by barring the forum proceedings, then a substantive classification is preferable. Yet, even if the foreign provision conferring immunity is considered substantive, a forum court can still find that it does not apply to proceedings in the forum as a matter of *interpretation*; which was the other basis of the decision of the Court of Appeal in *Al Jedda*. This approach was also taken in a more recent decision, *Harty v Sabre International Security Ltd*,[216] where a plea of immunity under CPA 17 in respect of personal injuries suffered in Iraq was found not to apply in English proceedings based on the interpretation of the provision. An approach to immunity based on statutory interpretation would be consistent with the Canadian and Australian cases discussed below,[217] where this method was used as an alternative to the substance / procedure

---

[213] [2011] 2 WLR 225, para 91 (Arden LJ), para 166 (Elias LJ).
[214] ibid.
[215] ibid para 169.
[216] [2011] EWHC 852 (QB).
[217] *Investors Group Trust Co Ltd v Capital City Savings and Credit Union Ltd* (1991) 118 AR 254 (Alta QB) (legislation not applied in the forum) and *Amaca Pty Ltd v Frost* (2006) 67 NSWLR 635 (legislation applied); see 6.51 and 6.58 below.

distinction to determine whether foreign legislation, which was alleged to restrict the jurisdiction of the forum courts, should be applied.

A statutory interpretation approach is also preferable in the context of a plea of foreign state and diplomatic immunity under *forum* law. Returning to the *Garsec* case, what would have been interesting is whether the Australian court would also have applied a substantive characterization in the context of a proceeding where its *own* statute on foreign state immunity had been invoked. Had such a characterization been adopted, it is arguable that the forum legislation on immunity could be bypassed in favour of applying the immunity rules of the foreign law of the cause of action. Such a conclusion, however, raises a number of difficulties. First of all, the principles of foreign state and diplomatic immunity are not simply limits on domestic court jurisdiction but are externally imposed restraints from public international law[218] which are designed to protect the sovereignty of nation states from foreign legal process. There are therefore sound public policy reasons why such rules should not be capable of evasion by the application of forum choice of law principles. While a procedural classification of immunity is hard to justify, given its often outcome determinative effect, a better argument would be to say that immunity, while substantive, should nevertheless be regarded as an overriding mandatory rule of the forum applicable in all cases. Some support for this view comes from the English decisions which have recognized that forum public policy in private international law includes principles of public international law.[219]

4.69

A further reason for treating forum rules on foreign state and diplomatic immunity as overriding mandatory provisions is the complexity and absurdity which may result from applying foreign law rules on this topic. Returning to the *Garsec* case, what would have happened if the Australian court had found the forum's rules of foreign state immunity to be inapplicable because the issue of such immunity was classified as substantive? The court would then have had to apply the immunity rules of Brunei, meaning presumably those rules that would be applied *if a foreign state were sued in its (Brunei's) courts*. So in *Garsec* it would not have been the principles of Brunei domestic law dealing with the legal status of the Sultan which would have been applicable but the rules which Brunei would apply to *foreign* sovereign defendants. Such an outcome would lead to odd results: the Australian court would have to apply immunity rules of Brunei law which a Brunei court itself would not have applied on the facts of *Garsec*, since the Sultan is not a foreign sovereign entity in that country.

4.70

---

[218] J Walker, '*Castillo v Castillo*: Closing the Barn Door' (2006) 43 Canadian Business LJ 487, 491–2.
[219] *Kuwait Airways Corp v Iraqi Airways Co (Nos 4 and 5)* [2002] 2 AC 883.

The goal of uniformity of outcome, which is a cardinal principle of Australian choice of law methodology after *Neilson*,[220] would therefore have been defeated. This conclusion is a further reason why foreign state and diplomatic immunity, though substantive, should not be governed by foreign law.

---

[220] *Neilson v Overseas Projects Corp of Victoria Ltd* (2005) 223 CLR 331.

5
Parties to Litigation

A.	Capacity	5.01
	1. Capacity to Sue and Be Sued	5.01
	2. Capacity to be a Party to Litigation/Name of Party to Litigation	5.05
B.	The Proper Party	5.09
C.	Individual Issues	5.16
	1. Standing	5.16
	2. Joinder	5.17
	3. Contribution and Indemnity	5.18
	4. Subrogation	5.20
	5. Proportionate Liability	5.21
	6. Vicarious Liability	5.22
	7. Inter-Spousal Liability	5.23
	8. Fatal Accident Cases	5.24
	9. Representative Actions	5.26
	10. Defendants: 'Sue Others First' Provisions	5.31
	11. Corporations and Derivative Suits	5.35
	12. Foreign State Entities	5.48

A number of distinct choice of law issues arise in the context of determining the status of parties to proceedings. The topic of parties is therefore an area which may not be neatly analysed in terms of the substance / procedure distinction as other choice of law rules and laws are often involved.

A. CAPACITY

1. Capacity to Sue and Be Sued

5.01 The first matter to consider is whether the claimant or defendant has separate legal personality and capacity to sue and be sued. This matter is governed in most legal systems by the law of the entity's domicile or country of formation or creation.[1] So in *Chaff and Hay Acquisition Committee v JA*

---

[1] I Szászy, 'The Basic Connecting Factor In International Cases in the Domain of Civil Procedure' (1966) 15 ICLQ 436, 453 and *International Civil Procedure: A Comparative Study* (Sijthoff, 1967) 234–8.

Hemphill & Sons Pty Ltd[2] an entity which under the law of the place of its formation was not a corporation but had a separate personality from those of its members, and could sue and be sued in its collective name, was held to be entitled to bring an action in the forum.[3] More startlingly, an abandoned Indian temple which had been recognized as having legal personality under its constituent law was permitted to sue in England to recover a statue even though the entity would not have been recognized as a legal person under the law of the forum.[4] The same principle was applied by a Canadian court to allow an unincorporated entity to sue which, although having no legal personality in Canada, had legal personality and a right to sue or be sued under the law of its country of formation.[5] The court explicitly relied upon the principle of comity in support of its view.[6]

5.02 Consistent with the principle that the legal personality of an entity is governed by the law of its place of formation is the rule that the existence of a corporation or its capacity to sue or be sued is referred to the law of the country of incorporation.[7] Such law also determines whether a company has been dissolved.[8] This rule has been applied in Australia to allow a foreign corporation to be sued in the forum despite its having been deregistered under Australian companies legislation.[9] There are also particular choice of law issues concerning derivative actions between members and officers of companies which are discussed at 5.35–5.47.

5.03 The same rule has also been applied to partnerships: in deciding whether such an entity may be sued in the forum the law of the place of creation or formation is applied to determine whether capacity to sue or be sued exists.[10]

---

[2] (1947) 74 CLR 375.
[3] See also *Von Hellfeld v Rechnitzer* [1914] 1 Ch 748 (CA) (foreign defendant with no separate legal personality under the law of the country of formation could not be sued in England).
[4] *Bumper Development Corporation v Commissioner of the Police of the Metropolis* [1991] 1 WLR 1362 (CA).
[5] *International Association of Science and Technology for Development v Hamza* (1995) 122 DLR (4th) 92 (Alta CA).
[6] ibid para 37; see also *Doe v Canada* (2001) 204 DLR (4th) 80 (Alta CA), where an action was dismissed against the Roman Catholic Church as the plaintiff failed to show that the defendant had capacity to sue or be sued under the law of its home jurisdiction.
[7] *Lazard Bros & Co v Midland Bank Ltd* [1933] AC 289; this is also the position in the US, see *Johnson v Helicopter and Airplane Services Corp* 404 F Supp 726, 730 (D Md 1975).
[8] *Banque Internationale de Commerce de Petrograd v Goukassow* [1923] 2 KB 682 (CA).
[9] *McIntyre v Eastern Prosperity Investments Pte Ltd (No 6)* (2005) 218 ALR 401 (Fed Ct); *Feng v GMS Fulfilment Service Ltd* (2004) 50 ACSR 527 (SC NSW).
[10] *Gerling Global General Insurance Co v Canadian Occidental Petroleum Ltd* 1998 ABQB 714; *Devon Canada Corp v PE-Pitsfield LLC* (2008) 303 DLR (4th) 460; 2008 ABCA 393.

A. Capacity

It is also useful to note that in European civil law countries it is also generally accepted that the law of an entity's domicile or country of formation applies to the question of whether the entity has capacity to sue and be sued in the forum. French law uses the term 'capacité pour agir',[11] Spanish law 'la capacidad para ser parte',[12] and German law 'Parteifähigkeit' and 'Prozessfähigkeit'.[13] However, in the context of a corporation's capacity to sue and be sued, German courts have applied the law of the administrative seat or headquarters of the entity. Note that this law may not be the same as the law of the place of incorporation.[14] The position under Swiss[15] and Belgian[16] law is similar to the French and Spanish view. The basic principle under Italian law for non-individuals is also that the law of the place of incorporation/formation applies but, exceptionally, Italian law will apply mandatorily if (a) the registered office of the entity is located in Italy, or (b) Italy is the main focus of the entity's activities.[17]

5.04

2. Capacity to be a Party to Litigation/Name of Party to Litigation

The second major issue involving parties to litigation which has arisen in Commonwealth law is whether the claimant or defendant is *the type of entity that can be a party to litigation* in the forum. This issue has traditionally been referred to the law of the forum, either on the basis that it pertains to the conduct of proceedings or because local public policy requires scrutiny of the range of actors who might be the subject of litigation. There is consistent US authority.[18] Consequently, an action could not be commenced against a dead person or a dissolved corporation[19] in the forum even though such a proceeding may have been permissible under the law

5.05

---

[11] B Audit, *Droit International Privé* (Economica, 3rd edn, 2005) para 443.
[12] A Calvo Caravaca and J Carrascosa González, *Derecho Internacional Privado Vol 1* (Editorial Comares, 6th edn, 2005) 397–9. Note that under Spanish law, however, the public policy of the forum may be applied in substitution of the party's personal law if such law imposes incapacity on discriminatory grounds.
[13] R Geimer, *Internationales Zivilprozeßrecht* (OUS Verlag Dr Otto Schmidt, 5th edn, 2005) para 326. 'Prozessfähigkeit' specifically refers to the capacity of a person to conduct a suit independently.
[14] Oberlandesgericht Frankfurt (23 June 1999) [2001] ECLY 890; Oberlandesgericht Brandenburg (31 May 2000) [2001] ECLY 464 (Irish private limited company found to have no capacity to sue under German law, the country of its headquarters).
[15] A Bucher and A Bonomi, *Droit International Privé* (Helbing and Lichtenbahn, 2nd edn, 2004) 50–1.
[16] F Rigaux and M Fallon, *Droit International Privé* (Larcier, 3rd edn, 2005) para 11.9.
[17] Legge di 31 Maggio 1995 n 218, art 25(1).
[18] *Re Estate of Agioritis* 80 Misc 2d 108 (Surr Ct NY 1974).
[19] *Hal Commodities Cycle Management v Krish* (1993) 17 CPC (3d) 320 (Ont Ct Gen Div).

governing the cause of action. An action against a corporation which is subsequently dissolved and merged into another corporation may, however, proceed in the forum where it would be permitted under the law of incorporation of the new entity.[20]

5.06 Similarly, it has been generally accepted that *the name* in which litigation is brought is a matter of procedure and governed by the law of the forum.[21] So in *Didisheim v London and Westminster Bank*[22] the question of whether a suit may be instituted in the name of a mentally ill person or his or her next friend was a procedural matter governed by the law of the forum. The same principle would presumably apply to determine whether an infant may bring or defend an action in its own name or whether a 'litigation friend' is required. Likewise, in *Oxnard Financing SA v Rahn*[23] a partnership which had legal personality under Swiss law nevertheless could be sued in England either in the name of the partnership or in the names of all the partners, since either course was permitted under English law as the law of the forum. Similarly in Canada, the 'method' of suing a partnership has been held to be a matter of procedure and governed by forum law, such that if a partnership does not carry on business in the forum, it must be sued in the names of the individual partners.[24] The same approach is applied in the United States under the Second Restatement.[25]

5.07 This principle has been applied to determine whether an assignee must sue in his or her name or in the name of or in conjunction with the assignor.[26] Application of forum law may also possibly be supported in this context as it is a matter of procedural convenience to have all relevant parties in one proceeding, yet it could perhaps equally be argued that where a rule operates to prevent third parties from facing multiple actions, it has a substantive dimension.[27]

---

[20] *Global Container Lines Ltd v Bonyad Shipping Co* [1999] 1 Lloyd's Rep 287 (Com Ct).

[21] Compare Szászy (n 1 above) (1966) 452, who would refer this issue to the law of the cause of action.

[22] [1900] 2 Ch 15.

[23] [1998] 1 WLR 1465 (CA).

[24] *Gerling Global General Insurance Co v Canadian Occidental Petroleum Ltd* 1998 ABQB 714, para 51. See also *NIFSMBC-V200651 Investment Ltd Partnership v Gainday Investments Ltd* [2009] HKCFI 17, where it was assumed that the proper name in which a foreign partnership may bring litigation as a claimant in Hong Kong was governed by Hong Kong law.

[25] Restatement (Second) of Conflict of Laws, §125 comment a.

[26] *Regas Ltd v Plotkins* (1961) 29 DLR (2d) 282, 286–8 (SCC). Again, the same principle applies in the US under the Second Restatement, see ibid.

[27] N Rafferty, M Baer, J Blom, E Edinger, G Saumier, and C Walsh, *Private International Law in Common Law Canada* (Edmond Montgomery Publications, 2nd edn, 2003) 557; L Collins (ed), *Dicey, Morris and Collins on the Conflict of Laws* (Sweet & Maxwell, 14th edn, 2006) para 7.012.

5.08 It is suggested, in any event, that the tenacity of the law of the forum may be waning in the area of parties to litigation. First of all, the principle of comity has greater resonance today than previously and has resulted in a much wider recognition of entities as subjects of litigation in Commonwealth countries, at least where such entities have legal personality under their constituent laws. As was said by the Court of Appeal in *Bumper Development*, it is necessary to 'avoid the danger of there being any fetter of an artificial procedural nature imported from the *lex fori* which might otherwise stand between a right recognised by and enforceable under the *lex causae*'.[28] Indeed, it is hard to imagine that before the *Bumper Development* case 'a pile of stones'[29] would have been entitled to sue in England. It appears that courts are increasingly unconcerned by the fact that a foreign unincorporated entity may gain an advantage in terms of capacity to sue over a local unincorporated entity. The recognition of foreign institutions is seen as a more important objective. The second reason why the influence of the law of the forum is diminishing in this area comes from the narrowing of the scope of procedure in Canada and Australia. It is obvious that the question of whether an entity may be the subject of litigation affects the rights and duties of the parties and may result in a liability being imposed or not imposed under local law which would not have occurred under the law of the place of the entity's formation.[30] Foreign rules on the subject are also unlikely to be difficult for the forum to administer. Therefore, once again, a blanket procedural characterization of the issue and automatic application of forum law is inappropriate; courts need to address the wider factors at work in assessing whether an entity should be entitled to sue or be sued in the forum.

B. THE PROPER PARTY

5.09 Further support for the view that the law of the forum is losing sway in this area comes from the line of cases which have emphasized that the question of whether the claimant or defendant is the proper party in the particular action before the court is governed by the *law of the cause of action*. A striking example of this principle would be where the law of the forum does not allow a third party to enforce rights under a contract but the law of the cause of action would. In such a situation the key element is not so much forum control over its own litigation practices but rather the

---

[28] *Bumper Development Corporation v Commissioner of the Police of the Metropolis* [1991] 1 WLR 1362, 1373.
[29] ibid 1371.
[30] Szászy reaches a similar conclusion based on his 'closest connection' test: Szászy (n 1 above) (1966) 452–3.

cause of action itself and whether an entity is entitled to invoke such cause or be afflicted with liability under it.[31] As such, the principle is clearly substantive on either the broad or the narrow views of the substance / procedure distinction, and this conclusion has been confirmed in commentary[32] and a number of decisions.

5.10 An example of this principle arose in *Lucas v Coupal*[33] where an action for damages was brought in Ontario by a child, arising from an accident which occurred in Quebec. Under Ontario law a child could sue in his or her own name but under the law of Quebec the action must be brought in the name of an appointed tutor with any damages awarded paid to the tutor and held in its name until the child attains adulthood. An Ontario court held that the issue in this case was not *in whose name* the litigation should be brought but rather *in which entity was the cause of action vested*. In other words, who was the proper claimant to invoke the action before the court? The court held that it was the tutor in accordance with the law of the cause of action. A further application of this principle occurred in *Sanderson v Halstead*.[34] There, a claimant was held entitled to bring an action against the parent of his deceased wife on the basis that under the law of the cause of action (Quebec) he was the direct successor in title to all the rights of the deceased, whereas under the law of the forum (Ontario) the claimant could only have sued as a personal representative under a grant of letters probate or administration (which had not occurred). In a slightly similar context, a Singapore court recently adopted this 'proper party' analysis in preventing the administrator of an estate from suing to enforce rights in respect of shares in a company held by the deceased.[35] The court found that under the law of cause of action, which was Egyptian, the rights and the shares vested only in the deceased's heirs, not his personal representative, and so no action could be brought by the representative.[36]

---

[31] In *Hartmann v Konig* (1933) 50 TLR 114 (HL) it was accepted that the question of whether third parties could enforce an agreement was a matter to be resolved by the law of the cause of action.

[32] *Dicey, Morris and Collins* (n 27 above) para 7.012; J Walker, *Castel & Walker Canadian Conflict of Laws* (LexisNexis Butterworths, 6th edn, 2005) para 6.3a; and J McLeod, *The Conflict of Laws* (Carswell Legal Publications, 1983) 222. R Graveson, *Conflict of Laws* (Sweet & Maxwell, 7th edn, 1974) 599 refers to the proper party concept as 'ownership of the right of action'; and E Crawford, 'The Adjective and the Noun: Title and Right to Sue In Private International Law' [2000] Juridical Review 347 speaks of 'title to sue'.

[33] [1931] 1 DLR 391.

[34] [1968] 1 OR 749 (Ont HCJ).

[35] *Shafeeg bin Salim Talib v Helmi bin Ali bin Salim bin Talib* [2009] SGHC 180, para 53.

[36] cf *Samson v Holden* [1963] SCR 373, where the question of the proper parties to the litigation was referred to the law of the cause of action but such law was not applied because under the choice of law rules of this law the issue was classified as procedural.

B. The Proper Party

Similarly, in the area of non-contractual obligations, EU law in the Rome II Regulation now recognizes that the law applicable to the obligation will determine 'the persons entitled to compensation for damage sustained personally'.[37] Such a rule will establish who is a proper claimant and, in particular, 'whether a person other than the "direct" victim may be compensated'.[38] In the case of defendants, the Regulation also provides that the law of the obligation should determine the 'persons who may be held liable for acts performed by them'[39] and the question of 'capacity to incur liability in tort/delict'.[40]

5.11

The 'proper party' analysis has been applied in classifying as substantive a claimant's right to 'directly' sue the tortfeasor's liability insurer.[41] The same position is taken in the Rome II Regulation,[42] English choice of law rules before the Regulation,[43] and in the majority of recent US decisions.[44] This conclusion is supported by the fact that such statutes create a new cause of action where none existed previously.[45]

5.12

Also, in Australia it has been held that the capacity of one member of an international organization to sue another for breach of the articles of association of the organization, which were governed by foreign law, was determined by the law of the cause of action.[46]

5.13

The principle of the proper party is also recognized in the United States in those jurisdictions which observe the substance / procedure distinction in choice of law matters. In *Clayton v Burnett*[47] the Court of Appeals of North Carolina held that the question of which party was entitled to institute a

5.14

---

[37] Rome II, art 15(f).

[38] *Dicey, Morris and Collins* (n 27 above) (4th Supplement to the 14th edn, 2010) para S35.260, citing Explanatory Memorandum to the Rome II Regulation.

[39] Rome II, art 15(a).

[40] ibid Recital 12.

[41] *Plozza v South Australian Insurance Co Ltd* [1963] SASR 122; *Sabell v Liberty Mutual Ins Co* (1973) 38 DLR (3d) 113 (BCSC).

[42] Rome II, art 18; see also in German law, Geimer (n 13 above) para 354a.

[43] In *Jones v Assurances Generales de France (AGF) SA* [2010] IL Pr 4 and *Thwaites v Aviva Assurances* [2010] IL Pr 47 (both decisions of the Mayor's and City of London Court) it was assumed that a direct action suit was substantive.

[44] Restatement (Second), §125 comment a; *Roberts v Home Insurance Indemnity Co* 48 Cal App 3d 313 (CA Cal 1975); *Hertz Corp v Piccolo* 453 So 2d 12 (SC Fla 1984); *Smith v Strongbuilt Inc* 393 F Supp 2d 1254 (WD Okla 2005); *Polensky v Continental Casualty Co* 397 F Supp 2d 1164, 1168 (DND 2005); L McDougal, R Felix, and R Whitten, *American Conflicts Law* (Transnational Publishers, 5th edn, 2001) 410. cf *Ford v State Farm Insurance Co* 625 So 2d 792 (Miss 1993) (direct action suit procedural because it concerns 'remedy').

[45] McDougal (n 44 above) 410.

[46] *Dachser v Waco* [2000] NSWSC 1049.

[47] 522 SE 2d 785 (CANC 1999).

wrongful death action arising from a wrong committed in another jurisdiction was substantive because it directly concerned the rights of the parties, namely who is entitled to recover damages, and so was governed by the law of the cause of action. Similarly, in *Siegel v Novak*[48] a Florida court held that the right and capacity of trustees to challenge certain trust distributions was governed by New York law as the law of the cause of action. The issue was clearly substantive since it 'relate[s] to whether a cause of action may proceed' not merely the 'machinery for carrying on the suit'. Further, 'the ability to bring an action at law is a most valuable attribute of a legal right'.[49] Once again, given that the right of the party to sue was closely linked to the cause of action rather than the mechanics of the court process, application of the law of the cause of action was warranted. It is also worth noting that the US Second Restatement broadly supports the above analysis, where it provides that forum law will not be applied 'when its application would substantially affect the rights and duties of the parties'.[50] In such a case the law of the cause of action will be applied.

5.15 Finally, the European civil law countries mentioned earlier also recognize the concept of the proper party, referring the issue to the law of the cause of action. Under French law, the matter is described as 'qualité',[51] under Spanish law as 'legitimacion',[52] and under German law as '"Activ" and "Passiv" Legitimation'.[53]

C. INDIVIDUAL ISSUES

1. Standing

5.16 The choice of law implications of 'standing' as an independent concept have not been considered in Commonwealth decisions. Under domestic law, standing refers to the idea that a claimant must have an interest in the litigation in the sense of being personally affected (as distinct from the public generally) to sue.[54] In US decisions, standing has been classified as a procedural matter and governed by the law of the forum.[55] The same

---

[48] 920 So 2d 89 (CA Fla 2006).
[49] ibid 94.
[50] Restatement (Second), § 125.
[51] Audit (n 11 above) para 444.
[52] Calvo Caravaca and Carrascosa González (n 12 above) 399.
[53] Geimer (n 13 above) para 326.
[54] See, in the public law context, Senior Courts Act 1981 (UK), s 31(3).
[55] *Jones v Prince George's County* 835 A 2d 632, 644 (CA Md 2003).

C. *Individual Issues*

approach has been taken under French[56] and Belgian[57] law where standing is described as 'interêt'. On balance, it is likely that Commonwealth courts would take a similar view, despite the fact that standing has a link to the outcome of the litigation. Since, however, the principal rationale of a standing requirement is to limit access to the courts and conserve judicial resources, it is more appropriately procedural as an integral part of the mode or conduct of court proceedings.

2. Joinder

All legal systems have rules whereby parties may 'join' others to pending litigation, for example a claimant may wish to add a second defendant to an action or a defendant may wish to implead a third party in a contribution or indemnity suit. While the power to join a party to litigation certainly has the potential to influence outcome, joinder is also closely connected with the court's processes of regulating litigation and determining the scope of a dispute. Consequently, it is most appropriately governed by forum law,[58] a view taken in the US Second Restatement.[59]

5.17

3. Contribution and Indemnity

In most Commonwealth countries, statutes have been enacted to confer a non-contractual right on one tortfeasor to obtain contribution from another tortfeasor. While it is clear that the right is substantive,[60] there remains some uncertainty as to whether it should be classified as restitutionary[61] or tortious.[62] The analogous right of a claimant to an indemnity from a

5.18

---

[56] Audit (n 11 above) para 444.

[57] Rigaux and Fallon (n 16 above) para 11.8.

[58] M Illmer, 'Neutrality Matters—Some Thoughts about the Rome Regulations and the so-called Dichotomy of Substance and Procedure in European Private International Law' (2009) 28 Civil Justice Quarterly 237, 247.

[59] Restatement (Second), § 127 comment a (4); McDougal (n 44 above) 409.

[60] *Fluor Australia Pty Ltd v ASC Engineering Pty Ltd* (2007) 19 VR 458, para 52; *Arab Monetary Fund v Hashim (No 9)* (1994) The Times, 11 October (EWHC); K Takahashi, *Claims for Contribution and Reimbursement in an International Context* (OUP, 2000) 45–67; M Pryles, 'Tort and Related Obligations in Private International Law' (1991) 227 *Hague Recueil* 9, 150. This is also the position in the US, see Restatement (Second) of Conflict of Laws, § 173.

[61] *Sweedman v Transport Accident Commission* (2006) 226 CLR 362 (statutory right of insurer to indemnity); *The Nominal Defendant v Bagot's Executor and Trustee Co Ltd* [1971] SASR 346, 365 (revd on other grounds (1971) 125 CLR 179); *Stewart v Honey* [1972] 2 SASR 585, 594; M Davies, A Bell, and P Brereton, *Nygh's Conflict of Laws in Australia* (LexisNexis Butterworths, 8th edn, 2010) para 20.47.

[62] *Baldry v Jackson* [1977] 1 NSWLR 496; the issue was left open in *Fluor Australia Pty Ltd v ASC Engineering Pty Ltd* (2007) 19 VR 458 para 55.

tortfeasor for loss caused to the claimant by the claim of a third party should be similarly regarded.[63] Interestingly, in England it has long been held that where a claim for contribution is brought under the Civil Liability (Contribution) Act 1978 (UK) the statute will apply on its own terms, as opposed to only when it is selected under the forum's choice of law rules.[64] In effect, the Act operates as an overriding mandatory rule and prevents resort to any right to contribution under foreign law where the statute applies.[65] Note, however, that this approach was not taken in respect of almost identical legislation by the Supreme Court of Victoria in *Fluor Australia Pty Ltd v ASC Engineering Pty Ltd*.[66] The court there instead concluded that the relevant forum statute was only applicable where the common law choice of law rules selected the law of the forum.

5.19 The position in English law must now take account of the Rome II Regulation. A logical starting point is article 20 which provides that 'if a creditor has a claim against several debtors who are liable for the one claim and one of the debtors has already satisfied the claim in whole or in part, the question of that debtor's right to demand compensation from the other debtors shall be governed by the law applicable to the debtor's non-contractual obligation towards the creditor'.[67] Since, however, under some Commonwealth laws, an obligation to contribute may arise before one of the persons liable has paid the common creditor, this provision will not be available. In such circumstances the better view seems to be that contribution relates to 'division of liability' under article 15(b) of the Regulation and so is also referred to the applicable law.[68] Thus the key question is whether the existing approach which applies forum law to contribution based on an overriding mandatory rule survives the adoption of Rome II. While overriding rules are expressly provided for in article 16, the limited role accorded to forum law under the Regulation may suggest that courts may hesitate before relying on the pre-existing law.[69] Better still, the lack of emphatic wording in the Civil Liability (Contribution) Act, together with the highly persuasive Victorian decision in *Fluor Australia*, may

---

[63] *Sweedman v Transport Accident Commission* (2006) 226 CLR 362.

[64] *Arab Monetary Fund v Hashim (No 9)* (1994) The Times, 11 October (EWHC); *The Baltic Flame* [2001] 2 Lloyd's Rep 203, para 36 (Potter LJ).

[65] For a critique, see A Briggs, 'The International Dimension to Claims for Contribution: *Arab Monetary Fund v Hashim*' [1995] LMCLQ 437.

[66] (2007)19 VR 458, para 56.

[67] See also, in the case of contribution pursuant to contract, the Rome I Regulation, art 16 and for contracts entered into before 17 December 2009, the Rome Convention, art 13(2).

[68] A Dickinson, *The Rome II Regulation* (OUP, 2008) para 14.119.

[69] ibid para 14.120.

C. Individual Issues

hopefully persuade English courts to reconsider their classification of the statute as an overriding mandatory rule.[70]

4. Subrogation

In personal injury cases where an insurer has indemnified an insured person for damage suffered by that person, a common provision in the insurance policy confers a right on the insurer to be subrogated to any claims that the insured person may have against the original tortfeasor. This right has always been considered substantive and governed by the applicable law of the insurance policy.[71] The same result is achieved under the Rome II Regulation[72] which provides that where a creditor has a non-contractual claim against a debtor and a third person has a duty to satisfy the creditor, the law which governs the third person's duty to satisfy the creditor shall determine whether the third person is entitled to exercise against the debtor the rights which the creditor had against the debtor. Hence, where an insured has a non-contractual claim against the tortfeasor and the insurer has a duty to satisfy the insured pursuant to a policy, the law of the policy will determine whether the insurer may proceed against the tortfeasor.[73]

5.20

5. Proportionate Liability

Recent civil liability legislation in Australia has introduced proportionate liability for claims for economic loss or property damage but not for personal injury. The basis of such liability is that a tortfeasor cannot be held liable for more than his or her proportionate share of responsibility for the harm incurred by the claimant, having regard to the relative responsibilities of others for the damage.[74] Under the laws of some Australian states and territories, the court is given power to (and in other jurisdictions is *required* to) have regard to the comparative responsibility of a concurrent tortfeasor who is not a party to the proceeding. Although the legislation confers an

5.21

---

[70] See A Briggs, *The Conflict of Laws* (OUP, 2nd edn, 2008) 215.

[71] *West Tankers Inc v Ras Riunione Adriatica Di Sicurta Sp A* [2005] EWHC 454 (Comm); *Drews v Insurance Corp of British Columbia* (1998) 55 BCLR (3d) 281, para 28; *Kingsway General Insurance Co v Canada Life Insurance Co* (2001) 149 OAC 303.

[72] Rome II, art 19.

[73] Dickinson (n 68 above) para 14.110; B Doherty, C Thomann, and K Scott, *Accidents Abroad International Personal Injury Claims* (Thomson Reuters, 2009) para 9.075; see also, in the case of subrogation pursuant to contract, the Rome I Regulation, art 15 and for contracts entered into before 17 December 2009, the Rome Convention, art 13(1).

[74] See eg Civil Liability Act 2002 (NSW), Part 4; Civil Liability Act 2003 (Qld), Ch 2, Part 2; Wrongs Act 1958 (Vic), Part IVAA and M Davies, 'Choice of Law After the Civil Liability Legislation' (2008) 16 Torts LJ 104.

express direction on the courts to assess such responsibility, its main focus is the ascertainment of the rights and liabilities of the parties rather than the mode, conduct, or regulation of court proceedings. Application of the provisions is also unlikely to involve great inconvenience for the machinery of the forum and so a substantive classification would be warranted.

6. Vicarious Liability

5.22 It is clear, both under common law choice of law principles[75] and the Rome II Regulation,[76] that the question of whether someone is liable for the acts of another person is governed by the law of the cause of action as it obviously concerns the rights of the parties rather than the conduct of court proceedings.

7. Inter-Spousal Liability

5.23 The laws of some countries (and US states) have had rules barring one spouse from suing another in a tort action. Once again, similarly to vicarious liability, it is strongly arguable both in proceedings under Commonwealth law and the Rome II Regulation that such an issue is substantive and governed by the law of the obligation.[77] One Australian court agreed with this classification but left the choice of law issue open as between the law of the cause of action (tort) or the law governing capacity of the parties, which would be the law of the place of their domicile.[78]

8. Fatal Accident Cases

5.24 It is suggested that the issue of whether a right to sue for damages for personal injury may survive the death of the victim and pass to his or her estate would be similarly treated as substantive under both the Rome II Regulation[79] and under common law principles of private international law on the basis that it has a direct impact on the rights and liabilities of the parties. This conclusion has been reached in the United States.[80]

---

[75] *The Halley* (1886) LR 2 PC 193; *Joss v Snowball* (1969) 72 SR (NSW) 218; Pryles (n 60 above) 148.

[76] Rome II, art 15(g).

[77] G Johnston, *The Conflict of Laws in Hong Kong* (Sweet & Maxwell Asia, 2005) para 2.025.

[78] *Warren v Warren* [1972] Qd R 386 (Sup Ct Qld); see also Pryles (n 60 above) 166.

[79] Rome II, art 15(e); Doherty (n 73 above) para 11.012.

[80] Restatement (Second), § 124 comment a and illustration 2; P Hardin and W Kaelin, 'Characterization of Survival of Tort Actions' (1954) 4 Duke Bar Journal 105 (criticizing the decision in *Grant v McAuliffe* 264 P 2d 944 (Cal 1953) which had held survival to be procedural).

C. *Individual Issues* 129

Similarly, the statutory right of a claimant to sue for the wrongful death of another person is substantive and governed by the law of the cause of action.[81] A related question, in the context of an action for wrongful death, is what law determines the persons who may be beneficiaries to proceeds of a suit and how much each beneficiary receives. In one US decision[82] a court held that the issue of the distribution of recovery to beneficiaries is 'remedial law' and so the law of the forum applies. Very properly, courts in later US decisions have rejected this view, holding instead that the designation of the class of beneficiaries within a statute creating a cause of action which did not exist at common law is substantive.[83] The same classification applies to determining the amount each beneficiary is to receive.[84] The Second Restatement also adopts a substantive approach to both issues.[85] Such a classification is justified since these rules do not implicate how courts are administered or concern the execution of a judgment but instead identify who benefits from a judgment.[86] It is hoped that a Commonwealth court would take a similar approach, since the matter is strongly outcome determinative and has little connection with the mode or conduct of court proceedings. **5.25**

9. Representative Actions

A more complex choice of law issue which has arisen in relation to parties to litigation is when a claimant seeks to sue in the forum in the capacity of a representative of another and relies on an appointment made under foreign law. The question is whether the forum will defer to the law of the place of the act (*lex loci actus*) or require compliance with the forum's own rules on representative actions. There remains an arguably arbitrary split in the authorities, with certain representatives such as trustees in bankruptcy, liquidators, receivers,[87] administrators of alien enemy property, and curators of mentally-ill persons[88] being recognized as having capacity to sue in the forum, while other persons such as administrators of deceased persons and of absentees' property[89] are excluded from recognition. In the **5.26**

---

[81] *Dyno Wesfarmers Ltd v Knuckey* [2003] NSWCA 375; *Kilberg v Northeast Airlines Inc* [1961] 2 Lloyd's Rep 406 (NYCA).
[82] *Walters v Rockwell International Corp* 559 F Supp 47, 49–50 (ED Va 1983).
[83] *Re Estate of Louis Riso* 48 Va Cir 352, 355 (Circ Ct Va 1999); *Estate of Blanton* 824 So 2d 558 (Miss 2002).
[84] *Re Estate of Gilmore* 946 P 2d 1130 (NM App 1997).
[85] Restatement (Second), § 177 and comment a.
[86] *Re Estate of Gilmore* 946 P 2d 1130, 1134 (NM App 1997).
[87] *Bargain Harold's Discount Ltd v Paribas Bank of Canada* (1992) 113 NSR (2d) 434 (NSSC).
[88] *Didisheim v London and Westminster Bank* [1900] 2 Ch 15.
[89] *Kamouh v Associated Electrical Industries International Ltd* [1980] 1 QB 199.

latter two cases foreign administrators could not sue in the forum unless leave was obtained to swear death and an English grant of administration made. Further, where a forum statute imposes mandatory requirements for the appointment of a representative (for example regarding the execution and filing of a power of attorney),[90] these rules apply regardless of the validity of the power under the law of the place of the act. Forum law can therefore apply again through the prism of an overriding mandatory rule and local public policy rather than through a procedural characterization.

5.27 Yet if the touchstones in this area are comity and the admission of foreign law where it affects the rights and duties of the parties, then arguably all such 'representatives' should be recognized. If such an approach were taken, it would be interesting to see if other foreign representatives—such as persons authorized to sue on behalf of a group of persons with common rights under group action legislation—might also be recognized as having capacity to sue in the forum.[91] Given that some jurisdictions, such as the United States, Canada, and Australia,[92] have more sweeping 'class-action'-type legislation than the common law 'representative action' procedure, a flexible approach on recognition could expand the scope of availability of such legislation beyond the forum courts. Such an approach may be particularly useful where the jurisdictional rules of the country of enactment may be difficult to satisfy. Courts in other jurisdictions may, however, baulk at applying such foreign group action legislation given the procedural complexity involved and the lack of familiarity of the 'non-home' jurisdiction in applying such a regime.

5.28 The law applicable to class action regimes has only been indirectly considered in the United States. First of all, there are cases which have examined the issue of what law applies to a 'class action waiver' provision in a contract. Such a term involves parties agreeing to waive any rights they may have to invoke the class action procedures of a given state's law. In one decision, *America Online Inc v Superior Court*,[93] a Californian court refused to give effect to such a waiver which was valid under the law of the cause of action on the basis that it offended Californian public policy as expressed in an overriding mandatory statute of the forum. In another Californian

---

[90] *SMBD-Jewish General Hospital v Kummermann* 2004 QCCS 13776 (applying art 59 of the Quebec Code of Civil Procedure).

[91] The authors of Nygh seem to support this view although the decision cited (*Anderson v Johnson* (1877) 1 Knox (NSW) 1 (SC NSW)) is equivocal on the point; see Davies (n 61 above) para 16.39.

[92] See eg Federal Court of Australia Act 1976 (Cth), Part IVA; Supreme Court Act 1986 (Vic), Part 4A.

[93] 90 Cal App 4th 1, 15 (CA Cal 2001).

C. Individual Issues

case, *Discover Bank v Superior Court*,[94] a court enforced such a waiver, holding that there was no breach of local public policy given the strong connections between the parties and the foreign law of the cause of action. Significantly also, the court found that the issue of enforcing a waiver provision was not to be classified as procedural for choice of law purposes. The question of whether a waiver should be enforced directly affected the rights and duties of the parties and so was substantive, a conclusion which was also assumed by the court in the *America Online* case. The court in *Discover Bank* did say, however, that the classification might have been different if a party had sought to enforce the class action *procedures* of the forum—such as joinder, certification requirements including whether there are common questions among the class, who may be a representative party, etc. Such matters are more likely to be procedural and governed by forum law. In a similar manner, the drafters of the International Law Association Report on Transnational Group Actions considered the requirements for 'certification' of a class to be governed by the law of the forum.[95]

Secondly, there have been US decisions which have examined the effect of provisions in class action legislation which prohibit the use of such actions in some cases.[96] In a series of decisions[97] US courts have held that such provisions are substantive because they take away a claimant's right to bring a class action and so are applicable whenever the place of enactment supplies the law of the cause of action. As such a provision obviously concerns the rights and duties of the parties more than the conduct of a court's proceedings, it would also be likely to be considered substantive by a Commonwealth court. **5.29**

The foregoing material suggests that while restrictions on the availability of class actions under foreign laws may be applied in the forum on the basis that they abrogate the rights of the parties, it is unlikely that a claimant would be able to invoke directly the class action regime of a foreign jurisdiction. Most provisions of such legislation are closely tied to a local court's control and management of its proceedings as well as being supported by local public policy. **5.30**

---

[94] 134 Cal App 4th 886, 897 (CA Cal 2005).
[95] International Law Association, *Report of the Seventy-Third Conference* (International Law Association, London 2008) 583 (comment by C Kessedjian); see also P Wood, *Conflict of Laws and International Finance* (Sweet & Maxwell 2007) para 3.040.
[96] See eg New York Civil Practice Law and Rules (CPLR), s 901(b) which removes the right to a class action for certain damages claims for breach of statute.
[97] *Weber v US Sterling Securities* 924 A 2d 816 (Sup Ct Conn 2007); *Landsman & Funk PC v Skinder-Strauss Associates* 636 F Supp 2d 359 (DNJ 2009).

10. Defendants: 'Sue Others First' Provisions

5.31 Also, in the case of defendants, there is a situation where a foreign rule requires that one person must be sued before another. One such case is where an individual partner cannot be sued in relation to the partnership's debts, unless the partnership has been sued and judgment entered against it first. Similarly, some foreign legal systems require a principal debtor to be sued before a guarantor or an uninsured, injured person to sue the tortfeasor insured before bringing an action against the tortfeasor's insurer.[98] In all of these situations, there is a well-established distinction between two types of case. The first is where the defendant has no liability unless other persons are sued first and the second is where the defendant's liability is clear and uncontested and the requirement to sue others first is a mere condition precedent. In the first situation, the direction to sue the other parties is substantive and governed by the law of the cause of action; in the second, the requirement is procedural and so not applicable in proceedings in the forum.[99]

5.32 One writer[100] has criticized this distinction on the basis that the second case really involves a rule of substantive law as well. The rule is said to be substantive because the premise of the sue others first requirement is to provide that their property be exhausted first ahead of the defendant's, an objective which would appear to be more than litigation mechanics, instead relating to the scope of liability of the respective defendants. Yet an argument along these lines was rejected in *Johnson Matthey & Wallace Ltd v Ahmad Alloush*.[101] In that case the court had to consider an action against partners in a Jordanian entity, which was based on the following provision in Jordanian law:[102]

> Every partner shall be liable jointly with the other partners as well as severally for all the debts and liabilities of the [entity] which were incurred while he was a partner provided always that no execution order shall be issued against any partner in respect of his several liability for the [entity's] debts or liabilities, unless the [entity] has been dissolved or unless a creditor has obtained judgment and the [entity] does not have sufficient funds to meet the judgment debt.

The defendant first argued (and the court agreed) that the personal liability of the Jordanian partners was a substantive matter governed by Jordanian law as the law of the cause of action. Next, the defendants argued that the

---

[98] See eg *Cruickshank v Mid-Continent Casualty Co* 355 BR 391 (D Mass Bank 2006).
[99] *General Steam Navigation Co v Guillou* (1843) 11 M & W 877; *Re Doetsch* [1896] 2 Ch 836.
[100] M Wolff, *Private International Law* (OUP, 2nd edn, 1950) 240.
[101] (1984) 135 NLJ 1012 (CA).
[102] Jordanian Companies Law (No 12 of 1964), s 19.

C. Individual Issues

requirement that no execution be issued unless certain preconditions were met was also substantive because, in reality, no liability could ever be enforced unless such events occurred. In effect, liability was dependent upon the preconditions being satisfied. The Court of Appeal, however, applied the distinction referred to at 5.31, finding that the preconditions were merely an example of a provision which required others to be 'sued first' but which did not remove the partners' liability. Consequently, the conditions were procedural and not applicable in the forum.

Under the more limited Canadian/Australian view of procedure, it is unlikely that this conclusion would be reached. Not only does this issue have little to do with a court's management or conduct of its own proceedings, it clearly has a direct bearing on the outcome in the litigation. In this regard, it is interesting to note that in an older Australian case[103] it was assumed that a foreign law provision which required a plaintiff to first 'levy execution against the goods of the principal debtor' before suing a guarantor was substantive and applicable in proceedings in New South Wales. The court did not rely on the distinction referred to at 5.31. **5.33**

The same comment may also be made about a foreign rule which provides that civil proceedings cannot be brought until a criminal prosecution has been instituted.[104] Where foreign law is the law of the cause of action, for the forum to ignore such a precondition on the ground that it is merely procedural is to denature the foreign law and to reach an outcome which would not be achieved by the courts of that country applying their own law. Where, by contrast, the foreign condition is not a prerequisite to a civil claim being brought but 'merely a practical hurdle . . . to be met for reason of court practice',[105] it can be more properly disregarded. **5.34**

11. Corporations and Derivative Suits

(a) England

As noted at 5.02, the main choice of law rule in respect of a corporation's capacity to sue or be sued is the law of the place of incorporation. An issue which has arisen is whether this rule also applies in the case of a statutory **5.35**

---

[103] *Subbotovsky v Waung* (1968) 72 SR (NSW) 242.
[104] But cf *Scott v Seymour* (1862) 1 H & C 219, 230, 234–7 and *Grupo Torras SA v Al-Sabah* [1999] CLC 1469, 1661–2.
[105] *Yugraneft v Abramovich* [2008] EWHC 2613 (Comm), paras 299–300. In *AK Investment CJSC v Kyrgyz Mobil Tel Ltd* [2011] UKPC 7, para 108 the Privy Council, on appeal from the Isle of Man, refused to determine, in the absence of further expert evidence, the status of a Kyrgyz rule which provided that a civil claim could only be brought after conflicting judgments were set aside following a criminal conviction.

derivative action, that is, an action by a minority shareholder against a company for a wrong done to the company. The derivative action is an exception to the rule in *Foss v Harbottle*,[106] whereby the company is the proper claimant in an action to redress harm done to the company.

5.36 In *Heyting v Dupont*[107] the Court of Appeal had to consider a derivative action brought by a minority shareholder of a Jersey company. Although the choice of law issue was not directly raised, Russell LJ said:[108] 'I daresay that the rule in *Foss v Harbottle* is a conception as unfamiliar in the Channel Islands as is the Clameur de Haro in the jurisdiction of England and Wales. But clearly this is a matter of procedure to be decided according to the law of the forum.' No reason was given for this conclusion and that—combined with the fact that the point did not directly arise for decision—meant that the matter was still open for resolution in England.

5.37 More recently, in *Konamaneni v Rolls Royce Industrial Power (India) Ltd*,[109] Lawrence Collins J (as he then was) had to consider a derivative suit brought against an Indian company. After making a full examination of the issue and paying particular regard to US authority, his Lordship concluded that the availability and right to a derivative action was governed by the law of the place of incorporation. According to Lawrence Collins J, a derivative action 'confer[s] a right on shareholders to protect the value of their shares by giving them a right to sue and recover on behalf of the company. It would be very odd if that right could be conferred on the shareholders of a company incorporated in a jurisdiction which had no such rule and under which they had acquired their shares'.[110] In essence then, a derivative action is a true substantive right, not a mere procedural mechanism or device, and should be governed by the law closest to the action, namely the law of the place of incorporation. This conclusion sits comfortably with the well accepted rule that matters of internal management of the corporation or disputes between members of the company are governed by the same law.[111] Yet it should be noted that in *Konamaneni* the choice of law issue again did not strictly arise for decision because there was no evidence that English and Indian law were different.

5.38 Later English decisions have, however, suggested that the law of the place of incorporation will not be applied to all aspects of a derivative action

---

[106] (1843) 2 Hare 461 (Ch).
[107] [1964] 1 WLR 843.
[108] ibid 848.
[109] [2002] 1 WLR 1269 (Ch).
[110] ibid para 50.
[111] *Pergamon Press Ltd v Maxwell* [1970] 1 WLR 1167.

involving a foreign company. In *Base Metal Trading Ltd v Shamurin*[112] Arden LJ suggested that the requirement under English law on a shareholder to serve notice on the company which is the object of a derivative suit will be applied in cases involving a foreign company as well on the basis that it is procedural and governed by forum law. Further, in *Harding v Wealands*,[113] Arden LJ gave a further example of a procedural matter in the context of a derivative action: 'compliance with Civil Procedure Rule 19.9' (now section 260 of the Companies Act 2006 (UK)). This provision contains a number of formal requirements which must be satisfied by claimants in derivative suits in English courts, including obtaining the permission (or leave) of the court to proceed with the claim.

5.39 Consequently, even under the *Konamaneni* analysis of derivative suits, it will not be all aspects of the derivative action which are subject to the law of the place of incorporation; only whether the claimant has a right to such action and the scope of such right.

(b) Other Commonwealth Countries

5.40 Unfortunately, decisions in other Commonwealth countries are not consistent on the question of choice of law in derivative actions. The Hong Kong Court of Final Appeal, in a dictum,[114] appears to endorse the English position, namely that the right to bring a derivative action is governed by the law of the place of incorporation but that any leave of the court requirement 'is a procedural question governed by the *lex fori*'. While the matter was expressly left open by the Hong Kong Court of First Instance,[115] in a more recent decision the same court assumed that the law of the place of incorporation applied to determine whether a derivative suit may be brought on behalf of a company.[116]

5.41 In Canada, the authorities are split on the issue. In *Axis Management Inc v Alsager*[117] a court held that the right to bring a derivative action against a foreign company had to be decided by the law of the place of incorporation. Such law governed issues relating to the internal management of the corporation, which included the right to bring a derivative suit. By contrast,

---

[112] [2005] 1 WLR 1157, para 68.
[113] [2005] 1 WLR 1539, para 62 (revd on other grounds [2007] 2 AC 1).
[114] *Waddington Ltd v Chan Chun Hoo Thomas* [2008] HKCFA 63, para 55, Lord Millett NPJ (with whom Li CJ, Bokhary PJ, and Chan PJ agreed).
[115] *Ming Lai Siu Fun v Tsang Hung Kong* [2010] HKCFI 381, paras 63–64 (in the context of a 'double' derivative action).
[116] *East Asia Satellite Television (Holdings) Ltd v New Cotai LLC* [2010] HKCFI 615, para 104.
[117] (2000) 197 Sask R 234.

136   Chapter 5: Parties to Litigation

and more recently, in *Everest Canadian Properties Ltd v CIBC World Markets Inc*[118] the British Columbian Court of Appeal held that a shareholder's right to bring a derivative suit against a US corporation was procedural and governed by the law of the forum. Interestingly, neither *Axis Management* nor *Konamaneni* were referred to, but instead the court relied on the earlier *Heyting* decision to support its conclusion. The court also relied on three Canadian cases in support of a procedural characterization which did not involve choice of law. Consequently the *Everest* decision appears to rest on rather unsafe foundations, especially given that the court committed the 'Cook heresy' of relying on decisions on the substance / procedure distinction where the distinction was drawn for purposes other than choice of law.

5.42 A similar observation may be made about the Australian decision *Virgtel Ltd v Zabusky*.[119] *Virgtel* concerned an application for leave to commence a derivative action in Queensland against a Nigerian company which was in receivership in Nigeria. The Australian court granted leave and held that the right of a shareholder to bring a derivative action was procedural and governed by the law of the forum. The court relied on a number of Australian decisions to support this conclusion but, similarly to the *Everest* case, all but one of them did not involve choice of law questions or foreign corporations. In *Ebbage v Manthey*[120] (the decision referred to in *Virgtel* which did consider the choice of law issue) the court had to consider whether an equitable owner of shares was able to bring a derivative action against a Vanuatu corporation. The court treated the question as one of 'standing' and therefore a matter of procedure. Standing was not a question 'relating to the rights and liabilities of members, officers or shareholders of a foreign corporation' which would be referred to the law of the place of incorporation under Australian choice of law rules.[121] Significantly, the court in *Ebbage* relied on two of the Australian cases involving the substance / procedure distinction in domestic law[122] which were also cited by the court in *Virgtel*, and so the Cook heresy point is apt here also. While the court in *Virgtel* at some points in the judgment seems to acknowledge that the availability of the right to bring a derivative proceeding is substantive and governed by the law of the place of incorporation,[123] ultimately it found that the availability of the right was not an issue on the

---

[118] 2008 BCCA 276.
[119] [2006] 2 Qd R 81 (SC Qld).
[120] [2001] QSC 4 (SC Qld).
[121] Foreign Corporations (Application of Laws) Act 1989 (Cth), s 7(3)(e).
[122] *Scarel Pty Ltd v City Loan and Credit Corp Ltd (No 2)* (1988) 17 FCR 344; *Karam v Australia and New Zealand Banking Group Ltd* (2000) 34 ACSR 545.
[123] [2006] 2 Qd R 81, para 60.

facts. What was in question was 'the manner of its exercise' or 'the manner of setting up such a proceeding'.[124] *Konamaneni* was cited but distinguished on the ground that its discussion of the choice of law issue was obiter, while *Hausman*, a US authority which clearly supports the application of the law of the place of incorporation to derivative actions[125] was distinguished on the ground that it concerned 'not *how* a derivative action might be brought but whether it might be brought at all'.[126] The distinction between the 'availability' of the right to a derivative action and the 'manner of its exercise' is, with respect, not obvious on the facts of *Virgtel*. Certainly if the issue involved determining whether a provision requiring leave before commencing an action was procedural or substantive, then it would be a matter of manner and form as suggested by Arden LJ in *Harding v Wealands*. But on the facts of *Virgtel* the question really was one of whether the action could be brought at all.

In the more recent decision of *Oates v Consolidated Capital Services Ltd*,[127] both the New South Wales Supreme Court and the Court of Appeal left the issue of the applicable law in derivative actions open.[128] The trial judge in *Oates* did, however, note without disapproval the comment of Lawrence Collins J in *Konamaneni* that the law of the place of incorporation determined the extent of duties owed by a director of a foreign company.[129] It is not clear, however, whether this reference indicates support for the view that such law also applies to the issue of the availability of a derivative action.

5.43

(c) United States

The US position gives a central but not exclusive role to the law of the place of incorporation in derivative suits. In *Hausman v Buckley*[130] (cited by Lawrence Collins J in the *Konamaneni* case) the law of the place of incorporation (Venezuela) was applied to determine whether a derivative suit could be brought in New York on the basis that the right to bring such an action is substantive not procedural. Under Venezuelan law, the shareholder could only bring a derivative suit with the approval of the majority of shareholders and so the action was barred on the facts.

5.44

---

[124] ibid paras 50–51.
[125] *Hausman v Buckley* 299 F 2d 696 (2nd Cir 1962).
[126] [2006] 2 Qd R 81, para 60 (emphasis added).
[127] [2008] NSWSC 464; affd (2009) 76 NSWLR 69.
[128] See (2009) 76 NSWLR 69, para 101.
[129] [2008] NSWSC 464, para 41.
[130] 299 F 2d 696 (2nd Cir 1962).

5.45 The continued relevance of *Hausman* can be seen in its recent application by the US District Court of Colorado in *Oteng v Golden Star Resources Ltd*[131] and by the Court of Appeal of California in *Vaughn v LJ International Inc*.[132] In *Oteng* the court applied the law of the place of incorporation (Ghana) to determine whether a shareholder in a foreign corporation could sue derivatively on the basis that this matter was an 'internal affair' of the corporation. In *Vaughn* the court gave an even wider scope of operation to the law of the place of incorporation. *Vaughn* concerned a shareholder of a British Virgin Islands company who had failed to obtain approval from the BVI courts to commence a derivative suit against the company, as was required by BVI law. The US court held that the leave/approval requirement was a substantive provision that applied in the forum as part of the law of the place of incorporation. The court found that the approval requirement was a condition precedent to the right to sue derivatively and thus itself part of the substantive right, not 'a matter of mere court administration or mode of proceeding'.[133] A similar approach and result was reached in *Taylor v LSI Logic Corporation*,[134] where a shareholder's derivative action against a Canadian company was held not to be capable of being brought in the United States because the law of the place of incorporation vested exclusive jurisdiction in the Canadian courts for such an action. The US court expressly rejected the argument that such a provision was procedural and not applicable to proceedings in the forum.

5.46 The findings in these cases go beyond the position under Commonwealth law which, as noted at 5.38, appears to treat leave requirements as purely procedural. Certainly, such an approach has the advantage of limiting dépeçage by seeking to ensure that a single law applies to all issues where possible.

5.47 By contrast, some US decisions have agreed that the law of the place of incorporation normally governs the right to bring a derivative action but that a 'public policy' exception may exist where foreign law is immoral or unjust.[135] There appears to be no reported case, however, where such an exception has been applied. Another suggested exception to the law of the place of incorporation is application of the law of the forum where it has the most significant relationship with the issue to be decided. The drafters

---

[131] 615 F Supp 2d 1228 (D Colo 2009).
[132] 174 Cal App 4th 213 (Cal Ct App 2009). See also *CMIA Partners Equity Ltd v O'Neill* 29 Misc 3d 1228A (Sup Ct NY 2010).
[133] ibid 220.
[134] 715 A 2d 837 (SC Del 1998).
[135] *Re BP plc Derivative Litigation* 507 F Supp 2d 302, 308–9 (SDNY 2007); *City of Harper Woods Employees Retirement System v Olver* 589 F 3d 1292, 1299 (DC Cir 2009).

of the Second Restatement suggested that forum law may have the most significant relationship where the corporation has little contact, apart from the fact of incorporation, with such country's law, but the great majority of contacts are with the forum.[136] Again, however, this exception seems to have been rarely, if ever, applied, which suggests that the law of the place of incorporation remains the fundamental rule in derivative actions in the United States. Certainly there seems to be little enthusiasm for application of the law of the forum pursuant to a procedural characterization.

12. Foreign State Entities

5.48 Another issue which has arisen in relation to parties concerns the status of entities or instrumentalities of a foreign state. The issue of foreign state immunity generally in terms of choice of law has already been considered at 4.64 and 4.69–4.70 in the context of jurisdiction but here the inquiry is what law should be applied to determine whether an entity is part of a foreign state so as to entitle the entity to immunity. The question has often arisen in North America, typically where an arbitration award or judgment has been obtained against an entity that has not been satisfied and the claimant then seeks to execute against the assets of a foreign state. Courts have therefore had to determine whether the entity is the alter ego of a foreign state, in which case execution against the state is permissible, or a distinct body, in which case execution would not be allowed. The issue has also arisen at the jurisdictional stage where a defendant seeks to claim immunity as an agency of a foreign state.

(a) Canada

5.49 Canadian courts are divided on the choice of law question in each case. In *University of Calgary v Colorado School of Mines*,[137] an Alberta court held that the question of whether a body was an agency of the United States for the purposes of an immunity from jurisdiction defence was governed by Canadian law as the law of the forum. No reference was to be made to any other law, such as the law of the foreign state in question. In that case the court purported to follow an earlier decision of an Ontario court, *Ferranti Packard Ltd v Cushman Rentals Ltd*,[138] although in that case the court relied upon both the laws of the foreign state and the forum to determine whether an entity was an 'alter ego' of the foreign state. By contrast, at the other end of the spectrum, is the decision of the Federal Court of Canada in

---

[136] Restatement (Second), § 302 comments b, c, and g.
[137] (1995) 179 AR 81.
[138] (1981) 115 DLR (3d) 691 (Ont HCJ).

Foresight Shipping Co v Union of India.[139] In that case, execution was sought against the assets of a company alleged to be an instrumentality of the state of India to enforce a debt incurred by India in an arbitration. Significantly, the court found that the questions (a) whether the company was the 'alter ego' of India, and (b) whether the circumstances would allow the corporate veil of the company to be pierced were both substantive and governed by the law of the cause of action. Although the court does not make it clear, presumably the cause of action here is the one which formed the basis of the original arbitration proceedings leading to the award. If so, then it seems slightly unusual to rely on such law at the stage of execution, given that the matter has been adjudicated and all that is left is enforcement, an issue which has traditionally been governed by the law of the forum.[140] So, the forum state has a clear interest in having its law applied in this context; this interest may probably best be recognized by the adoption of a tailored choice of law rule which takes into account *both* forum law and the law of the foreign state when a question arises as to whether an entity forms part of the state.

5.50 Such a nuanced approach is evident in two other Canadian decisions. In *TMR Energy Ltd v State Property Fund of Ukraine*[141] the Federal Court held that both the law of the forum and the law of the foreign state should be applied in determining whether an entity was the alter ego of the foreign state so as to allow execution of an arbitral award against the state directly. The court noted that while foreign law was relevant in determining the status of an entity—in particular, whether it is distinct from the state, in considering its duties and powers, ability to act independently, and capacity to sue and be sued—the law of the forum must also be considered.[142] Execution of judgments was normally governed by the law of the forum and so that law had a clear interest in establishing whether an entity was 'answerable to the process of the court'. Forum concepts of what constitutes a distinct legal entity and the criteria of the alter ego test must therefore also be examined, to ensure that the definition provided under foreign law is 'relevant to our execution process'. The approach taken in *TMR* was followed by an Alberta court in *Collavino Inc v Yemen (Tihama Development Authority)*.[143] *Collavino* also involved an attempt to execute an award, originally made against a company, against assets of a foreign state. The court endorsed the approach in *TMR* that both the laws of the foreign state and

---

[139] 2004 FC 1501.
[140] See 6.78.
[141] (2003) 244 FTR 1 (revd on other grounds (2005) 250 DLR (4th) 10).
[142] ibid para 116.
[143] (2007) 9 WWR 290.

the forum were relevant to the question of whether the entity was an alter ego of the state.[144]

5.51 While it is logical to refer to both laws on the issue of the status of a foreign entity, a problem may arise where the local and foreign laws are in conflict. It is suggested that in such a case the foreign law should prevail on the basis that it has the closest connection to the entity in question and is more consistent with the choice of law rule, that the nature and powers of an entity should be governed by the law of the place of its formation. Interestingly, in both the *TMR* and *Collavino* cases the courts found there to be no conflict between the local and foreign law, although in *TMR*, the court did not appear to consider the Canadian law principles in any detail but relied solely on evidence of foreign law.[145] Also, in *Collavino*, while Canadian law was briefly referred to, the issue was predominantly resolved by reference to the law of the foreign state.[146] Such approaches suggest that the law of the place of formation or incorporation will have great sway on this question.

(b) England

5.52 The issues of whether a body has the requisite 'governmental control' and 'government functions' to be a 'separate entity' of a foreign state under the UK State Immunity Act 1978 have not arisen frequently in litigation before English courts. While the general approach has been to apply English law to these questions, courts have also, on occasion, taken into account the laws of the country under which the body was incorporated.[147] So in *Kensington International Ltd v Republic of the Congo*[148] the court noted that the purpose of a Congolese State-owned oil company, according to its constituent legislation, was 'to undertake the exploitation of Congo's oil reserve on behalf of the Congo, to hold that State's oil related assets on its behalf and to represent the State on oil-related matters'.[149] The court concluded that the company was part of the foreign state.

(c) Australia

5.53 The Full Federal Court of Australia has recently considered the issue and appears to have applied a combination of both the law of the forum and

---

[144] ibid para 107.
[145] (2003) 244 FTR 1 para 134.
[146] (2007) 9 WWR 290 para 116.
[147] H Fox, *The Law of State Immunity* (OUP, 2nd edn, 2008) 254; P Webb, 'Some Thoughts on the Place of English Law as *Lex Fori* in Private International Law' (1961) 10 ICLQ 818, 819.
[148] [2005] EWHC 2684 (Comm).
[149] ibid para 55.

the law of the foreign state to determine whether a foreign entity is an 'agency or instrumentality of a foreign state'[150] under the Australian Foreign States Immunities Act 1985 (Cth). While the criteria employed for resolving this question were derived from Australian law principles, what was decisive in the case was that the foreign entity had been established under legislation designed for state-owned bodies which was intended to fulfil government functions and whose purpose was to benefit the public.[151]

(d) United States

5.54 A similar approach has been taken in the United States to that prevailing in Canada. In a series of US cases courts have looked to elements under both the law of the forum and the law of the foreign state to determine whether an entity is an alter ego of the foreign state for the purposes of both service of process and execution of judgments and awards.[152]

---

[150] *PT Garuda Indonesia Ltd v Australian Competition and Consumer Commission* [2011] FCAFC 52; (2011) 277 ALR 67.

[151] ibid para 49 (Lander and Greenwood JJ); para 169 (Rares J).

[152] See eg *S & R Davis v Yemen* 218 F 3d 1292, 1298–9 (11th Cir 2000); *Garb v Republic of Poland* 440 F 3d 579, 594–5 (2nd Cir 2006) and *Compagnie Noga d'Importation v Russian Federation* 361 F 3d 676, 685–6 (2nd Cir 2004); cf *Transaero Inc v La Fuerza Aera Boliviana* 30 F 3d 148, 152 (DC Cir 1994) (law of the forum only).

6
Judicial Administration

A. Court Proceedings	6.02
1. Constitution and Competence of Courts	6.02
2. Commencement of Proceedings	6.03
3. Pleading Requirements	6.04
4. Form and Classification of Action and Choice of Law Rules	6.05
5. Court Powers to Manage and Conduct the Proceedings	6.08
6. Pre-Trial Evidence Collection	6.11
7. Jury Trial	6.13
8. Right of Appeal	6.16
9. Right to a Public Hearing	6.20
10. Notice before Action and Other Condition Precedent Provisions	6.22
B. Costs and Lawyers' Fees	6.31
1. Costs	6.31
2. Contingency Fees	6.36
3. Security for Costs/Security Bonds	6.37
C. Statutory 'No Action' Clauses	6.40
1. Generic Court Provisions	6.40
2. 'Leave of the Court' Provisions	6.47
3. 'Named Court' Provisions: Vesting Jurisdiction	6.49
4. 'Named Court' Provisions: Divesting Jurisdiction	6.55
D. Priorities and Rights of Creditors	6.59
1. Priorities	6.59
2. Rights of Creditors	6.65
E. Judgments and Orders	6.77
1. Form and Requirements	6.77
2. Methods of Enforcement	6.78
3. Rules for Enforcement	6.82

This chapter examines a number of matters, all of which concern the operation and processes of the courts in some way. The constitution of the court, court room conduct, pleading requirements, pre-trial evidence collection, the right to a jury trial, the right to an appeal, pre-action notice requirements, costs, and the effect of legislative provisions limiting access to courts are all examples of such issues. Superficially, almost all such issues would appear to fall within the restrictive definition of procedure

6.01

articulated by the High Court of Australia in *John Pfeiffer Pty Ltd v Rogerson*,[1] that is, they are matters concerned with the mode or conduct of court proceedings or 'rules which are reasonable and necessary for the conduct of the action'.[2] Consequently, they should in principle be governed by forum law, a conclusion also reached by the drafters of the US Second Restatement who refer the broad topic of 'judicial administration' to this law.[3] In relation to some of the topics above, however, closer examination is required to assess whether this conclusion is accurate in all situations and also whether the application of forum law may be justified on grounds other than procedure (for example public policy).

A. COURT PROCEEDINGS

1. Constitution and Competence of Courts

6.02 It is likely to be universally accepted that a litigant must take the forum courts as it finds them[4] and cannot request a special court for trial of the action because such a court may have been available under the law of the cause of action.[5] Consequently, forum law exclusively will determine which of its courts will be competent to adjudicate an action, assuming jurisdiction exists under the rules of the forum.[6]

2. Commencement of Proceedings

6.03 The rules governing how an action may be commenced in a court (in Commonwealth law systems, by service of process) and how such process is to be served on the defendant are again exclusively those of the forum.[7]

---

[1] *John Pfeiffer Pty Ltd v Rogerson* (2000) 203 CLR 503, para 99 (Gleeson CJ, Gaudron, McHugh, Gummow, and Hayne JJ).
[2] ibid para 192 (Callinan J).
[3] US Restatement (Second), § 122.
[4] *John Pfeiffer Pty Ltd v Rogerson* (2000) 203 CLR 503, para 99 (Gleeson CJ, Gaudron, McHugh, Gummow, and Hayne JJ); J Carruthers, 'Substance and Procedure in the Conflict of Laws: A Continuing Debate in Relation to Damages' (2004) 53 ICLQ 691, 693.
[5] E Lorenzen, 'The Statute of Frauds and the Conflict of Laws' (1923) 32 Yale LJ 311, 328; E Morgan, 'Choice of Law Governing Proof' (1944) 58 Harvard L Rev 153, 159.
[6] Restatement (Second), § 123, A Dickinson, *The Rome II Regulation* (OUP, 2008) para 14.61; N Rafferty, M Baer, J Blom, E Edinger, G Saumier, and C Walsh, *Private International Law in Common Law Canada: Cases Text and Materials* (Edmond Montgomery Publications, 2nd edn, 2003) 535.
[7] *John Pfeiffer Pty Ltd v Rogerson* (2000) 203 CLR 503, para 192 (Callinan J); Restatement (Second), § 126; E Sykes and M Pryles, *Australian Private International Law* (Law Book Co, 3rd edn, 1991) 256; Australian Law Reform Commission, *Choice of Law* (Report No 58) (1992) para 10.9; Rafferty (n 6 above) 535.

A. Court Proceedings

This result was recently confirmed by the Court of Appeal of Nova Scotia in *Vogler v Szendroi*[8] which involved a claimant who was injured in the US state of Wyoming, the law of which was the law of the cause of action. The claimant commenced proceedings in Nova Scotia three years after the accident but did not serve the defendant for another three years, that is, six years after the accident. Under the Wyoming rules, an action is commenced by filing a complaint with the court but if this document has not been served within sixty days of filing, the action is not considered to have been commenced until the date of service. The court held the Wyoming provision—in requiring filing *and* service to initiate an action—to be procedural on the basis that it 'simply direct[ed] the manner in which an action is commenced'.[9] The foreign law was concerned with process[10] or the mode or conduct of court proceedings rather than substantive rights. Apart from the proximity of service to the mode and conduct of the forum's proceedings, another justification for applying forum law to the issue of how proceedings are to be commenced is that the law of the cause of action is not known at the initiation of proceedings and so the law of the forum is the only law 'available'. The *time* at which a proceeding is deemed to have commenced is also determined by the law of the forum.[11] Where service of process takes place outside the forum, however, the forum court may also have to take account of foreign laws, such as the law of country of service in certain circumstances.[12] Similarly, while the rules determining the existence of and exercise of jurisdiction by courts are predominantly those of the forum, reference may also be made to the laws of other countries in particular cases.[13]

3. Pleading Requirements

6.04 The form and requirements of pleadings, and scope for and manner of their amendment and challenge are matters exclusively governed by forum law.[14] Not only are such issues rarely likely to be outcome determinative, they clearly fall within the province of the forum court's control of its own proceedings.[15] Hence, in two Australian decisions the court used its procedural powers to amend a statement of claim to correct a mistake

---

[8] (2008) 290 DLR (4th) 642.
[9] ibid para 29.
[10] ibid para 36.
[11] *Kansas v Hartford Accident and Indemnity Co* 426 SW 2d 720 (Mo KC Ct App 1968).
[12] See Ch 4.
[13] See Ch 4.
[14] Australian Law Reform Commission (n 7 above) para 10.9; Restatement, Second, § 127 comment a (2), (3); *Boersma v Amoco Oil Company* 658 NE 2d 1173 (Ill App Ct 1995).
[15] Sykes and Pryles (n 7 above) 256.

Chapter 6: Judicial Administration

in the name of the defendant[16] and to add further claims,[17] both after the applicable foreign limitation periods had expired. There are English decisions to the same effect.[18] Arguably, however, where amendments are sought to avoid a foreign limitation period which is applicable in the forum as part of the law of the cause of action, they should be more properly classified as substantive and only available if the procedural rules of the foreign law of the cause of action so permit.[19]

4. Form and Classification of Action and Choice of Law Rules

6.05 It is widely accepted in common law countries that forum law determines the form in which an action must be brought, for example whether it be in tort or contract.[20] This proposition is essentially a restatement of the rule that matters of characterization (at least in respect of causes of action) are governed by the law of the forum. Hence, while a claimant may wish to sue in country A under the strict liability statute of country B, it will be for the law of country A to determine the category of cause of action in which the action falls (for example tort).[21] Once the classification is determined, the appropriate choice of law rule of country A will then be applied to establish whether the statute of country B is relevant. A claimant therefore will not be able to invoke a category under the law of the cause of action which does not exist under the law of the forum. So, in one US decision a plaintiff was not permitted to plead its case for wrongful dismissal from employment as a suit in contract, which was the appropriate classification under the law of the cause of action but was confined to the category recognized under forum law, which was tort.[22] Therefore, forum law supplies both the rules of classification and choice of law in cases with a foreign element (with the exception of the *renvoi* principle where the choice of law rules of the law of the cause of action may be consulted).

6.06 Still on choice of law matters, Commonwealth principles of private international law generally require a claimant or defendant to plead any rules of foreign law it wishes to rely upon to support its case.[23] Since foreign law is regarded as a question of fact in Commonwealth legal systems which

---

[16] *Nikolay Malakhov Shipping Co Ltd v Seas Sapfor Ltd* (1998) 44 NSWLR 371 (NSWCA).
[17] *Dyno Wesfarmers Ltd v Knuckey* [2003] NSWCA 375.
[18] See cases discussed at 9.32 below.
[19] See 9.33 below.
[20] Restatement (Second), § 124 and comment a; I Szászy, 'The Basic Connecting Factor in International Cases in the Domain of Civil Procedure' (1966) 15 ICLQ 436, 454.
[21] *Forsyth v Cessna Aircraft Co* 520 F 2d 608, 611 (9th Cir 1975).
[22] *Gouge v BAX Global Inc* 252 F Supp 2d 509, 521 (ND Ohio 2003).
[23] *Neilson v Overseas Projects Corp of Victoria Ltd* (2005) 223 CLR 331.

A. Court Proceedings

must be established before the legal rights and liabilities of the parties can be ascertained, the basis of such a rule of pleading is forensic and relates to the forum court's machinery for resolving the litigation. A procedural classification is therefore appropriate. This issue is also discussed in the context of presumptions at 7.23.

A related type of pleading issue involving choice of law concerns a claimant who has multiple causes of action arising from a single set of facts and whether it is entitled to plead all such causes in the one proceeding. Under domestic common law principles a claimant may 'accumulate' multiple causes[24] but the position may be different in civil law countries.[25] While, in *Base Metal Trading Ltd v Shamurin*[26] the English Court of Appeal implied that the question of whether concurrent causes of action may be pleaded was procedural, it is clear that such an issue has a direct impact on the rights and liabilities of the parties by allowing a claimant to maximize its chances of recovery. Such a rule therefore has little to do with the mode, conduct, or regulation of the forum court's proceedings and so should be considered substantive.[27]

6.07

5. COURT POWERS TO MANAGE AND CONDUCT THE PROCEEDINGS

Court powers to manage the proceedings are also clearly procedural and governed by forum law on any of the substance-procedure models.[28] From a broad perspective, practicality compels no other result since 'a French litigant could hardly require of an English judge applying French law to his case that he conduct inquisitorial rather than the English adversarial model of inquiry'.[29] More specifically, the rubric of court management of proceedings would include the powers to determine what constitutes an appearance[30] by the defendant, whether legal representation is required,[31] and the court's capacity to streamline proceedings by, for example, not allowing interrogatories to be used, or placing limits on discovery or the number of witnesses in a trial. So, where a power of a court to rectify an irregularity in the conduct of a proceeding is narrower under the law

6.08

---

[24] *Henderson v Merrett Syndicates Ltd* [1994] 2 AC 145.
[25] ibid 184 (Lord Goff).
[26] [2005] 1 WLR 1157.
[27] A Dickinson, 'Applicable Law Arbitrage—an Opportunity Missed?' (2005) 121 LQR 374, 378.
[28] Restatement (Second), § 127; Szászy (n 20 above) 454.
[29] C Fassberg, 'The Forum: Its Role and Significance in Choice-of-Law' (1985) 84 *Zeitschrift für Vergleichende Rechtswissenschaft* 1, 10.
[30] Australian Law Reform Commission (n 7 above) para 10.9.
[31] Szászy (n 20 above) 454; E Spiro, 'Forum Regit Processum' (1969) 18 ICLQ 949, 952.

of the forum than under the law of the cause of action, an applicant is confined to its rights under forum law.[32] The forum's rules as to when a summary or default judgment may be ordered also fall within the scope of the court's powers to manage its proceedings.[33] Consequently, such rules will be applied in the forum even where the law of the cause of action is foreign.[34] Note, however, that recognition and enforcement of a summary judgment in another country may be refused on public policy grounds where the forum's rules (that is, those of the country of origin) on summary judgments allow for no reasons to be given for the decision. Deference to forum law on this question is therefore not total.[35]

6.09 Many Commonwealth civil procedure rules provide a right to third parties to intervene in a proceeding between other parties. Such a right to intervene may exist, for example,[36] where an issue arises out of or relates to a claim in an existing proceeding and it is 'just and convenient' to determine such issue between the third party and any party to the proceeding. Under the mode or conduct of proceedings view, such a right is likely to be procedural as it is a mechanism by which relevant interests and persons can be heard in the one proceeding and issues resolved concerning such parties. Moreover, since third parties still possess the right to commence independent proceedings to protect their interests, the right of intervention is unlikely to be crucial to the outcome. Consistent with the above view, in an Australian decision it was held that the forum's provision on intervention applied even though the law of the cause of action was foreign.[37] By parity of reasoning, the rules on joinder by which a third party may be added by a claimant as a co-defendant or added as a third party defendant by the defendant to the original proceeding would also be considered procedural[38] even though the claim(s) against such an entity would be determined by the applicable law of the cause of action. The topic of parties and applicable law is discussed more fully in Chapter 5.

6.10 It is also well established that a court's powers to dismiss an action for abuse of process or malicious prosecution are governed by the law of the place where the proceeding complained of occurred.[39] Such a conclusion

---

[32] *Windsurf Holdings Pty Ltd v Leonard* [2009] NSWCA 6, para 14 (Bell JA) (with whom Beazley JA agreed) para 1.

[33] Australian Law Reform Commission (n 7 above) para 10.9.

[34] *Rockwell v Raytheon Corp* 2006 WL 305411 *2 (CA Mich 2006).

[35] *Society of Lloyds v X* (French Court of Cassation, 22 October 2008) [2009] IL Pr 12.

[36] See eg Supreme Court (General Civil Procedure) Rules 2005 (Victoria), r 9.06.

[37] *Wheeler v SDS Ausminco Ltd* [2001] VSC 261.

[38] Restatement (Second), § 127 comment a (4).

[39] *Yugraneft v Abramovich* [2008] EWHC 2613 (Comm), paras 425, 430; Restatement (Second), § 155; *Tripodi v Local Union No 38, Sheet Metal Workers International Association* 120 F Supp 2d 318, 321 (SDNY 2000).

A. Court Proceedings

flows from the fact that the purpose of the doctrine is the protection of the court's processes and the avoidance of harassment of defendants.[40] Abuse of process therefore squarely falls within the forum's power to control the conduct of its own proceedings.

6. Pre-Trial Evidence Collection

On one view, this issue is also part of the forum court's power to conduct its proceedings and so should be governed by local law.[41] Yet the matter is complicated by the fact that the availability of common law discovery or disclosure (particularly the wide US version) when compared to the European civil law model, where each party is limited to relying upon the evidence in its own possession, may have a potential impact on the outcome of the litigation. For example, critical evidence may be excluded from a civil law trial which would be unearthed in a common law proceeding. Again, on balance, such rules lie at the heart of a court's trial processes and it would be unwieldy and inefficient if a judge had to apply the evidence gathering rules of another jurisdiction without the supporting infrastructure for such rules. Such rules are properly subjected to forum law.[42] Note, however, that the act of taking evidence abroad may trigger conflict with foreign laws (such as a law of privilege) so that the application of forum law is qualified in such cases. This issue is explored in more detail in Chapter 8, and the question of admissibility of evidence is discussed in Chapter 7.   **6.11**

Statutory provisions, which require parties to provide information to each other, have also been held to be applicable to all proceedings in the forum, regardless of the governing substantive law.[43]   **6.12**

7. Jury Trial

The right to a jury trial (as opposed to having a judge as trier of fact) is often cited as an example of an issue which should be governed by the law of the forum.[44] One reason cited is the serious inconvenience and impracticality which would ensue if a country which had no tradition of such trials were forced to employ such a proceeding in a foreign case.[45] In effect, then, this approach is an example of impracticality operating as a public policy-type basis for the application of forum law. Under the right-remedy test, a   **6.13**

---

[40] *Yugraneft v Abramovich* [2008] EWHC 2613 (Comm), para 430.
[41] Restatement (Second), § 127 comment a (5).
[42] ibid § 122 comment a.
[43] *Hamilton v Merck and Co Inc* (2006) 66 NSWLR 48, para 36 (Spigelman CJ).
[44] Sykes and Pryles (n 7 above) 256–7.
[45] L Collins (ed), *Dicey, Morris and Collins on the Conflict of Laws* (Sweet & Maxwell, 14th edn, 2006) para 7.026.

right to a jury trial is clearly procedural as it does not relate to the existence or definition of any right under the cause of action in the litigation but only to the enforcement of such right. Under the more limited notion of procedure in Canadian and Australian decisions, a right to a jury trial may also be classified as procedural on the basis that it pertains to the mode or conduct of proceedings or litigation machinery. If this test of procedure is applied on its own then the position is clear but if it is employed in conjunction with the 'outcome determinative' principle from *Pfeiffer v Rogerson*, then the status of jury trials becomes less certain. Obviously the right to a jury trial, as opposed to a decision by a judge alone, may have a potential bearing on the result in the litigation[46] (for example in terms of the amount of damages awarded)[47] and so can be seen as substantive under this test. To that extent, this is an issue where the 'conduct of proceedings' and 'outcome determinative' principles appear to be in conflict and consequently, as argued in Chapter 2, the conduct of proceedings criterion should prevail; otherwise the scope and operation of forum law in an important matter of local court management would be unduly restricted.[48] Moreover, practicality and convenience support the application of forum law to this issue since the institution of a jury would be almost impossible to replicate in a civil law country with no such tradition.[49]

6.14 There have been surprisingly few cases which have considered the choice of law status of a jury trial, although in a recent Australian decision[50] it was held that the jury trial provision under the law of the forum applied to claims for defamation governed by foreign laws. In support of this conclusion the court relied[51] upon an earlier New South Wales decision, *Waterhouse v Australian Broadcasting Corporation*[52] but unfortunately this case based its procedural characterization on the outdated right-remedy approach and so a clear statement of the place of a jury trial under more contemporary principles is therefore required. The same observation may

---

[46] Australian Law Reform Commission (n 7 above) para 10.17; L McDougal, R Felix, and R Whitten, *American Conflicts Law* (Transnational Publishers, 5th edn, 2001) 407.

[47] For an extreme example, see *The Loewen Group Inc v United States* ICSID Case No ARB (AF)/98/3/(26 June 2003).

[48] Morgan (n 5 above) 171; cf this view with that of the Australian Law Reform Commission (n 7 above) para 10.18, which recommended that provision for a jury trial should remain procedural in international cases in Australia but substantive in interstate cases 'unless the demands of practicality and justice suggest otherwise'.

[49] Fassberg (n 29 above) 10; see also the discussion in relation to the Rome II Regulation at 11.29 below.

[50] *Dehsabzi v John Fairfax Publications Pty Ltd (No 2)* [2008] NSWDC 77.

[51] ibid para 16.

[52] (1990) A Def R 50–070.

A. Court Proceedings

be made about the obiter remark in a Canadian decision[53] that jury rights were procedural because they involved the enforcement of a substantive right not the creation or extinguishment of the right itself. In two English decisions the right to a jury trial on damages was suggested, obiter, to be a procedural matter on the basis that it was a method for assessment of damages which would be difficult to replicate in countries with no tradition of the institution.[54]

6.15 Under US law all questions relating to jury trials, including whether a party is entitled to such a trial,[55] whether a matter should be presented to the judge or jury for determination,[56] what instructions are to be given to the jury,[57] whether a party may waive a jury trial,[58] and the number of jurors required to reach a verdict[59] are considered to be procedural as they relate to the method by which a trial is conducted. Such a position strongly suggests that the same result would be reached under the Australian mode or conduct of court proceedings view.[60]

8. Right of Appeal

6.16 Forum law determines the time period within which an appeal must be lodged.[61] The question of what law determines whether a *right* of appeal exists is, however, more contentious. A number of text writers have suggested that such a right is a procedural matter and so governed by the law of the forum.[62] Yet, in all such cases, the definition of procedure relied upon may have been the traditional right-remedy formulation and

---

[53] *Hubbard v City of Edmonton* (1917) 37 DLR 458, 460 (Alta CA).

[54] *Harding v Wealands* [2005] 1 WLR 1539, para 57 (Arden LJ) (revd on other grounds [2007] 2 AC 1); *Re T & N Ltd* [2005] EWHC 2990, para 83.

[55] Restatement (Second), Conflict of Laws, § 129; *Vanier v Ponsoldt* 833 P 2d 949 (SC Kan 1992).

[56] *Hoeper v Air Wisconsin Airlines* 2009 WL 3764080 (CA Colo).

[57] *Naughton v Bankier* 691 A 2d 712, 716 (Ct Spec App Md 1997); *Meredith v Missouri Pacific Railroad* 467 SW 2d 79, 82 (Mo Sup Ct 1971); *Boersma v Amoco Oil Co* 658 NE 2d 1173 (App Ct Ill 1995).

[58] *World Wide Imports Inc v Bartel* 145 Cal App 3d 1006, 1012–13 (CA Cal 1983).

[59] *Owens-Corning Fiberglas Corp v Martin* 942 SW 2d 712, 721 (Ct App Tex 1997), A Lowenfeld, *Conflict of Laws: Federal, State and International Perspectives* (Lexis-Nexis, 2nd edn, 2002) 73.

[60] Dicey, Morris and Collins (n 45 above) para 7.026, also assert that the issue of jury trials should be governed by forum law.

[61] Spiro (n 31 above) 959.

[62] See eg R Graveson, *Conflict of Laws* (London, Sweet & Maxwell, 7th edn, 1974) 615; Sykes and Pryles (n 7 above) 257; J Fawcett and J Carruthers, *Cheshire, North and Fawcett Private International Law* (OUP, 14th edn, 2008) 80; Dickinson (n 6 above) para 14.61; Rafferty (n 6 above) 535; Spiro (n 31 above) 959–60.

so the question must be considered afresh in the context of the more recent, limited views on the scope of procedure. Here, similarly to the right to jury trial, the right to appeal would seem to fall squarely within the province of a court's conduct and management of its own proceedings. Yet, equally obviously, the existence or non-existence of such a right could be outcome determinative. Again, it is suggested that given the conflict between the two principles and the need to preserve some content in procedure the 'conduct of proceedings' view should be solely employed to determine the characterization of this matter. Given that rights of appeal are close to the heart of the judicial function, the law of the forum deservedly applies. This view is taken in the US Second Restatement in relation to rights of appeal and other proceedings to review a judgment.[63]

6.17 The application of forum law to rights of appeal is supported by the New South Wales Court of Appeal decision in *Julia Farr Services Inc v Hayes*.[64] This case concerned an action which was commenced by a claimant before the New South Wales Dust Diseases Tribunal arising out of a tort in South Australia, which was governed by that State's law. Under section 32 of the Dust Diseases Tribunal Act 1989 (NSW), an appeal from the Tribunal to the New South Wales courts lies only for a question of law. By contrast, an appeal under South Australian law (the law of the cause of action) was wider, being available for errors of fact and law. The defendant argued that South Australian law should be applied on the basis that the right to appeal was substantive, but the New South Wales court disagreed. According to the court, a right of appeal is related to 'the extent of a court's jurisdiction' and consequently concerns both the regulation of the 'mode or conduct of court proceedings' and 'the statement of the limits within which [a] court can act'.[65] The court also noted that although 'the extent of appellate rights has the potential to affect outcomes . . . so does any regulation of the mode or conduct of court proceedings'. Despite its potentially outcome determinative nature, the right was still 'fundamentally procedural'.[66] Finally, the court noted that 'while the label "procedural" is hallowed, it may be better to see appellate rights as governed by the law of the forum simply because they are "a given for litigation in the forum"'.[67]

---

[63] Restatement (Second), § 127 comment a (9).
[64] [2003] NSWCA 37.
[65] ibid para 51.
[66] ibid para 52; a procedural characterization of the right to appeal was also adopted in *Wallaby Grip Ltd v Gilchrist* [2007] NSWSC 1181, para 46.
[67] ibid para 53.

A. Court Proceedings

The above comments are important in a number of ways. First, there is a clear statement that the right to appeal is procedural and governed by forum law because it concerns an issue at the centre of the judicial function—the extent of the court's jurisdiction. Secondly, the court acknowledges the conflict, noted at 2.26, in the *Pfeiffer* definition of substance and procedure, that is, that a matter relating to the mode or conduct of proceedings, and thus procedural, can also be potentially outcome determinative and substantive. Consistent with the approach suggested in Chapter 2 for resolving such a conflict, the court gave preference to the 'conduct of proceedings' view. Thirdly, the court also significantly recognizes (perhaps as a result of the second point) that the 'procedural' and 'substantive' labels may sometimes be of limited utility in resolving choice of law questions in procedural matters. It may be better to identify the issue and then consider which law should be applied to the issue on the grounds of connection, policy, and interest. **6.18**

Before leaving the issue of appeals, it must be acknowledged that Callinan J of the High Court of Australia, in *BHP Billiton Ltd v Schultz*,[68] suggested obiter that a right of appeal was substantive, presumably on the basis of its outcome determinative effect. The judge was again specifically referring to section 32 of the Dust Diseases Tribunal Act 1989 (NSW) where such a right was restricted. It is suggested, however, that the views of the New South Wales Court of Appeal in *Julia Farr* should be preferred, given that Callinan J did not seek to reconcile the 'mode or conduct of proceedings' criterion with the outcome determinative concept. Moreover, there would be serious practical complications for the forum if it had to import provisions on appeals from other countries, which are likely to have been developed in the context of a particular judicial system or hierarchy. **6.19**

9. Right to a Public Hearing

Another matter which relates to the nature of court proceedings is the question of whether a court hearing must be conducted in public, or in other words, whether a party has a right to privacy in adjudication. The issue arose in an Irish decision *De Gortari v Smithwick*.[69] This case concerned a letter of request from a French tribunal to an Irish court for the taking of evidence from a witness, who was a third country national residing in Ireland. It was accepted by both parties that the equivalent proceedings, had they taken place in France, would have been heard in private and the **6.20**

---

[68] (2004) 221 CLR 400, paras 235, 247; see also Kirby J, para 148, n 259.
[69] [1999] IESC 51.

question for the Irish court was whether the same procedure should be followed in the Irish proceeding.

6.21 It should first be noted that the matter in *De Gortari*, being a request from a foreign tribunal to the forum court, is a proceeding of *the forum*. This position is to be contrasted with an examination of a witness on commission by a foreign court in the forum, which is a proceeding of *the foreign tribunal*. Consequently, the question was whether, as a matter of the Irish proceedings, the hearing should be conducted in private. The Supreme Court of Ireland[70] first noted the inconvenience/impracticality rationale for not applying foreign procedural rules but then noted that 'it is by no means apparent than any particular degree of confusion or difficulty would result from having the proceedings in this case heard *in camera*'.[71] Hence, unlike a jury trial, there is no necessary logistical obstacle to a court conducting proceedings in private. The court then noted that while it was arguable that the question of proceedings being held in public was 'more than merely procedural . . . one must not be misled by the fact that the rule, at least in the Irish context, has a significant constitutional dimension'.[72] The constitutional reference here is to article 34.1 of the Irish Constitution, which provides that justice should generally be 'administered in public'. To give weight to this constitutional aspect on the question of classification, the court said, would be 'to assume that a rule classified in one way for internal law purposes must be classified in the same way in order to resolve a conflicts of law issue'.[73] In other words, the court very properly recognized the danger of employing the 'Cook heresy' to make the classification. Ultimately, though, the court did not have to resolve the issue because it found that no choice of law issue arose and that Irish domestic law, expressed in article 34.1 of the Constitution, required the proceedings to be heard in public. In a separate judgment Denham J agreed,[74] although her Honour was prepared to hold more emphatically that the public hearing requirement was 'fundamentally procedural' for the purposes of the conflict of laws.[75] On balance, therefore, this conclusion is correct, given the issue's close link to the conduct of court proceedings.

---

[70] Keane J (with whom Hamilton CJ, Barrington J, and Murphy J agreed).
[71] ibid para 28.
[72] ibid para 29.
[73] ibid para 29.
[74] ibid para 60.
[75] ibid para 56.

A. Court Proceedings

10. Notice before Action and Other Condition Precedent Provisions

(a) Notice before Action Provisions

6.22 A more difficult issue which has arisen in a number of recent cases is the classification of statutory provisions that require a party to give notice, often as a precondition to commencing proceedings. In English and Commonwealth decisions, where the right-remedy approach to substance and procedure has been applied, notice requirements have been considered procedural on the basis that they relate to 'enforcement' of actions rather than the creation or extinguishment of rights.[76] So, in *Base Metal Trading Ltd v Shamurin*,[77] Arden LJ suggested that the requirement under English law that a shareholder serve a notice on the company which is the object of a derivative suit was procedural. Similarly, in an Australian decision,[78] the obligation in a contract on a claimant to give notice in writing to a carrier of loss or damage in respect of which a claim is to be made before commencing proceedings was held to be a matter of procedure.

6.23 In the United States, notice before action provisions have also been considered procedural but for the arguably more principled reason that they relate to a matter of important public policy of the forum, namely the ability to control access to its courts and to require plaintiffs to bring their actions in a particular manner.[79] One US commentator has, however, rejected this approach, saying that since the purpose of such provisions is to 'retard the ability of plaintiffs to succeed in prosecuting claims',[80] a substantive classification is more apposite.

6.24 The issue of statutory duties to provide notice before commencing proceedings has been more recently considered in Australia under the narrower 'mode or conduct of proceedings' definition of procedure. The provision in question was section 9(1) of the Personal Injuries Proceedings Act 2002 (Qld) (PIPA 2002) which provides that: 'Before starting a proceeding in a court based on a claim, the claimant must give written notice of the claim, in the approved form, to the person against whom the proceeding is proposed to be started.'

---

[76] See also *Dicey, Morris and Collins* (n 45 above) 4th Cumulative Supplement (2010) para 7.003.
[77] [2005] 1 WLR 1157, para 68.
[78] *Allan J Panozza and Co Pty Ltd v Allied Interstate (Q) Pty Ltd* [1976] 2 NSWLR 192, 196 (NSWCA).
[79] *Vest v St Albans Psychiatric Hospital Inc* 387 SE 2d 282 (W Va 1989).
[80] McDougal (n 46 above) 411.

6.25 The status of this provision was considered by the New South Wales Court of Appeal, in respect of a tort occurring in Queensland, in *Hamilton v Merck and Co Inc*.[81] The court was unanimous in its decision but two separate judgments were delivered. In the first, given by Spigelman CJ (with whom Tobias JA agreed),[82] it was first noted that a notice before action requirement was a matter 'capable of satisfying the [*Pfeiffer*] test for a substantive law expressed in terms of "enforceability" on the basis that, analogous to a statute of limitation, the effect of the notice not being provided was that the claimant was denied 'the right to institute proceedings at all'.[83] Further, the judge noted, the use of the language 'before starting a proceeding in a court' at the outset of section 9 suggested a condition precedent 'that can be characterised as substantive' at least 'if that formulation were employed in a legislative scheme that creates a new right or . . . entirely substitutes a legislative scheme for pre-existing common law rights'.[84] Spigelman CJ cited the example of New Zealand legislation which created a statutory no-fault liability scheme in place of common law rights.[85] The implication, therefore, is that had the present notice requirement been contained in legislation of this type, it would have been considered substantive. However, the Queensland legislation under consideration did not create a new right or substitute a legislative scheme for common law rights; the legislation was 'based on the pre-existing scheme for motor vehicle accidents' in an earlier statute.[86] This approach is a good example of both contextual and provision-specific analysis in application of the substance-procedure dichotomy. While the language of the provision may be considered substantive in isolation, according to Spigelman CJ, in the context of an enactment which does not take away common law rights, it becomes procedural. Yet this approach may also be questioned: why should the substance/procedure characterization of a provision be influenced by whether the rights in issue are new or 'existing'? Surely a precondition to the exercise of an existing common law right is just as burdensome or significant a barrier as one imposed on a new statutory right. Presumably, according to Spigelman CJ, had the notice provision been contained in legislation which created a new statutory right, he would have found it substantive.

---

[81] (2006) 66 NSWLR 48.
[82] ibid para 165.
[83] ibid para 39.
[84] ibid para 61.
[85] See Accident Rehabilitation and Compensation Insurance Act 1992 (NZ) considered in *James Hardie & Co Pty Ltd v Hall* (1998) 43 NSWLR 554.
[86] *Hamilton v Merck and Co Inc* (2006) 66 NSWLR 48, paras 67, 69. The earlier legislation was the Motor Accident Insurance Act 1994 (Qld).

A. Court Proceedings

Spigelman CJ then proceeded to apply the reasoning from a Queensland decision,[87] in which similar legislation had been interpreted, on the effect of the notice before action provision. In that case, it had been said that the aim of such a provision was 'to force the claimant toward negotiating a settlement of the claim before bringing an action in court. One of the objects of the [legislation] . . . is to encourage the speedy resolution of such claims. To that extent, the principal purpose or effect of those provisions is procedural or forensic'.[88] The encouragement of 'speedy resolution of claims' can clearly be seen as an aspect or function of judicial administration, and hence procedural. Next, Spigelman CJ found evidence in the PIPA 2002 legislative scheme that 'steps may [still] be taken in legal proceedings' despite the apparent prohibition on proceeding in the absence of satisfying the notice requirement.[89] Further, the power conferred in the statute to allow the proceedings to continue in the absence of a notice is not the same as the power of the court to grant an extension of time under a limitation statute given that the PIPA 2002 power is expressed in general terms.[90] What therefore appears decisive for Spigelman CJ in adopting a procedural classification of the notice requirement in the *Merck* case is that the absence of such a notice did *not* have the effect of extinguishing the plaintiff's cause of action in the same manner as non-compliance with a statute of limitation would have. Hence the impact on the capacity of the parties to enforce their rights and obligations was limited when compared with the strong connection between the notice requirement and the mode and conduct of court proceedings.[91]

6.26

There was a second judgment in the *Merck* decision, by Handley JA (again with whom Tobias JA agreed), that reached the same conclusion, although expressed more in the language of the right-remedy distinction. According to Handley JA, the notice provision here only regulated 'the manner in which the rights and duties of the parties are to be enforced or their enjoyment secured by judicial remedy'[92] and did not prevent the claimant from enforcing its rights in the way that resulted from non-compliance with a limitation provision. The second part of this sentence is the crucial

6.27

---

[87] *Young v Keong* [1999] 2 Qd R 335 (QCA).
[88] ibid 336–7 (McPherson JA) quoted by Spigelman CJ at para 86, with approval expressed at para 91.
[89] *Hamilton v Merck and Co Inc* (2006) 66 NSWLR 48 paras 94–95; eg under s 18(1)(a), after a certain time period has passed, the claimant may proceed with its action on the presumption that notice has been given and under s 18(1)(c) the court is given a general discretion to proceed despite non-compliance with the notice requirement.
[90] ibid para 101.
[91] ibid para 102.
[92] ibid para 143.

158   *Chapter 6: Judicial Administration*

element: the claimant's action was not extinguished by its failure to comply with the notice provision and so, on balance, a procedural classification was more appropriate.

6.28 Thus, overall, the *Merck* decision is not a general authority on the status of notice clauses: despite finding the requirement to be procedural on the facts of the case, the court appears to acknowledge that in certain circumstances, such a provision may be classified as substantive. So, for example, it is suggested that where a notice before action provision exists which if not complied with would result in the claimant's action being extinguished, then it should be considered substantive as such a provision has a direct impact on the enforceability of the rights and duties of the parties.[93]

6.29 The *Merck* case has since been applied in two more recent decisions, to declare procedural both the notice provision in the PIPA 2002[94] and a requirement that a claimant, 'before commenc[ing] court proceedings', provide the defendant with 'a pre-filing statement setting out particulars' of its claim.[95]

(b) Other Condition Precedent Provisions

6.30 Apart from notice before action provisions there are often other administrative hurdles such as medical certificates and mediation requirements with which a claimant must comply before an action can be brought. In the *Merck* case, the New South Wales Court of Appeal held that for the same reasons as applied in the case of the notice provision, a requirement that there be a conference of the parties before commencing an action was procedural.[96] Such a conclusion is consistent with the view that such requirements relate to the forum's management of its own proceedings[97] and assist in ensuring that only genuine cases proceed to trial. These measures may be distinguished from notice before action provisions which, if not complied with, would extinguish the claimant's cause of action.

---

[93] It is interesting to note that the Queensland District Court, in a case decided before *Merck*, held that a requirement to give notice under the Motor Accidents Act 1988 (NSW), s 42 was substantive and applicable to an action in Queensland in respect of a New South Wales tort; see *Hooper v Robinson* [2002] QDC 80. Similarly to the legislation in *Merck*, however, a failure to give notice did not extinguish the claimant's cause of action under the NSW statute.

[94] *Kok v Sheppard* [2009] NSWSC 1262, para 37.

[95] *Hodgson v Dimbola Pty Ltd* [2009] ACTSC 59, para 24. The legislative provision was the Workplace Injury Management and Workers Compensation Act 1998 (NSW), s 315.

[96] *Hamilton v Merck and Co Inc* (2006) 66 NSWLR 48, para 103 (Spigelman CJ), para 143 (Handley JA).

[97] R Mortensen, 'Homing Devices in Choice of Tort Law: Australian, British and Canadian Approaches' (2006) 55 ICLQ 839, 876 but see the comment of McDougal at 6.23.

B. COSTS AND LAWYERS' FEES

1. Costs

(a) Commonwealth

The position under the laws of Commonwealth countries regarding the classification of costs is reasonably settled. The term costs in this context generally refers to fees incurred by the lawyers representing the parties and in Commonwealth jurisdictions the normal rule is that costs follow the event, that is, the successful party is entitled to recover its costs from the losing side, although the forum court typically retains a discretion. Where the question relates to what law should be applied to the determination of costs at the time of judgment, the law of the forum has exclusive application. This proposition has been confirmed by Canadian,[98] Australian,[99] Scottish,[100] and African[101] courts and is also implicit in English[102] and Hong Kong[103] judgments. In *Somers v Fournier*[104] the Ontario Court of Appeal noted that the purpose of costs is to encourage settlement, penalize inappropriate conduct in proceedings, and generally facilitate the management and control of the litigation process. Costs are therefore 'an essential tool designed . . . to make the machinery of the forum court run smoothly' and to aid courts 'in administering their machinery'. Costs are also incidental to the rights of the parties[105] in that they are awarded at the conclusion of litigation and so not determinative of outcome (although, under Commonwealth law, they normally follow the outcome). Consequently, the court's power to award costs is best seen as a tool in the forum court's management of its proceedings and therefore properly subject to forum law.[106]

6.31

---

[98] *Somers v Fournier* (2002) 60 OR (3d) 225 (Ont CA); *Bachand v Roberts* (1996) 7 CPC (4th) 93, para 6 (Ont Gen Div).
[99] *Labuda v Langford* [2001] ACTSC 126, para 6.
[100] *Wimpey Construction (UK) Ltd v Martin Black & Co (Wire Ropes) Ltd* [1988] SLT 637.
[101] *Preferential Trade Area Bank v ESCOM* (High Court of Malawi 2003) cited in R Oppong, 'A Decade of Private International Law in African Courts 1997–2007 (Part I)' (2007) 9 YBPIL 223, 241.
[102] See eg *Union Discount Co Ltd v Zoller* [2002] 1 All ER 693 (CA).
[103] *Peregrine Fixed Income Ltd v JP Morgan Chase Bank* [2005] HKCFI 71, para 74.
[104] (2002) 60 OR (3d) 225, paras 17–18.
[105] ibid para 19.
[106] Spiro (n 31 above) 958.

(b) European Union

6.32 The principle that forum law applies to costs has been confirmed in a number of European decisions where challenges have been brought to costs orders by the court of origin at the stage of recognition and enforcement of the court's judgment in a foreign jurisdiction. The general approach taken in these cases has been to uphold a costs order of the court of origin[107] unless the amount of the award was so excessive and disproportionate as to offend the public policy of the law of the country of recognition.[108] In the *Pordea* case, the public policy of the law of the country of recognition was sourced in an international instrument, article 6(1) of the European Convention on Human Rights, which provides for a right of access to courts. Such access to justice was found to be denied where costs were set at a disproportionately high level. This decision is a rare example of forum law (in the sense of the law of the country of origin) on procedural matters being overridden by transnational standards. By contrast, the use of a different *basis* for awarding costs by the court of origin (for example a rule which provides no general right to reimbursement of costs as is the case generally in the United States) has been held not to offend the public policy of the country of recognition.[109] Furthermore, in a German decision, it was held that a party which had retained a foreign lawyer in litigation before the German courts, was only required to pay the amount of costs that would be charged by an equivalent German lawyer.[110] This conclusion flowed from the fact that the law of the forum applies to costs. The court also held, importantly, that restrictions on costs under forum law do not violate principles of EU law, specifically, articles 49 and 50 of the EU Treaty (dealing with freedom of movement of workers) and

---

[107] See eg *Re The Enforcement of a United States Judgment for Damages* (Bundesgerichthof Case IX ZR 149/91 4 June 1992) [1994] IL Pr 602; Oberlandesgericht Hamm (23 W 34/99 16 October 2000) [2002] ECLY 1191. The Supreme Court of Japan has taken a similar view, see *Judgment upon case concerning 'judgment of a foreign court' as provided in Article 24 of the Law on Civil Enforcement and the judgment of Hong Kong High Court ordering the payment of court costs* [1998] JPSC 24 (28 April 1998) (costs orders of the forum court are to be enforced provided they do not exceed the costs actually incurred).

[108] *Pordea v Times Newspapers Ltd* [2000] IL Pr 763 (Court of Cassation 16 March 1999) (English judgment for costs not enforced in France); *Coburn v The Auxiliary Insurance Fund for Covering Liability Arising from Car Accidents* [2008] IL Pr 9 (Areios Pagos 17 November 2006) (English judgment not enforced in Greece).

[109] *Re the Enforcement of a United States Judgment for Damages* [1994] IL Pr 602. The court there also suggested that the existence of rules in the country of origin which allow contingency fee arrangements would not violate the public policy of the country of recognition.

[110] Bundesgerichthof (VIII ZB 55/04 8 March 2005) [2005] ECLY 217.

Council Directive (EEC) 77/249 (facilitating the right of lawyers to provide services).

(c) United States

In the United States the issue of applicable law in respect of costs is complicated by the fact that different regimes for awarding lawyers' costs apply: some states adopt the Commonwealth 'loser pays' rule, while the majority provide that each party will bear its own costs regardless of outcome. There is also no consensus in the United States as to the approach to be taken on applicable law and costs. The US Second Restatement makes only a brief reference to the issue, suggesting that costs should be governed by forum law on the basis that they relate to the regulation of litigation.[111] Such an approach corresponds to the Commonwealth position referred to at 6.31, and has been applied by a number of US courts.[112]   **6.33**

By contrast, other US courts have classified lawyers' costs or 'attorneys fees' as substantive, and applied the law of the cause of action to determine whether they should be awarded.[113] According to this view, rules on attorneys' fees concern 'much more than the mere process of litigation' and instead grant certain substantive rights to the parties. For example, the Commonwealth loser-pays rule has been described as 'creat[ing] a quasi-right of action for "wrongful" legal costs. The prevailing plaintiff enjoys a right to recover attorneys fees for having needed to vindicate [its] rights through litigation' while 'the prevailing defendant enjoys a right to recover . . . fees for having . . . to defend . . . a claim that should not   **6.34**

---

[111] Restatement (Second), § 122 comment a.

[112] See eg under the law of *Florida*: *BDO Seidman LLP v British Car Auctions Inc* 802 So 2d 366 (CA Fla 2001); *Illinois*: *Midwest Grain Products of Illinois Inc v Productization Inc* 228 F 3d 784 (7th Cir 2000); *Louisiana*: *Wooley v Lucksinger* 14 So 3d 311 (CA La 2008); *New Jersey*: *Chin v Chrysler LLC* 538 F 3d 272, 279 (3rd Cir 2008) and *Mitzel v Westinghouse Electric Corp* 72 F 3d 414, 418 (3rd Cir 1995); and *Wyoming*: *Smithco Engineering Inc v International Fabricators Inc* 775 P 2d 1011 (Sup Ct Wyo 1989). cf *Minnesota*: *Bannister v Bemis Co Inc* 2008 WL 2002087 *3 (D Minn 2008) and *Nebraska*: *Dernick Resources Inc v Wilstein* 2007 WL 2688900 *3 (D Neb 2007) (forum law applied because attorney fees 'remedial').

[113] See eg under the law of *Arizona*: *Aries v Palmer Johnson Inc* 735 P 2d 1373 (Ariz CA 1987); *Arkansas*: *Calvert v Estate of Calvert* 259 SW 3d 456 (CA Ark 2007); *Georgia*: *Elberta Crate & Box Co v Cox Automation Systems LLC* 2005 WL 1972599 (MD Ga 2005); *Idaho*: *Boise Tower Associates LLC v Washington Capital Joint Master Trust Mortgage Income Fund* 2007 WL 4355815 (D Idaho); *Kansas*: *Atchison Casting Corp v DOFASCO Inc* 1995 WL 655183 (D Kan 1995); *New York*: *RLS Associates Inc v United Bank of Kuwait plc* 464 F Supp 2d 206 (SDNY 2006); *Oklahoma*: *Boyd Rosene and Associates Inc v Kansas Municipal Gas Agency* 174 F 3d 1115 (10th Cir 1999); *Texas*: *Fairmont Supply Co v Hooks Industrial Inc* 177 SW 3d 529 (Tex App 2005) and *Midwest Medical Supply Co LLC v Wingert* 317 SW 3d 530 (Tex App 2010).

have been brought'.[114] A party's right to recover attorney fees is therefore analogous to a civil cause of action. An alternative rationale for a substantive characterization is that it deters forum shopping by not making the award of attorney fees dependent upon choice of forum.[115] The consequence of the substantive view is that parties may stipulate by contract the applicable law in respect of lawyer fees either by a term expressly referring to such fees or by a general choice of law provision. A third approach classifies lawyer costs as substantive where they relate to the outcome of litigation but procedural where they are awarded for bad faith or vexatious conduct by a lawyer, such as for wilful violation of a court order.[116] A final approach classifies lawyers' fees as substantive but nevertheless applies forum law on the basis of overriding public policy. Specifically, non-reciprocal agreements whereby only one party to the litigation is entitled to an award of attorney fees or agreements which provide for recovery of fees only in limited circumstances, even where valid under foreign law, are unenforceable in the forum on the ground of unconscionability.[117]

6.35 The reason for including this extended discussion of costs in US law is that it may suggest an alternative pathway for Commonwealth courts in the future. As contingency fees become more widely accepted and costs awards become ever greater in proportion to the complexity of litigation, legislatures may choose to revisit the application of the loser pays rule in all litigation. At the same time and consequently, parties may increasingly seek to control the risk of costs by contractually selecting a certain law to determine the issue in advance of any dispute. For such a strategy to be effective, however, Commonwealth courts would need to reconsider their blanket procedural classification of lawyer costs or at least allow an exception to this rule where parties expressly choose the law to apply to the issue.

2. CONTINGENCY FEES

6.36 In the United States, there is widespread use of contingency fee agreements, whereby a lawyer acts for a party on the basis that he or she will only receive a fee for services if the litigation for which the lawyer is engaged is

---

[114] *RLS Associates Inc v United Bank of Kuwait plc* 464 F Supp 2d 206, 218 (SDNY 2006).

[115] *Boise Tower Associates LLC v Washington Capital Joint Master Trust Mortgage Income Fund* 2007 WL 4355815 (D Idaho).

[116] *Servicios Comerciales Andinos SA v GE del Caribe* 145 F 3d 463 (1st Cir 1998); *Boyd Rosene and Associates Inc v Kansas Municipal Gas Agency* 174 F 3d 1115, 1126 (10th Cir 1999).

[117] See eg in California, *ABF Capital Corp v Grove Properties Co* 126 Cal App 4th 204 (CA Cal 2005); *Kim v Hayes Lemmerz International Inc* 2007 WL 1566713 (CA Cal).

successful. In *Mitzel v Westinghouse Electric Co*[118] forum law was held to govern the regulation of contingency fee arrangements, since they are formed between lawyer and client, which is a fiduciary relationship involving an imbalance of power and so of special concern to the court in which the litigation was conducted. Public policy, rather than a procedural characterization, seems to be the basis for applying forum law. By contrast, in *Hoiles v Alioto*,[119] the validity and interpretation of a contingency fee agreement was treated as a substantive matter and governed by the law applicable to the contract. In Commonwealth countries both views would seem to be arguable, although a court may also consider the issue to be procedural given its proximity to the conduct of litigation and relatively slimmer connection to the rights and liabilities of the parties.

3. Security for Costs/Security Bonds

6.37 The issue of security for costs, where a defendant requests that a claimant post a bond in advance of any trial to cover the legal fees of the defendant (in the event that the claimant is unsuccessful), requires separate consideration in terms of applicable law. Again, the basic position in Commonwealth jurisdictions is that the rules of the forum exclusively determine whether an order for security should be made.[120] Occasionally, however, Commonwealth courts will, in determining whether to order security in the case of a non-resident claimant, look to the law of the claimant's country on enforcement of foreign judgments to determine whether a costs order of the forum would be enforced.[121] To that extent, therefore, foreign procedural law has some role to play in determining whether security should be ordered. Although orders for security for costs are not generally awarded by US courts, it is likely that this issue would also be governed by forum law on the basis that it is integral to a court's control of its own proceedings and is a method for securing obedience to a court's orders.[122] Accordingly, in one US decision, the English security for costs rule was not applied on the public policy ground that it would deny access to justice to poorer litigants in the US forum.[123]

6.38 Note, however, that there are treaty provisions which may operate to limit the monopoly of forum law in a given case. For example, an 'equality of

---

[118] 72 F 3d 414 (3rd Cir 1995).
[119] 461 F 3d 1224 (10th Cir 2006).
[120] See *Nasser v United Bank of Kuwait* [2002] 1 WLR 1868 (CA).
[121] *Letendre v SYSCO Food Service of Atlantic Canada* 2008 NSSC 105 (Sup Ct Nova Scotia); *Lesecq v Ottawa Montessori School* (2008) 89 OR (3d) 62 (Ont SCJ).
[122] Restatement (Second), § 130 comment a; see 6.80 below.
[123] *Standard Reserve Holdings Ltd v Downey* 2004 WL 3316264 (Md Cir Ct).

164 *Chapter 6: Judicial Administration*

treatment' provision may require that an English court should not order security against a foreign resident claimant where it would not do so against an English resident claimant.[124] German law also modifies the strict application of forum law to security by reference to the principle of reciprocity. The general rule is that a foreign claimant will be required to post security before a German court unless it can show that a German claimant would not be so compelled before the foreign party's own courts.[125]

6.39 A related matter is where a party is required to post a bond to cover the costs of potential harm to the other party in an application for an interim measure, such as an interlocutory injunction. US courts have unanimously held that the law of the forum has exclusive application to the question of whether a bond should be ordered.[126] The drafters of the Restatement support this conclusion on the basis that a bond is a method of securing obedience to court orders.[127] While the issue has not been raised before a Commonwealth court, the US view would almost certainly be adopted on the basis that the payment of a bond is central to the court's conduct and control of its own proceedings.

C. STATUTORY 'NO ACTION' CLAUSES

1. Generic Court Provisions

6.40 Within this category are statutory provisions which provide that 'no [court] action may be brought' in certain circumstances, such as where a contract is not in writing, where the claimant (for example an agent) is unlicensed, or where such action may only be brought with the leave of the court. A feature of these provisions is that that no specific court is mentioned but court action *in general* is proscribed. Some cases have involved forum legislation and others enactments of foreign jurisdictions.

6.41 The old English case of *Leroux v Brown*[128] is an example of a statutory provision of the forum in the above terms. In that case, the court found that an oral contract governed by and valid and enforceable under French law

---

[124] See eg *Pera Tourism Inc v Savile Row Tours and Travel Ltd* [1998] IL Pr 407 (Central London County Court) (United Kingdom-Turkey Convention 1931, art 12).

[125] Bundesgerichtshof (VIII ZR 198/80) [1984] ECLY 74; Oberlandesgerichthof Koblenz [1998] ECLY 1003.

[126] *Dombrovski v Sirius International Ins Corp* 2007 WL 2624804 (ND Oh); *Stephens v National Distillers and Chemical Corp* 1993 WL 228851 (SDNY); *Apache Village Inc v Coleman Co* 776 P 2d 1154 (Colo App 1989).

[127] Restatement (Second), § 130 comment a; see 6.80 below.

[128] (1852) 12 CB 801.

C. Statutory 'No Action' Clauses 165

(the law of the cause of action) nevertheless could not be enforced in England because it was not in writing as required by the Statute of Frauds. The reason for the court's conclusion was that the writing requirement was procedural and applied to the contract as part of the law of the forum. As noted in Chapter 7,[129] this decision has been criticized on this aspect, given that the imposition of a writing requirement for an enforceable contract plainly affects the rights and duties of the parties and so should be regarded as substantive. Such a classification has in fact been made in US, Australian, and Canadian decisions.[130] It is, however, noted at 7.30 that the application of forum law in cases involving similar statutory provisions to that in *Leroux v Brown* may sometimes be more defensible today under the doctrine of public policy and overriding forum mandatory rules. Instead of focusing upon whether the writing requirement was procedural a court could conclude, in certain circumstances, that a statutory provision is mandatory in character and must be applied in every action brought in the forum, regardless of the applicable law. Such a result could be justified by the fact that forum policy is contravened by allowing certain contracts to be enforced without writing given the risk of fraud and also as a legitimate basis on which the forum seeks to control access to its courts. Some US courts have reached this result.[131]

6.42 What position have other Commonwealth courts in more recent cases taken in respect of such provisions which prevent the institution of actions? In an Australian case involving a forum statute one judge suggested, pertinently, that to characterize such a provision as procedural 'might seem an altogether excessive manifestation of the inveterate tendency of the common law to conceal questions of substantive law under procedural masks'.[132] The judge did not consider in that case, however, whether the provision could have applied as an overriding mandatory rule. Similar statutory provisions of the forum have been considered in a number of Canadian cases. In *Bateman & Litman Real Estate Ltd v Big T Motel Ltd*[133] the court refused to apply a forum enactment to prevent an unlicensed agent from suing to recover a commission on the ground that the provision was substantive and not applicable where foreign law was the proper law of the contract. The court applied the right / remedy distinction, concluding that the statute did not merely bar the remedy but extinguished the right to recover by unlicensed persons. No reference was made to whether the

---

[129] See 7.27 below.
[130] See cases discussed ibid.
[131] See cases discussed at 7.30 below.
[132] *Australian Continental Resources Ltd v ATS* (1974) 8 SASR 127, 133–4 (SC SA Bray CJ).
[133] (1964) 44 DLR (2d) 474 (Sask QB) (affd 49 DLR (2d) 480).

enactment could have applied as an overriding mandatory rule of the forum.

6.43 In *Block Bros Realty Ltd v Mollard*[134] a British Columbia court had to consider a similar statutory provision of the forum and reached the same result as in the *Bateman* case, although by a more contemporary approach to substance and procedure. Instead of relying on the right / remedy distinction, the court stated that 'legislation should be categorized as procedural only if the question is beyond any doubt. If there is any doubt, [it] should be resolved by holding that the legislation is substantive'.[135] What was particularly influential on the court was the outcome determinative nature of the issue: here the decision on whether the legislation applied would determine whether the action could proceed.[136] In *Block Bros* the defendant also argued that the legislation should nonetheless apply on the basis of local public policy, the argument being that the court should not encourage suits by unlicensed agents, wherever they or the land may be located. The court disagreed, saying that to allow the action to proceed would not offend 'conceptions of essential justice and morality'.[137] A similar approach was taken in another Canadian decision in which forum legislation rendering void gambling contracts and prohibiting suits to enforce such agreements[138] was held not to apply to an action to recover a debt under a loan contract for gambling, which was governed by Nevada law.[139] The *Block Bros* case was applied in support of the view that an enactment should be presumed to be substantive in effect unless its terms are clearly procedural.[140] The court also gave two further reasons for applying forum law: the right / remedy distinction and, more appropriately, the fact that the local legislation was not intended to apply to events which took place outside the forum.

6.44 A different approach to an identical statute in the gaming context was taken by the Singapore Court of Appeal in *Star City Pty Ltd v Tan Hong Woon*.[141] This case involved a Singaporean resident who had been lent money to gamble at a casino in New South Wales, Australia, with the terms of the facility being governed by New South Wales law. In an action

---

[134] (1981) 122 DLR (3d) 323 (BCCA).
[135] ibid 328.
[136] ibid 327–8.
[137] ibid 330.
[138] Gaming Act 1845 (UK) applying with imperial force in Canada.
[139] *Horseshoe Club Operating Co v Bath* [1998] 3 WWR 128 (BCSC); see also *Boardwalk Regency Corp v Maalouf* (1992) 88 DLR (4th) 612 (Ont CA).
[140] ibid para 7.
[141] [2002] 2 SLR 22; this decision was followed by the High Court of Malaysia in *Jupiters Ltd v Lim Kin Tong* [2005] MLJU 534.

C. Statutory 'No Action' Clauses

to recover the unpaid loan in Singapore, the court refused to enforce the contract on the basis of section 5(2) of the Civil Law Act 1999 (Sing), which is very similar to section 18 of the Gaming Act 1845 (UK). The sub-section provides that 'no action shall be brought . . . in the court for recovering any sum of money . . . alleged to be won upon any wager'. The court applied the right / remedy distinction to hold that this provision was procedural, because it regulated proceedings and concerned the enforceability of rights rather than the validity or existence of the right itself. To buttress this conclusion in favour of forum law, the court then held in the alternative that the foreign cause of action should not be recognized in Singapore because it would be contrary to local public policy. While Singapore will enforce a transaction for a genuine loan, it will not allow foreign casinos to bring actions to recover gambling debts. This argument on public policy was reinforced by the 'mandatory wording' of section 5(2), requiring that *'no action shall* be brought', which was clearly intended to apply to all gambling contracts sought to be enforced in Singapore, whatever their governing law.

While opinions may differ as to the propriety of enforcing gambling contracts, the public policy and overriding mandatory rules approaches are certainly to be preferred as mechanisms for applying forum law over the procedural characterization, given their greater transparency. A limitation of the overriding mandatory rules approach, however, is that it has generally only been applied where legislation, not common law rules, is involved and a problem with public policy as an exclusionary doctrine is that it has traditionally received only a narrow interpretation in Commonwealth rules of private international law. **6.45**

A Canadian decision which also adopts an overriding mandatory rules approach to interpreting forum legislation is *Avenue Properties Ltd v First City Development Corporation Ltd*.[142] This case concerned a contract for the sale of land in Ontario between an Albertan company as vendor and a British Columbian company as purchaser which was governed by Ontario law. In an action by the vendor for specific performance of the contract, the purchaser argued that a provision of a British Columbian statute,[143] which required the vendor to submit a prospectus to a government authority and deliver it to the purchaser, had not been complied with. The court held that the provision applied to the proceedings in the forum but not because it was procedural. Rather, the provision was an overriding mandatory enactment which applied to all contracts where a person solicited **6.46**

---

[142] (1986) 32 DLR (4th) 40 (BCCA).
[143] Real Estate Act 1979 (BC), s 62.

168   *Chapter 6: Judicial Administration*

the sale of land to persons in British Columbia, whether the land was located in the forum or outside. The legislation could not be avoided by parties choosing the law of another country or province. Put in other terms, the court said it would be contrary to public policy to enforce a contract made in clear contravention of a forum statute. This approach is significant because it again shows a willingness to address directly the reasons why forum law should be applied in a given case. Instead of simply using a label or a badge such as procedural, with no other reasoning in support, the court considered that the legislation was intended to apply to transactions with a significant foreign element.

2. 'Leave of the Court' Provisions

6.47 Another type of statute is one which requires a party to obtain the leave of an unnamed court before commencing an action. Again, there has been no consistency of view as to whether such a requirement is substantive or procedural. In *Harding v Wealands*[144] Arden LJ of the English Court of Appeal suggested that the requirement (now expressed in section 260 of the Companies Act 2006 (UK)) to obtain the leave of an English court before commencing a derivative suit was procedural. Similarly, in an Australian decision[145] it was said, with little reasoning, that an injured plaintiff's right to enforce 'with the leave of the court' its charge against an insurer in respect of moneys payable by the insurer by way of indemnity against the liability of the insured was procedural. A contrary result in respect of very similar legislation was, however, reached in *Farquharson Pty Ltd v FAI General Insurance Co Ltd*,[146] although in this case, unlike *Dixon*, the leave requirement was found in foreign legislation, not a forum statute. In the *Farquharson* case the court held that the creation of the statutory charge and the requirement to obtain leave of the court were inseparably intertwined. As a grant of leave was essential to the enforcement of the charge and the institution of any action, it was characterized as substantive.[147] Given the close interrelationship between the leave requirement and the capacity to bring an action under this legislation, the view in *Farquharson* is to be preferred.

6.48 By contrast, in a Canadian case a requirement in foreign legislation that a claimant could only sue a defendant, who had been declared bankrupt, with the leave of the court was held to be procedural and so not applicable

---

[144] [20051 WLR 1539, para 62 (revd on other grounds [2007] 2 AC 1); this position was supported in *Waddington Ltd v Chan Chun Hoo Thomas* [2008] HKCFA 63, para 55.
[145] *Dixon v Royal Insurance Australia Ltd* (1991) 105 ACTR 1 (SC ACT).
[146] [1998] VSC 106 (SC Vic).
[147] ibid para 19.

C. Statutory 'No Action' Clauses

in the forum.[148] The procedural characterization was supported on the ground that a leave requirement was a jurisdictional matter and foreign law cannot be relied upon to determine the forum's jurisdiction.[149] In the Canadian context, at least, this statement is no longer strictly accurate in the light of *Muscutt v Courcelles*,[150] which, as discussed,[151] now instructs Canadian courts to refer to foreign law on jurisdiction as one of the criteria in determining whether jurisdiction exists in the forum.

3. 'Named Court' Provisions: Vesting Jurisdiction

6.49 A different category of cases from those already mentioned arises where legislation identifies a *specific* court in which a proceeding must be brought as opposed to courts in general. This issue has arisen in a number of Canadian decisions. In two such cases, the following provision[152] was considered (which is still in force): 'no action shall be commenced except by the leave of [Her Majesty's Court of Queen's Bench for Saskatchewan]'.

6.50 In *Toronto-Dominion Bank v Martin*[153] the court held the enactment of the forum to be substantive on the basis that application of the provision would destroy the claimant's rights to enforce a contract governed by foreign law. The court emphasized that the scope of procedure should be restricted 'so as not to frustrate the fundamental purposes of conflict laws',[154] a prominent example of which is the recognition of foreign rights. Such an approach certainly reflects the more contemporary Commonwealth view of substance and procedure. Significantly, the court also considered whether the forum provision should apply as a matter of statutory construction. Similarly to the approach taken to determine whether a forum enactment may apply as an overriding mandatory rule, the court here suggested that a forum statutory provision may, by contrast, *not* be applied in the forum *even where it is classified as procedural under the forum's rules of private international law*.[155] The novelty of this approach is that it subordinates the common law substance procedure distinction to the 'higher' goal of legislative intent.[156] Such an approach is to be welcomed in that it

---

[148] *Nemaha Energy Inc v Wood and Locker Inc* (1985) 68 BCLR 187 (BCSC).
[149] ibid para 13.
[150] (2002) 60 OR (3d) 20.
[151] See 4.43–4.44 above.
[152] Land Contracts (Actions) Act (1978) (Sask), ss 3(1) and 2(b).
[153] (1985) 39 Sask R 60 (Sask QB).
[154] ibid para 5.
[155] ibid para 14.
[156] There was also some evidence of this approach in *Horseshoe Club Operating Co v Bath* [1998] 3 WWR 128 (BCSC), discussed at 6.43 above.

again confronts directly the issue of whether forum law should be applied in preference to foreign law, as opposed to using characterization as a subterfuge. In the *Toronto-Dominion Bank* case itself the court concluded that 'it was not the legislature's intention to subject the mortgagee in a foreign mortgage to the process of seeking leave in this jurisdiction, particularly when, at the time of the mortgage, the mortgagor was a resident of the foreign jurisdiction'. The legislative intent was rather that 'the contract under which the action is to be taken must involve land within [the forum]'. Hence, quite properly, the court found that legislative intention pointed against applying the forum statute, even if it had been classified as procedural in choice of law terms. This approach provides an alternative and valuable path to determining the question of whether forum (and also foreign) legislation should be applied.

6.51 In a later decision,[157] considering the same Saskatchewan provision, an Albertan court in contrast to the conclusion of Walker J in *Toronto-Dominion Bank*, held that the enactment was procedural. On closer inspection, however, the court's analysis was based more on whether the legislature *intended* the provision to apply to courts in Alberta. To that extent, there is some similarity with the approach taken by Walker J. The Albertan court noted that:[158] 'The only court that is vested with jurisdiction by the Act is the Court of Queens Bench of Saskatchewan. The application of the Act to an action in an Alberta court would mean that a mortgagee who wishes to sue in debt in an Alberta court must first get leave of the Saskatchewan court to be able to sue in the Alberta court. That simply cannot be.' The court then went on to emphasize the relationship between 'named court' provisions and jurisdiction, saying that a foreign legislature has no power to oust or direct the forum court in the existence or exercise of its own jurisdiction: 'A foreign rule which circumscribes the jurisdiction of this court will not be recognized by this court. The doors to this court cannot be closed by foreign legislators.'[159] This approach is based on the forum's policy of protecting its jurisdiction from foreign intrusion but again may need to be slightly qualified in the light of the direction in *Muscutt v Courcelles*[160] for forum courts to consider foreign law of jurisdiction in determining whether jurisdiction exists. Nevertheless, the court is to be applauded for not simply reaching its conclusion that forum law applies on a finding that the provision was merely procedural but instead clearly

---

[157] *Investors Group Trust Co Ltd v Capital City Savings and Credit Union Ltd* (1991) 118 AR 254 (Alta QB).
[158] ibid para 48.
[159] ibid para 50.
[160] (2002) 60 OR (3d) 20.

C. Statutory 'No Action' Clauses

articulating the policies at work in applying forum law. The same result was reached in a later Canadian decision interpreting similar inter-provincial legislation.[161]

There is also US authority which has refused to recognize foreign statutory provisions that purport to preclude proceedings in any court other than in the foreign country itself, although here a procedural classification was the tool used. In *Randall v Arabian American Oil Co*[162] a provision stating that a foreign labour tribunal had exclusive jurisdiction over any claim by an employee was held to be procedural and not binding on US courts.

6.52

New Zealand courts have taken a similar approach. In *Rimini Ltd v Manning Management and Marketing Pty Ltd*[163] the New Zealand High Court had to decide whether it would exercise jurisdiction in respect of a dispute concerning a franchise agreement which was governed by New Zealand law but whose performance took place in Australia. One issue which arose was whether the Contractual Remedies Act 1979 (NZ), which made significant changes to the common law of contract, would apply in proceedings in Australia. While the Act stipulated that relief under the Act may be granted by a court, with 'court' defined to include certain New Zealand tribunals, the New Zealand court nevertheless found that the Act did not preclude a foreign court from hearing suits under its provisions; its purpose was merely to define 'for domestic purposes' which courts in New Zealand had jurisdiction to apply the Act.[164] Accordingly, the statute's application in an Australian court was ultimately a matter for that tribunal applying its own rules of private international law.[165] Such an approach therefore applies the notion of legislative intent to prevent the provision being used to bar proceedings in the foreign court.

6.53

A contrasting approach is taken in the area of derivative suits and oppression actions involving companies. In this context, Canadian courts have consistently held that a provision in corporations legislation which states that a named court has the power to determine breaches of such legislation will be classified as substantive with that court having exclusive jurisdiction. A substantive approach is arguably justified here because of the serious consequences of the statutory derivative and oppression action for shareholders. Application of the law of the place of incorporation is therefore appropriate. So, in *Nord Resources Corporation v Nord Pacific Ltd*,[166] a New

6.54

---

[161] *Stoeterau v Crowsnest Air Ltd* (1995) 5 BCLR (3d) 251 (BCSC).
[162] 778 F 2d 1146 (5th Cir 1998); see also McDougal (n 46 above) 410.
[163] [2003] 3 NZLR 22 (High Ct).
[164] ibid para 45.
[165] ibid para 52.
[166] (2003) 263 NBR (2d) 205 (NBQB).

Brunswick court held that an oppression suit against a New Brunswick corporation governed by New Brunswick law could only be brought in the forum, not in a US court, because the forum legislation under which the action was pursued *required* that such proceedings be brought in the forum courts. Likewise in *Voyage Co Industries Inc v Craster*,[167] an oppression suit against a foreign corporation, governed by foreign law, could not be brought in the forum because the foreign statute which was part of the law of the cause of action required suit to be commenced in that place. The same approach was taken with the same result in *Zi Corporation v Steinberg*.[168] The statutory provision in each case was found to be substantive and applied in the forum where the foreign law was the law of the cause of action. There is also US authority to the same effect. In *Taylor v LSI Logic Corporation*[169] an oppression suit in Delaware against a Canadian company was dismissed on the ground that a Canadian statutory provision reserved exclusive jurisdiction to Canadian courts and was substantive.

4. 'Named Court' Provisions: Divesting Jurisdiction

6.55 A slightly different type of named court provision is one which *prohibits* actions being brought in a certain court as opposed to an enactment which confers exclusive jurisdiction on that court. In Australia, courts in a few cases have interpreted these provisions where they have arisen under a foreign law of the cause of action. However, instead of applying the substance / procedure distinction to determine whether the enactment should be applied in the forum, courts have applied the uniquely Australian 'no advantage' principle from the *Neilson* case,[170] which requires the forum court to apply the same law as would be applied by the foreign court in the territory of the law of the cause of action. The result is that not only is the foreign statute applied in the forum but the courts disregard the implicit territorial limitation in the statute in favour of a general, generic prohibition on suits wherever commenced.

6.56 In *Breavington v Godleman*,[171] which concerned an action in Victoria arising out of a tort committed in the Northern Territory governed by that place's law, the suit was not allowed to proceed due to a Territory statute which

---

[167] 1998 BCSC 1776.

[168] 2006 ABQB 92 (Alta QB).

[169] 715 A 2d 837 (SC Del 1998); see also *Locals 302 and 612 of the International Union of Operating Engineers v Blanchard* 2005 WL 2063852 (SDNY). In the *Locals* case the court also specifically held that a provision whereby leave of a foreign court was required was substantive and prevented proceedings going forward in the forum: *3–*4.

[170] *Neilson v Overseas Projects Corp of Victoria Ltd* (2005) 223 CLR 331.

[171] (1988) 169 CLR 41 (High Ct).

C. Statutory 'No Action' Clauses

prevented common law actions being brought 'in the Territory'.[172] The High Court held that Northern Territory law applied as the law of the cause of action and specifically, according to two judges,[173] this law was to be applied in the manner in which it would be adjudicated by a court in the territory of the law of the cause of action. Since no action could be brought in the place of the law of the cause of action, the suit was also barred in the forum.[174]

More recently, in *Amaca Pty Ltd v Frost*,[175] the New South Wales Court of Appeal had to consider an action in New South Wales arising out of a tort committed in New Zealand. New Zealand had established a statutory no-fault compensation scheme, which abolished recovery of common law damages. The New Zealand statute[176] provided that 'no person may bring proceedings independently of this Act, whether under any rule of law or any enactment, in any court in New Zealand, for damages'. The New South Wales court had to determine whether the reference to 'court in New Zealand' would also have the effect of barring an action for common law damages in New South Wales. The Court held that it did have this result by two distinct, although mutually reinforcing, routes. The first approach acknowledged that New Zealand law was applicable in New South Wales as the law of the cause of action. In determining whether the reference to the named court applied to bar suit in Australia, the court applied the no advantage/uniformity of outcome approach from *Neilson* to declare that, once foreign law was found to be the law of the cause of action, the forum must strive to reach the same result as the foreign court would applying its own law. Here it was clear that a New Zealand court would not have allowed the claimant to sue for common law damages arising from a New Zealand tort had the case been brought there. Consequently, the claimant in New South Wales 'should receive no advantage from suing in the Australian forum which the plaintiff could not obtain in the courts of the *lex loci delicti*'.[177] The prohibition on suit in New Zealand courts therefore effectively meant a prohibition on suit in *any* courts. In consequence, as was discussed in Chapter 3,[178] the effect of this approach, once the forum's choice of law rules have selected foreign law as the law of the cause of action and classified the issue in dispute as substantive, is that the foreign law must be applied to the issue (subject only to forum

6.57

---

[172] Motor Accidents (Compensation) Act 1979 (NT), s 5.
[173] (1988) 169 CLR 41, 98 (Wilson and Gaudron JJ).
[174] See also, to the same effect, *Wayte v Wayte* [2005] WADC 192 (Dist Ct WA).
[175] (2006) 67 NSWLR 635.
[176] Accident Insurance Act 1998 (NZ), s 394(1).
[177] *Amaca Pty Ltd v Frost* (2006) 67 NSWLR 635, para 82.
[178] See 3.10.

public policy). The forum must apply the same law and in the same manner as it would be applied by the foreign court.

6.58 The second approach adopted in the *Amaca* case, which also supported the finding that the New Zealand 'named court' provision should be applied to prevent proceedings being brought in New South Wales, relied on statutory interpretation. In examining the legislative history of the New Zealand provision it was clear that the New Zealand Parliament intended the provision to apply in all cases where the tort occurred in New Zealand and was governed by New Zealand law regardless of where the suit was brought.[179] Therefore, once again, as an alternative to choice of law methodology, courts can use a process of statutory construction to determine if a 'named court' provision in foreign legislation should apply in the forum. This approach is reminiscent of that adopted by Walker J in the *Toronto-Dominion Bank* case and is useful because of its transparent appraisal of why foreign law should be applied in a given case. Sometimes, as has been seen throughout this work, an approach based solely on the substance / procedure distinction (particularly the right-remedy approach) can mask this reality. Yet an approach based on statutory interpretation and intent can normally only be adopted where legislative rules are involved.

D. PRIORITIES AND RIGHTS OF CREDITORS

1. Priorities

6.59 Another example of judicial administration arguably arises where property is being distributed by a court and the asset fund is insufficient to satisfy the claims of all creditors. Typically this situation occurs where a defendant has gone into bankruptcy, a deceased person's estate is being administered, or a ship has been sold after being arrested in the forum and a number of creditors make claims to the proceeds. It has long been held in English law that questions relating to the administration and distribution of a debtor's assets, including issues of priority between creditors, are procedural matters governed by the law of the forum. The rationale for this view has been that matters of administration are remedial, since they involve the means by which the rights of creditors are enforced, rather than the establishment of the rights themselves.[180]

---

[179] *Amaca Pty Ltd v Frost* (2006) 67 NSWLR 635, para 125 (Spigelman CJ), para 133 (Santow JA), para 134 (McColl JA).
[180] *Cheshire, North and Fawcett* (n 62 above) 93.

D. Priorities and Rights of Creditors

A key question to consider is whether the same view of classification would apply under more contemporary Australian and Canadian views of substance and procedure, which typically define procedure more restrictively. One of the suggested approaches to defining substance and procedure is to define substantive as an issue which impacts on the rights and obligations of the parties, that is, is outcome determinative. Applying this idea, resolution of priorities between creditors clearly affects their rights and so could arguably be substantive.[181] According to another criterion, an issue is more likely to be procedural if it relates to the mode, conduct, or regulation of court proceedings. Application of this concept to an administration of a debtor's assets and determination of priorities between creditors is not easy. On one view an administration, being court-supervised and in the case of a bankruptcy or liquidation involving a court-appointed officer to determine the distribution of property, is closely connected to the judicial function. Yet it could equally be argued here that the issue does not involve the mechanics or machinery of litigation, such as determining whether proper service of process has occurred or what forms of proceeding are adopted. Instead, the court in an administration of assets is merely the forum by which certain acts affecting the rights of the parties are performed. On balance, however, public policy supports a procedural classification: it would be very impractical and difficult for a court to have to apply foreign rules on administration or priorities, such as the appointment of court officers, particularly where the administration involves large numbers of claims by creditors from different jurisdictions. In such a context, it may be impossible to select a single law for the entire administration: 'setting a plan of distribution would become a matter of nightmarish complexity'.[182] Therefore, in the interests of simplicity, consistency, and 'doing evenhanded justice between competing creditors',[183] a single law—the law of the forum—must be applied to determine the distribution of proceeds and ranking of claims. Thus it is suggested that the older authorities, which support a procedural classification, remain correct in their conclusion that forum law applies, although today the outcome is reached by a different rationale.

6.60

---

[181] This point was made by both the South African Court of Appeal in *The Andrico Unity* [1989] 4 SA 325 (A), para 72 and R Mason, 'Choice of Law in Cross-Border Insolvencies: Matters of Substance and Procedure' (2001) 9 Insolvency LJ 69, 84, yet both ultimately conclude that the issue of priorities is procedural. See also I Fletcher, *Insolvency in Private International Law* (OUP, 2nd edn, 2005) para 2.78.

[182] *The Andrico Unity* [1989] 4 SA 325 (A), paras 72–73.

[183] *The Halcyon Isle* [1981] AC 221, 230–1.

6.61 *Pardo v Bingham*[184] involved a British national who executed a document in Venezuela creating a debt in favour of G, who registered the instrument. The effect of registration under Venezuelan law was that G became entitled to be paid his debt out of the general assets of the debtor in priority to other creditors. In administration of the debtor's estate in England, however, the English court held that the fund must be distributed exclusively according to the principles of English law with no regard to the position under the law of the cause of action of any individual transaction. The estate was therefore divided among creditors without regard to any priority to any individual claimant under foreign law.

6.62 A similar result was reached in *Re Melbourn*[185] where the claimant would have lost priority under the law of the cause of action.[186] That case involved a husband and wife married in the Dutch colony at Batavia, who entered into a pre-marriage contract by which the husband promised the wife a sum of money for her separate use. Under the law of Batavia such a contract had no effect as regards third parties unless registered, and no registration had occurred. After the husband and wife came to England, the husband became bankrupt and the wife made a claim in the administration for the sum agreed. The court allowed the wife's claim to proceed on the basis that the failure to register the contract under Batavian law did not affect the validity of the obligation but was merely procedural in depriving the wife of any priority as regards third party creditors in any future administration. Since, however, English law exclusively governed the question of priority, the failure to register the contract under the law of the cause of action was irrelevant.[187]

6.63 The principle that priorities are determined by the law of the forum of administration has also been consistently applied in cases where a ship has been sold after arrest and a number of creditors make claims to the fund.[188]

6.64 Finally, there are two exceptions to the rule on priorities: the resolution of competing claims with respect to a debt and to immovable property is governed by the proper law of the debt[189] and the law of the place where the immovable is situated[190] respectively.

---

[184] (1868) LR 6 Eq 485.
[185] (1870) LR 6 Ch App 64.
[186] See also *The Colorado* [1923] P 102 (CA).
[187] See also *Thorburn v Steward* (1871) LR 3 PC 478 (PC).
[188] *The Colorado* [1923] P 102 (CA); *The Halcyon Isle* [1981] AC 221 (PC); *Fournier v The Ship Margaret 'Z'* [1999] 3 NZLR 111 (HCNZ); *The Ioannis Daskalelis* [1974] SCR 1248 (Sup Ct Can).
[189] *Kelly v Selwyn* [1905] 2 Ch 117.
[190] *Norton v Florence Land and Public Works Co* (1877) 7 Ch D 332.

2. Rights of Creditors

(a) England

A distinction must arguably be drawn between priorities and administra- **6.65**
tion of assets on the one hand, and the nature and status of the right of the
creditor who makes a claim to the fund on the other. This issue has arisen
often in the context of ship sales, where creditors seek to have their interest recognized in the forum as a maritime lien to obtain a higher position
in the ranking of securities. It is strongly arguable that the nature and
validity of such a right should be classified as substantive and governed
by the law applicable to the right.[191] Unlike the issue of priorities, there is
no serious inconvenience to the court in determining the nature and existence of such a right any more than there would be in giving effect to foreign
rights under a contract or a tort. Recognition of such a right would also not
affect the mode or conduct of local court proceedings and would often be
outcome determinative. Even under the right-remedy view, it seems hard
to classify such a right as merely remedial. The English Court of Appeal
adopted a substantive classification of a creditor's security interest over
eighty years ago in *The Colorado*.[192] That case involved a priorities dispute
arising from the proceeds of sale of a French ship. One of the competing
interests was an 'hypothèque' registered under French law, which according to expert evidence accepted by the court, created rights and obligations
analogous to a maritime lien under English law. Having ascertained the
status of the French interest under its governing law, the court then applied
English law to give priority to the French interest over that of the repairsmen, despite the fact that under French law the hypothèque would have
been subordinate to their interests.

English courts in later decisions have, however, not been so clear in draw- **6.66**
ing a distinction between the substantive right and the issue of priorities/
administration and have suggested instead that the nature and existence
of foreign rights should also be assessed according to forum law. Hence,
on this view, it is irrelevant whether an interest would be classified as a
maritime lien under foreign law: the factual circumstances must satisfy
the conditions under forum law for the grant of such a lien for it to be so
recognized. So in *The Zigurds*[193] and *The Acrux*,[194] English courts made
obiter statements to the effect that even if certain interests had the status

---

[191] Cheshire, North and Fawcett (n 62 above) 93; P Carter, 'Priorities of Claims in Private International Law' (1984) 54 BYBIL 207, 208–9; Mason (n 181 above) 86.
[192] [1923] P 102.
[193] [1932] P 113.
[194] [1965] P 391.

of a maritime lien under foreign law, they would not be recognized under English law. Most significantly, a majority of the Privy Council in *The Halcyon Isle*[195] took this approach. That case involved a priorities dispute between an English registered mortgagee and US ship repairers whose interest under US law would have been entitled to the status of a maritime lien. It was agreed unanimously among the members of the Privy Council that questions of priority were procedural and subject to forum law but the court split as to what law should be applied to determine the nature of the US repairers' interest. The majority regarded this issue also as procedural on the basis that it was 'remedial'[196] and also because 'any question as to who is entitled to bring a particular kind of proceeding in an English court' was 'a question of jurisdiction'.[197] It has been suggested throughout this work that the use of the right-remedy distinction tends to obscure important policy choices and interests in classifying an issue as substantive or procedural and this tendency appears again here. Further, the accuracy of the statement, in suggesting that all questions regarding who may sue are procedural is also doubtful in the light of the analysis conducted in Chapter 5, where it was shown that the issue may be subject to a number of different laws other than that of the forum.

6.67 A possibly stronger argument in favour of a procedural classification is that there is a close connection between the recognition of foreign rights and the process by which priorities are determined in that the first issue may, for practical purposes, resolve the second.[198] While this observation has force, it is arguably less compelling than the arguments in favour of a substantive classification. As the minority judges said in *The Halcyon Isle*, 'the comity of nations, private international law and natural justice' all support this view.[199] In particular, a serious injustice would often result from a procedural classification since repairers would be deprived of the lien under the law in which they had contracted, simply because the ship travelled to and was sold in a country which did not recognize such an interest.[200] Application of foreign law is therefore supported by party expectations, respect for foreign laws, and the desirability of having a single law apply to the lien regardless of the location of the ship.[201] Later in their

---

[195] [1981] AC 221.
[196] ibid 238.
[197] ibid 235.
[198] *The Andrico Unity* [1989] 4 SA 325 (A), para 53.
[199] [1981] AC 221, 246.
[200] ibid 246–7.
[201] H Staniland, 'Foreign Maritime Liens Not to be Recognized in South Africa' [1990] LMCLQ 491, 492; W Tetley, 'Maritime Liens in the Conflict of Laws' in J Nafziger and S Symeonides (eds), *Law and Justice in a Multistate World: Essays in Honor of Arthur T. von Mehren* (Transnational Publishers Inc, 2002) 439–57.

D. Priorities and Rights of Creditors

judgment, Lords Scarman and Salmon reinforced this conclusion by emphasizing the fact that a lien is a property right.[202] The bulk of academic commentary clearly supports the minority position for its greater recognition of foreign rights.[203]

(b) Canada

Courts in Commonwealth countries have differed in their approach to this issue. In Canada, it has been the position since at least 1926[204] that contracts for necessaries or supplies entered into in the United States will be given the effect that they would receive under US law, namely treated as maritime liens and then ranked according to the Canadian law of priorities. Such a view is said to be consistent with 'the logic'[205] and the approach in *The Colorado*. Canadian courts have also addressed the possibly unspoken rationale for the non-recognition of foreign rights under the majority view in *The Halcyon Isle*: that is, the concern that it would lead to a flood of 'spurious claims for maritime liens purportedly created by legislative fiat in a foreign jurisdiction'.[206] The Canadian response to this concern has been to note that a foreign lien or right would not be enforced where it was contrary to forum public policy, thus preserving some control for forum law in the area.[207] An example of such a case would be where, under foreign law, the rights of a forum resident claimant would be subordinated to those of the foreign lien holder 'whose existence could not have been anticipated'.[208] Yet in no Commonwealth decision can it be said that the foreign right in question was spurious or acquired in bad faith, which casts some doubt on this fear. Almost all cases have involved claims by repairers or bodies seeking seamen's wages or benefits, claims which are hardly unforeseeable from the point of view of a shipowner or charterer with the claimants being likely to have the expectation that their rights would enjoy the same status as they would have in their country of creation.

6.68

---

[202] [1981] AC 221, 250.

[203] *Cheshire, North and Fawcett* (n 62 above) 93–4; M Davies, A Bell, and P Brereton, *Nygh's Conflict of Laws in Australia* (LexisNexis Butterworths, 8th edn, 2010) para 16.43 but cf *Dicey, Morris and Collins* (n 45 above) para 7.033, who appear, uncritically, to accept the current position.

[204] *The Strandhill* [1926] SCR 680; *The Ioannis Daskalelis* [1974] SCR 1248; *Marlex Petroleum Inc v The Har Rai* [1984] 2 FC 345 (affd [1987] 1 SCR 57); *Holt Cargo Systems Inc v ABC Containerline NV (Trustees of)* [2001] 3 SCR 907, para 41 (Binnie J); *Kent Trade and Finance Inc v JP Morgan Chase Bank* [2008] FCA 399.

[205] *Metaxas v Ship Galaxias (No 2)* (1988) 19 FTR 108, para 35.

[206] ibid para 40.

[207] ibid para 45 citing *The Strandhill* [1926] SCR 680.

[208] ibid para 43.

180   Chapter 6: Judicial Administration

As one Canadian judge said, an important effect of foreign liens being recognized is that 'in a competitive worldwide market an American necessaries man runs less risk in extending credit'.[209]

6.69 The Canadian authorities are also important because they provide a response to the objection that if Commonwealth courts were to recognize foreign lien rights, choice of law problems would arise. In fact, Canadian courts have devised highly flexible choice of law rules for determining when a foreign lien should be recognized. They have first noted that a maritime lien is a secured property right against a vessel which arises from operation of law—specifically when a debt is incurred by or on behalf of a ship—rather than from tort or contract.[210] Yet where the lien has arisen in the context of a contract to supply necessaries for a ship, a choice of law clause in such a contract will normally determine the existence and nature of the lien.[211] Where, by contrast, there is no contract between the parties or the transaction giving rise to the lien is more closely connected with another country, it may be more appropriate that that country's law be applied.[212] A 'closest connection test' therefore operates which, while occasionally difficult to apply, is a far more principled approach than simply applying forum law to the question pursuant to a procedural classification.

(c) New Zealand

6.70 The approach taken in other Commonwealth countries has varied, although it is possible to discern a general trend in favour of adopting a substantive classification to the issue of recognizing foreign rights. In New Zealand, the Court of Appeal in *The Betty Ott* case[213] confirmed that the priority of competing interests was governed by the law of the forum but then proceeded to hold that an Australian registered mortgage over a ship was to be treated under New Zealand law as an unregistered mortgage, because it had not been entered in the New Zealand register. The reasoning of the majority in *The Halcyon Isle* was relied upon to hold that the nature and status of a foreign security interest in a ship was not to be resolved by application of the applicable law of the interest but by forum law. The effect of this view is that a registered ship mortgage only enjoys such status in

---

[209] *The Ship Nordems* [2010] FC 332, para 14 (affd [2011] FCA 73).
[210] *Kent Trade and Finance Inc v JP Morgan Chase Bank* [2008] FCA 399, para 20.
[211] ibid paras 24, 26.
[212] ibid para 26; *Imperial Oil Ltd v Petromar Inc* 2001 FCA 391; *The Ship Nordems* [2010] FC 332.
[213] [1992] 1 NZLR 655.

D. Priorities and Rights of Creditors

the country of registration.[214] Consequently, the later New Zealand debenture was found to take priority over the earlier Australian 'unregistered' mortgage.

Two comments may, however, be made about *The Betty Ott* decision. The first observation is that the court's decision may have been influenced by the fact that decisions of the New Zealand Court of Appeal were still subject to appeal to the Privy Council in 1992, and so the New Zealand court may have felt bound by the Board's decision in *The Halcyon Isle*. Such a right of appeal no longer exists. Secondly, the precise decision on the facts of *The Betty Ott* was almost immediately reversed by legislation. Under section 70 of the Ship Registration Act 1992 (NZ), a foreign registered instrument creating securities or charges on ships is given the same status as a New Zealand registered mortgage. This provision was recently applied in *Keybank National Association v The Ship 'Blaze'*[215] to give recognition to a US registered mortgage in respect of a ship. If a generous interpretation of section 70 is maintained by New Zealand courts in future cases, then it is likely that further inroads will be made into the majority view in *The Halcyon Isle*, although not pursuant to the more comity-conscious private international law method.[216]

6.71

(d) South Africa

In South Africa, the Supreme Court in *The Andrico Unity*[217] followed the majority view in *The Halcyon Isle*, although the case concerned jurisdiction to bring an action *in rem* rather than priorities. The court nevertheless refused to recognize a foreign maritime lien for the purposes of establishing jurisdiction on the basis that only such liens accorded by the law of the forum conferred standing to sue.

6.72

(e) Australia

In Australia, there has only been one decision on the issue, *Morlines Maritime Agency Ltd v The Proceeds of Sale of the Ship 'Skulptor Vuchetich'*[218] and the court followed the majority in *The Halcyon Isle*, although with some hesitation. The court declined to treat a claim for moneys owing under a hire agreement as a maritime lien despite the fact that it would

6.73

---

[214] P Myburgh, 'Recognition and Priority of Foreign Ship Mortgages: *The Betty Ott*' [1992] LMCLQ 155, 159.
[215] [2009] 2 NZLR 271.
[216] P Myburgh, 'The New Zealand Ship Registration Act 1992' [1993] LMCLQ 444.
[217] [1989] 4 SA 325 (A).
[218] [1997] FCA 432.

have enjoyed that status under US law. This conclusion followed from the fact that the Privy Council majority view required the court to consider only whether the facts before the court amounted to a lien under Australian law as the law of the forum. It should also be noted, however, that the court in *Morlines* suggested that the position in Canada was consistent with the Privy Council majority when, as noted at 6.68, this observation is only true on the issue of priorities, not on recognition of foreign interests. Since that decision, the High Court of Australia has given judgment in *John Pfeiffer Pty Ltd v Rogerson*[219] and introduced the new mode or conduct of court proceedings and outcome determinative tests for classifying substance and procedure questions. It is obvious that recognition of foreign security interests in ships does not involve the conduct of court proceedings and is plainly outcome determinative.[220] In addition, there is no impracticality for a forum court in recognizing a discrete foreign right, whereas in the case of priorities, the forum has to establish a system for the administration of assets which may involve a diverse range of creditors. Recently, in *Elbe Shipping SA v The Ship Global Peace*,[221] Allsop J suggested that in a future case an Australian court might be willing to consider 'the recognition of foreign maritime liens by reference to principles of private international law different to those expressed by the majority of the Privy Council in *The Halcyon Isle*'. Hence, there now seems to be clear movement away from the procedural classification of maritime liens and other security interests in ships.

(f) The EU Impact

6.74 Finally, it is arguable that the majority position in *The Halcyon Isle* cannot be reconciled with EU instruments on choice of law, such as the Rome Convention on the Law Applicable to Contractual Obligations and the Rome I and Rome II Regulations. In the case of a maritime lien, which arises in the context of a contract between the parties to which the Convention or the Rome I Regulation applies, the applicable law of the contract will apply to 'the consequences of breach of the contract',[222] which would be likely to include maritime liens. A similar conclusion would apply in the case of a maritime lien derived from a non-contractual obligation under article 15(d) of the Rome II Regulation, since it would probably be regarded as a 'measure . . . to ensure the provision of compensation'.

---

[219] (2000) 203 CLR 503.
[220] M Davies and K Lewins, 'Foreign Maritime Liens: Should they be Recognised in Australian Courts?' (2002) 76 Australian LJ 775.
[221] [2006] FCA 954, para 131.
[222] Rome Convention, art 10(1)(c); Rome I Regulation, art 12(1)(c).

D. Priorities and Rights of Creditors

In a recent decision of the English Court of Appeal,[223] however, there is no suggestion of any change in approach to the treatment in private international law of maritime liens. *The Fesco Angara* involved an application for an injunction to restrain the pursuit of proceedings in a US federal court. The Court of Appeal refused the injunction, stating that the US proceedings involved a claim for a US maritime lien which could only be obtained in that country's courts. There was therefore nothing 'vexatious or oppressive' about bringing a claim for relief in a foreign court which could not be granted in English proceedings.[224] Both parties to the litigation conceded that an English court could not award a US lien, presumably on the basis that such rights were only procedural. It would have been interesting to see the court's reaction had the classification issue been directly raised.

6.75

(g) United States

The US position on priorities and maritime liens is broadly similar to the Canadian approach. First, on the question of priorities and administration of the debtor's assets generally, the law of the forum applies. Again this conclusion is reached by reason of practical necessity, since where creditors' claims are governed by different laws it would be very difficult to select a single law to govern the administration.[225] On the question of the nature of the creditors' rights in an administration, in particular whether a US court would recognize a foreign maritime lien, US courts have always treated such an issue as substantive and usually applied the law of the cause of action giving rise to the claim to determine it.[226] A few US courts have, however, gone further and applied a law other than the law of the cause of action to the issue of the availability of a maritime lien and so, for example, have granted a US lien despite the law governing the contract between the parties being foreign.[227] Such an approach appears to be based on 'a separate multi-factor choice of law inquiry', which makes the availability of the lien dependent on whether it is granted by the law which has the closest connection to the issue.[228] Yet, on either view, the nature and status of the claims of creditors in an administration are classified as substantive.

6.76

---

[223] *The Fesco Angara* [2010] EWCA Civ 1050.

[224] ibid para 56.

[225] See *Oil Shipping (Bunkering) BV v Sonmez Denizcilik ve Ticaret AS* 10 F 3d 1015, 1023–4 (3rd Cir 1993); *Fortis Bank (Nederland) NV v MV Shamrock* 379 F Supp 2d 2 (D Me 2005).

[226] See eg *Bominflot Inc v The MV Heinrich S* 465 F 3d 144 (4th Cir 2006); *Oil Shipping (Bunkering) BV v Sonmez Denizcilik ve Ticaret AS* 10 F 3d 1015 (3rd Cir 1993).

[227] See eg *Rainbow Line Inc v MV Tequila* 480 F 2d 1024, 1026–7 (2nd Cir 1973).

[228] M Davies, 'Choice of Law and US Maritime Liens' (2009) 83 Tulane L Rev 1435, 1456.

E. JUDGMENTS AND ORDERS

1. Form and Requirements

6.77 The form and requirements of a judgment are matters obviously falling within the rubric of the forum's power of management and control of its proceedings[229] and should therefore be determined by the law of the country in which the judgment was rendered, even in proceedings for recognition of such judgment in a foreign country.[230] The same principle would apply to the meaning of any terms used in a judgment.[231] Such a principle, along with convenience, would also determine whether a court may give an award of damages in a foreign currency.[232] However, the issue of the identification of the currency in which the loss is to be calculated is resolved by the law of the cause of action.[233] A different question is the classification of the measures a court may use to ensure compliance with its judgments or orders. A further issue, related but distinct, is what law should be applied to determine *whether* a foreign judgment should be recognized or enforced in the forum.

2. Methods of Enforcement

6.78 It has long been clear that the issue of execution or manner of enforcing a local or foreign judgment is governed by the law of the country of enforcement as a procedural matter.[234] This rule applies regardless of the law applied by the court of origin to the merits or the procedural law applied by that court.[235] Practicality and effectiveness underlie the choice of the law of the country of enforcement: only the local sovereign has the capacity to apply coercive measures to ensure compliance with a judgment.[236] Furthermore, the processes of the forum could not operate if forced to apply

---

[229] Restatement (Second), § 127 comment a (7).

[230] Szászy (n 20 above) 453.

[231] *Martyn v Graham* [2003] QDC 447 (Dist Ct Queensland).

[232] *Owners of Eleftheotria v Despina R* [1979] AC 685, 704; *Miliangos v George Frank (Textiles) Ltd* [1976] AC 443.

[233] *Kraut AG v Albany Fabrics Ltd* [1977] QB 192; Cheshire, North and Fawcett (n 62 above) 106–7.

[234] Dicey, Morris and Collins (n 45 above) para 7.008; K Kerameus, 'Enforcement in the International Context' (1997) 264 *Hague Recueil* 179, 379–95; Graveson (n 62 above) 614–15; Sykes and Pryles (n 7 above) 257; *John Pfeiffer Pty Ltd v Rogerson* (2000) 203 CLR 503, para 192 (Callinan J); *Royal Trust Co v Kritzwiser* [1924] 3 DLR 596, 598–9 (Sask CA).

[235] Kerameus (n 234 above) 385.

[236] ibid 380, 388.

E. Judgments and Orders

different and unfamiliar enforcement mechanisms.[237] In two old English cases it was held that the forum's powers of arrest of a defendant for a debt would be applied despite the fact that the debt may have been incurred in a foreign country or by the national of a country where such powers of arrest did not exist.[238] More recently, in *DSLangdale Two LLC v Daisytek (Canada) Inc*,[239] an Ontario court held that the question of whether a defendant may obtain a stay of execution and enforcement of a US judgment in Ontario was determined by local law. The principle was recently applied in a different context in *Vitol SA v Capri Marine Ltd (No 2)*.[240] In that case, a judgment had been obtained by Vitol against Capri in England and enforcement of such judgment was sought against two other entities, Spartacus and Primerose, in Maryland, United States, which were said to hold assets in common with Capri and so be available for execution of the judgment. Capri sought an anti-suit injunction in England to restrain Vitol from pursuing execution against Spartacus and Primerose in Maryland. One of the reasons given by the court for rejecting the injunction was that any question as to the enforceability or execution of an English judgment in a foreign country must be resolved in the courts of that country 'according to the applicable local law', here that of Maryland.[241]

6.79 A garnishee order has also been regarded as a form of execution and so governed by the law of the forum,[242] although in some Canadian cases there has been a reluctance to exercise jurisdiction to order garnishment of a debt situated in another province in aid of enforcement of a judgment in the forum.[243]

6.80 The position in respect of the execution and enforcement of judgments also applies in the United States, where it is well established that the local law of the forum applies generally to provide the methods of securing obedience to orders of the court.[244] Examples of such methods may be the arrest of the defendant, an order requiring a claimant to post a bond,[245] sanctions for contempt of court, measures for sequestration of property, and attachment (including what forms of property may

---

[237] J McLeod, *The Conflict of Laws* (Carswell Legal Publications Calgary, 1983) 224.
[238] *Flack v Holm* (1820) 1 Jac & W 405; *De la Vega v Vianna* (1830) 1 B & Ad 284.
[239] (2004) 6 CPC (6th) 363.
[240] [2010] EWHC 458 (Comm).
[241] ibid para 33.
[242] *Wayfarer Holidays Ltd v Hoteles Barcelo* (1993) 12 OR (3d) 208, para 12 (Ont Ct Gen Div).
[243] See eg *Delaire v Delaire* (1996) 147 Sask R 161 (SCQB).
[244] Restatement (Second), § 130.
[245] See discussion of security for costs at 6.37–6.39 above.

186   *Chapter 6: Judicial Administration*

be attached)[246] and freezing[247] or garnishment orders.[248] Further and more specifically, § 131 of the Restatement provides that the local law of the forum determines the manner and methods of enforcing a judgment,[249] including whether enforcement should be by way of levy of execution and sale, whether remedies such as appointment of a receiver and granting of an injunction are available, and whether the judgment debtor can be subjected to arrest[250] or its property exempted from execution.[251] In European civil law countries it is also well established that the methods for enforcement of a judgment[252] (including whether enforcement can be suspended)[253] and sanctions for non-compliance with court orders and judgments[254] are matters exclusively governed by the law of the forum which, in the case of a foreign judgment, is the law of the country of enforcement.

6.81 There is, however, one qualification which must be made to this analysis. Under article 15(d) of the EU Rome II Regulation, which applies to non-contractual obligations,[255] the law of the obligation governs the measures which may be awarded 'to ensure the provision of compensation' to the successful claimant. It is arguable that this provision would include measures designed to assist with enforcement of a judgment such as attachment, freezing, and garnishment orders. Yet the forum has no power to give relief which does not exist under its law. Hence, the suggested effect of this provision is that while the remedy must be available under the law of the forum and the law of the obligation, the conditions and principles under which it would be granted are those of the law of the obligation. Such an outcome represents a significant change from the common law position in that it would require a court, which has been asked to enforce a judgment, to apply the law of the obligation in the judgment to determine whether enforcement remedies should be granted.

---

[246] *Farmers Exchange Bank v Metro Contracting Services Inc* 107 SW 3d 381, 391 (CA Mo 2003).
[247] See further on freezing orders 10.13 below.
[248] *Phillips v Phillips* 285 SE 2d 52 (CA Ga 1981).
[249] See also Restatement (Second), § 99.
[250] ibid § 131 comment a; see *Baker v General Motors Corp* 522 US 222, 235 (US Sup Ct 1998); *Texaco Inc v Pennzoil Co* 784 F 2d 1133, 1156 (2nd Cir 1986).
[251] *Marine Midland Bank v Surfbelt Inc* 532 F Supp 728 (WD Pa 1982); Restatement (Second), § 132.
[252] *Office des Poursuites et des Faillites de Nyon (OPF) v Dumartheray* [2007] IL Pr 29 (French Court of Cassation First Civil Chamber, 30 October 2006).
[253] *Maurice Bidermann Zylberberg v RHI Holdings Inc* [1996] IL Pr 189 (Paris Court of Appeal 9 March 1995).
[254] For Germany, see R Geimer, *International Zivilprozessrecht* (OUS Verlag Dr Otto Schmidt, 5th edn, 2005) para 361.
[255] According to the majority of English courts, the Rome II Regulation applies to events giving rise to damage on or after 20 August 2007, although the matter is currently the subject of a reference to the ECJ. For a fuller discussion, see 11.01 below.

E. *Judgments and Orders* 187

3. Rules for Enforcement

Regarding the final issue referred to at 6.77, the law of the enforcing court **6.82** (the forum) principally provides the rules to determine *if* a foreign judgment should be recognized and enforced in the forum, but reference is also made to the law of the country where the judgment was rendered on certain issues. Such a balanced and nuanced approach to applicable law is appropriate in a context where comity and respect for foreign laws and institutions are important. Reference to foreign law is again not made pursuant to a substance / procedure distinction but out of recognition that within the procedural category the law of the forum should not have exclusive application. This reference to foreign law may therefore be seen as another example of Kahn-Freund's 'enlightened' application of the law of the forum. For example, the question of whether a judgment is for a monetary sum[256] or is penal[257] in nature is resolved by forum law but the issue as to whether the defendant submitted to the jurisdiction of the foreign court is assessed according to the standards of both the law of the forum and the law of the country of rendition. So, in *Akai Pty Ltd v People's Insurance Co Ltd*,[258] an English court held that if a step taken by the defendant would not be regarded as a submission under the law of rendition then it would not amount to a submission in enforcement proceedings in the forum, even if under the domestic law of the forum, such conduct would have constituted a submission. Yet by contrast, where conduct would have amounted to a submission under the law of rendition but not under the law of the forum, then the forum is not bound by the foreign court's characterization.[259] The law of the country of rendition has also been applied to determine whether the judgment is final and conclusive[260] and whether valid service of process took place.[261]

---

[256] cf *Poh Soon Kiat v Desert Palace Inc* [2009] SGCA 60, para 19, where the Singapore Court of Appeal said that the issue of whether the judgment was for a monetary sum was governed by the law of the country of rendition but then proceeded to reject the expert evidence and substitute its own interpretation of the judgment.

[257] *Huntington v Attrill* [1893] AC 150, 155.

[258] [1998] 1 Lloyd's Rep 90, 97 (applying the Civil Jurisdiction and Judgments Act 1982 (UK), ss 32 and 33).

[259] ibid.

[260] *Nouvion v Freeman* (1889) 15 App Cas 1; *Schnabel v Yung Lui* [2002] NSWSC 15; *Morgan Stanley & Co International Ltd v Pilot Lead Investments Ltd* [2006] HKCFI 497, para 18; Szászy (n 20 above) 453 (who refers to the '*lex loci actus*' of the judgment).

[261] Szászy, ibid; although this issue may also be subject to the public policy of the enforcing court in a given case, see 4.27 above.

6.83 In terms of the defences to enforcement, the question of whether a judgment was procured by fraud[262] or involved a breach of public policy[263] are to be determined exclusively according to the standards of the forum, although public policy may include the provisions of relevant conventions such as the right to a fair trial under article 6 of the European Convention on Human Rights.[264] The position in respect of the defence of breach of natural justice is less clear. While most recent Commonwealth authorities emphasize that, in determining whether 'minimum standards of fairness' or 'substantial justice' existed in the foreign proceedings, the forum will apply its own standards,[265] some courts have given weight to the law of the country of rendition on the issue of whether the defendant had been given due notice of the foreign proceedings.[266]

---

[262] See eg *Owens Bank Ltd v Bracco* [1992] 2 AC 443 (HL); *Yoon v Song* (2000) 158 FLR 295 (SCNSW).

[263] See eg *Stern v National Australia Bank* [1999] FCA 1421, paras 133–147.

[264] *X v Société JA Delmas Export* [2006] ECLY 136 (French Court of Cassation First Civil Chamber 31 January 2006).

[265] *Jet Holdings Inc v Patel* [1990] 1 QB 335, 345; *Adams v Cape Industries plc* [1990] Ch 433, 564–7; *Beals v Saldanha* [2003] 3 SCR 416, paras 60–64; *Cortes v Yorkton Securities Inc* (2007) 278 DLR (4th) 740, para 71.

[266] *Igra v Igra* [1951] P 404, 412; *Boele v Norsemeter Holding AS* [2002] NSWCA 363, para 28.

7
Evidence I: General Principles

A.	Introduction	7.01
B.	Admissibility	7.03
	1. General Principles	7.03
	2. Documentary Evidence	7.05
	3. Admissibility in Criminal Cases	7.08
	4. Interpretation Versus Variation of Documents	7.12
C.	Burden of Proof and Presumptions	7.15
	1. Burden of Proof	7.15
	2. Presumptions	7.18
D.	Individual Topics within Evidence	7.26
	1. Statutory Requirement of Written Evidence	7.26
	2. Witnesses	7.31
	3. Evaluation and Probative Force of Evidence	7.32
	4. Administration of Evidence	7.34
E.	Estoppel	7.36
	1. Issue and Cause of Action Estoppel	7.37
	2. *Henderson v Henderson* Estoppel	7.42
	3. The US Position	7.45
	4. Statutory Provisions Preventing Relitigation	7.47
	5. Other Estoppels	7.51

A. INTRODUCTION

The law of evidence is another area which has long been considered to fall exclusively within the realm of procedure and so is governed by the law of the forum.[1] Yet more recent developments arguably suggest a move towards greater flexibility in terms of choice of law in evidence, at least in respect of specific issues. Such movement is likely to increase with the advent of EU instruments such as the Rome I and Rome II Regulations on the applicable law in contractual and non-contractual obligations respectively, which have removed more matters from the scope of

7.01

---

[1] *Bain v Whitehaven and Furness Junction Railway* (1850) 3 HLC 1, 19.

forum law as well as the recent narrowing of the scope of procedure (or alternatively, broadening of the scope of substance) in Canada and Australia.

7.02 Enhanced flexibility surrounding the choice of law rules with respect to evidence has long been a feature of civil law systems, as can be seen, for example, from article 3130 of the Quebec Civil Code which provides that: 'Evidence is governed by the law applicable to the merits of the dispute, subject to any rules of the court seised of the matter which are more favourable to the establishment of evidence.' Interestingly, some Canadian common law commentators have expressed support for this approach,[2] in particular for the wider role given to the law of the cause of action, although not at the expense of the integrity of the adjudicative process. Such an analysis may be a pointer to future developments of the common law choice of law rules. Even before these developments, however, it would have been mistaken to conclude that in common law countries the law of the forum applied to all matters concerning evidence without exception. For example, it has long been accepted that the issue as to *what* are the material facts in a given case to prove, such as whether a contract exists or whether a breach of a duty of care has occurred, is determined by the law of the cause of action.[3] The same position applies in civil law countries where the 'object' of evidence is considered substantive.[4] By contrast, the matter of *how* the facts in issue are to be proved, including the methods of proof which may be used, such as oral or written evidence, has, at least in common law countries, traditionally been governed by the law of the forum.[5] The distinction between identifying the material facts and proving them is best analysed under the rubric of the following topics in evidence.

---

[2] See eg J Walker, *Castel & Walker Canadian Conflict of Laws* (LexisNexis Butterworths, 6th edn, 2005) para 6.3(c).

[3] *The Gaetano and Maria* (1882) 7 PD 137 (CA); *Owners of Sailing Ship 'Fortunato Figari' v Steamship 'Coogee'* (1904) 29 VLR 874, 900 (Sup Ct Vic).

[4] See eg France: B Audit, *Droit International Privé* (Economica, 3rd edn, 2005) para 447; Spain: A Calvo Caravaca and J Carrascosa González, *Derecho Internacional Privado Vol I* (Editorial Comares, 6th edn, 2005) 407; and Switzerland: A Bucher and A Bonomi, *Droit International Privé* (Helbing & Lichtenbahn, 2nd edn, 2004) 52.

[5] *Loutchansky v Times Newspapers Ltd (Nos 2 to 5)* [2002] QB 783, para 86 (proof of moral damage in libel is procedural).

B. ADMISSIBILITY

1. General Principles

It has long been asserted in common law jurisprudence that questions of the admissibility of evidence are to be determined by the law of the forum, presumably on the basis that admissibility relates more to the issue of how facts are to be proved rather than what the facts are.[6] The consequence of this view is that a document may be accepted into evidence in the forum even if it would be inadmissible under the law of the cause of action,[7] and the fact that the document is admissible under the law of the cause of action is irrelevant to its admissibility in the forum.[8] The US Second Restatement also adopts this approach on the basis that it accords with the efficiency and convenience of the court proceedings.[9]

7.03

A question may be raised, however, as to whether this rule should continue to exist in such absolute terms, especially given the recent Canadian and Australian reformulations of substance and procedure. Applying such tests, it is questionable whether rules on admissibility are a necessary part of the mode or conduct of court proceedings but it is certainly arguable that they can impact upon the result in litigation[10] where, for example, a crucial piece of evidence would be excluded under one law but not another. Adoption of a substantive classification should, therefore, assist in deterring forum shopping. There would also appear to be no particular inconvenience in a forum court applying the admissibility rules of a foreign country. Significantly, a substantive classification is supported in some civil law

7.04

---

[6] *Yates v Thompson* (1835) 3 Cl and F 544; *Bain v Whitehaven and Furness Junction Railway* (1850) 3 HLC 1. In *Wiedemann v Walpole* [1891] 2 QB 534 (CA) the court applied forum law to determine whether evidence of a person's silence, in not responding to a claimant's letters in which allegations were made, was admissible as corroboration of such allegations. Foreign law was not, however, pleaded and forum law was probably also the law of the cause of action.

[7] *Bristow v Sequeville* (1850) 5 Exch 275.

[8] *Brown v Thornton* (1837) 6 Ad and El 185.

[9] Restatement (Second), § 138 comment a applied in *Crafton v Union Pacific Railroad Co* 585 NW 2d 115 (Neb Ct App 1998).

[10] L McDougal, R Felix, and R Whitten, *American Conflicts Law* (Transnational Publishers, 5th edn, 2001) 416.

countries[11] and a few US decisions.[12] Where, however, the issue of admissibility arises in the context of a preliminary, procedural matter such as jurisdiction, forum law has a stronger claim to application, given its lesser proximity to the merits.[13]

2. Documentary Evidence

7.05 The particular status of documents in cross-border litigation also arguably calls for a more sophisticated choice of law approach to admissibility questions. Until recently, Commonwealth courts simply applied the law of the forum to all issues concerning the admissibility or evidential weight of documents. So, in *Wicken v Wicken*,[14] an issue arose as to the validity of a talaq divorce between Muslims of Gambian nationality where the husband relied on a letter, which was a permissible method of proof under the law of the cause of action, Gambia. The authenticity of the letter was disputed, however, on the basis that under Gambian law the evidence of two witnesses as to the husband's handwriting was required. The English court, however, regarded proof of authenticity of a document as a question of evidence and procedure, and so the Gambian requirements were not applicable. Under English law the letter was authentic and so admitted into evidence. Similarly, in *Banque Indosuez v Madam Sumilan Awal*[15] a Singapore court had to determine whether a person had authority to represent an Indonesian company in proceedings in Singapore. It was conceded that the issue of authority was governed by the law of Indonesia and the court was requested to accept a deed notarized in Indonesia as

---

[11] V Bellini, 'Evidence in Private International Law' [1953] University of Western Australia L Rev 330, citing French and Italian authors (at n 4); I Szászy, 'The Basic Connecting Factor In International Cases in the Domain of Civil Procedure' (1966) 15 ICLQ 436, 452. See also, for France, Audit (n 4 above) para 448 and for Belgium, F Rigaux and M Fallon, *Droit International Privé* (Larcier, 3rd edn, 2005) para 11.15. But, cf Spain, where the law of the forum seems to be preferred for the issue of admissibility: Caravaca and González (n 4 above) 407 and *AS Hydrema Danmark v Euman SA* (Supreme Court of Spain, 8 April 2005) noted in I Arevalo, 'Spain: Contract—Damages Claims' (2006) 17(6) International Company and Commercial L Rev N46. Switzerland also seems to favour the law of the forum: Bucher and Bonomi (n 4 above) 52.

[12] See eg *Diehl v Ogorewac* 836 F Supp 88 (EDNY 1993) where a rule of the (foreign) law of the cause of action that prohibited the admission into evidence of a claimant's failure to wear a seat belt in a tort case was applied. It must be acknowledged, however, that in the majority of US decisions in civil cases, forum law has been applied to the issue of admissibility, see eg *Mason v Lynch* 878 A 2d 588 (CA Md 2005); *Greenwood v Hildebrand* 515 A 2d 963 (SC Pa 1986); *Ford v Newman* 396 NE 2d 539 (Sup Ct Ill 1979).

[13] *The Kapitan Temkin* [1998] SGHC 427, para 5.

[14] [1999] 2 WLR 1166 (Fam D).

[15] [1997] SGHC 2.

conclusive evidence of the person's authority. The Singapore court, however, held that the issue of the admissibility and weight of such document had to be determined in accordance with forum law.[16] An Australian court took a similar approach in holding that a requirement under foreign law that a deed be stamped before being admitted into evidence was procedural and so not applicable in the forum.[17]

There are other authorities, however, which arguably adopt a more perceptive choice of law analysis. For example, there is the suggestion that where the issue of admissibility arises in relation to a written instrument such as a contract or a power of attorney, it should not be classified as a question of procedure but rather as one relating to the *formal validity* of the instrument. Formal validity is broadly defined in the Giuliano and Lagarde Report on the Rome Convention[18] as 'every external manifestation required on the part of a person expressing the will to be legally bound and in the absence of which such expression of will would not be regarded as legally effective'. The consequence of adopting this view is that if the document is formally valid according to the law of the place of its execution (*lex loci actus*), then it should be admitted into evidence in the forum, regardless of the view of the law of the forum. The rationale for this view is that the parties, at the time of executing the document, are more likely to have the place of execution in mind than the ultimate forum which will adjudicate the matter (which is likely to be unknown). This approach is generally recognized in the private international law rules of most civil law countries[19] and, if accepted in Commonwealth law,[20] would have resulted in a different outcome in the *Wicken*, *Banque Indosuez*, and *Rothwells* cases

7.06

---

[16] ibid para 50.

[17] *Rothwells Ltd (in liq) v Connell* (1993) 119 ALR 538 (Qld CA).

[18] Giuliano and Lagarde, 'Council Report on the Convention on the Law Applicable to Contractual Obligations' [1980] OJ C282/1, 29.

[19] See eg France: *Ollanescu v Culacov* (Court of Cassation 1e Ch Civ D, 5 January 1999) [1999] ECLY 1195; *Le Meilleur v Trehout* (Court of Cassation 1e Ch Civ, 23 January 2001) [2002] ECLY 1188 (donation) and Audit (n 4 above) para 448; Greece: *Erinodikeio Limiras* 25/2002 [2003] ECLY 729 (validity of power of attorney); Spain: Caravaca and González (n 4 above) 406; Belgium: *Al Mowahidine v Chatar* [1989] ECLY 161 (Trib Civ Liège, 30 November 1988) (contents of a power of attorney) and Rigaux and Fallon (n 11 above) para 11.16; the Netherlands: HR 31 January 1992 1993 NJ 261 (Supreme Court) cited in R van Rooij, M Polak, and L Steffens, *Private International Law in the Netherlands Supplement* (1995) 57 but cf Italy: *Fondazione Banco di Sicilia v Mauritius Commercial Bank Ltd* (Court of Cassation, 30 September 2005) [2006] ECLY 121 (forum law applies to validity of power of attorney).

[20] In support of this view, P Wood, *Conflict of Laws and International Finance* (Sweet & Maxwell, 2007) para 2.028.

discussed at 7.05.²¹ In the case of modern commercial contracts, however, the place of contracting can be fortuitous and uncertain and so reference to the law governing the contract is preferable for questions of formal validity arising in relation to such transactions.²² Note that the issue of formal validity also arises in the context of writing requirements for documents and the statute of frauds, and is considered at 7.26–7.29.

7.07 Some support for a substantive classification of the formal validity of documents can be found in the EU instruments referred to earlier. For example, under article 18(2) of the Rome I Regulation, 'a contract or act intended to have legal effect may be proved by any mode of proof recognised by the law of the forum or by any of the laws referred to in Article 11' (namely the law of the cause of action and the law of the place of the act) under which that contract or act is formally valid.²³ Any mode of proof available under foreign law must, however, be capable of being administered by the law of the forum. By contrast, where a question arises as to the mode of proof of an issue relating to a contract or an act other than its *validity or existence*, then the EU provisions do not apply. In such a case the matter is one of 'evidence' under article 1(3) and so falls outside the scope of the instruments. Consequently, determination of the applicable law will be left to the choice of law rules of the forum which, at least in common law countries, would result in the law of the forum being applied.²⁴

---

²¹ The applicable law to a foreign-executed power of attorney was left open by an Australian court in *Ghosn v Principle Focus Pty Ltd & Ors (No 2)* [2008] VSC 574, para 40 (Sup Ct Vic) but in *Li Yuen Ling v Tang Kwong Wai Thomas* [2009] HKCFI 1164, para 25 a Hong Kong court interestingly held that the formal validity of a power of attorney was governed by the law of the place where it was intended to be used rather than the country of execution.

²² L Collins (ed), *Dicey, Morris and Collins on the Conflict of Laws* (Sweet & Maxwell, 14th edn, 2006) para 32.177.

²³ Note that the choice of law rule for formal validity is varied slightly when the contract is entered into between parties who are in different countries: Rome I, art 11(2). See also Rome II, art 22(2).

²⁴ For a civil law decision in which this conclusion was also reached, see *AS Hydrema Danmark v Euman SA* (Supreme Court of Spain 8 April 2005) noted in I Arevalo, 'Spain: Contract—Damages Claims' (2006) 17(6) International Company and Commercial L Rev N46. There, it was held that the method of proof required (eg whether oral or written evidence) to prove the damages caused by a breach of contract was procedural under Spanish choice of law rules.

B. Admissibility

3. Admissibility in Criminal Cases

7.08 The rule that questions of admissibility are governed by the law of the forum is also generally supported by courts in Canadian and US criminal cases, although there are some signs of dissent. Typically, evidence has been collected in another jurisdiction to prosecute a defendant in the forum and the question has arisen of whether the forum court should apply its own law on admissibility or that of the place of collection. (Note that given that the cases involve criminal prosecutions, there is no cause of action and so no 'law of the cause'.)

7.09 In *R v Newall (No 1)*[25] evidence was obtained by wiretap in the United States, which would not have been admissible under US law. The evidence was nevertheless accepted by a Canadian court on the basis that admissibility was procedural and governed by the law of the forum. A similar approach and result was evident in the more recent Quebec Court of Appeal decision in *R v Thomas*.[26] At least one distinguished Canadian judge has, however, suggested that the forum law governs admissibility rule should be justified, at least in criminal cases, in terms of public policy rather than because admissibility is classified as procedural. In some cases, for example, it may be appropriate to admit evidence where it has been obtained in accordance with the law of the place of collection and there is no unfairness to the defendant. In other cases, even where there has been compliance with foreign law in obtaining the evidence, local public policy should be employed to prevent admission where there may be unfairness to the defendant.[27] Such an approach is a more sophisticated choice of law analysis in that it makes the application of forum law depend both upon compliance with the law of the place where the evidence was collected and the question of fairness to the defendant. In this way, forum law is applied in a more policy-oriented manner rather than simply because the whole issue of admissibility is procedural. Such a view is also arguably more consistent with the decisions and legislative instruments involving taking evidence abroad where, in certain circumstances, the law of the country where the evidence is collected is recognized and applied.[28]

7.10 In the United States, forum law has also been generally applied in criminal cases where evidence has been obtained in a foreign jurisdiction (for example a confession) and a question has arisen as to its admissibility in the

---

[25] (1982) 67 CCC (2d) 431 (BCSC).
[26] (2005) 199 CCC (3d) 188.
[27] *R v Harrer* (1995) 128 DLR (4th) 98, para 17 (La Forest J).
[28] See Ch 8.

forum, although again there are some opposing views. In some decisions application of the law of the forum is justified on the basis that questions of admissibility are procedural,[29] while in others forum law is applied for reasons of public policy, specifically because it provides greater protection to the defendant in denying admissibility,[30] or because the forum is the place where the crime occurred and is being prosecuted and so has the strongest interest in applying its law.[31] By contrast, in numerous other cases, the law of the place where the evidence was obtained has been applied on the basis that it has the closest connection to the issue of admissibility.[32]

7.11 A related issue which has arisen in a number of US decisions is what law should be applied where evidence was obtained *in breach* of the law of a foreign jurisdiction and then sought to be admitted in a prosecution in the forum. The question is whether the forum should use its exclusionary rules to suppress the evidence (in effect applying the foreign law as the law of the place of collection of the evidence) or ignore the foreign law and admit the material under forum rules on admissibility. Most US courts have applied forum law to admit the evidence, again on the basis that the forum has the closest connection to the issue of admissibility since it is the place where the crime occurred and is being prosecuted.[33] Hence the US position, especially in criminal cases, is not unanimously in favour of forum law on admissibility, and even in the cases where it is applied this is at least as much due to public policy reasons as to application of a procedural classification.

4. Interpretation Versus Variation of Documents

7.12 The arguable weakness in the current common law position on admissibility is well illustrated by the distinction drawn between extrinsic evidence relied upon to interpret a document, and extrinsic evidence which adds to, varies, or contradicts its terms. The first situation is classified as an issue of

---

[29] *State v Briggs* 756 A 2d 731 (RI 2000); *People v Burge* 443 SW 2d 720 (Tex Crim App 1969); *People v Ostas* 179 AD 2d 893 (SCNY 1992).

[30] *Davidson v State* 25 SW 3d 183 (Tex Crim App 2000); *State v Lynch* 969 P 2d 920 (Mont 1998); *People v Flores* 28 Misc 3d 1213A (SCNY 2010).

[31] *People v Saiken* 275 NE 2d 381, 385 (Ill 1971); *Commonwealth v Miller* 15 Mass L Rptr 11 (Mass Superior Court 2002); *People v Flores* 28 Misc 3d 1213A (SCNY 2010).

[32] *Commonwealth v Sanchez* 716 A 2d 1221 (Pa 1998); *Frick v Oklahoma* 634 P 2d 738 (Okla Crim App 1981); *Washington v Brown* 940 P 2d 546 (Wash 1997); *State v Bridges* 925 P 2d 357 (Hawaii 1996).

[33] *People v Orlosky* 40 Cal App 3d 935 (CA Cal 1974); *Commonwealth v Miller* 15 Mass L Rptr 11 (Mass Superior Court 2002); *Commonwealth v Cryer* 689 NE 2d 808 (Mass 1998).

B. Admissibility

interpretation of an instrument and governed by the law of the cause of action but the second example is seen as an issue of admissibility of evidence or proof and governed by the law of the forum. The consequence of this view is that the common law 'parole evidence' rule—by which oral statements may not be admitted to contradict the terms of a subsequent written agreement—will apply to a contract governed, for example, by the law of a civil law country, where no such rule exists. This was the outcome reached in *Korner v Witkowitzer*.[34]

It is hard to see why both the issues of interpretation and variation are not considered substantive and referred to the law of the cause of action, given that they plainly impact upon the rights of the parties by determining the meaning and existence of the terms of an agreement. Also, there would be little practical inconvenience to the forum court in admitting such evidence. The Australian Law Reform Commission, in its report on choice of law, advocated a substantive classification,[35] and this position is also generally adopted in the United States[36] and European civil law countries.[37] There is also some evidence of a move in this direction in the New Zealand decision in *Filter Solutions Ltd v Donaldson Australia Pty Ltd*.[38] In this case the court had to determine whether provisions of the Contractual Remedies Act 1979 (NZ) applied to a contract which was governed by New South Wales law. The Act allowed the court to imply terms into the contract which would not have been possible under the governing law of the agreement, given the presence of an 'entire contract' provision which prevented admission of further terms. The court, despite referring to the *Korner* case,[39] concluded that the capacity under the Act for implying terms into a contract was a substantive matter for choice of law purposes with the result that the statute would only apply if New Zealand law was the governing law.[40] Such an approach seems to be an implicit rejection of *Korner* since a power to imply terms into an agreement is arguably more

7.13

---

[34] [1950] 2 KB 128; see also *Brown v Thornton* (1837) 6 Ad and El 185.

[35] Australian Law Reform Commission, *Choice of Law* (Report No 58, 1992) para 10.48; See also M Davies, A Bell, and P Brereton, *Nygh's Conflict of Laws in Australia* (LexisNexis Butterworths, 8th edn, 2010) para 16.22 and M Illmer, 'Neutrality Matters—Some Thoughts about the Rome Regulations and the so-called Dichotomy of Substance and Procedure in European Private International Law' (2009) 28 Civil Justice Quarterly 237, 256.

[36] Restatement (Second) of Conflict of Laws, § 140; *Mueller v Hubbard Milling Co* 573 F 2d 1029, 1035 (8th Cir 1978); *Menendez v Perishable Distributors Inc* 329 SE 2d 149 (SC Ga 1985); *Southeastern Health Care Inc v Payton Health Care Facilities Inc* 1988 WL 71209 (ND Ill); McDougal (n 10 above) 419.

[37] Bellini (n 11 above) 340.

[38] [2006] NZHC 762.

[39] ibid para 71.

[40] ibid para 73.

akin to a variation, than an interpretation, of a contract.[41] Hopefully, this approach will be followed in future Commonwealth decisions, although the prognosis is not entirely clear.[42]

7.14 Further support for a reconsideration of the view in *Korner*, comes from article 18(2) of the Rome I Regulation which provides that a contract or an act intended to have legal effect may be proved by any means of proof recognized by the law of the forum or by any of the laws which govern formal validity under the Regulation, namely the law of the cause of action and the law of the place of the act.[43] The editors of *Dicey, Morris and Collins* suggest that this provision 'will in some cases render admissible evidence of the type declared inadmissible under English law in *Korner*...'.[44]

C. BURDEN OF PROOF AND PRESUMPTIONS

1. Burden of Proof

7.15 The issue of the burden of proof arises when a rule imposes a duty on a party to persuade the court of the existence of a certain fact in order to establish a claim or defence. While courts in some earlier decisions suggested that the question of the burden or onus of proof was governed by the law of the forum,[45] the preponderant view among commentators[46] is to consider it substantive and governed by the law of the cause of action. This conclusion is justified by the fact that since the burden of proof can have a plainly outcome determinative effect in certain cases, it should not be divorced from the substantive right which is sought to be established. An example of this situation is where a claimant can provide no evidence of a right which he or she claims, yet under the law of the cause of action,

---

[41] Interestingly, it was not argued that the Act could apply in New Zealand as an overriding mandatory rule.

[42] Unfortunately, an Australian court recently reaffirmed the traditional distinction from *Korner* in *Australian Zircon NL v Austpac Resources NL* (2010) 243 FLR 423, para 69 although, in that case, the issue was whether evidence of circumstances surrounding the contract were admissible which was held to be substantive even on the *Korner* view. In *Seaworld Parks and Entertainment LLC v Marineland of Canada Inc* 2011 ONSC 4084 an Ontario court applied foreign law to the question of whether parole evidence may be admitted to interpret or vary a contract but found it to be the same as forum law in any event.

[43] See also Rome II, art 22(2).

[44] *Dicey, Morris and Collins* (n 22 above) para 7.018.

[45] *The Roberta* (1937) 58 Lloyd's Rep 159, 177.

[46] A Briggs, *The Conflict of Laws* (Clarendon Press, 2nd edn, 2008) 234; R Graveson, *Conflict of Laws* (Sweet & Maxwell, 7th edn, 1974) 602, M Wolff, *Private International Law* (OUP, 2nd edn, 1950) 234–5; J Fawcett and J Carruthers, *Cheshire, North and Fawcett Private International Law* (OUP, 14th edn, 2008) 89.

C. Burden of Proof and Presumptions

which creates the right, the burden of proof would rest on the person denying the right to prevent the claimant succeeding.[47] A substantive classification would also be likely to be adopted in Australia and Canada under these countries' more restrictive conceptions of procedure/expansive views of substance. The same view has also been taken in civil law countries.[48] Recently, in *Fiona Trust and Holding Corporation v Privalov*,[49] Andrew Smith J noted that while 'generally as a matter of English private international law, the burden of proof is probably a procedural matter determined by the *lex fori*', he could not 'accept that, in determining whether harm was caused by the defendant's fault [under a provision of the Russian Civil Code] the English court would not give effect to the express provision in paragraph 2 of article 1064 [of the Code] that the burden of proof about this is upon the defendant'.[50] This statement suggests a move towards application of the law of the cause of action to the issue of burden of proof.

The dominant view among courts and commentators in the United States is now also to classify the issue of the burden of proof as substantive.[51] For example, under section 133 of the Second Restatement, Conflict of Laws, the law of the cause of action will be applied to burden of proof 'where the primary purpose of the rule . . . is to affect decision of the issue rather than regulate the conduct of the trial'. According to both English[52] and US authority,[53] an example of an outcome determinative burden would be

7.16

---

[47] Graveson (n 46 above) 602; Wolff (n 46 above) 234–5.
[48] Bellini (n 11 above) 339. See also for France: Audit (n 4 above) para 447; Spain: Caravaca and González (n 4 above) 407; Belgium: Rigaux and Fallon (n 11 above) para 11.15; Switzerland: Bucher and Bonomi (n 4 above) 52–3; Germany: Bundesgerichtshof 29 June 1989 [1990] ECLY 160; and the Netherlands: DC Utrecht, 30 August 1978 (affd CA Amsterdam 13 May 1982) 1983 NIPR 204, cited in R van Rooij and M Polak, *Private International Law in the Netherlands* (Kluwer, 1987) 104.
[49] [2010] EWHC 3199 (Comm).
[50] ibid para 94.
[51] For early decisions to this effect, see *Precourt v Driscoll* 157 A 525 (NH 1931) and *O'Leary v Illinois Terminal Railroad Co* 299 SW 2d 873 (Sup Ct Mo 1957). See also McDougal (n 10 above) 418, R Weintraub, *Commentary on the Conflict of Laws* (Foundation Press, 4th edn, 2001) 62 and E Morgan, 'Choice of Law Governing Proof' (1944) 58 Harvard L Rev 153, 185. cf *Shaps v Provident Life & Accident Insurance Co* 826 So 2d 250 (SC Fla 2002) where the burden of proof was classified as procedural but based on the outdated view of substance and procedure that the burden of proof only related to the enforcement of rights (the remedy) rather than the creation or extinguishment of rights.
[52] *Dawson v Broughton* (2007) 151 Sol Jnl 1167 (Manchester County Court); *Harding v Wealands* [2007] 2 AC 1, para 74 (Lord Rodger).
[53] *Fitzpatrick v International Railway* 169 NE 112 (1929) (NYCA); cf *Mudd v Goldblatt Bros Inc* 454 NE 2d 754 (App Ct Ill 1983) (burden of proof a matter of evidence and therefore procedural; see comment in relation to *Shaps v Provident Life & Accident Insurance Company* 826 So 2d 250 (SC Fla 2002) at n 51 above).

that placed on a defendant in proving contributory negligence in a tort case. By contrast, a burden of proof in relation to preliminary matters, such as on the question of establishing or challenging jurisdiction, should be governed by forum law.[54]

7.17 The substantive interpretation also receives support from the EU instruments on choice of law already mentioned. For example, under the Rome I and Rome II Regulations, the applicable law of the obligation in each case will apply to the extent that it contains, in the law of the obligation, rules which determine the burden of proof.[55] Interestingly, while these provisions purport to refer the issue of the burden of proof to the law of the obligation, as opposed to the law of the forum, such a result may not always be obtained. The problem is that the wording in the provisions does not simply refer the issue of the burden of proof to the law of the obligation; such law is applied only to the extent that, according to the choice of law rules of the law of the obligation, the matter would be classified as substantive and not procedural. The EU instruments therefore require the adjudicating court to classify the issue according to the law of the cause of action.[56] There is therefore the possibility that an English court may be required to apply the law of a foreign country to the issue of the burden of proof only to find that such country's choice of law rules treat the matter as procedural. Presumably in such a case the matter is then determined by application of the English common law choice of law rules on the basis that the EU instrument does not apply. If by application of such common law rules, the burden of proof is regarded as a substantive issue and governed by the law of the cause of action, such law will then be applied without regard to how the choice of law rules of such law classify the issue. Indeed, if the choice of law rules of the law of the cause of action were also engaged, the problem of 'gap' in the applicable law may arise where no law is found to govern the issue of burden of proof.[57] Avoidance of this problem is therefore a further reason for only applying the choice of law rules of the forum state at this point in the analysis. A different result may, however, be reached under the Australian 'no advantage/uniformity of outcome' test,[58] since in such a case the forum court would have

---

[54] *Tietloff v Lift-A-Loft Corp* 441 NE 2d 986 (CA Ind 1982).

[55] Rome I, art 18(1); Rome II, art 22(1).

[56] R Fentiman, *Foreign Law in English Courts* (OUP, 1998) 37–8; *Cheshire, North and Fawcett* (n 46 above) 89; R Plender and M Wilderspin, *The European Private International Law of Obligations* (Sweet & Maxwell, 3rd edn, 2009) paras 14.079, 17.062; cf E Schoeman, 'Rome II and the Substance-Procedure Dichotomy' [2010] LMCLQ 81, 84–6, 91 who argues that the law of the obligation has exclusive application in such a case.

[57] J McLeod, *The Conflict of Laws* (Carswell Legal Publications, 1983) 220.

[58] *Neilson v Overseas Project Corp of Victoria Ltd* (2005) 223 CLR 331.

C. *Burden of Proof and Presumptions* 201

to apply the law selected by the choice of law rules of the law of the cause of action and any *renvoi* doctrine under that law.

2. PRESUMPTIONS

Commentators have traditionally divided presumptions into two categories: **7.18** irrebuttable and rebuttable presumptions. An irrebuttable (or conclusive) presumption exists when, upon proof of a set of material facts in a case, the adjudicating court must reach a particular legal conclusion. Such rules are widely considered to be substantive and governed by the law of the cause of action because of their closeness to the substantive right at stake in the litigation and their plainly outcome determinative effect.[59] In addition, according to the distinction at 7.02,[60] such a presumption would seem to be an example of facts that are required to be proved (and so substantive) rather than a method of proving the facts themselves. For example, in *Re Cohn*[61] an English statutory rule provided that where two people died in circumstances where it was not possible to determine who died first, the elder was presumed to have died before the younger. The court held that this presumption was substantive because it was 'not directed to helping in the ascertainment of any fact' but was a rule which applied 'in all cases affecting title to property'. The rule therefore did not apply where foreign law was the law of the cause of action. Consequently, the German law or rule which provided that the deceased were presumed to have died simultaneously was applied. Interestingly, the court also made a characterization of the German rule and found it to be substantive. If a procedural classification had been reached, the problem of 'gap' in the applicable law may have arisen with the court unable to resolve the dispute. Fortunately, this problem did not arise.[62]

A *rebuttable* presumption of law by contrast arises when, after proof of a **7.19** set of facts, the court must reach a certain legal conclusion unless the contrary position is proven. The classification of such presumptions is less certain than with irrebuttable rules. A good argument nevertheless also exists for a substantive interpretation, given that a rebuttable presumption may still provide a claimant with a strong case in circumstances where he or she would otherwise lose, where, for example, there is little evidence to

---

[59] *Fiona Trust and Holding Corp v Privalov* [2010] EWHC 3199 (Comm), para 98; the US Restatement (Second), § 134 provides that where 'the primary purpose of the rule . . . is to affect decision of the issue rather than regulate the conduct of the trial' a presumption of the law of the cause of action will be applied in the forum. See also McDougal (n 10 above) 416.
[60] *The Gaetano and Maria* (1882) 7 PD 137 (CA).
[61] [1945] Ch 5.
[62] The problem of 'gap' and 'cumulation' in the applicable law is discussed at 3.02 above.

support the claim.⁶³ Such presumptions may therefore often be closely connected to the substantive right and also outcome determinative. Where a presumption has this character,⁶⁴ most Commonwealth courts, the US Second Restatement,⁶⁵ and US courts⁶⁶ have held it to be substantive. A good example of a rebuttable presumption is section 419(4) of the Merchant Shipping Act 1894 (UK) which provided that where a ship breached the International Regulations for the Prevention of Collisions at Sea 1897 and was involved in a collision with another vessel, the infringing ship would be presumed to be at fault unless proof was shown to the contrary. Such a provision was held to impact directly on the party's rights and liabilities and so was substantive.⁶⁷

7.20 Within the category of rebuttable presumptions are also those of more general application such as the validity of marriage, resulting trust, that a person has died, and that a child is legitimate. In the case of marriage, Commonwealth courts have routinely applied such a presumption existing under a (foreign) law of the cause of action, hence implicitly treating it as substantive.⁶⁸ For example, in a Hong Kong decision⁶⁹ the court refused to apply a presumption under forum law supporting the validity of an existing marriage over an earlier one where the law governing the parties' capacity to marry was foreign. According to the court, a presumption of marriage (relating to a party's capacity to marry) is a matter of substantive law and governed by the law of the party's pre-marriage domicile.⁷⁰ In the case of death, by contrast, courts have appeared to treat a foreign presumption as procedural without much analysis,⁷¹ although in

---

⁶³ McDougal (n 10 above) 415.

⁶⁴ cf Tetley, who regards all rebuttable presumptions as substantive: W Tetley, *International Conflict of Laws Common, Civil and Maritime* (International Shipping Publications: Blais, 1994) 606, 611.

⁶⁵ See Restatement (Second), § 134 discussed at n 59 above and Morgan (n 51 above) 193–4.

⁶⁶ *Rowe v Hoffmann-La Roche Inc* 892 A 2d 694 (NJ Superior Court 2006); *PPG Industries Inc v Central Industrial Maintenance Inc* 2006 WL 752982 (WD Pa); *De Santis v Wackenhut Corp* 732 SW 2d 29 (CA Tex 1987) (presumption of irreparable harm in permanent injunction application).

⁶⁷ *Owners of Sailing Ship 'Fortunato Figari' v Steamship 'Coogee'* (1904) 29 VLR 874, 900 (Sup Ct Vic). For two more recent US decisions involving shipping collisions in which a similar approach was taken and outcome reached, see *Ishikazi Kisen Co v US* 510 F 2d 875 (9th Cir 1975) and *Otal Investments Ltd v M/V Clary Mineral Shipping Co* 494 F 3d 40 (2nd Cir 2007).

⁶⁸ *Mahadervan v Mahadervan* [1964] P 233; *De Thoren v A-G* (1876) 1 App Cas 686.

⁶⁹ *Wong Zhong Lan-Xiang v Wong* [2002] HKCFI 50.

⁷⁰ ibid paras 79–80.

⁷¹ *In the Goods of Schulhof* [1948] P 66; cf Bellini (n 11 above) 340, n 26, who argues, by reference to civilian doctrine, that it should be substantive.

C. Burden of Proof and Presumptions

the United States a presumption against the suicide of an insured person has been found to be substantive.[72]

In recent civil liability legislation in Australia two new presumptions have been created: the first is that a person is presumed to be aware of the risk of injury if the risk was 'obvious' to a reasonable person in his or her position.[73] The intention of this provision was to make it easier for a defendant to succeed on the defence of voluntary assumption of risk than would be the case at common law and so is clearly directed at the rights and liabilities of the parties and would therefore be substantive.[74] Such a conclusion is supported by the observation of Lord Rodger in *Harding v Wealands*[75] that the defence of voluntary assumption of risk is substantive. The second new presumption in the Australian legislation is that contributory negligence will be presumed when an injured person is intoxicated.[76] Since it is well established that the defence of contributory negligence is substantive,[77] a presumption closely connected with this plea should be equally classified.   7.21

The status of an important evidentiary presumption in tort law—*res ipsa loquitur*—is unclear. Under this doctrine, which is applied in most common law jurisdictions, a court is permitted to infer negligence on the part of the defendant from the occurrence of the accident itself. While there are no Commonwealth cases on point, the US Second Restatement (and most US decisions)[78] provides that such a rule should generally be considered procedural and governed by forum law since it is no more than a matter of circumstantial evidence which only *invites* the tribunal to reach a conclusion on liability. Where, however, the doctrine is expressed as a *presumption* which a defendant must rebut to escape liability, then it should be classified as substantive.[79] On balance, this general conclusion in favour of the procedural view is probably correct: although *res ipsa loquitur* is related to the issue of substantive liability, it is more in the nature of a method of proof or strategy for the court in gathering relevant evidence. The doctrine does not direct the court on how the case should be decided; it simply   7.22

---

[72] *Melville v American Home Assurance Co* 584 F 2d 1306 (3rd Cir 1978).
[73] See eg Civil Liability Act 2002 (NSW), s 5G(1); Civil Liability Act 2003 (Qld), s 14(1); Civil Liability Act 1936 (SA), s 37(1).
[74] M Davies, 'Choice of Law after the Civil Liability Legislation' (2008) 16 Torts LJ 104, n 56.
[75] [2007] 2 AC 1, para 74.
[76] See eg Civil Law (Wrongs) Act 2002 (ACT), s 95(1); Civil Liability Act 2002 (NSW), s 50(1); Civil Liability Act 2003 (Qld), s 47(1)–(3).
[77] *Dawson v Broughton* (2007) 151 Sol Jnl 1167 (Manchester County Court); *Harding v Wealands* [2007] 2 AC 1, para 74 (Lord Rodger).
[78] See eg *Boersma v Amoco Oil Co* 658 NE 2d 1173 (Ill App Ct 1995).
[79] Restatement (Second), § 135 comment b.

offers the court an approach to achieving a certain result. A rule that silence on the part of a party with regard to facts alleged by the other party may be considered an admission of those facts should be similarly classified.[80] It follows that the same result should apply in the case of what is known in Australian law as the *Jones v Dunkel* principle;[81] that is, the inference that may arise against a party who elects not to adduce evidence on a matter in issue.

7.23 A rebuttable presumption of law can, however, also be linked to the conduct or regulation of the forum court's proceedings.[82] A rule, for example, which provided that a subsidiary of a foreign company carrying on business in the forum is presumed to be an agent of such company for the purpose of service and asserting jurisdiction over the company[83] should be applied as part of the law of the forum. Forum law also has the closest connection to the issue of service of process, a matter which would also be regarded as procedural under any of the applicable tests.[84] A rule whereby the claim of a party is considered substantiated if the other party fails to enter an appearance (such as in summary judgment proceedings) should also be considered procedural.[85] While obviously outcome determinative, the rule is closely tied to the court's management of its own proceedings and its concern with limiting costs and encouraging expedition in litigation. Similarly, a presumption which is used by a court to establish the facts to determine what legal issues are relevant should be regarded as procedural and governed by the law of the forum, since it is forensic in nature and arises at a preliminary stage of the litigation.[86] For example, the common law presumption that foreign law is identical to local law in the absence of proof to the contrary is best seen as procedural. There is no doubt that the application of such a rule may have 'outcome determinative' effect in a given case (because the claimant can rely upon forum law as the law of the cause of action as opposed to having its case dismissed for failure to prove the relevant foreign law). Yet because the rule is a method by which the court establishes the relevant facts and issues (here the applicable law), it is a form of 'machinery'. Indeed, all the rules governing proof of foreign law are best regarded as procedural, a conclusion which would especially follow in common law systems where foreign law is regarded as a question of fact which must be pleaded and proven by the parties, not applied

---

[80] Giuliano-Lagarde Report (n 18 above) 36.
[81] (1959) 101 CLR 298 (Aust H Ct).
[82] Australian Law Reform Commission (n 35 above) para 10.53.
[83] cf *Adams v Cape Industries Plc* [1990] Ch 433.
[84] See 4.01 above.
[85] Giuliano-Lagarde Report (n 18 above) 36.
[86] Walker (n 2 above) para 6.3(c).

C. Burden of Proof and Presumptions

ex officio by the court. Once again, the function of the rule here is forensic and mechanical: to assist the court in establishing 'the facts' so that the legal issues in dispute can be identified and resolved.[87] Furthermore, adoption of a substantive view of pleading and proof of foreign law would require the forum to engage in the circular task of first having to find the applicable law and (if foreign) then using such law to determine the rules governing how and whether such law must be pleaded and proven.

The EU law instruments on applicable law mentioned earlier contain the same provision in respect of presumptions as was seen in the case of burden of proof; that is, the law governing the obligation will apply to presumptions of law to the extent that such law classifies presumptions as substantive and not procedural.[88] Note again that this provision will require an English court to make reference to foreign rules of classification with respect to presumptions if such law is the law of the obligation. The other point to note about the EU provisions is that they draw no distinction between rebuttable and irrebuttable presumptions. Under the private international law rules of many civil law countries, presumptions are also considered substantive and governed by the law of the cause of action.[89] **7.24**

Before leaving the topics of the burden of proof and presumptions, it is important to note the role for public policy, which may sometimes operate as an unarticulated but influential choice of law rule in this area. For example, provisions which aim to deter fraud or undue influence are not obviously procedural in the sense of being connected with the remedy sought or because they concern the mode or conduct of court proceedings. Moreover, the application of such rules may clearly have an impact on the outcome of litigation and so arguably should be considered substantive. Yet in a number of cases it has been suggested that the rules of the forum on such matters should nevertheless be applied, given the need of the forum to uphold local standards and deter unconscionable conduct.[90] As an illustration of this principle, the policy underlying the rule in English law, which prevents witnesses to a will also being beneficiaries, could be regarded as sufficiently strong to be applied notwithstanding that the law **7.25**

---

[87] R Hausmann, 'Pleading and Proof of Foreign Law: A Comparative Analysis' (2008) The European Legal Forum I-2008 I-I.

[88] See 7.17 above, and the German decision reported at [2011] ECLY 16 where, under Rome II, art 22(1), the court applied the law of the obligation (the Netherlands) to the question of whether a presumption of fault existed.

[89] Giuliano-Lagarde Report (n 18 above) 36; for France: Audit (n 4 above) para 447; Spain: Caravaca and González (n 4 above) 407; Belgium: Rigaux and Tallon (n 11 above) para 11.15; and Switzerland: Bucher and Bonimi (n 4 above) 52–3.

[90] Davies (n 35 above) para 16.28.

of the cause of action was foreign.[91] This last point is a useful reminder, again, that the substantive and procedural categories should not be used to conceal choice of law decisions made on other policy grounds. A frank and transparent admission as to the policies underlying the choice of law determination should be encouraged.

D. INDIVIDUAL TOPICS WITHIN EVIDENCE

1. Statutory Requirement of Written Evidence

7.26 Another issue which, in Commonwealth countries, has historically been referred to the law of the forum but remains controversial is the status of statutory provisions which require that, for a transaction to be enforceable, it must be evidenced or proven by a written note or memorandum. The most famous example of such an enactment is the Statute of Frauds 1677 the legacy of which survives in English law in other statutory provisions which impose writing requirements.[92] According to the old English decision of *Leroux v Brown*,[93] such provisions are procedural where they merely render the contract unenforceable and so relate to the remedy, as opposed to rendering it invalid which would extinguish the parties' rights and therefore be substantive. In the *Leroux* case an oral contract which was formally valid under French law, the law of the cause of action, was not enforced in England due to the absence of writing. By logic, the reverse situation should also apply: a writing requirement under the law of the cause of action will not be applied in the forum where the contract is formally valid under local law.

7.27 The result in *Leroux v Brown* has been criticized by academic commentators for many years[94] but arguably is simply an orthodox application of the right-remedy view of substance and procedure.[95] Not surprisingly then, in more recent English decisions, where the same test of substance

---

[91] *Re Fuld's Estate (No 3)* [1968] P 675.
[92] See eg Law of Property Act 1925 (UK), s 53(1)(a) and (b).
[93] (1852) 12 CB 801.
[94] See eg AH Robertson, *Characterization in the Conflict of Laws* (Harvard University Press, 1940) 255; W Beckett, 'The Question of Classification in Private International Law'(1934) 15 BYBIL 46, 69–71; E Lorenzen, 'The Statute of Frauds and the Conflict of Laws' (1923) 32 Yale LJ 311; *Cheshire, North and Fawcett* (n 46 above) 77; *Dicey, Morris and Collins* (n 22 above) para 7.019; McLeod (n 57 above) 221; G Johnston, *The Conflict of Laws in Hong Kong* (Sweet & Maxwell Asia, 2005) para 2-007; see also Australian Law Reform Commission (n 35 above) para 10.50.
[95] Lorenzen (n 94 above) 324.

and procedure has continued to apply, the case has been followed,[96] although not universally.[97] Certainly, application of more contemporary notions of substance and procedure—in particular, an analysis which focuses on whether the issue is outcome determinative or relates to the mode or conduct of court proceedings—should yield a substantive classification. According to this view, there is no difference between a provision which declares a contract 'unenforceable' due to a lack of writing as opposed to 'invalid', as either results in the parties' rights under the contract being set aside. Also, there is little likelihood that applying a writing requirement under foreign law would inconvenience the forum. A substantive classification of writing formalities has consistently been adopted in the United States[98] and most recently has been accepted by the Western Australian Court of Appeal in *Tipperary Developments Pty Ltd v the State of Western Australia*.[99] In *Tipperary Developments* the Court applied the 'outcome determinative' test from *John Pfeiffer Pty Ltd v Rogerson* to reject the view that a writing requirement was procedural. Note, however, that the law of the cause of action was also the law of the forum in that case and so the ruling was not essential to the decision. The same result was reached in a recent Canadian decision where a forum statute which rendered a contract unenforceable without writing was held to be only applicable where forum law was the law of the cause of action.[100]

7.28 The conclusion in cases such as *Tipperary*, that writing requirements for contracts are substantive and governed by the law of the cause of action, may be compared with the view suggested at 7.06, that writing formalities in relation to contracts or other documents should be regarded as a matter of formal validity.[101] In terms of applicable law, however, the result is likely to be the same whichever classification is adopted. As noted at 7.06, in questions of formal validity, while the law of the place of execution (the *lex*

---

[96] See eg *G + H Montage GmbH v Irvani* [1990] 1 WLR 667 (CA); *Maddison v Alderson* (1883) 8 AC 467, 474; *Morris v Baron & Co* [1918] AC 1, 15 (both HL).

[97] *Monterosso Shipping Co Ltd v International Transport Workers Federation* [1982] 2 Lloyd's Rep 120, 129 (Lord Denning MR), 131–2 (May LJ).

[98] Restatement (Second), § 141; *Bernkrant v Fowler* 360 P 2d 906 (Cal 1961); *Paulson v Shapiro* 490 F 2d 1, 6 (7th Cir 1973); *Bushkin Associates v Raytheon Co* 473 NE 2d 662 (Sup Jud Ct Mass 1985); *Spink & Son Ltd v General Atlantic Corp Ltd* 167 Misc 2d 120 (NYSC 1996); *Trumpet Vine Investments NV v Union Capital Partners Inc* 92 F 3d 1110 (11th Cir 1996); *Samra v Shaheen Business & Investment Group Inc* 355 F Supp 2d 483 (DDC 2005); *Aramarine Brokerage Inc v OneBeacon Ins Co* 307 Fed Appx 562 (2nd Cir 2009).

[99] (2009) 38 WAR 488, para 81 (McLure JA with whom Wheeler and Newnes JJA agreed); see also Australian Law Reform Commission (n 35 above) para 10.50, which advocates a substantive classification.

[100] *Miller Farm Equipment (2005) Inc v Shewchuk* (2009) 335 Sask R 111, para 56 (Sask Ct QB).

[101] Cheshire, North and Fawcett (n 46 above) 747.

loci actus) has a strong claim to application in respect of documents such as powers of attorney, in the case of contracts the law governing the contract is preferable because the place of contracting is often fortuitous and difficult to identify. There is little Commonwealth authority on point, although in one Canadian decision a requirement that a notarial certificate be produced, before a guarantee could be enforced, was held to apply in the forum on the basis that the requirement existed under both the law governing the contract and the law of the place of execution (which were the same).[102] Under EU instruments, such as the Rome Convention[103] and the Rome I[104] and Rome II[105] Regulations, the question of writing requirements in relation to a contract or an act intended to have legal effect is described as one of formal validity. Such instruments provide that a contract or an act may be proved by any means of proof recognized by the law of the forum or by any of the laws which govern formal validity under the Regulation, namely the law of the obligation and the law of the place of the act. Under the EU instruments, therefore, the result in *Leroux v Brown* would appear to be avoided: evidence *other than writing* of a contract under either the law governing the contract or the place of execution will now be admissible to prove its existence or validity.[106]

7.29 A further problem with the *Leroux v Brown* distinction between enforceability (procedural) and invalidity (substantive) is that an awkward situation may arise where under the law of the forum a contract would be void but under the law of the cause of action it would only be unenforceable. In such a case the forum may have no option but to uphold the contract even though it is defective under all relevant laws, an incredible result which occurred in an old US decision.[107] This is another illustration of a 'gap' in the applicable law which was discussed at 3.02; it is hoped that a Commonwealth court would avoid this conundrum by simply classifying all writing requirements as substantive.

7.30 While the logic of a substantive classification for writing requirements is compelling, one final comment should be made, that is, that the result of applying forum law in *Leroux v Brown* could still be reached today on a more justifiable basis according to contemporary choice of law notions.

---

[102] *Lehndorff Property Management Ltd v McGrath* [1984] 3 WWR 187 (BCSC); Walker (n 2 above) para 6.3(c).

[103] Rome Convention, art 14(2).

[104] Rome I, art 18(2).

[105] Rome II, art 22(2).

[106] *Dicey, Morris and Collins* (n 22 above) paras 7.020, 32.179; Plender and Wilderspin (n 56 above) para 14.073.

[107] *Marie v Garrison* 13 Abb N Cas 210 (NY 1883).

D. Individual Topics within Evidence

If such a statutory requirement were seen instead as an application of forum public policy and overriding mandatory rules, aiming to deter fraud or to encourage parties to reflect before entering binding agreements,[108] the outcome of applying forum law is arguably more defensible. Such a result has been reached by US courts where the transaction is found to be closely connected to the forum.[109] Note that the operation of forum overriding mandatory rules is expressly preserved under both the Rome I[110] and Rome II[111] Regulations. The effect of statutory rules which purport to control access to courts is considered in Chapter 6.

2. Witnesses

7.31 It is also well established that the questions of whether a witness is competent or compellable to testify are governed by the law of the forum.[112] Given the closeness of this issue to the mode and conduct of the forum court's proceedings (and the more slender connection with the outcome of the litigation) such a view is defensible. The same position applies in the United States[113] where, in cases involving a 'dead man's statute'—that is, a law which prevents a witness from testifying concerning any statement or transaction made by a dead person—US courts have classified the statute as procedural and so applied it where it forms part of forum law[114] but not where it is part of a (foreign) law of the cause of action.[115] The question of what law applies to a witness's or party's claim of privilege is more complex and is discussed in detail in Chapter 8.[116]

---

[108] McDougal supports the application of forum law in such a case, see (n 10 above) 420–1 but cf Lorenzen (n 94 above) 335–7, who argues that the policy of enforcement of private rights under a contract should take precedence.

[109] See eg *Intercontinental Planning Ltd v Daystrom Inc* 248 NE 2d 576 (NYCA 1969) and *Williamson Pounders Architects PC v Tunica County* 597 F 3d 292 (5th Cir 2010) but cf *Spink & Son Ltd v General Atlantic Corp* 167 Misc 2d 120 (NYSC 1996) where the transaction was found to be more closely connected to the country of the law of the cause of action and so the forum statute was not applied.

[110] Rome I, art 9.

[111] Rome II, art 16.

[112] *Bain v Whitehaven and Furness Junction Railway* (1850) 3 HLC 1, 19; *Kennedy v Anderson* (1991) 50 DLR 105 (Sask CA); *Cheshire, North and Fawcett* (n 46 above) 80; Illmer (n 35 above) 256.

[113] Restatement (Second), Conflict of Laws, § 137.

[114] *Maltas v Maltas* 197 F Supp 2d 409, 425 (D Md 2002).

[115] *Equitable Life Assurance Society v McKay* 760 P 2d 871 (S Ct Ore 1988).

[116] cf *Dicey, Morris and Collins* (n 22 above) para 7.025, who see the issue of privilege as procedural and governed by the law of the forum.

3. Evaluation and Probative Force of Evidence

7.32 While there is no direct Commonwealth authority in point, the question of what weight or value is to be given to admitted evidence is almost certainly a procedural matter and governed by forum law as it directly relates to how a court conducts its trials.[117] The question of whether sufficient evidence existed to support a court judgment should be similarly classified.[118]

7.33 With more hesitation, it is suggested that the question of standard of proof—that is, the level a claimant or defendant must reach before a claim or a defence will be considered established—should be similarly classified despite its potential to affect outcome.[119] The standard (or 'quantum') of proof is a key element in the court's tools for the administration of litigation and the conduct of its proceedings. In essence, the court is using the standard to evaluate the weight to be accorded to facts which have already been established. Hence, in a number of US decisions, courts have held that a requirement that a party prove its case by 'clear and convincing evidence' (as opposed to 'the preponderance of evidence') is procedural.[120]

4. Administration of Evidence

7.34 Finally, questions relating to the 'administration' of evidence, for example the right to discovery,[121] subpoenas against third parties,[122] Anton Piller (search and seizure) orders or expert reports, and the means by which witness evidence is to be received (whether in documentary or oral form,[123]

---

[117] This is the view taken in civil law countries: for France see Audit (n 4 above) para 449 and Spain, Caravaca and González (n 4 above) 407. See also Illmer (n 35 above) 257. Note, however, that a French commentator has recently argued that as the questions of administration of evidence and probative force or weight are intrinsically linked to other issues concerning evidence (for example admissibility) they should all be subjected to the same law, in that writer's view, the law of the cause of action; see M-L Niboyet, 'Contre Le Dogme de la *Lex Fori* en Matière de Procédure' in *Vers de nouveaux équilibres entre ordres juridiques mélanges en l'honneur de Hélène Gaudemet-Tallon* (Dalloz, 2008) 363, 372–3.

[118] Restatement (Second), § 135; *Hystro Products Inc v MNP Corp* 18 F 3d 1384, 1388 (7th Cir 1994).

[119] Bellini (n 11 above) 338–9; Johnston (n 94 above) para 2.009.

[120] *Boone v Royal Indemnity Co* 460 F 2d 26, 29 (10th Cir 1972); *Computerized Radiological Services Inc v Syntex Corp* 595 F Supp 1495, 1503 (EDNY 1984). Note that in these cases the courts described the issue as one of 'burden of proof' but it is clear from the provisions discussed that the matter involved a question of *standard* of proof.

[121] Restatement (Second), § 127 comment a (5).

[122] ibid.

[123] Illmer (n 35 above) 256.

D. Individual Topics within Evidence

what oath (if any) is administered, whether the court or counsel may question witnesses,[124] whether cross-examination[125] or pre-trial communication with witnesses is allowed), are at the heart of a court's conduct of its proceedings and should be governed by forum law. This conclusion is also implicit in the provisions of the Rome I[126] and Rome II[127] Regulations which provide that an act or contract intended to have legal effect may be proved by any mode of proof recognized by the law of the forum or by any of the laws governing the formal validity of the act or contract, provided that such mode of proof can be *administered by the forum*. The question of the law to be applied to aspects of the administration of evidence has not been debated in a common law court but both civil law courts[128] and commentators[129] almost unanimously support the view that forum law applies. The principal exception to the application of forum law here may be where a defendant resists an order to produce evidence by pleading a privilege or duty not to disclose under foreign law, a topic which is discussed in Chapter 8. Further, even where such a privilege or duty not to disclose is not invoked by the defendant, it still may be necessary for a claimant to seek enforcement of such orders requesting evidence in the courts of the country where the evidence is situated (which may be difficult) or alternatively to seek orders for disclosure directly from such courts. In both such cases, the court of the country where the evidence is situated may apply its own law to determine whether the evidence should be produced, subject to the provisions of relevant treaties such as the Hague Evidence Convention.

7.35 In a recent US decision[130] it was argued that the question of whether a party had engaged in 'evidence spoliation' or destruction should be classified as procedural; but the court did not have to resolve the question as it found no conflict between the laws of the forum and the cause of action on the issue. In principle, however, the question of a party's conduct in relation to the preservation of evidence is closely connected with the court's powers of administration and so a procedural classification is

---

[124] Tetley (n 64 above) 612.
[125] Restatement (Second), § 127 comment a (6).
[126] Rome I, art 18(2).
[127] Rome II, art 22(2).
[128] See *Société Vandel v Sociétés ZF France and ZF Passau GmbH* (Court of Cassation Ie Ch Civ, 4 July 2007) [2008] ECLY 52 (right to preliminary expert report governed by forum law).
[129] Giuliano-Lagarde Report (n 18 above) 37. For France, see Audit (n 4 above) para 450 (but cf Niboyet (n 117 above); for Spain, Caravaca (n 4 above) 407; and for Belgium, Rigaux and Fallon (n 11 above) para 11.15.
[130] *Holiday v Ford Motor Co* 2006 WL 178011 (Ohio App Dist).

appropriate. This conclusion was recently reached by a German commentator in the context of the Rome I and Rome II Regulations.[131]

E. ESTOPPEL

7.36 The concept of estoppel exists in a number of forms in English common law, each of which must be addressed separately for applicable law purposes.

1. Issue and Cause of Action Estoppel

7.37 Issue estoppel arises where a particular matter has been decided in earlier proceedings and a party is estopped from raising it in subsequent proceedings. Cause of action estoppel or *res judicata* prevents a subsequent suit being brought on the same cause of action. Both issue and cause of action estoppel are sometimes referred to collectively as 'estoppel by record'. The question of the law to be applied to issue and cause of action estoppel has often arisen in the context of the recognition of foreign judgments. The leading English case is the decision of the House of Lords in *Carl Zeiss Stiftung v Rayner and Keeler Ltd (No 2)*[132] which concerned whether a foreign judgment could give rise to an issue estoppel in subsequent proceedings in England. Most textwriters cite the case as authority for the proposition that the law of the forum (that is, the country of recognition) applies to determine whether an issue estoppel arises on the basis that both issue and cause of action estoppel are matters of procedure.[133] This view is correct on any of the views of substance and procedure, given the relationship between the issue and the conduct of proceedings in the forum, in the sense that the forum does not want to expend resources on matters already determined elsewhere or reach a contradictory result to a foreign court. Public policy may therefore provide an alternative justification for the application of forum law in this context.

7.38 Yet forum law does not have exclusive application to estoppel by record. The requirements for both an issue and cause of action estoppel are that there is a final and conclusive judgment of the foreign court on the merits

---

[131] C Thole, 'Anscheinsbeweis und Beweisvereitelung im harmonisierten Europäischen Kollisionsrecht—ein Prüfstein für die Abgrenzung zwischen lex causae und lex fori' [2010] *Praxis des Internationalen Privat und Verfahrensrechts* 285, 288–9.

[132] [1967] 1 AC 853.

[133] See eg *Dicey, Morris and Collins* (n 22 above) para 7.031; T Yeo, *Choice of Law for Equitable Doctrines* (OUP, 2004) para 4.104; Illmer (n 35 above) 257.

E. *Estoppel*   213

and that the proceedings in the forum involve the same cause of action and the same parties (or privies). In the *Carl Zeiss* case Lord Reid examined most fully the question of applicable law. While he noted[134] that 'it is quite true that [issue] estoppel is a matter for the lex fori . . . the lex fori ought to be developed in a manner consistent with good sense'. Such a statement is reminiscent of the enlightened *lex fori* concept championed by Kahn-Freund, a view which is confirmed earlier in his speech when Lord Reid stated that regard must be had to the law of the country which rendered the judgment. Specifically, it must be shown by the parties seeking recognition of the issue estoppel that the judgment is final and conclusive under the law of the country of rendition, that is, the issue could not be relitigated under such law. 'It seems to me to verge on absurdity that we should regard as conclusive something in the German judgment which the German courts themselves would not regard as conclusive'.[135] The other members of the House of Lords agreed with Lord Reid on this point.[136] Consequently, on the facts of *Carl Zeiss*, no estoppel was found because the defendant failed to show that the German judgment was final and conclusive under German law. Such a view is consistent with the treatment of finality and conclusiveness in respect of recognition of foreign judgments more generally where the law of the country of rendition has long been applied to determine whether a foreign judgment was final.[137] This approach suggests that although issue and cause of action estoppel based on a foreign judgment are procedural matters and so principally governed by forum law, reference to the law of the country of rendition is also required to give proper recognition to the foreign interests involved. This issue is therefore either an example of a choice of law question arising *within* the field of procedure or a case of the forum limiting the application of its own rules by reference to foreign laws.

The majority of English decisions since *Carl Zeiss* have implicitly supported this view by applying the law of the country of rendition to the issue of whether the foreign judgment is final and conclusive, while employing the law of the forum to determine whether the causes of action and the parties are the same in both proceedings.[138] To this extent, therefore, the

7.39

---

[134] *Carl Zeiss Stiftung v Rayner and Keeler Ltd (No 2)* [1967] 1 AC 853, 919.
[135] ibid.
[136] See ibid 927 (Lord Hodson); 936 (Lord Guest); and 970 (Lord Wilberforce).
[137] *Nouvion v Freeman* (1889) 15 App Cas 1; *Schnabel v Lui* [2002] NSWSC 15; I Szászy, 'The Basic Connecting Factor in International Cases in the Domain of Civil Procedure' (1966) 15 ICLQ 436, 453.
[138] Note, however, that there have been occasional dicta suggesting that the law of the forum should have exclusive application to the issue; see eg *Vervaeke v Smith* [1983] 1 AC 145, 162 (Lord Simon of Glaisdale).

applicable law in issue and cause of action estoppel is a combination of foreign and forum law. So in *Black v Yates*,[139] while forum law was applied to determine if the causes of action were the same, it was conceded by the parties that the question of whether the foreign judgment was final was resolved by foreign law. More recently, in *Barrett v Universal-Island Records Ltd*,[140] it was reaffirmed 'that an English court should not give a foreign judgment greater conclusive effect than it would have in its home jurisdiction'[141] and so foreign law was applied to determine if the judgment was final and conclusive.[142] Finally, in the most recent English case on the question, the court appeared to go even further than the *Carl Zeiss* principle in its application of foreign law. In *Abdel Hadi Abdallah Al Qahtani & Sons Beverage Industry Co v Antliff*[143] the court applied foreign law both to the question of the finality of the foreign judgment and more broadly as to whether all the criteria for an issue estoppel were established under foreign law. If such a view were followed in later cases then forum law would be effectively excluded from the inquiry.

7.40 Therefore, it is clear from the English decisions that foreign law must be applied in issue and cause of action estoppel at least to the issue of finality. Such result is logical or else, as noted by Lord Reid, the law of the forum may give greater operation to a foreign judgment than the law of the country in which it was rendered.

7.41 The position in Commonwealth countries as regards applicable law in cause of action and issue estoppel is similarly unclear, with some courts applying foreign law (the law of the country of rendition of the judgment) to some or all aspects of the doctrine, while others apply the law of the forum (the law of the country of recognition) exclusively. While in Canada most courts[144] have taken the predominant English approach of applying the law of the country of rendition to the question of whether the foreign judgment was final and conclusive but leaving all other criteria for an estoppel to the law of the forum, in one case,[145] foreign law was applied in

---

[139] [1992] 1 QB 526.

[140] [2006] EWHC 1009.

[141] ibid para 189.

[142] See also, to the same effect, *The Good Challenger* [2003] EWHC 10 (Comm), para 31 (affd [2004] 1 Lloyd's Rep 67) and *HJ Heinz Co Ltd v EFL Inc* [2010] EWHC 1203 (Comm), paras 43–44.

[143] [2010] EWHC 1735 (Comm), paras 52–55; [2010] All ER(D) 172 (Jul).

[144] *Monteiro v Toronto Dominion Bank* 2006 Can LII 124 (ONSCDC), para 27 (affd (2008) 89 OR (3d) 565); *Gerling Global General Insurance Co v Canadian Occidental Petroleum Ltd* (1998) 230 AR 39, paras 21–23; *Four Embarcadero Center Venture v Mr Greenjeans Corp* (1988) 64 OR (2d) 746, 752–3 (affd (1988) 65 OR (2d) 160 (Ont CA)).

[145] *Consolidated Oil and Gas Inc v Suncor Inc* (1993) 140 AR 188, paras 27–32.

E. Estoppel

respect of all the elements of an estoppel, not merely the issue of finality. In Australia the question of issue/cause of action estoppel in relation to a foreign judgment has arisen in three decisions,[146] and in all of them the law of the forum was applied without any contrary argument from the parties. The same approach appears to have been taken in a recent Hong Kong decision, although in that case the finality of the foreign judgment was conceded by the defendant.[147] In Singapore the finality of a foreign judgment has been held to be governed by the law of the country of rendition.[148]

2. HENDERSON V HENDERSON ESTOPPEL

Another type of estoppel, although closely related to issue and cause of action estoppel, is that referred to under Australian law as 'Anshun' estoppel[149] and under English law as the rule in *Henderson v Henderson*.[150] According to this rule a party is precluded in subsequent proceedings from raising a cause of action or issue which they *could and should* have raised in the earlier proceedings. This doctrine is therefore related to issue and cause of action estoppel in that it operates as a method to ensure the finality of proceedings. While under issue and cause of action estoppel matters determined in previous proceedings cannot be reopened, under *Anshun* estoppel matters which should have been raised in previous proceedings cannot be subsequently aired. Where the conditions for the estoppel are established, which includes showing that the foreign judgment was final, any subsequent proceedings are an abuse of process. **7.42**

The question of what law applies to such an estoppel, where it is alleged in relation to forum proceedings subsequent to a foreign judgment, has been resolved in a similar way to issue and cause of action estoppel. While the existence of the doctrine itself, together with its sanction of abuse of process is clearly subject to forum law[151] on the basis of the public policy of protecting the forum's courts from vexatious proceedings, the English Court of Appeal has again held that the law of the country of rendition **7.43**

---

[146] *Nicholls v Michael Wilson and Partners Ltd* (2010) 243 FLR 177, para 392 (NSWCA Lindgren AJA); *Armacel Pty Ltd v Smurfit Stone Container Corp* (2008) 248 ALR 573, paras 80–81; and *Talacko v Talacko* [1999] VSC 81.
[147] *First Laser Ltd v Fujian Enterprises (Holdings) Co Ltd* [2011] HKCA 1, para 44.
[148] *Bellezza Club Japan Co Ltd v Matsumura Akihiko* [2010] 2 SLR 342, para 15 (Sing High Ct).
[149] *Port of Melbourne Authority v Anshun Pty Ltd* (1981) 147 CLR 589.
[150] (1843) 3 Hare 100; 67 ER 313.
[151] *Pacific International Sports Club Ltd v Soccer Marketing International Ltd* [2009] EWHC 1839 (Ch) paras 122–123; Yeo (n 133 above) para 4.104.

applies to determine the finality of the foreign proceedings.[152] In the *Charm Maritime* case, the court found that as there was a conflict of expert evidence, the finality requirement was not established, with the result that the forum proceeding was not an abuse of process. More recently, in *PCH Offshore Pty Ltd v Dunn (No 2)*,[153] the Australian Federal Court similarly held that the issue of finality must be resolved by foreign law but as no evidence had been led of such law, it would be inappropriate to find an abuse of process. By contrast, in two other Australian cases the law of the forum was solely applied to determine whether such an estoppel existed.[154] With respect, the same arguments that were raised in the English decisions to support at least a partial reference to foreign law on the question of finality should also apply in this context. It would seem illogical that an English or Commonwealth court should hold that a party should have raised a matter in earlier foreign proceedings when, under the law of the country where such proceedings took place, the matter could have been entertained in a subsequent action in the same court. Deference to foreign law is therefore appropriate on this issue.

7.44 Hence, the position with respect to issue, cause of action, and *Henderson v Henderson* estoppel is that they appear to be all clearly procedural matters, given that they are closely connected to the regulation of court proceedings in the forum. While the acceptance of such a plea may well have outcome determinative effect in a given case, the dominant aspect is the need to prevent re-litigation and preserve judicial economy. Yet, as the English and Canadian decisions show, despite being procedural, the matters are not exclusively resolved by forum law: for sound reasons of comity the law of the country of rendition of the judgment is also applied.

3. The US Position

7.45 Under US law issue estoppel is referred to as 'issue preclusion' and cause of action estoppel is known as 'collateral estoppel' or 'claim preclusion'. The US position as regards applicable law for each of these doctrines is relatively settled. According to § 95 of the Second Restatement of the Conflict of Laws, the law of the country where the judgment was rendered exclusively determines the effect of the judgment in any subsequent proceeding, in particular whether an estoppel may be raised based on the judgment (comment c). Such law also determines whether the foreign

---

[152] *Charm Maritime Inc v Kyriakou* [1987] 1 Lloyd's Rep 433.
[153] (2010) 273 ALR 167.
[154] *O'Brien v Tanning Research Laboratories Inc* (1988) 84 ALR 221, 228 (NSWCA Kirby P); *Talacko v Talacko* [1999] VSC 81.

judgment was final and conclusive (comment g). This approach has been applied in the vast majority of decisions since the Restatement was promulgated.[155] The Second Restatement also provides that the law of the state where the judgment was rendered should determine 'whether a defendant will be precluded from raising in a subsequent proceeding issues which he could have but failed to assert . . . in the original proceeding';[156] in other words, the English *Henderson v Henderson* estoppel. The US approach therefore goes beyond the predominant Commonwealth position in applying the law of the place of rendition of the judgment to all aspects of whether a cause of action or issue estoppel may be pleaded.

Finally, US law has a doctrine of 'judicial estoppel' which provides that where a party assumes a particular position in litigation and succeeds in persuading the court to accept that position, it may not be permitted to take an inconsistent position in later litigation.[157] Interestingly, an English court recently applied this doctrine under the rubric of abuse of process[158] in relation to a party which had taken a different stance in English proceedings to that which it had pursued in a prior action in the British Virgin Islands courts. The English court applied the law of the forum to the issue of whether such an estoppel existed, which is consistent with the practice of the US authorities that have addressed the issue.[159] US courts have emphasized that the doctrine aims to protect the integrity of the courts from duplicative proceedings and so is closely related to the forum court's control of its own processes. **7.46**

4. STATUTORY PROVISIONS PREVENTING RELITIGATION

A similar inquiry may arise where a legislature creates a specialist tribunal to resolve certain disputes with provisions included, which aim to expedite proceedings and reduce costs for claimants with limited means by providing that certain matters which have been determined in earlier litigation **7.47**

---

[155] See eg *Instituto Nacional de Commercializacion Agricola (Indeca) v Continental Illinois National Bank and Trust Co* 858 F 2d 1264, 1271 (7th Cir 1988); *Painewebber Inc v Ras* 767 F Supp 930, 932 (ND Ill 1991); *Kim v Co-operative Centrale Raiffeisen-Boerenleenbank BA* 364 F Supp 2d 346, 349 (SDNY 2005); *Garcia v GMC* 990 P 2d 1069, 1072–3 (CA Ariz 1999); *Harper v Delaware Broadcasters Inc* 743 F Supp 1076, 1082 (D Del 1990).

[156] Restatement (Second), § 95 comment g; but see *Harper v Harper* 600 SE 2d 659 (CA Ga 2004) where the court held that the rules of the forum applied to determine whether a defendant was obliged to bring a counterclaim in an earlier proceeding in a foreign court and so estopped from raising the plea in the forum.

[157] *Edwards v Aetna Life and Casualty* 690 F 2d 595 (6th Cir 1982).

[158] *Yugraneft v Abramovich* [2008] EWHC 2613 (Comm), paras 429–430.

[159] *Middleton v Caterpillar Industrial Inc* 979 So 2d 53, 60 (SC Ala 2007); *CSX Transportation Inc v Howell* 675 SE 2d 306, 309 (CA Ga 2009).

218   *Chapter 7: Evidence I: General Principles*

cannot be reopened. An Australian example is the Dust Diseases Tribunal Act 1989 (NSW) which was established to facilitate the bringing of personal injury proceedings by sufferers of asbestosis. Section 25B of the Act prevents the relitigation of issues of a general nature determined in previous proceedings in the Tribunal without leave, whether or not the proceedings were between the same parties.

7.48   The classification of this provision has divided Australian courts. For example, in *James Hardie & Co Pty Ltd v Barry*[160] Spigelman CJ of the New South Wales Court of Appeal considered that section 25B was a 'presumption' and was accordingly substantive[161] on the authority of *Re Cohn* and *Mahadervan*. Priestley JA agreed, although in his view the substantive characterization was justified by the outcome determinative effect of the provision.[162] By contrast, Mason P considered the provision both to be procedural[163] and an overriding mandatory rule of the forum which must be applied regardless of the applicable law.[164] In support of the procedural view, the judge noted that the provision was 'neutrally expressed, ambulatory and flexible in operation' and thus unlike the cases involving presumptions which 'operate in a single context with an identifiable outcome discernible on their face'. In later decisions, the courts have been no closer to agreement. In *BHP Billiton Ltd v Schultz*[165] Callinan J[166] of the High Court thought that section 25B did 'more than relax the rules of evidence. [It] would allow the Tribunal to depart from the audi alteram partem rule . . . by enabl[ing] the Tribunal to use against a party evidence and findings which it has had no opportunity of testing or controverting. However they may be expressed, provisions capable of producing that outcome, of denying natural justice, do not have the appearance of merely being procedural'. This view has been followed in some subsequent decisions.[167] By contrast, in other cases it has been suggested that the provision is procedural on the basis that its object is to expedite proceedings and reduce costs and duplication; it is therefore part of the 'mode or conduct of court proceedings'.[168] Other courts have simply left the issue open.[169]

---

[160] (2000) 50 NSWLR 357.
[161] ibid para 16.
[162] ibid para 123, citing *John Pfeiffer Pty Ltd v Rogerson* (2000) 203 CLR 503 paras 98–100, 102.
[163] (2000) 50 NSWLR 357 para 78.
[164] ibid para 77.
[165] (2004) 221 CLR 400.
[166] ibid para 253.
[167] See eg *Stavar v Caltex Refineries (NSW) Pty Ltd* [2008] NSWDDT 22, para 115.
[168] See eg *Hearn v Commonwealth* [2000] NSWDDT 12; see also *James Hardie & Co Pty Ltd v Barry* (2000) 50 NSWLR 357 para 111 (Mason P).
[169] *BI (Contracting) Pty Ltd v Haylock* [2005] NSWSC 592; *BHP Billiton Ltd v Utting* [2005] NSWSC 260, para 9; *Frodyma v Royal Adelaide Hospital* [2006] NSWDDT 11, para 13; *Caltex Refineries (Qld) Pty Ltd v Stavar* [2008] NSWSC 223.

E. *Estoppel*

A similar provision in the same legislation is section 25(3) which provides **7.49**
that where historical evidence and general medical evidence concerning
dust exposure and dust diseases has been admitted in any proceedings
before the Tribunal, such evidence may be received as evidence in any
other proceeding before the Tribunal whether or not the proceedings are
between the same parties. In *BHP Billiton Ltd v Schultz*[170] Callinan J again
suggested that the provision is substantive, for the same reasons he
expressed in relation to section 25B, and this view has been followed in
some subsequent decisions.[171]

While the question is not an easy one, and has plainly divided Australian **7.50**
courts, it may be argued that as both provisions are part of a legislative
scheme to create a new tribunal which operates under an express policy of
reducing costs and delays in order to enhance justice for claimants, their
connection with the mode or conduct of court proceedings is strong and
so a procedural classification is more appropriate. Again, this conclusion
is not to deny that the provisions may have outcome determinative effect.
Alternatively, it may be said that the provisions embody a sufficiently
strong forum public policy to be applied regardless of the applicable law.

5. Other Estoppels

There is very little Commonwealth authority on the applicable law with **7.51**
respect to other estoppels (for example estoppel by representation of existing fact, estoppel by convention, estoppel in agency, promissory estoppel,
and proprietary estoppel). Estoppel by representation of fact occurs where
a person asserts the truth of a set of facts to another and cannot later deny
the fact created by such representation. Promissory estoppel arises where
a person promises another not to enforce some pre-existing right in the
future and proprietary estoppel arises where a person promises to confer
an interest in property on another but fails to do so, with the promisee in
both cases relying on the promise. Given the close connection between
these estoppels and the rights and liabilities of the parties, a substantive
characterization would seem appropriate.[172] The doctrine of waiver, which
is analogous to such estoppels and often has an outcome determinative
effect, should be similarly treated.[173]

---

[170] (2004) 221 CLR 400, para 253.
[171] *Stavar v Caltex Refineries (NSW) Pty Ltd* [2008] NSWDDT 22, paras 38–39; *Amaca Pty Ltd v Aartsen* [2011] NSWSC 676, paras 50–52.
[172] Bellini (n 11 above) 340, n 25.
[173] Wolff (n 46 above) 456; in the case of statutes of limitations, see 9.34 below.

(a) Estoppel by Representation of Fact

7.52 In the case of estoppel by representation of existing fact it was held in a Canadian case that this was a substantive matter governed by the law of the cause of action. In *Allen v Hay*[174] a defendant in the US state of Washington gave a promissory note to give an appearance of ownership of assets in order to deceive a bank examiner in connection with the accounts of the company. When the bank commissioner later sued to recover on the note, the court held that the defendant was estopped from alleging a lack of consideration for the note under Washington law, which applied as the law of the cause of action. A possibly different approach was taken by the English Court of Appeal in *Janred Properties Ltd v Ente Nazionale Italiano per Il Turismo*.[175] In that case, the question of whether a defendant was estopped by its conduct and representation was determined by English law, although English law was both the law of the forum and the law of the cause of action. US law, which refers to estoppel by representation as 'equitable estoppel', also regards the issue as substantive and governed by the law of the cause of action.[176]

(b) Estoppel by Convention

7.53 This form of estoppel arises where both parties to a transaction act on an assumed state of facts or law the assumption being either shared by both or made by one and acquiesced in by the other party. The party against whom the estoppel is sought is prevented from denying the assumed facts or law.[177] Such an estoppel is therefore directly concerned with the rights and liabilities of the parties in the merits of the litigation and less obviously linked to the regulation of the mode or conduct of court proceedings. A substantive classification is therefore appropriate and was the view taken recently by the Hong Kong Court of Appeal.[178] In *Dornoch Ltd v Westminster International BV*[179] the English Admiralty Court tentatively agreed with this view but found it unnecessary to decide the issue, as English law was both the law of the cause of action and the law of the forum.

---

[174] (1922) 69 DLR 193.
[175] [1989] 2 All ER 444.
[176] *Norfolk Southern Railway Co v Trinity Industries Inc* 2009 WL 856340 (ND Tex) *6; *Annecca Inc v Lexent Inc* 345 F Supp 2d 897, 906 (ND Ill 2004).
[177] *Republic of India v Indian Steamship Co Ltd (No 2)* [1998] 1 AC 878, 913 (Lord Steyn) (with whom the other members of the House of Lords agreed).
[178] *First Laser Ltd v Fujian Enterprises (Holdings) Co Ltd* [2011] HKCA 1, para 86; see also Yeo (n 133 above) para 4.104 and Johnston (n 94 above) para 2.010.
[179] [2009] EWHC 1782 (Adm), para 21.

E. Estoppel

(c) Promissory Estoppel and Estoppel in Agency

The applicable law for promissory estoppel does not appear to have been considered by a Commonwealth court, although given that it is normally pleaded in connection with a contract, there would seem to be a good argument that it should be subjected to the law applicable to the contract. Significantly, this approach has been taken in the United States where the matter has arisen frequently,[180] although in a few cases the law of the place of reliance has been applied in preference to the law of the contract.[181] Another type of contract-based estoppel involves the issue of whether a principal is estopped from denying his or her agent's apparent authority to enter into contracts with third parties. Once again, given the clear connection between this issue and the rights and liabilities of the parties, the matter is best seen as substantive.[182]

7.54

(d) Proprietary Estoppel

While there is no direct Commonwealth or US authority on the question, comments have been expressed in favour of applying the law of the country where the property, which is said to form the basis of the estoppel, is situated.[183] Since again, this form of estoppel has a clear impact on the parties' rights and obligations in the litigation, this view is preferred.

7.55

---

[180] *The Limited Stores Inc v Pan America World Airways Inc* 600 NE 2d 1027 (Sup Ct Ohio 1992); *Eby v York-Division* 455 NE 2d 623, 626 (CA Ind 1983); *J-Squared Technologies Inc v Motorola Inc* 364 F Supp 2d 449, 453 (D Del 2005); *Trent Partners and Associates Inc v Digital Equipment Corp* 120 F Supp 2d 84, 95 (D Mass 1999); *PAE Govt Services Inc v MPRI Inc* 514 F 3d 856, 860 (9th Cir 2007).

[181] *NCC Sunday Inserts Inc v World Color Press Inc* 759 F Supp 1004, 1011 (SDNY 1991).

[182] *Rimpacific Navigation Inc v Daehan Shipbuilding Co Ltd* [2009] EWHC 2941 (Comm), para 34; *Britannia Steamship Insurance Association v Ausonia Assicurazioni SpA* [1984] 2 Lloyd's Rep 98, 100, 102; Yeo (n 133 above) para 4.104; *Dicey, Morris and Collins* (n 22 above) para 7.031.

[183] *Dornoch Ltd v Westminster International BV* [2009] EWHC 1782 (Adm), para 21.

8
Evidence II: Taking Evidence Abroad, Privilege, and Other Bars on Disclosure

A. Taking of Evidence Abroad	8.01
1. Introduction	8.01
2. Common Law Methods for Taking of Evidence	8.03
3. International Instruments for Taking of Evidence	8.11
4. Application of Foreign Rules on Taking of Evidence	8.16
B. Privilege and Other Bars on Disclosure	8.20
1. Lawyer-Client Communications	8.21
2. Witnesses: the Audio-Video Dimension	8.37
3. Privilege Against Self-Incrimination	8.38
4. Enforcement of Foreign Requests for Evidence	8.60

A. TAKING OF EVIDENCE ABROAD

1. Introduction

As was noted in Chapter 7, evidence is a topic similar to service of process where the law of the forum has been traditionally considered to exercise dominant, if not exclusive, control on the basis that all questions which arise fall within the domain of procedure. Yet it will be argued that, again, other laws may also need to be applied to qualify the operation of forum law in this area. This issue particularly arises where the claimant seeks to obtain evidence abroad for a proceeding in the forum, that is, requests testimony or documents from a person in a foreign jurisdiction. In such a case, the law of the place where the evidence is located arguably demands recognition, both out of respect for the sovereignty of the foreign country where the evidence is located and also because of the reality that any request for evidence may have to be enforced in that place to have practical effect.[1] There is some support for this view where proceedings

8.01

---

[1] J Dolinger and C Tiburcio, 'The Forum Rule in International Litigation—Which Procedural Law Governs Proceedings to be Performed in Foreign Jurisdictions: *Lex Fori* or *Lex Diligentiae*?' (1998) 33 Texas Intl LJ 425; and I Szászy, 'The Basic Connecting Factor in International Cases in the Domain of Civil Procedure' (1966) 15 ICLQ 436, 453, who refers the issue of the 'validity

are brought in the country where the evidence is located pursuant to a letter of request under international instruments such as the Hague Evidence Convention[2] and the EU Evidence Regulation.[3] As part of the cooperative processes of such instruments for the taking of evidence abroad, there is a relaxation and modification of the traditional rule that the law of the forum (for whose courts the evidence is required) exclusively governs the matter of taking evidence. Alternatively, the forum may choose to restrict the scope of operation of its evidence gathering laws out of deference to the sovereignty and enforcement concerns above. In this way, forum law continues to apply exclusively to the taking of evidence but in an 'enlightened' and sensitive fashion. This approach has been most evident in cases where a claimant has sought a unilateral order for the taking of evidence from the forum courts.

8.02 Conflicts between the law of the forum (for whose courts the evidence is required) and the country where the evidence is located are not surprising given the great differences in the procedures for taking evidence between common law and civil law countries. While common law procedures grant to the parties the right and power to collect evidence for a court action, in civil law systems the forum court itself gathers the evidence. As a result, civil law countries have often regarded the taking of evidence in their territory without the approval of the local courts as a breach of sovereignty.[4] In this chapter, the choice of law position in respect of a number of pretrial processes for the taking of evidence under English and Commonwealth law will first be considered before examining the approach taken under the Hague Convention and the EU Regulation. In addition, a detailed discussion will be made of the status of privilege and other prohibitions on disclosure, issues which arise commonly in the area of taking of evidence abroad.

---

of evidence administered abroad' to the '*lex loci actus*'. cf T Hartley, 'Jurisdiction in Conflict of Laws—Disclosure, Third-Party Debt and Freezing Orders' (2010) 126 LQR 194, 201–5, who argues that the law of the forum should exclusively apply to questions of disclosure of documents based on a concern that the party seeking disclosure may be denied a fair trial by a court accepting spurious objections to disclosure under foreign law.

[2] Convention of 18 March 1970 on the Taking of Evidence Abroad in Civil or Commercial Matters.

[3] Council Regulation (EC) 1206/2001 of 28 May 2001 on cooperation between the courts of the Member States in the taking of evidence in civil or commercial matters.

[4] D McClean, *International Co-operation in Civil and Criminal Matters* (OUP, 2002) 79.

2. Common Law Methods for Taking of Evidence

(a) Commonwealth

Discovery (now described under the English Civil Procedure Rules (CPR) **8.03** as disclosure and inspection of documents)[5] is one of the most significant pre-trial processes in the common law system. Under English and Commonwealth law, discovery has only generally been available against a party to the litigation, yet does extend to documents held by the party outside the jurisdiction.[6] It will, however, not be in every case that the party must make disclosure of such documents: for example this may be excused on the ground that it would violate the law of the place where the document is kept or a privilege of the defendant.[7] The circumstances in which foreign law may apply to prevent disclosure of material for forum proceedings are discussed later in this chapter.

Other important pre-trial measures in which evidence may be procured **8.04** include mareva injunctions (in England now described as 'freezing orders') and subpoenas (in England, 'witness summonses'). In the case of marevas, it is well established that they may be applied to prevent dissipation of assets both within and outside the forum and may require the defendant to disclose the location of assets and related documents.[8] Where a freezing order is sought in relation to proceedings abroad, English courts have been willing to grant such relief if the defendant has a sufficient connection to England, for example, where it is domiciled there.[9] The rationale for such a requirement is again both comity towards the foreign court and the need to ensure enforceability of the forum court's orders.[10] Such a position is further evidence of an 'enlightened *lex fori*' type approach, where access to the remedies of the forum is predicated on an English link. A similar position with respect to freezing orders has been taken in other Commonwealth countries.[11] Yet it is important to note that, as with disclosure, the cross-border operation of such relief raises the possibility of conflict with the law of the country where the evidence is located; in particular, where the defendant faces possible prosecution under that country's law by disclosure of such material.

---

[5] CPR, r 31.6.
[6] *Farquharson v Balfour* (1823) Turn & R 184, 190–1.
[7] *MacKinnon v Donaldson, Luffkin Jenrette Securities Corp* [1986] Ch 482.
[8] *Bank of Crete SA v Koskotas* [1991] 2 Lloyd's Rep 587.
[9] *Credit Suisse Fides Trust SA v Cuoghi* [1998] QB 818 and *Motorola Credit Corp v Uzan (No 2)* [2004] 1 WLR 113 (both Eng CA).
[10] L Merrett, 'Worldwide Freezing Orders in Europe' [2008] LMCLQ 71, 75.
[11] *Davis v Turning Properties Pty Ltd* (2005) 222 ALR 676 (NSW Sup Ct); *Obégi Chemicals LLC v Kilani* 2011 ONSC 1636.

8.05 In the case of subpoenas against third parties resident abroad, however, the scope for conflict between the law of the forum and foreign law is much less due to a conscious policy of abstention followed by English and Commonwealth courts. The general practice is that subpoenas will not be issued against third parties outside the forum unless 'exceptional circumstances' apply.[12] Two reasons are normally given for this restriction: first, that such orders may be perceived as an interference with the sovereignty of the foreign country and secondly, that they are generally incapable of enforcement and so futile. In any case, the rule against extraterritorial subpoenas may be seen as another example of the enlightened *lex fori* in procedural matters where a forum court unilaterally reduces the operation of its own law out of deference to foreign interests. Commonwealth practice is generally consistent with this position.[13] The *MacKinnon* 'exceptional circumstances' test does not apply where a liquidator seeks documents abroad in relation to the winding-up of an overseas company in the forum. In that case, to obtain such an order, the liquidator must show that there is no risk that the defendant would be exposed to liability under the law of the country where the documents are situated.[14] The power of the forum court to grant a subpoena in this category of case is therefore made expressly subject to compliance with the law of the place where the documents are located.

8.06 Apart from these pre-trial measures for collecting evidence, English and Commonwealth practice also provide mechanisms for taking evidence abroad during the course of a proceeding. One method involves the direct taking of evidence from a witness in a foreign country by appointment of a special examiner, and the other involves the issue of a request by the forum court to the court of the country in which the evidence is located. In the case of appointment of an examiner, Commonwealth practice has normally required evidence that the foreign country has no objection to such an order.[15] Some courts have gone further and required that, as a condition of an examiner being appointed, the applicant must obtain an order from the court in which the evidence is located giving the examiner the necessary coercive powers under local law.[16] Alternatively, if the forum court

---

[12] *MacKinnon v Donaldson, Luffkin Jenrette Securities Corp* [1986] Ch 482.

[13] *Arhill Pty Ltd v General Terminal Coy Pty Ltd* (1990) 23 NSWLR 545; *Gao v Zhu* [2002] VSC 64; *Stemcor (A/Asia) Pty Ltd v Oceanwave Line SA* [2004] FCA 391; cf *Walker v Newmont Australia Ltd* [2010] FCA 298.

[14] *Re Mid East Trading Ltd; Lehman Bros Inc v Phillips* [1998] 1 All ER 577 (CA); *Application of Robert William Whitton* [2007] NSWSC 606.

[15] See eg CPR, r 34.13(4); *Gould v State Bank of NSW* SC NSW, 28 February 1996; *Park v Citibank Savings Ltd* (1993) 31 NSWLR 219.

[16] *Harwood v Priestley* (1997) 6 Tas R 383.

A. Taking of Evidence Abroad

wants to give the greatest weight to comity and enforceability factors, it can issue a request to the foreign court asking that it take the evidence from the witness. In either case, the examination is conducted in accordance with any procedure permitted in the country in which the examination is to take place. Hence, the scope of operation of forum procedural law is limited in cases of examination of witnesses abroad: both by the requirement of consent of the home state and the need for any procedure adopted to conform to its law and practice.[17] The need to conform to local practice and procedure has, however, occasionally made courts hesitate before ordering personal examination. In particular, a key concern may be that the foreign procedures provide an adequate mechanism for testing the witnesses' evidence.[18] Hence, although the law of the foreign country is applied to the examination, if it does not meet the needs and requirements of the forum (for whose courts the evidence is required) an order may not be issued. To that extent, the law of the forum retains ultimate control.

Note, however, that despite the forum adopting principles sensitive to the law of the country where the evidence is to be taken, it still may be necessary for a claimant to seek enforcement of such orders in that country or alternatively to seek orders for disclosure directly from its courts. In both such cases, the court of the country where the evidence is situated is likely to apply its own law to determine whether the evidence should be produced, subject to the provisions of relevant treaties such as the Hague Evidence Convention, discussed at 8.12–8.14. Consequently, in that situation, the law to be applied to determine whether the evidence can be taken will not be the law of the country *seeking* the evidence but the place where the evidence is situated. 8.07

The situation regarding taking evidence abroad may, however, be different where the evidence is proposed to be taken by *audio or video link* from the foreign country for proceedings in the forum. In a very recent Australian decision,[19] it was held that where legislation of the forum confers a power on its courts to allow the taking of such testimony in a foreign country by video link,[20] then (in the absence of an express provision) the consent of the foreign state to such a process is not required. Where, however, it is shown that the law of such country *prohibits* a person within its borders from participating in such a process, it may not be appropriate for the forum court to take the evidence. In the audiovisual context, therefore, forum law appears to assert even greater control. 8.08

---

[17] *Idoport Pty Ltd v National Australia Bank Ltd* [2001] NSWSC 838, para 53.
[18] *Hardie Rubber Co Pty Ltd v The General Tire & Rubber Co* (1973) 129 CLR 521.
[19] *Joyce v Sunland Waterfront (BVI) Ltd* (2011) 281 ALR 54.
[20] Federal Court of Australia Act 1976 (Cth), s 47A.

(b) United States

8.09 In the United States, a similarly restrictive position applies to that in Commonwealth countries with respect to the granting of extraterritorial subpoenas. Under the Walsh Act[21] a US court may issue a subpoena requiring the appearance of a US citizen or resident who is in a foreign country but not a foreign national in a foreign country.[22] Such an approach both recognizes the enforcement limitations of US court orders abroad and the sovereignty of the foreign country in respect of evidence within its borders. Application of an unqualified law of the forum would again be inappropriate.

8.10 In one US decision, however, the choice of law question in matters of taking evidence abroad was more directly raised. It has been assumed in the discussion so far that, in the absence of the issue of a letter of request under an international instrument such as the Hague Evidence Convention, a party may have resort to the evidence taking rules and procedures of the law of the forum where evidence is required from abroad. While, as noted earlier, forum law has sometimes not been applied out of regard for the sovereignty of the foreign state or because foreign law prohibits disclosure,[23] it has never been suggested that the evidence collecting processes of the *foreign country* must be applied *in preference to* those of the forum. Yet, in *Re Vitamins Antitrust Litigation*,[24] it was argued that, in a request for discovery under the US Federal Rules of Civil Procedure against parties resident in Belgium and Japan, the law of the place of the evidence should be applied to the issue of discovery. The court found that US law applied but principally for reasons of public policy: the foreign laws were highly restrictive in their provision for discovery.[25] Such a conclusion does not therefore preclude possible application of foreign law in another case involving the taking of evidence, and it will be interesting to see in subsequent US (or Commonwealth) cases whether the choice of law issue is revisited.

3. International Instruments for Taking of Evidence

8.11 The taking of evidence abroad is also governed by two important international instruments: the Hague Evidence Convention ('the Convention') and the EU Evidence Regulation. The main focus of the discussion of the

---

[21] 28 USC, § 1783.
[22] *Gillars v US* 182 F 2d 962, 978 (DC Cir 1950).
[23] See further discussion at 8.20 et seq below.
[24] 120 F Supp 2d 45 (DDC 2000).
[25] ibid 55–7.

A. Taking of Evidence Abroad

instruments in this work will be on the possible choice of law issues which arise under them.

(a) Hague Evidence Convention

It should be noted first that in both Commonwealth countries[26] and the United States,[27] the Convention does not have exclusive or mandatory effect. In other words, a party seeking evidence does not have to make 'first resort' to the Convention but may rely on unilateral measures under the law of the forum to obtain evidence.[28] The forum law on the taking of evidence therefore continues to operate, even where the dispute falls within the scope of the Convention. In some commentary[29] the application of forum law to the taking of evidence abroad, even to bypass the Convention, has been justified on the basis that it would enable evidence to be taken remotely by audio or video means. As discussed at 8.08, however, the efficacy of such 'remote' procedures (indeed any procedures for taking evidence abroad under forum law) may still depend in some cases upon whether the law of the country where the witness is located would allow the taking of such evidence. To that extent, therefore, the forum does not have complete control. **8.12**

Assuming that the Convention is invoked, its key aspect is that it provides a cooperative mechanism for the taking of evidence abroad by means of letters of request. Article 1 provides that a court in a contracting state may request the competent authority of another contracting state by means of a letter of request to obtain evidence. If the letter of request satisfies the requirements of the Convention, then under article 12 a central authority of the requested state may only reject the request where such a state considers that the subject matter of the request does not fall within the area of judicial power and its sovereignty or security would be thereby prejudiced.[30] Article 12 therefore provides an example of where the taking of evidence is made expressly subject to compliance with the law of the requested state.[31] This approach is also evident in article 9 which provides that the court executing the request applies its own laws and procedures **8.13**

---

[26] *The Heidberg* [1993] 2 Lloyd's Rep 324.
[27] *Société Nationale Industrielle Aerospatiale v US District Court for the Southern District of Iowa* 482 US 522 (1987).
[28] See eg in the US context, *Re Vitamins Antitrust Litigation* 120 F Supp 2d 45 (DDC 2000).
[29] M Davies, 'Bypassing the Hague Evidence Convention: Private International Law Implications of the Use of Audio or Video Conferencing in Transnational Litigation (2007) 55 AJCL 205, 206–9.
[30] *Rio Tinto Zinc Corp v Westinghouse* [1978] AC 547.
[31] Dolinger and Tiburcio (n 1 above) 434.

and article 10 where measures of compulsion of the requested state may be used to secure compliance with the request for evidence. Where, however, the request requires the court to follow a special method of procedure under the law of the requesting state, then this must be applied by the court of the requested state, unless it is incompatible with, or performance is impossible under, local law.[32] Commentators, however, have insisted that this last reservation for the law of the requested state is strictly limited: 'incompatible' with such law does not simply mean different; there must be a constitutional or statutory prohibition on production.[33] English decisions under the Convention are consistent with this view. In *J Barber & Sons v Lloyds Underwriters*[34] it was stated that a request by a foreign court for a particular mode of taking evidence should be accepted unless what was asked for was contrary to established procedures. So a request to an English court to order the production of documents and oral depositions from third parties for US litigation was not accepted where it was clearly contrary to English procedure because, for example, 'particular' documents were not sought.[35] Application of the rules of the requested state also may arise under the Convention where a person in the requested country seeks to claim privilege from disclosure. This issue is addressed in art 11 of the Convention which is discussed later.[36]

8.14 The practice under the Convention shows, therefore, that requested states have generally tried to accommodate and defer to procedures of the requesting state where specifically asked to do so unless there is likely to be serious incompatibility with the law of the requested state.[37] Such an approach suggests support for a continued controlling role to the law of the forum (the law of the requesting state) in matters of taking of evidence under the Convention despite the references to the law of the requested state.[38] In the same manner, English and Commonwealth courts have also been reluctant to determine whether the procedural rules of the requesting state have been or will be complied with in the taking of evidence. Specifically, it is well established that a requested state's courts should not

---

[32] Hague Evidence Convention, art 9.
[33] McClean (n 4 above) 118.
[34] [1987] QB 103.
[35] *Genira Trade and Finance Inc v CS First Boston and Standard Bank (London) Ltd* [2001] EWCA Civ 1733. Canadian decisions on letters of request (although not under the Convention) are to the same effect; *Connecticut Retirement Plans and Trust Funds v Buchan* 2007 ONCA 462.
[36] See 8.62 below.
[37] McClean (n 4 above) 118.
[38] cf Dolinger and Tiburcio (n 1 above) 434, who suggest that the Convention creates a dual choice of law rule consisting of the law of the forum (the requesting state) and the *lex diligentiae* or the law of the place where the relevant act is to be performed (the requested state); see also Szászy (n 1 above).

A. Taking of Evidence Abroad

adjudicate upon the likely relevance or admissibility of evidence to the proceedings in the requesting country, except in the 'clearest' of cases.[39] Later English cases appear to have relaxed this rule slightly by saying that the requested court may look at the issue of relevance of the requested testimony if 'raised in broad terms' but not whether particular answers to questions would constitute relevant admissible evidence.[40] A policy of general deference to the law of the requesting state on matters of admissibility and relevance of evidence is therefore again noticeable, a point made explicitly by the Hong Kong Court of Appeal in *Prediwave Corporation v New World TMT Ltd*.[41] The New South Wales Court of Appeal has further noted that, apart from choice of law considerations, there is also the question of practicality: 'It would unduly lengthen the course of proceedings in the country where the evidence was located if it was necessary to prove the foreign law of evidence as a fact with respect to the admissibility of the question and answer in the foreign jurisdiction. This is meant to be a practical scheme of international cooperation.'[42] A similar policy of deference to foreign law can be seen in the reverse case, where a challenge is brought to the issue of a letter of request in the *requesting* state's courts on the ground that the witnesses are not competent to testify under the law of the *requested* state. In *Chan Mei Yiu Paddy v Secretary for Justice (No 2)*[43] the court held that an order to issue a letter of request should only be refused where there was 'overwhelming evidence' under the law of the requested state that the witnesses were neither competent nor compellable.[44] In almost all such cases, therefore, the issue of admissibility should be left to the courts of the requested state.

(b) EU Evidence Regulation

8.15 Within the European Union there is now a Council Regulation dealing with the taking of evidence abroad in civil and commercial matters. While the Regulation was strongly influenced by the Hague Evidence Convention, it provides for the direct transmission of requests from court to court rather than using central authorities. From a choice of law perspective,

---

[39] *Rio Tinto Zinc Corp v Westinghouse* [1978] AC 547.

[40] *Re Asbestos Insurance* [1985] 1 WLR 331, 339 (Lord Fraser); *Genira Trade and Finance Inc v CS First Boston and Standard Bank (London) Ltd* [2001] EWCA Civ 1733, para 14; *Gredd v Arpad Busson* [2003] EWHC 3001, para 27. Canadian practice, outside the context of the Convention, is similar: *Re Friction Division Products Inc and EI Du Pont de Nemours & Co Inc* (1986) 56 OR (2d) 722, para 25; *Treat America Ltd v Nestlé Canada Inc* 2011 ONSC 617.

[41] [2006] HKCA 391, paras 36–37.

[42] *British American Tobacco Services Ltd v Eubanks* (2004) 60 NSWLR 483, para 70.

[43] [2008] HKCFI 337.

[44] ibid paras 22–24.

the Regulation is almost identical to the Convention in that any request for the taking of evidence is to be executed in accordance with the law of the requested state unless a special procedure is provided by the law of the requesting state which will be employed, where it is not incompatible with the law of the requested state.[45]

4. Application of Foreign Rules on Taking of Evidence

8.16 So far it has been assumed that, under Commonwealth law at least, the taking of evidence is carried out in accordance with the rules of the forum where the principal proceeding is taking place, subject to any special provisions in international instruments such as the Convention or possible defences under the law of the place of the evidence. This position is consistent with the proposition that matters of evidence are generally governed by the law of the forum. A line of English authority has, however, qualified this approach to allow a party to litigation in England to have access to more generous discovery procedures under foreign law, specifically that of the United States, in addition to any procedures available under forum law. In *South Carolina Insurance Co v Assurantie Maatschappij de Zeven Provincien NV*[46] the House of Lords had to consider an application by a defendant to inspect documents located in the United States in the possession of a non-party to litigation, who had no presence in England. While disclosure under English law was not available, the defendant approached a US court, relying on 28 USC § 1782 of the US Code, which allows a US court to order the production of documents for use in foreign proceedings.[47] The House of Lords refused to issue an anti-suit injunction to restrain the defendant from seeking such relief. While evidence gathering was traditionally a matter for the law of the forum, this did not mean that other laws could not be relied upon. Parties to English litigation could therefore have resort to foreign procedures where they did not interfere with the forum's process or rights of the other party. Foreign procedural rules may therefore be used to supplement and extend forum law on this issue.

8.17 In recent decisions both English and other Commonwealth courts have been more circumspect about allowing litigants to have recourse to US procedures out of a concern to avoid interference with local processes.

---

[45] Art 10(2), (3), and (4).
[46] [1987] AC 24.
[47] The generosity and scope of § 1782 can further be seen from the fact that an order may be made under this provision even where the material sought is not discoverable under the law of the foreign country, see *Intel Corp v Advanced Micro Devices Inc* 542 US 241 (2004).

A. Taking of Evidence Abroad

In *Omega Group Holdings Ltd v Kozeny*[48] the Commercial Court granted an injunction to restrain a party from pursuing a § 1782 application to depose individuals who would also be giving evidence in England. The US application would have exposed the witnesses twice to cross-examination and so was abusive. Similarly, in *Bankers Trust International plc v PT Dharmala*[49] the Commercial Court restrained a party from using § 1782 to obtain depositions and documents after the English trial had been completed and where many of the documents had already been the subject of applications for discovery before the English courts. Significantly, however, the courts in both decisions assumed that a litigant could invoke § 1782 to obtain both documents and pre-trial witness testimony which extends the reach of *South Carolina*. Concerns regarding the effect of the § 1782 procedure on the conduct of proceedings in the forum were also expressed by the Federal Court of Australia in *Allstate Life Insurance Co v Australia and New Zealand Banking Group Ltd (No 4)*.[50] In that case an anti-suit injunction was granted to restrain a party from taking an oral deposition of an employee of the opposing party in the United States under § 1782 on the ground that the procedure was oppressive, for two reasons. First, the process would interfere with the opposing party's preparation and conduct of the trial in Australia[51] and secondly, an 'adverse procedural discrimination' would occur since certain employees of the opposing party, resident in the United States, would be subject to the § 1782 procedure, while others, resident in Australia, would not. This would lead to a 'disparity' in the Australian court proceedings.[52] Interestingly the applicant for the injunction did not seek to restrain the use of § 1782 insofar as it required the employee in the United States to produce documents.[53] It was therefore effectively conceded that the § 1782 procedure was available *in principle* to supplement the Australian court's procedural rules and so was not 'inconsistent with the forum's power over its own processes'.[54]

By contrast, in *Nokia Corporation v Interdigital Technology Corporation*[55] the Patents Court refused to restrain a party from pursuing applications in the US courts to obtain documents and witness depositions. While the court felt that the applications might not yield any useful information, they were

8.18

---

[48] [2002] CLC 132.
[49] Com Ct, 19 October 1995.
[50] (1996) 64 FCR 61.
[51] ibid 70.
[52] ibid 70–1.
[53] ibid 67–8.
[54] ibid 71–2.
[55] [2004] EWHC 2920 (Pat).

not abusive in the sense of causing unfair prejudice to the other party. Questions of admissibility of any evidence gained will be a matter for the English forum but *how* that evidence is obtained is not limited to English law methods. In other words, foreign procedural law may be relied upon to gather evidence for English litigation and, to that extent, the law of the forum does not have exclusive operation but may be supplemented by more expansive or generous foreign procedures.[56]

8.19 Interestingly, a similar issue may arise before a Commonwealth court in relation to the English equivalent of § 1782, namely section 1 of the Evidence (Proceedings in other Jurisdictions) Act 1975, which gives English courts the power to order discovery of evidence for use in foreign civil proceedings. While the scope of English discovery is not as broad as under US law, such a provision may nevertheless provide an alternative to a letter of request where a claimant before a Commonwealth court seeks documents from an English resident for the purposes of trial. Once again, therefore, forum procedures may be supplemented by those under the law of the country where the evidence is located.

B. PRIVILEGE AND OTHER BARS ON DISCLOSURE

8.20 The issue of privilege and other restrictions on disclosure of information has arisen commonly in cases of taking evidence abroad and pre-trial disclosure (discovery), as well as where a defendant is called to testify in the forum regarding events occurring elsewhere and seeks to raise privilege under foreign law as a defence. The two most frequently invoked types of privilege have been legal professional privilege, where a party seeks to prevent admission of lawyer-client communications, and the privilege against self-incrimination, where a party seeks to resist a request for evidence on the ground that disclosure will either amount to or reveal an offence. In the context of transnational litigation, there are important choice of law issues relevant to privilege which have so far been little explored in the authorities or the literature. Such questions are important in knowing which law a Commonwealth court would have to apply to determine a defendant's claim to privilege in a request for witness testimony or

---

[56] See also *American Endeavour Fund Ltd v Trueger* [1997] JLR 18 where the Royal Court of Jersey refused to restrain a party from using a § 1782 application to take depositions from a third party witness where the application was brought before discovery had taken place in the Jersey proceedings and, most recently, *Royal Bank of Scotland v Hicks* [2011] EWHC 287, para 96 where a § 1782 application was also allowed to proceed because the English proceedings had not yet reached the stage where such an application could be said to be abusive.

B. Privilege and Other Bars on Disclosure

production of documents. The topic of prohibitions on disclosure will be examined both from the perspective of the court for which the evidence is required (normally outside the country where the evidence is located) and from the position of the court in the country where the evidence is located.

1. Lawyer-Client Communications

(a) Substantive or Procedural?

A preliminary question to consider is whether privilege is classified as substantive or procedural for choice of law purposes. If the doctrine were classified as substantive then a party would only be able to claim privilege if it were available under the law governing the cause of action. If privilege were regarded as procedural by contrast, then the law of the forum would determine whether it existed or could be claimed.[57] **8.21**

Traditionally, English law has regarded privilege—both legal professional and the right to non-incrimination—as procedural and governed by the law of the forum. Such a conclusion is reached due to the fact that evidentiary questions are considered procedural and privilege forms part of the law of evidence.[58] Such a view, however, now seems contestable in a number of Commonwealth countries, such as Australia and Canada, where a narrow conception of procedure has been advocated, focusing on the mode or conduct of proceedings. While privilege is commonly asserted at the time of pre-trial discovery and in witness testimony at trial, events which are themselves part of the court proceedings, the doctrine does not dictate the form or conduct of such proceedings.[59] Also, privilege has a significant impact on the rights and duties of the parties and may well influence the outcome of litigation. Finally, unlike the case of a right to a jury trial, it is unlikely to be inconvenient or impractical for a court to apply foreign privilege rules. There is therefore a good argument that privilege should be treated as substantive for choice of law purposes. **8.22**

---

[57] Note that the choice of law position with respect to 'evidentiary privileges' is expressly left open in the American Law Institute/UNIDROIT Rules and Principles of Transnational Civil Procedure (2004) R 27.1.1, P18A.

[58] L Collins (ed), *Dicey, Morris and Collins on the Conflict of Laws* (Sweet & Maxwell, 14th edn, 2006) paras 7.015, 7.025.

[59] cf Illmer, who argues that legal professional privilege is 'concerned with the protection of privacy and secrecy, not with the decision on the merits', see M Illmer, 'Neutrality Matters—Some Thoughts about the Rome Regulations and the so-called Dichotomy of Substance and Procedure in European Private International Law' (2009) 28 Civil Justice Quarterly 237, 256.

8.23 The anomaly of the existing procedural characterization of privilege is clearly apparent in an Australian decision, *Kennedy v Wallace*,[60] where the court assumed that legal professional privilege was procedural despite describing it in the judgment as a 'substantive right'.[61] A similarly contradictory position was evident in a Canadian decision where legal professional privilege was described as a 'substantive right' of the client yet also as a 'rule regulating the production of evidence' and so procedural for private international law purposes.[62] The same reasoning was relied upon by another Canadian court to deny the operation of the Fifth Amendment to the US Constitution in Canadian proceedings.[63] This position does, however, pre-date the redefinition of substance and procedure by the Supreme Court of Canada in *Tolofson v Jensen*,[64] and so its current status in Canada may be questionable. A Hong Kong court has, however, also adopted this conflicting approach. Despite describing the privilege against self-incrimination as 'not a matter of procedure or evidence . . . [but] a substantive right',[65] it nevertheless unquestioningly applied forum law to the question of whether such privilege applied. Academic writing has noted the inconsistency of describing privilege as a substantive right, yet applying the law of the forum because it should be classified as procedural for private international law purposes.[66] A more nuanced view, while still advocating the application of the law of the forum to privilege, was expressed by an Australian court in *Michael Wilson and Partners Ltd v Nicholls*.[67] The court there said that matters of discovery and privilege were governed by the law of the forum because they were both part of the local procedure. Yet the 'foreign interests' involved called for a sensitive and calibrated application of forum law, in other words, an 'enlightened *lex fori*'.[68]

8.24 One of the few English decisions to consider the issue was *Bourns Inc v Raychem Corporation*[69] where the Court of Appeal implicitly accepted that the issue of privilege was governed by the law of the forum without

---

[60] (2004) 213 ALR 108 (Fed Ct).
[61] ibid para 199 (Allsop J), para 62 (Black CJ and Emmett J).
[62] *Circosta v Lilly* (1967) 61 DLR (2d) 12, 15 (Ont CA).
[63] *Oilworld Supply Co v Audas* BCSC, 23 May 1985.
[64] (1994) 120 DLR (4th) 289, 321.
[65] *Salt and Light Development Inc v Sjtu Sunway Software Industry Ltd* 2006 HKCFI 384, para 35.
[66] J McComish, 'Foreign Legal Professional Privilege: A New Problem for Australian Private International Law'(2006) 28 Sydney L Rev 297, 311, 320; J Weinstein, 'Recognition in the United States of the Privileges of another Jurisdiction' (1956) 56 Columbia L Rev 535, 541.
[67] (2008) 74 NSWLR 218.
[68] ibid para 11.
[69] [1999] 3 All ER 154 (CA).

B. Privilege and Other Bars on Disclosure

directly deciding the question.[70] In that case a party to English proceedings sought to use a document which had been produced for litigation in the United States. The claimant argued that English law should not be applied to confer legal professional privilege, where privilege had been lost or waived under the law of the place where the documents were located. The Court, however, considered that, in applying the English law of privilege, 'the fact that under foreign law the document is not privileged or that the privilege that existed is deemed to have been waived is irrelevant'.[71] Strictly speaking, therefore, the case concerns the scope of the operation of *English domestic law* and whether it should be qualified by reference to foreign law rather than whether the issue of privilege itself may be governed by foreign law. *Bourns* was applied by the Court of Appeal in *British American Tobacco (Investments) Ltd v United States*[72] where it was held that privilege under English law was not lost merely because under foreign law privilege would have been waived.

An alternative approach would be to see the question of privilege as substantive but nevertheless governed by the law of the forum for reasons of public policy. This view appears to have been taken by the English Court of Appeal in the context of the privilege to protect 'without prejudice' communications.[73] The Court saw the public policy lying in the need to promote the settlement of disputes. That case concerned an application to restrain a party from using correspondence and other communications in foreign proceedings. The court refused the application, saying it was a matter for the courts in other countries to apply their own rules of privilege 'based on their own perception of where the greater public interest lies'. While this decision maintains the forum dominance in the area of privilege, it at least has the advantage—by use of the mechanism of public policy—of frankly acknowledging the interests at stake and not concealing them under a blanket procedural characterization.[74] Such an analysis still, however, excludes any possibility of foreign privilege law applying in the forum, which is arguably unprincipled and hostile to comity. By contrast, in other cases, it has been held that a right to privilege under foreign law may be an important discretionary factor in refusing to

8.25

---

[70] cf *Dicey, Morris and Collins* (n 58 above) para 7.015, who cite *Bourns* for the proposition that privilege is procedural.
[71] [1999] 3 All ER 154, 167.
[72] [2004] EWCA Civ 1064, para 34.
[73] *Prudential Assurance Co Ltd v Prudential Insurance Co of America* [2003] EWCA Civ 1154.
[74] cf *Sodeca NA v NE Investments* [2002] EWHC 1700 (holding that the without prejudice doctrine is procedural for choice of law purposes and so is governed by the law of the forum).

238   *Chapter 8: Taking Evidence Abroad, Privilege*

order the examination of a foreign resident.[75] Also, as will be seen at 8.62, article 11 of the Hague Evidence Convention allows a party to assert a privilege under the law of the requesting and/or requested states. Hence, there is already some scope for the recognition of foreign privilege laws under Commonwealth choice of law principles.

8.26 There may, however, be a problem with the conclusion that privilege is 'substantive' and governed by the law of the cause of action. Such a finding may be of little assistance where no cause of action exists, such as in a criminal proceeding or in the context of a governmental inquiry. Suppose, for example, a court in country X may seek information from a person in country Y to determine if offences were committed against the law of country X. The resident of country Y asserts a privilege from disclosure arising under that country's law. Similarly, an issue may arise as to the admissibility of certain lawyer-client communications in an inquiry conducted by governmental authorities. As there is no 'cause of action', in each case the court cannot recognize and apply foreign law pursuant to any substance-procedure dichotomy. Also, in a case there may be multiple causes of action each governed by the law of a different country, and for a court to have to apply multiple laws of privilege may be cumbersome. Another problem with treating privilege as substantive and governed by the law of the cause of action is that this outcome may not match party expectations. At the stage of drafting a contract, for example, it seems unlikely that parties, when choosing the governing law, would have been considering the issue of privilege.

8.27 A further problem of applying the substance / procedure distinction or forum public policy is that both deny the entitlement of a third state's law of privilege to apply. In a given case it may be that the communication between lawyer and client has little to do with either the forum or the country the law of which governs the cause of action. A choice of law rule which at least allowed for the possibility of a third country's law being applied would be beneficial.

8.28 What options are then open to a Commonwealth court? One approach to consider would be that predominantly adopted in the United States and at least one Canadian decision:[76] dispense with the substance / procedure distinction and apply instead the law of the place which has 'the most significant relationship' with the communication or a variant of this rule to determine whether privilege applies. Note that the US rules only apply

---

[75] *Volksbank Schwabisch Gmund eG v Werner* Qld CA, 1 September 1999.
[76] See eg *Cook v Parcel* BCSC, 11 July 1996. (affd on other grounds (1997) 143 DLR (4th) 213 (BCCA)).

B. Privilege and Other Bars on Disclosure

to the situation of lawyer-client privilege or, slightly more broadly, privileges arising from a relationship (such as doctor-patient). The privilege against self-incrimination is assumed to be governed by the law of the forum exclusively and not subject to choice of law analysis. Before making a specific recommendation for Commonwealth countries, the US position should be examined more closely.

(b) US: Most Significant Relationship

8.29 In the United States, the most significant relationship test has been defined in a number of ways. In the case of lawyer-client privilege, one approach has been to apply US law if the communication between lawyer and client 'touches base' with the forum, such as where the communication occurred in the United States and involved US attorneys and advice on US law. Where, however, the communication took place in a foreign country and involved foreign lawyers and law, the US court will have less interest in applying its law.[77] In such cases, the relationship giving rise to the communication is not centred in the United States and so foreign law is applied. The US states which follow versions of the 'interest analysis' choice of law model take a similar approach. So, in one decision,[78] Californian law was applied because the communication between lawyer and client occurred there, and so the forum had the greatest interest in applying its law, and in another case, Illinois law was applied as the place of communication.[79] However, the most significant relationship test can prove difficult and arbitrary to apply where the contacts between lawyer and client are spread across a number of jurisdictions.[80]

8.30 A variation on the most significant relationship principle is found in § 139 of the Second Restatement, which has been applied by a number of US courts. Interestingly, the Restatement rules apply to a whole series of relationships. including attorney-client, patient and doctor, penitent and confessor, and between spouses. While the drafters of the Restatement saw a broader interest in protecting certain relationships and 'encourag[ing] socially desirable confidences',[81] the effect of its principles is to favour the

---

[77] *Golden Trade Srl v Lee Apparel Co* 143 FRD 514, 522 (SDNY 1992); *VLT Corp v Unitrode Corp* 194 FRD 8 (D Mass 2000); *Astra Aktiebolag v Andrx Pharmaceuticals Inc* 208 FRD 92 (SDNY 2002); *Eisai Ltd v Dr Reddy's Laboratories Inc* 406 F Supp 2d 341 (SDNY 2005).
[78] *Connolly Data Sys Inc v Victor Technologies Inc* 114 FRD 89 (SD Cal 1987).
[79] *Lego v Stratos Lightwave* 224 FRD 576 (SDNY 2004); *Super Tire Engineering Co v Bandag Inc* 562 F Supp 439 (ED Pa 1983); *Pepsico Inc v Baird, Kurtz and Dobson LLP* 206 FRD 646 (ED Mo 2002) (the place of communication has the most significant relationship).
[80] See eg *Bamco 18 v Reeves* 685 F Supp 414 (SDNY 1988).
[81] Restatement (Second), § 139 comment b.

admission of evidence over recognition of the privilege. Under § 139(1), 'even if a communication would be privileged under the law of the forum, evidence that it is not privileged under the local law of the state with the most significant relationship with the communication should be admitted in the forum unless admission would be contrary to the strong public policy of the forum'; and § 139(2) provides for the admission of evidence 'where it is not privileged in the forum but privileged under the law of the state with the most significant relationship with the communication, unless there are "special reasons" for not admitting the evidence'.

8.31 In determining which state or country has the most significant relationship with the communication, the drafters of the Restatement suggested that it may be the place where an oral interchange between persons occurred, or where a document was received, unless a prior relationship existed between the parties, in which case it will be where the relationship was centred.[82] Primary emphasis is therefore placed on the country of communication. Where the communication is between residents of the same jurisdiction the test has been easy to apply.[83] A state has also been found to have the most significant relationship with a communication between client and adviser, where the client was only temporarily present in the jurisdiction.[84] Where, however, the contacts are spread across a number of states, the most significant relationship test can be difficult to apply,[85] a point which has led some academic writers[86] and courts[87] to be strongly critical of the principle.

8.32 However, § 139 is not simply a most significant relationship test. Under § 139(1) deference is accorded to the state with the most significant relationship where, under such law, the evidence would be admitted (as compared to the forum which would have excluded it). Courts have almost always followed this direction and applied foreign law to admit

---

[82] ibid § 139 comment e.

[83] See *Re Teleglobe Communications Corp* 392 BR 561 (Bank D Del 2008); *People v Allen* 336 Ill App 3d 457 (CA Ill 2003); *Equity Residential Properties Management Corp v Kendall Risk Management Inc* 246 FRD 557 (ND Ill 2007); *Sterling Financial Management LP v UBS Paine and Webber* 336 Ill App 3d 442 (2002).

[84] *State v Heaney* 689 NW 2d 168 (Sup Ct Minn 2004); *Iowa v Eldrenkamp* 541 NW 2d 877 (Iowa 1995); *Washington v Donahue* 18 P 3d 608 (Wash CA 2001).

[85] *Allianz Ins Co v Guidant Corp* 869 NE 2d 1042 (CA Ill 2007).

[86] McComish (n 66 above) 329; S Bradford, 'Conflict of Laws and the Attorney-Client Privilege: A Territorial Solution' (1991) 52 University of Pittsburgh L Rev 909, 936.

[87] *Blanton v Kenneth Littlefield* 2010 RI Super Lexis 107 (Super Ct RI) *14.

B. Privilege and Other Bars on Disclosure 241

the evidence.[88] Under § 139(2), by contrast, deference is accorded to the law of the forum where it would admit the evidence (as compared to the law of the state with the most significant relationship which would exclude it), unless 'special reasons' exist. The drafters noted that the forum state should be more reluctant to give effect to a foreign privilege if the contacts with the forum state are 'numerous and important'. The forum, however, should be more inclined to recognize the foreign privilege if the facts established by the evidence would be unlikely to affect the outcome or could be proved in some other way.[89] Yet again, courts in almost all cases have followed the general direction to apply forum law to admit the evidence.[90] In *Allianz*, *Allen*, *Kos*, and *Lipham* the courts expressly rejected the argument that a 'special reason' existed for applying foreign law, finding that the forum had strong contacts with the parties and the relationship and that the evidence was material to the litigation. In the *Major* case a Kentucky court went further, saying that even if the foreign jurisdiction had the most significant relationship with the parties and the communication, an independent 'special reason' needed to be found to displace forum law.[91] While some US commentators have criticized § 139 for being excessively forum-centred,[92] the results in the decided cases, especially under § 139(1) do not support this conclusion. A more accurate view may be to see § 139 as favouring the law of the jurisdiction which admits the evidence (whether that happens to be the forum or not) at the expense of the law providing the privilege.[93]

---

[88] *State v Heaney* 689 NW 2d 168 (Sup Ct Minn 2004); *Saint Anne's Development Coy LLC v Trabich* 2009 WL 324054 (D Md); *Gonzalez v State* 45 SW 3d 101 (Tex Crim App 2001) (penitent and confessor); *Washington v Donahue* 18 P 3d 608 (Wash CA 2001) (patient-doctor); *Ford Motor Co v Leggatt* 904 SW 2d 643 (Tex 1995); *Iowa v Eldrenkamp* 541 NW 2d 877 (Iowa 1995); *Independent Petrochemical v Aetna Cas and Sur Co* 117 FRD 292 (DDC 1987); *Mazzella v Philadelphia Newspapers Inc* 479 F Supp 523 (EDNY 1979) (journalist privilege).

[89] Restatement (Second), § 139 comment d.

[90] *Sterling Fin Management LP v UBS Paine-Webber* 336 Ill App 3d 442 (2002); *People v Allen* 336 Ill App 3d 457 (2003); *Re Teleglobe Communications Corp* 392 BR 561 (Bank D Del 2008); *Allianz Ins Co v Guidant Corp* 869 NE 2d 1042 (CA Ill 2007); *Kos v State* 15 SW 3d 633 (CA Tex 2000) (physician-patient privilege); *Major v Commonwealth* 275 SW 3d 706 (SC Ky 2009); *Danklef v Wilmington* 429 A 2d 509 (Super Ct Del 1981); *Kuhn & Kogan Chtd v Jeffrey C Mensh & Assocs Inc* 77 F Supp 2d 52 (DDC 1999); *Saleba v Schrand* 300 SW 3d 177 (SC Ky 2009); *Rawat v Navistar International Corp* 2010 WL 1417840 (ND Ill); *State v Lipham* 910 A 2d 388, 391–2 (Sup Jud Ct Me 2006) (spousal privilege).

[91] *Major v Commonwealth* 275 SW 3d 706, 714 (SC Ky 2009); see also *Saleba v Schrand* 300 SW 3d 177 (SC Ky 2009). But cf *Equity Residential Properties Management Corp v Kendall Risk Management Inc* 246 FRD 557 (ND Ill 2007) and *Compuware Corp v Moody's Investors Services Inc* 222 FRD 124 (ED Mich 2004) in which the foreign law of privilege was applied where the forum had almost no contact with the parties and the communication.

[92] R Weintraub, *Commentary on the Conflict of Laws* (Foundation Press, 4th edn, 2001) 78.

[93] Bradford (n 86 above) 939.

8.33 In evaluation, it is acknowledged that the US most significant relationship approaches provide significantly more scope for the operation of foreign privilege law in the forum than is possible under the prevailing Commonwealth law approach, which treats privilege as procedural. US courts have in fact chosen to avoid the substance-procedure dichotomy altogether and sought to address directly the issue as to which law should be applied. Unfortunately, however, the most significant relationship test (in all its variations) is too broad and uncertain and, in the case of the Second Restatement, arguably too unbalanced in its preference for the admission of evidence over privilege rights.

(c) An Appropriate Choice of Law Rule?

8.34 In this regard, an alternative to all the approaches discusssed would be to develop a narrowly framed and specific choice of law rule for privilege questions, not based on the substance / procedure distinction. For example, writers in the context of legal professional privilege have suggested that the court should apply the law of the place in which the lawyer or adviser was admitted to practice,[94] while another has supported the law of the country where the attorney-client relationship has its 'predominant effects'.[95] The second view is justified on the basis that a lawyer may form a relationship with a client in a country other than the one in which he or she principally practises. While such a situation may arise, it is likely in most cases that a lawyer will only give advice on the law of the country in which he or she habitually practises. If a lawyer did give advice on the law of a jurisdiction in which he or she is admitted, but in which he or she does not reside or normally practise, then exceptionally that law can be applied. It would be undesirable, however, to use a term such as 'predominant effects', as this arguably suffers from the same imprecision as the most significant relationship formulation.

8.35 The clarity and ease of application of the 'law of the country of admission' rule, as well as the scope for application of foreign privilege law (either the law of the cause of action or a third country's law), make it an attractive candidate. The proposed rule is, however, confined to the lawyer-client context and cannot apply in the context of other privileges where other choice of law rules would have to be developed.

---

[94] McComish (n 66 above); Bradford (n 86 above); see also, in the international arbitration context, D Kozlowska, 'Privilege in the Multijurisdictional Area of International Arbitration' (2011) 14 International Arbitration L Rev 128, 130.

[95] K Berger, 'Evidentiary Privileges: Best Practice Standards versus/and Arbitral Discretion' (2006) 22 Arbitration International 501, 510–11.

B. Privilege and Other Bars on Disclosure

As a final word on legal professional privilege, it has been noted that **8.36** forum law has been applied almost exclusively with little regard for whether such a right exists under foreign law. Possibly to make up for the absence of a choice of law rule, Commonwealth courts have occasionally interpreted the domestic law of the forum on privilege as including advice given by foreign lawyers on foreign legal matters,[96] or documents produced for foreign court proceedings.[97] The effect of such an approach is to treat foreign lawyers as the 'mirror image' of local lawyers.[98] To that extent, there is some evidence of an 'enlightened' application of the law of the forum at work as rights provided under local law are extended to embrace foreign situations and actors. Arguably, though, a more principled and even-handed approach would be to apply the foreign law of privilege directly pursuant to a choice of law rule rather than simply taking it into account in determining the scope of forum law. The possibility of some choice of law analysis being applied to privilege appears to have been left open by the Full Federal Court of Australia in *Kennedy v Wallace*.[99] There, the court made it clear that while the Australian law of privilege applied to advice given by foreign lawyers, the position may well be different where no privilege attached under either the legal system governing the foreign lawyer (the country of admission) or the legal system of the state where the advice was given.[100] In such cases, presumably, foreign law may be indirectly applied to deny the claim to privilege.

2. Witnesses: the Audio-Video Dimension

The situation where a witness gives evidence by way of audio or video **8.37** link from another country in proceedings in the forum raises interesting issues from a choice of law perspective. Specifically, there is the question of whether a witness, resident in country A, may claim privilege under that country's laws from answering a question in proceedings being conducted in country B, where no such privilege is recognized. The overall Commonwealth position on this matter is debatable, although under

---

[96] *Kennedy v Wallace* (2004) 213 ALR 108; *Re Duncan, Garfield v Fay* [1968] 2 All ER 395, 398; *Hartz Canada Inc v Colgate-Palmolive Co* (1988) 27 CPC (2d) 152.
[97] *Minnesota Mining & Manufacturing Co v Rennicks (UK) Ltd (No 1)* [1991] FSR 97 (Ch D); *Société Française Hoechst v Allied Colloids Ltd* [1991] RPC 245 (Pat Ct).
[98] McComish (n 66 above) 319.
[99] (2004) 213 ALR 108.
[100] ibid para 214 (Allsop J), para 62 (Black CJ and Emmett J). See also Australian Law Reform Commission and New South Wales Law Reform Commission, *Uniform Evidence Law* (Report No 102, 2006) para 14.99.

Australian law[101] it seems clear that the privilege of the foreign country (A in the example) would not be recognized, as the laws of the forum ('for the purposes of . . . evidence, procedure, contempt of court or perjury') apply exclusively to a person giving evidence from a remote location. One way in which this provision could be avoided and foreign law applied is if the issue of privilege were classified as substantive. Yet, if the foreign law containing the privilege upon which the claimant relies is not the law of the cause of action (or there is no such law) then such an argument would presumably not be of assistance. Commentary has therefore been justifiably critical of the exclusive application of the law of the forum in the case of audio/video delivered evidence, with the suggestion made that application of the 'dual' choice of law rule in article 11 of the Hague Evidence Convention would be preferable.[102] Article 11 provides that a party may resist disclosure in the context of a request for oral testimony where a privilege exists under either the law of the requesting or requested states. While such a provision is perhaps overgenerous to the witness in its application of privilege laws, it may be the most appropriate method, apart from adopting a US-type 'most significant relationship' test, for recognizing a foreign privilege in such circumstances.

3. Privilege Against Self-Incrimination

8.38 In the case of the privilege against self-incrimination the law of the forum has also been exclusively applied in Commonwealth countries, with the only possible alternative—the law of the country where the offence took place or would take place—being ignored. Similarly to legal professional or lawyer-client privilege, the only qualification to this approach has been to extend the forum law of privilege in certain cases to embrace offences under foreign law. Such a conclusion raises the possibility that a Commonwealth court may apply its own law of privilege in respect of foreign offences in circumstances where the foreign law itself would recognize no such privilege. Yet the exclusive application of forum law has rarely been questioned.[103]

8.39 Under the rubric of the privilege against self-incrimination, a number of different categories of case may be identified. The first situation is where a

---

[101] See eg Evidence (Audio and Audio Visual Links) Act 1998 (NSW), s 5C (2) and Evidence (Miscellaneous Provisions) Act 1958 (Vic), s 42E.

[102] Davies (n 29 above) 232.

[103] But see Dolinger and Tiburcio (n 1 above) 445, who argue that any issue regarding a privilege or prohibition on disclosure under the law of the country of the location of the evidence should be decided by that country's courts and law on the basis of national sovereignty.

B. Privilege and Other Bars on Disclosure

party facing a request for evidence complains that disclosure would involve *an admission of a past criminal offence* under foreign law. This type of case more obviously fits within the idea of protection against self-incrimination. The second type of case is where the requested party complains that *the act of disclosure itself* would amount to a criminal offence in a foreign country. Two commonly cited foreign legislative provisions in this regard are article 273 of the Swiss Penal Code and article 47 of the Swiss Bank Law. Article 273 provides: 'whoever seeks out any commercial or business secret in order to disclose it to a foreign authority or to a foreign organisation . . . or whoever discloses [any such] secret to a foreign authority or to a foreign organisation will be punished with jail'. Article 47 imposes penal sanctions on officers and employees of a bank who disclose a customer's identity or information about a customer. Another commonly cited foreign provision which imposes sanctions on disclosure of evidence is the French 'blocking statute', article 1*bis* of July 1980, which provides that 'it is forbidden for any person to request, seek or produce in writing orally or by any other means economic, commercial, industrial, financial or technical documents or information with a view to it being used as evidence in foreign judicial . . . proceedings'. The use of the term 'blocking statute' refers to the fact that the French legislation expressly purports to block access by foreign courts to local documents. The Swiss provision, by contrast, is more in the nature of a general secrecy obligation.

Some Commonwealth courts have explicitly suggested that the two categories of case identified in 8.39 should be kept separate—with the second type of case, where disclosure itself breaches foreign law, not really involving privilege at all.[104] Most cases have involved complaints of disclosure as an offence and it is this category of case which will first be examined.

8.40

(a) Disclosure as an Offence

English decisions

An early view, which gives widest application to the law of forum, comes from the decision of the Privy Council in *The Consul Corfitzon*.[105] The defendant objected to an order for discovery on the ground that compliance would render him liable to a penalty under Swedish law. The court, however, stated that foreign law was irrelevant as 'the practice and procedure are governed by the municipal law of the state from which it derives

8.41

---

[104] *Michael Wilson and Partners Ltd v Nicholls* (2008) 74 NSWLR 218, para 5; *The Canada Trust Co v Stolzenberg* The Times, 10 November 1997 (Ch D).
[105] [1917] AC 550.

its jurisdiction and cannot be modified by the municipal legislation of any other state'.[106]

8.42 The absoluteness of this view, however, which applies the law of the forum without regard at all for foreign law, is unlikely to represent current English law. More recently, in *MacKinnon v Donaldson, Luffkin Jenrette Securities Corporation*,[107] Hoffmann J noted that a defendant could 'be excused from having to produce a document on the grounds that this would violate the law of the place where the document is kept'.[108] While in that case the judge did not have to address in what circumstances foreign law would be recognized to excuse disclosure,[109] the issue was more directly addressed by the Privy Council in *Brannigan v Davison*.[110] In *Brannigan* the defendants refused to give evidence to a commission of inquiry on the ground that to do so would render them liable to prosecution under the secrecy laws of a foreign state, laws similar to article 273 of the Swiss Penal Code, referred to at 8.39. The Privy Council (on appeal from New Zealand) ordered that they make disclosure. The court first found that the English law of privilege against self-incrimination does not apply to a case where disclosure would either amount to an offence under foreign law or reveal past offences under foreign law. Equally, however, the court rejected the approach taken in the *Consul* case (see 8.41) that the forum should ignore the fact that disclosure could breach or reveal breaches of foreign laws. An appropriate middle ground was that the court retained a discretion to excuse a witness from giving evidence which may incriminate him or her under foreign law. The discretion involves a balancing exercise where all the circumstances are taken into account; in particular, the adverse consequences to the forum proceeding if the questions are not answered and the detriment to the witness and to comity if the witness is compelled to answer.[111] Obviously, therefore, this is a less rigid and more enlightened application of the law of the forum than the previous approach and provides some scope for recognition of foreign law.

8.43 English decisions since *Brannigan* have continued to apply this discretionary, balancing test to determine whether a defendant must comply with a

---

[106] ibid 555–6 (Lord Parker of Waddington).
[107] [1986] Ch 482.
[108] ibid 494.
[109] See also *The Heidberg* [1993] 2 Lloyd's Rep 324 (discovery was not excused because it was unlikely to be a breach of foreign law and there was little risk of prosecution in any event).
[110] [1997] AC 238.
[111] ibid 251.

request for evidence where it is said that disclosure will violate foreign law. Yet, in the vast majority of cases, courts have ordered that the evidence be taken despite the possible breach of foreign laws. In *The Canada Trust Co v Stolzenberg*[112] the court had to consider an objection to a disclosure order in a mareva injunction application on the basis that it violated article 273 of the Swiss Penal Code. The court first confirmed that it was proper to take into account, in determining whether a defendant should make disclosure, that he or she may be put in the position of having to commit a criminal offence in another country. Such a matter was said to go to the court's discretion, as had been stated in *Brannigan v Davison*. The court also noted that there was a difference between the disclosure *as* an offence and disclosure *of* an offence cases. A court should be 'more reluctant to require a defendant to do something which would of itself be a criminal offence in another jurisdiction than it would be to require the defendant to do something which would reveal that he had in the past committed an offence in the foreign jurisdiction'. Presumably in such a case comity and sovereignty concerns are raised more acutely; the forum should have greater regard to foreign laws in the disclosure *as* an offence situation. Yet, despite this view, the court in *Stolzenberg* nevertheless ordered disclosure. While the court found that there was a possible breach of article 273, it accepted expert evidence of the plaintiff that the defendant might have a defence to such a charge under Swiss law and that, in any event, the risk of prosecution was low. Most importantly, the court was swayed by the purpose for which the evidence was sought: that is, 'the need to take prompt pre-emptive and effective steps to counter multi-million pound transnational crime' in which the defendant 'appears to have been closely involved'. Such a conclusion suggests that the nature of the case will also be relevant to the strength of the forum's interest in applying its law in favour of disclosure. In *Re Mid East Trading Ltd*[113] the Court of Appeal also ordered disclosure where there was 'no real risk' that the defendant would be exposed to liability under foreign law for producing the documents.[114]

8.44 The French blocking statute referred to earlier[115] was considered in *Morris v Banque Arabe et Internationale d'Investissement SA*.[116] The *Morris* case concerned a request for discovery by an English liquidator against a French company which was alleged to have participated in a fraud by the

---

[112] The Times, 10 November 1997 (Ch D).
[113] [1998] 1 All ER 577 (CA).
[114] See also, to the same effect, *Re Casterbridge Properties* [2002] BPIR 428 (Ch D).
[115] See 8.39 above.
[116] [2001] IL Pr 37 (Com Ct).

company in liquidation. The French company relied on the blocking statute. The court ordered disclosure noting that (a) the law of the forum should be given predominant operation in matters of discovery, (b) the documents in question were crucial to the liquidator's investigation, and (c) there was little risk of prosecution under the French statute. Most recently, in *Masri v Consolidated Contractors International Company SAL*,[117] the English Commercial Court again ordered disclosure in circumstances where there was no evidence to suggest that criminal prosecution[118] or civil liability[119] for such an act was likely under foreign law. In a later stage of this litigation[120] Clarke J held that it was not appropriate for an English court to determine whether or not to exercise its contempt jurisdiction by reference to whether such an order would place the person alleged to be in contempt in breach of foreign law, including foreign criminal law.[121] Such a prospect may, however, be a reason for the English court not treating the breach as worthy of sanction or diminishing the penalty that may otherwise have been imposed.[122] In that case, orders for contempt were made where a number of defendants deliberately refused to honour an English judgment requiring disclosure of certain information and there was little risk that they would be exposed to criminal prosecution or suffer penalty under foreign law for non-compliance with the English court orders.[123]

8.45 All of the aforementioned decisions suggest that English courts give almost no weight to foreign law prohibitions on producing evidence where there is little likelihood of prosecution for disclosure. Such a view is to be supported, for otherwise 'unscrupulous litigants'[124] may use the remote prospect of prosecution to deny the claimant crucial documents it may need for a fair trial. Where the prospect of criminal liability is real, as opposed to fanciful, however, a much stronger argument exists for recognition of the prohibition under foreign law, both to protect the interests of the defendant and the sovereignty of the foreign state.

Australia

8.46 The bulk of Commonwealth decisions have followed the *Brannigan* approach, where the complaint is that disclosure *itself* would amount to

---

[117] [2008] EWHC 2492 (Comm).
[118] ibid para 26.
[119] ibid para 28.
[120] [2011] EWHC 1024 (Comm).
[121] ibid para 249.
[122] ibid para 247.
[123] ibid para 429.
[124] Hartley (n 1 above) 202.

a breach of foreign law. While the courts have applied a discretionary test which in theory gives weight to the foreign law, in practice, in almost all cases, the courts have come down in favour of production. So, in *Bank of Valetta plc v National Crime Authority*,[125] the Australian Federal Court held that a foreign bank had to comply with a notice to produce even though to do so would possibly infringe the banker-customer confidentiality duty under foreign law. The court noted that the balancing approach, as articulated in *Brannigan v Davison*, required a weighing of the interests of the foreign party and respect for the sovereignty and laws of the foreign state, on the one hand, with the needs of the country requesting the evidence, on the other. Here the Australian public interest in the investigation of criminal activity was found to be more significant and so the risk of violating foreign law was held not to be a reasonable excuse to avoid production. Interestingly, the *Valetta* decision implicitly suggests that where the request for evidence is sought for a criminal investigation as opposed to for civil litigation between private parties, then the forum's interest in mandating disclosure and ignoring the breach of foreign law will have a greater claim to exclusive application.

A court in another Australian decision, *Australian Securities Commission v Bank Leumi Le-Israel*,[126] took a similar approach. That case involved a request by an Australian government body for information as to the ownership of shares by two Swiss companies. The Swiss companies objected on the ground that disclosure would violate article 273 of the Swiss Penal Code. Again, however, the Australian court held that the purpose of the request for evidence here was to comply with the mandatory requirements of Australian statutory company law which compelled disclosure of shareholdings. The legislative scheme so established would be undermined by allowing foreign parties to be exempt from disclosure obligations. Most recently, in *Michael Wilson and Partners Ltd v Nicholls*,[127] Brereton J of the Supreme Court of New South Wales noted that the existence of foreign law obligations of confidentiality will not provide an 'absolute objection to an order for production' but will, at most, only bear on the court's discretion to make the order given that disclosure, being procedural, is predominantly a matter for the law of the forum. The judge then proceeded to order disclosure in a civil proceeding between private parties after finding, in any event, that there was neither criminal liability nor civil liability (on the facts) under foreign law.

8.47

---

[125] (1999) 164 ALR 45; (affd [1999] FCAFC 1099).
[126] (1995) 134 ALR 101; (affd (1996) 69 FCR 531).
[127] (2008) 74 NSWLR 218, para 11.

8.48 So, similarly to the English position, Australian courts have been generally reluctant to allow persons to resist orders for disclosure of documents on the ground that production of the evidence may involve a criminal offence or other breach of foreign laws, at least in the absence of a clear likelihood of prosecution.

Canada

8.49 Canadian courts have also been generally unwilling to allow parties to avoid disclosure on the ground that to do so would violate the law of a foreign country, at least where the complainant is a party to the litigation rather than a third party. While in *Frischke v Royal Bank of Canada*[128] the Ontario Court of Appeal refused to compel a third party witness, resident in Panama, to violate Panamanian laws of secrecy by disclosure of information, in all cases since, Canadian courts have required disclosure. For example, in *Spencer v The Queen*,[129] the Crown sought evidence from an employee, then a resident and citizen of Canada, who had formerly been manager of the Royal Bank of Canada in its branch in the Bahamas, in connection with an income tax prosecution in Canada. The employee objected on the ground that he would be subjected to criminal prosecution in the Bahamas if he testified. The court ordered disclosure finding that 'to permit a foreign jurisdiction to shape the laws of Canada on a matter of fundamental principle has no support historically or legally. It must be for the Canadian courts or the legislatures to determine on clearly defined grounds whether a privilege exists exempting a witness from the basic obligation to give evidence'.[130] Consequently, to allow a party 'to refuse to give evidence in the circumstances of this case would permit a foreign country to frustrate the administration of justice in this country'. The *Frischke* case was distinguished on the ground that the witness in that case resided outside the forum, in the country whose laws it alleged prohibited disclosure. The risk of prosecution was therefore greater.

8.50 In later cases the approach in *Spencer* has generally been followed, with the *Frischke* case being distinguished on the further ground that the person resisting disclosure there was a third party witness, not a party to litigation in the Canadian forum. Hence, in all cases where a party to litigation has objected to disclosure on the basis of foreign law, production

---

[128] (1977) 17 OR (2d) 388.
[129] (1983) 145 DLR (3d) 344; (affd [1985] 2 SCR 278).
[130] ibid 353.

B. Privilege and Other Bars on Disclosure

has been ordered.[131] A possible departure from this unanimity appears in *Comaplex Resources International Ltd v Schaffhauser Kantonalbank*,[132] where an Ontario court did appear to accept in principle, in the case of a party to litigation, that disclosure could be excused on the basis that it was prohibited under foreign law. Yet the court nevertheless ordered disclosure on the facts of the case, noting that in the case of article 273 of the Swiss Penal Code, the provision did not apply to prohibit the answering of questions in a civil action or producing relevant documents which disclose the identity of customers. The risk of prosecution was therefore minimal.

United States

8.51 Historically, there has been great scope for conflict between US and foreign laws in the taking of evidence, given the very broad powers under US law for obtaining evidence, both from parties and non-parties. Consequently, US courts have often been confronted with the argument that a request for documents or testimony is said to violate foreign law. The early view, derived from the First Restatement on the Conflict of Laws, was that US courts had no power to order disclosure of evidence in violation of the law of the country where the evidence was located.[133] A strict *lex loci actus* or *lex situs* choice of law rule (the law of the place where the evidence is to be taken) was therefore applied in the area of taking evidence abroad.

8.52 This approach was, however, jettisoned by the Supreme Court in *Société Internationale pour Participations Industrielles et Commerciales SA v Rogers*.[134] The *Rogers* case concerned an action by a Swiss company to recover property seized by a US government agency, the Alien Property Custodian, under the Trading with the Enemy Act (US). The US defendant sought certain documents from the Swiss plaintiff which it refused to provide, citing article 273 of the Swiss Penal Code and article 47 of the Swiss Bank Law. The US Supreme Court upheld the order for disclosure but, interestingly, refused to sanction the Swiss plaintiff for failure to produce the documents. In upholding the disclosure order, the court noted that all the circumstances of the case had to be considered, including the policies underlying the action for which disclosure was sought. Here the policies of the US Trading with the Enemy Act were strong in supporting disclosure. In refusing to

---

[131] See eg *ED Miller Sales & Rentals Ltd v Caterpillar Tractor Co* (1988) 22 CPR (3d) 290 (Alta CA); *Laxton v Coglon* (2006) 61 BCLR (4th) 127 (BCSC); *Comexter Inc v Westminster County (Official Administrator)*, BCCA, 17 July 1987.
[132] (1991) 84 DLR (4th) 343 (Ont CJ).
[133] Restatement (First) of the Conflict of Laws, § 94 (1934).
[134] 357 US 197 (1958).

impose sanctions, however, the court first noted that the plaintiff had not been in collusion with the Swiss authorities to block discovery and had made good faith efforts to provide discovery.[135] Secondly, the impact of foreign law could not be discounted: 'fear of criminal prosecution constitutes a weighty excuse for non-production and this excuse is not weakened because the laws preventing compliance are those of a foreign sovereign'.[136] Hence, according to the Supreme Court, foreign law does operate to qualify the law of the forum in matters of discovery but only at the stage of ordering sanctions for non-disclosure, not in determining whether disclosure should be ordered at all.

8.53 Later US lower court decisions have taken a less rigid view of the role of foreign law and have instead applied an overall 'balancing of interests' test in determining whether disclosure should be ordered in the face of alleged breaches of foreign law.[137] The balancing test, which is similar in some respects to the *Brannigan* formulation under Commonwealth law, is derived from § 40 of the 1965 Restatement (Second) of the Foreign Relations Law of the United States. Among the interests to be considered under § 40 are the parties' interests, the nature of the discovery that is to be sought, the territory in which the demanded conduct would occur, the nationality of the person ordered to act in relation to the sovereign that is prohibiting the demanded conduct and the extent to which the nation is in a position to enforce compliance or penalise non-compliance with its law. The terms of § 40 were largely replicated in the more recent § 442 of the 1987 Restatement (Third) of the Foreign Relations Law of the United States, which added two further matters to be considered in the balancing of interests: 'the importance to the investigation or litigation of the documents or other information requested' and 'the availability of alternative means of securing the information'.[138]

8.54 The breadth of the discretion given to courts would suggest that US courts will reach a variety of results on the question of disclosure. Yet, overall, it is clear that US interests in favour of disclosure have more commonly prevailed over foreign interests, which confirms the strength of the law of the forum (already noted in Commonwealth countries) in matters of taking evidence.[139] Also, while US courts have not always framed the issue

---

[135] ibid 208.
[136] ibid 211.
[137] G Born and P Rutledge, *International Civil Litigation in United States Courts* (Aspen Publishers, 4th edn, 2007) 951.
[138] Restatement (Third) of the Foreign Relations Law of the United States, § 442(1)(c).
[139] L Collins, 'The United States Supreme Court and the Principles of Comity: Evidence in Transnational Litigation' (2006) 8 YBPIL 53, 56.

B. *Privilege and Other Bars on Disclosure*

explicitly as one of a choice between US and foreign laws, in practice, the question of applying US law on discovery or deferring to a foreign prohibition on disclosure on the ground of 'comity' is arguably a form of choice of law analysis.

At the risk of oversimplifying the large body of US decisions, the following general propositions can be made. First, where the case involves a private civil action, as opposed to criminal or civil enforcement proceedings in which the US government is seeking information, the 'balance' usually, but not always, comes down in favour of disclosure.[140] Where, however, a private civil action also involves important US governmental interests, such as the prevention of financing of terrorism, disclosure will be ordered even if it would place the defendant in breach of its own country's laws.[141] Here the strength of the governmental interest provides a powerful public policy reason in support of application of the law of the forum. Secondly, where the entity requested to make discovery is a party to the litigation as opposed to a third party witness, a stronger case for disclosure is made.[142] Thirdly, where the consequence of disclosure is at most civil liability under foreign law (for example for breach of bank or corporate secrecy) as opposed to penal sanctions, especially with imprisonment, then disclosure will generally be ordered on the basis that the hardship suffered by the foreign party is not great.[143] Fourthly, where the foreign law prohibiting disclosure is sought to be applied extraterritorially to conduct in the United States rather than to activities within the foreign state, disclosure is more likely to be ordered.[144] Finally, foreign penal laws which are *designed to protect against disclosure generally, both within and outside the country of enactment*, will be given greater deference than measures simply enacted to protect local parties from having to comply with foreign discovery laws. Hence, the French blocking statute (noted at 8.39), has been routinely ignored by US courts in decisions to

8.55

---

[140] *Société Internationale pour Participations Industrielles et Commerciales SA v Rogers* 357 US 197 (1958); *US v First National City Bank* 396 F 2d 897, 904 (2nd Cir 1968); *US v Davis* 767 F 2d 1025, 1035 (2nd Cir 1985); *Re Grand Jury Subpoena* 218 F Supp 2d 544 (SDNY 2002); cf *Minpeco SA v Conticommodity Services Inc* 116 FRD 517, 523 (SDNY 1987).

[141] *Strauss v Credit Lyonnais SA* 242 FRD 199 (EDNY 2007); *Weiss v National Westminster Bank* 242 FRD 33 (EDNY 2007); *Linde v Arab Bank plc* 463 F Supp 2d 310 (EDNY 2006).

[142] *Minpeco SA v Conticommodity Services Inc* 116 FRD 517, 526–7 (SDNY 1987).

[143] *US v First National City Bank* 396 F 2d 897, 901 (2nd Cir 1968); *Minpeco SA v Conticommodity Services Inc* 116 FRD 517, 524 (SDNY 1987); *US v Chase Manhattan Bank* 584 F Supp 1080, 1086 (SDNY 1984) (civil bank secrecy laws); *Garpeg Ltd v US* 583 F Supp 789, 796 (SDNY 1984); *US v First National City Bank of Chicago* 699 F 2d 341 (7th Cir 1983).

[144] *Re Vivendi Universal SA Securities Litigation* 618 F Supp 2d 335 (SDNY 2009).

order discovery[145] on the basis that it is seen as an 'overly broad and vague'[146] obstruction to the proper exercise of justice. By contrast, provisions such as the article 273 of the Swiss Penal Code and article 47 of the Swiss Bank Law, which prohibit disclosure in absolute terms and focus on maintaining secrecy of banking and corporate data, are more often applied to deny production.[147] Other foreign statutes which give discretionary authority to government agencies not to comply with US disclosure orders (such as the Protection of Trading Interests Act 1980 (UK)) have also generally been given short shrift by US courts in favour of ordering production under the law of the forum.[148]

8.56 Overall then, the position under US law is not so different from that in the Commonwealth: while a broad discretion exists with respect to exempting disclosure due to foreign prohibitory laws, in practice, in the clear majority of cases, courts will give the law of the forum wide application and order production of the material.

(b) Disclosure of an Offence

8.57 The second type of case under the broad heading of privilege against self-incrimination is where a party complains that giving evidence would force him or her to disclose past offences under foreign law. As far as the application of the privilege against self-incrimination is concerned, in this situation, English legislation makes it clear that the privilege only applies to offences under local law.[149] Consequently, the discretionary balancing test from *Brannigan v Davison* will need to be relied upon in this context also, as the Privy Council suggested. So in *Credit Suisse Fides Trust SA v Cuoghi*[150] the *Brannigan* test was applied to refuse disclosure of information

---

[145] *Compagnie Francaise d'Assurance v Phillips Petroleum Co* 105 FRD 16, 30 (SDNY 1984); *Valois of America v Risdon Corp* 183 FRD 344 (D Conn 1997); *Remington Products Inc v N Am Philips Corp* 107 FRD 642, 651 (D Conn 1984); *Rich v Kis-California Inc* 121 FRD 254 (MDNC 1988); *Bodner v Paribas* 202 FRD 370, 374 (EDNY 2000). The similarly worded Quebec Business Concerns Records Act has been treated in the same manner: *Lyons v Bell Asbestos Mines Ltd* 119 FRD 384, 389–90 (DSC 1988).

[146] *Rich v Kis-California Inc* 121 FRD 254, 258 (MDNC 1988).

[147] *Minpeco SA v Conticommodity Services Inc* 116 FRD 517, 524 (SDNY 1987); *Trade Development Bank v Continental Insurance Co* 469 F 2d 35 (2nd Cir 1972); *Cochran Consulting Inc v Uwatec USA Inc* 102 F 3d 1224, 1230 (Fed Cir 1996). See also *Reinsurance Co of America Inc v Administratia Asigurarilor de Stat* 902 F 2d 1275, 1280, 1282 (7th Cir 1990) (Romanian state secrets law absolute in its application); *US v First National City Bank of Chicago* 699 F 2d 341 (7th Cir 1983) (Greek law the same).

[148] See eg *Re Uranium Antitrust Litigation* 480 F Supp 1138 (ND Ill 1979).

[149] Civil Evidence Act 1968 (UK). s 14(1)(a).

[150] [1998] QB 818.

B. Privilege and Other Bars on Disclosure

which might have revealed past offences under foreign law. A Hong Kong court, however, recently qualified the scope of this principle, saying that the discretion would only be applied to refuse disclosure where serious offences were involved, not 'regulatory . . . offences against the minor fiscal interests of the State'.[151] A New Zealand court also ordered disclosure, despite the defendant's possible incrimination under foreign law, because of the forum's greater interest in the conduct of its litigation.[152] Academic writing is supportive of this view, asserting that the privilege should apply to prevent the disclosure of offences under foreign law but only if the jeopardy under such law is near certain, not merely speculative.[153] The *Brannigan* principle has also been recognized as a basis for refusing disclosure, where documents may be used in foreign criminal proceedings against the defendant, although again the risk of prosecution must be real.[154]

Finally, in Australia legislation has been enacted which in one respect goes beyond the *Brannigan* principle in its recognition that foreign offences may fall under the forum's privilege against self-incrimination. Section 128(4)(a) of the Evidence Act 1995 (Cth) provides: 'the court may require the witness to give the evidence if the court is satisfied that: (a) the evidence does not tend to prove that the witness has committed an offence against or arising under, or is liable to a civil penalty under a law of a foreign country . . .'. While this provision contemplates that the forum's law on privilege against self-incrimination may be extended to prevent disclosure of past offences under foreign law,[155] it should be noted that this provision only applies to witness testimony or affidavit evidence at trial.[156] No privilege applies in the situation where documents are sought pursuant to pre-trial discovery and the risk of commission of a foreign offence is raised to resist disclosure. In this latter context, Australian courts will need to rely on the *Brannigan* principle to determine whether disclosure is warranted.[157]

8.58

---

[151] *Salt and Light Development v Sjtu Sunway Software Industry Ltd* [2006] HKCFI 384, para 82.
[152] *Waller v Max Resources Ltd (in liq)* HCNZ, 21 June 2004.
[153] C Theophilopoulos, 'The Anglo-American Legal Privilege Against Self-Incrimination and the Fear of Foreign Prosecution' (2003) 25 Sydney L Rev 305, 322.
[154] *Bank Gesellschaft Berlin International SA v Raif Zihnal* 16 July 2001 (Com Ct) (no real risk of prosecution, so disclosure ordered); cf *Beckkett Pte Ltd v Deutsche Bank AG* [2005] SGCA 34 (significant risk of prosecution, so disclosure refused).
[155] A privilege against self-incrimination arising under foreign law was recognized under the Evidence Act 1995 (Cth), s 128 in *Re Application concerning s 80 of the Supreme Court Act and sections 119 and 128 of the Evidence Act* [2004] NSWSC 614, para 32.
[156] *Lifetime Investments Pty Ltd v Commercial (Worldwide) Financial Services Pty Ltd* [2006] FCA 696.
[157] *X v Australian Crime Commission* (2004) 212 ALR 596, para 44.

8.59 In the United States, by contrast, the position with regard to the privilege against self-incrimination and foreign offences is clear: the privilege is not available to avoid disclosure of material which may lead to prosecution under foreign law.[158] To that extent, there is little deference to foreign law in the US 'disclosure of an offence' cases.

4. Enforcement of Foreign Requests for Evidence

8.60 The earlier discussion on privilege and prohibitions on disclosure of evidence considered the problem where a defendant seeks to resist an application for production of evidence *in the forum in which the trial was to take place* on the basis that to do so would expose it to prosecution under foreign laws. As was noted, Australian and other common law courts have been generally reluctant to accede to this argument. The position changes dramatically, however, when the prohibition on disclosure is raised as a defence in proceedings in the country where the evidence is located and the prohibition is part of local law. In the absence of a formal letter of request to a Commonwealth court under an instrument such as the Hague Evidence Convention, courts have generally been reluctant to enforce subpoenas issued against third parties resident in the forum, especially where to do so would breach local laws preventing disclosure. In *XAG v A Bank*[159] the English Commercial Court was confronted with a subpoena issued by a New York court against the London branch of a US bank, requiring production of documents concerning UK bank accounts of a company for a tax avoidance investigation. The English court noted that a balancing of interests exercise was involved but still granted an injunction to the company to restrain the bank from making disclosure. The court held that the English law principle of bank secrecy from the *Tournier* case[160] prevailed over the interest of assisting the New York court with evidence. The Court was influenced in its decision by the 'improbability' that the bank would face contempt sanctions in New York. An identical result on very similar facts was reached by a Hong Kong court in *FDC Co Ltd v The Chase Manhattan Bank*[161] and more recently a Canadian court invoked one of its own 'blocking statutes'[162] to refuse to enforce a US court order for examination of a witness and production of documents.[163]

---

[158] *US v Balsys* 524 US 666 (1998).
[159] [1983] 2 All ER 464.
[160] *Tournier v National Provincial and Union Bank of England* [1924] 1 KB 461.
[161] [1990] 1 HKLR 277.
[162] Business Concerns Records Act (Quebec), s 2.
[163] *Southern New England Telephone Co v Zrihen* 2007 QCCS 1391.

B. Privilege and Other Bars on Disclosure

These decisions all show that where a request for disclosure of information is brought before the courts of the country whose laws would prohibit or render unlawful such disclosure, the deference to the law of the country seeking the evidence is much less. The weight to be given to the anti-disclosure laws is greater given that in this context they are not foreign but *local* laws. Relevant to the issue of recognition of a forum court's disclosure orders is the recent *Gambazzi* litigation. This case involved an action against a Swiss national, Gambazzi, in England, in which he was ordered to make disclosure of assets and documents. He refused to make disclosure and was found guilty of contempt of court and barred from taking any further part in the proceeding, which led to a default judgment being given against him. Enforcement of the judgment was sought in Italy and Gambazzi relied on the defence of public policy under article 27 of the Brussels Convention. A reference was made to the European Court of Justice,[164] which held that while a Member State's court may make orders to ensure the proper conduct of proceedings and the fair administration of justice, such orders must be 'proportionate' given the importance of the defendant's right to be heard. A 'manifestly disproportionate' order would thus be contrary to public policy. The Italian court therefore had to determine whether the order barring Gambazzi from participating in the proceeding because of his failure to comply with the disclosure order was proportionate. The Italian court found that it was, with one reason (relevant to the present discussion) being that Gambazzi had no proper reason for resisting the original disclosure order, such as violating a professional secrecy obligation or foreign (Swiss) criminal law.[165]

8.61

Where the evidence sought is the subject of a letter of request to a Commonwealth court under the Hague Evidence Convention, there is also scope for refusing production under local law. Articles 9 and 12 of the Convention, which allow the courts of the requested state to refuse a request where it violates local law in certain circumstances have already been noted. Further, and of possibly wider scope, is article 11 which provides that a party may resist disclosure in the context of a request for oral testimony and/or production of documents[166] where a privilege exists

8.62

---

[164] Case C-394/07 *Gambazzi v Daimlerchrysler Canada Inc* (2 April 2009) [2009] 1 Lloyd's Rep 647.
[165] Judgment of Milan Court of Appeal, 24 November 2010; see G Cuniberti, at <http://www.conflictoflaws.net/2011/gambazzi-looses-in-milan>(sic) (accessed, 1 March 2011).
[166] See Hague Evidence Convention, arts 1 and 3 where both acts are regarded as the 'giv[ing] of evidence under the Convention'.

under the law of the requesting or requested states[167] or where there is a 'duty' or obligation not to provide evidence under either or both such laws. The concept of 'privilege' appears to cover both legal professional privilege and the privilege against self-incrimination.[168] It is not clear how broadly the term 'duty' should be interpreted but it is at least arguable that the narrow view taken by common law courts to the effect that provisions such as article 273 of the Swiss Penal Code allow a party to avoid disclosure while the French blocking statute (for example) does not, may be inconsistent with the article. Surely a statutory provision which requires a party not to provide evidence in response to a request from another jurisdiction is just as much a 'duty' as a wider obligation not to produce evidence for any purpose, provided of course that the provision in each case is consistent with the Convention. An Australian example of such a 'blocking statute' is section 42(1)(a) of the Foreign Evidence Act 1994 (Cth) which provides that the Attorney-General may make an order prohibiting the production of a document. Overall, therefore, there is considerable scope for the operation of privileges and prohibitions on disclosure under the Convention.

8.63 Additionally, it is also worth noting that article 11 of the Hague Evidence Convention goes further in its recognition of foreign privileges. Under the optional article 11(2) the drafters allowed contracting states to declare that they will respect privileges under the laws of third states. Perhaps because of its radical nature, the UK and other Commonwealth countries have made no such declaration but it is an interesting innovation in the context of applicable law. Article 14 of the EU Evidence Regulation, referred to at 8.15, is of similar effect. Under the Regulation 'a request . . . shall not be executed when the person concerned claims the right to refuse to give evidence or to be prohibited from giving evidence'. Such a provision therefore clearly extends to the circumstance where a witness has an obligation not to produce evidence as well as where he or she has a right not to do so.

8.64 Finally, it should also be noted that even where there is no specific prohibition under the law of the country in which the evidence is located, it may be difficult for a claimant to enforce any order of the forum court to obtain evidence where no letter of request is used. Commonwealth rules on the recognition and enforcement of foreign judgments generally only require

---

[167] This provision was applied in *Rio Tinto Zinc Corp v Westinghouse* [1978] AC 547 to allow certain witnesses to claim privilege under English law (the requested state) and other witnesses to claim privilege under US law (the requesting state). See also *Renfield Corp v E Remy Martin & Co SA* 98 FRD 442, 444 (D Del 1983).

[168] *Rio Tinto Zinc Corp v Westinghouse* [1978] AC 547.

B. Privilege and Other Bars on Disclosure

courts to enforce final and conclusive judgments on the merits of a foreign court; not interlocutory orders.[169] While there is some scope in English law for courts to make orders 'in aid of' foreign proceedings, such as freezing orders,[170] the position in respect of other types of interlocutory relief (for example to obtain evidence) is less clear. Consequently, therefore, there is at least some risk that the courts in the country where the evidence is located will use their own law to prevent enforcement of the request for evidence regardless of whether local law has been breached. In that respect, therefore, the law of the forum in which the trial is to take place may in practice be thwarted by application of the law of the country in which the evidence is located simply because of the need to enforce the forum's orders.

---

[169] *Nouvion v Freeman* (1889) 15 App Cas 1.
[170] *Credit Suisse Fides Trust SA v Cuoghi* [1998] QB 818 (Eng CA).

9
Statutes of Limitation

A. The Common Law Position	9.01
1. The Right-Remedy Approach	9.01
2. The Substantive Trend	9.05
3. The South African *Via Media*	9.08
4. Limitations and Overriding Mandatory Rules	9.11
B. The UK Statutory Regime	9.12
1. The Foreign Limitation Periods Act	9.12
2. Public Policy	9.20
3. The EU Instruments	9.24
4. *Renvoi* and Limitations	9.27
5. Filling the Gaps in the UK Statutory Regime	9.31
C. Further Issues	9.35
1. Choice of Law and Limitations in Jurisdictional Disputes	9.35
2. Avoiding a Foreign Limitation by Displacing the Applicable Law	9.37
3. A Legislative Return of the Law of the Forum?	9.39
4. Time Provisions Other Than Limitations	9.43
5. The US Position	9.45

A. THE COMMON LAW POSITION

1. THE RIGHT-REMEDY APPROACH

It was noted in Chapter 2 that the traditional common law approach to the classification of substance and procedure was based on the right / remedy distinction. According to this distinction, where a law merely prevents enforcement of a remedy it was considered procedural but where the law extinguished the right it was classified as substantive. The right / remedy distinction had its most direct application in the area of statutes of limitation. Certain statutory provisions (especially from European civil law countries) were considered to be 'prescriptive' and to extinguish the claimant's cause of action ('the right') if not complied with, while others were thought only to bar a claimant's right to relief in respect of the right ('the remedy'). Most Commonwealth statutes were regarded as barring the remedy only, as they were usually expressed in terms such as 'an action

9.01

shall not be brought except within the time stated after the action arose'.[1] Application of forum law may also have been justified by a more general concern that access to forum courts was an exclusively local matter.[2] There were, however, statutory exceptions, such as where a provision provided that a right of ownership by virtue of adverse possession extinguished the claimant's right.[3] Such a provision, classified as substantive, was accordingly applied by the forum when it was part of the law of the cause of action. Another exception was where a limitation provision was included in a statute which created a new cause of action such as a right to workers' compensation. In a number of decisions courts held that such a limitation provision, because it was annexed to a new statutory right, was substantive.[4]

9.02 The consequence of the right-remedy view and the fact that most Commonwealth limitation provisions were considered procedural meant that claimants could bring actions in the forum under a local, unexpired limitation statute even where the action was barred under the limitation law of the cause of action.[5] Clearly this position encouraged forum shopping as claimants would seek out common law jurisdictions with the most attractive limitation periods, regardless of the position under the law of the cause of action. A defendant could only circumvent this result by persuading the forum court that the limitation statute of the law of the cause of action was substantive. In such a case the matter could not then proceed in the forum because the claimant's right, not merely their remedy, was extinguished.[6]

9.03 Two other situations which could arise under the traditional common law view could lead to absurd results. The first situation was where the forum limitation statute was classified as substantive and the provision in the law of the cause of action procedural. Such a case raises the problem of 'gap' in choice of law, discussed in Chapter 3,[7] where application of the rules on classification yields no applicable law, with the result that no limitation period applies. Such a result was reached by a German court in

---

[1] *Pederson v Young* (1964) 110 CLR 162, 166–7 (Menzies J).

[2] L McDougal, R Felix, and R Whitten, *American Conflicts Law* (Transnational Publishers, 5th edn, 2001) 427.

[3] *Beckford v Wade* (1805) 17 Ves J 87; *Re Peat's Trusts* (1869) LR 7 Eq 302; *Inglis v Commonwealth Trading Bank of Australia* (1972) 20 FLR 30, 43 (ACTSC).

[4] *Australian Iron and Steel v Hoogland* (1962) 108 CLR 471, 488 (Windeyer J); *Byrnes v Groote Eylandt Mining Co Pty Ltd* (1990) 19 NSWLR 13 (NSWCA).

[5] *Huber v Steiner* (1835) 2 Bing NC 202; *Harris v Quine* (1869) LR 4 QB 653; *McKain v RW Miller & Co (South Australia) Pty Ltd* (1991) 174 CLR 1.

[6] *Harris v Quine* (1869) LR 4 QB 653, 658; *Subbotovsky v Waung* (1968) 72 SR (NSW) 242, 251 (NSWCA).

[7] See 3.02 above.

A. The Common Law Position

an 1882 decision.[8] The problem of 'gap' has, however, frequently arisen in recent decisions in South Africa.[9] The second situation is where the forum limitation period was classified as procedural but the provision in the law of the cause of action substantive, with the result that both periods could apply. Such a case raises the issue of 'cumulation' in choice of law, also discussed in Chapter 3.[10]

The common law approach was not, however, adopted in most European civil law countries, where all forms of limitation—whether barring the right or the remedy—have long been considered substantive and governed by the law of the cause of action, subject to a public policy exception where the foreign period was too brief or too long.[11] The European position has also been adopted in a number of major international conventions.[12]

9.04

2. The Substantive Trend

The traditional common law position on limitation statutes is, however, fast disappearing in the Commonwealth. In a series of decisions by the Supreme Court of Canada in *Tolofson v Jensen*[13] and the High Court of

9.05

---

[8] Reichsgericht 4 January 1882 RGZ 7, cited in O Kahn-Freund, *General Problems of Private International Law* (Sijthoff, 1976) 226.

[9] See 9.08–9.10 below.

[10] See 3.02 above.

[11] For Quebec see the Civil Code, art 3131: 'prescription is governed by the law applicable to the merits of the dispute'. For France see B Audit, *Droit International Privé* (Economica, 3rd edn, 2005) para 445; *Société Nationale de Recouvrement v Y* [2003] ECLY 724 (Court of Cassation, First Civil Chamber, 3 June 2003); F Hage-Chahine, 'La Prescription Extinctive en Droit International Privé' (1995) 255 *Hague Recueil* 229; and B Fauvarque-Casson, 'La Prescription en Droit International Privé' in *Droit International Privé Travaux du Comité Français de Droit International Privé Année 2002–2004* (Editions Perdone, 2005) 235. For Germany see R Geimer, *Internationales Zivilprozeßrecht* (OUS Verlag Dr Otto Schmidt, 5th edn, 2005) para 351. For Belgium see F Rigaux and M Fallon, *Droit International Privé* (Larcier, 3rd edn, 2005) para 11.13. For Switzerland see Statute of Private International Law, art 148(1). For the Netherlands see HR 24 January 1986 NJ 1987 56 (Dutch Supreme Court), cited in R Plender and M Wilderspin, *The European Private International Law of Obligations* (Sweet & Maxwell, 3rd edn, 2009) para 14-051, n 105. cf Italy, however, where *Italian* statutes of limitation appear to be classified as procedural and applicable where the law of the cause of action is foreign (Cass 1 August 2000, n 10026 Foro it Rep (2000) Diritto Internazionale Privato, n 59) unless there is pleaded a *foreign* limitation law which would be classified under its own choice of law rules as substantive, in which case, that law will be applied (App Firenze, 5 October 1989, Foro it Rep (1991) Trasporto marittimo, n 88). See also V Sinisi and A Sculli, 'Italian Conflict-of-Law Rules' (2007) 29 The Comparative Law Yearbook of International Business 207, 211.

[12] See eg Hague Convention of 4 May 1971 on the Law Applicable to Traffic Accidents, art 8(8) and the Hague Convention of 2 October 1973 on the Law Applicable to Products Liability, art 8(9) (1972) 1 ILM 1283.

[13] (1994) 120 DLR (4th) 289.

Australia in *John Pfeiffer Pty Ltd v Rogerson*[14] the courts stated that, henceforth, all statutes of limitation will now be classified as substantive. The reasoning was that since all statutes of limitation, whether barring the remedy or the right, have a direct impact on the rights and liabilities of the parties to the litigation[15] (in that they determine whether an action may proceed), application of the law of the cause of action is appropriate. Uniformity of result and the discouragement of forum shopping are both enhanced by such an approach. Moreover, statutes of limitation have little connection to the mode or conduct of court proceedings and foreign limitation provisions are not especially difficult or inconvenient to find or apply. While such statutes may also reflect important forum policies in preventing stale claims and encouraging expeditious litigation, such concerns can be accommodated, in exceptional cases, through the public policy defence.[16]

9.06 In Canada, lower courts in decisions since the *Tolofson* case have dutifully and uniformly treated limitation periods as substantive.[17] Similarly, in Australia, while the conclusion in *Pfeiffer* on the status of limitation provisions was strictly only obiter, the decisions of lower courts have unanimously confirmed that foreign limitation laws are substantive.[18] In the Australian context, the position taken in *Pfeiffer* was also partially pre-empted by legislation enacted in the early 1990s which requires an Australian court to apply the limitation law of the law of the cause of action where such law is that of another Australian State or Territory or New Zealand.[19] Public policy is not likely to be available to exclude a limitation period of the law of the cause of action under such legislation, at

---

[14] (2000) 203 CLR 503.

[15] ibid paras 99–100; see also *Dyno Wesfarmers Ltd v Knuckey* [2003] NSWCA 375, paras 45–46 (Handley JA) and E Lorenzen, 'The Statute of Limitations and the Conflict of Laws' (1919) 28 Yale LJ 492, 496: 'a right which can be enforced no longer by an action at law is shorn of its most valuable attribute'.

[16] P Stone, 'Time Limitation in the English Conflict of Laws' [1985] LMCLQ 497, 501; see 9.20–9.23 below.

[17] See eg *Stewart v Stewart* (1997) 30 BCLR (3d) 233 (BCCA); *Michalski v Olson* (1997) 123 Man R (2d) 101, para 23; *Caspian Construction Inc v Drake Surveys Ltd* (2004) 184 Man R (2d) 284, para 19; *Brill v Korpaach Estate* (1997) 200 AR 161, paras 7, 23 (CA); *Pawlus v Banque Nationale de Paris (Canada)* (2001) 277 AR 80, para 44 (CA); *Ferguson v Arctic Transportation Ltd* (1998) 147 FTR 96, para 52; *Wong v Lee* (2002) 58 OR (3d) 398, para 20 (CA); *Bank of America v Maas* 2010 ONSC 4546 (affd 2010 ONCA 833).

[18] *O'Driscoll v J Ray McDermott SA* [2006] WASCA 25; *Darcy v Medtel Ltd (No 3)* [2004] FCA 807, para 18; *HWC v The Corp of the Synod of the Diocese of Brisbane* [2008] QSC 212, para 37.

[19] See eg Choice of Law (Limitation Periods) Act 1993 (NSW); Choice of Law (Limitation Periods) Act 1993 (Vic).

A. The Common Law Position

least where such law is that of an Australian sister-state.[20] The principle in *Pfeiffer* remains relevant, however, where the law of the cause of action is not from Australia or New Zealand.[21]

In the case of other Commonwealth countries, New Zealand has recently enacted legislation which requires its courts to apply the limitation period of the law of the cause of action,[22] subject to the defence of public policy, although this exception is not available in the case of an Australian limitation period.[23] However, the traditional right-remedy approach to statutes of limitation appears still to apply in Hong Kong,[24] Singapore,[25] and India, although in 2005 the Indian Law Commission recommended the adoption of a general substantive classification.[26]

9.07

3. THE SOUTH AFRICAN *Via Media*

The position in South Africa is worthy of special consideration both given the significant number of recent decisions in which the issue of choice of law and limitation has arisen and the distinctive approach which has been applied. The starting point is South Africa's own limitation legislation, the Prescription Act 1969, which has been universally interpreted, under the traditional common law view of characterization, as substantive because it extinguishes the cause of action.[27] The problem for South African courts, however, is that the traditional common law classification of limitations is still followed with the result that *foreign* limitation provisions of the law of the cause of action must still be examined to determine whether they bar the right (substantive) or only the remedy (procedural). Where a foreign limitation law is found to bar the right, according to the classification rules

9.08

---

[20] *John Pfeiffer Pty Ltd v Rogerson* (2000) 203 CLR 503, paras 63, 91; *Merwin Pastoral Co Pty Ltd v Moolpa Pastoral Co Pty Ltd* (1933) 48 CLR 565.
[21] *Fleming v Marshall* [2011] NSWCA 86, para 46.
[22] Limitation Act 2010, s 55(2).
[23] ibid s 56(3).
[24] *Peregrine Fixed Income Ltd v JP Morgan Chase Bank* [2005] HKCFI 71, para 32 and *Botanic Ltd v China National United Oil Corp* [2008] HKCFI 721, para 91.
[25] *O'Driscoll v J Ray Mcdermott SA* [2006] WASCA 25 (Western Australian Court of Appeal referring to the expert evidence of TM Yeo on Singapore law, paras 10, 31).
[26] See Law Commission of India, *193rd Report on Transnational Litigation—Conflict of Laws—Law of Limitation* (2005) at <http://lawcommissionofindia.nic.in/reports/Report193.pdf> (accessed October 2011) which proposes a new s 11(2) to the Limitation Act 36 of 1963.
[27] See eg *Kuhne & Nagel AG Zurich v APA Distributors (Pty) Ltd* 1981 3 SA 536 (High Court of Witwatersrand); *Laconian Enterprises Ltd v Agromar Lineas Ltd* 1986 3 SA 509 (Durban High Court); *Laurens v von Hohne* 1993 2 SA 104 (High Court of Witwatersrand).

of the law of the cause of action,[28] then no conflict arises: the court must apply the foreign limitation. Where the foreign law, however, is found only to bar the remedy, then the South African courts are confronted directly with the problem of 'gap'. Their response has been to devise a method known as the *'via media'* to resolve this situation which, according to the South African Supreme Court of Appeal, involves application of the limitation law with 'the closest and most real connection with the legal dispute'.[29] Such law has, however, in most cases been found to be the law of the cause of action, with the result that the claimant's rights are unenforceable in the forum.[30]

9.09 A number of comments may be made about the South African position. The first observation to note is that much of the legal development in this area has been arguably based on a false assumption. Three of the principal South African (and one Zimbabwean) decisions since 1981[31] have involved English law as the law of the cause of action and the assumption has been that England still classifies limitation periods as procedural, despite the enactment of the Foreign Limitation Periods Act 1984 (FLPA 1984) which, as discussed at 9.12, was intended to alter the common law in requiring English courts to apply the limitation of the foreign law of the cause of action. This point, combined with the fact that the Rome Convention (in force in England since 1991 and applicable to contracts entered into before 17 December 2009) considers limitation periods to be part of the law of the obligation, means that it is questionable whether an English court would have classified an English limitation period as procedural but a foreign period as substantive, as has been inferred by the South African courts.[32] It is arguable that a substantive classification would be applied by English courts to both limitation laws, with the result that no 'gap' would exist in the South African proceeding and English limitation law would be applied as part of the law of the cause of action.

---

[28] South African courts have generally classified the limitation period of the foreign law of the cause of action according to that country's rules of classification: see eg *Laurens v von Hohne* 1993 2 SA 104. The same analysis would apply, however, even if the forum's rules of classification were employed.

[29] *Society of Lloyds v Price* 2006 5 SA 393, para 26; *Monokandilos v Générale des Carriers et des Mines SA* [2010] ZAGPPHC 184, para 15 (Pretoria High Court). The *'via media'* approach is derived from the writings of the Canadian scholar Falconbridge, see J Neels, 'Falconbridge in South Africa' (2008) 4 JPIL 167, 170.

[30] *Society of Lloyds v Price* 2006 5 SA 393, paras 28, 32.

[31] *Laconian Enterprises Ltd v Agromar Lineas Ltd* 1986 3 SA 509; *Society of Lloyds v Romahn* 2006 4 SA 23 (Cape High Court); *Society of Lloyds v Price* 2006 5 SA 393; and *Coutts & Co v Ford* 1997 1 ZLR 440 (Harare High Court).

[32] See especially *Society of Lloyds v Price* 2006 5 SA 393, para 19.

A. The Common Law Position

A second criticism of the South African law is that arguably it reaches the correct result—that the law of the cause of action applies to limitation—but by an unnecessarily convoluted and complex means. Instead of undertaking the onerous and probably inexact task of classifying foreign limitation laws according to the foreign law's own rules and then weighing this law against the law of the forum to determine which law has the closest connection to the limitation issue, the courts could adopt a simpler and more direct method. This approach would be to adopt a general substantive classification for all limitation statutes, whether barring the right or the remedy, as the Australian and Canadian courts have done.[33] Indeed, two judges[34] went very close to adopting this approach despite framing their analysis in terms of the *via media*. A response to this contention may be to say that the *via media* approach does not necessarily *compel* the court to apply the law of the cause of action to limitation in every case; it is instead a flexible mechanism which admits the possibility of other laws being applied. While this view may be acknowledged, the reality is that in almost every South African decision since 1981 the law of the cause of action has been applied where a conflict of limitation law was found to exist.[35] Consequently, it is suggested that South Africa should now be added to the countries where the substantive classification of limitations has been adopted, despite the veneer of the *'via media'*.

9.10

4. LIMITATIONS AND OVERRIDING MANDATORY RULES

The further question of whether limitation provisions may be considered overriding mandatory rules of the forum which must be applied, regardless of the applicable law, has arisen in some European civil law countries, with the prevailing view appearing to be that such provisions are not mandatory

9.11

---

[33] This view has been advocated by some South African commentators; see Neels (n 29 above) 192, 196–7 and S Eiselen, 'Laconian Revisited—A Reappraisal of Classification in Conflicts Law' (2006) 123 South African LJ 147, 158–9 but cf C Forsyth, 'Mind the Gap Part II: the South African Court of Appeal and Characterisation' (2006) 2 JPIL 425, 429, n 14, who acknowledges the trend in favour of the law of the cause of action in limitation cases but still sees a role for the *via media* approach in other conflicts disputes.

[34] *Society of Lloyds v Romahn* 2006 4 SA 23, para 86 (Van Zyl J) and *Coutts & Co v Ford* 1997 1 ZLR 440, 446 (Chidyausiku J).

[35] *Kuhne & Nagel AG Zurich v APA Distributors (Pty) Ltd* 1981 3 SA 536; *Laurens v von Hohne* 1993 2 SA 104; *Society of Lloyds v Price* 2006 5 SA 393; *Society of Lloyds v Romahn* 2006 4 SA 23; *Coutts & Co v Ford* 1997 1 ZLR 440; *Monokandilos v Générale des Carriers et des Mines SA* [2010] ZAGPPHC 184. cf *Laconian Enterprises Ltd v Agromar Lineas Ltd* 1986 3 SA 509 where the law of the forum was applied although in that case the action was proscribed under neither the law of the forum nor the law of the cause of action, a point noted by the Supreme Court of Appeal in *Society of Lloyds v Price* 2006 5 SA 393, para 24.

either because they are capable of being waived by the parties[36] or because they lack a clear intent to apply irrespective of the law of the cause of action.[37] This observation will have relevance in the case of the Rome Convention and the Rome I and Rome II Regulations (discussed more fully at 9.24–9.26) where a court may apply overriding forum mandatory rules as an exception to the law of the obligation.[38] In common law countries, the argument that limitation provisions are overriding mandatory rules has not, at least until very recently in Canada,[39] been raised but the view expressed in respect of the European civil law countries would arguably apply equally. One interesting Australian case[40] did not involve a conflict between a common law choice of law rule and an overriding mandatory rule but instead a possible conflict between two forum statutes, one requiring application of the law of the (foreign) cause of action to limitation questions (pursuant to which the claim was barred) and the other decreeing that, because the proceedings in the forum were brought before a specialist tribunal, no limitation period applied.[41] The court held that the statute selecting the limitation period of the law of the cause of action must be applied to bar the action, which perhaps again suggests a reluctance to classify forum laws as overriding mandatory rules in this area.

B. THE UK STATUTORY REGIME

1. THE FOREIGN LIMITATION PERIODS ACT

9.12 Far reaching legislation was enacted in England in the FLPA 1984[42] which has now been supplemented by the Rome Convention[43] and the Rome I[44] and Rome II[45] Regulations which, on the issue of limitation, are in broadly

---

[36] Hof's-Hertogenbosch [2008] *LJN* BD3905 (Dutch Court of Appeal) examining the Dutch Civil Code, art 3:322(2), cited in Plender and Wilderspin (n 11 above) para 14-051, n 105.

[37] M Bonell, 'Limitation Periods' in A Hartkamp et al (eds), *Towards a European Civil Code* (Kluwer Law International, 3rd edn, 2004) 517; see also *Trans Grupo Vialle Iberica (Société) v X* [2011] ECLY 29 (French Court of Cassation, 12 July 2010).

[38] See Rome Convention, art 7(2); Rome I, art 9; and Rome II, art 16.

[39] See 9.40–9.41 below.

[40] *Brear v James Hardie & Co Pty Ltd* (2000) 50 NSWLR 388 (NSWCA).

[41] Dust Diseases Tribunal Act 1989 (NSW), s 12A.

[42] The legislation was passed on the recommendations of the Law Commission; see England and Wales Law Commission, *Classification of Limitation in Private International Law* [1982] EWLC 114. See, for Scotland, the Prescription and Limitation (Scotland) Act 1984.

[43] Convention on the Law Applicable to Contractual Obligations 1980.

[44] Regulation (EC) 593/2008 of 17 June 2008 on the law applicable to contractual obligations.

[45] Regulation (EC) 864/2007 of 11 July 2007 on the law applicable to non-contractual obligations.

B. The UK Statutory Regime

similar terms. In the case of contracts entered into before 17 December 2009, the Convention applies and for contracts after that date, the Rome I Regulation. According to the majority of commentators and courts, the Rome II Regulation applies to a tort where the events giving rise to the damage occurred on or after 20 August 2007 and where legal proceedings in respect of such events are commenced on or after 11 January 2009.[46] The issue of the temporal operation of Rome II is, however, currently pending before the European Court of Justice.

Under the FLPA 1984 the general rule is that the limitation provision of the law of the cause of action will be applied in an English court.[47] An English limitation period will therefore only be applied where English law is the law of the cause of action. The consequence of this position is that a claimant cannot proceed in England if the action is barred under the foreign law of the cause of action but can bring proceedings in England even if barred under English law, provided that the limitation period of the law of the cause of action has not expired. This second situation has been described as 'more controversial'[48] because it could lead to English courts being saddled with stale or perpetual claims and the establishment of truth being compromised, particularly in cases where oral evidence is significant. It was concluded, however, that the defence of public policy would be available to respond to such circumstances where injustice would result. Where a foreign tort of defamation is involved or any other foreign tort committed before 1 May 1996,[49] the 'double actionability' test exists as the choice of law rule, which requires that for a suit to proceed in England, the tort must be actionable under both the law of the forum and the law of the place of the wrong. The FLPA 1984 provides that in such a case, the limitation rules of both England and the foreign country must be applied, with the expiry of either period being enough to defeat the action.[50]

9.13

Note also that under section 3 of the FLPA 1984, where a court in a foreign country has determined any matter by reference to the law of that or any other country (including England and Wales) relating to limitation, the

9.14

---

[46] For more detailed reference to the decisions and commentary on this issue, see 11.01 below.

[47] FLPA, s 1.

[48] J Fawcett and J Carruthers, *Cheshire, North and Fawcett Private International Law* (OUP, 14th edn, 2008) 81.

[49] The Private International Law (Miscellaneous Provisions) Act 1995 (PILA 1995) applies to torts committed after that date but before the date when the Rome II Regulation came into force. Defamation, however, remains excluded from both instruments and the common law choice of law rules continue to apply; see PILA 1995, s 13.

[50] FLPA 1984, s 1(2); *Yugraneft v Abramovich* [2008] EWHC 2613 (Comm), para 342; *Bank of Credit and Commerce International SA v Ali* [2006] EWHC 2135 (Ch), para 30.

foreign court shall be deemed to have determined the matter on its merits. This provision reverses the effect of *Harris v Quine*,[51] whereby it was possible to bring subsequent proceedings in England on a cause of action which had been dismissed by the foreign court due to the expiry of a statute of limitation, since such statute was only procedural in the English forum. The effect of section 3 is to bar such subsequent proceedings. The same result would also be reached in those Commonwealth countries (such as Australia and Canada) which classify limitation periods as substantive.

9.15 The FLPA 1984 also importantly provides that an English court will apply the foreign provision even if it would be classified as procedural under the choice of law rules of the law of the cause of action.[52] In Canada the same result has been reached under common law principles, with one court noting that it was 'irrelevant' that a limitation statute of the law of the cause of action would be characterized as procedural under the choice of law rules of such law.[53] Under the *Neilson* 'no advantage' principle in Australian law, by contrast, regard may be had to the classification rules of the foreign law of the cause of action in order for the Australian court to apply the same law as would be applied by a court in that country. The impact of the *Neilson* test on statutes of limitation is explored more fully at 9.28–9.29.

9.16 Further, the law of the cause of action also applies to determine the event which causes the limitation period to commence, for example the breach of obligation or the suffering of injury,[54] and also the event or circumstance which causes the limitation period to be extended or suspended.[55] Moreover, if a discretion exists under the foreign law of the cause of action to suspend or extend the limitation period, then an English court must attempt to exercise that discretion in the manner in which it would be exercised in a comparable case by the courts of that country.[56] An almost identical approach applies under the Australian[57] and New Zealand[58] legislation referred to above where, in addition, the right to extend time has been held to be substantive under common law principles because of its

---

[51] (1869) LR 4 QB 653.
[52] FLPA 1984, s 4(2); Law Commission Report (n 42 above) para 4.4.
[53] *Bank of America v Maas* 2010 ONSC 4546, para 9 (affd 2010 ONCA 833).
[54] FLPA 1984, s 4(1)(a).
[55] ibid.
[56] ibid s 1(4).
[57] See eg Choice of Law (Limitation Periods) Act 1993 (NSW), s 6; *Mason v Murray's Charter Coaches and Travel Services Pty Ltd* (1998) 88 FCR 308, 320 (Drummond J), and 330 (Sackville J); *Pulido v RS Distributions Pty Ltd* [2003] ACTSC 61, para 59; *Berriman v Cricket Australia* (2007) 17 VR 528, para 25; and *Carslake v Gadens Lawyers* [2006] SASC 9, para 12.
[58] Limitation Act 2010 (NZ), s 55(3).

direct impact on the enforceability of the rights and duties of the parties to the litigation.[59] The same position applies in Canada.[60]

Note, however, that even under the FLPA 1984 there is still some residual operation left to the law of the forum. First, the time of and manner in which proceedings have been commenced for the purpose of stopping the running of the limitation period is resolved by English law as the law of the forum.[61] Consequently, it will be the issue of the writ in the action rather than its service upon the defendant which will be the relevant act. This approach has been justified[62] on the ground that considerable delays can be involved where service is required on a defendant located abroad, for example under the procedures of the Hague Service Convention, and it would be unjust to subject the claimant to the rules of the law of the cause of action on this question.[63] The same position was adopted by the Nova Scotia Court of Appeal in *Vogler v Szendroi*.[64] That case involved a claimant who was injured in the US state of Wyoming, the law of which was the law of the cause of action. The claimant commenced proceedings in Nova Scotia three years after the accident but did not serve the defendant for another three years, that is, six years after the accident. Under the Wyoming rules, an action is commenced by filing a complaint with the court but if the pleading has not been served within sixty days of filing, the action is not considered to have been commenced until the date of service. The court held the Wyoming provision—in requiring filing and service to initiate an action—to be procedural on the basis that it 'simply direct[ed] the manner in which an action is commenced'.[65] The Wyoming law was thus concerned with process[66] or the mode or conduct of court proceedings rather than with substantive rights. The court also found that the characterization of the law of the cause of action was irrelevant to the question.[67]

9.17

---

[59] *Berriman v Cricket Australia* (2007) 17 VR 528, para 26; *Wall v Toll Transport Pty Ltd* [2010] VSC 522, para 27.

[60] *Stewart v Stewart* (1997) 30 BCLR (3d) 233 (BCCA).

[61] FLPA 1984, s 1(3); *Barros Mattos v MacDaniels Ltd* [2005] EWHC 1323 (Ch), para 131.

[62] J Walker, 'Twenty Questions (about Section 23 of the Limitations Act, 2002)' in W Gray, L Kerbel-Caplan, and J Ziegel (eds), *The New Ontario Limitations Regime: Exposition and Analysis* (Ontario Bar Association, 2005) 95, 110.

[63] Law Commission Report (n 42 above) para 4.19; for an analysis of the choice of law position in relation to service of process, see Ch 4.

[64] (2008) 290 DLR (4th) 642.

[65] ibid para 29.

[66] ibid para 36.

[67] ibid para 30.

9.18 A second recognition of the law of the forum under the FLPA 1984 is the provision which allows an English court to ignore any foreign rules which require the interruption of the running of the limitation period because of the absence of a party from a given country.[68] Such a provision is important to encourage claimants to bring proceedings expeditiously and so prevent defendants from being subjected to almost indefinite liability.[69]

9.19 Next, where equitable relief (such as an injunction) is sought in an English proceeding, the FLPA 1984 allows the defendant still to rely on discretionary defences under English law, such as laches, to defeat the action even where the law of the cause of action is foreign.[70] Where, however, the claim is time barred under the foreign law, it must be dismissed, regardless of the circumstances. Where the claim is not time barred or no period of limitation exists under the foreign law, the English court must take the foreign rules into account in exercising its discretion. It is not entirely clear what this last provision means but, arguably, this equitable defences exception is otiose in the light of the public policy defence.[71]

2. Public Policy

9.20 The public policy defence to the application of foreign limitation periods is the most significant recognition of forum law under the FLPA 1984. While the FLPA 1984 is silent on the issue, it is clear that where the public policy defence applies, the 1984 Act is excluded and the limitation period of the forum applies. Courts have taken the view that the effect of the public policy defence is to remove the foreign limitation law and insert the relevant English limitation period which applies as part of the procedural law of the forum.[72] While such view is no doubt practical and avoids the problem of there being no limitation period at all, it does sit awkwardly with the more contemporary view that limitation periods are substantive because of their impact on the parties' rights. Consequently, an alternative view may be to say that public policy has the effect of not only disapplying the foreign limitation period but also attracting local limitation law to fill the gap. This approach is consistent with the analysis adopted elsewhere in this work to the effect that public policy is an additional (and often preferable) pathway to forum law in conjunction with the procedural

---

[68] FLPA 1984, s 2(3).
[69] Law Commission Report (n 42 above) para 4.27.
[70] FLPA 1984, s 4(3).
[71] Stone (n 16 above) 511.
[72] *The Komninos S* [1991] 1 Lloyd's Rep 370, 377 (Bingham LJ); *Arab Monetary Fund v Hashim* [1996] 1 Lloyd's Rep 589, 600 (Saville LJ); B Doherty, C Thomann, and K Scott, *Accidents Abroad International Personal Injury Claims* (Thomson Reuters, 2009) para 11.030.

B. The UK Statutory Regime

characterization. Note that the same argument could also be made in the case of the public policy defence to foreign limitations under the Rome Convention and the Rome I and Rome II Regulations. The practice of applying forum limitation law pursuant to public policy also avoids absurdity and confusion in the case of Commonwealth countries, such as Canada and Australia, where limitation periods are classified as substantive. If, for example, in those countries, a foreign limitation period were to be disapplied on public policy grounds, forum limitation law could never be applied in default because it would also be treated as substantive and so not applicable where foreign law was the law of the cause of action. The consequence, therefore, is that no limitation period would apply at all. The only way for forum limitation law to be applied in such circumstances is if public policy itself has the effect of 'selecting' such law.[73]

Turning to the content of the public policy defence under the FLPA 1984, it is first important to note that the doctrine cannot be used to exclude an *English* limitation period in favour of a foreign one when English law is the law of the cause of action.[74] The doctrine only operates to exclude foreign limitation periods and is provided in the legislation in two, interrelated parts. Section 2 provides that '(1) In any case in which the application of [a foreign limitation provision] would to any extent conflict (whether under sub-section (2) below or otherwise) with public policy, that [provision] shall not apply . . . (2) The application of [the foreign provision] shall conflict with public policy to the extent that its application would cause undue hardship to a . . . party to the action'. The first aspect of public policy, in section 2(1), is the general exclusionary doctrine in private international law which provides that foreign law will not be enforced in an English court where it violates a fundamental principle of justice.[75] A limitation provision which was based on racial or other discrimination would be an example.[76] In keeping with the narrow scope of this doctrine in

9.21

---

[73] The editors of *Dicey, Morris and Collins* are slightly ambiguous on this point. They note that the effect of public policy on disapplying a foreign limitation is that 'the issue is then governed by the common law principles under which the limitation principles prescribed by English law as the *lex fori* will be applied'; L Collins (ed), *Dicey, Morris and Collins on the Conflict of Laws* (Sweet & Maxwell, 14th edn, 2006) para 7.050. This statement could indicate support for the view expressed in *The Komninos* above (ie that English limitation applies by default because it is procedural) or the alternative view proposed here that public policy attracts forum law by itself.

[74] *Chagos Islanders v The Attorney-General* [2003] EWHC 2222 (QB), para 608 (affd on different grounds [2004] EWCA Civ 997).

[75] Law Commission Report (n 42 above) paras 4.43–4.44; *Loucks v Standard Oil Co of New York* 224 NY 99, 111 (1918) (Cardozo J); *Kuwait Airways Corp v Iraqi Airways Co (Nos 4 and 5)* [2002] 2 AC 883, para 18 (Lord Nicholls).

[76] ibid para 4.45; cf *Oppenheimer v Cattermole* [1976] AC 249 (HL).

English private international law, the defence was intended to be an exceptional one, only available in 'the most unusual circumstances'.[77] Such circumstances would be present where a foreign limitation period was relied upon by a thief or other recipient of stolen property who was not a purchaser in good faith.[78] The position, however, may be otherwise if the victim of the theft had delayed in seeking recovery after it had discovered the facts relevant to its cause of action. A foreign period may also be disapplied on general public policy grounds where the defendant's deliberate concealment of key facts resulted in the action being time barred.[79]

9.22 The second, more specific, aspect of the public policy defence in section 2(2) of the FLPA 1984 is where application of the foreign limitation would 'cause undue hardship' to a person who might be a party.[80] Undue hardship may be pleaded by either a claimant arguing that an excessively short period deprives them of a claim or a defendant contending that an unreasonably long period results in a loss of a defence. The 'undue hardship' principle, like the general public policy defence, was, however, intended to have a narrow application and to be available only in exceptional circumstances.[81] The addition of the word 'undue' before hardship means more than just hardship, it 'means excessive, that is greater hardship than the circumstances warrant'.[82] In decisions which have considered the hardship defence the courts have generally maintained this strict line and focused on the effects of applying the foreign rule in a given case, especially by reference to the comparable English limitation provision. The focus is on the party alleging hardship, however, with no 'balancing' of interests between claimant and defendant to be undertaken.[83] The circumstances in which 'undue hardship' may be present have been considered in a number of English cases. In *Durham v T & N Noble plc*[84] the Court of Appeal held that a foreign limitation period is not contrary to public policy simply because it is less generous than the comparative English period.[85] Some reason other than the mere length of the period

---

[77] ibid para 4.39 cited in *City of Gotha v Sotheby's* The Times, 8 October 1998 (QBD).
[78] *City of Gotha v Sotheby's* The Times, 8 October 1998 (QBD).
[79] ibid.
[80] FLPA 1984, s 2(2).
[81] *Arab Monetary Fund v Hashim* [1993] 1 Lloyd's Rep 543, 592 (Comm) (affd on this point [1996] 1 Lloyd's Rep 589 (CA)) and *City of Gotha v Sotheby's* The Times, 8 October 1998 (QBD).
[82] *Arab Monetary Fund v Hashim* [1993] 1 Lloyd's Rep 543, 592 (Comm); see also *Jones v Trollope Colls Cementation Overseas Ltd* The Times, 26 January 1990 (CA).
[83] *Jones v Trollope* ibid; *Harley v Smith* [2010] EWCA Civ 78, para 55.
[84] CA, 1 May 1996.
[85] See also *Harley v Smith* [2010] EWCA Civ 78, para 55.

B. The UK Statutory Regime

must be identified.[86] However, the court in the *Durham* case did note that, in the case of personal injury, if the foreign limitation period ran from the date of sustaining personal injury irrespective of whether the claimant knew or even could have known of his or her injury at that time, it would be 'strongly arguable' that such a rule would cause a claimant undue hardship. On the facts, that test was not satisfied because the foreign law allowed the claimant one year from the date of knowledge in which to bring an action, which was considered reasonable. Similarly, in *Yugraneft v Abramovich*[87] the court saw nothing unjust, by itself, in a foreign time limit of three years from knowledge of the violation of a person's right. In *Arab Monetary Fund v Hashim*[88] a claimant was also unable to invoke the defence where the foreign limitation period was three years and the claimant had all the material it needed to bring the proceedings and was fully aware of the foreign limitation law before the expiry of the period. Further, it has been held that the absence, in the foreign law, of an escape provision similar to section 33 of the Limitation Act 1980 (UK) (under which a limitation period may, in the court's discretion, not be applied in actions for personal injury or death) is not sufficient to amount to undue hardship.[89] Hardship has, however, been established where the foreign limitation period was only twelve months and the claimant had been led to believe, while recuperating in hospital for the bulk of the limitation period, that her claim would be honoured.[90] In another case of reliance, hardship was proven when the parties had agreed to an extension of time which ultimately was not effective under the foreign law of the cause of action.[91] By contrast, in another decision involving a twelve-month foreign period,[92] a claimant was unable to invoke the defence where the party could *not* show that it had been misled by legal advice into delaying commencement of its claim until after the period had expired.[93] While, on the facts, there was some doubt as to whether the claimant's advisers were aware of the period, there was no evidence that such lack of awareness caused prejudice to the claimant. Additionally, the court said, the mere fact that there was 'uncertainty' about the limitation period was insufficient to amount to hardship; rather the existence of such uncertainty should 'have made it necessary to

---

[86] Law Commission Report (n 42 above) para 4.46.
[87] [2008] EWHC 2613 (Comm), para 323.
[88] [1996] 1 Lloyd's Rep 589 (CA).
[89] *Connolly v RTZ Corp plc (No 3)* [1999] CLC 533.
[90] *Jones v Trollope Colls Cementation Overseas Ltd* The Times, 26 January 1990; see also Law Commission Report (n 42 above) para 4.46.
[91] *The Komninos S* [1990] 1 Lloyd's Rep 541 (reversed at [1991] 1 Lloyd's Rep 370 but the Court of Appeal agreed with the judge's conclusion on this issue).
[92] *Harley v Smith* [2010] EWCA Civ 78.
[93] ibid para 53.

bring proceedings sooner rather than later to avoid the risk ... of being out of time'.[94] Finally, as already noted, the hardship exception may also apply where the foreign law of the cause of action has no limitation period at all or where the period is substantially *longer* than the one under English law. But if, in such a case, the defendant has 'been aware of the matters put against him, has done little or nothing to contest liability and has sought to evade the effects of a judgment' then the defence is unlikely to apply.[95] Factors of reliance by the party seeking to avoid the limitation or waiver by the party seeking to enforce it seem, therefore, to be a common element in successful hardship pleas.

9.23 By contrast, the defence of public policy has rarely been invoked in Commonwealth cases to exclude an otherwise applicable foreign limitation period. In *Tolofson v Jensen*[96] La Forest J suggested that for an individual defendant to be protected from stale claims under foreign law would involve 'policy considerations unrelated to the manner in which a court must carry out its functions and the particular balance may vary from place to place. To permit the forum to impose its views over those of the legislature endowed with power to determine the consequences of wrongs that take place within its jurisdiction would invite ... forum shopping...'. Although the judge does not refer to the other situation in which public policy has been commonly invoked—where the claim is time barred under the law of the cause of action but not the forum—the message is clear that primacy must be given to the limitation law of the cause of action with public policy to be applied only in exceptional cases.[97]

3. The EU Instruments

9.24 It is important to note first that under section 8 of the FLPA 1984, sections 1, 2, and 4 of that Act will have no application where the rules of the Rome I or Rome II Regulation apply. The FLPA also does not apply to proceedings under the Rome Convention. Nevertheless the position under the Convention and the Regulations with respect to limitation is likely to produce similar outcomes to those produced by the FLPA 1984 in most cases. Under the Convention and the Rome I Regulation, the applicable law of the contract will 'govern the various ways of extinguishing obligations and prescription and limitation of actions',[98] while under the Rome II

---

[94] ibid para 54.
[95] *Dubai Bank Ltd v Abbas* Commercial Court, 15 October 1997; Law Commission Report, (n 42 above) para 4.47.
[96] (1994) 120 DLR (4th) 289, 322.
[97] *Michalski v Olson* (1997) 123 Man R (2d) 101.
[98] Rome Convention, art 10(1)(d); Rome I, art 12(1)(d).

B. The UK Statutory Regime

Regulation the applicable law of the obligation will 'govern . . . the manner in which an obligation may be extinguished and rules of prescription and limitation of actions, including rules relating to the commencement, interruption and suspension of a period of limitation'.[99] It is suggested that this reference to 'commencement' in Rome II refers only to the issue discussed at 9.16, under the FLPA 1984, that is, the event which causes the limitation period to commence (such as breach of obligation or incurring of injury) rather than the means of commencing proceedings in a court (the event which *stops* the running of the limitation period). This second matter remains governed by English law as the law of the forum,[100] an analysis which would accord with both the FLPA 1984 and the common law discussed earlier. Two additional points should be noted which may limit the role of the law of the forum in limitation cases under the Convention and the Regulations when compared to the 1984 Act. First, there is no express provision in the EU texts that allows a forum court to ignore any foreign rules which require the interruption of the running of the period because of the absence of a party from a given country. Dickinson suggests that such a foreign rule could possibly be classified as procedural and so outside the scope of the Regulations;[101] alternatively, in an extreme case where a defendant relied upon such a provision to wilfully obstruct the proceedings public policy could presumably be applied to exclude the foreign rule. Secondly, it is likely that the 'equitable defences' exception mentioned at 9.19 would not apply to proceedings under the Regulations, unless English law was the law of the obligation, given that rules relating to the grant of a remedy would fall within the scope of both texts.[102]

It is most likely that the classification of limitation periods under the Convention and the Regulations will, at least before English courts, be conducted in accordance with the rules of the forum, as is the case with the FLPA 1984, although there is no express provision to that effect. Other EU Member States, however, may choose to classify foreign limitations according to the rules of the law of the cause of action. Such an approach will not yield differences in result because under the Convention and the Regulations, in contrast to the FLPA 1984, limitation periods are designated as part of the applicable law of the obligation, that is, they are substantive. Another EU court applying English limitation law under the **9.25**

---

[99] Rome II, art 15(h).
[100] A Dickinson, *The Rome II Regulation* (OUP, 2008) para 14.50.
[101] ibid para 14.49.
[102] See Rome II, art 15(c); Rome I, art 12(1)(c); Dickinson (n 100 above) para 14.49.

278   *Chapter 9: Statutes of Limitation*

Convention or the Regulations can assume, therefore, that an English court would also classify the period as substantive.[103]

9.26 The application of a provision of the law of any country specified by the Convention or the Regulations on limitation may be precluded where to do so would be 'manifestly incompatible with' English public policy.[104] Public policy is not defined in the European instruments but some commentators have felt that the use of the word 'manifestly' in the Convention and the Regulations means that a higher standard for parties to satisfy has been created compared to the FLPA 1984, at least as regards the 'undue hardship' defence.[105] Yet, even if this view is correct, it is suggested that English courts should still look to the decisions under the 1984 Act on 'undue hardship' for assistance in determining whether or not to disapply a foreign limitation under the Convention and the Regulations. English courts have generally been circumspect in their application of the public policy/undue hardship defence under the FLPA 1984 and such caution would seem consistent with the text and spirit of the EU instruments. In addition, hardship is arguably a useful criterion for identifying breaches of public policy in the context of foreign limitations.

4. *Renvoi* AND LIMITATIONS

9.27 The issue of *renvoi* under the FLPA 1984 and the Regulations requires some consideration. Section 1(1) of the Act provides that 'where in any action . . . in a court in England and Wales the law of any other country falls in accordance with the rules of private international law applicable by any such court to be taken into account in determination of any matter—(a) the law of that country relating to limitation shall apply'. Section 1(5) then provides that '"law" in relation to any country shall not include rules of private international law applicable by the courts of that country'. The effect of these provisions is to exclude reference to foreign choice of law rules on the issue of limitation, that is, once an English court has determined the

---

[103] Plender and Wilderspin (n 11 above) paras 14-052, 16-082.
[104] Rome Convention, art 16; Rome II, art 26; Rome I, art 21.
[105] See Doherty (n 72 above) paras 11.028, 11.035; Dickinson (n 100 above) para 14.49. But cf *Dicey, Morris and Collins* (n 73 above) paras 7-052, n 19, 32-209, where it is argued that public policy should receive no stricter interpretation under the Regulations compared to the FLPA 1984. This position may, however, have been qualified in the recent Fourth Cumulative Supplement (2010) para 7.049, where the authors state: 'the public policy exception in s 2 of the [FLPA] . . . does not apply where the Rome I or II Regulation is applicable; and it will be necessary to refer exclusively to the public policy derogations in the Regulations'. See also *Fiona Trust and Holding Corp v Privalov* [2010] EWHC 3199 (Comm) para 133, where it was said that the public policy exception under the EU instruments is 'in different terms from those of the 1984 Act'.

applicable law on the substance of the dispute, as a hypothetical example, Mollovian law, then it must apply the domestic limitation law of Mollovia without regard to whether a Mollovian court would apply its limitation law on the facts of the case. Hence, if Mollovia had a rule that provided that its limitation provision should only apply to proceedings in the *courts of Mollovia*, an English court should ignore the restriction and apply the provision. A slightly different position operates where the English choice of law rule on the substance of the case itself includes *renvoi*, that is, it requires the application of the choice of law rules of Mollovia, such as in the area of succession to property. Where application of Mollovian choice of law rules would lead to Mollovian domestic law, then again Mollovian law and limitation would be applied as in the earlier example. Where, however, application of Mollovian choice of law rules would select *English* domestic law as the law of the cause of action, then the English court must apply its own law both to the cause of action and to the issue of limitation even if the Mollovian court would *not* apply the English limitation law because, for example, that court regarded the English provision as procedural. Similarly, where application of Mollovian choice of law rules would select the domestic law of a third country, Espirita, as the law of the cause of action, then the English court must apply Espiritan law both to the cause of action and to the question of limitation even if the Mollovian court would *not* apply the Espiritan limitation law because, again for example, that court regarded the provision as procedural. Such conclusions flow from the fact that the FLPA 1984 requires the English court to ignore the choice of law rules of the foreign law on the issue of limitation.

The approach of the FLPA 1984 to *renvoi* has been criticized on the ground that it impedes 'the objective of uniformity of decision'[106] and would almost certainly not apply in Australian law under the *Neilson* 'no advantage test'[107] of choice of law. Consistent with *Neilson*, an Australian court, for example the Western Australian Supreme Court, would apply Espiritan law (in the above example) to the cause of action and to the limitation but only if the Mollovian court would *itself* have applied Espiritan limitation law, because, for example, that court would have classified it as substantive (rather than procedural),[108] would not have excluded the law on public policy grounds, and Mollovian law recognized no doctrine of *renvoi*. Similarly, if Mollovian choice of law rules had selected the law of the

9.28

---

[106] Stone (n 16 above) 507; P Carter, 'The Foreign Limitation Periods Act 1984' (1985) 101 LQR 68, 72–4.

[107] *Neilson v Overseas Projects Corp of Victoria Ltd* (2005) 223 CLR 331.

[108] If the Mollovian court classified the Espiritan limitation as procedural, then presumably the Western Australian court would apply Espiritan law to the cause of action but Mollovian limitation law as this would be the result reached by the Mollovian court.

forum (Western Australia) as the law of the cause of action, then the Western Australian court would apply Western Australian law to the cause of action and to the issue of limitation but again only if Mollovia classified the Western Australian limitation provision as substantive.[109] While the *Neilson* approach yields a sensible result in the examples discussed, in other situations it may cause confusion. For example, what would have happened under the example above if Mollovia (like Australia) had also adopted the double *renvoi* principle and referred the matter to Espiritan law which included its choice of law rules and approach to *renvoi*? An inextricable circle would potentially be created with no domestic law of the cause of action or statute of limitation capable of being selected. In *Neilson* itself this problem could have arisen since the action in that case was time barred under the law of the cause of action (China) but not the law of the forum (Australia). The dilemma was, however, avoided by a majority of the Australian High Court rather contentiously finding that a Chinese court would not apply *renvoi* and would only remit the matter back to Western Australian domestic law and its statute of limitation with the result that the action was not barred. In the later decision of *O'Driscoll v J Ray McDermott SA*[110] the problem of the inextricable circle was also avoided where an Australian claimant sued in Western Australia for breach of his employment contract which was entered into in Singapore but involved working on a barge in Indonesian territorial waters. The defence was that the claim was barred by Singapore limitation law. The court first determined that the governing law of the contract was Singaporean and that under Australian choice of law rules, the Singapore limitation was substantive. Applying the *Neilson* 'no advantage' test, the court then considered how a Singapore court would have handled the claim. The court found that, under Singapore choice of law rules, limitations statutes were classified as procedural and applicable in Singapore regardless of the law of the cause of action. Hence the Singapore limitation applied in Australia and there was no conflict between Australian and Singaporean choice of law rules. Similar to the Mollovia-Espirita example at 9.27, however, the matter could have become much more complex if Singapore choice of law rules had selected the law of a third country (for example Indonesia) as the law of the cause of action.

---

[109] Similar to the Espiritan example above, if Mollovian law classified the Western Australian limitation as procedural, then the Western Australian court would apply its own law to the cause of action but Mollovian law to the issue of limitation because, again, this would be the result reached by the Mollovian court.

[110] [2006] WASCA 25.

B. The UK Statutory Regime

The other difficulty with applying the 'no advantage' principle in cases of limitation is that it may be very difficult to replicate precisely what the foreign court would do in a given situation. Assume, on the example discussed earlier, that an Australian court applied Mollovian choice of law rules which selected Espiritan law as the law of the cause of action and the Espiritan limitation period. Assume also that the Espiritan period was very short, for example three months, compared to a Mollovian period of three years and an Australian period of six years and that there is no public policy defence to the application of unjust laws under the law of Mollovia. Would an Australian court be able to rely upon the public policy defence under Australian law to exclude the Espiritan limitation period or would it have to adopt, as far as possible, the approach of Mollovia, in which case the Espiritan limitation law would have to be applied? Such complexities are best avoided by restricting the operation of *renvoi* in limitations cases as much as possible, as has occurred under the FLPA 1984. **9.29**

In the Rome Convention and the Rome I and Rome II Regulations, the exclusion of *renvoi* goes further than under the FLPA 1984, given that those texts deal with more than simply the question of limitation. Under all three instruments[111] it is provided that 'the application of the law of any country specified by this [Convention/Regulation] means the application of the rules of law in force in that country other than its rules of private international law'. The result of this, according to the example discussed, is that if an English court, applying the choice of law rules of the Convention or the Regulations, selected the law of Mollovia to govern the substance of the dispute, there would be no scope for the operation of Mollovian choice of law rules on either the cause of action or the issue of limitation. Mollovian limitation law would be applied by the English court in every case where Mollovia was the law of the obligation subject to the defence of public policy under forum law. **9.30**

5. Filling the Gaps in the UK Statutory Regime

There are also other matters concerning limitations and applicable law not fully covered by the FLPA 1984 or Rome I and II where judicial decisions may be relevant. For example, the New South Wales Court of Appeal has allowed a claimant to amend its statement of claim to correct a mistake in the name of the defendant[112] and to add claims under foreign law[113] even though the claims were time barred under the foreign law of the cause of **9.31**

---

[111] Rome Convention, art 15; Rome I, art 20; Rome II, art 24.
[112] *Nikolay Malakhov Shipping Co Ltd v Seas Sapfor Ltd* (1998) 44 NSWLR 371 (NSWCA).
[113] *Dyno Wesfarmers Ltd v Knuckey* [2003] NSWCA 375.

action. In both cases, the original statement of claim had been filed within time under that law but the amendment was filed after the time bar. The court described the right to obtain leave to amend a claim as a rule which 'touch[ed] the conduct of forum proceedings'.[114] Handley JA dissented on this point in both decisions, saying that the duty on the forum court to treat foreign limitation periods as substantive meant that the original period must be applied without alteration by the procedural rules of the forum. In both of these cases, the majority judges identified the key issue as a matter of *pleading* rather than a question of limitation and so it was properly the subject of forum law. In the *Dyno* decision, it should perhaps also be noted that the claims under foreign law which were sought to be added were identical in substance to those originally pleaded under forum (New South Wales) law, being actions under the Papua New Guinea equivalent of the Lord Cairns Act. A question may be raised as to whether the majority judges would have been so willing to allow the amendment had the claims been radically different in nature from the original pleadings. In such a case the majority might have been more inclined to adopt a substantive classification of the amendment issue.

9.32 The position under English law is more restrictive than in Australia but is likely to yield the same results in most cases. Section 1(3) of the FLPA 1984 refers to section 35 of the Limitation Act 1980 (UK) (LA 1980) which addresses the inclusion of new claims introduced by amendment to a statement of case. Similarly to the position in Australia, if such new claims or parties are accepted, they are considered as having been brought on the date of the original filed claim for the purposes of the applicable limitation law, which includes a foreign limitation under the FLPA 1984. Yet section 35(3) of the LA 1980 then provides that such amendments will only be permissible to add new claims or parties if the relevant rules of court are satisfied. The Civil Procedure Rules (CPR), rule 17.4 allows amendments to statements of case after the end of the limitation period and CPR, rule 19.5 similarly allows the addition or substitution of a party after the expiry of the period where certain conditions are satisfied. The requirements of CPR, rule 17.4 have been liberally applied by English courts in the context of applications to amend claims which had expired under foreign limitation provisions applicable under the FLPA 1984.[115] The question that arises is whether it is appropriate for the forum to use its procedural rules effectively to extend the limitation period, bearing in mind that both the FLPA

---

[114] ibid para 38.
[115] See eg *Barros Mattos v MacDaniels Ltd* [2005] EWHC 1323 (Ch) and *Latreefers Inc v Hobson* [2002] EWHC 1696 (Ch). cf *BP plc v AON Ltd* [2005] EWHC 2554 (Comm) (amendment refused).

B. The UK Statutory Regime

1984 and the Australian legislation (for example the Choice of Law (Limitation Periods) Act 1993 (NSW)) have indicated that the statutory powers to extend a limitation period are substantive. The view of Handley JA at 9.31, to the effect that forum procedural rules should not be applied to undermine foreign limitation periods, is also apposite. While the power to amend a statement of claim is an integral part of the administration of litigation, whether involving local or foreign elements, the act of doing so plainly has outcome determinative effect and, most importantly, weakens the impact of the foreign limitation.[116]

Consideration should therefore be given to requiring a claimant to adduce evidence of the procedural rules of the foreign law of the cause of action on the question of whether an amendment should be granted. Only if such rules permitted an amendment or at least did not prohibit it could a Commonwealth court grant the request. In effect, the issue of amendment in the context of expired limitation periods would cease to be one of pleading (procedural) and become one of limitation (substantive). This situation would seem to be a highly appropriate one for the admission in the forum of foreign procedural rules, a general point advocated throughout this work, which in any case is already provided for under the FLPA 1984 on the issue of extending the limitation period. This approach also addresses the issue raised by Dickinson that foreign limitation periods applicable under article 15(h) of the Rome II Regulation are not the subject of the statutory rights to amendment under section 35 of the LA 1980. According to this argument, such an omission is of no consequence since the right to amend after expiry of a limitation period would be a matter to be resolved by the procedural rules of the law of the obligation. 9.33

Another issue not covered by the FLPA 1984 or the Rome Convention and Regulations is waiver of the limitation period. In Canadian decisions it has been held that the requirement to plead a limitation period is a procedural matter governed by the law of the forum,[117] since it is again considered to be a matter of pleading. Canadian courts have also held that the consequence of a failure to plead a limitation period, namely the waiver of the right to rely on the defence, is also a matter governed by forum law.[118] Given the clear trend in favour of applying a substantive classification to most issues concerning limitations, due to their direct impact on the rights and liabilities of the parties, a good argument may be 9.34

---

[116] See Doherty (n 72 above) para 11-034.
[117] *Tolofson v Jensen* (1994) 120 DLR (4th) 289, 322.
[118] ibid *Hrynenko v Hrynenko* (1997) 37 BCLR (3d) 35 para 10 (affd (1998) 168 DLR (4th) 437 (BCCA)).

made that waiver should be similarly treated.[119] Support for a substantive view may also be found in the analogous cases of estoppel by representation and convention discussed in Chapter 7.[120]

C. FURTHER ISSUES

1. Choice of Law and Limitations in Jurisdictional Disputes

9.35 Under the traditional English test of *forum non conveniens* from the *Spiliada* case,[121] adopted in all Commonwealth countries (with a variation in Australia), it is well established that a claimant can avoid a stay of forum proceedings if it can show that it would be denied a legitimate personal or juridical advantage by the court declining to exercise jurisdiction. Lord Goff in *Spiliada* gave an example of such an advantage as the situation where a claimant was time barred in the jurisdiction which the defendant alleged to be the 'more appropriate forum' but whose action could proceed in the forum.[122] Such an analysis appears to assume that statutes of limitation are procedural and that each forum will apply its own; a view which of course no longer applies in England after the FLPA 1984, the Rome Convention and the Rome I and Rome II Regulations. The effect of these instruments, as already noted, is that an English court, subject to public policy, must apply the limitation of the law of the cause of action. In theory, therefore, a claimant should no longer be able to argue that it would be denied the 'advantage' of English limitation law if a stay were granted, where English law is not the law of the cause of action, since foreign law should apply wherever the case is adjudicated. Where English law, by contrast, is the law of the cause of action (as was the case in *Spiliada*), the claimant also should likewise not be able to rely on the fact that English limitations law will be applied in England but not in the foreign court unless it can produce clear evidence that the foreign court would not apply English law. Another effect of the FLPA 1984, the Convention, and the Regulations has therefore been to reduce jurisdictional disputes over limitation matters, a trend which is both desirable and noticeable in recent English litigation.

9.36 Interestingly, however, in other Commonwealth countries such as Canada, where it is also well established that questions of limitation are generally

---

[119] W Tetley, *International Conflict of Laws Common, Civil and Maritime* (International Shipping Publications, Blais, 1994) 689.
[120] See 7.52–7.53 above.
[121] [1987] AC 460.
[122] ibid 483–4.

substantive, in a number of cases involving applications for a stay of proceedings on *forum non conveniens* grounds, courts have assumed without argument that forum law applies to limitation issues. For example, in *Kelner Pilatus Center v Charest*[123] an Ontario court made no reference to the principle in *Tolofson* concerning limitations and accepted that the action would be barred in the interprovincial (Quebec) court but not in the forum. Yet it should have been relatively easy for the court to establish that Quebec would apply the law of the cause of action to limitations,[124] with the result that as Ontario law was the law governing the cause of action, its limitation law was likely to be applied in either jurisdiction. Consequently, a key assumption upon which the Ontario court refused the stay—that the matter was time barred in the Quebec court—was almost certainly incorrect. The same comment may be made about an earlier Ontario decision, *Gotch v Ramirez*,[125] where a stay in favour of litigation in Pennsylvania was refused on the assumption that the action would be statute barred in the foreign court but not in the forum, despite the law of the cause of action being that of the foreign country, with the result that the foreign bar should also have applied in Ontario (subject to public policy). The position would, however, be different if forum law governed the cause of action and under this law the matter was not barred but it was shown that the foreign court would apply its own law in any event to bar the action. Canadian courts in other stay cases[126] have shown an awareness of the rule that limitation questions are substantive and consequently placed little reliance on limitation as a factor in the stay determination since the same result would be reached in either of the competing jurisdictions.

2. Avoiding a Foreign Limitation by Displacing the Applicable Law

9.37 An alternative mechanism for avoiding a foreign limitation period and reinstating the law of the forum exists in the area of torts or non-contractual obligations in most Commonwealth countries except Australia. This avenue is important to consider because, if widely available, it would represent

---

[123] 2007 ONSC 20782.

[124] *Tolofson v Jensen* (1994) 120 DLR (4th) 289.

[125] (2000) 48 OR (3d) 515; see also *Lilydale Cooperative Ltd v Meyn Canada Inc* (2007) 84 OR (3d) 621 (affd 2008 ONCA 126) where a stay was refused with again the key reason being that the action would be statute barred in the courts of the law of the cause of action (Alberta) but not in the forum (Ontario). A similar false assumption seems to have been made in *Bulmer Aircraft Services Ltd v Bulmer* 2005 NBQB 396, para 17 and *Dempsey v Staples* 2011 ONSC 1709, paras 48–50.

[126] See eg *Schreiber v Mulroney* (2007) 88 OR (3d) 605, para 84 (stay granted in favour of trial in Quebec).

a further method of forum control in the area of limitation in Commonwealth countries and would further qualify the shift towards the law of the cause of action. First, in jurisdictions which still apply the double actionability rule to foreign torts there is a flexible exception to the law of the place of the wrong which enables the forum to apply its law to any issue with which it has the most substantial connection.[127] Conceivably, the issue to be displaced could be a foreign limitation period, and this occurred in at least one decision. In *Ennstone Building Products Ltd v Stanger*[128] the court would have applied English law to allow the action to proceed instead of the law of the place of the tort, where it was barred, because the advice which formed the basis of the claim was rendered in England and both parties were English companies.[129] By contrast, in *Durham v T & N Noble plc*,[130] the exception was not applied since all relevant connections were with the foreign law of the cause of action. A similar exception may exist in Canada, where the double actionability choice of law rule for torts has been replaced by presumptive application of the law of the place of the wrong. So in *Tolofson v Jensen* it was suggested that, at least in the case of international as opposed to interprovincial torts, rigid application of the law of the place of the wrong may be avoided only where it would cause 'an injustice'.[131] Yet, this exception was held not to apply to the situation where a claimant was seeking to rely on forum law to circumvent an expired foreign limitation period in *Roy v North American Leisure Group Inc*.[132] In the *Roy* case the claimant was an Ontario resident who suffered personal injury while on a cruise in the Caribbean and sued (among others) the English owner of the vessel. The court held that English law was the law of the place of the wrong and so its limitation law must also be applied. Conceivably, had there been more facts connecting the issue with Ontario, the court might have taken a different view on the applicable law.

9.38 In the case of proceedings under the Rome II Regulation, a similar approach is likely to prevail to that existing under the previous legislation, the Private International Law (Miscellaneous Provisions) Act 1995. Under section 11 of the PILA 1995 the basic choice of law rule in torts cases was the law of the country in which the relevant events occurred, but under section 12 this law could be displaced in favour of another law (such as the law of the forum) where the connections between the tort and the forum were so significant that it was substantially more appropriate for forum law to be

---

[127] *Boys v Chaplin* [1971] AC 356.
[128] [2002] 1 WLR 3059 (CA).
[129] ibid para 50.
[130] CA, 1 May 1996.
[131] *Tolofson v Jensen* (1994) 120 DLR (4th) 289, 314 (La Forest J), 326 (Major J).
[132] (2004) 73 OR (3d) 561, para 12.

C. Further Issues

applied to issues arising in the case or any of those issues. This test is similar to the common law 'flexible exception', since it allows the court to identify a particular issue in the litigation, such as limitation, and displace the foreign law on this matter. Alternatively, the forum court may consider that the circumstances of the case, such as the residence of the parties and the place where the relevant events that constituted the tort occurred, require displacement of the entire foreign law. Section 12 was applied to displace the law of the place of the tort (where the action was barred) in favour of the law of the forum in one English decision,[133] involving an English claimant who was recruited to work in the UAE by an English employment agency and suffered injury there while working for a German contractor. The court held, in proceedings against both companies, that since the claimant's presence in the UAE was purely temporary, his contract of employment was governed by English law and all of the parties to the litigation had little connection with the UAE, it would be more appropriate to apply English law, with the result that the claim was not time barred. It is suggested that such a result could equally be reached under article 4(2) of the Rome II Regulation where the law of the parties' common habitual residence must be applied in preference to the law of the place of the wrong, and article 4(3) which allows a court to displace the law of the place of the wrong where the tort is 'manifestly more closely connected' with another country. English law would have been the law of the common habitual residence in the action against the English company and England would also arguably have been 'manifestly more closely connected' with the claim against the German company.

3. A Legislative Return of the Law of the Forum?

Finally, it is also appropriate to note legislative developments in Canada, some of which have undermined the rule that limitations are substantive. These enactments suggest that, despite the earlier discussion, the law of the forum may possibly stage a resurgence in Commonwealth countries in the future. The first such provision is section 13(1) of the British Columbia Limitation Act 1996 which provides that:

9.39

If it is determined in an action that the law of a jurisdiction other than British Columbia is applicable and the limitation law of that jurisdiction is, for the purposes of private international law, classified as procedural, the court may apply British Columbia limitation law or may apply the limitation law of the other jurisdiction if a more just result is produced.

---

[133] *Hornsby v James Fisher Rumic Ltd* [2008] EWHC 1944 (QB).

Some Canadian scholars[134] have argued that this provision is redundant after the *Tolofson* decision, given that all Canadian provinces now classify the issue of limitation as substantive. This view is only correct if (a) a limitation provision of another Canadian province is before a British Columbian court, in which case it will always be applied (subject to public policy), or (b) a limitation provision of any other jurisdiction is before the court and the court applies its own rules of classification, ignoring the classification rules of the law of the cause of action.[135] If, however, such foreign rules are applied by the British Columbian court and the limitation provision is from a Commonwealth jurisdiction or US state where limitations are still generally regarded as procedural, then section 13(1) will be relevant. This precise situation arose in *Ruwenzori Enterprises v Waji*,[136] where a British Columbian court applied the limitation law of the law of the cause of action—Texas—under section 13(1) after finding that the provision would have been classified by Texan courts as procedural. The Court found it unjust to apply British Columbian law, given the paucity of contacts that the forum had with the parties and the action.[137]

9.40 The second relevant Canadian enactment is found in a number of provinces. For example, section 12 of the Albertan Limitations Act (before amendment in 2007) provided:

> The limitations law of the Province shall be applied whenever a remedial order is sought in this Province, notwithstanding that, in accordance with conflict of law rules, the claim will be adjudicated under the substantive law of another jurisdiction.

Legislative provisions in Saskatchewan[138] and Newfoundland and Labrador[139] are to the same effect. The Albertan provision was the subject of an important and controversial decision of the Supreme Court of Canada in *Castillo v Castillo*.[140] The *Castillo* case concerned a husband and wife, both residents of Alberta, who were involved in a single car accident in California. The wife brought an action against her husband in Alberta within the province's limitation period but after the California limitations period had expired. The wife argued that although the law of the place of

---

[134] J McEvoy, 'Characterization of Limitation Statutes in Canadian Private International Law: the Rocky Road of Change' (1996) 19 Dalhousie LJ 425, 433.
[135] This was the view taken in *Bank of America v Maas* 2010 ONSC 4546, para 9 (affd 2010 ONCA 833).
[136] 2004 BCSC 741, para 265 (affd (2006) 274 DLR (4th) 696, para 46).
[137] 2004 BCSC 741, para 273.
[138] Limitations Act 2004 (Sask), s 27.
[139] Limitations Act 1995 s 23.
[140] [2005] 3 SCR 870.

C. Further Issues

the wrong was California, which meant that after *Tolofson* California limitation law should be applied, this outcome was statutorily reversed by section 12 of the Alberta Limitations Act. The Supreme Court of Canada, however, held that the Californian limitation statute must be applied pursuant to *Tolofson* to bar the action and that section 12 does not revive an action time barred by the substantive law of the place of the wrong.[141] In addition, a majority of the court said, the effect of section 12 is to create a *further and additional* time bar to that under the law of the cause of action so that if a suit, for example, is within time under the foreign applicable law, it may still be subject to a shorter period in Alberta which would bar the suit.[142] The reasoning of the court, with respect, is brief and conclusory and seems to underplay the fact that a legislature can (subject to constitutional constraints) enact overriding mandatory rules to alter common law choice of law rules. Also, to give section 12 the double-barrelled operation suggested seems hard to justify on the text of the provision. It is submitted instead that the provision is an overriding mandatory rule, which requires Albertan courts to apply Albertan limitation law to all proceedings in Alberta regardless of the law of the cause of action.[143] Properly read, the provision therefore reverses the decision in *Tolofson* and a similar analysis would apply in the case of the Saskatchewan and Newfoundland enactments, particularly since those provisions appear to have all been enacted subsequent to the *Tolofson* decision.

Further support for this contention can be found in observations made in two lower court Canadian decisions. In *Caspian Construction Inc v Drake Surveys Ltd*[144] the Manitoba Court of Appeal suggested that the effect of section 12 of the Alberta Limitations Act was 'to override, at least in part, the application of the limitations law of the law of the *lex loci delicti* that was confirmed for tort litigation in *Tolofson*' and in *Bank of America v Maas*,[145] decided after *Castillo*, the Ontario Superior Court of Justice noted that 'some provinces [for example Alberta] did not codify the rule in *Tolofson* and chose to legislatively reverse it by expressly providing that all proceedings brought within the province are subject to the local limitation period'. In support of this view, the court in *Maas* referred to the 2010 Supreme Court decision in *Yugraneft Corporation v Rexx Management*

9.41

---

[141] ibid para 4.
[142] ibid para 6; Bastarache J, while concurring in the result, found the Limitations Act 2004 (Alta), s 12 to be inapplicable to the case on the basis that it was unconstitutional on either the claimant's or the defendant's suggested construction of the provision.
[143] See, in support of this view, G Robertson, '*Castillo v Castillo*: Limitation Periods and the Conflict of Laws' (2002) 40 Alberta L Rev 447.
[144] (2004) 184 Man R (2d) 284, para 21.
[145] 2010 ONSC 4546, para 15 (affd 2010 ONCA 833).

Corporation[146] where the court had to determine the applicable limitation period in respect of an application to enforce a foreign arbitral award in Alberta. Rothstein J, who gave the judgment of the court, said that:[147]

> The comprehensive nature of the [Albertan] Act is reinforced by s 12, a provision that appears specifically designed to *counteract the effects of this Court's decision* in *Tolofson* in a conflict of laws situation . . . [Section 12] ensures that all proceedings brought within the province are subject to the local limitation period, notwithstanding that any other limitation period may also be applicable pursuant to a conflict of laws analysis like that performed in *Tolofson*.

These observations, however, must be read in the light of the fact that in 2007 (after *Castillo* but before *Yugraneft*) section 12 was amended to embody the decision in *Castillo*. A new section 12(2) was added which provides that where a matter arises before an Albertan court in which foreign law is the law of the cause of action, the limitation period of that country or province will apply where it is shorter in length than the period provided under the law of the forum. Hence, it now appears (at least in Alberta) that although section 12(1) still on its face reverses the effect of *Tolofson* (as noted by the Supreme Court in *Yugraneft*), section 12(2) effectively restores the common law position by providing that foreign law will apply in every case where it provides a shorter limitation period (presumably subject to forum public policy).

9.42 Finally it is worth noting that another Canadian province, Ontario, has enacted legislation which gives statutory recognition to the *Tolofson* principle. Section 23 of the Ontario Limitations Act 2002 provides that 'for the purposes of applying the rules regarding conflict of laws, the limitations law of Ontario or any other jurisdiction is substantive law'. In most cases, such a provision will be unnecessary since Ontario courts, applying *Tolofson*, would reach the same result. Yet the provision may be useful where, for example, a foreign limitation period is before an Ontario court, yet under the choice of law rules of the foreign country, the provision would be classified as procedural. Presumably section 23 will have the effect of directing an Ontario court to ignore such a characterization and apply the foreign limitation law regardless. Also, section 23 may have some utility as a 'self-characterizing statute' (see 3.07) with foreign courts, in deciding whether to apply Ontario limitation law, given clear instruction that according to Ontario choice of law rules, it is to be considered substantive. Such an instruction may be particularly useful in jurisdictions such as Australia, where the 'no advantage' approach to

---

[146] [2010] 1 SCR 649; 2010 SCC 19.
[147] ibid para 38.

C. *Further Issues* 291

choice of law may require an Australian court to determine whether the foreign court would apply its own limitation period if the matter arose before that court.[148]

4. Time Provisions Other Than Limitations

Time limits in rules of court governing issues arising during the pre-trial and trial stages of a proceeding, such as a period for the filing of a defence, complying with an order for disclosure, or filing an appeal, are governed by forum law as they are part of the court's powers to manage litigation.[149] The same position is adopted in most European civil law countries.[150]   **9.43**

Another issue which may arise is where parties to a contract include a provision which contains a shorter time period for bringing claims than the relevant limitation period of the law of the cause of action. Since such a time period is incorporated in a document governing the rights and obligations of the parties rather than being in legislation enacted by the state, it is appropriately considered to be substantive and governed by the applicable law of the contract.[151] Notice before action requirements in legislation, at least where they extinguish obligations, should be treated similarly.[152]   **9.44**

5. The US Position

The US position on choice of law and limitation is too diverse to be fully treated in a work of this nature and so an outline of the main approaches must suffice, again with an eye to an overall assessment of the degree of forum control in this area. The starting point for consideration of US law in this area is the Supreme Court decision in *Sun Oil Co v Wortman*.[153] In that case it was decided that the adoption by one state of a procedural characterization of statutes of limitation was entirely consistent with the   **9.45**

---

[148] *Neilson v Overseas Project Corp of Victoria Ltd* (2005) 223 CLR 331.

[149] *Tolofson v Jensen* (1994) 120 DLR (4th) 289, 322; *Stern v Dill* 442 NW 2d 322, 324 (Minn 1989); A Lowenfeld, *Conflict of Laws: Federal, State and International Perspectives* (LexisNexis, 2nd edn, 2002) 73.

[150] See eg for France: Audit (n 11 above) para 445; for Belgium: Rigaux and Fallon (n 11 above) para 11.12; and for Germany: Geimer (n 11 above) para 353.

[151] *Dicey, Morris and Collins* (n 73 above) para 7.54; Law Commission (n 42 above) para 4.52. It is acknowledged that in *Allan J Panozza and Co Pty Ltd v Allied Interstate (Q) Pty Ltd* [1976] 2 NSWLR 192, 196 the New South Wales Supreme Court held that a provision in a contract requiring a person to give notice of loss to a carrier within five days of the date of delivery, before bringing proceedings, was procedural. Yet the authority of this case is doubtful as it pre-dates the redefinition of substance and procedure in *Pfeiffer v Rogerson*.

[152] See 6.28 above.

[153] 486 US 717 (1988).

state's obligation to confer full faith and credit on the laws of other states under the US Constitution. Consequently, each US state may either adopt a substantive or procedural characterization of limitation legislation of other states consistently with its constitutional obligations.

9.46 Statutes of limitation have been, in a similar way to Commonwealth law, traditionally classified in US law as procedural, unless they are annexed to a statutory cause of action or are in the form of a 'statute of repose' which bars an action (typically against a product manufacturer) after a stated number of years, regardless of when the cause of action accrued.[154] However, from the 1970s, some US courts began to adopt a substantive characterization of all limitation statutes,[155] while others, applying more flexible choice of law methodologies, applied the law which has the closest connection to, or greatest interest in, the issue of limitation.[156] This last, issue-specific approach departs from the strict choice of law dichotomy seen in Commonwealth countries, where only the law of the forum or the law of the cause of action can apply to limitations. Such a view, by isolating limitations as a distinct issue for choice of law purposes, raises the possibility of a law being applied other than the two mentioned. Section 142 of the Restatement (Second) of the Conflict of Laws (1988 revised version) adopts neither a substantive nor procedural characterization with regard to statutes of limitation but provides that they should be subject to the law of the state with the most significant relationship to the limitation issue, regardless of the law of the cause of action. Yet the provision then qualifies this open-ended direction by stating a general preference for the application of forum law. Specifically it is provided in §142(1) that, in the absence of exceptional circumstances which would make the result unreasonable, the forum will apply its own statute of limitation to bar the claim. This view is justified by the need to ensure accurate determinations in forum litigation by precluding adjudication of stale claims[157] and to give defendants peace from possibly indeterminate litigation under foreign law. By contrast, the Restatement then provides in § 142(2) that the forum's statute of limitation will be applied to *allow* an action to proceed unless there is no substantial forum interest and the claim would be barred by a statute of limitations of a state (or country) having a more significant

---

[154] *Rice v Dow Chemical Co* 875 P 2d 1213 (Wash 1994).

[155] See eg *Heavner v Uniroyal Inc* 305 A 2d 412, 418 (NJ 1973).

[156] See eg *Ashland Chemical Co v Provence* 181 Cal Rptr 340, 342 (CA Cal 1982); *Merkle v Robinson* 737 So 2d 540, 542 (Fla 1999).

[157] McDougal (n 2 above) 427; but see R Weintraub, *Commentary on the Conflict of Laws* (Foundation Press, 4th edn, 2001) 76 and E Scoles, P Hay, P Borchers, and S Symeonides, *Conflict of Laws* (Thomson West, 4th edn, 2004) 130, who criticize the provision for being too forum-biased.

C. Further Issues

relationship to the parties and the occurrence. In applying this provision, US courts have been equally divided in selecting forum or foreign law.[158] By contrast, the 1982 Uniform Conflict of Laws Limitations Act (UCLLA), adopted in six states,[159] classifies statutes of limitations as substantive and governed by the law of the cause of action,[160] subject to a hardship-type defence.[161]

9.47 Another important inroad into forum control in limitation matters in the United States has been made by 'borrowing' statutes, which have been enacted by a majority of US states. While such statutes are not uniform in their terms, they generally operate to bar an action in the forum if it is already barred by the corresponding law of the place where the cause of action arose or accrued or alternatively the place where the defendant or both parties resided. In effect, the forum is required to 'borrow' the limitation statute of the other jurisdiction to prevent forum shopping by plaintiffs. Such statutes, however, may be criticized as one-sided as they allow the forum court only to borrow a *shorter* limitation period of the foreign jurisdiction. Borrowing statutes do not therefore address the issue of whether it might be unjust for a claimant to be subjected to an expired foreign limitation when its claim is still permissible under forum limitations law.[162] The other weakness of borrowing statutes is that they also borrow the 'tolling' provisions of the other jurisdiction. Tolling provisions normally operate to stop the running of the limitation period where the defendant is absent or not resident in the forum state.[163] While some US courts[164] have held that the tolling rules do not apply where the defendant is amenable to personal service, the result is often burdensome for defendants (where they apply) and, as noted at 9.18, was wisely avoided in the English FLPA 1984.

---

[158] cf *De Loach v Alfred* 960 P 2d 628 (Sup Ct Ariz 1998); *Weitz Company LLC v Travellers Cas & Suty Co* 266 F Supp 2d 984 (SD Iowa 2003) and *Jackson v Chandler* 61 P 3d 17 (Az 2003) (forum law applied) with *Nierman v Hyatt Corp* 808 NE 2d 290 (Sup Jud Ct Mass 2004); *Washburn v Soper* 319 F 3d 338 (8th Cir 2003) and *Huynh v Chase Manhattan Bank* 465 F 3d 992 (9th Cir 2006) (foreign law applied).

[159] Washington, Colorado, Oregon, North Dakota, Montana, and Minnesota. See *Hein v Taco Bell Inc* 803 P 2d 329 (Wash Ct App 1991). Note that in Louisiana, its 1991 Conflict of Laws Code includes a provision (art 3549) which allows application of the law of the cause of action to the issue of limitation as an exception to the law of the forum where there are 'compelling considerations of remedial justice.'

[160] UCLLA, s 2.

[161] ibid s 4.

[162] Weintraub (n 157 above) 70.

[163] McDougal (n 2 above) 438.

[164] See eg *Meyer v Paschal* 498 SE 2d 635 (SC 1998).

9.48 Another restriction on forum control in this area is found in those US states which, despite adopting a procedural classification of limitations, recognize the right of parties to choose the law applicable to the issue of limitation in their contract. Some courts have construed general choice of law clauses ('this contract is governed by the laws of New York') as implicitly embracing issues of limitation,[165] while others have required an express intention by the parties to apply a certain limitation law in their contract on the basis that questions of limitation are still classified as procedural and a general choice of law clause only governs 'substantive' matters.[166]

9.49 Overall the US experience is broadly consistent with the Commonwealth practice in terms of the diminishing degree of forum control over limitations matters. While the procedural characterization still holds sway as a presumptive rule, its application is so qualified by exceptions as to make the application of forum law (particularly to allow a suit barred under the law of the cause of action) less frequent than might have been expected. While the various approaches to choice of law and limitations under US law are more nuanced and factually responsive, arguably the simpler Commonwealth approach, where the law of the cause of action is applied directly, is preferable both from a practical perspective and in serving the important policy interests involved. Limitations may therefore be an area where the relevant choice of law options are properly confined to the law of the cause of action and the law of the forum.

---

[165] *Hughes Electronics Corp v Citibank Delaware* 15 Cal Rptr 3d 244 (CA Cal 2004); *Hatfield v Halifax plc* 564 F 3d 1177, 1183 (9th Cir 2009).

[166] See eg *Diamond Waterproofing Systems Inc v 55 Liberty Owners Corp* 826 NE 2d 802 (NY 2005); *Smither v Asset Acceptance LLC* 919 NE 2d 1153, 1157–8 (CA Ind 2010).

10
Remedies I: General Principles, Non-Monetary Relief, and Statutory Restrictions

A. The Nature of the Remedy	10.01
B. Interim and Provisional Remedies	10.06
1. Anti-Suit Injunctions	10.07
2. Interlocutory Injunctions	10.08
3. Freezing Orders	10.13
4. Search Orders	10.14
5. The EU Dimension	10.15
C. Final Non-Monetary Relief	10.20
1. Specific Performance, Rescission, and Injunctions	10.20
2. Constructive Trusts and Tracing	10.21
3. The EU Dimension	10.23
D. Set-Off and Counterclaim	10.25
E. Statutory Restrictions on Remedies	10.32

A. THE NATURE OF THE REMEDY

It has long been the position in the common law of Commonwealth countries that a claimant can only obtain remedies which are available under the law of the forum.[1] Yet such a principle needs to be carefully evaluated to assess whether it reflects contemporary notions of procedure based on the mode or conduct of court proceedings and practicality, as opposed to simply being a manifestation of the outdated right / remedy distinction. Certainly the statement is true to the extent that it suggests that the forum has no power to award relief existing under foreign law which has no counterpart under the law of the forum. Such a conclusion flows from the fact that remedies are part of the court's machinery for resolving disputes and it would be impractical for the forum to have to implement

10.01

---

[1] L Collins (ed), *Dicey, Morris and Collins on the Conflict of Laws* (Sweet & Maxwell, 14th edn, 2006) para 7.006.

foreign remedies alien to the forum's traditions and processes. Hence, the form of the remedy sought is at least partly a procedural issue. The well known decision in *Phrantzes v Argenti*,[2] where an English court refused to make an order against a claimant's father requiring him to execute and enter into a dowry contract on behalf of the claimant (which was a valid remedy under Greek law), is a good example. According to Greek law, before the court could make an order it had to determine the father and daughter's financial positions. The English court noted that not only did English law not contain such a remedy but 'the machinery by way of remedies here is so different from that in Greece as to make the right sought to be enforced . . . a different right'.[3] Putting the language of right and remedy to one side, what the court is suggesting here is that English law cannot admit a foreign remedy where no equivalent exists under the law of the forum and which the forum lacks the machinery and competence to bring into effect.[4] The Australian High Court has more recently endorsed this view in *Pfeiffer v Rogerson*, where it noted that a claimant cannot obtain remedies of a kind which the forum is unable to provide.[5]

10.02 Once, however, it is established that the remedy sought exists under forum law, it will be argued that it is then for the law of the cause of action to determine whether such relief may be granted on the facts of the case. In effect, therefore, the remedy sought by the claimant must also have a counterpart or equivalent under the law of the cause of action (even if it is referred to there under a different label), to give proper recognition to the fact that remedies often have a direct impact on the rights and liabilities of the parties. Consequently, if the remedy in question does not also exist or have a functional equivalent under the law of the cause of action then it cannot be awarded by the forum court. Once it is established that a similar type of relief is available under foreign law, it is that law which determines whether it should be granted on the facts. For forum law, by contrast, also to determine whether the remedy should be granted would effectively denude the foreign substantive right of any value since the remedy is 'an inseparable part'[6] of the substantive right. Where possible the same law should apply to both right and remedy to prevent unnecessary fragmentation

---

[2] [1960] 2 QB 19.

[3] ibid 35–36.

[4] Briggs also refers to the powers of contractual variation and rewriting under the Australian Trade Practices Act 1974 (Cth) (now Competition and Consumer Act 2010 (Cth)) as an example of orders which may not be easily applied by a foreign court: A Briggs, 'Conflict of Laws and Commercial Remedies' in A Burrows and E Peel (eds), *Commercial Remedies Current Issues and Problems* (OUP, 2003) 271, 275.

[5] (2000) 203 CLR 503, para 99 (Gleeson CJ, Gaudron, McHugh, Gummow, and Hayne JJ).

[6] G Panagopoulos, 'Substance and Procedure in Private International Law' (2005) 5 JPIL 69, 77.

A. The Nature of the Remedy

of choice of law and dépeçage. It is suggested that this analysis equally applies to proceedings under the Rome I Regulation and the Rome Convention where the applicable law of the obligation shall govern 'the consequences of a total or partial breach of obligations',[7] and the Rome II Regulation where it is stated that the applicable law (of the obligation) 'will govern measures which are designed to prevent or terminate injury or damage or to ensure the provision of compensation'[8] but in all such cases the forum court is 'only required to grant remedies which are "within the limits of . . . its procedural law"'.[9] The effect of these provisions is that the question of whether a remedy may be granted in particular litigation is primarily one for the law of the cause of action, subject to the relief being part of the forum's machinery.

10.03 The essentially limited scope of the decision in *Phrantzes* is confirmed by the later Canadian decision in *Khalij Commercial Bank Ltd v Woods*.[10] There, a claimant successfully enforced a banking debt under an instrument governed by Dubai law despite the fact that this law (unlike the law of the forum) provided for separate determinations of liability and enforcement with considerable discretion given to the court at the enforcement stage. The *Phrantzes* case was distinguished on the basis that the relief sought there could not be practically granted by the forum, whereas in *Khalij* all that was sought to be recovered was payment of a fixed sum. Indeed, the court in *Khalij* suggested that the result in *Phrantzes* might have been different had that case only concerned recovery of a sum of money.[11]

10.04 Consequently, there is little support for two further propositions which are often said to flow from the view that the forum can only grant its own remedies.[12] The first is that the claimant is entitled to a remedy under forum law even where such relief is not available under the law of the cause of action,[13] and the second is that the claimant cannot obtain an injunction, for example, where it would not be granted under forum law even if the remedy was available under the law of the cause of action.[14] The recent decision of the English Commercial Court in *Fiona Trust and Holding Corporation v Privalov*[15] suggests a tentative step in favour of the

---

[7] Rome Convention, art 10(1)(c); Rome I, art 12(1)(c).
[8] Rome II, art 15(d).
[9] Rome Convention, art 10(1)(c); Rome I, art 12(1)(c); Rome II, art 15(d).
[10] (1985) 17 DLR (4th) 358 (Ontario High Court).
[11] ibid 365.
[12] Briggs (n 4 above) 275; Panagopoulos (n 6 above) 77–8, 86–7; cf *Dicey, Morris and Collins* (n 1 above) para 7.006.
[13] *Baschet v London Illustrated Standard Co* [1900] 1 Ch 73; *Liverpool Marine Credit Co v Hunter* (1868) LR 3 Ch App 479, 486.
[14] *Warner Brothers Pictures Inc v Nelson* [1937] 1 KB 209.
[15] [2010] EWHC 3199 (Comm).

above contention that foreign remedies can be recognized and available in Commonwealth courts, at least where the form of relief exists in the forum. In the *Fiona Trust* case the English court had to consider an action under the Russian Civil Code which broadly equated to the English tort of trespass to property. The claimant argued that it was entitled to the English law remedy of an account of profits for such conduct as the question of remedy was wholly governed by English law as the law of the forum. The court rejected this argument, stating that the decision to award remedies under English law is not one that can be made in isolation from the foreign substantive right. Instead, in determining the appropriate remedy, the court must examine 'what is the nature of the liability under the foreign law and what remedy or remedies would English law provide for English law liability similar or analogous to the kind of liability established under the foreign law'.[16] In *Fiona Trust* this test required the court to analyse the nature of liability under Russian law, which it found to be similar to the English tort of trespass, and then to award what would be the appropriate English remedy—compensatory damages. The remedy of account of profits could not be awarded because it did not accord with the foreign substantive right said to have been infringed.

10.05 While this decision did not involve the court granting a remedy under *foreign* law this could simply be because no such relief was sought by the claimant. The court revealed a possible sympathy to recognizing foreign remedies in the way that it used the foreign law on liability to 'shape' the available relief under forum law. It will be interesting to see in a later case whether the court will be persuaded to take the next logical step and award a foreign remedy directly where it represents the equivalent of relief available in the forum. In the absence of the considerations which confronted the court in the *Phrantzes* case, there should be no obstacle and, indeed, the greater receptiveness towards foreign law coupled with the more restrictive conception of 'procedure' evident in most Commonwealth countries should dictate such a course. As will be further discussed at 10.15–10.19 the effect of the EU instruments arguably gives much clearer and more direct authorization to courts to apply foreign remedies.

B. INTERIM AND PROVISIONAL REMEDIES

10.06 It has long been assumed in Commonwealth countries that the availability of all interim orders—such as interlocutory injunctions, freezing or mareva

---

[16] ibid para 158.

B. Interim and Provisional Remedies

relief, Anton Piller or search orders,[17] and anti-suit injunctions—are governed by forum law as matters of procedure. Such a view may be defended on the ground that most such remedies are integrally related to the conduct of proceedings in the forum, specifically to manage the case and preserve the parties' rights until trial.[18] Additionally, the applicable law on the merits may be unknown at the time a provisional remedy is sought and so it may be premature and inaccurate for the forum to apply foreign law to the grant of such relief when such law may not ultimately be found to be the law of the cause of action.[19] Such a blanket classification of interim or provisional relief is, however, coming under increasing challenge.

1. Anti-Suit Injunctions

First, in the case of anti-suit injunctions, it was noted earlier[20] that the enforcement of contractual rights of the parties may be involved, such as where an injunction is sought to enforce an exclusive jurisdiction clause or equitable rights where the foreign proceeding is deemed unconscionable. In such cases a substantive classification of the remedy is more appropriate. A procedural classification should, however, apply when the remedy is sought to protect the processes of the forum court, for instance when a liquidation or administration of assets is being conducted by the forum.

10.07

2. Interlocutory Injunctions

Secondly, in the case of interlocutory injunctions, such as orders to restrain a trespass or an infringement of an intellectual property right, there is at least a provisional adjudication of the rights of the parties which can in practice lead to the resolution of the dispute without the need for a trial on the merits. For example, it will be necessary to show that the relevant tort, infringement of intellectual property right, or breach of contract occurred at least to the level of an arguable case. In resolving whether each cause of action is provisionally made out, the law of the cause is applied but once this is done the principles of forum law are employed to determine whether the injunction will be granted. This approach is followed in most US decisions.[21]

10.08

---

[17] *Anton Piller KG v Manufacturing Processes Ltd* [1976] Ch 55 (CA).
[18] Briggs (n 4 above) 285.
[19] ibid 284.
[20] See 4.62–4.63 above.
[21] See eg *Modern Computer Systems Inc v Modern Banking Systems Inc* 871 F 2d 734 (8th Cir 1989); *Rimkus Consulting Group Inc v Cammarata* 255 FRD 417 (SD Tex 2008); *Vital State Canada Ltd v Dreampak LLC* 303 F Supp 2d 516 (DNJ 2003).

10.09 A recent Singaporean decision suggests, however, that the principles of the law of the cause of action should also be applied to determine whether an interim injunction should be *granted* which would give the remedy a further substantive aspect. In *Shanghai Electric Group Co Ltd v PT Merak Energi Indonesia*[22] the court had to consider whether to grant an injunction to restrain a beneficiary (the defendant) of an on-demand bond from making a call on the bond. The bond had been issued by the plaintiff to the defendant pursuant to a contract where the defendant provided funds for the construction of a power plant. Both the contract and the bond were governed by English law. The court noted that the issue in dispute was not whether the remedy of injunction was *available* to the claimant; this question would have been governed by forum law since 'the court can only give its own remedies as opposed to alien remedies'.[23] Rather, the question was whether the injunction should be *granted* in this particular case. This issue involved the vindication of a substantive right and so should be governed by the law of the cause of action.[24] Here the effect of granting the injunction would be to impose a restraint on a beneficiary's right to receive payment on an on-demand bond, which would effectively deprive the beneficiary of its right to immediate payment. In such circumstances the defendant would lose a substantive right under the bond.[25] What is notable about this decision is that the court resolved the substance/procedure classification not by reference to whether the relief sought was interlocutory or final but by an assessment of the commercial purpose and impact of the remedy on the parties' rights. Such a view is consistent with the narrow, 'mechanics', view of procedure advocated above; once it was clear that the remedy existed under the law of the forum, then the law of the cause of action determined whether it should be awarded in the given case.

10.10 A comparison may be made between the *Shanghai Electric* case and a recent decision from Canada. In *Telesis Technologies Inc v Sure Controls Systems Inc*[26] a claimant sought an interlocutory injunction in an Ontario court to restrain the defendant from breaching a non-competition clause in a distributorship agreement. The agreement was governed by Ohio law but also contained a provision allowing the claimant to seek an injunction in the court of its choosing. The court applied Ontario law as the law of the forum to determine whether the preliminary injunction should be granted

---

[22] [2010] SGHC 2.
[23] ibid para 20 applying *Phrantzes v Argenti* [1960] 2 QB 19.
[24] ibid para 21.
[25] ibid para 30.
[26] 2010 ONSC 5288.

on the basis that the issue was procedural. The court's conclusion was strongly influenced by this provision, allowing the claimant to sue to obtain an interim remedy in any court it wished, holding that this clause amounted to a choice by the parties of the procedural law of the chosen court for any applications for provisional remedies. The position would have been different, the court said, had the parties chosen foreign law to govern procedural matters, such as by use of a foreign exclusive jurisdiction clause. Hence, although the result in this case confirms the orthodox view that interim relief should be classified as procedural, the court's approach nevertheless lays the way open for foreign law to be applied in a given case.

There is also US authority which supports the growing trend that the granting of an interlocutory injunction should be governed by the law of the cause of action. In *Sim Snowboards Inc v Kelly*[27] a claimant sought a preliminary injunction to restrain the defendant from endorsing the products of a corporation, an act which amounted to a breach of his contract with the claimant, which was governed by Californian law. Under the law of the forum, Oregon, such an injunction could have been granted but under the law of California a statute existed which barred the issuing of injunctions in certain personal services contracts. The court applied the Californian statute to defeat the action, finding that the question of whether the remedy should be granted was substantive, as it affected the rights of the parties 'not merely the methodology of the litigation'.[28]

10.11

Finally, there is also evidence in European civil law countries of a substantive classification being made of interlocutory injunctions. Decisions from the Netherlands[29] and Switzerland[30] both involved a defendant in country A distributing material to consumers in country B in breach of the rights of the claimant under the latter country's laws. In both cases, the courts held that the law of country B applied to determine whether provisional measures to restrain the distribution of such material would be ordered, on the basis that such law was the law of the cause of action.

10.12

3. Freezing Orders

A third example of where the exclusive control of forum law in the area of interim remedies may be waning is freezing or mareva orders. The basic

10.13

---

[27] 863 F 2d 643 (9th Cir 1988).
[28] ibid 645.
[29] *Lowland Yachts BV v Firma Dahm International GmbH* (District Court of The Hague) (23 February 1989) [1991] IL Pr 350.
[30] *Kantonsgerichtpräsident, Zug* (19 April 1990) [1992] ECLY 4330.

position, of course, is that forum law is fundamental to this type of relief since the object of such orders is to prevent abuse of the forum's processes by protecting assets of the defendant from dissipation in advance of trial.[31] A procedural classification of the order, based on its connection to the conduct and regulation of the forum court's proceedings, is therefore appropriate.[32] Yet, even in the context of this relief, there are signs of a more nuanced choice of law analysis developing. The first such sign is the requirement—to obtain such an order—that the claimant show a good arguable case on the merits against the defendant.[33] Although no Commonwealth court has yet said so explicitly, such a question must surely be classified as substantive and governed by the law of the cause of action, given its direct connection to the rights of the parties. Interestingly, a civil law commentator has recognized this aspect.[34] The second piece of evidence reflecting a relaxation of the strict application of forum law arises in circumstances where a Commonwealth court has been asked to make such orders 'in aid of' foreign proceedings. In this situation, the forum court has typically required a connection with the forum before making the order sought (for example that the defendant was domiciled there)[35] which is possibly an example of the 'enlightened *lex fori*' concept at work, with the strict operation of forum law modified to take account of foreign circumstances. One English commentator has, however, suggested that such an application of forum law is still insufficiently 'enlightened' given the intrusion on the jurisdiction of the foreign court of such orders. Instead, comity requires that before the forum makes an interim order in aid of foreign proceedings, the remedy in question should at least also exist under the law of the foreign country.[36]

4. SEARCH ORDERS

10.14 The treatment of search orders, which are granted to allow a claimant to enter premises for the purpose of search and inspection of documents, is

---

[31] *Cardile v LED Builders Pty Ltd* (1999) 198 CLR 380, paras 25, 40 (Gaudron, McHugh, Gummow, and Callinan JJ); *Aosta Shipping Co Ltd v Gulf Overseas General Trading LLC* 2007 BCSC 354; see 6.80 above, where it is noted that under the US Restatement (Second), § 130 freezing orders are considered to be 'methods of securing obedience to the orders of the court'.

[32] T Yeo, *Choice of Law for Equitable Doctrines* (OUP, 2004) para 4.43.

[33] *Cardile v LED Builders Pty Ltd* (1999) 198 CLR 380, para 68 (Gaudron, McHugh, Gummow, and Callinan JJ); *Talacko v Talacko* [2009] VSC 349, paras 25, 27.

[34] K Kerameus, 'Provisional Remedies in Transnational Litigation' in International Association of Procedural Law, *Trans-national Aspects of Procedural Law* vol 3 (Giuffrè Editore, 1998) 1169, 1193–4.

[35] *Credit Suisse Fides Trust SA v Cuoghi* [1998] QB 818 (CA).

[36] Briggs (n 4 above) 282–3, 286.

B. Interim and Provisional Remedies

likely to be generally similar to freezing orders, since the rationale of the remedy is to preserve evidence. A procedural classification is therefore apt, especially where the order is sought in aid of proceedings in the forum, as there the protection of local processes is paramount.[37] Again, where the search order is sought in aid of foreign proceedings, arguably it is necessary that some connection with the forum is demonstrated before it can be granted or, even further, that it should be shown that the remedy also exists under the law of the foreign court.

5. The EU Dimension

10.15 Recent developments under EU law lend support to the view that the grip of the forum on interim and provisional remedies is declining. In the case of the Rome II Regulation, article 15(d) provides that the applicable law of the obligation will govern 'the measures which are designed to prevent or terminate injury or damage or to ensure the provision of compensation'. Interim remedies such as interlocutory injunctions to restrain an infringement of a party's rights are clearly designed to prevent or terminate injury or damage.[38] This conclusion is reinforced by article 2 of the Regulation which states that the instrument applies equally to non-contractual obligations that are 'likely to arise', which would include such forms of interlocutory relief. Further, the Explanatory Memorandum speaks of 'ways of preventing or halting the damage such as an interlocutory injunction'.[39]

10.16 Further, an anti-suit injunction, at least where it involves the enforcement of contractual or equitable rights, would also fall within article 15(d) of the Rome II Regulation as a 'measure designed to prevent or terminate injury or damage'. Where, by contrast, the order is invoked to protect the forum court's processes it should be considered procedural and governed by the law of the forum.[40]

10.17 The objective of a freezing order is to maintain the status quo until trial and to prevent abuse of the forum court's processes by a defendant removing assets from the jurisdiction which may be used to satisfy a judgment. Such orders therefore have a direct connection to the conduct and regulation of the forum court's proceedings and a lesser link to the merits of the

---

[37] Yeo (n 32 above) para 4.47.
[38] European Commission, *Proposal for a Regulation on the law applicable to non-contractual obligations* COM(2003)427 final (21 February 2006) 24.
[39] Explanatory Memorandum, 24.
[40] For a fuller discussion, see 4.62–4.63 above.

action.[41] Article 15(d), however, also includes 'measures . . . to ensure the provision of compensation', which would appear to embrace such relief since a freezing order aims to prevent a defendant from depriving a claimant of the fruits of recovery. Yet, as already noted, the forum can only grant remedies within its own armoury and so perhaps the best interpretation of this provision is to say that, for a freezing order to be issued, it must exist *as a remedy* under both the laws of the forum and the law of the obligation but the conditions for its grant are those imposed by the law of the obligation. An approach may be taken similar to that of the Singapore court in *Shanghai Electric Group Co Ltd v PT Merak Energi Indonesia*.[42]

10.18 The status under the Rome II Regulation of search orders and relief designed to ensure compliance with a judgment, such as remedies of attachment and garnishment, is likely to be the same as freezing orders since all are likely to be 'measures . . . to ensure the provision of compensation'.

10.19 The provisions of the Rome I Regulation and the Rome Convention are in different terms to Rome II. Article 12(1)(c) of the Rome I Regulation (and article 10(1)(c) of the Rome Convention) provides that the applicable law of the obligation shall govern 'the consequences of a total or partial breach of obligations'. Most commentators agree that this provision does not embrace any forms of interlocutory relief,[43] which means that if such a remedy is sought in an action in an English court where the Rome I Regulation or the Convention applies, then the applicable law will be determined by the English rules of private international law. As discussed earlier, though, it is no longer a foregone conclusion that forum law will apply in every case or at least without modification where an interim remedy is sought under the common law rules.

C. FINAL NON-MONETARY RELIEF

1. Specific Performance, Rescission, and Injunctions

10.20 The classification of final, non-monetary relief has also moved in a substantive direction recently. Most recent commentary and the clear majority of US courts have argued that final relief clearly connected to the merits of

---

[41] A Rushworth, 'Remedies and the Rome II Regulation' in J Ahern and W Binchy, *The Rome II Regulation on the Law Applicable to Non-Contractual Obligations* (Martinus Nijhoff, 2009) 199, 202.

[42] [2010] SGHC 2.

[43] R Plender and M Wilderspin, *The European Private International Law of Obligations* (Sweet & Maxwell, 3rd edn, 2009) para 14.039.

the case, such as orders for specific performance,[44] rescission,[45] and an injunction to restrain a breach of contract or a tort,[46] should be governed by the law of the cause of action. Given the clear impact on the rights and liabilities of the parties and limited connection with the conduct of the forum's proceedings of such orders, this view is compelling. Such a conclusion may have particular significance in the case of specific performance, which has traditionally been awarded on a more restricted basis in common law systems than in civil law countries, for example only in cases where damages are inadequate.[47] In principle, the right to declaratory relief should be similarly classified,[48] given its clear connection to the rights and liabilities of the parties. The substantive classification approach emphatically rejects the rather extreme position adopted until recently in Australian law that all equitable remedies, whether final or interim, should be governed by the law of the forum. As discussed above, this approach to equitable relief rests on the concept that equity operates *in personam* on the conscience of the defendant, but the view that forum law applies exclusively to such relief is now seriously questioned in Commonwealth jurisdictions, including Australia.[49] Yet forum law is not entirely irrelevant in this context since, as already noted, the particular remedy must first exist under that law and the forum does not have to grant foreign relief where this would impose an unreasonable burden of supervision or administration on the forum.[50] Public policy would also be available to prevent the application of a foreign remedy in circumstances where, for example, it would be unjust.

---

[44] Briggs (n 4 above) 275; Yeo (n 32 above) paras 4.24, 4.27; Panagopoulos (n 6 above) 86–7. Relevant US decisions include *Allegheny Energy Inc v DQE Inc* 171 F 3d 153, 159 (4th Cir 1999); *Ringfree USA Corp v Ringfree Co Ltd* 2008 WL 4691046 (CD Cal) *3; *Dynasty Apparel Industries Inc v Rentz* 2007 WL 641825 (SD Ohio) *6; *Odishelidze and Employee Benefits Associates Inc v Agora Inc* 1996 WL 655787 (D Puerto Rico) *2.

[45] Yeo (n 32 above) para 4.80; relevant US decisions are *Re Commercial Money Center Inc* 627 F Supp 2d 786, 799 (ND Ohio 2009); *Pinnacle Communications International Inc v American Family Mortgage Corp* 417 F Supp 2d 1073, 1081 (D Minn 2006); *Kase v Salomon Smith Barney Inc* 218 FRD 149, 158 (SD Tex 2003).

[46] Briggs (n 4 above) 279–80; Yeo (n 32 above) para 4.31.

[47] M Wolff, *Private International Law* (OUP, 2nd edn, 1950) 238.

[48] But cf Wolff (n 47 above).

[49] See eg *Rickshaw Investments Ltd v Nicolai Baron von Uexkull* [2007] 1 SLR 377; *Yugraneft v Abramovich* [2008] EWHC 2613 (Comm); *Douglas v Hello! Ltd (No 3)* [2006] QB 125, para 97; and *Murakami v Wiryadi* (2010) 268 ALR 377.

[50] *Phrantzes v Argenti* [1960] 2 QB 19.

2. Constructive Trusts and Tracing

10.21 A constructive trust is a form of remedy imposed by the court in respect of property that has been acquired by a defendant through conduct regarded as unconscionable in equity, with such property declared to be held on trust for the claimant. The classification of a constructive trust is best regarded as substantive since such an order is closely linked to the rights and liabilities of the parties as it involves the imposition of an interest over property and has limited relevance to the conduct of court proceedings.[51] A substantive classification was expressly adopted, obiter, in *Chase Manhattan Bank NA v Israel-British Bank (London) Ltd*[52] and assumed to be correct in *Bank of Ireland v Pexxnet Ltd*,[53] *Murakami v Wiryadi*,[54] and *To Group Co Ltd Xiamen King v Eton Properties Ltd*.[55] Canadian authority is split on the question, with the Ontario Superior Court of Justice taking a substantive view[56] but the British Columbia Supreme Court opting for a procedural classification.[57] In the latter case, it is suggested, however, that the court was too heavily influenced by the right-remedy view of substance and procedure, with the court noting that it was 'not persuaded that a constructive trust remedy is indissolubly connected to the [right of] unjust enrichment arising from the breach of confidence that both must be seen as two sides of one substantive coin'.[58] Instead of trying to fit constructive trusts into the right-remedy framework it would have been preferable if the court had considered broader questions such as the impact of such an order on the merits of the litigation and its connection with the forum court's processes. Also, while a possible objection which may be raised to a substantive classification is that in certain countries, especially those with a civil law tradition, the constructive trust does not exist, it should not, however, be difficult in most cases to locate an equivalent form of relief under foreign law. Significantly, again, in the majority of recent

---

[51] J Walker, *Castel & Walker Canadian Conflict of Laws* (LexisNexis Butterworths, 6th edn, 2005) para 28.7; *Dicey, Morris and Collins* (n 1 above) para 7.010; Panagopoulos (n 6 above) 82–3.
[52] [1981] Ch 105.
[53] [2010] EWHC 1872 (Comm).
[54] (2010) 268 ALR 377.
[55] [2010] HKCFI 236, para 107.
[56] *Cooper-Standard Automotive Canada Ltd* 2009 ONSC 51188, para 25.
[57] *Minera Aquiline Argentina SA v IMA Exploration Inc* 2006 BCSC 1102, paras 248–9 (affd on different grounds 2007 BCCA 319).
[58] ibid para 248.

C. Final Non-Monetary Relief

US decisions, a substantive classification of constructive trusts has been adopted.[59]

Tracing is a device whereby property in the hands of the defendant is identified as belonging to the claimant after it has been mixed with or substituted by other property. Since the object of tracing is to locate property in support of actions, such as for breach of trust, and is a necessary precondition for the bringing of some actions, it should also be regarded as substantive and governed by the law of the cause of action.[60] Some judicial support for this view can be found in *Chase Manhattan Bank NA v Israel-British Bank (London) Ltd*.[61]

3. THE EU DIMENSION

The provisions of both the Rome I and Rome II Regulations (and the Rome Convention) clearly extend to include final non-monetary orders. In the case of Rome I, article 12(1)(c) (and Rome Convention, article 10(1)(c)) provides that the law of the obligation applies to 'the consequences of a total or partial breach of obligations'. Commentators have noted that such an expression would include all final remedies in relation to contracts, such as specific performance, repudiation, rescission, and injunctions to restrain breach.[62] In the case of non-contractual obligations, the principal final, non-monetary remedy is the injunction to restrain commission of a wrong and this would certainly be a measure designed to prevent or terminate injury or damage under article 15(d) of the Rome II Regulation. It has also been suggested that the effect of both article 12(1)(c) of Rome I and article 15(d) of Rome II is that the determination of when a particular remedy should be awarded, for example an injunction as opposed to damages, is also a matter for the law of the obligation.[63] Such a contention would be consistent with the view expressed above regarding the common law position but is of course subject to the wording in article 12(1)(c) of Rome I and article 15(d) of Rome II which requires that the remedy sought be 'within the limits conferred by the forum's procedural law', that is, available under that law.[64] In other words, the law of the obligation determines which remedy is appropriate on the facts of the case but such relief must

---

[59] See eg *Amusement Industry Inc v Stern* 693 F Supp 2d 327, 342 (SDNY 2010); *United States of America v One Silicon Valley Bank Account* 549 F Supp 2d 940, 954 (WD Mich 2008).

[60] *Dicey, Morris and Collins* (n 1 above) para 7.010; Panagopoulos (n 6 above) 84–6; J Harris, 'Tracing and the Conflict of Laws' (2002) 73 BYBIL 65, 68–70.

[61] [1981] Ch 105, 127–8.

[62] Plender and Wilderspin (n 43 above) para 14.037; Yeo (n 32 above) para 4.27.

[63] Plender and Wilderspin (n 43 above) para 16.064.

[64] Rome I, art 12(1)(c); Rome Convention, art 10(1)(c); Rome II, art 15(d).

also be available under the law of the forum. This reservation made for the operation of forum law would also operate to exclude the application of a foreign remedy which would require constant supervision of the forum court or cause hardship.[65] The public policy exception under the EU instruments would arguably be an alternative basis for excluding such a foreign remedy.

10.24 Finally, the reference in article 15(c) of the Rome II Regulation to the law of the obligation applying to 'the remedy claimed' would also be likely to include final declaratory orders if such relief were not considered to be a measure designed 'to prevent or terminate injury or damage' within article 15(d).[66]

D. SET-OFF AND COUNTERCLAIM

10.25 The position of set-off is less clear in terms of classification and so requires more extended consideration. Set-off involves a defendant seeking to deduct a debt owed to it by the claimant from an amount owed by the defendant to the claimant with the debts arising from connected claims. The leading decision on what law applies to whether set-off is available in an action is an old English case, *Meyer v Dresser*,[67] where it was suggested by two judges that set-off is a matter of procedure and governed by the law of the forum.[68] The force of this view may, however, be weakened by the fact that English law may also have been the law of the cause of action in that case, with the substance / procedure distinction not referred to by the other two judges.[69] In any event, one of the judges who favoured a procedural interpretation[70] suggested that a different view on classification may be taken where the effect of the defendant's claim of set-off was to discharge or extinguish its liability to the claimant on the original claim as opposed to merely being a claim brought by the defendant in the same proceeding which takes effect as a set-off from the date of court judgment. The distinction is between set-off arising *outside* legal proceedings and set-off declared by one party *during* legal proceedings.[71] In *Meyer v Dresser* the

---

[65] Plender and Wilderspin (n 43 above) para 14.039.
[66] A Dickinson, *The Rome II Regulation* (OUP, 2008) para 14.25.
[67] (1864) 16 CB (NS) 646.
[68] ibid 665 (Willes J) and 665 (Byles J).
[69] Erle CJ and Keating J; see P Wood, *English and International Set-Off* (Sweet & Maxwell, 1989) para 23.20 and see also P Wood, *Set off and Netting, Derivatives and Clearing Systems* (Sweet & Maxwell, 2007) para 6.005.
[70] Willes J.
[71] U Magnus, 'Set-Off and the Rome I Proposal' (2006) 8 YBPIL 113, 115, n 6, 118, n 17.

D. Set-off and Counterclaim

defendant's claim against a carrier for damages for inadequate delivery of goods was held not to be one which would discharge its liability for freight and so was a procedural issue.

10.26 The idea that the right to set-off is substantive where it extinguishes or discharges the defendant's original liability is based on the traditional effect of set-off in European civil law countries as compared to common law jurisdictions.[72] The principle has been endorsed by some commentators on English[73] and Scottish[74] private international law, although many of the other commonly cited old English decisions are inconclusive on the point. Either these cases involved both English law as the law of the cause of action and law of the forum[75] or the content of the law of the forum and the foreign law of the cause of action on set-off was identical (a 'false conflict').[76] In *Prekons Insaat Sanayi AS v Rowlands Castle Contracting Group Ltd*[77] the English Commercial Court applied the above distinction between a set-off which would discharge or extinguish liability as opposed to merely being a claim brought by the defendant in the same proceeding. The court found that the question of whether the defendant was entitled to plead a set-off which would have extinguished the original obligation was substantive and governed by the law of the claimant's cause of action.

10.27 The position in the United States is broadly similar. Section 128 of the Second Restatement provides that the law of the forum will apply 'in determining whether a claim may be pleaded by way of set-off, counterclaim or other defense unless under the otherwise applicable law the defendant's claim, if allowed, would operate to qualify the plaintiff's claim in whole or in part'. While this provision fails to identify 'the otherwise

---

[72] Set-off is considered substantive under European rules of private international law. For Germany, see R Geimer, *International Zivilprozeßrecht* (OUS Verlag Dr Otto Schmidt, 5th edn, 2005) para 352; Magnus (n 71 above) 118, n 17; and I Szászy, 'The Basic Connecting Factor In International Cases in the Domain of Civil Procedure' (1966) 15 ICLQ 436, 452. For the Netherlands, see R Bertrams, 'Set-Off in Private International Law' in K Boele-Woelki, F Grosheide, E Hondius, and G Steenhoff, *Comparability and Evaluation: Essays in Honour of Dimitra Kokkini-Iatridou* (Martinus Nijhoff, 1994) 153. See also R Zimmermann, *Comparative Foundations of a European Law of Set-Off and Prescription* (CUP, 2002) 23.

[73] Dicey, Morris and Collins (n 1 above) para 7.032; Wolff (n 47 above) 233–4; cf J Fawcett and J Carruthers, *Cheshire, North and Fawcett Private International Law* (OUP, 14th edn, 2008) 95 who support a procedural classification.

[74] E Crawford and J Carruthers, *International Private Law: A Scots Perspective* (Thomson West, 3rd edn, 2010) para 8.26.

[75] See eg *Allen v Kemble* (1848) 6 Moo PC 314 (PC) and *Maspons v Mildred, Goyeneche & Co* (1882) 9 QBD 530 (CA).

[76] *MacFarlane v Norris* (1862) 2 B & S 783.

[77] [2006] EWHC 1367 (Comm), para 12.

applicable law', it does support a substantive classification in the case where the set-off would wholly or partly extinguish the defendant's liability. Hence, where a counterclaim brought by the defendant not only arose out of the same transaction which gave rise to the plaintiff's claim but would have altered the rights of the parties to that transaction,[78] the law of the cause of action was applied to determine whether the defendant's plea amounted to a set-off. Such law was found to be the law of the state with the most significant relationship to the contract and the parties.

10.28 Under the Rome I Regulation,[79] however, it is arguable that the distinction between set-off which extinguishes the original liability (the traditional Roman law set-off) and set-off merely based on a claim brought in the same proceedings does not apply. Article 17 provides that 'where the right to set-off is not agreed by the parties, set-off shall be governed by the law applicable to the claim against which the right to set-off is asserted'. The provision does not appear to distinguish between types of set-off in classifying them as substantive.[80]

10.29 Given the lack of certainty in the current law, the precise choice of law position under Commonwealth law would seem open to argument, guided by contemporary notions of substance and procedure. Where set-off has the effect of discharging or extinguishing the defendant's original obligation to the claimant, its connection with the mode or conduct of the forum court's proceedings is less significant compared to its impact on the rights of the parties. A substantive classification in this case is therefore appropriate, with the law governing the original obligation of the defendant to be applied to determine whether set-off is available.[81] Choice of such law is justified on the basis that whether a claim has been discharged by subsequent payment (the set-off) is referable to the law applicable to that claim.[82] This view accords with article 17 of the Rome I Regulation (see 10.28). The other situation is where the defendant's claim has some connection to the original obligation and some set-off effect arising by court judgment but does not extinguish or discharge the primary claim, such as in *Meyer v*

---

[78] *Wear v Farmers and Merchants Bank of Las Cruces* 605 P 2d 27 (SC Alaska 1980).

[79] Regulation (EC) 593/2008 of 17 June 2008 on the law applicable to contractual obligations.

[80] Magnus (n 71 above) 120; cf *Dicey, Morris and Collins* (n 1 above) para 32.208, where it is asserted that 'set-off' under the Regulation would be 'that type of set-off which extinguishes the obligation'.

[81] *Dicey, Morris and Collins* ibid; Magnus, ibid 118–19; Wolff (n 47 above) 234.

[82] Wood (2007) (n 69 above) para 6.002; cf Tetley, who favours the application of the law of the country with the closest connection to the parties' relationship: W Tetley, *International Conflict of Laws Common, Civil and Maritime* (International Shipping Publications, Blais, 1994) 661.

Dresser. Given the increasing trend to narrow the scope of procedure and the desirability of avoiding dépeçage and applying one law to all aspects of the case, this issue should also now be treated as substantive, especially in the light of the apparently broad approach in the Rome I Regulation.[83] Arguably, also, the focus on whether set-off extinguishes rights or not as a test for whether it is substantive has echoes of the discredited right-remedy distinction. Since all forms of set-off are in essence forms of payment or discharge[84] they clearly have a direct impact on the rights and liabilities of the parties. Some support for a broader view of what is substantive in the area of set-off comes from a decision of the Saskatchewan Court of Appeal in *Lashburn AG Ventures Ltd v Western Grain Cleaning & Processing Ltd.*[85] The case concerned an action by a seller of goods against a purchaser for failure to pay on the contract, with the purchaser claiming a right to set-off an amount which it was owed by the plaintiff's agent. The court held that the right to set-off was substantive and governed by the law of the contract against which set-off is claimed.[86]

10.30 A distinct question is whether a defendant has a right to plead set-off or to raise a counterclaim in the same proceedings or whether it must bring a separate action in respect of the plea. This matter should be left to forum law as it pertains to the court's control and management of its own proceedings.[87]

10.31 Finally, where forum legislation (such as in the area of insolvency) grants a right to set-off, this right will apply regardless of the law of the cause of action as an overriding mandatory rule of the forum.[88]

E. STATUTORY RESTRICTIONS ON REMEDIES

10.32 Also within the category of legislation affecting choice of law in matters of substance and procedure are provisions which limit a claimant's rights to

---

[83] Wood (1989) (n 69 above) paras 23.3–23.9; Bertrams (n 72 above) 159; Yeo (n 32 above) para 4.107; in *SecretHotels2Ltd v EA Traveller Ltd* [2010] EWHC 1023 (Ch) English law was applied to determine whether such a set-off existed but it is likely that it was also the law of the cause of action and no foreign law was pleaded.

[84] P Wood, *Conflict of Laws and International Finance* (Sweet & Maxwell 2007) para 13.012.

[85] (2003) 241 Sask R 97.

[86] ibid para 11.

[87] Magnus (n 71 above) 120; Crawford and Carruthers (n 74 above) para 8.26; M Illmer 'Neutrality Matters—Some Thoughts about the Rome Regulations and the so-called Dichotomy of Substance and Procedure in European Private International Law' (2009) 28 Civil Justice Quarterly 237, 247; Wood (n 84 above) para 13.013.

[88] *Re Kaupthing Singer and Friedlander Ltd (in Administration)* [2010] EWCA Civ 518; *Re Bank of Credit and Commerce International SA (No 10)* [1997] Ch 213.

312   Chapter 10: Remedies I: General Principles, Non-Monetary Relief

certain remedies, for example that a mortgagee may only recover from the mortgagor the land or the goods in an action on a mortgage but not the deficiency in the purchase price. Such legislation, which is still in force in some common law jurisdictions, has been the subject of consideration in a number of Canadian decisions. In *Canadian Acceptance Corporation v Matte*[89] the court held that the above provision, where part of forum legislation[90] did not apply to a mortgage contract that was governed by foreign law. The court, applying the right-remedy distinction, found the provision to be substantive because it extinguished the claimant's rights. The court also found that there was no offence to local public policy in allowing a foreign mortgagee to recover, on a foreign mortgage, any deficiency after the goods had been sold. The same result was reached in another Canadian decision[91] where the court again took the view that where a forum statute[92] barred the mortgagee's right to recover amounts under the mortgage, it could not apply to a mortgage governed by foreign law. Forum public policy was also not offended by allowing a foreign mortgagee to recover on a personal covenant to pay contained in a mortgage governed by foreign law in respect of foreign land. Similar results would almost certainly be reached under more contemporary versions of the substance / procedure distinction, where the scope of procedure is narrower than under the right-remedy view. No reference was made in either case, however, to whether the statute might have applied by overriding mandatory force or legislative intent.

10.33   A similar approach has also been taken when courts have considered *foreign* legislative provisions of this type. In *243930 Alberta Ltd v Wickham*[93] the Ontario Court of Appeal applied an Albertan provision[94] to an action on a mortgage governed by Albertan law. The court held the provision to be substantive and so to be applied as part of the law of the cause of action. The legislation extinguished rights by removing the personal liability of the mortgagor and so was clearly more than procedural.[95] Lacourcière JA gave a conferring judgment but expressed himself in more contemporary notions of the substance-procedure dichotomy. He applied the Cook

---

[89] (1957) 9 DLR (2d) 304 (Sask CA).
[90] Limitation of Civil Rights Act 1953 (Sask), s 18(1) re-enacted in the Limitation of Civil Rights Act 1978 (Sask), s 18(1).
[91] *Sigurdson v Farrow* (1981) 121 DLR (3d) 183 (Alta Ct QB).
[92] Judicature Act 1970 (Alta), s 34(17) re-enacted in Law of Property Act 2000 (Alta), s 40(1).
[93] (1990) 75 OR (2d) 289.
[94] Law of Property Act 1980 (Alta), s 41.
[95] *243930 Alberta Ltd v Wickham* (1990) 75 OR (2d) 289, 305 (McKinlay JA with whom Blair JA agreed).

E. Statutory Restrictions on Remedies

'inconvenience/impracticality' test, stating that foreign law should generally be applied in the forum unless it was too inconvenient to do so. Here, the foreign statute directly impacted on the parties' rights and would not be too inconvenient for the forum court to apply.[96] The same result as in *Wickham* was reached in respect of similar foreign legislation[97] in *The Bank of Nova Scotia v Beynon*,[98] where the court said that as the provision 'define[d] aspects of the rights and obligations of the parties' it was part of the substantive law.[99]

10.34 To show, however, that the issue of classification in mortgage legislation is not entirely resolved, even in an era where the category of 'procedural' matters for choice of law purposes is diminishing, attention should be drawn to a recent decision of the Saskatchewan Court of Queen's Bench in *Chrysler Financial Canada v Morris*.[100] There, a claim was brought by a mortgagee for the balance of the purchase price on a contract for the sale of a chattel which had been seized. The contract was governed by Ontario law. The question for the court was whether the remedies provision in Saskatchewan legislation[101] applied to the transaction in circumstances where it was alleged to have been breached by the mortgagee, because of its failure to serve notice on the purchaser before seizing the chattel. The relevant section provides that 'if a secured party takes possession of an implement . . . in contravention of this Part . . . (a) the agreement is deemed to be cancelled with respect to the implement (b) the farmer is released from all liability with respect to the implement under the agreement and (c) the farmer is entitled to recover from the secured party an amount equal to 1½ times the fair market value of the implement'. The court, in considering whether the provision was procedural for choice of law purposes, took a surprisingly wide view of the concept, stating that it embraced matters affecting the enforcement of the rights of a secured party[102] and 'all matters relating to the nature of a plaintiff's remedy',[103] although the court did acknowledge that there may be cases 'where right and remedy are indissolubly connected'. Here, however, the court concluded

---

[96] ibid 293–4; N Rafferty, M Baer, J Blom, E Edinger, G Saumier, and C Walsh, *Private International Law in Common Law Canada* (Edmond Montgomery Publications, 2nd edn, 2003) 543.
[97] Chattel Mortgage Act 1979 (BC), s 23.
[98] Ontario District Court, 3 April 1987.
[99] There is also US authority to the same effect, see *Stricklin v Soued* 936 P 2d 398 (CA Ore 1997).
[100] 2009 SKQB 510.
[101] Saskatchewan Farm Security Act (1989), s 55.
[102] 2009 SKQB 510, para 121.
[103] ibid para 122.

that the provision was procedural, although it did note that the remedy of giving the purchaser 1½ times the value of the chattel 'comes perilously close to affecting substantive rights'.[104]

10.35 Arguably, the court was influenced in its characterization by an unstated policy of consumer protection and the need to give recovery to a local individual with lesser bargaining power. If this view is correct, then this case may be another example where the procedural classification (here based on the right / remedy distinction) is used as a mask to conceal other policy reasons for applying forum law. An approach to applying forum law based more explicitly on legislative intention, overriding mandatory rules or public policy, is preferable.

---

[104] ibid para 164.

11

Remedies II: Damages and Statutory Compensation

A. The Common Law Position	11.02
1. Heads of Damages	11.02
2. Interest	11.03
3. Deductibility of Benefits	11.09
4. Alternative Compensation Schemes	11.14
5. Remoteness of Damage	11.16
6. Quantification of Damages	11.17
7. Public Policy	11.37
8. Overriding Mandatory Rules	11.38
9. Rules for Displacement of the Applicable Law	11.39
10. Conditions Precedent/Notice before Action Requirements	11.48
11. Jurisdictional Control?	11.50
B. The EU Instruments	11.52
1. Applicable Law and Damages	11.53
2. Public Policy and Overriding Mandatory Rules	11.60
3. Applicable Law and Displacement	11.62
4. Recent English Decisions on Rome II	11.65
C. The US Position	11.68
1. Damages	11.68
2. Interest	11.72

11.01 Under common law cases of tort and contract, the distinction between substance and procedure has arisen frequently in relation to a number of issues concerning damages, in particular, limitations on damages and the issue of quantification or assessment. Questions have also arisen about the proper role of public policy in protecting the interests of the forum. In the United Kingdom, in the case of tort and contract, EU instruments now apply: specifically, in the case of contracts entered into before 17 December 2009, the Rome Convention and, on or after that date, the Rome I Regulation. In the case of torts or 'non-contractual obligations' there is some uncertainty as to precisely when the Rome II Regulation operates, although the preferred view among English courts[1] and commentators[2] is that it applies where the events giving rise to the damage occurred on or after 20 August 2007 and where legal proceedings in respect of such events were commenced on or after 11 January 2009. The matter is, however, currently the subject of a reference to the European Court of Justice.[3] Despite these developments the common law principles are likely to remain relevant in torts cases in England, both for events giving rise to damage before the operational date of the Rome II Regulation and also as a background in Rome II cases, at least until the courts reach a settled interpretation.[4] Since the main focus of this work is on Commonwealth law principles, a detailed examination will first be made of the common law position before assessing the impact of the EU instruments in English law.

A. THE COMMON LAW POSITION

1. Heads of Damages

11.02 It is now well established in the laws of Commonwealth countries that the issue of what heads of damages may be recovered in an action in tort[5]

---

[1] *Maher v Groupama Grand Est* [2009] EWHC 38 (QB) para 16 (obiter) (affd [2010] 1 WLR 1564); *Jacobs v Motor Insurers Bureau* [2010] EWHC 231 (QB) (assumed) (revd on different grounds [2011] 1 All ER 844); *Bacon v Nacional Suiza Cia Seguros y Reseguros SA* [2010] EWHC 2017 (QB), para 61; *Bonsall v Cattolica Assicurazioni* [2010] IL Pr 45 (Winchester County Court); cf *Homawoo v GMF Assurance SA* [2010] EWHC 1941 (QB), para 49 where the 'preliminary' view was expressed that the Regulation only applies to events giving rise to damage occurring on or after 11 January 2009. (See also, to the same effect, the decision of the German Bundesgerichtshof in *Decision XaZR 19/08* (9 July 2009) referred to in A Dickinson, *The Rome II Regulation: Updating Supplement* (OUP, 2010) para 3.319A).

[2] A Dickinson, *The Rome II Regulation* (OUP, 2008) paras 3.317, 3.322; L Collins (ed), *Dicey, Morris and Collins on the Conflict of Laws* (Sweet & Maxwell, Fourth Supplement, 2010) para S35.168; cf L Heffernan, 'Rome II: Implications for Irish Tort Litigation' in J Ahern and W Binchy, *The Rome II Regulation on the Law Applicable to Non-Contractual Obligations* (Martinus Nijhoff, 2009) 257, 258, 267, who appears to favour the 11 January 2009 view.

[3] The reference was made in *Homawoo v GMF Assurance SA* [2010] EWHC 1941 (QB). Note that on 6 September 2011 the Advocate General, Mengozzi, delivered his opinion on the question referred, stating that the Regulation only applies to events giving rise to damage which occurred on or after 11 January 2009: Case C-412/10 *Homawoo v GMF Assurance SA* [2011] ECJ para 55.

[4] B Doherty, C Thomann, and K Scott, *Accidents Abroad International Personal Injury Claims* (Thomson Reuters, 2009) para 7.018 but cf A Briggs, 'When in Rome Choose as the Romans Choose' (2009) 125 LQR 191, who sees little role for the common law principles of private international law in cases under the EU instruments.

[5] *Boys v Chaplin* [1971] AC 356.

A. The Common Law Position

or contract[6] is classified as substantive and governed by the law of the cause of action. For example, in *Boys v Chaplin*[7] a majority of the House of Lords held that the right to recover damages for pain and suffering was substantive. Similar views have been expressed in other Commonwealth countries.[8] In principle, the same approach should also apply to the availability of punitive or exemplary damages,[9] at least where the recipient of such an award is a private plaintiff[10] or where an award relates to the defendant's deliberate and callous disregard of the plaintiff's rights as opposed to being a punishment for non-compliance with court orders.[11] In the latter context, a foreign law providing such damages should not be enforced in the forum on the ground that it is penal.

2. Interest

(a) Right to Pre-Judgment Interest

It is well accepted in all Commonwealth countries that the right to claim interest on a contractual debt is a matter of substance governed by the law applicable to the contract.[12] There is also support for the view that pre-judgment interest, that is, interest by way of damages dating from the time of accrual of the cause of action, is substantive and governed by the law of the obligation.[13] The position is the same in civil law countries.[14] In *Somers*

11.03

---

[6] *Livesley v Horst* [1924] SCR 605 (Sup Ct Can).
[7] [1971] AC 356.
[8] *Breavington v Godleman* (1988) 169 CLR 41.
[9] *Travelers Casualty and Surety Co of Europe Ltd v Sun Life Assurance Co of Canada (UK) Ltd* [2004] EWHC 1704 (Comm), para 77; *SA General Textiles v Sun & Sand Ltd* [1978] 1 QB 279, 299–300 (Lord Denning MR).
[10] *SA General Textiles v Sun & Sand Ltd* [1978] 1 QB 279, 299–300.
[11] *Benefit Strategies Group Inc v Prider* (2005) 91 SASR 544, paras 68, 72, 73.
[12] *Mount Albert Borough Council v Australasian Temperance and General Mutual Life Assurance Society* [1938] AC 224 (PC).
[13] In the case of torts, see eg *Maher v Groupama Grand Est* [2010] 1 WLR 1564, para 33 but note the court's findings in relation to the Senior Courts Act 1981, s 35A (discussed at 11.05 below) which arguably undercut the conclusion that interest is substantive; *Knight v Axa Assurances* [2009] EWHC 1900 (QB), para 32; *Somers v Fournier* (2002) 60 OR (3d) 225; *Gosche v Boucher* 2009 ABQB 277, para 15; *Labuda v Langford* [2001] ACTSC 126, para 6; *Goldamere v Metso Minerals* [2007] NSWSC 980, para 23; and in the case of contracts, *Miliangos v George Frank Textiles Ltd (No 2)* [1977] QB 489, 496–7. See also L Collins (ed), *Dicey, Morris and Collins on the Conflict of Laws* (Sweet & Maxwell, 14th edn, 2006) paras 7.039, 33.396; J Fawcett and J Carruthers, *Cheshire, North and Fawcett Private International Law* (OUP, 14th edn, 2008) 100; English Law Commission, *Private International Law: Foreign Money Liabilities* Law Comm No 124 (1983) paras 2.27–2.33; G Johnston, *The Conflict of Laws in Hong Kong* (Sweet & Maxwell, 2005) para 2.015.
[14] K Kerameus, 'Enforcement in the International Context' (1997) 264 *Hague Recueil* 179, 396.

318   Chapter 11: Remedies II: Damages and Statutory Compensation

v Fournier[15] the Ontario Court of Appeal described pre-judgment interest as 'akin to a head of damage, which is available to respond to a delay in the delivery of awarded compensation'.[16] A substantive classification is therefore appropriate, even though the award of such interest may be at the discretion of the court and so be 'displaced, varied or reduced where the conduct of the claimant has adversely affected the speedy process of the litigation'.[17] Pre-judgment interest is therefore an item of compensation which forms part of the award of damages for which the defendant is liable.

11.04 It has to be acknowledged, however, that a line of English authority has rejected this consensus. In *Midland International Trade Services v Sudairy*[18] (in the context of contracts) and *Kuwait Oil Tanker Co SAK v Al Bader*[19] (in the context of torts) it was held that section 35A of the Senior Courts Act 1981, which gives English courts a discretion to award interest on a debt or damages was procedural and applicable regardless of the law of the obligation. The rationale expressed for this view was that because the provision is discretionary and enables a court to take account of a variety of factors, it is appropriate to apply it in any case before an English court.[20] Yet, it is hard to see why the presence of discretion in a provision should automatically render it procedural and unfit for application by any courts other than those in the country of enactment. In this regard, the Brunei Court of Appeal[21] thought that the discretionary nature of section 35A was no impediment to that court applying the provision to award interest in relation to a contract governed by English law. According to the Brunei court, where the claimant has a 'right' to interest under foreign law 'he can insist on the court considering his claim, as a matter of law, even though [under that foreign law] the court has a discretion to refuse an award'.[22] An overriding mandatory rule, backed by local public policy, stands in a different position. Yet, in another part of the judgment in *Midland*, the court reveals perhaps the real reason for the procedural classification, which is the need to protect claimants: 'the award of interest under the statutory power reflects a broader justice and a broader power of the court to remedy injustice'.[23] Indeed, in the *Midland* case, interest was awarded

---

[15] (2002) 60 OR (3d) 225.
[16] ibid para 28.
[17] ibid para 30.
[18] Financial Times, 2 May 1990.
[19] The Independent, 11 January 1999.
[20] This view is supported by Doherty (n 4 above) para 7.027.
[21] *Brunei LNG Sendirian Berhad v Interbeton BV* [1996] BNHC 32.
[22] ibid.
[23] *Midland International Trade Services v Sudairy* Financial Times, 2 May 1990.

A. The Common Law Position

under English law in circumstances where it was forbidden under the Sharia law applicable in Saudi Arabia. Public policy therefore is arguably the true basis of the decision.[24] Unfortunately, however, as has been noted elsewhere in this work, the use of the procedural classification to apply forum law is a more blunt and opaque instrument than public policy because it has the effect of applying forum law in all cases rather than in the exceptional ones where justice so demands.

Regrettably, the procedural view of interest was recently adopted by the English Court of Appeal in *Maher v Groupama Grand Est*.[25] The argument in favour of procedural classification in that case rested on two premises. The first is that section 35A of the Senior Courts Act 1981 gives a discretion to the court, a view which has already been addressed,[26] and the second is that section 35A 'creates a remedy'[27] under the anachronistic right / remedy distinction. Yet, even if this classification of interest is accepted (which it is not), this conclusion seems hard to square with the court's comments at other points in the judgment that 'the right to recover interest [is] a head of damage', and so substantive.[28] As noted at 11.02, ever since the House of Lords decision in *Boys v Chaplin*, matters relating to heads of damages have been considered substantive. So while the court acknowledges the right of foreign law to determine whether interest is recoverable, it largely renders such law irrelevant by allowing section 35A to be used to give the 'remedy' of interest under English law in any event.

11.05

(b) Right to Post-Judgment Interest

The position with respect to 'post-judgment' interest, that is, interest payable on a judgment debt, is also controversial. According to one view, the recovery of such interest should be governed by the same principles as pre-judgment interest since it also represents 'compensation for being kept out of the money due'.[29] The consequence of this approach is that a substantive classification should be adopted, presumably with the law of the cause of action in the judgment being applied to determine whether such

11.06

---

[24] The same may also be said of the decision in *Abdel Hadi Abdallah Al Qahtari & Sons Beverage Industry Co v Antliff* [2010] EWHC 1735 (Comm), para 58.

[25] [2010] 1 WLR 1564, para 37 followed in *Abdel Hadi Abdallah Al Qahtari & Sons Beverage Industry Co v Antliff* [2010] EWHC 1735 (Comm).

[26] See 11.04 above.

[27] [2010] 1 WLR 1564, para 37.

[28] ibid paras 33, 40.

[29] Singapore Academy of Law Law Reform Committee, Report on Pre- and Post-Judgment Interest (2005) para 180, at <http://www.agc.gov.sg/publications/docs/LRC_Report_on_Interest-August_2005.pdf> (accessed October 2011); *Livesley v Horst* [1924] SCR 605, 610.

interest should be awarded. Yet it can also be argued that post-judgment interest is less a matter of compensation to the claimant and more a means by which the forum enforces or sanctions compliance with its judgments,[30] similar to a form of execution, as discussed at 6.78–6.80. Seen in this way, post-judgment interest would be classified as procedural but governed by the law of the country where the judgment was rendered, in the case of a forum judgment and the law of the place of enforcement in the case of a foreign judgment which is sought to be enforced in the forum. English authority appears to support this view.[31]

(c) Rate of Interest

11.07 The question of the right to pre-judgment interest on damages must also be distinguished from the *rate* at which such interest may be charged. Here there again appears a split within the Commonwealth countries. In Canada, there is support for the position that the rate of interest on damages is substantive.[32] Under the Australian mode or conduct of court proceedings or outcome determinative tests of substance and procedure the same result is likely to be reached. Not only could a different rate of interest under the law of the obligation alter the final quantum of damages considerably, there is no particular connection between interest and the regulation of court proceedings, and the application of foreign rules on the rate of interest would hardly be impractical. In England, however, it has long been considered that the rate of interest on a debt is procedural and governed by forum law by analogy with the issue of assessment of damages.[33] The conclusion that the rate of interest was procedural was also assumed in the tort context in *Harding and Wealands*,[34] where the House of Lords had to consider whether New South Wales legislation, which included provisions providing for a larger discount rate on damages than would be available under English law, applied in English proceedings. The court held that such a provision, along with others limiting the right to damages, was procedural and not applicable in England. This finding suggests an unwillingness to import the rate of interest under New South Wales law on the basis that it was a matter of assessment of damages, and

---

[30] ibid.

[31] *Gater Assets Ltd v NAK Naftogaz Ukrainy* [2008] EWHC 1108, (Comm) para 27; see also Doherty (n 4 above) para 7.028; and Johnston (n 13 above) para 2.015.

[32] *Livesley v Horst* [1924] SCR 605, 610; *Viktor Overseas Ltd v Deuilemar Compagnia di Navigazione SpA* 1997 FC 6298.

[33] *Miliangos v George Frank (Textiles) Ltd (No 2)* [1977] QB 489, 497; *Lesotho Highlands Development Authority v Impregilo Sp A* [2002] EWHC 2435 (Comm); *Rogers v Markel Corp* [2004] EWHC 1375 (QB); *Dicey, Morris and Collins* (n 13 above) R 226(2).

[34] [2007] 2 AC 1.

A. The Common Law Position

so procedural. As will be argued, the concept of 'assessment' should have no application to the content or amount of the damages award, any aspect of which is substantive; rather it should refer (at most) to the mechanical or factual process by which the award is established. Applying this view, the rate of interest on damages must accordingly be substantive and it is interesting to note that Kerr J (obiter), in *Helmsing v Malta Drydocks*,[35] reached the same conclusion.

Finally, some English judges have noted that even a finding that English law applies to the rate of interest does not mean that foreign law principles are irrelevant. There is scope here, again, for the application of an 'enlightened *lex fori*' under section 35A of the Senior Courts Act 1981, which gives courts a wide discretion to determine the appropriate rate, including taking note of the position under foreign law.[36] While such an approach has the scope to temper the forum-centredness of the procedural classification, this is surely a less certain and predictable route than applying the foreign law on interest directly. **11.08**

3. Deductibility of Benefits

Another issue of uncertainty in respect of the classification of damages in private international law is the reduction of, or deductibility from, an award of damages of benefits already received by the claimant. This issue arose in the Court of Appeal decision in *Roerig v Valiant Trawlers Ltd*.[37] That case involved a Dutch woman bringing a claim under the Fatal Accidents Act 1976 (UK), in respect of the death of her Dutch husband, who was killed in an accident involving a ship owned by the defendants while the ship was in English territorial waters. The claimant, having already received benefits under Dutch law, was successful on her primary argument that English law (including the Act) applied to the wrong, but the court found that even if Dutch law had governed the action, section 4 of the Act would have applied in the English proceedings as a procedural provision. Section 4 provides that, in assessing damages in respect of a person's death under the Act, benefits which have accrued to any person from the deceased's estate or otherwise as a result of his or her death shall be disregarded in any award of damages. Consequently, the benefits that accrued to the deceased under Dutch social security law would not be taken into account in awarding damages under English law, unlike under **11.09**

---

[35] [1977] 2 Lloyd's Rep 444, 449–50.
[36] *Maher v Groupama Grand Est* [2009] EWHC 38 (QB), para 33; *Dicey, Morris and Collins* (n 13 above) para 33.398
[37] [2002] 1 WLR 2304 (CA).

Dutch law where such benefits would have been deducted. Interestingly, while the court based its application of forum law on the fact that the issue of deductibility of benefits was procedural, it did note that 'policy considerations'[38] played a role in this conclusion, although the nature of these was unstated. Possibly the court was concerned not to limit the claimant's scope for redress but further development of this point would have been valuable. Alternatively, the 'policy considerations' to which the court was referring may have been the fact that section 4 must be applied as an overriding mandatory rule of English law.[39] Again, if this interpretation is correct, it would be a preferable means of applying forum law than the procedural classification but the reasoning is not completely clear.

11.10 The outcome reached in the *Roerig* case regarding the classification of benefits is consistent with the earlier English decision in *Coupland v Arabian Gulf Petroleum Co*,[40] where Hodgson J held that a Libyan rule pursuant to which social security and labour benefits were not deductible from an award of damages was a matter of quantification, and so not applicable in an action in England. The position in *Roerig* still probably represents English common law. Given the very broad interpretation made by the House of Lords in *Harding v Wealands* regarding the concept of quantification as including any limits on damages, a provision under foreign law which reduced damages by reference to benefits received would almost certainly be classified as procedural and not applicable in English proceedings.

11.11 The approach in *Roerig* differs from the position taken in other Commonwealth countries. For example, in Canada it is well established that the deductibility of benefits under a no-fault compensation scheme is not a matter of quantification but is classified as a head of damage and so is substantive. The result therefore is that a claimant's award of damages under foreign law is unaffected by the fact that it has received benefits under the law of the forum.[41] In Australia a slightly different approach is taken to that in Canada, although the same outcome has been reached.

---

[38] ibid para 26.

[39] ibid paras 28–30; this was the view taken of the decision by Arden LJ in *Harding v Wealands* [2005] 1 WLR 1539, para 48.

[40] [1983] 1 WLR 1136.

[41] *Britton v O'Callaghan* (2002) 62 OR (3d) 95, para 10 (Ont CA); *Salminen v Emerald Taxi Ltd* OSCJ 14 Oct 1999; *George v Gubernowicz* (1999) 44 OR (3d) 247, 251. cf D Garrow, D Hansen, and M Parkes, 'Damages for Personal Injury or Wrongful Death in Canada' (2004) 69 Journal of Air Law and Commerce 233, 248, n 61 who argue that a procedural classification of benefits is warranted because they 'offset rather than increase the loss suffered by the plaintiff' and so are a matter of quantification.

A. The Common Law Position

As will be discussed,[42] Australian common law, at least in the case of interstate torts, considers all matters relating to damages (including quantification) as substantive. Consequently, in *BHP Billiton Ltd v Schultz*[43] two judges of the Australian High Court[44] declared that a provision which provides that a successful plaintiff's damages for non-economic loss should not be reduced for workers' compensation that he or she has received[45] is substantive.

11.12 Australian courts have also considered the slightly different question of how to classify a provision which has the effect of reducing an award of damages due to the fraud or other bad conduct of the claimant. For example, section 66 of the Motor Accidents Act 1988 (NSW) provides '(1) that if a claimant, for the purpose of obtaining a financial benefit did or omitted to do anything concerning a motor accident or any claim relating to a motor accident with the knowledge that the doing of the thing or omission to do the thing was false or misleading . . . (2)(a) a person who has a liability in respect of a payment, settlement compromise or judgment is relieved from that liability to the extent of the financial benefit so obtained by the claimant'. In *Zardo v Ivancic*[46] the Australian Capital Territory Supreme Court held that the effect of the above provision is that it 'relieves a person of liability to the extent mentioned' and so is 'plainly substantive'. The reduction of damages for fraud or other bad conduct of the claimant arguably operates in a similar way to the defence of contributory negligence in that it provides for the reduction and apportionment of the claimant's damages. It was noted at 7.21 that the plea of contributory negligence is considered substantive under English law.[47]

11.13 Reduction of damages also used to occur under Australian law in the context of multi-jurisdictional defamation litigation, where a claimant had already recovered damages in a previous action in respect of the same publication.[48] Statutory provisions operated to reduce the amount of recoverable damages in the forum where there existed matters which may 'mitigate or reduce the damages that may be recovered' and were held to be substantive.[49]

---

[42] See 11.20 and 11.32 below.
[43] (2004) 221 CLR 400.
[44] ibid para 148, n 257 (Kirby J); para 251 (Callinan J).
[45] Dust Diseases Tribunal Act 1989 (NSW), s 12D.
[46] (2001) 161 FLR 228, para 19.
[47] *Dawson v Broughton* (2007) 151 Sol Jnl 1167 (Manchester County Court); *Harding v Wealands* [2007] 2 AC 1, para 74 (Lord Rodger).
[48] See eg Civil Law (Wrongs) Act 2002 (ACT), s 135.
[49] *Lewincamp v ACP Magazines Ltd* [2008] ACTSC 69, para 346.

324 Chapter 11: Remedies II: Damages and Statutory Compensation

4. Alternative Compensation Schemes

11.14 A different situation which can arise in tort claims is where alternative compensation arrangements, such as an administrative no-fault scheme, operate. Such schemes operate in a number of Commonwealth jurisdictions, including New Zealand, the Canadian provinces of Quebec and Ontario, and the Australian state of Victoria and typically apply to traffic and/or workplace accidents. Where the particular scheme entirely abolishes the common law right to sue then it is clearly substantive and applicable as part of the law of the cause of action. In two early Privy Council decisions on appeal from Canada, it was held that the existence of a no-fault workers' compensation scheme, which removed the right to bring a civil claim in tort under the law of the place of the wrong, meant that no action could be brought in the forum.[50] This conclusion was reached in the context of interpreting the second limb of the double actionability choice of law rule[51] (which required that a wrong be actionable under the law of the place where it was committed). Arguably, however, this reasoning would equally apply in the context of a choice of law rule which presumptively selects the law of the place of the wrong (as is the case in England, Canada, and Australia) to bar suit on the foreign wrong in the forum, on the basis that the bar is substantive.[52] Such a conclusion can be supported on the basis that the claimant's right to sue in respect of all or any[53] heads of damages has been extinguished.

11.15 More recent decisions in Australia and Canada have confirmed that no-fault compensation schemes are substantive and can operate to bar suit in the forum where the scheme is part of the law of cause of action. Although, as has been noted throughout this work, Canadian and Australian courts apply a more limited concept of procedure to that generally accepted under English common law, it is suggested that a substantive classification should be universally adopted. In *Lucas v Gagnon*,[54] the Supreme Court of Canada held on appeal from Ontario that the Quebec no-fault insurance scheme, which removed the right to sue for traffic accidents, applied to an accident which occurred in Quebec. The same result has

---

[50] *McMillan v Canadian Northern Railway Co* [1923] AC 120; *Walpole v Canadian Northern Railway Co* [1923] AC 113.
[51] *Phillips v Eyre* (1870) LR 6 QB 1.
[52] R Tobin and E Schoeman, 'The New Zealand Accident Compensation Scheme: the Statutory Bar and the Conflict of Laws' (2005) 53 AJCL 493, 499, 503–4, 512–13.
[53] Note that the New Zealand scheme allows a claimant to sue to recover exemplary damages in certain circumstances but removes the right to recover compensatory damages: Tobin and Schoeman (n 52 above) 503–4.
[54] (1994) 120 DLR (4th) 289.

A. The Common Law Position

been reached in respect of a bar on recovery of pecuniary damages under the Ontario statutory no-fault scheme.[55] Similarly, in *Amaca Pty Ltd v Frost*,[56] the New South Wales Court of Appeal applied the New Zealand statutory no-fault scheme to a tort committed in that country with both parties accepting that the effect of the no-fault scheme was substantive.[57] The willingness of Commonwealth courts to classify no-fault administrative schemes as substantive is also evident from the Ontario Court of Appeal decision in *Chomos v Economical Mutual Insurance Co*.[58] In that case the court held that a forum no-fault scheme was substantive despite the fact that the scheme contained provisions dealing with quantification of damages which, according to Canadian law principles, would be considered as procedural. For example, section 267(1) of the Insurance Act (Ontario) provides immunity from actions in Ontario for loss or damage for bodily injury arising out of motor vehicles subject to an exception for damages for non-pecuniary losses which meet a numerical threshold. The presence of this quantification provision in the no-fault scheme was held not to alter the fundamentally substantive nature of the scheme; indeed the sub-section was described as 'integral' to it.[59] The court in *Chomos* therefore took the 'holistic' approach to characterization referred to at 3.04–3.05, a tendency which is also evident in the judgments of Waller LJ[60] and Sir William Aldous[61] (but not Arden LJ)[62] of the English Court of Appeal in *Harding v Wealands*. Instead of focusing on a specific provision and considering its classification in isolation, the court considers its place in the legislation as a whole, which avoids choice of law fragmentation and dépeçage.[63] Such an approach seems entirely appropriate in the context of a no-fault scheme which would be undermined and unduly complicated if a law other than that which enacted the scheme were to be applied to individual parts of the scheme. In the case of legislation, however, which does not constitute a single codified scheme but addresses a number of distinct issues, a more provision-specific approach to classification, such as that advocated by Arden LJ in *Harding v Wealands*, is more desirable.

---

[55] *Wong v Lee* (2002) 58 OR (3d) 398, para 21 (Ont CA).
[56] (2006) 67 NSWLR 635.
[57] This was also the conclusion reached in the earlier decision of the New South Wales Court of Appeal in *James Hardie & Co Pty Ltd v Hall* (1998) 43 NSWLR 554.
[58] (2002) 216 DLR (4th) 356.
[59] ibid para 51.
[60] *Harding v Wealands* [2005] 1 WLR 1539, paras 30, 33 (revd on other grounds [2007] 2 AC 1 (HL)).
[61] ibid para 85.
[62] ibid para 66.
[63] See also *Plamondon v Aviva Canada Inc* 2008 ONSC 61240, para 11.

5. REMOTENESS OF DAMAGE

11.16 It is well established in Commonwealth countries, that the question of remoteness of damage is classified as substantive and governed by the law of the action.[64] *D'Almeida Aranjo Ida v Sir Frederick Becker & Co Ltd*[65] concerned a contract governed by Portuguese law whereby the claimant seller agreed to purchase goods from a third party supplier in Portugal, agreeing to open a letter of credit in favour of the supplier and to pay the supplier an indemnity in the event of breach of contract. The defendant purchaser had also agreed with the claimant to make payment by opening a letter of credit in the seller's favour but failed to do so. The result was that the claimant was liable to the supplier for the amount of the indemnity and sought this amount in a suit against the defendant. Pilcher J held that the issue of whether the claimant could recover the indemnity depended on whether the damage was too remote, which was a substantive matter, governed by the law applicable to the parties' contract. Such a conclusion is consistent with either the narrow 'machinery of litigation' or the remedial view of procedure.

6. QUANTIFICATION OF DAMAGES

(a) Legislative or Judicial Limitations on Damages

11.17 The issue of quantification is arguably the most contentious and uncertain in the whole topic of damages. It is also highly significant because the rules and practices of quantification, particularly in personal injury claims, vary widely from country to country. One of the difficulties concerns definition and identifying exactly what matters the term quantification embraces. Historically, Commonwealth courts have considered quantification to embrace both the status of legislative or judicial limitations or 'caps' on damages and the methods of computation or assessment of damages, for instance by periodical or 'once and for all' payments. It is strongly argued that a limitation on damages is not a matter of quantification, since it may have the effect of significantly altering the scope of the defendant's liability and is often a reflection of a carefully considered policy determination by the particular legislature to limit the price of insurance. The issue of nomenclature in the context of quantification is important because it may have subtly contributed to some Commonwealth courts making an

---

[64] *D'Almeida Aranjo Ida v Sir Frederick Becker & Co Ltd* [1953] 2 KB 329; *Livesley v Horst Co* [1924] SCR 605; *Harding v Wealands* [2005] 1 WLR 1539, para 56 (Arden LJ) (revd on other grounds [2007] 2 AC 1 (HL)).

[65] ibid.

A. The Common Law Position

erroneous application of the substance / procedure distinction in relation to this issue.

The leading English decision on the status of limitations on damages is *Harding v Wealands*.[66] There the House of Lords, reversing the Court of Appeal, held that all matters relating to the quantification of damages are classified as procedural at common law and governed by the law of the forum and that a statutory limitation on damages was an issue of quantification. The same conclusion applied in respect of proceedings under the Private International Law (Miscellaneous Provisions) Act 1995 (UK) (PILA 1995). This case has already been criticized, in Chapter 2 for its reliance on the outdated right-remedy view of substance and procedure and its reluctance to consider whether the concept of 'procedure' may have been updated since the enactment of the PILA 1995. Further, on the specific question of caps or limits on damages, the House of Lords was content to treat this issue as a matter of quantification—and so procedural—with little discussion.

11.18

The *Harding* case involved an accident in New South Wales and under section 11 of the PILA 1995, New South Wales law applied as the law of the cause of action which included the Motor Accidents Compensation Act 1999 (MACA 1999). A key object of the MACA 1999 was to reduce the compensation for injuries in motor accidents and so maintain the affordability of insurance for New South Wales residents. To implement this objective, limits are placed on the amounts recoverable for general damages for non-economic loss, for loss of earnings, and for gratuitous care, as well as prohibiting any award for the first five days' loss of earning capacity. Also, the discount rate on damages in respect of future economic loss was twice that available under English law. The result was that the claimant stood to gain 30 per cent more in terms of damages under English law than he would have obtained under the law of New South Wales. The House of Lords held that all of the above provisions of the MACA 1999, in imposing limitations on the amount of damages available to the claimant, were procedural and so not applicable in the English proceedings. As discussed in Chapter 2, a major reason for the court's conclusion was its insistence that in interpreting the word 'procedure' in section 14(3)(b) of the PILA 1995, the court had to apply the meaning that existed at the time of enactment of the legislation.[67] According to the court, the concept of 'procedure' in 1995 embraced all aspects of quantification of damages,

11.19

---

[66] [2007] 2 AC 1.
[67] ibid para 51 (Lord Hoffmann).

including limitations on damages, on the basis that this issue relates to the 'remedy' rather than the right.

11.20 In adopting a procedural characterization of the provisions in the New South Wales legislation the House of Lords also relied heavily[68] on the majority decision of the High Court of Australia in *Stevens v Head*,[69] which involved an action in Queensland arising out of a traffic accident in New South Wales. In that case, the majority held that statutory provisions in New South Wales which limited the right to damages were matters related to quantification and so procedural and not applicable in the Queensland proceedings. The decision in the *Stevens* case was, however, expressly rejected by the High Court in the later case of *John Pfeiffer Pty Ltd v Rogerson*,[70] where it was held that provisions of New South Wales legislation, which limited damages payable to an injured employee, applied in an action in the Australian Capital Territory (ACT) in respect of an accident in New South Wales. The court in *Pfeiffer* considered that the issue of limitation of damages was substantive because it was outcome determinative and did not relate to the mode or conduct of court proceedings. Furthermore, the court said, 'all questions about the . . . amount of damages that may be recovered would . . . be treated as substantive issues'.[71] While this last observation went beyond the precise issue for determination in the case—that is, the status of limitations on damages—to apparently declaring that all aspects of quantification were substantive, its intention as far as limitations were concerned was clear.

11.21 Consequently, in later cases involving interstate torts in Australia involving a cap on damages under the law of the cause of action, courts have unhesitatingly treated such provisions as substantive and applicable in proceedings in the forum.[72] The High Court, however, suggested in the later decision in *Regie Nationale des Usines Renault v Zhang*[73] that it would reserve, for a future occasion, the applicability of the statement from *Pfeiffer* for *international* as opposed to interstate torts. The House of Lords in the *Harding* case seized on this concession in *Zhang* to declare that both the narrow *Pfeiffer* interpretation of 'procedure' and its statement on quantification of damages were dictated by constitutional demands unique to federal systems and so inapplicable in England.[74] Yet the House of Lords

---

[68] ibid paras 39–40 (Lord Hoffmann); para 72 (Lord Rodger).
[69] (1993) 176 CLR 433.
[70] (2000) 203 CLR 503.
[71] ibid para 100 (Gleeson CJ, Gaudron, McHugh, Gummow and Hayne JJ).
[72] See eg *McNeilly v Imbree* [2007] NSWCA 156; *Godin v Godin* [2003] WADC 21, para 8.
[73] (2002) 210 CLR 491, para 76 (Gleeson CJ, Gaudron, McHugh, Gummow, and Hayne JJ).
[74] [2007] 2 AC 1, para 48 (Lord Hoffmann).

A. The Common Law Position

may have been mistaken on both issues. First, on the question of the definition of 'procedure', as already argued,[75] the reservation in *Zhang* was not directed at this issue but only the question of damages. Secondly, as discussed later,[76] even on the issue of quantification, Australian courts in later cases appear to have applied the statement in *Pfeiffer* on damages to international cases, regardless of the qualification in *Zhang*.

Interestingly, the House of Lords in *Harding v Wealands* rejected[77] the interpretation of the *Cope v Doherty*[78] decision made by the editors of *Dicey, Morris and Collins*. The *Cope* case involved a statute which imposed a contractual term limiting the amount of damages, which was properly held to be substantive but, the court said in *Harding*, where a statute does not create a contractual term it should instead be deemed procedural. It is frankly hard to see why the applicable law in relation to limitation on damages should depend upon the cause of action pleaded by the claimant, particularly where in the case of tort and contract it will often be possible to plead interchangeably (such as in employment cases).[79] Such a result only encourages adroit pleading and 'cause of action shopping'. Yet the House of Lords appeared content to accept different choice of law rules for contract and tort damages, not simply derived from *Cope v Doherty* but also the Rome Convention, pursuant to which a cap on damages is clearly governed by the applicable law of the contract.[80] **11.22**

Of course, the House of Lords in the *Harding* case could have rejected the breadth of the *Pfeiffer* statement on damages and still found that statutory limitations on damages were substantive, given their closer proximity to the issue of liability. Yet it preferred to place this matter within the rubric of quantification, which meant that a procedural classification was easier to justify. Policy discussion, other than an insufficiently articulated concern to provide an English resident claimant with full compensation, was rather lacking in the House of Lords decision in *Harding*. Only one member of the court, Lord Rodger, appeared mindful of the danger of an expansive interpretation of procedure in the area of quantification of damages, noting that it 'may be criticised as being liable to encourage forum shopping'.[81] **11.23**

---

[75] See 2.37 above.
[76] See 11.32 below.
[77] [2007] 2 AC 1, para 46 (Lord Hoffmann).
[78] (1858) 4 K & J 367.
[79] A Gray, 'Loss Distribution Issues in Multinational Tort Claims: Giving Substance to Substance' (2008) 4 JPIL 279, 294.
[80] See Rome Convention, art 10(1)(c) and Rome I, art 12(1)(c).
[81] [2007] 2 AC 1, para 64.

Yet, in the judge's view, 'the policy of the legislature' must prevail.[82] Lord Rodger also acknowledged the consequences for the defendant's insurers of applying English law to the question of quantification but felt that 'the impact on the [NSW] scheme of applying a different scale of damages . . . is unlikely to be anything other than marginal'.[83] While such a conclusion may be true of the New South Wales legislative scheme *as a whole* it is unlikely that the individual insurer in this case would see the matter in such terms.

11.24 The status of limitations on damages has also arisen in Canada, although slightly curiously, despite the narrow 'machinery of litigation' view of procedure espoused in the *Tolofson* case, courts have generally classified the issue as procedural. It is slightly ironic, then, that the House of Lords in *Harding* implicitly referred to Canadian law as supporting a substantive characterization of limitations on damages;[84] in fact its true position is closer to the House of Lords' own preferred view. In *Wong v Wei*[85] the British Columbia Supreme Court held that a judicially-imposed limitation on the amount of non-pecuniary damages under British Columbian law applied to a tort that was governed by the substantive law of California. The limitation on damages was a matter of quantification or assessment and so procedural and applicable as part of the law of the forum.[86] The court relied on *Stevens v Head* to support this conclusion. In *Somers v Fournier*[87] the Ontario Court of Appeal approved the decision in *Wong v Wei* and applied a judicial limitation on non-pecuniary damages under Ontario law to an action arising from an accident in New York. The court noted that the judicial restriction on damages was a 'device developed in Canada to avoid excessive and unpredictable damages awards concerning non-pecuniary losses and the corresponding burden on society which follows from such awards'.[88] The limitation was therefore said to be a matter of quantification of damages and so procedural.

11.25 Two points should, however, be noted about these decisions. First, these are cases in which the limitation on damages existed under the law of the *forum* not the law of the cause of action and the limitation seems to have been applied at least, according to the Ontario court, more for policy reasons than because it was procedural. If this analysis is correct, then the Canadian cases may be distinguished from *Harding, Stevens,* and *Pfeiffer,*

---

[82] ibid.
[83] ibid para 77.
[84] ibid para 69 (Lord Rodger).
[85] (1999) 65 BCLR (3d) 222.
[86] ibid para 40.
[87] (2002) 60 OR (3d) 225.
[88] ibid para 57.

A. The Common Law Position

where a claimant was suing in the forum to avoid a cap on damages under the law of the cause of action. Accordingly, in *Wong* and *Somers*, the Canadian courts may well have felt that they were causing no offence to the foreign state by not applying its unlimited law on damages. By contrast, there was a clear forum policy that needed vindication. Such decisions may therefore be seen as more consistent with an overriding mandatory rule/public policy analysis for applying forum law.

The same justification cannot, however, be made of the Ontario Court of Appeal decision in *Craig v Allstate Insurance Co of Canada*.[89] *Craig* involved an action in Ontario arising out of a road accident in Florida which was subject to a cap on damages under Florida sovereign immunity legislation. The court refused to apply the limitation on the basis that it did not 'remove or extinguish all liability of a tortfeasor or its insurer'.[90] 'A limitation on the ability of an injured motorist to recover damages from a tortfeasor or its insurer is not the equivalent of a statutory bar to an action, a statutory ... immunity from suit provision or other absolute disentitlement to sue or seek relief through the courts.'[91] The court therefore seems to be limiting the substantive category in the context of damages to available heads of damages and total abrogation of the right to sue. Limitations or restrictions on liability, by contrast, are procedural. Such a view corresponds closely to that taken by the House of Lords in *Harding* and the High Court in *Stevens*. As argued at 11.20, however, it is clearly inconsistent with a limited definition of procedure based on the mode or conduct of court proceedings or an expanded concept of substance based on impact on the rights of the parties.[92]

11.26

(b) Numerical Assessment and Methods

In all Commonwealth countries apart from Australia the quantification of damages in terms of the numerical or factual process of computation and the method of assessment to be adopted are considered procedural and governed by the law of the forum. So, in a number of cases involving British holidaymakers who suffered personal injury abroad and then returned to England to sue, English provisions on quantification of damages were routinely applied in preference to those under foreign law on the basis that they were procedural.[93] Such a finding has had great practical significance

11.27

---

[89] (2002) 59 OR (3d) 590.
[90] ibid para 19.
[91] ibid paras 20, 26.
[92] *Dicey, Morris and Collins* (n 13 above) para 7.041.
[93] *Edmunds v Simmonds* [2001] 1 WLR 1003 (QBD); *Hulse v Chambers* [2001] 1 WLR 2386, para 9; *Kohnke v Karger* [1951] 2 KB 670.

given that English damages awards are substantially higher than those available in other European countries. No evidence was led in those cases to suggest that application of the foreign rules on quantification would be unduly impractical or onerous for the English court; it seems more likely that English courts felt that English habitual residents were entitled to receive damages under English law wherever they were injured. In effect, therefore, the procedural classification was arguably used to conceal a law of habitual residence rule being applied to quantification. Lord Rodger admitted as much in *Harding v Wealands* when he stated that quantification should, where possible, correspond to the social environment of the place where the claimant resides, presumably taking into account cost of living and career expectations.[94]

11.28 There are also methods of assessment under foreign law which, at least before the Rome II Regulation, an English court was not thought capable of adopting. For example, section 32A of the Senior Courts Act 1981 (UK) provides that an English court must award damages on a 'once and for all' basis except in cases where provisional damages are awarded in a personal injury case. There has traditionally been no scope for the award of periodical payments or revision of awards in the light of events subsequent to the delivery of judgment, although in the case of periodical payments at least, there is some evidence that this position has recently changed.[95] There is also scope for the award of revised damages under some Australian legislation.[96] Yet, while some writers[97] and courts[98] have suggested that such foreign provisions should not apply in proceedings in the forum because they are procedural, it is hard to see an obvious connection with the machinery of litigation or a particular reason of inconvenience in applying such approaches to awarding damages under foreign law. There should, therefore, be no obstacle to a Commonwealth court relying on foreign law to impose conditions on damages awards or to allow parties to bring subsequent proceedings for the alteration of quantum.[99] Interestingly, four judges of the High Court of Australia recently

---

[94] [2007] 2 AC 1 para 70.

[95] See eg *Cobham Hire Services Ltd v Eeles* [2009] EWCA Civ 204.

[96] See eg Dust Diseases Tribunal Act 1989 (NSW), s 11A.

[97] *Dicey, Morris and Collins* (n 13 above) para 7.038; T Petch, 'Substance and Procedure' (2005) 121 LQR 370, 373.

[98] *Harding v Wealands* [2005] 1 WLR 1539, para 57 (Arden LJ) (revd on other grounds [2007] 2 AC 1); *Stevens v Head* (1993) 176 CLR 433, 449 (Mason CJ). In *Hulse v Chambers* [2001] 1 WLR 2386, para 7 it was conceded by the defendant that an English court could not make an order for instalment payments, which was capable of subsequent review, similar to that which existed under Greek law, because it would be too inconvenient.

[99] A Briggs, 'Conflict of Laws and Commercial Remedies' in A Burrows and E Peel (eds), *Commercial Remedies Current Issues and Problems* (OUP, 2003) 271, 275; *Cheshire, North and*

A. The Common Law Position

suggested that the provision referred to earlier[100] which allows for the revision of damages awards is substantive since it deprives the defendant of the right of having damages finally assessed.[101]

Provisions, by contrast, which relate to the *institution* or body which conducts the assessment, whether by judge, jury, or special assessor, arguably stand in a separate category, given the difficulties for the forum court in replicating such bodies.[102] As was stated by David Richards J:[103] 'There is no question of an English court empanelling a jury to assess the damages [in accordance with foreign law].' **11.29**

Next, the mechanical or computational process of assessment in which monetary value is assigned to individual items of loss is essentially a question of fact which must be determined by the forum. Yet there seems to be no reason why, even in relation this issue, the forum court could not receive evidence from foreign experts as to the likely ranges of recovery and formulae of calculation in the event that the matter went to trial in the foreign country. Commonwealth courts routinely take this approach in the case of a settlement on behalf of a minor in domestic litigation. In such a case a court will not approve a settlement unless it is shown to be in the best interests of the minor, which is established by counsel producing figures of what a claimant in the minor's position would reasonably expect to obtain at trial.[104] Moreover, the forum court has the flexibility when assessing damages to take into account the particular social and economic circumstances of the claimant, including the living standards of the country in which he or she resides. To that extent, even the 'factual' process of assessment may be informed by foreign elements. There is evidence of this approach being taken by courts in civil law countries. So, in a Danish decision,[105] compensation was calculated in the context of a Hungarian resident claimant who was injured in Denmark on the basis of the cost of living in Hungary, and in a Swiss decision,[106] assessment of damages for a Serbian resident claimant injured in Switzerland was based on the fact that the normal cost of **11.30**

Fawcett (n 13 above) 847 (said in the context of the Rome II Regulation but arguably expressing a general view about the capacity of an English court to award periodical payments).

[100] Dust Diseases Tribunal Act 1989 (NSW), s 11A.
[101] *BHP Billiton Ltd v Schultz* (2004) 221 CLR 400, para 79 (Gummow J); para 147 (Kirby J); para 177 (Hayne J); para 226 (Callinan J); see also (more recently) *Wallaby Grip Ltd v Gilchrist* [2007] NSWSC 1181, para 40; *Amaca Pty Ltd v Aartsen* [2011] NSWSC 676, para 45.
[102] *Harding v Wealands* [2007] 2 AC 1, para 11 (Lord Woolf); *Re T & N Ltd* [2005] EWHC 2990 (Ch), para 83.
[103] *Re T & N Ltd* [2005] EWHC 2990 (Ch) para 83.
[104] In the Australian context, see *Yu Ge v River Island Clothing Pty Ltd* [2002] NSWSC 28.
[105] *Doczi v Zurich Forsikring* [1992] ECLY 2398.
[106] *Obergericht Thurgau* [2001] ECLY 1315.

334   *Chapter 11: Remedies II: Damages and Statutory Compensation*

living in Serbia was significantly lower than that prevailing in Switzerland. The court noted that where, by contrast, living costs differed only marginally from those in Switzerland, the forum's standards of calculation must be used. Similarly, in a Japanese decision,[107] the damages for Sri Lankan claimants who brought an action arising out of the wrongful death of a Sri Lankan resident in Japan were assessed according to the dramatically lower cost of living in Sri Lanka compared to that of Japan. As discussed at 11.58, a similar approach may be taken in cases under the Rome II Regulation, namely that a court can take into account as 'facts' in assessing quantum the 'social and economic conditions' of a country.[108]

11.31 It is therefore contended that it is no more difficult to apply foreign rules of calculation or assessment of damages than other foreign provisions on damages, in the absence of any unique institutional features. Moreover, expanding the scope given to the applicable law can be justified on the ground that fragmentation and dépeçage of laws in the context of damages should be avoided for the sake of simplicity and coherence and deterring forum shopping.[109] The law of damages in each country is normally conceived of as an entire, indivisible 'package' with heads of damages and rules of assessment to be applied together, not separated. As has been noted, civil liability has little value unless it also embraces quantum of damages, especially in personal injury where damage is the gist of the action.[110] This last observation falls within the broader argument in this work,[111] that right and remedy are indissolubly connected and should not be divided for choice of law purposes.[112] The link between liability

---

[107] *X1, X2 and X3 v Y* Tokyo High Court 25 January 2001 (2002) 45 Japanese Annual of International Law 155.

[108] *Cheshire, North and Fawcett* (n 13 above) 844 but cf the view of the Singapore Court of Appeal in *Goh Suan Hee v Teo Cher Teck* [2009] SGCA 52, paras 21, 23 where it was suggested that it would be improper for a court to take into account the circumstances of the claimant in awarding damages (eg where he or she comes from a developed country but is injured in a developing country). While such an approach aims for total fidelity to the law of the obligation in the assessment of damages it perhaps underestimates the (legitimate) desire of some courts to do justice in the individual circumstances of the case.

[109] See especially R Mortensen, 'Homing Devices in Choice of Tort Law: Australian, British and Canadian Approaches' (2006) 55 ICLQ 839, 859.

[110] *John Pfeiffer Pty Ltd v Rogerson* (2000) 203 CLR 503, para 194 (Callinan J): 'To separate a head of claim from the question of quantum appears to be wholly artificial'; *Goh Suan Hee v Teo Cher Teck* [2009] SGCA 52, para 21. See also Gray (n 79 above) 286 and P Beaumont and Z Tang, 'Classification of Delictual Damages: *Harding v Wealands* and the Rome II Regulation' (2008) 12 Edinburgh L Rev 131, 133.

[111] See Ch 2.

[112] *Goh Suan Hee v Teo Cher Teck* [2009] SGCA 52, para 21; G Panagopoulos, 'Substance and Procedure in Private International Law' (2005) 1 JPIL 69, 77 and A Scott, 'Substance and Procedure and Choice of Law in Torts' [2006] LMCLQ 44, 57, citing *Chase Manhattan Bank NA v Israel-British Bank (London) Ltd* [1981] Ch 105, 124 (Goulding J).

A. The Common Law Position

and quantum is particularly salient when it is remembered that jurisdictions will often lower the threshold of liability for a civil wrong in exchange for reduced damages[113] and that insurance premiums in a particular country will usually be a reflection of common levels of damages awarded under local law. For a forum court routinely not to apply such foreign laws on damages on the basis of a procedural classification undermines the policy of foreign legislatures and insurance schemes. Such an approach also has the effect of a law being applied which is an artificial amalgam of both countries' rules, and of a result being reached which could not be achieved in a wholly domestic case in either jurisdiction.[114]

Consequently, the general statement by the High Court of Australia in the *Pfeiffer* case, at 11.20, that all questions relating to the amount of damages should be treated as substantive, is sensible and avoids difficult and artificial questions of delineation within the concept of damages. A substantive classification of quantification is also justified because the matter does not concern the mode or conduct of court proceedings[115] and is clearly outcome determinative. Moreover, on the supposed inconvenience in applying foreign rules of quantum, it should be noted that Australian courts since *Pfeiffer* have regularly applied the rules of quantification of other Australian states and territories with little difficulty.[116] While the application of foreign rules of assessment may present more challenges forensically, this difference is not significant enough to warrant a separate and distinct choice of law rule for quantification.[117] While it is true that the High Court in *Zhang* expressly left open the choice of law position with regard to damages in international tort cases, in later decisions, no Australian court has held or suggested that matters of quantification are procedural. For example, in *McGregor v Potts*,[118] Brereton J stated that 'it is likely, though not concluded, that if the matter [concerning a tort in England]

11.32

---

[113] C Dougherty and L Wyles, 'Harding v Wealands' (2007) 56 ICLQ 443, 452; I Curry-Sumner, 'An Age-old Dilemma: Is It Time for a Revolutionary Approach? A Comment on Harding v Wealands' (2006) 8 YBPIL 321, 332.

[114] Briggs (n 99 above) 278.

[115] *Goh Suan Hee v Teo Cher Teck* [2009] SGCA 52, para 21.

[116] Among many cases may be cited: *Thompson v Evanoss* [2000] ACTSC 73, para 28; *Labuda v Langford* [2001] ACTSC 108, para 38; *FAI Allianz Insurance Ltd v Lang* [2004] NSWCA 413, para 23; *Randwick Labor Club v Amalgamated Television Services Pty Ltd* [2000] NSWSC 906, para 190; *Andrews v Traynor* [2003] QSC 292, para 3; *Villet v Bosch* [2006] WADC 8, para 13.

[117] cf the view of the Australian Law Reform Commission, which described the task for an Australian court in assessing damages for pain and suffering under foreign law as 'a practical impossibility': Australian Law Reform Commission, *Choice of Law* Report No 58 (1992) para 10.44. Such an opinion surely exaggerates the problem.

[118] (2005) 68 NSWLR 109, para 54.

were litigated in New South Wales, questions of . . . quantum of damages would . . . be governed by English law'. Further, in the later High Court decision in *Neilson*,[119] which also involved a foreign tort, the High Court did not suggest that any aspect of damages available under Chinese law was procedural. While the law of Western Australia was ultimately applied, this outcome was reached pursuant to the no advantage/uniformity of result principle.

11.33 Further support for the view that Commonwealth courts are competent to apply the rules on assessment of damages of foreign countries comes from the Canadian decision in *Metaxas v Ship Galaxias (No 5)*.[120] This case involved the assessment of severance payments for members of a ship's crew, and the court, while acknowledging that the question of assessment of damages was normally considered procedural, chose instead to apply the law of the cause of action, Greek law. Part of the reason for this conclusion was that 'it would be unjust and unfair of the crews of ships to expect that . . . the compensation . . . [for] a breach of contract by the ship's owners . . . might vary with each port at which the vessel may call'.[121] Significantly, the court also found that there would be no inconvenience or difficulty in applying the Greek rules of assessment.[122] Interestingly, this decision does not seem to have been referred to in later Canadian cases, which have instead taken the view that matters of quantification are procedural.[123]

11.34 It is also worth noting that the adoption of foreign rules of quantification also overcomes another potential problem which may arise in those Commonwealth countries, such as England, Australia, and Canada, where the tort choice of law rules allow the application of foreign law in circumstances where foreign law provides a cause of action or a head of damages which does not exist under the law of the forum.[124] In such cases it may be impossible to quantify damages according to forum precepts and, in the interests of avoiding absurd and artificial results, there is much to be said for importing foreign rules of quantification and assessment where possible.

---

[119] (2005) 223 CLR 331.
[120] (1990) 35 FTR 40 (Fed Ct Can).
[121] ibid para 20.
[122] ibid para 10.
[123] See eg *Somers v Fournier* (2002) 60 OR (3d) 225.
[124] *Dicey, Morris and Collins* (n 13 above) para 35.056; Scott (n 112 above) 59; J Carruthers, 'Substance and Procedure in the Conflict of Laws: A Continuing Debate in Relation to Damages' (2004) 53 ICLQ 691, 699–700.

A. The Common Law Position

There is therefore a strong argument in favour of a substantive classification in respect of almost all questions relating to the assessment of damages.[125] While such a conclusion removes assessment from the grip of forum law (subject to public policy, overriding mandatory rules, and displacement of the applicable law), it does raise the question of whether the only law that can be applied to assessment is the law of the cause of action or obligation. In England, with the advent of the Rome II Regulation, this issue may now be hypothetical, since the law of the obligation will almost certainly apply, by legislation, to questions of damages but in Commonwealth countries still governed by the common law, other options may be available.

11.35

In this regard, it is noteworthy that a French scholar[126] (with some common law supporters)[127] has argued that the law of the country of reparation should be applied to questions of damages on the basis that this law is best suited to accommodating the relevant social and economic factors concerning the claimant post-injury. Such a rule is, in effect, a law of habitual residence test which, as already noted, appears to have been the unofficial choice of law rule applied by English courts in cases under the PILA 1995, at least where English claimants were involved. While adopting such a rule 'officially' would have the advantage of transparency and closer calibration to the post-accident needs of the claimant, such a rule should not be employed in Commonwealth countries. The major concern is again the disruption to the coherence of applicable law in personal injury cases in that one law will be applied to liability (the law of the obligation) and another to damages (the law of the claimant's habitual residence).[128] While this form of dépeçage proceeds from a more principled and logical position than the separation of right and remedy under the procedural classification, it does lead to the same problem of a foreign law of obligations,

11.36

---

[125] Note that in *Goh Suan Hee v Teo Cher Teck* [2009] SGCA 52, paras 16, 21 the Singapore Court of Appeal recently left open the status of quantification of damages but hinted that it now favoured a substantive classification.

[126] O Boskovic, *La Réparation du Préjudice en Droit International Privé* (LGDJ, 2003).

[127] See eg Briggs (n 99 above) 271, 272–3; 'Decisions of British Courts on Private International Law' (2006) 77 BYBIL 554, 566; Scott (n 112 above) 55; and also *Cheshire, North and Fawcett* (n 13 above) 805.

[128] A Rushworth, 'Remedies and the Rome II Regulation' in J Ahern and W Binchy, *The Rome II Regulation on the Law Applicable to Non-Contractual Obligations* (Martinus Nijhoff, 2009) 199, 216–17; see also J Von Hein, 'Article 4 and Traffic Accidents' in Ahern and Binchy (n128 above) 153, 161, citing A Malatesta, 'The Law Applicable to Traffic Accidents' in A Malatesta (ed), *The Unification of Choice of Law Rules on Torts and Other Non-Contractual Obligations in Europe* (Padova CEDAM, 2006) 85, 96–9, who stresses that 'the tortfeasor's legitimate interest in foreseeability of the applicable law' should be the overriding principle.

which was designed to be engaged in its entirety, being applied in a piecemeal fashion. In any event, as noted at 11.30, it is likely that the specific facts and circumstances of the claimant's country of residence can be taken into account as 'factual' matters during the process of assessment in the forum. Hence, even under a law of the obligation test, reference to such law is not absolute but does allow some leeway to accommodate individual cultural and residential circumstances, which appears to be the main rationale of a law of habitual residence rule. Another issue is that in an increasingly mobile world, the losses suffered by a claimant may not be felt in his or her place of habitual residence, for instance where a claimant is injured while employed on a fixed-term contract in the law of the country of obligation.[129] The argument in favour of a presumptive application of the law of the obligation to the assessment of damages is also reinforced when it is recalled that the doctrines of public policy, overriding mandatory rules and displacement of applicable law (discussed at 11.37–11.47) all provide some scope for removal of a case from the law of the obligation where justice so demands. Another possible advantage of this approach is that it comes closest to reconciling the common law principles with those under Rome II and so assists the goal of uniformity of outcome.[130]

7. Public Policy

11.37 Public policy may provide an alternative basis to a procedural classification for resort to forum law in cases involving foreign law which provides few or no heads of damage for a claimant.[131] While the public policy exception to the law of the cause of action has typically been reserved in common law rules of private international law for serious cases,[132] in Canadian cases involving international torts it has been applied where the claimant would suffer 'an injustice'. Examples of injustice are where the claimant would be denied a remedy under foreign law[133] or where no suit could be brought because of a guest statute.[134] Such injustice will not, however, be present where the claimant is merely unable to obtain government benefits under foreign law[135] or where there is a mere difference in quantum

---

[129] Rushworth (n 128 above) 216.
[130] See 11.58 below.
[131] See PILA 1995, s 14(3)(a)(i).
[132] See 3.17–3.18 above.
[133] *Hanlan v Sernesky* (1998) 38 OR (3d) 479 (Ont CA).
[134] *Gill v Gill* [2000] BCSC 870.
[135] *Somers v Fournier* (2002) 60 OR (3d) 225, para 42.

A. The Common Law Position

of damages between forum and foreign law.[136] By contrast, the position may be different 'where a cap on damages falls alarmingly short of the damages actually sustained by the victim'[137] or where the defendant would be subjected to unlimited liability in terms of damages.[138] Consequently, it could be argued that where a damages award under the law of the cause of action is likely to be extremely and oppressively high or absurdly low and inadequate compensation by forum standards, then the public policy defence should be available to exclude the foreign law in favour of local rules.[139] As argued elsewhere in this work, public policy is often a more transparent and principled basis for applying forum law than the traditional procedural characterization, which can mask unarticulated policy concerns. Public policy is also a more precise tool, allowing for calibration to the facts of an individual case, compared to the all or nothing, blanket procedural approach. In this regard the Canadian 'injustice' test, while potentially vague and unpredictable, does at least identify the protection of claimants as a legitimate policy in awarding damages.[140] So, while the quantum of damages under New South Wales law in *Harding v Wealands* would have been insufficiently low to trigger the public policy exception,[141] it would have been useful if the House of Lords had at least acknowledged the policy issues at stake in the applicable law determination. The nearest the court came to such an analysis was the reference to the concern expressed in Parliament during the passage of the PILA 1995

---

[136] *Wong v Lee* (2002) 58 OR (3d) 398, para 17; *Gill v Conamex Trucking System Inc* (2001) 16 CPC (5th) 320, para 13.

[137] *Bezan v Van der Hooft* [2004] ABCA 44, para 10.

[138] Cf *Wong v Lee* (2002) 58 OR (3d) 398, para 17.

[139] For supporting views, see Carruthers (2004) (n 124 above) 702; Briggs (n 99 above) 276; and 'Decisions of British Courts Involving Questions of Public or Private International Law' (2004) 75 BYBIL 537, 586; M Keyes, 'Substance and Procedure in Multistate Tort Litigation' (2010) 18 Torts LJ 201, 226; G Davis, 'Damages in Transnational Tort Litigation: Legislative Restrictions and the Substance/Procedure Distinction in Australian Conflict of Laws' in J Berryman and R Bigwood (eds), *The Law of Remedies New Directions in the Common Law* (Irwin Law, 2010) 639, 662; and A Mills, 'The Dimensions of Public Policy in Private International Law' (2008) 4 JPIL 201, 218 (applied to foreign judgments). cf R Weintraub, 'Choice of Law for Quantification of Damages: A Judgment of the House of Lords Makes a Bad Rule Worse' (2007) 42 Texas Intl LJ 311, 320, who suggests that public policy goes only one way, ie to enable an English court to *reduce* excessive awards under foreign laws but not to *increase* seriously inadequate ones. Yet surely the 'injustice' which requires the intervention of public policy should run both ways.

[140] For a similar view, see *Harding v Wealands* [2005] 1 WLR 1539, para 52 (Arden LJ).

[141] This point was made by the trial judge, who noted that while English and NSW policy differed on the level of damages, it could not be said that NSW law infringed 'fundamental principles of English justice'; *Harding v Wealands* [2004] EWHC 1957 (QB), para 73 (Elias J).

that English courts should not be forced to award the excessively high levels of damages available under US law.[142]

8. Overriding Mandatory Rules

11.38 Another situation in which forum law may be applied to questions of damages is where it is embodied in overriding mandatory rules[143] which may be in statutory or common law[144] form. Rather surprisingly, this argument has been relied upon rarely in Commonwealth decisions, although it was successful in the Australian case *Buckby v Lloyd Aviation Jet Charter Ltd*.[145] This case concerned an employee, habitually resident in South Australia, who was injured in Queensland and sued his employer in South Australia. While the common law choice of law rule for torts would have required application of the law of Queensland to available heads of damage, the court held that this rule was ousted by the operation of the Workers Rehabilitation and Compensation Act 1986 (SA), an overriding forum statute. Section 6 applied the Act to a worker who was injured outside South Australia but who was 'predominantly employed' in that State. Section 54 of the Act abolished recovery for economic loss. The court held that the combined effect of sections 6 and 54 was to 'vary the common law conflicts rules and direct South Australian courts to apply South Australian law to the extent specified in the Act'.[146] The court reached this conclusion based on the terms of the Act 'and its evident policy'. In *McNeilly v Imbree*,[147] which was referred to at 11.21, the New South Wales Court of Appeal applied a Northern Territory statute to assess damages in respect of an accident in the Territory which resulted in a higher damages award than would have been achieved under the New South Wales Motor Accidents Compensation Act 1999. Interestingly, the defendant did not seek to argue that the MACA 1999 should apply as an overriding mandatory rule,[148] despite section 123(1) of the Act which provides that 'a court cannot award damages to a person in respect of a motor accident contrary to this Chapter'.

---

[142] *Harding v Wealands* [2007] 2 AC 1, para 37.
[143] See PILA 1995, s 14(4).
[144] *Cheshire, North and Fawcett* (n 13 above) 850.
[145] (1992) 58 SASR 269.
[146] ibid 274.
[147] [2007] NSWCA 156.
[148] *Dicey, Morris and Collins* (n 2 above) 4th Cumulative Supplement (2010) para 7.043.

A. The Common Law Position

9. Rules for Displacement of the Applicable Law

A further important question to consider is whether forum law may be applied by an alternative means other than pursuant to a procedural classification. At 11.37, reference has already been made to forum public policy and how it may arguably be available to disapply foreign law on heads of damages and quantification. This inquiry is important to the present study, because if mechanisms are available to displace foreign law in favour of the forum relatively freely, then changes to the substance-procedure classification to give more effect to foreign law may well be of limited effect and utility. The primary focus of the inquiry will be on displacement measures in relation to tort law, since it is in this area that cross-border damages disputes have most commonly arisen.

11.39

In English law under the PILA 1995, which probably still applies to torts committed before 20 August 2007[149] (except defamation which remains governed by the double actionability rule),[150] the general choice of law rule requires the application of the law of the country in which the events constituting the tort in question occur,[151] which is the place of injury in a personal injury case.[152] This rule may, however, not be applied in section 12(1) where 'it appears . . . from a comparison of the significance of the factors connecting the tort with the country in s 11 and those with another country (normally England) that it is "substantially more appropriate" for the applicable law for determining the issues arising in the case or any of those issues' to be (English) law. The possible inspiration for section 12 was the House of Lords decision in *Boys v Chaplin*,[153] where the court found that English law should apply to the heads of recoverable damage in the context of an action between two British nationals and English habitual residents arising out of an accident in Malta. England was much more closely connected to the issue of recoverable damages and Malta was found to have no interest in applying its law to an action between two English residents.

11.40

Section 12 of the PILA 1995 has been applied in a number of cases to displace the presumptively applicable foreign law under section 11 in favour of English law, and in each case the issue was either heads of damages or quantification. *Edmunds v Simmonds*[154] involved a claim for damages for

11.41

---

[149] For a full discussion of the temporal scope of the Regulation, see 11.01 above.
[150] PILA 1995, s 13.
[151] PILA 1995, s 11(1).
[152] ibid s 11(2).
[153] [1971] AC 356.
[154] [2001] 1 WLR 1003 (QBD).

personal injury arising out of a road traffic accident in Spain. The claimant and defendant were both British nationals and English residents, on holiday in Spain when the accident happened, and were travelling in the same car. Before trial, it was agreed between the parties that there was no difference in liability between English and Spanish law but that the laws differed on quantification with English law likely to produce a higher damages award. When the claimant sued the defendant in England the defendant's insurer argued that because it was Spanish (as was the driver of the other vehicle and its insurer) Spanish law should be applied. The English court disagreed, holding that the factors connecting the dispute with England, namely the domicile and nationality of the parties, the fact that they were only temporarily in Spain for a holiday, and that the claimant's damages arose wholly in England, 'overwhelmingly' outweighed the factors linking the action to Spain. English law was therefore applied to the issue of quantification. The court approved the earlier unreported High Court decision in *Hamill v Hamill*,[155] which reached the same conclusion although in that case the facts were even more closely connected with England as the accident did not involve a third party Spanish driver. In *Dawson v Broughton*[156] English law was again applied to a tort occurring in a foreign country, this time France, where the parties were both British nationals, although in that case the claimant was domiciled in France. The same result occurred in *B v B*,[157] where both claimants and defendant were British nationals domiciled in England, who had an accident while on holiday in Spain. English law was again applied under section 12, with the court following the *Edmunds* decision. The court again disregarded the fact that the defendant's insurer and hire car were Spanish, seeing these factors as 'background circumstances not immediately connected' to the tort.

11.42 Only one case appears to buck the trend of giving a generous interpretation to section 12 of the PILA 1995 in order to refer the matter back to English law. This decision was *Harding v Wealands*[158] which involved a claimant who was a British national, resident in England, who sued the defendant, his former partner, who was an Australian national but resident in England at the time of the accident, which occurred in New South Wales. While the first instance judge held that English law should apply to the wrong,[159] the Court of Appeal disagreed, finding that the coincidence between the nationality of the defendant and the place of the accident

---

[155] 24 July 2000.
[156] (2007) 151 Sol Jnl 1167.
[157] 29 July 2008 (QBD).
[158] [2005] 1 WLR 1539 (revd on other grounds [2007] 2 AC 1).
[159] [2004] EWHC 1957 (QB).

A. The Common Law Position

resulted in the presumptively applicable law under section 11 having the strongest claim to application.[160] Waller LJ, however, made the interesting observation that given 'the settled relationship' between the parties 'if they had been on holiday in France when this accident occurred, England might have been found to be substantially more appropriate and to have displaced French law'.[161] The editors of *Dicey, Morris and Collins* also speculate whether the defendant's Australian nationality would have been 'less prominent' if the parties had lived together in a 'settled relationship' in England for several years before the accident.[162] Arguably, however, there was already an adequate factual basis for applying English law, given that the defendant's domicile at the time of the accident was almost certainly England,[163] with this connecting factor being of greater relevance than nationality in an increasingly mobile and globalized community. Also, as the trial judge noted, the consequences of the accident were to be felt in England where the claimant would continue to live and receive care.[164] Nevertheless, despite this division over the result in *Harding v Wealands*, it is clear that English courts have exhibited a keenness to apply section 12 where possible in what may be described as the 'common domicile' cases.[165] Such an approach is also likely to be followed in cases under the Rome II Regulation.[166]

The thread running through these cases is that where both parties to the litigation are English domiciliaries or habitual residents, British nationals, and only temporarily present in a country where the accident occurs,[167] there is a good chance that foreign law will be displaced in favour of English law, even if the insurer or another driver involved in the accident is foreign. If, however, one of the parties is a foreign resident, the argument

11.43

---

[160] Waller LJ also noted that the location of the insurance policy might be a relevant consideration in determining whether English law should be applied; in *Harding* it was a New South Wales policy. By comparison, courts in all the other decisions mentioned gave this factor little weight.

[161] [2005] 1 WLR 1539, para 20.

[162] *Dicey, Morris and Collins* (n 13 above) para 35.108.

[163] E Schoeman, '*Harding v Wealands*: Substance and Procedure in the English Courts' (2007) 13 New Zealand Business Law Quarterly 3, 7–8; Weintraub (n 139 above) 317–18; Scott (n 112 above) 62 but contrast Briggs (n 139 above) 585.

[164] [2004] EWHC 1957 (QB), para 34.

[165] Interestingly in *Hulse v Chambers* [2001] 1 WLR 2386, in the context of an action between English habitual resident claimants and their father (also an English resident) and a Greek insurer, arising out of an accident in Greece, the parties accepted that Greek law applied to liability with no scope for displacement under PILA 1995, s 12. The judge, however, hinted that the concession might have been wrongly made in the light of the decisions in *Edmunds* and *Hamill*, which involved 'markedly similar facts' (para 4).

[166] See 11.62 below.

[167] Mortensen (n 109 above) 865.

for avoiding foreign law will be harder to make. While this conclusion seems reasonable, given that the bulk of personal injury cases before English courts in recent years have involved holiday accidents, where a British person has been injured by the negligence of another family member, it does mean that the substance / procedure distinction has little role to play since forum law has been applied in any event. Indeed, for those claimants wanting to secure the application of English law to the issue of available heads of damages (such as in *Boys v Chaplin*), the displacement argument is infinitely preferable since, under common law principles, an English court must apply foreign law heads of damages as they are substantive. Where, under the Rome II Regulation, the scope of foreign law in relation to damages is even greater, extending to issues of quantification,[168] then the rules of displacement may become an even more vital path to claimants seeking the greater protection of forum (English) law. The issue of displacement under the Rome II Regulation is discussed later.[169]

11.44 Finally, and just to show that section 12 of the PILA 1995 is much more likely to be available to English claimants seeking to avoid foreign law than *foreign* parties seeking to avoid *English* law, the decision in *Roerig v Valiant Trawlers*[170] is of interest. This case concerned a Dutch wife suing, on behalf of her deceased Dutch husband, an English shipowner, and arose out of an accident in English waters. As noted at 11.09, English law, unlike Dutch law, provided that any benefits received by the claimant would not be deducted from any award of damages and the English court refused to displace English law, given that there were important connections between the action and England. It seems, therefore, that it will be a rare case in which English law as the law of place of the wrong will be displaced in favour of foreign law. This outcome is consistent with the view expressed above that English courts still generally prefer to apply English law to damages, where possible.

11.45 Some observations should also be made about the position regarding displacement in other Commonwealth countries. In a number of jurisdictions, such as Singapore, Hong Kong, and New Zealand,[171] which have retained the double actionability choice of law rule, the 'flexible exception' from *Boys v Chaplin* continues to operate. By contrast, in Canada, as noted at 11.37, in international[172] tort cases an 'injustice' exception has been

---

[168] See 11.57–11.59 below.
[169] See 11.62–11.64 below.
[170] [2002] 1 WLR 2304 (CA).
[171] *Baxter v RMC Group plc* [2003] 1 NZLR 304.
[172] There is no 'injustice' exception in inter-provincial tort cases: *Tolofson v Jensen* (1994) 120 DLR (4th) 289.

A. The Common Law Position

recognized which is closer to a public policy-type exclusion than the English displacement principle, since it focuses on the injustice of applying a particular rule on damages rather than on the connections with the issue.

11.46 Different again is the position in Australia, where there is no displacement mechanism available in either international or interstate tort cases.[173] Instead, in international tort cases, Australian courts apply the *Neilson* 'no advantage' principle, which requires the application of the choice of law rules of the law of the cause of action (the law of the place of the wrong) and any *renvoi* rules under that law. The consequence of this approach is that an Australian court will normally apply foreign law to all issues which an Australian court would regard as substantive (for example available heads of damages) regardless of whether the foreign law would classify the issue as substantive or procedural. In most tort cases the same result will be reached as under Australian choice of law rules since the choice of law rules of the place of the wrong would in practice rarely select a law other than their own to a local tort. Consequently there will be no scope for remission or transmission to another legal system. If however, as in *Neilson*, the foreign choice of law rules would refer the matter back to Australian substantive law, the Australian court would apply its own law, substantive and procedural, but only if the foreign law classified all issues as substantive. If the foreign choice of law rules classified an issue as procedural, then an Australian court would apply foreign law to that issue and Australian law to all matters which the foreign law considered substantive. A further problem may arise if the choice of law rules of the place of the wrong recognize a doctrine of *renvoi* or would select the law of a *third country* as the substantive law, for in those situations the law to be applied by the Australian court becomes very unclear. As has been argued elsewhere in this work, the complexity and uncertainty of this exercise[174] makes it undesirable for adoption in other Commonwealth jurisdictions.

11.47 On balance, therefore, under the pre-existing English law and current Commonwealth principles there is some scope for reversion to the law of the forum by displacement of the applicable law but it will normally only be in cases where the parties share the same habitual residence. When coupled with the earlier, similar conclusions with respect to the scope of

---

[173] *John Pfeiffer Pty Ltd v Rogerson* (2000) 203 CLR 503; *Regie Nationale des Usines Renault SA v Zhang* (2002) 210 CLR 491; the absence of a flexible exception has been criticized, see R Garnett, '*Renault v Zhang*: A Job Half Done?' (2002) 10 Tort L Rev 145 and R Anderson, 'International Torts in the High Court of Australia' (2002) 10 Torts LJ 132, 140–141.

[174] Mortensen (n 109 above) 874.

10. Conditions Precedent/Notice before Action Requirements

11.48 This issue has been discussed earlier,[175] where it was noted that pre-action notices, certificates, mediation requirements,[176] or other administrative hurdles have been generally classified as procedural under Commonwealth law. Such a conclusion has been justified on the basis that those requirements relate to the forum's management of its own proceedings. In the case of notice before action provisions, however, it was suggested that a substantive characterization is more appropriate where a failure to provide such notice would extinguish the claimant's cause of action. In this situation, there is a clear and direct impact on the rights and liabilities of the parties.[177]

11.49 One particular pre-action requirement of specific relevance to damages should be noted. Section 132(1) of the Motor Accidents Compensation Act 1999 (NSW) provides that if there is a dispute about whether the degree of permanent impairment of an injured person is sufficient for an award of damages for non-economic loss, the court may not order any such damages unless the degree of impairment has been assessed by a medical assessor under Part 3.4 of the Act. The New South Wales Court of Appeal, in *Fuller v K & J Trucks*,[178] suggested obiter that section 132(1) was procedural, as it establishes an administrative process to be followed before the court may award damages for non-economic loss and does 'not enact any underlying or general principle about entitlement [to such damages]'. The court suggested that although the High Court in the *Pfeiffer* case had indicated that all matters relating to the assessment of damages was substantive, it is unlikely that the High Court would have intended provisions for 'machinery for medical assessment' before damages to be similarly classified.[179] Since the institution of a medical assessor may be difficult for a foreign court to replicate, a procedural classification would

---

[175] See 6.30 above.

[176] Mortensen (n 109 above) 876.

[177] See 6.28 above. See also the US commentator McDougal, who supports a substantive classification of pre-action requirements on the basis that their intention is to 'retard the ability of plaintiffs to succeed in prosecuting claims': L McDougal, R Felix, and R Whitten, *American Conflicts Law* (Transnational Publishers, 5th edn, 2001) 411.

[178] [2006] NSWCA 88, para 33 (Bryson JA) (with whom Handley JA agreed (para 1); Ipp JA expressly reserving his view (para 2)).

[179] ibid para 34.

A. The Common Law Position

appear to be justified. In a US decision a similar approach was taken where a requirement that a claimant submit medical malpractice claims to a review panel before suing was held to be procedural.[180]

11. JURISDICTIONAL CONTROL?

As discussed at 2.35, it was suggested that a robust use of forum jurisdictional devices to ensure that matters are heard in the courts of the country of the law of the cause of action could make resort to the substance-procedure dichotomy unnecessary in cross-border damages disputes.[181] Yet in this area, particularly in cases involving personal injury, English and Australian courts have both been reluctant to use their discretionary powers to stay proceedings brought by local claimants in respect of foreign causes of action. In early proceedings in *Harding v Wealands* the English courts rejected a stay on *forum non conveniens* grounds, and in the later case of *Cooley v Ramsey*[182] an English court allowed service outside England in an action brought by a British national and domiciliary against an Australian defendant arising out of an accident in New South Wales. While the judge noted that in the *Spiliada* case Lord Goff had said that a stay of English proceedings should not simply be refused because of a likely higher damages award under English law,[183] England was nevertheless found to be the appropriate forum in this case. The key factor was that preparation of the claimant's case would be far easier if the trial took place in England, especially given his injuries and incapacity. This case may therefore suggest a reluctance to use jurisdictional principles to resolve the issue of choice law.

11.50

Similar results were recently reached in Singapore, where courts refused to stay proceedings brought by Singapore-resident claimants against Malaysian defendants arising out of accidents in Malaysia, with the location of witnesses being the primary consideration.[184] In Canada, where there exists both a real and substantial connection test for establishing jurisdiction[185] and a *Spiliada*-like *forum non conveniens* principle for declining

11.51

---

[180] *Vest v St Albans Psychiatric Hospital Inc* 387 SE 2d 282 (W Va 1989).
[181] See A Briggs, 'Decisions of British Courts During 2006 Involving Questions of Public or Private International Law' (2006) 77 BYBIL 554, 572; Scott (n 112 above) 61.
[182] [2008] EWHC 129 (QB).
[183] *Spiliada Maritime Corp v Cansulex* [1987] AC 460, 483.
[184] *Goh Suan Hee v Teo Cher Teck* [2009] SGCA 52 and *Ismail bin Sukardi v Kamal bin Ikhwan* [2008] SGHC 191.
[185] *Beals v Saldanha* (2003) 234 DLR (4th) 1 (SCC).

348   Chapter 11: Remedies II: Damages and Statutory Compensation

jurisdiction,[186] the same trend is likely to be evident.[187] In Australia, the bias in favour of local claimants is even more palpable: under the 'clearly inappropriate forum' test a defendant must show, in order to obtain a stay of proceedings, that it would suffer vexation or oppression if trial took place in Australia. Not surprisingly, in three High Court decisions, local claimants were successful in resisting stay applications brought by foreign defendants arising out of personal injuries suffered abroad.[188] Finally, such discretionary jurisdictional measures as exist under the common law will be unavailable, in any event, in cases to which the Brussels I Regulation or Lugano Convention apply,[189] which further limits their utility.

B. THE EU INSTRUMENTS

11.52 Attention now turns to the position under the EU instruments, specifically the Rome II Regulation, the Rome Convention, and the Rome I Regulation. Primary focus will be on Rome II since, as mentioned at 11.01, questions of applicable law and damages have arisen commonly in the tort/non-contractual obligation context and, in any case, similar principles apply in contract. As mentioned already,[190] Rome II is likely to apply only in respect of events, giving rise to damage, which occur on or after 20 August 2007, where legal proceedings in respect of such events are commenced on or after 11 January 2009.

1. Applicable Law and Damages

11.53 Article 4 of the Rome II Regulation is the basic rule for determining the applicable law of the non-contractual obligation which will, in a similar way to section 11 of PILA 1995, normally select the law of the place of injury in personal injury cases, subject to the rules of displacement in article 4(2) and (3).[191] Once this law has been located, the next question is which issues concerning damages must it be applied to? The key provision in Rome II is article 15(c) which provides that the law applicable to non-contractual obligations under the Regulation 'shall govern, in particular . . .

---

[186] *Amchem Products Inc v British Columbia (Workers Compensation Board)* [1993] 1 SCR 897.
[187] See eg *Byers v Higgen* (1993) 80 BCLR (2d) 386 (BCSC); *Penny (Litigation Guardian of) v Bouch* (2009) 310 DLR (4th) 433 (NSCA).
[188] *Regie Nationale des Usines Renault SA v Zhang* (2002) 210 CLR 491; *Oceanic Sunline Special Shipping Co v Fay* (1988) 165 CLR 197; *Puttick v Tenon Ltd* (2008) 238 CLR 265.
[189] *Owusu v Jackson* [2005] QB 801.
[190] See 11.01 above.
[191] See 11.62–11.64 below.

the existence, the nature and the assessment of damage or the remedy claimed'. This provision should be read with article 15(d) which provides that the law of the obligation will govern 'within the limits of powers conferred on the court by its procedural law, the measures which a court may take to . . . ensure the provision of compensation'.

The first point to note is that it is clear under article 15(c) of Rome II that the issue of available heads of damage is a matter for the law of the obligation. The availability of non-compensatory damages, such as an award of exemplary damages or an account of profits, would also fall within this provision subject to any possible public policy objection.[192] It also seems clear that the question of limitations or caps on damages, either legislative or judicial, should be similarly treated. Consequently, the opposite result to that reached by the House of Lords in *Harding v Wealands* would be achieved under article 15(c).[193] Such a conclusion may, alternatively, be reached under article 15(b) which applies the law of the obligation to 'any limitation of liability'.[194]

11.54

The uncertain status of interest under the pre-existing English rules was considered earlier.[195] However, in the light of the breadth of the wording in article 15(c) of Rome II, 'the assessment of damage or the remedy claimed', it is strongly arguable that all questions relating to the award of pre-judgment interest, including the right to claim interest and at what rate, are governed by the law applicable to the non-contractual obligation.[196] Post-judgment interest, however, given its role in facilitating the enforcement of judgments, may continue to be regarded as procedural[197] and to be governed by the law of the country in which the judgment was rendered. Yet, to complicate things, article 15(d) refers to the law of the obligation a 'measure which a court may take to prevent or terminate injury or damage or to ensure the provision of compensation' which would appear to embrace such interest. Obviously, though, this conflict of classification will only be relevant where the law of the country where the judgment is rendered and the law of the obligation in the judgment itself are different.

11.55

The issue of deductibility of benefits was said to be governed by forum law in England in proceedings under the PILA 1995,[198] although it was

11.56

---

[192] Rushworth (n 128 above) 201; R Plender and M Wilderspin, *The European Private International Law of Obligations* (Sweet & Maxwell, 3rd edn, 2009) para 16.039.
[193] ibid para 16.056.
[194] *Cheshire, North and Fawcett* (n 13 above) 845.
[195] See 11.03–11.08 above.
[196] Dickinson, *The Rome II Regulation Updating Supplement* (OUP, 2010) para 14.35C.
[197] See 11.06 above.
[198] *Roerig v Valiant Trawlers Ltd* [2002] 1 WLR 2304 (CA).

Chapter 11: Remedies II: Damages and Statutory Compensation

not entirely clear whether this law was applied pursuant to a procedural classification, public policy, or overriding mandatory rules. In other Commonwealth countries, by contrast, the matter is clearly regarded as substantive and it is likely that this view will be applied under article 15(c) of Rome II.[199]

11.57 A much more difficult question, however, is whether all questions relating to the assessment of damages are now to be referred to the applicable law and so treated as implicitly substantive. In particular, does article 15(c) of Rome II require an English court to use all methods for calculating damages under the applicable law? It was suggested at 11.28, in the discussion on the common law principles, that applying foreign law rules on matters such as periodical payments or adjustments to damages awards in the light of later circumstances should not be too difficult for a Commonwealth court, especially since, in the case of periodical payments, English courts now have greater powers to award such relief under domestic law. It is therefore unlikely that the exception in article 15(d), that the forum is only obliged to act within the limits of its procedural powers, will be needed on this issue.[200] Where, however, the assessment of damages under foreign law requires an institution or body which would be difficult to emulate in the forum, such as a jury or special assessor, then article 15(d) may well be engaged to relieve the forum of the obligation to apply such a provision.[201] Such an outcome would be consistent with the common law principles mentioned at 11.29.

11.58 The distinction between facts and law in awarding damages was discussed at 11.30 in the common law material. While the Rome Convention[202] and the Rome I Regulation[203] make specific reference to this issue where it is stated that the law of the obligation shall govern assessment of damages 'in so far as it is governed by rules of law' (as opposed to when assessment involves questions of fact),[204] article 15(c) of Rome II contains no such reference. Nevertheless, most commentators consider that the omission was 'inadvertent' and that the distinction between facts and law should equally apply in cases under Rome II.[205] Under the rubric of facts,[206] courts should

---

[199] *Cheshire, North and Fawcett* (n 13 above) 845.
[200] ibid 847.
[201] Dickinson (n 2 above) para 14.34.
[202] Rome Convention, art 10(1)(c).
[203] Rome I, art 12(1)(c).
[204] Giuliano and Lagarde, Report on the Convention on the Law Applicable to Contractual Obligations [1980] OJ C282/1, 33.
[205] *Cheshire, North and Fawcett* (n 13 above) 845; J Carruthers, 'Has the Forum Lost Its Grip?' in Ahern and Binchy (n 128 above) 25, 42; Rushworth (n 128 above) 205–6.
[206] ibid 844.

aim to take into account the social and economic circumstances of the victim in assigning value to individual items of loss, and also, where possible, receive evidence from foreign experts as to the guidelines and likely ranges of quantum in the event that the matter goes to trial in the foreign country.[207] Discount rates on damages, however, are more akin to limitations or caps on damages and so should be determined by the applicable law.[208] In the context of the Rome Convention, the Giuliano-Lagarde Report[209] suggested that 'rules of law' would include the situation where the contract prescribes the amount of damages in cases of non-performance or there is an international convention fixing the amount of compensation.

The presence of Recital 33 in Rome II has also given rise to some controversy but it is suggested that its effect is consistent with the aforementioned view. Recital 33, which apparently arose out of a compromise between the European Council and Parliament, provides: **11.59**

> According to the current national rules on compensation awarded to victims of road traffic accidents, when quantifying damages for personal injury in cases in which the accident takes place in a state other than that of the habitual residence of the victim, the court seised should take into account all relevant circumstances of the specific victim, including in particular the actual losses and costs of aftercare and medical attention.

While on its face the effect of the recital is not completely clear, most commentators have suggested that the recital merely 'highlights the problem' involved with potential undercompensation of the claimant where a traffic accident takes place in a country outside his or her own place of habitual residence but 'does little more'.[210] Specifically, the recital does not go so far as to propose an alternative choice of law rule which would refer questions of quantification to the law of the victim's habitual residence but, at most, allows a forum court to take into account the factual circumstances

---

[207] cf Dickinson (n 2 above) para 14.19, who considers such 'tariffs, guidelines or formulae' to form part of the applicable law. Doherty (n 4 above) para 9.064 argues that the classification of law or fact depends upon the material which would be used by the court of the country of the law of the cause of action to determine quantification: if based on 'comparable cases previously decided' then it is a question of fact but if based on 'some statutory scale' then it would be a question of law. In essence, however, whether the guidelines emanate from the legislature or the judiciary, the process is the same. In *Re T & N Ltd* [2005] EWHC 2990 (Ch) (a case decided under the PILA 1995) David Richards J expressed some reluctance to receiving evidence of the levels of awards made by foreign courts.

[208] Plender and Wilderspin (n 192 above) para 16.043; cf A Rushworth and A Scott, 'Rome II: Choice of Law for Non-Contractual Obligations' [2008] LMCLQ 274, 294, who consider such rates to be a question of fact.

[209] Giuliano and Lagarde Report (n 204 above) 33.

[210] See eg P Kozyris, 'Rome II: Tort Conflicts on the Right Track—A Postscript to Symeon Symeonides' Missed Opportunity' (2008) 56 AJCL 471, 483.

confronting the victim in an attempt to ensure that such person is adequately compensated.[211] Two reasons are offered for this conclusion. The first is that any other interpretation would conflict with the express wording of article 15(c) which clearly refers the issue of assessment to the law of the obligation. The second reason is that the European Parliament had already proposed a choice of law rule requiring application of the law of habitual residence of the claimant which was rejected by the Commission and Council. For Recital 33 to be a true 'compromise' therefore, the basic applicable law rule must be maintained, subject to some flexibility. Such an interpretation would also have the effect of keeping Rome II consistent with the Rome Convention. Yet, as noted at 11.30 in the discussion on the common law principles, the reservation of factual questions to the forum may in practice give English courts wide powers to make damages awards which reflect the social and economic circumstances of the claimant, particularly if he or she is an English resident. Such an approach may be attractive to English judges with their 'instinct for a pragmatic solution',[212] and desire to compensate such persons' 'actual losses and costs' using the terms of Recital 33.

2. Public Policy and Overriding Mandatory Rules

11.60 The other bases for exclusion of the applicable law on damages in favour of forum law under the Rome II Regulation are public policy and overriding mandatory rules. Under article 26 of Rome II public policy may be invoked to exclude foreign law where its application would be 'manifestly incompatible' with forum values. While, as noted at 11.37 under the Commonwealth and pre-existing English law rules, public policy may possibly be available to supplant a foreign damages regime which provides grossly excessive or inadequate damages, the 'manifestly incompatible' threshold in article 26 may make it even more difficult to invoke the exception in cases under Rome II, at least for compensatory damages.[213] Relevant to this issue is Recital 32 which states that a national court may invoke public policy to exclude a law which provides for 'non-compensatory exemplary or punitive damages of an excessive nature'. The omission of compensatory damages here may be significant,[214] although the key

---

[211] Dickinson (n 2 above) para 14.31; Rushworth (n 128 above) 209.
[212] M Chapman, 'The Rome II Regulation and a European Law Enforcement Area: Harmony and Discord in the Assessment of Damages' [2010] Journal of Personal Injury Law 10, 18.
[213] Carruthers (n 205 above) 33; *Cheshire, North and Fawcett* (n 13 above) 852.
[214] Beaumont and Tang (n 110 above) 136.

question will always be whether, in a given case, the application of foreign law offends a fundamental principle of justice of the forum.

11.61 Provision for overriding mandatory rules is made in article 16 of Rome II[215] and it is clear that the application of such rules should only occur in 'exceptional circumstances'.[216] It is therefore likely that a similarly narrow approach will be taken to overriding rules as occurred under the pre-existing English and Commonwealth law.

3. Applicable Law and Displacement

11.62 The general provision on choice of law in the Rome II Regulation is article 4(1) which provides that 'unless otherwise provided in the Regulation the law applicable to the non-contractual obligation shall be the law of the country in which the damage occurs'. Article 4(2) and (3), however, introduce important qualifications to the general rule in article 4(1). Article 4(2) provides that where the claimant and the defendant both have their habitual residences in the same country at the time when the damage or injury occurs, then the law of their country of residence shall apply. Note that, unlike section 12 of the PILA 1995, article 4(2) appears to operate as a mandatory (not discretionary) rule of displacement so that where both parties habitually reside in a country other than the place of the damage, the law of that common residence shall apply.[217] Such a rule is therefore a more certain basis for applying English law in the 'family holiday'-type cases than section 12 and will mean that in all such cases (subject to an unlikely exception in article 4(3)) foreign law will be excluded.[218] Yet, in another respect, article 4(2) (and 4(3)) is different from section 12. While under section 12 the law of a country which is substantially more appropriate *to a particular issue* in the case (for example quantification of damages) may be applied as an alternative to the law of the place of the wrong, article 4(2) instead suggests that displacement will apply to all aspects of the tort action. Where both parties are found to share a common habitual residence, therefore, foreign law is excluded from the entire obligation, not simply a single issue such as assessment of damages. While some commentators have criticized the Regulation's lack of flexibility on this point,[219] the entire obligation approach does have the virtue of limiting the scope

---

[215] See also Rome I, art 9.
[216] Recital 32 to Rome II.
[217] *Cheshire, North and Fawcett* (n 13 above) 799.
[218] For an argument that the rule is too rigid and may not always accord with party expectations, see Dickinson (n 2 above) paras 4.81–4.82.
[219] S Symeonides, 'Rome II and Tort Conflicts: A Missed Opportunity' (2008) 56 AJCL 173, 204–5; R Fentiman, 'The Significance of Close Connection' in Ahern and Binchy (n 128 above) 85, 88.

354   *Chapter 11: Remedies II: Damages and Statutory Compensation*

for fragmentation of choice of law in damages cases and enhancing legal certainty.[220]

11.63 The same approach applies in the case of article 4(3) of Rome II which operates as an exception to both articles 4(1) and (2). Article 4(3) provides that 'where it is clear from all the circumstances that the tort is manifestly more closely connected with a country other than that indicated in (1) or (2) the law of that country shall apply'. A manifestly closer connection with another country might be based, in particular, on a pre-existing relationship between the parties, such as a contract that is closely connected with the tort in question. It will be particularly interesting to see whether English and other EU Member State courts apply article 4(3) broadly so as to encompass situations beyond the dual national/domicile holiday cases. It will be recalled that in *Harding v Wealands* Waller LJ refused to apply English law to displace New South Wales law under section 12 of the PILA 1995 because of the fact that the defendant was an Australian national but he may have applied English law had the accident occurred in France instead. While article 4(2) would be likely to cover the latter situation, could it be argued that article 4(3) may be satisfied and English law applied in the first case despite the Australian connections present? If this conclusion is correct, then it may be that English law will be available in a wider range of cross-border tort cases than before, which again means less need for the substance-procedure dichotomy. Indeed, it may be that English judges will respond to the loss of forum control on quantification of damages (see the earlier discussion of article 15(c))[221] with a greater impetus to use their powers of displacement[222] despite article 4(3) being expressed by the European Commission to be only available in 'exceptional' cases.[223] While it has been suggested[224] that article 4(3) may be interpreted narrowly so as only to apply the law of a country *other than* the law of the obligation (in article 4(1)) or the law of the common habitual residence (in article 4(2)), the express wording of the text does not support such an analysis.[225] Hence, conceivably, article 4(3) could be used to apply the law of the place of damage instead of the law of the parties' common habitual residence in article 4(2).[226] The only judicial guidance so far on this point

---

[220] Dickinson (n 2 above) para 4.78.
[221] 11.57–11.59 above.
[222] Carruthers (n 205 above) 41.
[223] Dickinson (n 2 above) paras 4.84–4.85.
[224] Fentiman (n 219 above) 89.
[225] Dickinson (n 2 above) para 4.89; Doherty (n 4 above) para 9.048; *Cheshire, North and Fawcett* (n 13 above) 803; P Stone, 'The Rome II Regulation on Choice of Law in Tort' (2007) 4 Ankara L Rev 95, 115.
[226] Stone (n 225 above) 115; *Cheshire, North and Fawcett* (n 13 above) 804.

B. The EU Instruments

comes from *Jacobs v Motor Insurance Bureau*,[227] where Owen J suggested, obiter, in an action between an English claimant and a German national defendant, resident in Spain, arising from an accident in Spain, that article 4(3) would not operate to displace Spanish law in favour of English law.

It appears, therefore, that the position under Rome II as far as displacement of the applicable law is concerned is likely to be no more generous than under the PILA 1995 or Commonwealth rules. Yet, given the significant changes effected to the substance-procedure classification in relation to damages by Rome II, with almost all issues now reserved to the law of the obligation, claimants may certainly seek to persuade English courts to interpret article 4(2) and (3) as widely as possible to attract English law.

11.64

4. Recent English Decisions on Rome II

Interestingly, in three recent English cases so far decided concerning the Rome II Regulation, only one has suggested that English courts may be receptive to approaches to bypass the requirement to apply foreign law to matters of quantification in article 15(c). In the first case, however, the court did not have to strictly address the issue but showed signs that it would have applied foreign law to the quantum question. In *Bacon v Nacional Suiza Cia Seguros y Reseguros SA*[228] Tomlinson J found that under the Rome II Regulation Spanish law applied to determine the liability of a Spanish driver who was sued by an English claimant in a case arising out of an accident in Spain. Yet, since the judge found the claimant to be 'entirely to blame for the accident', the issue of quantum was not reached. While it had been admitted by the parties that damages would be assessed at a higher rate under English law than Spanish law, the court did suggest that had it found in favour of the claimant on liability, it would also have concluded that Spanish law applied to the assessment of damages under article 15(c). Such a result was justified by the need expressed in Recital 6 of the Regulation 'to improve the predictability of the outcome of litigation [and] certainty as to the law applicable'. In other words, the needs of justice in the individual case were subordinate to systemic certainty in all matters concerning non-contractual obligations. The clear implication here is that foreign law would have been applied despite the fact that the claimant would have received less compensation than under English law. In *Homawoo v GMF Assurance SA*[229] Slade J also suggested that in the

11.65

---

[227] [2010] EWHC 231 (QB), para 46 (revd on other grounds [2011] 1 All ER 844).
[228] [2010] EWHC 2017 (QB).
[229] [2010] EWHC 1941 (QB), para 7.

context of an action against the insurer of a tortfeasor arising out of an accident in France, French law would apply to the question of assessment of damages.

11.66 By contrast, in *Jacobs v Motor Insurers Bureau*[230] the Court of Appeal suggested that the provisions of the Rome II Regulation can be avoided entirely if the claimant is a victim of a road traffic accident in an EU country caused by an uninsured driver. The claimant was a British national on holiday in Spain when, as a pedestrian, he was injured by an uninsured vehicle. The car was driven by a German national who may have been a resident in Spain. The claimant chose to sue the Motor Insurance Bureau (MIB), acting as the United Kingdom's compensation body under the Fourth Motor Insurance Directive ((EC) 2000/26). Liability was not in issue and the MIB argued that Spanish law applied to the issue of quantification of damages as the law of the place of the accident under article 15(c) of Rome II. The English Court of Appeal, reversing the decision of the first instance judge, held that English law applied to the issues of assessment and quantification. The rules under which a claim may be brought against the MIB in its capacity as compensation body are found in the Motor Vehicles (Compulsory Insurance Information Centre and Compensation Body) Regulations 2003. Regulation 13(1) provides that the claimant must reside in the United Kingdom and have been the victim of an accident in an EEA member state, caused by a vehicle normally based in an EEA state where it has proved impossible to identify the vehicle which is alleged to be responsible for the accident or an insurer of the responsible vehicle. Regulation 13(2)(a) allows a claim to be made for compensation from the compensation body (the MIB) and regulation 13(2)(b) provides that the compensation body shall compensate the injured party in accordance with the provisions of article 1 of the Motor Insurance Directive as if it were the body authorized under paragraph 4 of that article and the accident had occurred in Great Britain. The Court of Appeal agreed with the claimant that its cause of action did not involve a choice of law under Rome II but was derived from the provisions of the Fourth Motor Insurance Directive. Such provisions required English law to be applied to the assessment of damages without regard to the apparently contrary position in article 15(c) of Rome II.

11.67 The result of the case, therefore, was that the English claimant received a higher damages award, under English law, than he would have obtained under Spanish law. Indeed, in criticism of the decision, Dickinson[231] notes

---

[230] [2011] 1 All ER 844.
[231] 'Rome-ing Instinct?' conflictoflaws.net 9 November 2010.

that its effect will be that a claimant 'will receive more compensation from the MIB in cases of insurance delinquency than if he or she had sued the driver or made a direct claim against the insurer', since in both such situations the provisions of the Rome II Regulation (and hence the law of the obligation) would have clearly applied. The commentator does, however, note the 'conundrum' of Spanish law applying to the question of compensation in the *Jacobs* case. Spanish law imposes no obligation to compensate on the MIB, as a UK body, but only on the Spanish equivalent. Consequently, had Spanish law been applied, the claimant would have received nothing at all. This point appears not to have been appreciated by Owen J at first instance. The judge, despite finding that Spanish law would govern the issue of assessment, nevertheless assumed that the MIB would have an obligation to compensate the claimant under regulation 13(2)(b). Dickinson does, however, suggest a path by which English law can be applied to the assessment issue consistently with the application of Rome II. Article 16 of Rome II could be invoked to give 'overriding mandatory effect' to the UK Compensation Body Regulations, with English law thereby applying to the issue of compensation. Interestingly, therefore, both Dickinson and the Court of Appeal agree that English law should apply to the question of quantification although by different routes. Such an outcome suggests that the earlier expressed view that English courts may strive, as far as possible, to apply their law of damages to cases involving English habitual resident claimants will remain a persistent theme even in the Rome II landscape.

C. THE US POSITION

1. Damages

11.68 In the United States it is generally accepted that most questions relating to damages are considered to be substantive and governed by the law of the cause of action. Section 171 of the Restatement (Second) of Conflict of Laws provides that 'the law having the most significant relationship to the issue determines the measure of damages'. 'Measure of damages' includes 'what items of loss can be included in the damages, and what limitations, if any, are imposed upon the amount of recovery'.[232] US court decisions have confirmed that the issue of available heads of damages falls within the concept of measure of damages and so is governed by the law of the

---

[232] US Restatement (Second) of Conflict of Laws, § 171 comment a.

state with the most significant relationship.[233] Similarly, the issue of a legislative or judicial limitation on damages is regarded as an example of measure of damages and hence substantive.[234]

11.69 The right to recover damages must, however, be distinguished from the method of assessing damages, for instance whether by court or jury, which is governed by forum law. Forum law also appears to apply in most cases of quantification of damages in the sense of the numerical process of assessment. Such a conclusion is said to follow from the provision in the Restatement which states that 'the forum will follow its own practices in determining whether the damages awarded by a jury are excessive'[235] and is a major reason for foreign claimants in tort cases being attracted to the US courts.[236]

11.70 What is important to note, though, is that the US 'most significant relationship' choice of law rule is sufficiently open-textured and flexible to apply the law of any one of a number of places as substantive law—whether it be forum law, the law of the place of injury, or a third jurisdiction. Note also that the test is issue-specific, similar to section 12 of the PILA 1995, in that it refers to the country having the most significant relationship to the *issue* of damages, not the obligation as a whole. Normally this country will be the place of the offending conduct and injury[237] unless another state has a greater interest in the issue.[238] The classic situation where another state (normally the forum) has a greater interest than the place of injury is where the plaintiff and defendant are domiciled in that state.[239] Indeed, in many decisions US courts have displaced the law of the place of injury where damages are capped in favour of the law of the common domicile, which awards full compensation on the basis that the place of injury has little interest in restricting compensation to non-residents.[240] Further, some US courts have even been prepared to bypass the law of the place of injury in

---

[233] *Kammerer v Western Gear Corp* 618 P 2d 1330 (CA Wash 1980); *Goede v Aerojet General Corp* 143 SW 3d 14 (CA Mo 2004).
[234] *Brewer v Dodson Aviation* 447 F Supp 2d 1166, 1178 (WD Wash 2006); *Butler v Stagecoach Group plc* 72 AD 3d 1581 (SCNY App Div 2010); *Livingston v Baxter Health Corp* 313 SW 3d 717 (Mo App 2010).
[235] Restatement (Second), § 171 comment f.
[236] For a criticism of this position see R Weintraub (n 139 above) 313; and McDougal (n 177 above) 423.
[237] *Goede v Aerojet General Corp* 143 SW 3d 14 (CA Mo 2004); *Herbert v District of Columbia* 808 A 2d 776 (DC 2002).
[238] US Restatement (Second), § 171 comment b.
[239] ibid.
[240] *Lemons v Cloer* 206 SW 3d 60 (CA Tenn 2006); *Marillo v Benjamin Moore & Co* 32 AD 3d 1313 (NYAD 2006); *Reach v Pearson* 860 F Supp 141 (SDNY 1994).

C. The US Position

favour of forum law where the parties are not domiciled in the same place. Such an analysis goes beyond the Commonwealth rules on displacement and shows the influence of policy on US choice of law determinations. For example, in *Jones v Winnebago Industries Inc*,[241] forum law, which provided unlimited damages, was applied to an accident in Idaho, which had a cap on damages, where the plaintiff was from Idaho but the defendant was a forum-registered corporation. The court held that forum law had the most significant relationship to the issue of compensation in a case involving one of its companies which had manufactured and distributed its products abroad. The forum's interest was in holding its corporations fully accountable for their wrongs wherever their effects occurred.[242]

An even more stark example of policy being used to apply forum law to avoid a foreign limitation on damages arose in *Townsend v Sears, Roebuck & Co*.[243] The court there noted that in an earlier decision it had held that a cap on damages under forum law was unconstitutional in that it violated the doctrine of separation of powers by improperly delegating to the legislature the power of disregarding jury verdicts on damages, which was a 'judicial' function. The court in *Townsend* then applied this policy to a foreign cap on damages, choosing to displace it in favour of forum law. The forum was said to have a strong interest in protecting against another state's legislative encroachment on judicial power to determine quantification of damages. Yet it should not be thought that the flexibility of the US approach runs only in favour of the forum. In other cases courts have opted to apply caps on damages provisions under the law of the place of injury out of deference to the fact that the lawmakers in that state had adopted such a law to establish certainty and predictability in damages awards.[244] While it is true that the US 'most significant relationship' approach does inevitably lead to less predictable results than under Commonwealth law, its explicit and transparent acknowledgement as to why forum law should apply to a question of damages (including the policies involved) is certainly refreshing when compared to the occasional opaqueness of the substance-procedure dichotomy. Some evidence of this greater candour can be seen in the Commonwealth decisions discussed at 11.62 on displacement and, to a lesser extent, public policy but the US decisions go further.

11.71

---

[241] 460 F Supp 2d 953 (ND Iowa 2006).
[242] See also *Bacci v Kaiser Permanente Foundation Health Plan* 278 F Supp 2d 34 (DDC 2003).
[243] 858 NE 2d 552 (Ill App Ct 2006).
[244] *Mastondrea v Occidental Hotels Management SA* 918 A 2d 27 (NJ Super Ct App Div 2007); see also *Brewer v Dodson Aviation* 447 F Supp 2d 1166 (WD Wash 2006).

2. Interest

11.72 Section 171 of the Restatement (Second) also states that the right to claim prejudgment interest and the rate of such interest is substantive and governed by the law which has the most significant relationship to the issue. While the Restatement suggests that the issue of the right to prejudgment interest should be considered discretely and so should not necessarily be governed by the law which applies to the measure of damages more generally, US courts have normally applied the law governing damages to the issue of whether prejudgment interest may be claimed.[245] So, in the recent case *Lou v Lotis Elevator Co*,[246] forum law (which allowed prejudgment interest) was applied to a product liability injury in China between a forum-resident plaintiff and a US company which designed the product. The forum's interest in providing compensation to its habitual residents was stronger than that of the place of injury.

---

[245] *AE Inc v Goodyear Tyre & Rubber Co* 168 P 3d 507, 511 (SC Colo 2007); *Johnson v Continental Airlines Corp* 964 F 2d 1059, 1064 (10th Cir 1992); *Schwartz v Twin City Fire Insurance Co* 492 F Supp 2d 308, 323 (SDNY 2007); the *rate* at which such interest may be claimed has also been held to be substantive: *Travelers Casualty and Surety Co v Insurance Co of North America* 609 F 3d 143 (3rd Cir 2010).

[246] 933 NE 2d 140 (Mass App Ct 2010).

12

Conclusion

The primary focus of this work has been on the distinction between substance and procedure in private international law. All legal systems have long acknowledged a distinction between procedural and substantive matters, with the former governed by forum law and the latter category by the law of the cause of action. Common law countries have traditionally taken a very wide view of procedure based on the right / remedy distinction, with all matters pertaining to the rights of the parties being deemed substantive and any issue concerning the 'remedy' regarded as procedural. The result of such an approach has been to expand significantly the scope and reach of forum law in cross-border litigation, particularly in the areas of damages, non-monetary remedies, and statutes of limitation. By contrast, in civil law countries, the concept of procedure has long been linked to the processes of the court and the mechanics of litigation, which has resulted in a narrower subjection of matters to forum law. Nevertheless, as noted throughout this work, there is clear evidence in some Commonwealth countries, such as Australia and Canada (and possibly also Singapore), of the more restrictive civilian view of procedure now being accepted, although the approaches which have been taken by courts and legislatures in those countries have not always been uniform. A similar trend in expanding the reach of substance relative to procedure is also occurring in English law, although unlike Australia and Canada the impetus for such change has come less from the courts and more through the United Kingdom's implementation of EU instruments on choice of law, particularly in the areas of contractual and non-contractual obligations, which have allocated a wider range of matters to the substantive law. While in the United States a single, universally accepted position on choice of law in procedure is difficult to identify, there is an increasing general acceptance of the view that the application of forum law in a given case should depend less on whether a matter is classified as procedural as such and more on the forum's connections and interests with the issue. While such an analysis may not have resulted in a lesser application of forum law overall, this is at least a more transparent approach than simply applying forum law because the issue concerns 'the remedy'. For Commonwealth lawyers the proper delineation of substantive and procedural matters remains critical and so much of this work has been devoted

12.01

to this question. The narrow mode or conduct of court proceedings definition of procedure was endorsed and applied in various circumstances with the aim of providing practitioners with clear guidance not only as to the current state of the law but also as to its likely future application.

12.02 In determining the appropriate division between procedure and substance it is also important to examine the choice of law system as a whole, in particular the other methods by which an issue may be subjected to forum law, apart from the procedural classification. Concepts such as public policy, overriding mandatory rules, and rules for the displacement of the applicable law are important reminders of the various and diverse interests which the forum seeks to protect in the choice of law process in parallel with, and in addition to, procedure. Also, it is valuable to consider these doctrines alongside procedure, to ensure that the classification does not exceed its proper scope. Hence, where the application of forum law to a particular question may be more appropriately justified on a ground other than the procedural classification (for example public policy in the context of foreign law limits on damages), then this has been suggested. Awareness of the other bases of reference to forum law is also important because in a number of cases the procedural classification has arguably been used as a device to conceal other, unarticulated policy bases for applying forum law, such as in the House of Lords decision in *Harding v Wealands*.[1] The goals of transparency and clarity therefore also demand that procedure should receive an appropriate interpretation.

12.03 It was also noted in this work that the substance-procedure dichotomy alone cannot resolve all choice of law questions that may arise in the area of procedure. There is a need for other choice of law rules or approaches to be developed where an issue cannot easily be subjected to either the law of the forum or the law of the cause of action. Examples given in this work include the capacity of individuals and corporations, legal professional privilege, formal validity of documents, and (possibly) the quantification of damages. A second category of cases where the substance / procedure distinction does not provide a complete coverage in terms of choice of law is where a conflict occurs within the domain of procedure itself. Issues such as service of process, taking of evidence abroad, or issue estoppel in relation to a foreign judgment are all clearly procedural due to their link to the mode or conduct of the forum court's proceedings, yet it will often not be appropriate to apply the law of the forum *exclusively* in each case. Foreign law may also be relevant, for example the law of the country where service is to be performed, where the evidence is located, or where

---

[1] [2007] 2 AC 1.

Conclusion 363

the judgment said to give rise to the estoppel was rendered. While it is not suggested in these cases that forum law should be displaced by foreign law, the application of forum law may have to be modified or qualified to take account of the foreign system to produce a hybrid or 'enlightened' version of forum law. Such a result is motivated by the same concerns which justify the need for choice of law rules more generally, namely, recognition of foreign interests and comity, uniformity of outcome, and doing justice equally between local and foreign parties. While the enlightened forum law analysis does not strictly involve a choice between the law of country A and country B, an analogous process is at work which is important to recognise.

12.04 It is to be hoped that through a consideration of these different perspectives a realization can be reached of the complex and varied choice of law issues in procedure, with an understanding gained of the practical relevance and importance of these principles to the modern era of transnational litigation.

Bibliography

BOOKS

Ahern, J and Binchy, W (eds), *The Rome II Regulation on the Law Applicable to Non-Contractual Obligations* (Martinus Nijhoff, 2009)
Audit, B, *Droit International Privé* (3rd edn, Economica, 2005)
Born, G and Rutledge, P, *International Civil Litigation in US Courts* (4th edn, Aspen Publishers, 2007)
Boskovic, O, *La Réparation du Préjudice en Droit International Privé* (LGDJ, 2003)
Briggs, A, *Agreements on Jurisdiction and Choice of Law* (OUP, 2008)
—— *The Conflict of Laws* (2nd edn, Clarendon Press, 2008)
Bucher, A and Bonomi, A, *Droit International Privé* (2nd edn, Helbing & Lichtenbahn, 2004)
Caravaca, AC and González, JC, *Derecho Internacional Privado: Vol I* (6th edn, Editorial Comares, 2005)
Collins, L (ed), *Dicey, Morris and Collins on the Conflict of Laws* (14th edn, Sweet & Maxwell, 2006)
—— *Dicey, Morris and Collins on the Conflict of Laws* (4th supp, 14th edn, Sweet & Maxwell, 2010)
Crawford, E and Carruthers, J, *International Private Law: A Scots Perspective* (3rd edn, Thomson West, 2010)
Currie, B, *Selected Essays on the Conflict of Laws* (first published 1963, William S Hein & Co, 1990)
Davies, M, Bell, A, and Brereton, P, *Nygh's Conflict of Laws in Australia* (8th edn, LexisNexis Butterworths, 201)
Dickinson, A, *The Rome II Regulation* (OUP, 2008)
Doherty, B, Thomann, C, and Scott, K, *Accidents Abroad International Personal Injury Claims* (Thomson Reuters, 2009)
Einhorn, T, *Private International Law in Israel* (Wolters Kluwer, 2009)
Fawcett, J and Carruthers, J, *Cheshire, North and Fawcett Private International Law* (14th edn, OUP, 2008)
Fentiman, R, *Foreign Law in English Courts* (OUP, 1998)
Fletcher, I, *Insolvency in Private International Law* (2nd edn, OUP, 2005)
Fox, H, *The Law of State Immunity* (2nd edn, OUP, 2008)
Geimer, R, *Internationales Zivilprozeßrecht* (5th edn, Verlag Dr Otto Schmidt, 2005)
Graveson, R, *Conflict of Laws* (7th edn, Sweet & Maxwell, 1974)
Jaeckel, F, *Die Reichweite der lex fori im internationalen Zivilprozeßrecht* (Duncker & Humblot, 1995)
Johnston, G, *The Conflict of Laws in Hong Kong* (Sweet & Maxwell, 2005)
Kahn-Freund, O, *General Problems of Private International Law* (Sijthoff, 1976)
Lorenzen, E, *Selected Articles on the Conflict of Laws* (Yale University Press, 1947)
Lowenfeld, A, *Conflict of Laws: Federal, State and International Perspectives* (2nd edn, LexisNexis, 2002)

Maine, H, *Dissertations on Early Law and Custom* (first published 1886, Arno Press, 1975)
Mayer, P and Heuze, V, *Droit International Privé* (9th edn, Montchrestien, 2007)
McClean, D, *International Co-operation in Civil and Criminal Matters* (OUP, 2002)
—— and Beevers, K, *The Conflict of Laws* (6th edn, Sweet & Maxwell, 2005)
McDougal, L, Felix, R, and Whitten, R, *American Conflicts Law* (5th edn, Transnational Publishers, 2001)
McLeod, J, *The Conflict of Laws* (Carswell Legal Publications, 1983)
Mortensen, R, Garnett, R, and Keyes, M, *Private International Law in Australia* (2nd edn, LexisNexis Butterworths, 2011)
Nafziger, J and Symeonides, S (eds), *Law and Justice in a Multistate World: Essays in Honor of Arthur T von Mehren* (Transnational Publishers, 2002)
Petrochilos, G, *Procedure in International Arbitration* (OUP, 2004)
Plender, R and Wilderspin, M, *The European Private International Law of Obligations* (3rd edn, Sweet & Maxwell, 2009)
Rafferty, N et al, *Private International Law in Common Law Canada* (2nd edn, Edmond Montgomery Publications, 2003)
Raphael, T, *The Law of Anti-Suit Injunctions* (OUP, 2008)
Rigaux, F and Fallon, M, *Droit International Privé* (3rd edn, Larcier, 2005)
Robertson, A, *Characterization in the Conflict of Laws* (Harvard University Press, 1940)
Scoles, E, Hay, P, Borchers, P, and Symeonides, S, *Conflict of Laws* (4th edn, Thomson West, 2004)
Sparka, F, *Jurisdiction and Arbitration Clauses in Maritime Transport Documents: A Comparative Analysis* (Springer-Verlag, 2010)
Stone, P, *EU Private International Law* (Edward Elgar, 2006)
Stumberg, G, *Principles of the Conflict of Laws* (3rd edn, Foundation Press, 1963)
Sykes, E and Pryles, M, *Australian Private International Law* (3rd edn, LBC, 1991)
Szászy, I, *International Civil Procedure: A Comparative Study* (Sijthoff, 1967)
Takahashi, K, *Claims for Contribution and Reimbursement in an International Context* (OUP, 2000)
Tetley, W, *International Conflict of Laws Common, Civil and Maritime* (International Shipping Publications: Blais, 1994)
Tilbury, M, Davis, G, and Opeskin, B, *Conflict of Laws in Australia* (OUP, 2002)
Van Rooij, R and Polak, M, *Private International Law in the Netherlands* (Kluwer, 1987)
—— and Steffens, L, *Private International Law in the Netherlands Supplement* (Kluwer, 1995)
Walker, J, *Castel & Walker Canadian Conflict of Laws* (6th edn, LexisNexis, Butterworths, 2005)
Weintraub, R, *Commentary on the Conflict of Laws* (4th edn, Foundation Press, 2001)
Whincop, M and Keyes, M, *Policy and Pragmatism in the Conflict of Laws* (Ashgate, 2001)
Wolff, M, *Private International Law* (2nd edn, OUP, 1950)
Wood, P, *English and International Set-Off* (Sweet & Maxwell, 1989)
—— *Conflict of Laws and International Finance* (Sweet & Maxwell, 2007)
—— *Set Off and Netting, Derivatives and Clearing Systems* (2nd edn, Sweet & Maxwell, 2007)

Yeo, T, *Choice of Law for Equitable Doctrines* (OUP, 2004)
Zimmermann, R, *Comparative Foundations of a European Law of Set-Off and Prescription* (CUP, 2002)

Book Chapters

Baratta, R, 'Processo Civile (Legge Regolatrice)' in R Baratta (ed), *Dizionari del Diritto Privato Diritto Internazionale Privato* (Giuffrè Editore, 2010) 290

Bertrams, R, 'Set-Off in Private International Law' in K Boele-Woelki et al (eds), *Comparability and Evaluation: Essays in Honour of Dimitra Kokkini-Iatridou* (Martinus Nijhoff, 1994) 153

Bonell, M, 'Limitation Periods' in A Hartkamp et al (eds), *Towards a European Civil Code* (Kluwer Law International, 3rd edn, 2004) 517

Briggs, A, 'Conflict of Laws and Commercial Remedies' in A Burrows and E Peel (eds), *Commercial Remedies: Current Issues and Problems* (OUP, 2003) 271

Buxbaum, H, 'Improving Transatlantic Cooperation in the Taking of Evidence' in A Nuyts and N Watté (eds), *International Civil Litigation in Europe* (Bruylant, 2005) 343

Carruthers, J, 'Has the Forum Lost Its Grip?' in J Ahern and W Binchy (eds), *The Rome II Regulation on the Law Applicable to Non-Contractual Obligations* (Martinus Nijhoff, 2009) 25

Davis, G, 'Damages in Transnational Tort Litigation: Legislative Restrictions and the Substance/Procedure Distinction in Australian Conflict of Laws' in J Berryman and R Bigwood (eds), *The Law of Remedies New Directions in the Common Law* (Irwin Law, 2010) 639

Fauvarque-Casson, B, 'La Prescription en Droit International Privé' in *Droit International Privé Travaux du Comité Français de Droit International Privé Année 2002–2004* (Editions Perdone, 2005) 235

Fentiman, R, 'The Significance of Close Connection' in J Ahern and W Binchy (eds), *The Rome II Regulation on the Law Applicable to Non-Contractual Obligations* (Martinus Nijhoff, 2009) 85

Forner, J, 'Service of Judicial Documents Within Europe and in Third States' in A Nuyts and N Watté (eds), *International Civil Litigation in Europe* (Bruylant 2005) 391

Heffernan, L, 'Rome II: Implications for Irish Tort Litigation' in J Ahern and W Binchy (eds), *The Rome II Regulation on the Law Applicable to Non-Contractual Obligations* (Martinus Nijhoff, 2009) 257

Kerameus, K, 'Provisional Remedies in Transnational Litigation' in International Association of Procedural Law, *Trans-National Aspects of Procedural Law* (Giuffrè Editore, 1998) vol 3, 1169

Niboyet, M-L, 'Contre le dogme de la *lex fori* en matière de procédure' in *Vers de nouveaux équilibres entre ordres juridiques mélanges en l'honneur d'Hélène Gaudemet-Tallon* (Dalloz, 2008) 363

Rushworth, A, 'Remedies and the Rome II Regulation' in J Ahern and W Binchy (eds), *The Rome II Regulation on the Law Applicable to Non-Contractual Obligations* (Martinus Nijhoff, 2009) 199

Tetley, W, 'Maritime Liens in the Conflict of Laws' in J Nafziger and S Symeonides (eds), *Law and Justice in a Multistate World: Essays in Honor of Arthur T von Mehren* (Transnational Publishers, 2002) 439

Von Hein, J, 'Article 4 and Traffic Accidents' in J Ahern and W Binchy (eds), *The Rome II Regulation on the Law Applicable to Non-Contractual Obligations* (Martinus Nijhoff, 2009) 153

Walker, J, 'Twenty Questions (about Section 23 of the Limitations Act, 2002)' in W Gray, L Kerbel-Caplan, and J Ziegel (eds), *The New Ontario Limitations Regime: Exposition and Analysis* (Ontario Bar Association, 2005) 95

ARTICLES

Ailes, E, 'Substance and Procedure in the Conflict of Laws' (1941) 39 Michigan L Rev 392

Anderson, R, 'International Torts in the High Court of Australia' (2002) 10 Torts LJ 132

Arevalo, I, 'Spain: Contract—Damages Claims' (2006) 17(6) International Company and Commercial L Rev N46

Beale, J, 'The Jurisdiction of Courts over Foreigners' (1913) 26 Harvard L Rev 283

Beaumont, P and Tang, Z, 'Classification of Delictual Damages: *Harding v Wealands* and the Rome II Regulation' (2008) 12 Edinburgh L Rev 131

Beckett, W, 'The Question of Classification in Private International Law' (1934) 15 BYBIL 46

Bellini, V, 'Evidence in Private International Law' [1953] University of Western Australia L Rev 330

Berger, K, 'Evidentiary Privileges: Best Practice Standards versus/and Arbitral Discretion' (2006) 22 Arbitration Intl 501

Bradford, S, 'Conflict of Laws and the Attorney-Client Privilege: A Territorial Solution' (1991) 52 University of Pittsburgh L Rev 909

Briggs, A, 'The International Dimension to Claims for Contribution: *Arab Monetary Fund v Hashim*' [1995] LMCLQ 437

—— 'The Unrestrained Breach of an Anti-Suit Injunction: A Pause for Thought' [1997] LMCLQ 90

—— 'The Legal Significance of the Place of a Tort' (2002) 2 OUCLJ 133

—— 'Decisions of British Courts during 2004 Involving Questions of Public or Private International Law' (2004) 75 BYBIL 537

—— 'Decisions of British Courts during 2006 Involving Questions of Public or Private International Law' (2006) 77 BYBIL 554

—— 'When in Rome Choose as the Romans Choose' (2009) 125 LQR 191

Brilmayer, L, 'The Role of Substantive and Choice of Law Policies in the Formation and Application of Choice of Law Rules' (1995) 252 *Hague Recueil* 9

Campos, JG, 'Les Liens Entre La Competénce Judiciaire et La Compétence Législative en Droit International Privé' (1977) 156 *Hague Recueil* 227

Cappelletti, M, 'Review of I Szászy, *International Civil Procedure: A Comparative Study*' (1968) 16 AJCL 624

Carruthers, J and Crawford, E, 'Kuwait Airways Corp v Iraqi Airways Co' (2003) 52 ICLQ 761

Carruthers, J, 'Substance and Procedure in the Conflict of Laws: A Continuing Debate in Relation to Damages' (2004) 53 ICLQ 691

—— 'Damages in the Conflict of Laws—The Substance and Procedure Spectrum: *Harding v Wealands*' (2005) 1 JPIL 323

Carter, P, 'Priorities of Claims in Private International Law' (1984) 54 BYBIL 207

—— 'The Role of Public Policy in English Private International Law' (1993) 42 ICLQ 1

Chapman, M, 'The Rome II Regulation and a European Law Enforcement Area: Harmony and Discord in the Assessment of Damages' [2010] Journal of Personal Injury Law 10

Collins, L, 'The United States Supreme Court and the Principles of Comity: Evidence in Transnational Litigation' (2006) 8 YBPIL 53

Cook, W, '"Substance" and "Procedure" in the Conflict of Laws' (1933) 42 Yale LJ 333

Crawford, E, 'The Adjective and the Noun: Title and Right to Sue in Private International Law' [2000] Juridical Rev 347

Curry-Sumner, I, 'An Age-old Dilemma: Is It Time for a Revolutionary Approach? A Comment on *Harding v Wealands*' (2006) 8 YBPIL 321

Davies, M and Lewins, K, 'Foreign Maritime Liens: Should they be Recognised in Australian Courts?' (2002) 76 Australian LJ 775

Davies, M, ——'Case Note *Neilson v Overseas Projects Corporation of Victoria Ltd* Renvoi and Presumptions about Foreign Law' (2006) 30 Melbourne University L Rev 244

—— 'Bypassing the Hague Evidence Convention: Private International Law Implications of the Use of Audio or Video Conferencing in Transnational Litigation' (2007) 55 AJCL 205

—— 'Choice of Law after the Civil Liability Legislation' (2008) 16 Torts LJ 104

—— 'Choice of Law and US Maritime Liens' (2009) 83 Tulane L Rev 1435

Davis, G, 'Case Note: John Pfeiffer Pty Ltd v Rogerson: Choice of Law at the Dawning of the 21st Century' (2000) 24 Melbourne University L Rev 982

De Boer, T, 'Facultative Choice of Law: The Procedural Status of Choice of Law Rules and Foreign Law' (1996) 257 *Hague Recueil* 223

Dickinson, A, 'Applicable Law Arbitrage—An Opportunity Missed?' (2005) 121 LQR 374

Dolinger, J and Tiburcio, C, 'The Forum Rule in International Litigation—Which Procedural Law Governs Proceedings to be Performed in Foreign Jurisdictions: *Lex Fori* or *Lex Diligentiae*?' (1998) 33 Texas Intl LJ 425

Dougherty, C and Wyles, L, '*Harding v Wealands*' (2007) 56 ICLQ 443

Eiselen, S, '*Laconian* Revisited: A Reappraisal of Classification in Conflicts Law' (2006) 123 South African LJ 147

Fassberg, C, 'The Forum: Its Role and Significance in Choice-of-Law' (1985) 84 *Zeitschrift für Vergleichende Rechtswissenschaft* 1

Feuillade, M, 'Ley que Rige el Proceso en Casos Iusprivatistas Internacionales' 72 (165) *La Ley*, 28 August 2008

Forsyth, C, 'Characterisation Revisited: An Essay in the Theory and Practice of the English Conflict of Laws' (1998) 114 LQR 141

—— 'Mind the Gap Part II: the South African Court of Appeal and Characterisation' (2006) 2 JPIL 425

Garnett, R, '*Renault v Zhang*: A Job Half Done?' (2002) 10 Tort L Rev 145

—— 'The Hague Choice of Court Convention: Magnum Opus or Much Ado about Nothing?' (2009) 5 JPIL 161

Garrow, D, Hansen, D, and Parkes, M, 'Damages for Personal Injury or Wrongful Death in Canada' (2004) 69 Journal of Air Law and Commerce 233

Graveson, R, 'Review of I Szászy, *International Civil Procedure: A Comparative Study*' (1968) 17 ICLQ 534

Gray, A, 'Loss Distribution Issues in Multinational Tort Claims: Giving Substance to Substance' (2008) 4 JPIL 279

Griffith, G, Rose, D, and Gageler, S, 'Choice of Law Rules in Cross-Vested Jurisdiction: A Reply to Kelly and Crawford' (1988) 62 Australian LJ 698

Gummow, Hon Justice W, 'Form or Substance?' (2008) 30 Australian Bar Rev 229

Hage-Chahine, F, 'La Prescription Extinctive en Droit International Privé' (1995) 255 *Hague Recueil* 229

Hardin, P and Kaelin, W, 'Characterization of Survival of Tort Actions' (1954) 4 Duke Bar J 105

Harris, J, 'Anti-Suit Injunctions—A Home Comfort?' [1997] LMCLQ 413

—— 'Tracing and the Conflict of Laws' (2002) 73 BYBIL 65

—— 'Does Choice of Law Make Any Sense?' (2004) 57 Current Legal Problems 305

Hartley, T, 'Mandatory Rules in International Contracts: The Common Law Approach' (1997) 266 *Hague Recueil* 337

—— 'Jurisdiction in Conflict of Laws—Disclosure, Third-Party Debt and Freezing Orders' (2010) 126 LQR 194

Hausmann, R, 'Pleading and Proof of Foreign Law: A Comparative Analysis' (2008) Eur LF I-2008 I-I

Higgins, P, 'Some Aspects of Substance and Procedure in the Conflict of Laws' [1965] Australian Yearbook of International Law 53

Hodges, C, 'Europeanisation of Civil Justice: Trends and Issues' (2007) 26 Civil Justice Quarterly 96

Illmer, M, 'Neutrality Matters—Some Thoughts about the Rome Regulations and the so-called Dichotomy of Substance and Procedure in European Private International Law' (2009) 28 Civil Justice Quarterly 237

Kay, H, 'Foreign Law as Datum' (1965) 53 California L Rev 47

Kelly, D and Crawford, J, 'The Cross-Vesting Scheme' (1988) 62 Australian LJ 589

Kerameus, K, 'Enforcement in the International Context' (1997) 264 *Hague Recueil* 179

Keyes, M, 'Substance and Procedure in Multistate Tort Litigation' (2010) 18 Torts LJ 201

Kozlowska, D, 'Privilege in the Multijurisdictional Area of International Arbitration' (2011) 14 International Arbitration L Rev 128

Kozyris, P, 'Rome II: Tort Conflicts on the Right Track—A Postscript to Symeon Symeonides' Missed Opportunity' (2008) 56 AJCL 471

Kramer, L, 'Rethinking Choice of Law' (1990) 90 Columbia L Rev 277

Lorenzen, E, 'The Statute of Limitations and the Conflict of Laws' (1919) 28 Yale LJ 492

—— 'The Statute of Frauds and the Conflict of Laws' (1923) 32 Yale LJ 311

Lowenfeld, A, 'Introduction: The Elements of Procedure: Are They Separately Portable?' (1997) 45 AJCL 649

Magnus, U, 'Set-Off and the Rome I Proposal' (2006) 8 YBPIL 113
Main, T, 'The Procedural Foundation of Substantive Law' (2010) 87 Washington University L Rev 801
Mason, R, 'Choice of Law in Cross-Border Insolvencies: Matters of Substance and Procedure' (2001) 9 Insolvency LJ 69
McComish, J, 'Foreign Legal Professional Privilege: A New Problem for Australian Private International Law' (2006) 28 Sydney L Rev 297
—— 'Pleading and Proving Foreign Law in Australia' (2007) 31 Melbourne University L Rev 400
McEvoy, J, 'Characterization of Limitation Statutes in Canadian Private International Law: the Rocky Road of Change' (1996) 19 Dalhousie LJ 425
Merrett, L, 'Worldwide Freezing Orders in Europe' [2008] LMCLQ 71
Mills, A, 'The Dimensions of Public Policy in Private International Law' (2008) 4 JPIL 201
Morgan, E, 'Choice of Law Governing Proof' (1944) 58 Harvard L Rev 153
—— 'Rules of Evidence—Substantive or Procedural?' (1957) 10 Vanderbilt L Rev 467
Mortensen, R, 'Homing Devices in Choice of Tort Law: Australian, British and Canadian Approaches' (2006) 55 ICLQ 839
Mosk, R and Ginsburg, T, 'Evidentiary Privileges in International Arbitration' (2001) 50 ICLQ 345
Myburgh, P, 'Recognition and Priority of Foreign Ship Mortgages: *The Betty Ott*' [1992] LMCLQ 155
—— 'The New Zealand Ship Registration Act 1992' [1993] LMCLQ 444
Neels, J, 'Falconbridge in South Africa' (2008) 4 JPIL 167
Niederländer, H, 'Materielles Recht und Verfahrensrecht im Internationalen Privatrecht' (1955) 20 *Rabels Zeitschrift* 1
Opeskin, B, 'Statutory Caps on Damages in Australian Conflict of Laws' (1993) 109 LQR 533
Oppong, R, 'A Decade of Private International Law in African Courts 1997–2007 (Part I)' (2007) 9 YBPIL 223
Panagopoulos, G, 'Substance and Procedure in Private International Law' (2005) 1 JPIL 69
Petch, T, 'Substance and Procedure' (2005) 121 LQR 370
Pryles, M, 'Tort and Related Obligations in Private International Law' (1991) 227 *Hague Recueil* 9
Risinger, D Michael, 'Substance' and 'Procedure' Revisited: With Some Afterthoughts on the Constitutional Problems of Irrebuttable Presumptions' (1982) 30 UCLA L Rev 189
Robertson, G, '*Castillo v Castillo*: Limitation Periods and the Conflict of Laws' (2002) 40 Alberta L Rev 447
Rogerson, P, 'Quantification of Damages—Substance or Procedure?' [2006] Cambridge LJ 515
Rushworth, A and Scott, A, 'Rome II: Choice of Law for Non-Contractual Obligations' [2008] LMCLQ 274
Schoeman, E, '*Harding v Wealands*: Substance and Procedure in the English Courts' (2007) 13 New Zealand Business LQ 3

—— 'Rome II and the Substance-Procedure Dichotomy' [2010] LMCLQ 81
Scott, A, 'Substance and Procedure and Choice of Law in Torts' [2006] LMCLQ 44
Sedler, R, 'The *Erie* Outcome Test as a Guide to Substance and Procedure in the Conflict of Laws' (1962) 37 NYU L Rev 813
Sinisi, V and Sculli, A, 'Italian Conflict-of-Law Rules' (2007) 29 Comparative Law Yearbook of International Business 207
Spigelman, J, 'Proof of Foreign Law by Reference to the Foreign Court' (2011) 127 LQR 208
Spiro, E, 'Forum Regit Processum' (1969) 18 ICLQ 949
Staniland, H, 'Foreign Maritime Liens Not to be Recognized in South Africa' [1990] LMCLQ 491
Stone, P, 'Time Limitation in the English Conflict of Laws' [1985] LMCLQ 497
——'The Rome II Regulation on Choice of Law in Tort' (2007) 4 Ankara L Rev 95
Symeonides, S, 'Rome II and Tort Conflicts: A Missed Opportunity' (2008) 56 AJCL 173
Szászy, I, 'The Basic Connecting Factor in International Cases in the Domain of Civil Procedure' (1966) 15 ICLQ 436
Theophilopoulos, C, 'The Anglo-American Legal Privilege against Self-Incrimination and the Fear of Foreign Prosecution' (2003) 25 Sydney L Rev 305
Thole, C, 'Anscheinsbeweis und Beweisvereitelung im harmonisierten Europäischen Kollisionsrecht—ein Prüfstein für die Abgrenzung zwischen lex causae und lex fori' [2010] *Praxis des Internationalen Privat und Verfahrensrechts* 285
Tobin, R and Schoeman, E, 'The New Zealand Accident Compensation Scheme: The Statutory Bar and the Conflict of Laws' (2005) 53 AJCL 493
Totterman, R, 'Functional Bases of the Rule *Locus Regit Actum* in English Conflict Rules' (1953) 2 ICLQ 27
Walker, J, '*Castillo v Castillo*: Closing the Barn Door' (2006) 43 Canadian Business LJ 487
Webb, P, 'Some Thoughts on the Place of English Law as *Lex Fori* in English Private International Law' (1961) 10 ICLQ 818
Weinstein, J, 'Recognition in the United States of the Privileges of Another Jurisdiction' (1956) 56 Columbia L Rev 535
Weintraub, R, 'Choice of Law for Quantification of Damages: A Judgment of the House of Lords Makes a Bad Rule Worse' (2007) 42 Texas Intl LJ 311
Yackee, J, 'Choice of Law Considerations in the Validity and Enforcement of International Forum Selection Agreements: Whose Law Applies?" (2004) 9 UCLA Journal of Intl Law and Foreign Affairs 43

GOVERNMENT REPORTS

Australian Law Reform Commission and New South Wales Law Reform Commission, *Uniform Evidence Law* (Report No 102, 2006)
Australian Law Reform Commission, *Choice of Law* (Report No 58, 1992)
English Law Commission, *Classification of Limitation in Private International Law* (Law Com No 75, 1982)

English Law Commission, *Private International Law: Foreign Money Liabilities* (Law Com No 124, 1983)
English Law Commission and Scottish Law Commission, *Private International Law: Choice of Law in Tort and Delict* (Law Com No 87, 1984)
European Commission, 'Proposal for a Regulation on the Law Applicable to Non-Contractual Obligations' COM (2003)
Hague Conference on Private International Law, Conclusions and Recommendations of the Special Commission (2009) <http://www.hcch.net/upload/wop/jac_concl_e.pdf> (accessed 3 October 2011)
Law Commission of India, 193rd Report on Transnational Litigation: Conflict of Laws—Law of Limitation (2005) <http://lawcommissionofindia.nic.in/reports/Report193.pdf> (accessed 3 October 2011)
Singapore Academy of Law Reform Committee, Report on Pre- and Post-Judgment Interest (2005) <http://www.agc.gov.sg/publications/docs/LRC_Report_on_Interest-August_2005.pdf> (accessed 3 October 2011)

OTHER PUBLICATIONS

Carlier, P, L'Utilisation de la Lex Fori dans La Résolution des Conflits de Lois (PhD thesis, Université de Lille 2 2008)
Dickinson, A, 'Rome-ing Instinct?' (Conflict of Laws.Net: News and Views in Private International Law, 8 November 2010) <http://conflictoflaws.net/2010/rome-ing-instinct/> (accessed 3 October 2011)
Giuliano, M and Lagarde, P, Report on the Convention on the Law Applicable to Contractual Obligations [1980] OJ C282
International Law Association, Report of the Seventy-Third Conference (International Law Association, 2008)

Index

administration *see* judicial administration
admissibility of evidence
   in criminal cases 7.08–7.11
   documentary evidence 7.05–7.07
   general principles 7.03–7.04
   use of extrinsic evidence 7.12–7.14
agency estoppel 7.54
alternative methods of forum reference
   forum law-specific choice of law rules 3.23–3.27
   overriding mandatory rules 3.22
   overview 3.15
   pleading and proof of foreign law 3.28–3.29
   public policy 3.16–3.21
   uniformity of outcome 3.30
***Anshun* estoppel** 7.42–7.44
anti-suit injunctions 4.62–4.63, 10.07
   EU law 10.16
appeals 6.16–6.19
applicable law
   damages and compensation
     displacement to avoid foreign damages 11.39–11.47
     Rome II 11.53–11.59, 11.62–11.64
   displacement to avoid foreign limitations 9.37–9.38
audio evidence 8.08, 8.37
Australia
   characterization
     self-characterization 3.07
     uniformity of outcome 3.09
   choice of proper parties 5.13
   damages and compensation
     alternative compensation schemes 11.14–11.15
     conditions precedent 11.49
     deductibility of benefits 11.11–11.13
     displacement of applicable law 11.46
     jurisdictional control 11.50
   estoppel
     Anshun estoppel 7.42–7.44
     provisions preventing relitigation 7.47–7.50
   evidence
     admissibility 7.04
     burden of proof 7.15
     enforcement of foreign requests for disclosure 8.60
     rebuttable presumptions 7.21
     use of extrinsic evidence 7.13
   judicial administration
     appeals 6.16–6.19
     costs and fees 6.31
     creditors' rights 6.73
     'no action' clauses 6.41
     notice before action provisions 6.22, 6.24–6.29, 11.48
   jurisdiction
     immunities from jurisdiction 4.66, 4.69–4.70
     personal jurisdiction 4.47–4.48
   limitations 9.05–9.06
     amendment of claims and 9.31, 9.33
     uniformity of outcome 9.28–9.29
   'named court' provisions 6.55–6.58
   parties to litigation
     derivative actions 5.42–5.43
     foreign state entities 5.53
     proportionate liability 5.21
     'sue others first' provisions 5.33
   privilege
     audio-video evidence from abroad 8.37
     lawyer-client communications 8.22–8.23
     self-incrimination 8.46–8.48, 8.58
     substance and procedure 8.22–8.23
   quantification of damages
     legislative or judicial limitations 11.19–11.20
     numerical assessment and methods 11.27, 11.32
   service of process 4.28–4.30
   substance/procedure distinction
     case-by-case approach 2.18
     further significant developments 2.31–2.35
     new principles for procedure 2.22–2.24
     new principles for substance 2.25–2.27
   taking of evidence abroad 8.04–8.06, 8.08, 8.17

burden of proof
   characterization 3.08
   EU law 7.17
   general principles 7.15–7.16

Canada
   costs and fees 6.31
   damages and compensation
     alternative compensation schemes 11.14–11.15
     deductibility of benefits 11.11
   estoppel

Canada *(cont.)*
    by representation of fact 7.52
    issue and cause of action
        estoppel 7.41
  evidence
    admissibility 7.04
    burden of proof 7.15
    writing requirements 7.27–7.28
  interest on damages
    pre-judgment interest 11.03
    rate of interest 11.07
  interlocutory injunctions 10.10
  judicial administration
    creditors' rights 6.68–6.69
    'leave of the court' provisions 6.48
    'named court' provisions 6.50–6.51, 6.54
    'no action' clauses 6.41–6.43, 6.46
  limitations 9.05–9.06, 9.39–9.42
  parties to litigation
    derivative actions 5.41
    foreign state entities 5.49–5.51
    'sue others first' provisions 5.33
  personal jurisdiction 4.44–4.45
  privilege
    lawyer-client
        communications 8.22–8.23
    self-incrimination 8.49–8.50
  quantification of damages
    legislative or judicial
        limitations 11.24–11.26
    numerical assessment and
        methods 11.33
  service of process 4.33
  statutory restrictions on
      remedies 10.32–10.35
  substance/procedure distinction
    adoption of new principles 2.28–2.30
    case-by-case approach 2.18
capacity
  to be a party to litigation 5.05–5.08
  to sue and be sued 5.01–5.04
case management 6.08–6.10
characterization
  applicable law 3.06
  avoidance by legislation 3.08
  individual or global provision
      approach 3.04–3.05
  rule of law or issue 3.02–3.03
  self-characterizing provisions 3.07
  uniformity of outcome/'no
      advantage' 3.09–3.14
choice of court clauses
  Commonwealth countries 4.54–4.58
  United States 4.59
choice of law rules
  harmonization to avoid 3.31–3.33

  lawyer-client privilege 8.34–8.36
  limitations 9.35–9.36
  method of forum reference 3.23–3.27
  pleadings 6.05–6.07
  service of process
    Australia 4.28–4.30
    Canada 4.33
    English law 4.16–4.27
    EU Service Regulation 4.15
    Hague Service Convention 4.09–4.14
    Hong Kong 4.31
    Singapore 4.32
    United States 4.34–4.40
  taking of evidence abroad
    EU law 8.15
    Hague Evidence
        Convention 8.12–8.14
comity
  capacity to sue and be sued 5.01, 5.08
  characterization 3.06
  enforcement of foreign decrees 6.82
  Henderson, issue and cause of action
      estoppel 7.44
  importance 2.08
  inconsistency with convenience 2.10
  jurisdiction 4.44
  representative actions 5.27
  rights of creditors 6.67
  service of process 4.19, 4.21, 4.24, 4.37
commencement of proceedings 6.03
compensation *see* **damages and compensation**
condition precedent provisions
  notice before action
      provisions 6.22–6.29
  other requirements 6.30
constructive trusts 10.21
contingency fees 6.36
contribution and indemnity 5.18–5.19
convenience
  approach to substance and
      procedure 2.19–2.20
  rationale for application of forum
      law 2.09–2.10
corporations
  capacity to be a party to litigation 5.05
  capacity to sue and be sued 5.02
  derivative actions
    Commonwealth countries 5.40–5.43
    English law 5.35–5.39
    United States 5.44–5.47
costs and fees
  Commonwealth countries 6.31
  contingency fees 6.36
  EU law 6.32
  security for costs 6.37–6.39
  United States 6.33–6.35

Index

counterclaims 10.30
courts
  appeals 6.16–6.19
  case management 6.08–6.10
  choice of court clauses
    Commonwealth countries 4.54–4.58
    United States 4.59
  commencement of proceedings 6.03
  condition precedent provisions 6.22–6.30
  constitution and competence 6.02
  disclosure of evidence 6.11–6.12
  jury trials 6.13–6.15
  'no action' clauses
    generic court provisions 6.40–6.46
    'leave of the court'
      provisions 6.47–6.48
    'named court' provisions 6.49–6.58
  notice before action provisions 6.22–6.29
  pleadings 6.04–6.07
  public hearings 6.20–6.21
creditors
  nature and status of rights
    Australia 6.73
    Canada 6.68–6.69
    English law 6.65–6.67
    EU law 6.74–6.75
    New Zealand 6.70–6.71
    South Africa 6.72
    United States 6.76
  priorities 6.59–6.64

damages and compensation
  alternative compensation
    schemes 11.14–11.15
  conditions precedent 11.48–11.49
  deductibility of benefits 11.09–11.13
  displacement of applicable
    law 11.39–11.47
  heads of claim 11.02
  interest on damages
    post-judgment interest 11.06
    pre-judgment interest 11.03–11.05
    rate of interest 11.07–11.08
    US approach 11.72
  jurisdictional control 11.50–11.51
  overriding mandatory rules 11.38
  overview 11.01
  public policy 11.37
  quantification
    legislative or judicial
      limitations 11.17–11.26
    numerical assessment and
      methods 11.27–11.36
  remoteness of damage 11.16
  Rome II
    applicable law 11.53–11.59
    deductibility of benefits 11.56
    displacement of applicable
      law 11.62–11.64
    heads of claim 11.54
    interest 11.55
    limitations on damages 11.54
    overriding mandatory rules 11.61,
      11.67
    public policy 11.60
    quantification of damages 11.57–11.59
    recent English case law 11.65–11.67
  US approach
    general principles 11.68–11.71
    interest on damages 11.72
deductibility of benefits 11.09–11.13
derivative actions
  Commonwealth countries 5.40–5.43
  English law 5.35–5.39
  United States 5.44–5.47
diplomatic immunity 4.65, 4.69–4.70
disclosure of evidence
  administrative requirements 6.11–6.12
  enforcement of foreign requests 8.60–8.64
  judicial administration 7.34
  privilege
    lawyer-client
      communications 8.21–8.36
    self-incrimination 8.38–8.59
documentary evidence 7.05–7.07
domicile, law of the
  capacity to sue and be sued 5.01–5.04
  inter-spousal liability 5.23

enforcement
  choice of court clauses 4.57–4.58
  foreign requests for disclosure 8.60–8.64
  judgments and orders
    methods 6.78–6.81
    rules 6.82–6.83
English law
  characterization 3.03
  creditors' rights 6.65–6.67
  damages and compensation
    deductibility of benefits 11.09–11.10
    displacement of applicable
      law 11.40–11.44
    jurisdictional control 11.50
  historical approach to matters of
    procedure 2.03–2.08
  interest on damages
    post-judgment interest 11.06
    pre-judgment interest 11.04–11.05
    rate of interest 11.07–11.08
  issue and cause of action
    estoppel 7.37–7.40
  lawyer-client privilege 8.22, 8.24–8.25
  limitations
    amendment of claims and 9.32–9.33

English law *(cont.)*
  displacement of applicable law 9.37
  Foreign Limitation Periods Act
    1984 9.12–9.19
  impact of EU law 9.24–9.26
  judicial development of the
    law 9.31–9.34
  jurisdictional disputes 9.35
  public policy defence 9.20–9.23
  renvoi 9.27, 9.30
  parties to litigation
    derivative actions 5.35–5.39
    foreign state entities 5.52
  personal jurisdiction 4.46
  privilege
    lawyer-client communications 8.22,
      8.24–8.25
    self-incrimination 8.41–8.45, 8.57
  quantification of damages
    legislative or judicial limitations 11.18–
      11.19, 11.21–11.23
    numerical assessment and
      methods 11.27–11.29
  service of process 4.16–4.27
  set-off 10.25–10.26
  substance/procedure distinction
    application of right-remedy
      approach 2.03–2.08, 2.36
    case-by-case approach 2.18
    Harding v Wealands 2.37–2.47
  taking of evidence abroad 8.03–8.08
equity
  constructive trusts and
    tracing 10.21–10.22
  forum law-specific choice of law
    rules 3.23, 3.26–3.27
  specific performance and rescission 10.20
estoppel
  agency estoppel 7.54
  by convention 7.53
  Henderson estoppel 7.42–7.44
  issue and cause of action 7.37–7.41
    US law 7.45–7.46
  promissory estoppel 7.54
  proprietary estoppel 7.55
  provisions preventing
    relitigation 7.47–7.50
  by representation of fact 7.52
EU law
  see also **Rome I**; **Rome II**
  avoidance of characterization 3.08
  damages
    applicable law 11.53–11.59
    displacement of the applicable
      law 11.62–11.64
    overriding mandatory rules 11.61
    public policy 11.60

evidence
  burden of proof 7.17
  documentary evidence and formal
    validity 7.06–7.07
  presumptions 7.24
  use of extrinsic evidence 7.14
  writing requirements 7.28
judicial administration
  costs and fees 6.32
  creditors' rights 6.74–6.75
personal jurisdiction 4.53
public policy 3.18
remedies
  anti-suit injunctions 10.16
  interlocutory injunctions 10.15
  final non-monetary relief 10.23–10.24
  freezing orders 10.17
  search orders 10.18
  set-off 10.28
service of process 4.15
substance/procedure distinction
  choice of law instruments 2.51–2.53
taking of evidence abroad 8.15
evidence
  admissibility
    in criminal cases 7.08–7.11
    documentary evidence 7.05–7.07
    general principles 7.03–7.04
    use of extrinsic evidence 7.12–7.14
  burden of proof
    characterization 3.08
    EU law 7.17
    general principles 7.14, 7.15–7.16
  disclosure
    enforcement of foreign
      requests 8.60–8.64
    judicial administration 7.34
    lawyer-client
      communications 8.21–8.36
    self-incrimination 8.38–8.59
  judicial administration 7.34–7.35
  overview 7.01–7.02
  pre-trial collection 6.11–6.12
  presumptions
    classification 7.18
    EU law 7.24
    irrebuttable presumptions 7.18
    public policy 7.25
    rebuttable presumptions 7.19–7.23
  standard of proof 7.33
  taking of evidence abroad
    application of foreign law 8.16–8.19
    Commonwealth approach 8.03–8.08
    EU law 8.15
    Hague Evidence Convention 8.12–8.14
    overview 8.01–8.02
    US approach 8.09–8.10

evidence *(cont.)*
  weight or value 7.32
  witnesses 7.31
  writing requirements 7.26–7.30

fatal accident claims 5.14, 5.24–5.25
fees *see* **costs and fees**
final injunctions 10.20
foreign judgments
  rules for enforcement 6.82–6.83
  service of process and 4.26–4.27, 4.38
foreign law
  pleading and proof 3.28–3.29, 7.23
  public policy to exclude 3.16–3.21
  remedies 10.05
  taking of evidence abroad 8.16–8.19
foreign state entities
  immunities from jurisdiction 4.64–4.70
  parties to litigation
    Australia 5.53
    Canada 5.49–5.51
    English law 5.52
    overview 5.48
    United States 5.54
formal validity 7.06–7.07
forum law
  see also **characterization**
  alternative methods of reference
    forum law-specific choice of law rules 3.23–3.27
    overriding mandatory rules 3.22
    overview 3.15
    pleading and proof of foreign law 3.28–3.29
    public policy 3.16–3.21
    uniformity of outcome 3.30
  importance 1.03
  limitations 9.39–9.41
  matters of procedure
    Australian approach 2.21–2.24, 2.31–2.35
    Canadian approach 2.28–2.31
    case-by-case approach 2.18
    convenience approach 2.19–2.20
    convenience rationale 2.09–2.10
    English approach 2.36–2.47
    European civil law approach 2.02
    EU instruments 2.51–2.53
    natural justice rationale 2.11–2.12
    new approach 2.48–2.50
    public law rationale 2.13
    right-remedy approach 2.03–2.08
    territorial sovereignty rationale 2.14–2.16
    US approach 2.54–2.58
  substance/procedure distinction
    Australian approach 2.21–2.24, 2.31–2.35

  Canadian approach 2.28–2.30
  case-by-case approach 2.18
  conclusions 2.59
  convenience approach 2.19–2.20
  English approach 2.36–2.47
  EU law 2.51–2.53
  new approach 2.48–2.50
  right-remedy approach 2.03–2.08
  US approach 2.54–2.58
forum law-specific choice of law rules 3.23–3.27
freezing orders 10.13
  EU law 10.17

Harmonization
  overview 1.05
  to avoid choice of law rules 3.31–3.33
Henderson **estoppel** 7.42–7.44
Hong Kong
  costs and fees 6.31
  displacement of applicable law to avoid damages 11.45
  estoppel
    by convention 7.53
    issue and cause of action estoppel 7.41
  rebuttable presumptions 7.20
  self-incrimination 8.57
  service of process 4.31

immunities from jurisdiction 4.64–4.70
in rem **jurisdiction** 4.60–4.61
indemnity *see* **contribution and indemnity**
injunctions
  anti-suit injunctions 4.62–4.63, 10.07, 10.16
  final injunctions 10.20
  freezing orders 8.04, 10.13, 10.17
  interlocutory injunctions 10.08–10.12
insolvency
  creditors
    nature and status of rights 6.65–6.76
    priorities 6.59–6.64
  forum law-specific choice of law rules 3.23
  set-off 10.31
insurance
  direct action against insurer 5.12
  subrogation 5.20
inter-spousal liability 5.23
interest on damages
  post-judgment interest 11.06
  pre-judgment interest 11.03–11.05
  rate of interest 11.07–11.08
interim and provisional remedies
  anti-suit injunctions 4.62–4.63, 10.07
  freezing orders 10.13
    EU law 10.17

380   Index

interim and provisional remedies *(cont.)*
  interlocutory injunctions 10.08–10.12
  overview 10.06
  Rome I 10.19
  Rome II 10.15–10.19
  search orders 10.14
    EU law 10.18
interlocutory injunctions 10.08–10.12
irrebuttable presumptions 7.18
issue and cause of action
  estoppel 7.37–7.41

joinder 5.17
judgments and orders
  enforcement
    methods 6.78–6.81
    foreign judgments
      rules for enforcement 6.82–6.83
      service of process and 4.26–4.27, 4.38
  form and requirements 6.77
judicial administration
  costs and fees
    Commonwealth countries 6.31
    contingency fees 6.36
    EU law 6.32
    security for costs 6.37–6.39
    United States 6.33–6.35
  courts
    appeals 6.16–6.19
    case management 6.08–6.10
    commencement of
      proceedings 6.03
    condition precedent
      provisions 6.22–6.30, 11.48–11.49
    constitution and competence 6.02
    disclosure of evidence 6.11–6.12
    jury trials 6.13–6.15
    notice before action
      provisions 6.22–6.29
    pleadings 6.04–6.07
    public hearings 6.20–6.21
  creditors
    nature and status of
      rights 6.65–6.76
    priorities 6.59–6.64
  evidence 7.34–7.35
  judgments and orders
    enforcement methods 6.78–6.81
    form and requirements 6.77
    rules of enforcement 6.82–6.83
  'no action' clauses
    generic court provisions 6.40–6.46
    'leave of the court'
      provisions 6.47–6.48
    'named court' provisions 6.49–6.58
jurisdiction
  anti-suit injunctions 4.62–4.63

  Australian approach to sub-
    stance/procedure distinction 2.35
  choice of court clauses
    Commonwealth countries 4.54–4.58
    United States 4.59
  damages and compensation 11.50–11.51
  immunities from jurisdiction 4.64–4.70
  in rem jurisdiction 4.60–4.61
  limitations 9.35–9.36
  'named court' provisions
    divesting jurisdiction 6.55–6.58
    vesting jurisdiction 6.49–6.54
  personal jurisdiction
    Australia 4.47–4.48
    Canada 4.44–4.45
    English law 4.46
    establishment 4.43
    EU law 4.53
    Singapore 4.49
    United States 4.50–4.52
  relevance 4.41
  subject matter jurisdiction 4.42, 4.64
  various meanings 4.42
jury trials 6.13–6.15

lawyers
  communications privilege
    choice of law rules 8.34–8.36
    substance/procedure
      distinction 8.21–8.28
    US approach 8.29–8.33
  costs and fees
    Commonwealth countries 6.31
    contingency fees 6.36
    EU law 6.32
    security for costs 6.37–6.39
    United States 6.33–6.35
'leave of the court' provisions 6.47–6.48
legal professional privilege *see* **lawyers**
lex fori see **forum law**
liability
  inter-spousal liability 5.23
  proportionate liability 5.21
  vicarious liability 5.22
limitations
  amendment of claims 9.31–9.33
  Canada
    legislative developments 9.39–9.42
  choice of law rules 9.35–9.36
  common law position
    overriding mandatory rules 9.11,
      9.40–9.41
    right-remedy approach 9.01–9.04
    South African *via media* 9.08–9.10
    substantive trend 9.05–9.07
  displacement of applicable law 9.37–9.38
  jurisdictional disputes 9.35–9.36

limitations *(cont.)*
  time provisions other than
    limitations 9.43–9.44
  UK statutory regime
    Foreign Limitation Periods Act
      1984 9.12–9.19
    impact of EU law 9.24–9.26
    judicial development of the
      law 9.31–9.34
    public policy defence 9.20–9.23
    renvoi 9.27, 9.30
    US approach 9.45–9.49
    waiver 9.34

mandatory rules *see* **overriding mandatory rules**
matters of procedure
  English law 2.03–2.08
  EU approach 2.02
  importance 1.01
  rationale for application of forum law
    convenience 2.09–2.10
    judicial administration 2.13
    natural justice 2.11–2.12
    territorial sovereignty 2.14–2.16
  role of *lex fori* 1.02
  substance/procedure distinction
    Australian approach 2.21–2.24, 2.31–2.35
    Canadian approach 2.28–2.30
    case-by-case approach 2.18
    conclusions 2.59
    convenience approach 2.19–2.20
    English approach 2.36–2.47
    European civil law approach 2.02
    EU instruments 2.51–2.53
    new approach 2.48–2.50
    right-remedy approach 2.03–2.08
    US approach 2.54–2.58
  universal acceptance of criteria for choice of law 2.01
matters of substance *see* **substance/procedure distinction**

'named court' provisions
  divesting jurisdiction 6.55–6.58
  vesting jurisdiction 6.49–6.54
natural justice 2.11–2.12
New Zealand
  alternative compensation schemes 11.14–11.15
  creditors' rights 6.70–6.71
  displacement of applicable law to avoid damages 11.45
  limitations 9.07
  'named court' provisions 6.53, 6.57–6.58
  use of extrinsic evidence 7.13

'no action' clauses
  generic court provisions 6.40–6.46
  'leave of the court' provisions 6.47–6.48
  'named court' provisions 6.49–6.58
no advantage *see* **uniformity of outcome**
notice before action provisions 6.22–6.29, 11.48–11.49

orders *see* **judgments and orders**
overriding mandatory rules
  damages and compensation 11.35, 11.38, 11.61, 11.67
  insolvency 10.31
  limitations 9.11, 9.40–9.41
  method of forum reference 3.22
  'no action' clauses 6.45–6.46
  set-off 10.31
  writing requirements 7.30

parties to litigation
  capacity
    to be a party to litigation 5.05
    to sue and be sued 5.01–5.04
  choice of proper parties 5.09–5.15
  contribution and indemnity 5.18–5.19
  derivative actions
    Commonwealth countries 5.40–5.43
    English law 5.35–5.39
    United States 5.44–5.47
  fatal accident claims 5.24–5.25
  foreign state entities
    Australia 5.53
    Canada 5.49–5.51
    English law 5.52
    overview 5.48
    United States 5.54
  joinder 5.17
  liability
    inter-spousal liability 5.23
    proportionate liability 5.21
    vicarious liability 5.22
  name of party to litigation 5.06–5.07
  representative actions 5.26–5.30
  standing 5.16
  subrogation 5.20
  'sue others first' provisions 5.31–5.34
personal jurisdiction
  Australia 4.47–4.48
  Canada 4.44–4.45
  English law 4.46
  establishment 4.43
  EU law 4.53
  Singapore 4.49
  United States 4.50–4.52
pleading and proof of foreign law
  method of forum reference 3.28–3.29, 7.23

pleadings
  administrative requirements 6.04–6.07
presumptions
  characterization 3.08
  EU law 7.24
  irrebuttable presumptions 7.18
  public policy 7.25
  rebuttable presumptions 7.19–7.23
privilege
  audio-video evidence from abroad 8.37
  lawyer-client communications
    choice of law rules 8.34–8.36
    substance/procedure
      distinction 8.21–8.28
    US approach 8.29–8.33
  self-incrimination
    disclosure as an offence 8.41–8.56
    disclosure of an offence 8.57–8.59
    overview 8.38–8.40
procedure *see* **matters of procedure**
promissory estoppel 7.54
proof
  burden of proof
    characterization 3.08
    general principles 7.15–7.17
    public policy 7.25
  foreign law 3.28–3.29, 7.23
proportionate liability 5.21
proprietary estoppel 7.55
provisional remedies *see* **interim and provisional remedies**
provisions preventing relitigation 7.45–7.46
public hearings 6.20–6.21
public policy
  damages and compensation 11.35, 11.37, 11.60
  final non-monetary relief 10.20
  fraud and undue influence 7.25
  lawyer-client privilege 8.25, 8.27
  limitations 9.20–9.23
  method of forum reference 3.16–3.21
  'no action' clauses 6.44–6.45
  presumptions 7.25
  priorities 6.60
  writing requirements 7.30

quantification of damages
  legislative or judicial
    limitations 11.17–11.26
  numerical assessment and
    methods 11.27–11.36

rebuttable presumptions 7.19–7.23
relitigation *see* **provisions preventing relitigation**

remedies
  constructive trusts 10.21
  damages and compensation
    alternative compensation
      schemes 11.14–11.15
    conditions precedent 11.48–11.49
    deductibility of benefits 11.09–11.13
    displacement of applicable
      law 11.39–11.47
    heads of claim 11.02
    interest on damages 11.03–11.08
    jurisdictional control 11.50–11.51
    overriding mandatory rules 11.38
    overview 11.01
    public policy 11.37
    quantification 11.17–11.36
    remoteness of damage 11.16
    Rome II 11.53–11.67
    US approach 11.68–11.72
  final non-monetary relief
    constructive trusts and
      tracing 10.21–10.22
    injunctions 10.20
    Rome I 10.23
    Rome II 10.23–10.24
    specific performance and
      rescission 10.20
  general principles 10.01–10.05
  interim and provisional remedies
    anti-suit injunctions 4.62–4.63, 10.07, 10.16
    freezing orders 10.13, 10.17
    interlocutory injunctions 10.08–10.12
    overview 10.06
    Rome I 10.19
    Rome II 10.15–10.19
    search orders 10.14, 10.18
  set-off 10.25–10.31
  specific performance and rescission 10.20
  statutory restrictions 10.32–10.35
  tracing 10.22
remoteness of damage 11.16
renvoi **and 'no advantage'** 3.09–3.14, 6.57, 9.27–9.30, 11.46
representative actions 5.26–5.30
rescission 10.20
right-remedy approach
  conclusions 12.01
  condemnation by most
    contemporaries 2.17
  continuing application by English
    courts 2.37, 2.43–2.47
  history of English law 2.03–2.08
  limitations 9.01–9.04
Rome I
  avoidance of characterization 3.08

Index

Rome I (cont.)
  evidence
    burden of proof 7.17
    judicial administration 7.34
    presumptions 7.24
    use of extrinsic evidence 7.14
    writing requirements 7.28
  interim and provisional remedies 10.19
  limitations 9.24–9.26
  public policy 3.18
  remedies
    final non-monetary relief 10.23
    set-off 10.28–10.29
  temporal effect 11.01

Rome II
  avoidance of characterization 3.08
  choice of proper parties 5.12
  contribution and indemnity 5.19
  damages and compensation
    applicable law 11.53–11.59
    deductibility of benefits 11.56
    displacement of applicable law 11.62–11.64
    heads of claim 11.54
    interest 11.55
    limitations on damages 11.54
    overriding mandatory rules 11.61, 11.67
    public policy 11.60
    quantification of damages 11.57–11.59
    recent English case law 11.65–11.67
  direct action against insurer 5.12
  evidence
    burden of proof 7.17
    judicial administration 7.34
    presumptions 7.24
    writing requirements 7.28
  final non-monetary relief 10.23–10.24
  interim and provisional remedies 10.15–10.19
  limitations 9.24–9.26
  parties to litigation
    contribution and indemnity 5.19
    subrogation 5.20
    vicarious liability 5.22
  public policy 3.18
  temporal effect 11.01

search orders 10.14
  EU law 10.18
security for costs 6.37–6.39
self-characterizing provisions 3.07
self-incrimination
  disclosure as an offence
    Australia 8.46–8.48
    Canada 8.49–8.50
    English law 8.41–8.45
    US approach 8.51–8.56
  disclosure of an offence 8.57–8.59
  overview 8.38–8.40
service of process
  Australia 4.28–4.30
  Canada 4.33
  English law 4.16–4.27
  EU Service Regulation 4.15
  Hague Service Convention 4.09–4.14
  Hong Kong 4.31
  overview 4.01–4.07
  personal jurisdiction, as basis for 4.43
  Singapore 4.32
  United States 4.34–4.40
set-off 10.25–10.31
Singapore
  damages and compensation
    displacement of applicable law 11.45
    jurisdictional control 11.51
  interlocutory injunctions 10.09
  'no action' clauses 6.44
  personal jurisdiction 4.49
  service of process 4.32
South Africa
  creditors' rights 6.72
  limitations and *via media* 9.08–9.10
sovereignty
  rationale for application of forum law 2.14–2.16
  service of process abroad 4.02–4.03
specific performance 10.20
standard of proof 7.33
standing 5.16
statutes of limitations *see* **limitations**
statutory interpretation
  Canadian approach to substance-procedure distinction 2.29–2.30, 6.50–6.51
  immunities from jurisdiction 4.68–4.69
subrogation 5.20
substance/procedure distinction
  Australian approach 2.22–2.24, 2.31–2.35
  Canadian approach 2.28–2.30
  case-by-case approach 2.18
  conclusions 12.01–12.04
  convenience approach 2.19–2.20
  English approach 2.36–2.47
  European civil law model 2.02
  EU law
    choice of law instruments 2.51–2.53
  importance 1.02
  lawyer-client privilege 8.21–8.28
  new approach 2.48–2.50
  US approach 2.54–2.58
'sue others first' provisions 5.31–5.34

taking of evidence abroad
application of foreign law 8.16–8.19
Commonwealth approach 8.03–8.08
EU law 8.15
Hague Evidence Convention 8.12–8.14
overview 8.01–8.02
US approach 8.09–8.10
territorial sovereignty
rationale for application of forum law 2.14–2.16
service of process abroad 4.02–4.03
time limits 9.43–9.44
see also **limitation of actions; limitations**
tracing 10.22

uniformity of outcome and 'no advantage'
alternative methods of forum reference 3.30
characterization 3.09–3.14
damages 11.46
importance 1.03
limitations 9.27–9.30
'no action' clauses 6.55–6.57
United States
choice of proper parties 5.14
damages and compensation
general principles 11.68–11.71
interest on damages 11.72
estoppel
by representation of fact 7.52
issue and cause of action estoppel 7.45–7.46
promissory estoppel 7.54
evidence
admissibility 7.10–7.11
burden of proof 7.16
rebuttable presumptions 7.19, 7.22
spoliation 7.35
writing requirements 7.27, 7.30
judicial administration
commencement of proceedings 6.03
costs and fees 6.33–6.36
creditors' rights 6.76
enforcement of judgments 6.80
jury trials 6.15
'named court' provisions 6.52
'no action' clauses 6.41
notice before action provisions 6.23
priorities 6.76
security bonds 6.39
jurisdiction
choice of court clauses 4.59
personal jurisdiction 4.50–4.52
limitations 9.45–9.49
parties to litigation
derivative actions 5.44–5.47
fatal accident claims 5.25
foreign state entities 5.54
joinder 5.17
representative actions 5.28–5.29
privilege
lawyer-client communications 8.29–8.33
self-incrimination 8.51–8.56, 8.59
remedies
interlocutory injunctions 10.08, 10.11
set-off 10.27
service of process 4.34–4.40
substance/procedure distinction 2.54–2.58
taking of evidence abroad 8.09–8.10, 8.16–8.18

vicarious liability 5.22
video evidence 8.08, 8.37

witnesses
competence and compellability 7.31
privilege for audio-video evidence from abroad 8.37
writing requirements 7.26–7.30